The Early Barth—Lectures and Shorter Works

The Early Barth—Lectures and Shorter Works

Volume 1, 1905–1909

Karl Barth

Edited by
Hans-Anton Drewes and Hinrich Stoevesandt
in conjunction with Herbert Helms

Translated by
The Translation Fellows of the Center for Barth Studies,
Princeton Theological Seminary

Darrell L. Guder, English Editor
Matthias Gockel, German Editor
David C. Chao, Project Editor

WESTMINSTER
JOHN KNOX PRESS
LOUISVILLE • KENTUCKY

Original German-language edition, *Vorträge und kleinere Arbeiten: 1905–1909*, 1992, copyright © 1992 Theologischer Verlag Zürich

First English-language edition
Published by Westminster John Knox Press
Louisville, Kentucky

22 23 24 25 26 27 28 29 30 31—10 9 8 7 6 5 4 3 2 1

Book design by Drew Stevens
Cover design by Marc Whitaker / MTWdesign.net

Scripture is translated from Luther Bibel.

Library of Congress Cataloging-in-Publication Data

Names: Barth, Karl, 1886–1968, author. | Drewes, Hans-Anton, editor.
Title: The early Barth—lectures and shorter works / edited by Hans-Anton Drewes and Hinrich Stoevesandt in conjunction with Herbert Helms ; translated by the Translation Fellows of the Center for Barth Studies, Princeton Theological Seminary ; Darrell L. Guder, English editor, Matthias Gockel, German editor, David C. Chao, Project editor.
Other titles: The early Barth—lectures and shorter works
Description: First English-language edition. | Louisville, Kentucky : Westminster John Knox Press, 2022– | Includes bibliographical references and index. |
   Contents: volume 1. 1905–1909 — | Translated from German. | Summary: "These volumes contain essays, lectures, academic papers, correspondences, editorials, and other writings that were not previously translated into English and that provide insight into the development of Barth's theology during this crucial period of his life"— Provided by publisher.
Identifiers: LCCN 2022040036 (print) | LCCN 2022040037 (ebook) | ISBN 9780664264383 | ISBN 9781646982523 (ebook)
Subjects: LCSH: Barth, Karl, 1886–1968.
Classification: LCC BX4827.B3 A25 2022 (print) | LCC BX4827.B3 (ebook) | DDC 230/.044—dc23/eng/20221011
LC record available at https://lccn.loc.gov/2022040036
LC ebook record available at https://lccn.loc.gov/2022040037

Contents

Editors' Preface

For a long time, section III of Barth's Gesamtausgabe, under the title *Vorträge und kleinere Arbeiten*, has left a gap on the shelf, and likewise section IV (*Gespräche*) [*Barth in Conversation*], while numerous volumes from sections I, II, and V were released. In the planning of the Gesamtausgabe [Collected Works], the extensive and thematically diverse body of essays, lectures, articles, reviews, and drafts of papers was treated as a unified whole as soon as the collection had assumed its final contours. The first volume of the section—comprising the works of this genre that originated from 1922 to 1925, which finally appeared in 1990—is fourth in the chronological organization of the series. The writings span sixteen years from 1905—when Barth, as a first-year student, produced a small independent work (in the field of history of religions!)—until 1921, when he moved for the second time from parish ministry in Safenwil (Aargau) to the academic milieu, having been called to a newly established honorary professorship for Reformed theology in Göttingen. These writings will comprise a total of three volumes.

The beginning of the planning goes way back. It coincides with that memorable conference in the summer of 1970 in the Leuenberg Conference Center at Hölstein in the canton of Basel-Landschaft, where an ad hoc group of family members, friends, and students of Barth, as well as representatives of Theologischer Verlag Zurich, gathered to share thoughts on the possibilities for publishing Barth's unprinted literary estate [*Nachlass*], or parts of it, when after long consultation professor Ernst Wolf finally made the motion: not a selection, and not merely an edition of the literary estate either, but rather to go all out—a Gesamtausgabe (the complete works)!

In the euphoria of the response that this proposal evoked, under which it was immediately brought to a decision but with no clear vision of a sensible arrangement of the immense volume of material, initial editorial commissions were authorized at once. Two of them concerned groups of texts not yet closely inspected at that time, which two years later, as decided by the same circle of advisers that determined the definitive plan of the edition, found their place together with many others in section III. According to the 1970 comprehensive plan, quite vague at first, each group of texts was to have comprised one volume. Hence, the theological works, narrowly defined and beginning in 1909, were gathered into one volume, as long as they were not included in one of the collections arranged by Barth himself (each of these collections would be published again as a volume of the Gesamtausgabe, according to the tentative plan), and in the other volume the lectures and reports of a more political content were gathered, including the numerous notes that Barth collected in an envelope he labeled with the title "Socialist Speeches." Each was assigned to one editor: the first to Herbert Helms, the second to Friedrich-Wilhelm Marquardt.

Professor Wolf presented a first draft for the ordering of the Gesamtausgabe at a second conference in the summer of 1971. He arranged an outline of the entire material in accordance with the canon of the theological disciplines. The Karl Barth Archive, established shortly thereafter, at first received the assignment for the detailed execution of this plan. With that, however, considerable difficulties immediately arose: on the one hand, the disciplinary boundaries for the material at hand were too fuzzy to enable a clear-cut assignment in each case; on the other hand, for considerable portions a place would have been found only in an additional section under the uninviting title "Varia." For this reason, the aforementioned third conference in the summer of 1972 unanimously decided on a new plan for the edition, in force since then, according to which the sections received content-neutral titles by literary genre. For what is now called section III, the new plan rendered obsolete the original parceling of the two groups of texts mentioned and brought about their recombining, along with all material from the years 1905–1921 not already assigned to an editor in 1970. The latter material, already exceeding the two other groups, grew considerably as the view soon prevailed that despite or precisely because of its somewhat great scope, the academic work of the student Karl Barth should not be disregarded. Hans-Anton Drewes was willing to be engaged as an editor for this entire remainder.

When the basic decision was made at the conference of 1970 to take on the Gesamtausgabe, the further question arose as to whether Barth's printed works and his unpublished literary estate were each to be treated separately within this series or collated without regard to publication status. The follow-up conference decided in favor of the second option. That is how it has been handled in all the volumes affected by this decision and published to date—those of section I (Sermons), III (Smaller Works), and V (Letters). Among the smaller works, the proportion of texts from the period 1905–1921 that exist only in handwritten form is greater than in later years; in the years 1905–1909 it outweighs the printed texts by far. The arrangement of the pieces follows the chronology of their writing,[1] which can be reconstructed in almost all cases.[2] The sometimes considerably later printing dates of the pieces already published will therefore not determine their order.

For everything unprinted, the editorial work had to begin with sometimes difficult deciphering. High demands were made, especially given the great thematic diversity, also by the tracing of supporting material for Barth's remarks, preferably to the sources he actually used; the verification of citations; and the elucidation of some historical settings. Herbert Helms did the helpful groundwork for

---

1. Pieces like this—in this first volume, the essay, "Modern Theology and the Work of the Kingdom of God," with rejoinders from Ernst Christian Achelis and Paul Drews, Barth's reply, and Martin Rade's editorial final word—belong together and form an exception to the rule of chronological arrangement. In all such cases, the placement shall be based on the writing date of the first piece in the series.
2. In every case in this volume.

the specifically theological pieces mentioned above. In this first volume, these are the essays "Modern Theology and the Work of the Kingdom of God" and "The Cosmological Proof for the Existence of God." The important contribution of Friedrich-Wilhelm Marquardt, which begins in the second volume, will be appreciated there. Both editors handed over their manuscripts years ago to Hinrich Stoevesandt to produce the final version. Except for the two works mentioned, all the pieces in this volume were overseen by Hans-Anton Drewes.

In its first three-quarters, this first volume contains works by Barth from his years of study in Bern (1904–6), Berlin (1906–7), and Tübingen (1907–8), mainly contributions to seminars he attended; a thesis written for his theological examination; two lectures given for different collegiate audiences; and the oldest of Barth's texts meant for publication, a newspaper report on the Aarau Student Conference of 1906. The pieces in the last quarter, with one exception written for print, are from Barth's time as an editorial assistant for the journal *Die Christliche Welt*, headed by Martin Rade in Marburg (November 1908 to August 1909). The publication or republishing of these texts in the Gesamtausgabe thus goes back to the beginning of Karl Barth's life as a theologian. Writings from his grammar school years, mainly dramatic poems, are reserved for later publication in section VI, *Aus Karl Barths Leben*.

The two undersigned editors share the responsibility for this and the next two volumes, the second of which is to follow very soon, and the third likewise in short order. In addition to years of continuous communication on the nature of the process, they have made a large number of decisions together in many days of long work sessions. Despite the effort toward standardization in the technicalities, which goes far beyond the conventions only set out broadly in writing, minor individual peculiarities in the application of editorial criteria have not been eliminated. As is likewise the case in the broader framework of the Gesamtausgabe as a whole, room for editorial individualities, albeit narrowly defined, has always been kept open.

Chief Working Principles Employed by the Editors

For reprinting Barth's published texts, as elsewhere in the Gesamtausgabe, *punctuation* and *spelling* were adjusted to the rules in effect today, or were even then, but not strictly observed by Barth.

Some texts were previously only handwritten manuscripts, so they were handled differently (especially with regard to those that were only sketches, as abundant in the next two volumes). The aim is to give readers as accurate an impression as possible of the original state of the manuscript. Thus the *layout*, with varying size of the indentations, reflects that of the original as closely as possible. *Abbreviations* used by Barth are not always spelled out. Word elements omitted by abbreviations are supplemented in *square brackets* when they appear within a text for the first time; when repeated, they remain unresolved, with only the period (usually missing with Barth) being supplied by the editors.

Parts of the text that Barth emphasized by straight or wavy or double *underlining* are rendered in italics. The editors disregarded subsequent (pencil-made) underlines: some of them may have been added by Barth himself when he read them again, and some appear to be made by critical readers from the family or friends or from Barth's academic proofreaders.

In some of his works here, Barth uses *square brackets* in addition to the round ones. Since square brackets in this edition refer to additions made by the editors, however, the symbols { . . . } are used for those made by Barth.

Obvious *spelling errors* are corrected as a matter of course. In cases where there is doubt, or when the instance otherwise appears to be worth noting, a footnote will draw attention to it. Of these cases, the odd example of older orthography and certain of Barth's—even later—uniformly cultivated idiosyncrasies are distinguished in the writing of specific individual words. In both instances the manuscript's spelling remains preserved.

Where *punctuation marks* are missing with Barth (e.g., almost always at the end of a manuscript line) and would be helpful for the easier readability of sentences, and where an existing comma calls for a second one as a counterpart, they were supplied but sometimes (in the German ed.) distinguished by square brackets as additions of the editors.

Barth's own *corrections* are recorded without further comment. The text is thus offered in the final form redacted by Barth; preliminary versions are only mentioned in exceptional cases, since they are rather seldom found in the manuscripts. Remarks and corrections of external origin, such as those of Adolf von Harnack or Barth's father, are occasionally recorded in footnotes, simply in recognition of the prominence of the reviser.

When *quotations* show clear transcription errors (grammatical or orthographic), the text is normally aligned with the original that Barth cited; yet apart from that, where appropriate in spelling and punctuation and even with omission and inversion of words, the uncommon form may be left as is. Where, at most, an intentional change of the given wording might be suspected (i.e., in cases that are not quite obviously just a slip of the pen), or where circumstances otherwise seem somehow to be remarkable, the difference between citation and quoted original is given in a footnote.

The problem of *errors in content* also called for an editorial decision. It was an exaggeration when Karl Barth once anticipated the exclamation, "A couple of times you really missed the mark," as his father's expected reaction.[3] Still, he has, of course, occasionally run into mistakes. Tacit emendation was obviously ruled out. In some instances, a note appeared appropriate, especially if misunderstandings could thereby be avoided effortlessly. Elsewhere—especially where a succinct remark would not have been able to clarify the matter, and a detailed note would have given it disproportionate weight—the editors were generally not disposed to do so, and were as good as warned by the example of the otherwise meritorious Heinrich Düntzer ("Here Goethe is mistaken") against laying a finger on such altogether rare passages, on which Barth himself likely in a suitable place would have commented cheerfully ("How could I [write this]?")[4] and corrected them.

For both groups of texts, the ones printed earlier and the works published here from the manuscript for the first time, a particular convention used in the

---

3. See page 175 below.
4. *CD* IV/1: x [*KD* IV/1: viii, translation revised].

Gesamtausgabe also had to be applied in this volume (esp. the German ed.), even though it changed the typeface slightly. Barth would use Latin script, and less often quotation marks, to differentiate *Latin* or other foreign language *elements*, including entire citations, from the text written in German script.[5] In printed texts, he had put foreign-language words, phrases, and quotations in Antiqua, within Gothic type (later, in Antiqua type, he had put them into italics). Since the italic font in the Gesamtausgabe is used for *emphasis* (for the reproduction of underlines in Barth's manuscripts or the spacing out of letters in his printed texts), there is no corresponding typographic means for indicating foreign language text. Alternatively, the editors will use *quotation marks* or extract style for citations.

Just as in the *Vorträge und kleinere Arbeiten, 1922–1925* [*Barth's Lectures and Shorter Works, 1922–1925*], each individual piece is preceded by an editorial *introduction* identifying the background and implications of the document as well as immediate reactions to the oral presentations or to the publication of the texts in question. Where not otherwise indicated, the sources—mainly correspondence, on which these descriptions are based—are located in the Karl Barth Archive in Basel. The introductions are consistently put in italics; what would normally be in italics is in roman type there.

In the course of their work, the editors have received valuable help on various fronts. Some names are to be mentioned, such as Robert Develey, Doctor of Medicine, in Basel; and Ulrich Im Hof, Doctor of Philosophy, in Bern. Both are outstanding in their knowledge of the student association Zofingia and its history and have answered numerous specific questions. At various stages of the work, Jörg-Michael Bohnet has given his flair and keen eye to the service of the edition. Caren Algner, assistant at the Karl Barth Archive, and Eva Köpf in Tübingen helped with the reading of the proofs. Pastor Em. Hermann Schmidt in Oldenburg selflessly relieved the editors of the great task of preparing the indexes so that readers can orient themselves within the volume more easily. From the beginning, Dr. Eberhard Jüngel supported the work of the edition. The editors found the Theologischer Verlag Zurich and its director Werner Blum most accommodating. To them and to others who have provided information or assisted in individual phases of the work, the editors express their sincere thanks for support, without which the readers would have had to wait even longer for the appearance of the volume.

Tübingen and Basel, October 1991
Hans-Anton Drewes
Hinrich Stoevesandt

---

5. Barth also used abbreviations in Latin for biblical books and occasionally other text elements, such as the abbreviation "UV" for "Unser Vater" ["Our Father" as in the Lord's Prayer].

Translators' Preface

This translation of Karl Barth's *Lectures and Shorter Works* (*Vorträge und kleinere Arbeiten*), from section III of the German edition of the Gesamtausgabe (Collected Works), continues the Barth translation project of the Center for Barth Studies at Princeton Theological Seminary. The previous project resulted in the 2017–2019 publication, by Westminster John Knox Press, of three volumes of Barth's late conversations: *Barth in Conversation, 1959–1962*; then *1963*; and *1964–1968*. The gratifying outcome led to a strong interest on the part of the eighteen translators who worked on the project to tackle the translation of another section of the Collected Works. That enthusiasm for continuing the project was shared by the editorial team, which guided the *Conversations* through to completion: David Chao (project editor), Matthias Gockel (German editor), and Darrell Guder (English editor). The editorial team at Westminster John Knox Press was also supportive of tackling this next level of the Barth legacy.

Under the shared leadership of Kaitlyn Dugan, now Director of the Center for Barth Studies, and David Chao, a grant was successfully sought from the National Endowment for the Humanities, which specifically focused on the translation of major works in the humanities from other languages into English. The grant is making it possible for the translators of *Lectures and Shorter Works* to meet more often; it is providing stipends for all those working on the project; and it is providing a subsidy for publication. This is the first of three volumes made possible by this grant; if further funding is approved, it is hoped that many more of Barth's *Lectures and Shorter Works* will be translated.

The Barth translation project began in the mid 1990s, when the Center for Barth Studies at Princeton Theological Seminary invited Barth scholars interested in the challenges of translating Barth to meet once a year for three to four days to work on actual texts. This informal working group gradually turned its attention to the three German volumes of *Conversations*. The group's work focused on the accuracy and readability of translations, with particular concern for consistency in the translations of Barth's terminology. An online glossary was initiated, to which all the participants have direct access. All the experience gained in translating the three volumes of *Conversations* is now being applied to the work on the *Lectures and Shorter Works*.

The reader of *Barth in Conversation* will recognize the importance of the editorial introductions to each volume supplied by the German-speaking editors (both German and Swiss). The italicized introductions provide a documentary history of the evolution of each piece and locate them within the emerging world of Barth's thought. There is a wealth of important insight in this editorial material. The English translations prepared by this project are intended to be accurate and accessible in rendering all this content from the actual documents and footnotes.

The editors of the German original edition (Hans-Anton Drewes and Hinrich Stoevesandt) provide in their Preface (above) detailed information about their editorial policies, especially with regard to punctuation. As far as feasible, the English translators have followed the practices of the German edition.

Certain practices developed in the translation of the three *Conversations* volumes are continued in the *Lectures and Shorter Works*. With regard to bibliographical citations, our practice is to cite from English translations of cited works if they exist. If there is no English version, we provide a full bibliographical reference in German or Latin (normally in a footnote), and the translator may opt to insert an English translation of the title (in square brackets) if that information is deemed to be of interest to the English-speaking reader. The content and sequence of all footnotes is the same in the translated version so that the numbers mostly correspond, although some references were moved out of the text to footnotes to fit consistent style. Translators may decide to insert an additional footnote, in which case a numerical code (so footnotes stay in order) and an asterisk (e.g., [3*]) or a letter (e.g., [4a]) are used. Occasionally we use single square brackets for additions. The double brackets in the German text, changed to curly brackets { . . . } here, indicate additions by Barth that he himself put into single square brackets.

In the text and notes, Barth means Karl Barth (1886–1968) unless specified with a first name for someone else.

The reader of this volume will quickly and gratefully recognize the thorough and thoughtful work done by the two German-language editors, Hans-Anton Drewes and Hinrich Stoevesandt. They have set a high standard for all further work on Barth's theological legacy. It is our hope that the English translations will prove to be a reliable resource for the study of Barth in the years ahead.

We thank Kait Dugan for her untiring support of the project and the Center of Barth Studies for providing the necessary logistical and administrative framework. A special word of thanks goes to the entire group of translators, whose enthusiasm for the project continues to be invaluable.

David C. Chao, Project Editor, Princeton
Matthias Gockel, German Editor, Basel
Darrell Guder, English Editor, Seattle

Introduction to the English Edition

This work presents a translation of the first volume of *Lectures and Shorter Works* from the critical edition of the Collected Works of Karl Barth. The volumes within this division of the Collected Works contain lectures and shorter works in which Barth deals not only with theological issues but also with broader topics and problems; they are usually texts of a manageable length and generally directed to a larger and less specialized audience than his diverse academic works. They mainly take the form of public lectures or essays, but now and then they also include expert opinion pieces, reviews, and sundry other writings. Often the topics for these texts were chosen for him—sometimes with, sometimes without consultation—but almost always they are texts in which Barth seeks to express himself in a manner suitable to his audience and his time. The texts regularly make reference to early twentieth-century questions and conversations and correspondingly contain many allusions to contemporaneous culture and quotations from other writings.

In the publication of texts such as these, it is clear that a critical edition with detailed commentary is important and necessary, indeed perhaps even more important and necessary than in the case of the publication of lengthy monographs or lectures series, in which similar allusions and quotations also appear but do not play nearly such an important role in relation to the text as a whole and to the intention of what is written. This is all the more the case in relation to the *translations* of these texts, in which certain features of the text can simply become lost in translation. Moreover, today's readers, at a distance of more than one hundred years from the original version, let alone today's readers from a non-German-speaking context, do not generally possess the sufficient knowledge of German literary classics or contemporaneous German ecclesiastical and theological discussions needed to recognize such finer references on their own. For this reason, and especially with a view toward the ongoing and accurate reception of Karl Barth's theology in non-German-speaking contexts, this translation of the first volume of *Lectures and Shorter Works* is based on the original critical edition and includes both the latter's detailed introductions to the texts and its annotation apparatus. Beyond these, it also includes translators' remarks at various relevant points in order to illuminate further features of the cultural or literary context in which Barth was writing.

The present volume is the first volume chronologically in this division of Barth's Collected Works, and brings together Barth's earliest academic writings in theology, spanning the years 1905 through 1909. The larger part of the volume is occupied by texts written for the seminars he attended during his studies in Bern (1904–1906), Berlin (1906–07), and Tübingen (1907–08). From this period there also arises his "qualifying thesis [*Akzessarbeit*]," as well as two other lectures and his first text intended for publication—a report on the Aarau Students' Conference of 1906. The second, smaller part of the volume contains the texts— mainly reviews—that Barth wrote in Marburg in 1908 and 1909, in the course of his work as editorial assistant for the journal *Die Christliche Welt* (The Christian World), which was edited by Martin Rade.

The texts as a whole reflect the early formation and development of Barth's theological thinking. They shed light on his path over these years: from being a young student, trying out his craft on various subjects and beginning to make the discipline his own, through his time as an ardent follower of Adolf Harnack, all the way to becoming a dedicated pupil of Wilhelm Herrmann, by which point Barth, while certainly cutting his own profile, was still a long way off from the insights that would later become fundamental to him. Especially when seen from the perspective of Barth's later, mature theology, these early works are but "theological finger-exercises" (Eberhard Busch). It would consequently be impossible to expect from their publication and reception any fundamentally new insights with respect to the interpretation of Barth's later theology. Nonetheless, these texts open up interesting fresh perspectives in at least three important respects.

1

First, the volume leaves a strong impression of the *intellectual horizon* of the young Barth and the great *curiosity* with which he devotes himself to the most varied subjects. The panorama of the first four works alone spans essays on topics as diverse as the character of the religion of ancient India, the stigmata of Francis of Assisi, an exegetical work on the centurion at Capernaum, and an essay on the relationship between his student association and certain current issues, titled "Zofingia and the Social Question." Thoughts on the relationship between ecclesial practice and academic theology, as well as on questions of religious pedagogy, also appear in the volume. A few of these issues are no longer in the immediate foreground in Barth's later works, and some scholars have attributed this to—and at the same time criticized Barth for—the absence of highly topical perspectives of contemporary relevance from the horizon of his thinking. Yet this is not true of Barth's later career, and, as can be gleaned from this volume, it is particularly inaccurate as a statement concerning Barth's theological beginnings. Barth prepared meticulously for the wider subjects of topical interest on which he was asked to speak and write and, as the editorial introductions to the various texts evidence, he strove on each occasion to be up to date with contemporaneous discussion and relevant literature.

On the basis of the texts gathered here, and prior to the sharp break in his theology that occurred later, the way in which Barth in these early writings increasingly considered himself to be a "modern," liberal theologian can be easily understood. There is a certain pleasure in noting the vigor with which Barth adopts—and defends against critics—positions that he will reject years later with at least the same vehemence. Clearly, then, and despite all the contestable sweeping judgments in subsequent years, Barth knew his later "adversary" very well; and if he can speak of it later, it is precisely because he too started out from the same point. Here is the proof that this is true: here one can authentically encounter the early Barth, who in his heart—and even more so in his mind—was authentically neo-Protestant.

2

Second, and this ought not be understood as a contradiction, the texts in this volume also show how much in general Barth himself is already at work *shaping* his own theology, how many of his *characteristic thoughts* can already be found in these early, "liberal" texts, apart from dependence on any existing school of thought, claimed by himself or ascribed to him by others. Of course, such thoughts are never at this stage formed into a theological edifice comparable to the structures of his later work. Yet Barth's nonconformism—his pronounced refusal quickly to categorize himself or to prescribe for himself certain thoughts and his refusal to forbid others on the basis of adherence to a particular theological direction or principle—is already clearly evident in his theologically liberal phase.

To be sure, throughout these years Barth is deeply influenced by the foundations of liberal theological thinking, by the historical relativism of all knowledge as well as by the subjectivity and individualism of faith and of religion, and not least by the importance and indispensability of historical criticism. Nevertheless, at the close of his essay for the Harnack seminar, he can still write a sentence concerning the New Testament tradition such as this: "the really valuable thing about such a piece of evangelical tradition can neither be given to us nor taken from us by historical criticism" (p. 104).

There is another way that the young Barth stands out, not so much from his contemporaneous liberal theologians, but from many who seek today to emulate the liberal theologians in the academy and who correspondingly have a rather problematic relationship with the ecclesial nature of the profession. Even for Barth as a student, the close connection between church and theology—beyond any criticism of a dusty or triumphant churchiness—is just as self-evident as for the author of *Church Dogmatics*. There is hardly any difference in this respect between the Barth who, at the beginning of *Church Dogmatics* I/1, explains and expounds the idea that "Theology is a function of the church" and the editorial assistant of the *Die Christliche Welt*. Thus in 1909, albeit a little less practiced than a good twenty years later, Barth wrote similarly,

> I think that a student who has attended the school of historical and systematic theology with enthusiasm and love and not merely for the sake of passing examinations—such a student will not go to work in the church without some guidelines to build upon. And vice versa: the historical and systematic work of a teacher who is in touch with the life of the church and knows the latter's needs not only from a distance—such a teacher will, without confusing scholarship with "edification," provide students with the liveliness and the skills required for their future tasks. (pp. 231–32)

The choice of topic for the lecture that Barth had to give in January 1906 to his student association, the Bern branch of Zofingia, also indicates a direction that would remain important for him all his life. The "social question" was for him a question of great importance, far more so than for many of his fellow students in Zofingia; but more than this, Barth considered the question of great importance for the group as a whole, even though it probably had no existential meaning for most. It was a question that could not be ignored simply by deeming it irrelevant to student life or too much bound up with a purely material problem:

> ... [P]recisely because more than one generation has worked on the solution to this question, it has always been considered important and relevant, and thus it appears to me to be a problem intimately related to the whole broad question of the *work and significance of the Zofingia Association.* This is why every good member of Zofingia should and must have taken a position in one way or another. (p. 51, italics original)

Even in this earliest public treatment of this topic, Barth already shows himself to be well informed, using figures and election results to make clear how pervasive the problem already is in other countries, how socially explosive it can be, and how even Switzerland can by no means be certain of being spared from a lasting division of society and the associated dangers. He quotes the leading Swiss religious socialist, Leonhard Ragaz, and uses his words to portray a possible path of events that in fact almost became a reality just a few years later, at the time of the great National Strike of 1918:

> Our people threaten to separate themselves into two combative battle camps, exactly like in the worst times of our history, and once the military, furnished with live ammunition, pulls through the streets of our towns, the specter of a bloody civil war is already before us. On both sides, the struggle produces phenomena that do us harm and prophesy nothing good. (p. 52)

But then he argues in a different way, namely from the self-understanding of Zofingia, and not least from the special Christian perspective, from the commandment to love one's neighbor. Here, too, a point appears that arises again later in a comparable way: it is not the actuality of a particular problem that has to determine all action, and to which all other thinking and acting must be subordinated. No, this problem calls the Christian students to act because it cannot be tolerated from the Christian point of view, specifically, from Jesus' commandment to love one's neighbor. Social action is motivated and dominated by faith, by one's existence as a Christian:

> *The modern social question is more than a danger.* Anyone who goes a little deeper sees in it a link in the evolution of a problem—or, better, *the* problem—of humanity with which Jesus confronted the ancient world, and which found its religious solution in the *Reformation* and its political solution in the *Revolution,* the task which Jesus formulated as "You shall love your God with all your heart and your neighbor as yourself" (Matthew 22:37,39). In other words, this shows the problem of the *dual responsibility of the individual person: on the one hand to the Godhead, and on the other hand to humanity.* Mark my

words, the opinion is not that the solution to the social question would bring the end of that development, or putting it religiously, would bring about the "kingdom of God," as one so often hears it said today. I think of this solution, in common with those brought by Reformation and Revolution, only as *necessary premises* for achieving that goal, but exactly necessary ones. . . . (p. 53, italics original)

The attentive listener may hear in these lines a hint of the argument in which Barth, almost fifteen years later in his Tambach lecture, asserts his great reservation about religious socialism. It is likewise typical that, in the remainder of the text here, Barth opposes the view that such a large, comprehensive problem cannot adequately be addressed in one's own small environment. He simply points out what one might be able to do in the context of Zofingia in terms of small and perhaps—at first glance—not at all decisive things, in order to do and to implement whatever is possible, at least here, in one's own domain.

One cannot speak of more than an echo of the later course of Barth's work even in the last and perhaps most substantial text of the volume, "The Cosmological Proof for the Existence of God," a text that was critically annotated by his brother Heinrich, a student of philosophy. Nevertheless, here once again we see the extent to which a theme can accompany Barth throughout the various stages of his theological journey. The prospect of an ontological proof of God, with which Barth deals fundamentally and formatively more than twenty years later in his book on Anselm, already follows here the decisive rejection of a Thomistic construction of the proof, a construction that Barth would later label as "natural theology." The peculiar characteristic of the later work—namely, that Barth presupposes out of ontic and rational necessity the existence of God that he wants to prove—is, however, still regarded critically by the young Barth in 1909.

A final, perhaps not quite so surprising parallel to the later Barth, under which many a reader of Barth suffers, also emerges in these texts. His qualifying thesis—"The Concept of Christ's Descent to the Underworld in Church Literature until Origen"—and, above all, the seminar paper written for Harnack—"Paul's Missionary Activity according to Its Portrayal in the Acts of the Apostles"—easily reach the standard of many of the Licentiate (postgraduate) works of his time—if not in terms of the necessary depth and originality, then certainly in terms of the length of the expositions. Even these early works signal that someone is entering the theological arena who has a lot to say in more than one sense!

3

Finally, in addition to illuminating these important aspects of Barth's theological thinking and its development, there is a third area in which the texts brought together and translated in this volume offer interesting insights: *Barth's biography*, specifically, as they offer *a portrait of the path of his studies* from Bern via Berlin and Tübingen to Marburg. In this volume, as in the subsequent volumes of *Lectures and Shorter Works*, the numerous allusions to current topics and events or to literary style that can be discovered in the texts reveal some of Barth's influences and preferences. Many impressions from his travels and elsewhere have left their traces, which are elucidated, as far as possible, by the editors in the explanatory footnotes. Above all, the most important source for Barth's biography are the introductions written for each of the texts, which describe and reproduce from the sources the occasions and the circumstances of preparation, possible consultations made in advance, the specific characteristics of a lecture, or important reactions to a text.

Whether one is interested in the accuracy of Barth in the implementation and use of exegetical methods and steps (which many liked to doubt in view of later printed publications; but Barth knew exegesis, and he applied it, not only in those early years!); or in the energy and meticulousness with which the young student throws himself into particular works and tries to avoid every conceivable distraction, especially in a city like Berlin; or in the way in which, beyond his actual studies and apart from the essays to be written, theological questions and discussions again and again pervaded and shaped his everyday life, all this can be retraced and consulted here. Often the letters from his only correspondence that are extensively preserved from this time—that with his father—serve as an important source. In particular, his semester in Berlin appears in a new light here. It is often rumored, even by Barth himself, that his time in Berlin was at best a tolerable compromise, because he had really wanted to study in "liberal" Marburg, whereas his father would have preferred to see him in "moderate-conservative" Greifswald. However, the enthusiasm with which Barth reports on his academic encounters with Adolf Harnack and the enthusiasm with which he also writes the extensive seminar paper for Harnack present a somewhat different, more nuanced picture of events from a contemporaneous source.

For all the distinctive characteristics that this first volume of *Lectures and Shorter Works* and the texts gathered within in it have in comparison with later volumes, one thing is clear: the translation of a critical edition of these works is both necessary and significant. It is by no means a superfluous undertaking to attend to these texts from the pen of the young student and the great theologian in the making.

Peter Zocher
Karl Barth Archive, Basel
January 2022

List of Translators and Assignments

[The translation team cooperated in translating various pieces.]

Clifford Anderson, Associate University Librarian for Research and Digital Strategy and Professor of Religious Studies, Vanderbilt University: "The Stigmata of Francis of Assisi," "The Cosmological Proof for the Existence of God."

Matthew J. Aragon Bruce, adjunct professor, Calvin University Prison Initiative and Western Theological Seminary: "Review of Gustav Mix, *Toward the Reform of Theological Studies*"; "Review of A. Von Broecker, *Protestantische Gemeinde-Flugblätter*"; "Review of P. Mezger, *Eigenart und innere Lebensbedingungen einer protestantischen Volkskirche*"; "Review of Fr. A. Voigt, *Was sollen wir tun?*"; "Review of R. Jahnke, *Aus der Mappe eines Glücklichen*"; "Review of O. Pfister, *Religionspädagogisches Neuland*"; "The Belgian Mission Church"; "Review of *Zeitschrift für Wissenschaftliche Theologie*, vol. 51, nos. 1–2."

David C. Chao, Director of the Center for Asian American Christianity, Princeton Theological Seminary: "Paul's Missionary Activity according to Its Portrayal in the Acts of the Apostles."

Terry L. Cross, Professor of Systematic Theology and Dean, School of Religion, Lee University: "Zwingli's Sixty-Seven Articles of the First Disputation on Religion at Zurich 1523."

Sven Ensminger, PhD (University of Bristol): "The Character of the Religion of Ancient India," "Zofingia and the Social Question," "Modern Theology and Work for the Kingdom of God."

David A. Gilland, "Paul's Missionary Activity according to Its Portrayal in the Acts of the Apostles," "The Concept of Christ's Descent to the Underworld in Church Literature until Origen."

Darrell L. Guder, Emeritus Professor of Missional and Ecumenical Theology, Princeton Theological Seminary: "The Stigmata of Francis of Assisi," "Brief Communique."

Judith J. Guder, Retired musician and translator, "Brief Communique."

Thomas Herwig, Assistant Professor, Honors College of the University of Alabama: "Paul's Missionary Activity according to Its Portrayal in the Acts of the Apostles."

Cambria Kaltwasser, Assistant Professor of Theology, Northwestern College: "Introduction to the English Edition" by Peter Zocher, "Paul's Missionary Activity according to Its Portrayal in the Acts of the Apostles."

Oliver Keenan, OP, Director of the Aquinas Institute and Fellow in Systematic Theology, Blackfriars Hall, Oxford University: "Zofingia and the Social Question," "The Concept of Christ's Descent to the Underworld in Church Literature until Origen."

David MacLachlan, Associate Professor of New Testament, Atlantic School of Theology: "The Original Form of the Lord's Prayer."

Amy Marga, Associate Professor of Systematic Theology, Luther Seminary: "The Stigmata of Francis of Assisi."

Arnold Neufeldt-Fast, Associate Professor of Theology, Tyndale Seminary: "Zofingia and the Social Question," "Paul's Missionary Activity according to Its Portrayal in the Acts of the Apostles."

Travis Niles, Postdoctoral Researcher and Assistant, Institute for New Testament Studies, University of Basel: "Zofingia and the Social Question."

Paul T. Nimmo, King's Chair of Systematic Theology, University of Aberdeen: "The Centurion at Capernaum."

Patricia L. Rich, Translator: "Preface."

Ross Wright, Rector, The Church of the Good Shepherd; adjunct professor, Randolph-Macon College: "The Tenth Christian Students' Conference in Aarau," "Paul's Missionary Activity according to Its Portrayal in the Acts of the Apostles," "The Concept of Christ's Descent to the Underworld in Church Literature until Origen."

List of Abbreviated Works

AFranc	Analecta Franciscana
BGl	*Beweis des Glaubens*
BSGR	*Bibliothek der Symbole und Glaubensregeln der alten Kirche*. Edited by A. Hahn. 3rd ed. Breslau, 1897
BSLK	*Bekenntnisschriften der evangelisch-lutherischen Kirche*. Edited by Deutschen evangelischen Kirchenausschluss. 10th ed. Göttingen, 1986
Bw. B.	K. Barth and R. Bultmann. *Briefwechsel, 1922–1966*. Edited by B. Jaspert. Karl Barth Gesamtausgabe, Part 5: Letters. Zurich, 1971
Bw. R.	K. Barth and M. Rade. *Ein Briefwechsel*. Edited by Chr. Schwöbel. Gütersloh, 1981
CD	K. Barth. *Church Dogmatics*. Translated by G. W. Bromiley et al. 4 vols. in 12 parts. London: T&T Clark, 1936–69. Translation of *KD*
CR	Corpus Reformatorum. Halle/Braunschweig/Berlin; Leipzig; Zurich, 1834–
CW	*Die Christliche Welt*. Marburg
DS	*Enchiridion symbolorum, definitionum et declarationum de rebus fidei er morum*. Edited by H. Denzinger and A. Schönmetzer. 35th ed. Rome, et al., 1973
EA	Erlangen Ausgabe. M. Luther. Sämtliche Werke. Erlangen, 1826–
EKG	*Evangelisches Kirchengesangbuch*. Various editions. 1853–
GCS	Die griechischen christlichen Schriftsteller der ersten drei Jahrhunderte. Berlin, 1897–
GERS	*Gesanguch für die evangelische-reformirte Kirche der deutschen Schweiz*. 1891–
GThW	Grundriss der theologischen Wissenschaft. Tübingen, 1893–
HBLS	*Historisch-biographisches Lexikon der Schweiz*. Neuenburg, 1921–34
HC	Hand-Commentar zum Neuen Testament. Freiburg, 1889–
JDTh	*Jahrbücher für deutsche Theologie*. Stuttgart, 1856–
JPTh	*Jahrbücher für protestantische Theologie*. Braunschweig, 1875–
KD	K. Barth. *Kirkliche Dogmatik*. 4 vols in 12 parts. Zollikon: Verlag der Evangelischen Buchhandlung; et al., 1932–67
KK	Kurzgefasster Kommentar zu den heiligen Schriften Alten und Neuen Testamentes. Munich, 1886–

KNT	Kommentar zum Neuen Testament. Leipzig, 1903–
LThK	*Lexikon für Theologie und Kirche.* 2nd ed. 1957–68
MPTh	*Monatsschrift für Pastoraltheologie zur Vertiefung des gesamten pfarramtlichen Wirkens.* Göttingen
PG	Patrologiae cursus completes. Series Graeca. Paris, 1857–
PhB	Philosophische Bibliothek. Leipzig, 1868–
RBMAS	Rerum Britanicarum medii aevi scriptores; or, Chronicles and Memorials of Great Britain and Ireland during the Middle Ages. London, 1858–
RE³	*Realencyklopäedie für protestantische Theologie und Kirche.* 3rd ed. Leipzig: Hinrichs, 1896–1913
RGG[1,2,3]	*Die Religion in Geschichte und Gegenwart.* 1st ed., 1909–13. 2nd ed., 1927–32. 3rd ed., 1957–62. Tübingen: Mohr Siebeck
RV	Religionsgeschichtle Volksbücher für die deutsche christliche Gegenwart. Halle/Tübingen, 1904–
SgV	Sammlung gemeinverständlicher Vorträge und Schriften aus dem Gebiet der Theologie und Religionsgeschichte. Tübingen, 1896–
SNT	Die Schriften des Neuen Testaments neu übersetzt und für die Gegenwart erklärt. Göttingen, 1905–
SPAW	*Sitzungsberichte der preussischen Akademie der Wissenshaften.* Berlin, 1882–
SQS	Sammlung ausgewählter kirchen- und dogmengeschichtlicher Quellenschriften. Tübingen, 1901–
SThZ	*Schweizerische theologische Zeitschrift.* Zurich.
TaS	Texts and Studies. Cambridge, 1891–
ThB	Theologische Bücherei. Munich. 1953–
TLZ	*Theologische Literaturzeitung*
ThStKr	*Theologische Studien und Kritiken*
WA	Weimarer Ausgabe. M. Luther. Werke. Kritische Gesamtausgabe. Weimar, 1883–
WA DB	WA Deutsche Bibel. New Testament, 1522. Old Testament, 1534
ZKG	*Zeitschrift für Kirchengeschichte*
ZKWL	*Zeitschrift für kirchliche Wissenschaft und kirchliches Leben*
ZNW	*Zeitschrift für die neutestamentliche Wissenschaft*
ZTK	*Zeitschrift für Theologie und Kirche*
ZWT	*Zeitschrift für wissenschaftliche Theologie*

The Character of the Religion of Ancient India
1905

*Karl Barth began his studies of theology at the University of Bern in the winter semes-
ter of 1904–5. During his first semester he took a course on "General Religious History.
Part I (Prof. D. Steck)," besides "Introduction to the Study of Theology" with his father,
Fritz Barth, as well as lectures and courses in Old and New Testament (Karl Marti,
Rudolf Steck, and Fritz Barth), Church History (Fritz Barth, Wilhelm Hadorn), and
Philosophy (Hermann Lüdemann). During the summer semester of 1905, he took the
second part of the course on General Religious History. Barth's minutes or notes are not
preserved. This religious history-missiology piece, for which we have no direct supporting documents or background, seems to have emerged in that context. It was probably
written during the winter holidays, soon after the end of the winter semester. It cannot
be determined whether it was given as a presentation during the second part of the
course in the summer semester, or whether we are dealing with—just as with the later
investigation of the Lord's Prayer—a work for the Academic Evangelical-Theological
Association [Akademischen evangelisch-theologischen Verein]. The remarks are mostly
based on Paul Wurm's* Handbuch der Religionsgeschichte *(Handbook of the History of Religion) (see n. 2).*

*The manuscript is one of the pieces collected in "Excerpts I," a Halbkaliko volume
[common book-binding cloth], in which we find also two texts by Barth himself, besides
various excerpts such as "from the NT writings," from Luther's works or from the
church books of Pratteln and Frenkendorf: his report on the religion of ancient India
and his investigation of the stigmata of Francis of Assisi (see the next chapter). Just
like his lecture notes, Barth had the various pieces, written in ink on double pages, later
bound as a book.*

The task in front of us today consists in getting clarity, in broad brushstrokes,
regarding the *character of the religion of ancient India.*

One has already called the land of Indus and Ganges the "classical land
of the history of religion,"[1] and rightly so: for we do not know any people in
whose character, way of thinking, and history has religion engrained itself
more deeply than in that of the inhabitants of the Indian subcontinent. Here,
religion is not a mere area of public life next to other areas; much rather, the latter is founded in all of its relationships on the former.[2] But let us not get ahead

---

1. This characterization is found in Karl Barth's lecture notes: "History of Religion. Prof. D[octor
Fritz] Barth. Prima–Ob. Prima. Freies Gymnasium Bern. October 1903–July 1904" (Karl Barth Archive,
Basel), 123.
2. Cf. P. Wurm, *Handbuch der Religionsgeschichte* [Handbook of the history of religion] (Calwer/
Stuttgart: Calwer Verlagsverein, 1904), 150–51.

1

of ourselves! During the period of which we will need to talk, the circumstances were still different, and only in the course of millennia, after a series of changes, did what we call the Hindu religion emerge.

Let us put ourselves mentally back into the time when the Aryans, or rather a group of Aryans, left their dwellings in the hill countries in Central Asia and took possession of the Indian subcontinent. By doing so, their historical role as "Indians"[3] (*Indier*) begins. Determinative for the unhistorical character of this people is the circumstance that the date of this very important event today can only be construed, while the Indian sources do not contain any temporal data.[4] These Aryan immigrants, with their hardly significant culture—they were mostly ranchers—also brought with them their own language and religion. The different dialects of the Dravida tribes were confronted by the language of the Aryan people; the demon worship of the natives was confronted by the polytheism of the foreigners. Here we observe the interesting process in which the language of the natives held its ground, while simultaneously their religion was almost completely absorbed into that of the immigrants.[5] Yet even the immigrants' religion was not preserved in purity: a change is assessed to have happened so that their religion would find its parallel in the transformation of the entire character of the Indian people at the time. If the conquerors had been a forceful nature-loving people of the mountains, their offspring would now, under the influence of the tropical climate and a favorable nature, be effortlessly satisfying all demands of life; but they become this frail, passive race that we know as today's Hindu [people]. And the same happened in the religious area: Under the impression of an outside world that presented itself to the individual in a thousand different ways in lavish complexity, the Aryans' polytheistic worship of nature became more and more adventurous and turned finally into that conspicuous firmament of gods without any order, from which Brahman pantheism would emerge by necessity.[6] As *Duhm* says: "The richness of the spirit generated that sultry abundance of religious figures, metaphysical speculations, and mystical aspirations, which caused admiration as well as pity among the more energetic Europeans."[7]

Today we need to speak about the period between Aryan immigration, on the one hand, and the explicit display of Brahmanism, on the other hand; yet a clear separation is actually impossible, given the blurriness of the whole development.

The sources for all examinations in this area are found in the literary collection of the four Vedas, which is the reason why the Indian religion of that time is also called the "Veda religion."

Veda (= knowledge) refers in India not only to the four collections of religious songs that are important to us here, but also to the ritual literature belonging to them, containing all sorts of "theological drivel," as Max Müller from

3. Cf. Wurm, *Handbuch*, 151, 153.
4. Wurm, *Handbuch*, 151.
5. Wurm, *Handbuch*, 155.
6. Wurm, *Handbuch*, 151–52, 153, 172, 178–79.
7. Barth quotes from (the dictations) of Bernhard Duhm's Basel lecture on "General History of Religion" (§23). With minor variation, the sentence can be found in the transcript, produced by Walther Huber in 1902, based on a handwritten duplicate of the lecture during the winter semester 1901–2 (Manuscript Collection of Basel University Library).

Oxford calls it.[8] Yet [pieces of] this ritual literature, just as the first beginnings of philosophical speculation to be found here, often originate in later times and are therefore not relevant to us.

The religious events of the oldest period are much rather found in the original Vedas, the Veda-Sanhita (in contrast to the Veda-Brahmana, etc.), which can be classified into four collections: three canonically valid ones that are said to be inspired: the Rig-Veda, Sama-Veda, and the Jadjur-Veda, and one additional one that is not canonical, the Atharva-Veda.[9]

Let us now briefly examine the most central religious traits of this Veda literature, in order to consider briefly the stance toward Christianity that they imply for their followers.

The Indians' oldest *teachings about the gods* are more complicated than that of any other people; one might say considerably more on this topic than is possible in the quarter of an hour here. The difficulty of this polytheism lies in the fact that it is actually not really polytheism, for every one of the gods is described in the songs of the Veda respectively as the highest and mightiest one, although the existence of the other ones, sharing in this same characteristic, is not denied, {a reality that can similarly be found, for example, in the view of God at the times of the book of Judges.}[10] The Vedas keep us completely in the dark about the competences and functions of the individual deities, as we know them, for example, from Greek mythology.[11] A further difficulty arises from the number of Indian gods. Usually, 33 of them are counted, yet one later source already counts 3,339, and modern Hinduism even knows 330,000,000 of them, next to an unlimited number of demons.[12] From there, the move to the Brahmanic universal deity [*All-Gottheit*] is hardly surprising![13] From the same consideration, we arrive at the conclusion that the Hindus' position regarding the gods of their religion cannot be a serious hindrance to the acceptance of Christianity: pantheism is closer to monotheism than polytheism.

More important than the teaching on the gods is the Indian *cult*, the religious order that forms a downright great power [*Grossmacht*] in public life. Surely the Vedas do not yet know anything of temples or images of gods: the worship service happens in any place, so that the importance of sacrifice increases even more, happening in manifold forms and requiring a whole army of priests.[14]

In the Vedas as well can be found a *cosmology* in a confusion similar to the doctrine of the gods. The most varied gods are called creators and rulers of the world. It is telling that the problems of the "How?" of the creation of the world are raised yet are left without an answer.[15]

However, the most interesting trait in the religion of the Vedas is undeniably to be found not in the religious but in the *social sphere*: I am referring to the caste

8. Cf. Wurm, *Handbuch*, 152; Friedrich Max Müller, *Das Aitareya Brâhmana*, in Müller's *Essays*, vol. 1, *Beiträge zur vergleichenden Religionswissenschaft* (Leipzig: Wilhelm Engelman, 1869), 105.
    9. Wurm, *Handbuch*, 152–53.
    10. In the margin we find a later comment by Barth himself (see below, "Die Stigmata," n. 7): "prrr! airesia." The brackets seem to have been added to the text to clarify to what the exclaim of dislike refers. Cf. further Wurm, *Handbuch*, 151, 153, 155.
    11. Wurm, *Handbuch*, 171–72.
    12. Wurm, *Handbuch*, 158–59.
    13. Wurm, *Handbuch*, 154, 169, 171–72, 178–79.
    14. Wurm, *Handbuch*, 150–51, 152, 172–74.
    15. Wurm, *Handbuch*, 174.

system, which certainly looked quite different at the time of the Vedas than it looks today. Here as well, we notice the move from the simple to the exorbitant, which is typically Indian. The Vedas only know four main castes: priests, warriors, farmers, and slaves; today there are hundreds of castes, whose members are not allowed to eat together or marry each other.[16]

Those differences between the castes do not necessarily coincide with differences in social rank; rather, the castes today consist of members of the same trade. They might be called "corporate associations with a religious foundation."[17] It can be easily perceived what sort of complication of public life is caused by this system! This is where an open conflict arises between the ancient Indian worldview and the Christian worldview. The actual religious aspect of the Vedas' religion, the service of Agni, Indra, or Waruna,[18] is of little importance compared to this practically almost irresolvable difference: the Christian religion says that we are all sinners and the same before God [cf. Rom. 3:22–23]; the Veda religion recognizes people of privilege and slaves. How can [people holding] these [different] positions get along with one another? It is well known that some missionary associations avoid the difficulty even today by keeping the differences in caste, for example, [by assigning different seats] in worship,[19] and in terms of quantity [of results], they supposedly run well with that, which is understandable: if this deeply engrained offense is removed, it becomes relatively easy for the Hindu to become a Christian. Yet may opportunism be the driving force in this case? Basically, this is the missionary method of the Jesuits, pursued by them in China in the sixteenth century, for example, in the famous system of accommodation![20] The way in which the Basel Mission positions itself against the caste system is more dignified by comparison, even if it is perhaps less opportunistic.[21] The fact that they have a hard time with that is plausible; even in Europe there would be annoyed faces, if not worse, if one were to touch the privileged church seats of the nobility and the dignitaries! A third approach—if one were allowed to make suggestions without knowledge of specific circumstances—would maybe consist in recognizing the castes but trying to transform them in a Christian sense into mere trade associations, thus

---

16. Cf. Wurm, *Handbuch*, 153, 158.

17. Wurm, *Handbuch*, 158.

18. Cf. Wurm, *Handbuch*, 160–69, 179.

19. The continuation of the subordinate clause (written by Barth at the bottom as a later insertion) was cut off when the "Excerpta" were bound. Going by the sparse remains at the top of the letters, the continuation likely was along the lines in the main body of the text (cf. J. Richter, *Die deutsche Mission in Südindien: Erzählungen und Schilderungen von einer Missions-Studienreise durch Ostindien* [Gütersloh: Bertelsmann, 1902], 11). Here Barth probably thinks mostly of the Leipzig Mission, whose work among the Tamils led to the "Leipzig Caste Argument," since it respected, by and large, the belonging to different castes (cf., e.g., Chr. E. Luthardt, "Graul, Karl," in *RE3* 9:72, lines 60–73, esp. line 47). A description of the conditions and the missionary praxis is given by Richter in *Mission in Südindien*, 11–13, 128–41; see also J. Richter, *Nordindische Missionsfahrten: Erzählungen und Schilderungen von einer Missions-Studienreise durch Ostindien* (Gütersloh: Bertelsmann, 1903), 279–94; and cf. C. Ihmels, "Kaste. II. Kastenfrage in der Mission," in *RGG3* 3: cols. 1163–64.

20. Cf. R. Grundemann, "Mission unter den Heiden: 1. Katholische," in *RE³* 13:116, lines 20–48.

21. Cf. Richter, *Mission in Südindien*, 18–19: "People from Basel have realized from the beginning that the caste is simply irreconcilable with the Christian religion; thus, it must not be tolerated in the Christian community under any circumstances; . . . with them, the demonic force of the castes truly is broken. I have personally come to know and experience in detail so many surprising and pleasant traits in this respect that I do no longer doubt the reality and solidity of this success and take great joy in this success, albeit it is bought with great sacrifices."

eliminating the class restrictions. The good about it would then be preserved, and the sting of it would be removed. Yet these are considerations from the academic lectern.

Notwithstanding the last point, if we were to be asked for an overall assessment of the Veda religion, we might mark it with a big question mark. The eternal problem of humanity runs like a red thread through the many things that are unclear, confused, and fantastic in these ancient Indian poems: What is truth? The Veda religion offered one solution, and we have considered some aspects of it; but we also realize that such a profound, speculative people did not want to stop there. Brahmanism, starting already in the later parts of the Veda religion, was a further attempt in this direction, as was the religion of the Buddha, which came to surpass all its predecessors in regard to the earnestness of its views.

Bern, March 20, 1905

The Stigmata of Francis of Assisi
1905

In the summer semester of 1905 (as in the winter semester of 1905–6), Karl Barth attended his father Fritz Barth's "Lessons in Church History." The essay on the "Stigmata of Francis of Assisi" was probably composed for this class. Unfortunately, no materials remain that might provide information about Barth's approach to the work, its occasion and context, or the reception that it found.

As the commentary indicates in detail, Barth based his presentation above all on P. Sabatier (see n. 1) and K. von Hase (see n. 50). He likely used the first edition of Hases's monograph, not the reprint in the Collected Works, as a particular observation can confirm: the misunderstanding in footnote 52 and 103 probably arises from the fact that in the first edition the citations from Bonaventure and Thomas of Celano appear right next to each other on page 144, while in the Collected Works they follow each other on sequential pages (105 and 106). For that matter, it must remain open whether Barth's otherwise unsubstantiated change to the source text, which in fact contradicts what might be anticipated, was a mistake made on account of the haste detectable in the detail described (to which also the dating of this piece at the end of the essay testifies) or should be considered a conscious correction.

The manuscript is the first of the bound pieces in Excerpts I (see page 1 above), where it bears the subtitle "Essay for the Church History Seminar, Summer Semester 1905."

Praised be You, my Lord,
through those who give pardon for Your Love,
and bear infirmity and tribulation.
Blessed are those who endure in peace,
for *by You, Most High, shall they be crowned!*[1]

Introduction

"In the year 1509 on the last day of May, four preaching monks were burned alive in great agony on the *Schwellimatten* in Bern due to the abominable, diabolic phenomena and other heresies that they *presumed to level* against other monks in order to assert their doctrine of the immaculate conception of Mary." With these

---

1. Regis J. Armstrong, J. A. Wayne Hellmann, and William J. Short, eds., *The Saint*, Francis of Assisi: Early Documents 1 (New York: New City Press, 1999), 114; cf. Francis of Assisi, *Canticum Fratris Solis*, in *Analekten zur Geschichte des Franciscus von Assisi*, edited by H. Boehmer, 3rd ed., SQS, 2nd Series, vol. 6 (Tübingen/Leipzig, 1904), p. 66, lines 14–18 (= 1961, reviewed by Fr. Wiegand, with a postscript by C. Andresen, SQS, NF, 4:44, lines 37–45, line 2); see also P. Sabatier, *Leben des heiligen Franz von Assisi*, German trans. M. Lisco, New Edition (Berlin, 1897), 224–25, 242–43.

words, Meyer, the Chronicler of Zurich, relates the tragic conclusion to the "Jetzer Case."[2] Whether the deceit [may] redound in that instance to the Dominicans or, as newer research demonstrates, to the tailor journeyman [Hans] Jetzer, the story is at any rate typical for the declining [Roman Catholic] Church of the Middle Ages. The effect of this and similar incidents, the mistrust sown thereby against the church and monastics in the widest circles, cannot be estimated highly enough as a prefatory event for the ensuing Reformation. The church and its institutions had outlived themselves. And if today we page through a compendium of Catholic miracle stories like Görres's *Christian Mysticism*,[3] we find ourselves astonished at the hodgepodge of monstrosities and lapses of taste, but then come to understand why, in the eyes of the cultured world, the cloister's tales of "miraculous" events eo ipso had been regarded as shams or stupidities for centuries. It truly did the church no honor that it did not take measures against such "history" writing, but rather supported it and made it fruitful for its purposes, to the extent that modern historical critics find it necessary to strike out 90 percent of it. In view of these facts, who will wonder that people fell prey to the opposite extreme and basically up to the present day deny historical factuality to all "miracles," that is, to everything that lies beyond our ordinary world of appearances? It may be a sign of the times that people in our day, including those in the circle of modern historical theology, are slowly, but quite clearly, beginning to abandon this viewpoint. They do so not despite, but precisely in concert with, the findings of natural science. Today more than ever it dawns on us:

> There are more things in heaven and earth, . . .
> Than are dreamt of in our philosophy.[4]

Today we can no longer consider a "miracle" heavy-handedly as an absolute breach of the laws of nature, because we do not believe at all in *absolute* natural laws, as it was still regarded in the old worldview. This change in perspective may belong to the celebrated "transvaluation of all values" of the present age,[5] but the fact itself that we have overcome the earlier aversion to "miracles" of previous ages has not changed. We must thus consider and regard the historical material of bygone times from this perspective. It hardly needs to be said that we, especially when dealing with the Middle Ages, must, as previously, apply great caution to carve out the facts from the lavishly proliferating phantasies of the Cloister. Only the criterion of our criticism has changed from what it was fifty or a hundred years ago. None other than Adolf von Harnack attests to us: "The habit of condemning a narrative, or of ascribing it to a later age, only because it includes stories of miracles, is a piece of prejudice."[6]

---

2. See R. Steck, "Der Berner Jetzerprozess in neuer Beleuchtung nebst Mitteilungen aus den noch ungedruckten Akten," in *SThZ* 18 (1901): 13–29, 65–91, 129–51, 193–210, esp. 13.

3. J. Görres, *Die christliche Mystik*, vol. 1 (Regensburg/Landshut, 1836); vol. 2 (Regensburg, 1837); vol. 3 (Regensburg, 1840); vol. 4, parts 1 and 2 (Regensburg, 1842).

4. W. Shakespeare, *Hamlet, Prince of Denmark*, 1.5.

5. See the title of F. Nietzsche's posthumous studies and fragments first published in 1901: *The Will to Power: Attempt at a Transvaluation of All Values*, Nietzsche's Works 15, ed. P. Gast and E. and A. H. Horneffer (Leipzig, 1901). This formulation goes back to Nietzsche himself; see F. Nietzsche, *Posthumous Fragments: Autumn 1885 to Autumn 1887*, Nietzsche's Works, Critical Edition, ed. G. Colli and M. Montinari, part 8, vol. 1 (Berlin: de Gruyter, 1974), p. 107, lines 9–11.

6. See A. Harnack, *What Is Christianity?* (Philadelphia: Augsburg Fortress, 1987), 26.

Our approach to our topic today, "The Stigmata of Francis of Assisi," shall also be impartial and unbiased by the foundations of "rationality" and "knowledge," which we, in the end, must always regard as fragmentary. Maybe it is possible here, too, despite the manifold difficulties, to find a satisfactory solution in line with the remarks above.[7]

To this end, we will need to describe *"The Events according to the Sources"* in Part One, to present our *"Histor[ical] Cri[tical] Results"* in Part Two, and to add a concluding *"General Evaluation"* in Part Three.

Quad felix, faustum fortunatumque sit![8]

I. The Events according to the Sources

1. The Sources

By way of introduction to the matter, we start off by giving an abbreviated overview of the source materials that come under consideration.

a. From the beginning it may be regarded as a suspicious circumstance and at any rate a bad omen for our research that the oldest report we possess about the stigmata of Francis of Assisi flows from the pen of the Judas of his circle of disciples, as he has already been named,[9] that is, *Elias of Cortona*, the man, who, in the company of the *fratres minores* already acted during the lifetime of the founder of the order against his intentions and in the interests of the Roman Curia, which leveled all distinctions in favor of uniformity.[10] At issue here is a letter that he sent immediately after the death of Francis in 1226 to *Gregorius*, minister of the [Franciscan] Order in France.[11] We shall arrive at the conclusion, when treating its content later, that the apparent suspicion actually is a reason for its credibility.

b. More directly, a fragment of parchment interests us that *Francis himself* already handed over in 1224,[12] shortly after the stigmatization, to *Brother Leo*, one of his most true and resolute followers, who figured among the Three Companions [*Tres Socii*].[13] It contains the *Laudes Dei*, a doxology to the triune God in his different attributes and potencies, composed under the immediate impression of that event. Then, on the backside of the page and also in Francis's hand, follows the well-known Mosaic benediction from Numbers 6:24–26 directed to *Leo*, along with a later *annotation in red ink* below by the latter, which contains a short report about the occasion for the *Laudes*.

---

7. Barth later marked the last two sentences with red pen in the margins, writing next to it in red pen as well: "Prrr!"

8. "Let this be blessed, favorable, and fortunate." On this frequently used formula, which appears in varying forms, see M. Tullius Cicero, *De divinatione* 1.45, 102.

9. Presumably, Barth is thinking about Karl von Hase's description of Elias as "Francis's most beloved and yet his false disciple," in *Kirchengeschichte auf der Grundlage akademischer Vorlesungen*, part 2, *Germanische Kirche*, Mittlere Kirchengeschichte (Leipzig: Breitkopf & Härtel, 1890), 391.

10. See von Hase, *Kirchengeschichte*; Sabatier, *Franz von Assisi*, 149.

11. *Frater Elias ad Gregorium ministrum Franciae a. 1226 Oct. 4*; in Boehmer, *Analekten*, p. 90, lines 3–5; p. 92, line 23 (= 3rd ed., 1961, p. 61, lines 20–63, line 17).

12. *Cartula fratri Leonis data a. 1224*; in Boehmer, *Analekten*, p. 69, lines 9–p. 70, line 6 (= 3rd ed., 1961, p. 47, lines 2–27).

13. That is, the three monastic brothers, Leo, Rufinus, and Angelus, from whom the *Legenda trium sociorum* originates.

c. We find the third report about the matter in the *Legenda prima de Thomas de Celano*, circa 1230.[14] Sabatier has the impression that it is a frequently told, canonical story and thus judges it to be of little historical value.[15] It does not seem absolutely necessary to me to draw that conclusion, and less so since it stems from a period four years after Francis's death, during which years the tradition in its essential characteristics could very well have been kept unadulterated.

d. We find the next preserved source in Gregory IX's bull *Confessor Domini* from March 31, 1237, directed against certain circles, probably the Dominicans in particular, who were skeptical about the quality of the miracle of the stigmata.[16]

e. In 1246, the *Legenda trium sociorum*[17] was completed[18] in the Greccio Cloister in the Valley of Rieti, a work that, as a report of eyewitnesses, should have been of primary significance if Paul Sabatier had not, on weighty grounds, contested the authenticity precisely of the section that deals with the stigmatization.[19] Our task here cannot be to grapple with this problem of specialists, but we vouchsafe our decision to give only secondary consideration to the so-called Three Companions and their report to the major biographer of Francis.

f. The next oldest witness for the stigmata is once more an official document: the *Bulle Benigna operatio Alexander IV* of October 29, 1255.[20] It follows the same trend as the document of Gregory IX mentioned above without, however, bringing new content to the fore.

g. In 1260, we find a mention of the stigmata in the *Historia major of Matthew of Paris*.[21] It stands out for its temporal shifting of the events as well as by multiple bizarre additions, yet without warranting deeper consideration.

h. Naturally, the story does not go unmentioned in the *Legend of Saint Bonaventure*,[22] the official ecclesiastical biography of Francis, which was completed in 1263.[23] It essentially repeats the account of Thomas of Celano, though with the addition of new details that admittedly do not seem credible.[24]

i. In the year 1264, a certain Simon, Count of Tuscia, founded a special *Church of the Stigmata* on Mount La Verna, the founding charter of which is worthy of notice due to its likewise shifted date.[25]

k. Moreover, we shall consider the English monastic chronicler *Thomas of Eccleston*, who claims a direct tradition from Brother Leo for his report.[26]

14. Reprinted in the *Acta Sanctorum Octobris: Collecta, Digesta, Commentatriisque & Observationibus illustrata a C. Suyskeno, C. Byeo, J. Bueo, J. Ghesquiero*, vol. 2, *Quo dies tertius, & quartus continetur* (Antwerp, 1768), 683–723.

15. See Sabatier, *Franz von Assisi*, 260.

16. *Magnum Bullarium Romanum, a beato Leone Magno usque ad S. D. N. Benedictum XIV* (Luxemburg, 1742), 1:79.

17. Reprinted in *Acta Sanctorum Octobris* (1768), 2:723–42.

18. See Sabatier, *Franz von Assisi*, xxxv.

19. See Sabatier, *Franz von Assisi*, xxxvi–xxxvii.

20. *Magnum Bullarium Romanum* (1742), 1:109–10.

21. Matthaeus Parisiensis, *Chronica majora*, ed. H. R. Luard, RBMAS 57.3 (London, 1876).

22. Reprinted in *Acta Sanctorum Octobris* (1768), 2:742–98.

23. See Sabatier, *Franz von Assisi*, lxvii, 260.

24. See Sabatier, *Franz von Assisi*, lxvii, 260.

25. Reported in the introduction to *Speculum perfectionis seu s. Francisci Assisiensis Legenda Antiquissima*, ed. P. Sabatier, Collection of Studies and Documents on the History of the Religions and Literature of the Middle Ages 1 (Paris, 1898), ccxiii.

26. Thomas de Eccleston, *Liber de Adventu Fratrum Minorum in Angliam*, in AFranc 1 (Quaracchi Friers, 1885), 215–56.

l. Finally, there is a rich selection of legends about the stigmata and its won-drous effects in *Actus B. Francisci et Sociorum (Fioretti)*.[27]

Our next task will now be to put the material, as contained in the indicated sources, next to one another in order to take note of their developments.

2. Presentation of the Reports

Our reports may be divided into *two primary groups*: reports about the *act of stigmatization* and those about the *nature and quality of the stigmata* before and after the death of Francis. A third group might perhaps encompass those *legend-ary works* of Franciscan literature that bear on the stigmata of the founder of the [Franciscan] Order.

a. Reports about the Act of Stigmatization

We will present these in chronological order in the same manner as we previ-ously presented the sources, primarily because, by doing so, we obtain the best view of the development that they underwent over the course of time.

We thus begin again with the letter of *Elias of Cortona* to Gregory, the leader of the French branch of the Order. As previously mentioned, it was composed immediately after the death of Francis and, in its *first* and *third* parts, contains the report of these facts to distant brothers, combined with well-formulated words of comfort and encouragement, continually interspersed with citations and allusions from the Old and New Testaments. The *second* part contains a report about the miracle of the stigmata, words of *good tidings* for the faithful Minorites, which apparently stand in conscious contradiction to the sorrowful news [of his death] preceding it. Triumphantly, it begins: "And now, after tell-ing you these things, *I announce to you a great joy* and the news of a miracle. Such *a sign* that *has never been heard of from the dawn of time except in the Son of God, who is Christ the Lord*. Not long before his death, our brother and father appeared crucified, *bearing in his body* five wounds, which are truly *the marks of Christ*."[28] Then an extensive description of the marks of the wounds follows, which we will come to speak about again below. The simple phrase may be noted provi-sionally: "apparuit crucifixus quinque plagas portans" [He appeared crucified, bearing the five wounds].

Let us next hear the report in *The Autographs on the "Cartula" of St. Francis of Assisi* with the *Laudes Dei*:

> Two years before his death, the blessed Francis spent forty days on Mount La Verna from the Feast of the Assumption of the holy Virgin Mary until the September Feast of Saint Michael, in honor of the Blessed Virgin Mary, the Mother of God, and the blessed Michael the Archangel. And the Lord's hand

27. P. Sabatier, ed., *Actus beati Francisci et Sociorum ejus*, Collection of Studies and Documents on the Religious History and Literature of the Middle Ages 4 (Paris: Fischbacher, 1902); see also P. Sabatier, ed., *Floretum S. Francisci Assisiensis: Liber aureus, qui italice dicitur I Fioretti di San Francesco* (1902; Paris: Kessinger Reprints, 2010).

28. Regis J. Armstrong, J. A. Wayne Hellmann, and William J. Short, eds., *The Founder*, Francis of Assisi: Early Documents 2 (New York: New City Press, 2000), 490; Boehmer, *Analekten*, p. 91, lines 9–13 (= 3rd ed., 1961, p. 62, lines 18–21).

was upon him. After the vision and message of the seraph, and the impression of Christ's stigmata upon his body, he composed these praises written on the other side of this page and wrote them in his own hand, thanking God for the kindness bestowed on him.[29]

Here we already receive a determinate date for our event: Francis carries out a *fasting exercise* on *Mount La Verna* in the autumn *two years before his death*, thus in *1224*. A *seraph* appears to him, addressing him and impressing the *stigmata* on him. That becomes the occasion for the *Laudes Dei* found on the other side of the page.

We learn even more detailed information in the *Legenda Prima of Thomas of Celano* (1230):

> While he was staying in that hermitage called La Verna, after the place where it is located, two years prior to the time that he returned his soul to heaven, he saw *in the vision of God* a man, *having six wings like a seraph, standing over* him, *arms extended and feet joined*, affixed to a cross. *Two of his wings* were raised up, *two were stretched out over his head as if for flight*, and *two covered his whole body*. When the blessed servant of the most High saw these things, he was filled with the greatest awe, but could not decide what this vision meant for him. Moreover, he greatly rejoiced and was much delighted by the kind and gracious look that he saw the seraph gave him. The seraph's beauty was beyond comprehension, but the fact that the seraph was fixed to the cross and the bitter suffering of that passion thoroughly frightened him. Consequently, he got up both sad and happy as joy and sorrow took their turns in his heart; concerned over the matter, he kept thinking about what this vision could mean, and his *spirit was anxious* to discern a sensible meaning from the vision. While he was unable to perceive anything clearly understandable from the vision, its newness very much pressed upon his heart. Signs of the nails began to appear on his hands and feet, just as he had seen them a little while earlier on the crucified man hovering over him.[30]

Francis made a *stay* on *Mount La Verna two years before his death*, where a *crucified seraph*, with *six wings* that were extended in different ways, appeared to him. He remained *clueless* about the meaning of the vision until the *marks of the wounds* on the seraph were carried over to his own body. Here, too, a description of the same follows next.

The *Bull of Gregory IX* (*Confessor Domini*) *1237* reports the following: "This saint, while he was still following the course of this life and after he had blessedly consummated it, was divinely marked by the form of the stigmata on his hands, side, and feet."[31] Corresponding to the official character of the papal document, it merely makes a sheer *recital of the fact* without ornamental additions. In *1255*, the credibility of the stigmata is newly confirmed in the *Bull of*

---

29. Armstrong, Hellmann, and Short, *The Saint*, 108; Boehmer, *Analekten*, p. 69, lines 24–32 (= 3rd ed., 1961, p. 47, lines 15–21).

30. Armstrong, Hellmann, and Short, *The Saint*, 263–64; Thomas of Celano, *St. Francis of Assisi*, 2.1, 94; in *Acta Sanctorum Octobris* (1768), 2:709AB; Boehmer, *Analekten*, p. 92, line 26–p. 93, line 14 (= 3rd ed., 1961, p. 63, lines 19–35).

31. *Magnum Bullarium Romanum* (1742), 1:79, §1; translated by Christian Mouchel, *Les femmes de douleur: Maladie et sainteté dans l'Italie de la Contre-*Réforme (Besançon: Presses universitaire de Franche-Comté, 2007), 76.

Alexander IV (*Benigna operatio*), where we read about "those gratifying insignia of the Lord's passion, which should be frequently recalled and greatly admired, and which the hand of divine operation impressed on the body of this saint while he was still alive."[32] In somewhat other words, [these are] almost the same remarks as Gregory IX's.

From the *Historia Major of Matthew of Paris* (1260), for which I do not have the text before me, we may highlight that, according to Sabatier, it puts the act of the stigmatization fourteen days before Francis' death.[33]

Ever more entering into the half darkness of the tradition tinted by the church, we encounter the *Legend of Saint Bonaventure*. There we hear: "Christ looked upon him under the appearance of the seraph, . . . so that the friend of Christ might learn in advance that he was to be totally transformed into the likeness of Christ crucified, not by the martyrdom of his flesh, but by the enkindling of his soul."[34] And furthermore, the report is about the event itself: "One of those days, withdrawn in this way, while he was praying and all of his fervor was totally absorbed in God, Christ Jesus appeared to him as fastened to a cross. His *soul melted* at the sight, and the memory of Christ's passion was so impressed on the innermost recesses of his heart. From that hour, whenever Christ's crucifixion came to his mind, he could scarcely contain his tears and sighs, as he later revealed to his companions when he was approaching the end of his life."[35]

What is characteristic about his description is that in it *Christ himself*, under the form of a *seraph*, appears to Francis to bring the *stigmata* to him, which, by the way, is only *implied* and not told. We also gather something from this, apparently from Francis's own mouth, about the form of address during the appearance: "that the one who had appeared to him had told him some things that he would never disclose to any person as long as he lived. We should believe, then, that the utterances of that sacred seraph marvelously appearing to him on the cross were so *secret* that *people are not permitted to speak of them*."[36]

The inscription on the Church of the Stigmata on Mount La Verna, which dates from 1264, states: "After the Feast of the Assumption of the glorious Virgin Mary, Count Simone, son of the illustrious Guido, by the Grace of God, Count Palatine of Tuscany, founded this oratory in honor of the Blessed Francis, to whom in this same place the seraph appeared in the year of our Lord 1225, within the octave of the birth of the Virgin, and impressed upon his body and signed him with the stigmata of Jesus Christ by the grace of the Holy Spirit."[37]

Thomas of Eccleston knows the following about the appearance: "that the apparition of the seraphim took place whilst St. Francis was in ecstasy, and that the evidence was greater even than that written in the Saint's life. Moreover, many things, said Brother Leo, had been revealed to St. Francis of which he had never

---

32. Armstrong, Hellmann, and Short, *The Founder*, 780; *Magnum Bullarium Romanum* (1742), 1:109, §3.

33. See Sabatier, *Franz von Assisi*, 260.

34. Armstrong, Hellmann, and Short, *The Founder*, 632; *Legend of Saint Bonaventura* 13.192; in *Acta Sanctorum Octobris* (1768), 2:777E.

35. Armstrong, Hellmann, and Short, *The Founder*, 534; *Bonaventura* 1.12; in *Acta Sanctorum Octobris* (1768), 2:745AB.

36. Armstrong, Hellmann, and Short, *The Founder*, 633; *Bonaventura* 13.194; in *Acta Sanctorum Octobris* (1768), 2:778A.

37. Sabatier, *Speculum perfectionis*, 213; ET by Ella Noyes in *The Casentino and Its Story* (London: E. P. Dutton, 1905), 168.

spoken to any living man; but this the Saint did tell Brother Ruffino, his companion, that when he saw the angel from afar, he was exceedingly terrified, and that the angel had treated him stiffly. And the angel said that the Order should endure until the end of the world. . . ."[38] He promises him still more of the same for the future of his Order, then the report closes with the indication of its source: "These things were written down by Brother Warin of Sedenfeld from the lips of Brother Leo."[39] Due to this remark, one might be inclined to number this piece among the sources of the first rank, and it is not out of the question that a genuine kernel goes back to Leo. Yet the entirely *reflective nature* of the piece and very particularly the *panegyric to the Order* at the conclusion indicates, at any rate, a *later composition*, and therefore we have mentioned it here.

It now may also be appropriate to let the *plagiarist* in the *Tres Socii* be heard, since he probably was not temporally distant from the sources just cited. In this piece, excluded by Sabatier, we read: "While he was still alive in the flesh, the Lord adorned him with a wonderful prerogative of a unique privilege, wishing to show the whole world the fervor of love and the incessant memory of the passion of Christ, which he carried in his heart." The *appearance* is described in the following way: "Within its six wings there was the form of a very beautiful, crucified man, whose hands and feet were extended after the manner of a cross, and whose features were clearly those of the Lord Jesus."[40] Thus a *crucified human*, arms and legs *spread out as on a cross*, who resembles Christ, for so we likely have to understand the "features of the Lord Jesus"! In chapter 99 of the *Speculum perfectionis*, we find this interesting note: "Likewise, at the time he received on his body the stigmata of the Lord on the holy mountain of La Verna, he suffered so many temptations and afflictions from the devil that he was unable to appear his former joyful self."[41]

If we now glance at the notes of the *Actus B. Francisci*, we must, of course, be aware that we are strolling on grounds where the question of reliability more than ever can only be answered according to its probability, for here possible and impossible, original or naive traits from life, and baroque legends stand closely together. The best example is precisely *Chapter IX*, which is important for us here. We hear how Francis and his [Franciscan] brothers *Leo*, *Masseo*, and *Angelus* set out for Mount La Verna, where "our sisters, the birds"[42] show him a place, where they set up camp, and where Francis now wants to make a *forty-day exercise of penance and fasting* in honor of Saint Michael. Just once during the week Leo is allowed to provision him with bread and water. Francis concentrates his entire soul on his resolution: "Sometimes he was in such an ecstasy of spirit and so absorbed in God that he was not able to speak throughout the day or night."[43] The curious disciple, however, cannot help but eavesdrop on the master in his

38. Thomas of Eccleston, *The Chronicle of Thomas of Eccleston: "De Adventu Fratrum Minorum in Angliam,"* trans. Father Cuthbert (London: Sands, 1909), 95; *Collatio* XIII (alias XII), in Thomas of Eccleston, *The Chronicle*, 245.

39. *Collatio* XIII (alias XII), in Thomas of Eccleston, *The Chronicle*, 245.

40. Armstrong, Hellmann, and Short, *The Founder*, 108; see Leo, Rufinus, and Angelus, *Legenda trium sociorum* 5.69; in *Acta Sanctorum Octobris* (1768), 2:741D; see Sabatier, *Franz von Assisi*, xxxvi–xxxvii, 259.

41. Regis J. Armstrong, J. A. Wayne Hellmann, and William J. Short, eds., *The Prophet*, Francis of Assisi: Early Documents 3 (New York: New City Press, 2001), 346; Sabatier, *Speculum perfectionis* 99; in Armstrong, Hellmann, and Short, *The Prophet*, p. 194, line 22–p. 195, line 1.

42. *Actus* 9.26; in Armstrong, Hellmann, and Short, *The Prophet*, 34.

43. Armstrong, Hellmann, and Short, *The Prophet*, 454; 34 for *Actus* 9.

devotion, encountering him several times in ardent prayer no longer standing, but *floating* up into the clouds. Another time, he hears him speaking with someone and intervenes with the naive shout that Francis is a great saint too. The latter reprimands Leo sharply, yet at his insistence telling him about his conversation with God, who appeared to him as flames of fire. Finally, he warns him against similar interventions, closing with the words: "For in a few days on this mountain, God will perform an astonishing miracle, which the whole world will admire. For he will do something new, which he has never done before to any creature in this world."[44] Then Leo leaves him and the report goes on: "During that very same forty days and on that same mountain around the feast of the Exaltation of the Holy Cross, Christ appeared under the form of a winged seraph as though crucified and impressed both the nails and the stigmata on the hands and feet and side of Saint Francis, just as it says in his *Legend*."[45] The appearance had produced such luminosity that mountain and valley reflected them, to which the shepherds tarrying nearby were witnesses. "Why these sacred stigmata had been impressed on Saint Francis has not become entirely clear. But as Francis himself said to his companions, this great mystery is being put off for the future."[46] Then follows a quasi-genealogy of the *transmission of the sources*, which does not exactly make the story, meaning its details, more credible in our eyes. The writer indeed ascribes his facts to *Hugolino*, who got them from *James of Massa*, who got them from Brother *Leo*. It cannot be made plausible to us that a report of around nine printed pages could be kept unadulterated under such circumstances, even if it did not appear in the *Fioretti*. Still, a few of the details remain valuable to us, above all the fact that Francis already found himself in a state of extraordinary *ecstasy* for some time before the stigmatization.

We thereby come to the end of the reports about the act of stigmatization on Mount La Verna. Later we will carry out a comparison and critique of them in a larger context. But next we need to turn our attention to the different *descriptions of the stigmata themselves*, which may perhaps claim our attention even more acutely than the preceding reports.

b. Reports about the Stigmata

The first depiction of the stigmata we find already in the frequently mentioned letter of *Elias of Cortona*. It gives us valuable information, not only about the stigmata, but also about Francis's general *bodily condition*:

> His hands and feet had, as it were, the openings of the nails and were pierced front and back, revealing the scars and showing the nails' blackness. His side, moreover, seemed opened by a lance and often *emitted* blood.
>
> As long as his spirit lived in the body, *there was no beauty in him for his appearance was that of a man despised.* No part of his body was without great suffering. By reason of the contraction of his sinews, his limbs were stiff, much like those of a dead man. But after his death, his appearance was *one of great beauty*, gleaming with a dazzling white brightness and giving joy to all who looked upon him. His limbs, which had been rigid, became marvelously

44. Armstrong, Hellmann, and Short, *The Prophet*, 457; 38 for *Actus* 9.67.
45. Armstrong, Hellmann, and Short, *The Prophet*, 457; 39 for *Actus* 9.68.
46. Armstrong, Hellmann, and Short, *The Prophet*, 458; 39 for *Actus* 9.70.

soft and pliable, so that they would be turned this way and that, like those of a young child.[47]

The matter is fairly clear: his *hands* and *feet* showed the *stab wounds* on both sides, with the *black* left behind by the nails, and on his side a bleeding *lance wound* was also visible.

The description of Thomas of Celano is much more extensive:

> His hands and feet seemed to be pierced through the middle by nails, with the heads of the nails appearing on the inner part of his hands and on the upper part of his feet, and their points protruding on opposite sides. Those marks on the inside of his hands were round, but rather oblong on the outside; and small pieces of flesh were visible like the points of nails, bent over and flattened, extending beyond the flesh around them. On his feet, the marks of nails were stamped in the same way and raised above the surrounding flesh. His right side was marked with an oblong scar, as if pierced with a lance, and this often dripped blood, so that his tunic and undergarments were frequently stained with his holy blood.
>
> Sadly, only a few merited seeing the sacred wound in his side during the life of the crucified servant of the crucified Lord. Elias was fortunate and did merit somehow to see the wound in his side. For one time, when the same brother Rufino put his hand onto the holy man's chest to rub him, his hand slipped, as often happens, and it chanced that he touched the precious scar in his right side. As soon as he had touched it, the holy one of God felt great pain and pushed Rufino's hand away, crying out for the Lord to spare him. He hid those marks carefully from strangers, and concealed them cautiously from people close to him, so that even the brothers at his side and his most devoted followers for a long time did not know about them.[48]

In this report, our eyes fall immediately on (1) the strong emphasis on the peculiar form of the *wounds to hand and foot*. They really are not wounds at all, but a kind of *outgrowth* of the inner and outer hand and surface of the foot, respectively, in the form of *nails*, which are *twisted* at their tips. (2) The care with which the saint tried to *hide* the stigmata, even from his trusted companions.

The second papal *bull of confirmation* by *Alexander IV*, who, as Cardinal Hugolin, in his day had been an eyewitness in the retinue of Gregory IX, explains:

> Eyes looking closely saw, and touching fingers became most sure, that in his hands and feet a truly formed likeness of nails grew out of the substance of his own flesh or was added from some newly created material. While he was still living, the Saint zealously hid these from the eyes of men whose praise he shunned. After he had died, a wound in his side, which was not inflicted or made by man, was clearly seen in his body. . . . It could not be hidden from certain brothers who were his close companions, because it exuded fluid.[49]

47. Armstrong, Hellmann, and Short, *The Founder*, 490; Boehmer, *Analekten*, p. 91, lines 14–25 (= 3rd ed., 1961, p. 62, lines 22–30).

48. Armstrong, Hellmann, and Short, *The Saint*, 264–65; Thomas of Celano, *St. Francis of Assisi* 2.95; in *Acta Sanctorum Octobris* (1768), 2:709BC; Boehmer, *Analekten*, p. 93, lines 14–p. 94, line 6 (= 3rd ed., 1961, p. 63, line 35–p. 64, line 16).

49. Armstrong, Hellmann, and Short, *The Founder*, 780; *Magnum Bullarium Romanum* (1742), 1:109, §3; *Benigna operatio of Alexander IV* (1255).

Here as well we find an emphasis on both named points: nail-like *outgrowths* that Francis carefully *hides* and that are found after his *death*.

Matthew of Paris writes about the *side wound*: "His right side also was laid open and sprinkled with blood, so that the secret recesses of his heart were plainly visible";[50] and later, "After his death no marks of the wounds appeared either in his side, hands, or feet."[51] Both are highly fantastical details, which can hardly be taken seriously. Nevertheless, we will encounter the first of them again later.

In the *Legend of Saint Bonaventure*, we read: "People considered it a great gift to be allowed to kiss or even to see the sacred marks of Jesus Christ which Saint Francis bore in his own body."[52]

"He could not prevent at least some from seeing the stigmata in his hands and feet; . . . a number of the brothers . . . confirmed under oath . . . that this was so and that they had seen it."[53] "[He] covered with his left hand the wound in his right side, lest it be seen."[54] And as a specific confirmation of the truth of his statements, he goes on: "One of them, a knight who was educated and prudent, Jerome by name, a distinguished and famous man, had doubts about these sacred signs and was unbelieving like Thomas. Fervently and boldly, in the presence of the brothers and the citizens, he did not hesitate to move the nails and to touch with his hands the saint's hands, feet, and side. While he was examining with his hands these authentic signs of Christ's wounds, he completely healed the wound of doubt in his own heart and the hearts of others."[55]

The *nail form* of the stigmata is highlighted most expressly by the *plagiarist of the Three Companions*: "They saw in his hands and feet, not just the holes of the nails, but the nails themselves formed by his own flesh, taking shape from it, and showing the dark color of iron."[56] And in agreement with all the other reports, he says about the stigmata: "Until his death, the man of God, unwilling to divulge God's sacrament, concealed it to the best of his ability, although he was unable to cover it completely since it became known to at least his intimate companions."[57]

---

50. M. Parisiensis, *Chronica majora*, 134–35; *Roger of Wendover's Flowers of History: Comprising the History of England from the Descent of the Saxons to A.D. 1235 / Formerly Ascribed to Matthew Paris*, trans. J. A. Giles (London: Henry G. Bohn), 496; Barth is probably citing him, according to K. von Hase, *Franz von Assisi: Ein Heiligenbild* (Leipzig: Breitkopf & Härtel, 1856), 168 n. 42; reprinted in K. von Hase, *Gesammelte Werke*, vol. 5, *Heilige und Propheten* (Leipzig: Breitkopf & Härtel, 1892), 1–143, 121 n. 42.

51. *Roger of Wendover's Flowers of History*, 496; M. Parisiensis, *Chronica majora*, 135; K. von Hase, *Gesammelte Werke*, 5:185 n. 65; or 132 n. 65.

52. Armstrong, Hellmann, and Short, *The Saint*, 281; rather see Thomas von Celano, *St. Francis of Assisi* 2.4, p. 113; in *Acta Sanctorum Octobris* (1768), 2:715A (where it actually reads: "non solum ad osculandum [trans. note: *deosculandum*?], et [forte sed] ad videndum"; see. K. von Hase, *Gesammelte Werke*, 5:144 n. 3; or 105 n. 3).

53. Armstrong, Hellmann, and Short, *The Founder*, 636; Bonaventura 13.200; in *Acta Sanctorum Octobris* (1768), 2:778DE [trans. note: Barth seems to be citing a note in K. von Hase, *Gesammelte Werke*, 5:144, rather than the original edition].

54. Armstrong, Hellmann, and Short, *The Founder*, 715; see Bonaventura 14.208; in *Acta Sanctorum Octobris* (1768), 2:780E.

55. Armstrong, Hellmann, and Short, *The Founder*, 490, 646–47; Bonaventura 15.218; in *Acta Sanctorum Octobris* (1768), 2:782D.

56. Armstrong, Hellmann, and Short, *The Founder*, 108; Leo, Rufinus, and Angelus, *Legenda trium sociorum* 5.70; in *Acta Sanctorum Octobris* (1768), 2:741E.

57. Armstrong, Hellmann, and Short, *The Founder*, 108; Leo, Rufinus, and Angelus, *Legenda trium sociorum* 5.69; in *Acta Sanctorum Octobris* (1768), 2:741E.

The *Actus B. Francisci* speak at special length about this careful concealment of the stigmata. We read there in Chapter 34:

> Our blessed Father Francis so diligently concealed from the eyes of all those most holy wounds that Christ, the Son of God, had miraculously impressed in his hands and feet and side that, while the saint was living, hardly anyone was able to see them plainly. From that time onward, he went about with his feet covered, and only the tips of his fingers were visible to his companions, for he hid his hands in his sleeves, remembering what was said to the holy Tobias by the angel: *It is good to keep the secret of a king.* While he was still living, Saint Francis especially hid the wound in his side at all times so that, except for Brother Rufino, who managed to see it by a pious strategy, no one else was able to see it. By threefold evidence Brother Rufino assured himself and others about the most holy wound on the right side.[58]

Reports follow about how Rufinus happened to see the side wound on three occasions. The accounting of one of these episodes agrees internally with that of the already cited mention in *Th. v. Celano*. Chapter 39 of the *Actus* provides yet an additional supplement: "Saint Francis allowed only Brother Leo to touch his stigmata, while Leo was changing the bandages that he applied between those marvelous nails and the rest of the flesh in order to hold the blood and ease the pain."[59] On certain days, Francis admittedly rejected medical treatment, so that "on the day of the crucifixion, truly crucified by the pains of the cross, he might hang with Christ."[60]

The *actual documentary sources* for the stigmatization and the stigmata are thus *exhausted*. As already mentioned, some *legendary additions from later times* might be adduced, which are interesting to the extent that they shed light on the *assessment* and evaluation of the "miracle" by *contemporaries*. Yet *historically*, they remain entirely without merit and thus may conveniently be left *out of consideration* for our purposes.

We therefore now turn immediately to the task of subjecting the source material we have just gone through to a thorough appraisal.

3. Comparison and Critique

In the introduction we have already discussed the difficulty of being completely dependent, for a historical investigation, on monastic or ecclesial sources. This difficulty does sometimes occur, and it certainly must catch our attention in the case of the reports on the stigmata of Saint Francis. *Tholuck* says this about these reports: "To a large extent, we miss the character of sobriety in the biographies of Francis. Even in their tone every description is in many ways a poetic, hyperbolic panegyric."[61]

Source criticism is therefore an irrefutable *necessity* also in this case. Without criticism, there is no historical science. Yet if we now proceed along these lines,

---

58. Armstrong, Hellmann, and Short, *The Prophet*, 509; 116–17 for *Actus* 34.1–3.
59. Armstrong, Hellmann, and Short, *The Prophet*, 513; 129 for *Actus* 39.8.
60. Armstrong, Hellmann, and Short, *The Prophet*, 513; 129 for *Actus* 39.9.
61. See A. Tholuck, Über die Wunder der katholischen Kirche und insbesondere über das Verhältniss dieser und der biblischen Wunder zu *den Erscheinungen des Magnetismus und Somnambulismus*, in *Vermischte Schriften grösstentheils apologetischen Inhalts*, part 1 (Hamburg: Perthes, 1839), 28–148, 101.

we must be very clear that we are thereby treading on completely *subjective* and *relative* ground, which in and by itself can be as unscientific as remaining content with the earliest manuscript, for example. Indeed, it would be a different matter if there really were an absolute measure for science, for example, a[62] "twofold canon for thought and experience."[63] However, we do not have such a thing, and we will not have it—and it is perhaps better that way. Should someone claim to possess such an infallible measure—whether that be on the banks of the Tiber or the Rhine River[64]—it will turn into a *Procrustean bed*. The latter, however, should in no case become a symbol of source criticism, even if this occasionally seems to be the case.

By the same token, we ought not be held back, by the awareness that "our knowledge is only partial" (1 Cor. 13:9), from producing a *subjective perspective and measure*. An unhealthy *quietism* or *agnosticism* would be the result, which would have most fateful consequences not only for the field of science but also for our entire view of life.

Our critical examination of the stigmata of Saint Francis must therefore be understood in this light, as we now refer to the *relative* grounds of the sources and upon the *just-as-relative* field of historical investigation and hypothesis. According to the nature of things, this is split into two parts: (1) the *comparison and criticism of the sources*, with which we will first deal; and (2) the laying out of our *own perspectives*, which we will attempt to construe in the second main part of the paper.

For the sake of clarity, we will occupy ourselves with enumerating the major aspects of the report, as we did in the previous section.

a. Place, Time, and Occasion

Remarkable *differences* among the sources already become apparent here, not only in relation to *place* and *occasion*, which overall are in general agreement, but rather more in relation to the *time*.

Let us first compare the information about the *place* and the *occasion* and then approach the *primary issue* of the *time*.

Our oldest source, *Elias of Cortona*, is completely *silent* on these two aspects. This does not need to be interpreted as a suspicious sign. Rather, it is easy to explain based on the *character* and *style* of his letters. Elias does not want to share *dates* with the French monks but rather a *joyous fact* that he knows will evoke faith and resonance without needing further, more precise details. By contrast, *Brother Leo* writes on the paper with the *Laudes*: "*fecit quadragesimam in*

---

62. Here Barth added "Bolligers," then crossed out the name and substituted it with the indefinite article. See H. Mulert, "Bolliger, Adolf," in the *RGG*[1] 1: col. 1287. For information about the Swiss theologian Adolf Bolliger, see *RGG*[2] 1: cols. 1179–80.

63. In his book *Der Weg zu Gott für unser Geschlecht: Ein Stück Erfahrungstheologie*, 2nd ed. (Frauenfeld: Huber, 1900), and in a series of essays, Bolliger sought to "prove" that "experience and thought lead to theism"; see "Zu Schutz und Trutz," in *SThZ* 17 (1900): 1–11. He thought that in theology, as it is the case in general, "experience, specifically the logical working through of an experience," must be the "yardstick" of knowledge; see "Zur Bedeutung der Erkenntnis *für die Religion*," in *SThZ* 21 (1904): 201–27, esp. 201.

64. Bolliger was professor of systematic theology in Basel in 1891–1905.

loco Aluerne": he held a *forty-day practice of penance and fasting* [*quadragesima*] on *Mount La Verna*. This coincides with the details in *Thomas of Celano*, who only reports of a *mora*, a stay in a *hermitage* on *Mount La Verna*.[65] Both papal *bulls of confirmation* report nothing about the place or the occasion, while *Bonaventure* speaks of a lengthy prayer service without giving a definite place. The construction of the Church of the Stigmata on Mount La Verna must be particularly relevant for us, even though it happened forty years after the event. It is evidence that Mount La Verna, even back then, was generally seen as the location of this event, despite the silence of some sources. Finally, the *Speculum perfectionis* as well as the *Actus*, the former in close correspondence with *Celano*, mention Mount La Verna and the *quadragesima*.

Despite the silence in *Thomas of Celano*[66] and the *bulls of confirmation*, the motivation of which is easy to understand, we may take note of the *unanimity of the sources*.

More complicated is comparing the *dates*, in particular the setting of the *year*. Regarding the exact time frame, we may accept the uncontroverted details from the *Cartula* of Brother Leo, who claimed that Francis took up his *quadragesima* from the *Feast of the Assumption of Mary* until the *Feast of St. Michael*.[67] That would have been from the fifteenth of August until the twenty-ninth of September. This indeed makes *forty days*, excluding Sundays because they are not counted as days of fasting.

But what about the year itself?

Elias of Cortona says: "Not long before death."[68]

Brother Leo: "Two years before death."[69]

Thomas von Celano: "Two years before his soul returned to heaven."[70]

Gregory IX: "After that period of his life came to a happy end."[71]

Alexander IV: "While he was still alive."[72]

Matthew of Paris: *"Fourteen days before his death."*[73]

The inscription in the Church of the Stigmata: "In the year 1225."[74]

Meanwhile, the remaining sources do not give a definite date!

As we see, we have the choice between the years 1224, 1225, and 1226. Out of seven reports, two give the first year (1224), one gives the second year (1225), and four give the third year (1226) with more or less clarity. It is highly tempting to look for a *tendency* behind the fact that precisely all four curial or at least curially influenced sources place the stigmatization directly before Francis's death, just as *Karl von Hase* regards especially the position of Elias of Cortona as

65. Boehmer, *Analekten*, p. 69, lines 24–25 (= 1961, 3rd ed., p. 47, lines 15–16). See also Thomas von Celano, *St. Francis of Assisi*, 2.94; in *Acta Sanctorum Octobris* (1768), 2:709A; Boehmer, *Analekten*, p. 92, lines 26f–27 (= 1961, 3rd ed., p. 63, lines 19–20).

66. Perhaps a mixup here with Elias von Cortona.

67. Boehmer, *Analekten*, p. 69, line 25 (= 1961, 3rd ed., p. 47, line 15).

68. Boehmer, *Analekten*, p. 91, line 11f (= 1961, 3rd ed., p. 62, line 20).

69. Boehmer, *Analekten*, p. 69, line 24 (= 1961, 3rd ed., p. 47, line 15).

70. Thomas von Celano, *St. Francis of Assisi*, 2.94; in *Acta Sanctorum Octobris* (1768), 2:709A; Boehmer, *Analekten*, p. 92, lines 27–28 (= 1961, 3rd ed., p. 63, line 21).

71. *Magnum Bullarium Romanum* (1742), 1:79, §1.

72. *Magnum Bullarium Romanum* (1742), 1:109, §3.

73. Cf. Sabatier, *Franz von Assisi*, 260; M. Parisiensis, *Chronica majora*, 134.

74. Cf. Sabatier, *Speculum Perfectionis*, ccxiii.

a reason *against the veracity* of the stigmata.[75] From our perspective, both ways are *blind alleys*.

1. The statements of the papal bulls do not definitely indicate the year 1226. The *"postquam . . . consummavit . . ."* of Gregory IX[76] can also refer to the visitation of the body with the stigmata *after* Francis's death, a visit that he carried out during his time as Cardinal Hugolino in Assisi. (Then again, the other interpretation of the grammar does seem more probable to me.) Just as unreliable is the bull from Alexander IV. Earlier, when we took the bull as referring to 1226, the *"adhuc"* [yet] was pivotal: "while he was *very much alive*." The expression *". . . vitali spiritu foveretur"* also appears to us to refer to a sickly, exhausted body. The latter could just as well be a *poetic expression* where the *"adhuc"* simply corresponds to a *"yet."*[77] Both reports are in any case *doubtful*.

2. The main reason for the year 1226 falls away if a *variant in the letter of Elias*, cited by Sabatier, were genuine (Abbot Amoni, 1880), according to which we would need to read *"nam diu"* [for long] instead of *"non diu"* [not long]!?[78]

3. Regarding the unique detail in *Matthew of Paris*, fourteen days before his death, I hold this to be a simple misunderstanding in which for some reason or another the *"quadragesima"* [forty] turned into *"quarto decimo"* [fourteen].[79] Likewise, the year 1225 stands in the inscription in the Church of the Stigmata, without there being any support for it in the sources known to us!

And so we come to the year *1224* that is jointly attested by *Brother Leo* and *Thomas of Celano*. It seems that Bonaventure and the *plagiarist* of the Three Companions follow suit, while it is accepted definitively in the *Actus*. The opposing statement by both of the popes, if it is indeed that, can possibly rest upon Elias's false reading of *"not long."*

Now, of course, a few *internal contradictions* about the year 1224 still need to be eliminated: It can be asked, How is it possible that the stigmata, however they came about, could last for a full two years?

How should Francis's success at keeping this a relative secret for so long be explained?

How is it that, from the time of the stigmatization until his death, so little is said about them, while one would expect it to be a sensation, at least within the circle of his disciples?

The answer to all these objections will reveal itself in the second section; here we are only giving an introduction so that no one might believe that, with the obtained *concordance between the sources*, we might have already concluded our investigation.

Result: According to the sources, the stigmata occurred during an event of a *fasting-and-penance exercise on Mount La Verna*, during the time frame of August fifteenth through September twenty-ninth in the year 1224 (1225, or 1226, respectively).

---

75. K. von Hase, *Gesammelte Werke*, 5:170–78, esp. 122–27.

76. *Magnum Bullarium Romanum* (1742), 1:79, §1.

77. *Magnum Bullarium Romanum* (1742), 1:109, §3.

78. Cf. Sabatier, *Franz von Assisi*, 266 n. 1.

79. Cf. Sabatier, *Franz von Assisi*, 260. In M. Parisiensis, *Chronica majora*, 134, however, we read about "quintadecima die ante exitum suum." K. von Hase translates it the same way, *Gesammelte Werke*, 5:168 and 121: *"on the fifteenth day before his passing away."*

b. The Vision

I have already laid out the details of what the *Actus* has recounted about the process of the stigmatization on Mount La Verna. A small difference could occur in that Thomas of Celano spoke of a small place *that already had* a hermitage on it, while the *Actus* speaks of an *improvised shelter* made of tree branches. The thing in and of itself is irrelevant, but the *first* account appears to have represented the general assumption, as the famous image of the artist *Giotto* shows.[80]

What is more valuable to us is the passage we already highlighted, "he was sometimes in so long an ecstasy of the soul that night and day he could not speak, so absorbed was he in God";[81] and likewise the one in Bonaventure, where the vision came to him "while he was praying in a place set apart and was wholly absorbed into God, with superexceeding excess of fervour";[82] and according to Thomas of Eccleston, "in a certain seizure of contemplation."[83] We see the saint sunk deep in prayer upon a lonely mountain, a bit apart from the three disciples, who, in awestruck reverence, were watching the master on high. The object of his prayer was the *passion of Christ*, which yet had never come so close to him. Francis was prepared for great things, which we heard from his own mouth in the *Actus*. Who would want to deny that such an event cast a shadow in advance? The supposed Three Companions are fully correct to place this event into a casual nexus of the entire previous life of Francis: "and so from that time," namely, his conversion, "his heart was wounded and melted at the memory of the Lord's passion, which he always as long as he lived carried the wounds of the Lord in his heart, just as latterly appeared splendidly [luculenter] from the new impression of those same wounds made miraculously in his own body."[84]

"Do not come near, take off your shoes, for the ground that you stand on is holy ground!" [Exod. 3:5]. Must not this feeling overcome everyone who has dug deeply into the event that we shall now describe, an event that appropriately can be compared to the events at Horeb and Gethsemane. It was one of the rare moments in the life of humanity that *God* and *humanity* step within touch of each other. A "description according to the sources" of such a moment is nonsense: The relative nature of all historiography becomes clear here more than ever.

If we therefore undertake to present a *comparison of the reports* here, we still cannot expect in any way a disclosure of the actual being of the event. In its innermost core, it will always remain an enigma to us. This is all the more so because the reports which we have about it, in their overwhelming majority, are to be seen as being a *later addition*, a fact that is clear as their *differences* become greater and greater. Today we can no longer recognize how much this is due to the (not very detailed) narration that Francis gave to his disciples. Such a judgment is impossible in regard to dreams and visions.

---

80. See H. Thode, *Franz von Assisi und die Anfänge der Kunst der Renaissance in Italien*, 2nd ed. (Berlin: Grote, 1904), 144–51, esp. 148, plate 3, image 6; and plate 13, image 19.
81. *Actus* 9.31; in Armstrong, Hellmann, and Short, *The Prophet*, 34.
82. *Bonaventura* 1.12; in *Acta Sanctorum Octobris* (1768), 2:745A.
83. Thomas de Eccleston, *Collatio* XIII (XII), 245.
84. Leo, Rufinus, and Angelus, *Legenda trium sociorum* 1.14; in *Acta Sanctorum Octobris* (1768), 2:727 CD.

Elias of Cortona is silent about the particulars on this point as well, as he is about the earlier ones: "he appeared crucified, bearing five wounds."[85] That is all we hear.

Brother Leo says, the stigmatization happened "after the vision and address of the Seraph."[86]

By contrast, the description by *Thomas of Celano* is very detailed. The saint caught above him a glimpse of a "man of God" like a *seraph*.[87] The latter is only vaguely described: He is *crucified*, but has *six wings*, two raised up over his head, two to fly with, and two *covering his whole body*, so that no one could see anything of him, never mind his wounds.

Bonaventure already says about this: "he knew he saw Christ under the appearance of the Seraph"; this seems then to have become the primary interpretation of the seraph, again, as can be seen in the paintings of *Giotto*, which clearly show the head of Christ.[88] And further down, Bonaventure explicitly says, "Christ appeared to him as if nailed to the Cross."[89] Here we also hear that the apparition addresses Francis. Obviously, we are unable to make out anything of the content: "so eloquent had been the secrets!"[90]

The *inscription in the Church of the Stigmata* mentions only the seraph, as does *Thomas of Eccleston*, who explicitly speaks of an "angel."[91] Yet another variation is given by the so-called Three Companions, who describe the figure like this: between the wings there is the form of an absolutely *beautiful, crucified person*, arms and legs *spread out like a cross*, and whose face *looked like Christ*. According to the *Actus*, there appeared "Christ in the form of a winged Seraph, as if crucified,"[92] which corresponds to the description of Bonaventure almost word for word.

We have thus far *three versions* of the Vision:

1. A seraph (Leo, Thomas of Celano, Thomas of Eccleston, inscription in the Church of the Stigmata)
2. A *Christ figure* in the form of a seraph (*Bonaventure, Actus*)
3. A crucified *human* that looks like Christ (Three Companions)

It seems to us that the *first* one is most thoroughly attested to, because it is easy to explain how the others grew out of it, and not the other way around. By the way, it is also not out of the question that Francis himself had already given different versions, which is easily possible with highly emotive and imaginative personalities.

Result: During his exercise in penance and prayer, Francis receives an *apparition* who speaks to him, perhaps through a dream or a vision. It remains unclear

85. Boehmer, *Analekten*, p. 91, lines 12–13 (= 1961, 3rd ed., p. 62, lines 20–21).

86. Boehmer, *Analekten*, p. 69, line 29 (= 1961, 3rd ed., p. 47, lines 18–19).

87. Thomas von Celano, *St. Francis of Assisi* 2.94; in *Acta Sanctorum Octobris* (1768), 2:709A; Boehmer, *Analekten*, p. 92, line 28 (= 1961, 3rd ed., p. 63, line 21).

88. *Bonaventura* 13.192; in *Acta Sanctorum Octobris* (1768), 2:777E; see also H. Thode, plate 3, image 6; plate 13, image 19.

89. *Bonaventura* 1.12; in *Acta Sanctorum Octobris* (1768), 2:745AB.

90. *Bonaventura* 13.194; in *Acta Sanctorum Octobris* (1768), 2:778A.

91. See Sabatier, *Speculum Perfectionis*, ccxiii; Thomas de Eccleston, *Collatio* XIII (XII), 245.

92. *Actus* 9.68; in Armstrong, Hellmann, and Short, *The Prophet*, 39.

in the reports whether this was a *seraph, Christ*, or a *crucified person*. The first version seems to be the most acceptable.

c. The Stigmatization

Most of our sources agree that the imprinting of the stigmata stands *in connection* with the *vision* just described. This is not the case among the official and semiofficial file papers such as the letter of Elias and the two bulls of confirmation, which just report only the *fact*, not the how and where.

Brother *Leo* speaks of an "impression of the marks [*stigmatum*] on his body."[93] With this expression, we could think about a *direct transmission*, that is, an imprinting by the apparition, something like they claim[94] that Jetzer experienced in the Jetzer case in the monastery in Bern. But it also matches the description of *Thomas of Celano* and the later ones, just as it is also depicted in *Giotto's* painting. The apparition floats at a bit of a distance from the saint, and at the same time, magnetic lines stream from his hands, his feet, and his side onto the limbs of Francis. Thomas of Celano recounts that Francis went rigid from awe and terror and did not know what to make of the apparition. While he was still trying to make sense of it, the *marks of wounds* appeared on his limbs, as he saw them earlier on the limbs of the apparition.

Bonaventure's account of the stigmatization is interesting. If it were not Bonaventure himself who speaks here, one could come to the conclusion, because his report about it is so veiled and allusive, that someone is speaking here who does not believe in the stigmatization at all, or at most, only in a very *spiritualized* way. Here we read that at a glimpse of the apparition, "so impressed down to the marrow was the memory of Christ's passion on the inwards of his heart,"[95] so that from then on, whenever he remembered the passion, he had to weep.

This "down to the marrow," like another aforementioned line, "such that the friend of Christ knew beforehand that he would be transformed into the likeness of Christ crucified by the total immolation of his soul,"[96] shows that the author is thinking about the stigmata indeed. The *inscription in the Church of the Stigmata* and *Thomas of Eccleston* assume a more direct transference, likewise in the *Actus*.

Who wants to decide here? It is difficult to conduct historical investigations of visions. By contrast, it seems to us that, even on this point, the description of *Thomas of Celano* is older and more reliable, primarily because it has the visual arts on its side, as already mentioned.

Result: Looking at the apparition, Francis is initially shocked and speechless, and the stigmata appear on his limbs. Once again, it remains questionable in the sources whether this was thought of as a *direct transference* of them or a kind of magnetizing *effect from afar*.

---

93. Boehmer, *Analekten*, p. 69, lines 29–30 (=1961, 3rd ed., p. 47, line 19).
94. See R. Steck, "Der Berner Jetzerprozess," 68, 70.
95. *Bonaventura* 1.12; in *Acta Sanctorum Octobris* (1768), 2:745B.
96. *Bonaventura* 13.192; in *Acta Sanctorum Octobris* (1768), 2:777E.

d. The Stigmata

We have already spoken of the oldest and most straightforward description of the stigmata: it is that of *Elias of Cortona*. Here they are described as *symmetrical puncture wounds*, in which the *blackness of the nails* is still visible. The side appears like a *lance pierced through it*, and *it exudes blood*.

Already the account of *Thomas of Celano* is substantially different. According to him, Francis's limbs appear in the middle *as if nailed*, such that the *heads of the nails* protrude out of the inner and outer surfaces of the hands and feet, but on the other side are *"caruncula," pieces of flesh;*[97] Thomas compares them to unbent points of nails. The right side shows a *lance puncture*, with hematoma pressed onto the *clothes*.

The account of Alexander IV follows this account closely. It speaks as well of the *"expressa undique similitude clavorum,"* except with the difference that he leaves the question open whether the *excrescences* are out of *flesh* or *"de materia novae creationis."*[98] He emphasizes that the *side wound* is *not* somehow a *fraud*, as might seem especially likely.

According to *Matthew of Paris*, the *side wound* was so deep that one could see all the way to the heart, a remark that seems to me, in my understanding, to be unseemly already for anatomical reasons. A second remarkable characteristic is that all the wounds *disappear in his death*, which seems to be clearly an arbitrary *increase of the miraculous*. The series of witnesses concludes with the so-called Three Companions. With them, the later view was already so hardened that even a *clear polemic* against the account of Elias emerges:

Elias: "His hands and feet had *as it were the punctures of the nails* impressed on either side."[99]

Three Companions: "They could perceive in his hands and feet not just, as it were, the punctures of the nails but the nails themselves."[100]

Obviously, as time went on, the authors put forth effort to make the *later view* the only valid one and to *canonize* it at any price.

The evaluation of the entire question revolves substantially around the evaluation of this point. The natural thing to do here is that we primarily hold on to the *oldest account* by Elias of Cortona, because here we are dealing with supposed or actual *realities* that are accessible by a purely historical investigation. The other accounts are to be understood as based on this one.

One would have already noticed the nub of the matter in *Elias's* account, which the others follow suit. It is especially the observation *"clavorum nigredinem ostendentes,"*[101] "the wounds display the black of the nails," with which Elias obviously means the traces of the black iron in the bloody and then scabby wounds, or, that of which the stigmata were reminiscent, as we will see later. Yet the next historical account, by *Thomas of Celano*, abstracts in a different way: where the black of the nails is, there the nails are themselves—and then he depicts the latter in a rather fantastical manner, whereby, of course, it cannot be

---

97. Thomas of Celano, *St. Francis of Assisi* 2.95; in *Acta Sanctorum Octobris* (1768), 2:709B; Boehmer, *Analekten*, p. 93, line 19 (=1961, 3rd ed., 62, line 2).

98. *Magnum Bullarium Romanum* (1742), 1:109, §3.

99. Boehmer, *Analekten*, p. 91, lines 14–15 (= 1961, 3rd ed., p. 62, lines 22–23).

100. Leo, Rufinus, and Angelus, *Legenda trium sociorum* 5.70; in *Acta Sanctorum Octobris* (1768), 2:741E.

101. Boehmer, *Analekten*, p. 91, lines 15–16 (= 1961, 3rd ed., p. 62, line 23).

excluded that perhaps a few things about the appearance of the wounds fit with his description. This also seems to be pulled out of the writing of Alexander IV, who with Cardinal Hugolino was a former eyewitness, but whose papal bull apparently relies on the account of Celano. In this way, one misunderstanding is built upon another. By the time of the plagiarist of the Three Companions, the account already suggests that the author, who clearly understands his own social role, wants to argue against the details of Elias's account and for a *reduction in the glory of the master.*

Result: The stigmata are shown on the *hands* and *feet* and on the *side*; but what remains uncertain in the sources is whether they were only *scars* or *scars with the ends of nails sticking out on both sides.* This brings up the other question of whether these consist of the *flesh* or *foreign matter.* Here too, the sources show a remarkable *climactic movement* from the more straightforward, relatively *explainable* toward the more complicated and *supernatural.*

e. The Witnesses

A primary issue arises here. It shows up in most accounts, especially in the later ones, that Francis indeed tries to *conceal* the stigmata as well as he could. But he is *not successful* in doing so, especially because of the temporarily streaming blood from the *side wound* that wets his clothing. This occurrence is already highlighted by *Elias* and likewise by *Thomas of Celano.* Celano cites *Helias* and *Rufinus* as eyewitnesses during Francis's lifetime, while he apparently accepts that, after Francis's death, more of them came forward. *Rufinus* in particular appears to have made a great effort to gain knowledge of the wounds. A certain case shows him appearing to have caused Francis great pain by taking it upon himself, in rather juvenile fashion, to touch the wounds while making the contact appear unintentional. The *Actus* recounts this same story along with two other similar ones about him. *Alexander IV* apparently recounts, with Hugolino, that during the visitation of the body certain people would have seen the occurrence and would have touched the wounds: "handled,"[102] that is, evidently, the supposed nails of flesh. He also highlights how much the saint concealed his wounds during his lifetime; only the bloody effluence out of his side would have occasionally given it away. Here again *Bonaventure*'s witness appears to be suspect. After he recounts how seeing and kissing[103] the stigmata counted as great luck among the people, he continues: "he could not avoid people seeing the stigmata" and right after that: "very many people have affirmed on oath that they saw them."[104]

By the aforementioned example of the doubt of the knight *Hieronymus*, who otherwise does not appear in Francis's story, *we* will not be strengthened in our belief in the existence of the stigmata either. *Von Hase* is perhaps not wrong when he excludes this second Thomas as *unhistorical.*[105]

In the *Actus* we found that after the stigmatization, Francis even went around with *shoes* and *gloves.* This too, we can confidently refer to the field of invention,

---

102. *Magnum Bullarium Romanum* (1742), 1:109, §3.
103. See n. 52 above.
104. *Bonaventura* 13.200; in *Acta Sanctorum Octobris* (1768), 2:778DE.
105. See K. von Hase, *Gesammelte Werke*, 5:179–80, 128–29; see also 146, 107.

an invention that liked to adorn the master with a supernatural rich wreath of noble traits, in this instance with humility. *Francis did not need this*. And wearing any [extra] piece of clothing would have first and foremost contradicted the basic law of the Minor Friars: *"nihil tuleritis in via."*[106] Of course, the stigmata must have been obtained in some way other than we have seen in the majority of the sources. According to them, Francis would have been conspicuous in such a way that he would have needed such protective measure. What only remains in question is whether he still could have *walked* at all!!

Incidentally, the *Actus* gives us a few more eyewitnesses with names: Brother *Leo*, who apparently was entrusted with the—if only very rudimentary—medicinal treatment for the wounds.

Result: Despite Francis's efforts to keep the stigmata a secret even from his inner circle, the stigmata are noticed by them and soon by a wider circle, and they are widely revered.

We thus stand at the *end* of our first, *primarily historical, main section*. First, we quickly read through the sources that were to be considered; then we did a critical rereading of the individual sources. Now the *individual results* that were discovered will be collated into a historical-critical *final result*. To this end, we now leave the sources with which we have been dealing, in order to move toward a more *general perspective* on our problem.

II. Historical-Critical Results

It would not surprise me if someone who has been following our investigations thus far would interject the following *question*: "Of what use to me are your ten reports that assert the stigmatization and the stigmata themselves? They are all prejudiced or at least ecclesiastically colored, and you yourself have pointed out their many discrepancies. I regard the entire matter as superstition and monastic deception."

Such reservations would be understandable. But that alone does not dispose of the problem. We are dealing with a question to which, in their works, the most notable Francis of Assisi biographers K. Hase and P. Sabatier[107] have devoted a special appendix, which does merit "the sweat of the noble"[108] and a closer investigation.

Yes, if we were to find ourselves with our fact outside of any context of nature and the history of humanity, if it stood there in *isolation*, then that objection could appear to be justified although even then nothing would be proven! But that is not the case. Even though our event is certainly not of the daily sort, all that it will need is to be *located within that great context* in order to put it in another light historically. A comet that flies through the starry heavens

---

106. Sabatier, *Speculum Perfectionis* 2.3.8, line 20; cf. *Regula non bullata quae dicitur prima* 14, in Boehmer, *Analekten*, p. 13, lines 19–20 (= 1961, 3rd ed., p. 9, line 23).

107. See K. von Hase, *Gesammelte Werke*, 5:143–202, esp. 105–43; Sabatier, *Franz von Assisi*, 256–62, 266–67.

108. See Fr. G. Klopstock, "Der Zürcher See," lines 50–52, in *Friedrich Gottlob Klopstocks Oden*, ed. Fr. Muncker and J. Pawel (Stuttgart: G. J. Göschen, 1889), 1:85: "Immortality is a great thought, worthy of the sweat of the noble!"

that we know is certainly not a daily occurrence, but still we do not for that reason remove it from the realm of the possible—because its *existence* has been frequently *noted*. Historical science follows this very same principle. It knows of *nothing* that is *intrinsically impossible* but has the right to test all the appearances that it encounters against the world of appearance of both the *past* and the *present*, and to draw *provisional conclusions* from that testing. It must exercise care, as we emphasized in the introduction, not to move out of this provisional framework, for the *world of experience* is not a closed entirety, but rather experiences its daily *corrections* in every aspect. As soon as we have arrived at clarity about this, we will cease to speak of "impossibilities" and "miracles," that is, events that go *contra, praeter aut supra naturam*[109] [against, beyond, or above nature]. It is the modern progress of the natural sciences that justifies us in this: they have demonstrated results that would have rendered a person dizzy a hundred years ago. This *deepening of the knowledge of nature* must generate, as a necessary consequence, the insight that we cannot too quickly close the reports of stories that have "supernatural" content.

This is especially true in the relationships between *spirit* and *body*, a subtle area that only recently has received more in-depth scientific attention (*Forel, Dubois*,[110] and others). This is where the question of the stigmata belongs too.

By way of introduction to the problems that require consideration here, we will be best served by briefly surveying the views of the two great antipodes in this question, Hase and Sabatier, confronting the arguments that they advance to prove their views.

Hase, whom we encounter as the representative of a rationalizing view, believes that he has found the key to the riddle with Elias of Cortona, *who, during the night in which the saint died, branded the stigmata on him with a heated iron*. As a proof Hase refers to the following:

1. The *doctor with the glowing iron*, probably following a medieval medical practice, branded Francis, who was sick, on the forehead; Francis then followed this with the fire verse in his *Canticum solis* [Song of the Sun].
2. The blackness of the wounds as attested by several resources that were passed down.
3. The *zealous drive for relics*, a widespread aspect of that period of time, which reminds us of the raw mutilation of St. Elizabeth of Hungary.
4. The noticeably *rapid interment*.[111]

Sabatier, who assumes that *the origin of the stigmata was through neuropathic causes*,[112] also lists a series of negative factors:

---

109. Regarding this traditional definition of "miracle," see Chr. E. Luthardt, *Kompendium der Dogmatik* (Leipzig: Dörffling & Franke, 1873), 109; following A. Quenstedt, *Theologia didactico-polemica, sive Systema theologicum*, 4th ed. (Wittenberg, 1701), part. I, chap. XIII, sec. I, thesis XXVII, p. 535.

110. On the research and publications of the medical doctor and psychiatrist August Forel, see his *Rückblick auf mein Leben* (Zurich: Europa, 1935); on the neuropathologist Paul Dubois, see his work *The Psychic Treatment of Nervous Disorders* (New York: Funk & Wagnalls, 1908).

111. See K. von Hase, *Gesammelte Werke*, 5:176–81, as well as 126–31; see also 131–32, 97.

112. See Sabatier, *Franz von Assisi*, 257–58.

1. The *rapid interment* (see above)
2. The fact that the body was placed in a coffin
3. The later lack of knowledge of the location of the grave
4. The lack of any mention [of the stigmata] in the canonization bull
5. The contradiction [of the stigmata] by some contemporaries

He then *refutes* each of these one after another:

Ad 1. The Middle Ages provide *more examples* of such rapid interments.
Ad 2. The coffin, otherwise rarely used, served here as *a cautionary move*, in order that Francis, who was already canonized in the eyes of the people, should not experience at his death what happened to Saint Elizabeth.
Ad 3. The concealed gravesite was also chosen *out of caution* because they feared an attempt at robbery of the holy corpse by the Perugian neighbors, which actually happened occasionally.
Ad 4. The silence of the canonization bull proves nothing, since the stigmata were already *confirmed officially* in a special papal bull.
Ad 5. The objection of some bishops was merely one aspect of the major *conflict between the clergy of the religious order and the secular clergy.*

The contradiction of the Dominicans was obviously an expression of their *competitive envy.*[113]

As far as *Hase's hypothesis* is concerned, it appears to me to be best refuted by the fact that the alleged counterfeiter *Elias* would have necessarily had to make his opponents in the order, Brothers *Leo* and *Rufinus*, into coconspirators in this instance. *The fact that the reports of both agree with each other appears to me to be the most important historical witness to the genuineness of the stigmata.*

In yet another way the Catholic historian *Hurter*, in his *History of Innocent III* (4:267), seeks to explain the stigmata: He relates them to Francis's *illness*, as a result of which wounds appeared in his hands and feet, which he *compares* with the wounds of Christ. "Thus ultimately we may not even call upon a vital faith and the power of imagination to explain that saga."[114] This explanation might at first appear to be somewhat illuminating, yet [we must ask]: (1) Is it conceivable that the honest disciples, not to speak of Francis himself, would have regarded *ulcers* as *stigmata*? (2) In view of the resource materials that we have cited, may one speak of a *"saga"*? With the same justification, Hurter could have degraded every Gospel account of a miracle to a "saga": There are none that are as well documented as the stigmata of S. Francis of Assisi!

On the whole, we rather may build upon our sources, *chiefly* for the reason of the aforementioned *agreement of the sources, which come from entirely different circles.* We may do so all the more since a critic who is otherwise as sharp as *Sabatier* sees the reports about the stigmata as *quite genuine* and corresponding with the truth. He goes so far as even to accept the emphasis upon the *nail-like shape of the stigmata* in the sources from Thomas of Celano onward,[115] where,

113. See Sabatier, *Franz von Assisi*, 261–62.
114. Fr. Hurter, *Geschichte Papst Innocenz des Dritten und seiner Zeitgenossen*, vol. 4 (= *Kirchliche Zustände zu Papst Innocenz des Dritten Zeiten*, vol. 2) (Hamburg: Perthes, 1834), 167.
115. See Sabatier, *Franz von Assisi*, 338 n. 482.

however, we cannot follow him for both historical as well as general reasons. In our treatment of the sources, we have shown how this version emerged from the original report. Would it be conceivable that Francis could have *concealed* the stigmata, shaped in such a way, *for two years*? This was possible with a simple wound, but not with fleshly nails, which would also have prevented the saint from walking, as we have already mentioned.

To this extent, we concur without hesitation with the Catholic *Görres*: "Without the core structure and without the formative law, there is no crystallization; and thus without truth in the deepest roots and without the formative law, there is no saga."[116]

What then remains for us as the core, the kernel form of the narrative of the stigmata? We find *Tholuck's* definition of the process of stigmatization to be the best: he explains the process as *"the embodying of affects."*[117] In the sources we have seen how Francis, in a forty-day spiritual exercise in honor of St. Michael, immersed himself with intensified fervor *in the sufferings of Christ*, and this not for the first time but, according to the *Tres Socii*, apparently often since the hour of conversion. In an hour of especially intimate *mystical immersion* in this object, he receives the vision of the *crucified seraphim*, which *Sabatier* insightfully describes as the combination of the ideational complexes of the *Archangel Michael* and the *passion*.[118] We call to remembrance once more the extremely significant comment of the *Actus*: "Sometimes he was in such an ecstasy of spirit and so absorbed in God that he was not able to speak throughout the day or night!"[119] "Should it be unthinkable," says *Tholuck*, "that through the constant fixation upon the cross of Christ by an ecstatic person of such a disposition, in a moment where this intensifies, that the vision of this imagined content could be physically engraved upon him?"[120]

Modern physiology has demonstrated that such a thing is possible; in much the same sense, Harnack states: "We see that a strong will and a firm faith exert an influence upon the life of the body, and produce phenomena that strike us as marvelous."[121] "It is the spirit that builds itself a body," says *Schiller* somewhere.[122] *The stigmatization of Saint Francis* does not stand alone as an event of this kind.

We want to stay entirely away from those hysterical women of the first half of the nineteenth century: *Margareta Ebner*, the Beguine *Gertrudis* in Delft, and the most notorious case, *Catharine Emmerich*, for whom the stigmatization was also claimed. In the case of the person mentioned last, for whom medical certifications were produced, deception appears finally to have been discovered.[123]

---

116. J. Görres, "Der heilige Franziskus von Assisi ein Troubadour," in *Der Katholik: Eine religiöse Zeitschrift zur Belehrung und Warnung* 20 (Year 6, IV–VI, Strasbourg, 1826): 14–53, 36, n. *. See Tholuck, *Wunder der katholischen Kirche*, 103–5.

117. See Tholuck, *Wunder der katholischen Kirche*, 106.

118. See Sabatier, *Franz von Assisi*, 258.

119. Armstrong, Hellmann, and Short, *The Prophet*, 454; 34 for *Actus* 9.31.

120. See Tholuck, *Wunder der katholischen Kirche*, 106–7.

121. A. Harnack, *What Is Christianity?*, 27.

122. See Fr. von Schiller, *Wallenstein's Death* 3.13 (V. 1813).

123. See K. von Hase, *Kirchengeschichte auf der Grundlage akademischer Vorlesungen*, sec. 3.2 (Leipzig: Breitkopf & Härtel, 1892), 926–29; K. von Hase, *Franz von Assisi*, 129–30, 95–96; Tholuck, *Wunder der katholischen Kirche*, 98, 111–33; Tholuck, *Vermischte Schriften* (Hamburg: Perthes, 1839), 2:477–78. Görres, *Die christliche Mystik*, 2:424–25, 437, 453–56.

The case of *St. Catherine of Siena* seems to merit somewhat more trust, although it defies more precise control because her stigmata were *not externally visible* and were *experienced* by her only as pain.[124] We certainly are better off by *forgoing analogous references to other stigmatized persons*, of which Görres enumerates many,[125] since the observations of such cases are at the least *uncertain.* On the other hand, there would be available many other examples of such a *tangibly formative effect* of the spirit upon the body, without our having to take recourse to a "history of Christian mysticism."

I would like to remind us of an Old Testament example, the story of *Jacob*, who *wrestles with God* at the Jabbok Brook and whose *thigh was put out of joint* (Gen. 32:25–26).

These connections of spirit and body seem to be very meaningful for *embryonic life.* A rather unusual case, known to me personally, can illustrate this. A mother, several weeks before the birth of her child, experienced a powerful shock when the arm of a valuable statue broke off. The child is born—but *without an arm!*

More recently, some have gone so far as to conduct *experiments* in which *wounds*, blisters, and the like were generated using the power of *suggestion*. The only thing that would need to be addressed would be whether such a thing is also possible using *auto-suggestion.* If such a case is not known till now, that does not prove anything over against the reality of our case, because for good reasons it is *unique.*

Of course, it must not be assumed that, with the stigmatization, Francis's *ecstatic predisposition* disappeared. Quite the opposite: from then on it really came to a major *breakthrough*; until his death he found himself "in the rapture of contemplation."[126] How otherwise would the stigmata have lasted for two more years? We have no choice but to assume a continuing *conservation of the stigmata* through the same powers that had generated them to begin with. The wound in his side, which continued to bleed, also points to this.

We can thus summarize our results:

1. By virtue of a very special physical and psychic sensitivity, Francis of Assisi, from his conversion onward, was predisposed toward extraordinary neuropathic incidents.
2. This sensitivity was intensified on Mount La Verna
   a. by a forty-day episode of prayer and spiritual exercises, and
   b. by an especially intensive mystical immersion in the fact of the passion of Christ.
3. At a moment when this contemplation had attained its climax, Francis received a vision, and the continuing spiritual concentration on the suffering of Christ expressed itself physically with the generation of stigmata on the body of the saint.
4. The composition of the stigmata remains unclear for us. The visible representation in the reports from Thomas of Celano onward appear to be out of the question.

124. See K. Hase, *Franz von Assisi*, 199, 141–42.
125. See Görres, *Die christliche Mystik*, 2:410–56.
126. See Thomas of Eccleston, *Collatio* XIII (XII), 245.

III. General Assessment

A person with whom I recently discussed our theme gave me his opinion about it, which was that even if the matter were true, we would be dealing with a purely *pathological* case, with a process from the lowest levels of life, which from a *moral-religious perspective* would be completely *irrelevant*.

In a similar way *Hase*, at the conclusion of his special study of the stigmata, returns to the real world and states: "God does not look at cassocks or stigmata but at the inward person."[127] This is undoubtedly correct; still, the matter is not resolved by making such authoritarian remarks.

Isn't it curious how much we like to engage within *extremes*?! Either it must be an instance of a *supranatural miracle* or merely a *banal event* "from the lowest levels of life"!

We don't want to deny that there are some supporting factors for the latter view. One might ask us how we would evaluate the significance of the stigmas if now the alleged stigmatization of an *Emmerich* and people like her should be shown to be *factual*, which can't be ruled out at all. And how do we respond when, according to the most recent assumption by Prof. Steck,[128] even a notorious swindler like *Jetzer* might in fact have had stigmata?! —Now, first, none of it has been proven; and second, if it were the case, then the old proverb applies here: *Duo, cum faciunt idem, non est idem* [when two are doing the same thing, it is not the same thing].[129]

In the previous section we have shown how we could conceive of a relatively "natural" explanation of the stigmata miracle. In doing so, we mentioned the concept of "suggestion." So, someone might call out, "That's it!" and then begin to enumerate a great mass of cases from the broad area of hypnosis and suggestion, which have absolutely nothing in common with saints and holiness.

The important thing here is to oppose the error as though a so-called "miracle," that is, an event in which we believe that *God's will* is active in a special way, loses its religious value for us in that we arrive at the knowledge of the particular means that God uses in this act of will, or we discover *analogies* for the event in question, in which a special activity of God's will appears to us to be ruled out.

The narratives of the New Testament have not become less valuable for us because we understand the causes of some things, such as healings, better now than they did in earlier times.

For the fact is that God, up to this very day, *intervenes in and guides the history of humanity*; thus it is a matter of complete *indifference* whether or not we know *the means* that God uses for this. It is in essence just as irrelevant whether we want to call something a *"miracle"* or a *hypnotic appearance*, or whatever. Both are similarly inexplicable for normal thought.

---

127. K. von Hase, *Franz von Assisi*, 202, esp. 143.

128. R. Steck, "Kulturgeschichtliches aus den Akten des Jetzerprozesses" [Cultural-historical content from the files of the Jetzer trial], 21 [Barth appears to cite the essay, which starts off the third issue of the journal dated "August 1905," using the manuscript, or galley proofs, or some other separate document, in which the pagination differs]. See R. Steck, "Kulturgeschichtliches aus den Akten des Jetzerprozesses," in *Blätter für bernische Geschichte, Kunst, und Altertumskunde*, Year 1 (1905): 161–86, esp. 176–78.

129. See P. Terentius Afer, *Adelphoe* 5.3 (5.37–39).

And that is also the situation with our case.

However we may construe the so-called "natural" causes of the stigmata of Francis of Assisi, we recognize here a higher hand, which should indicate to the faithful servant of the Lord: You do not stand alone in your striving for the kingdom of God; the crucified Master is always near to you!

And in this sense we also undersign these words of St. Bonaventure:

"The seal of Christ crucified was impressed on his body not through any natural power or by human craft, but rather by the spirit of the living God in a marvelous power!"[130]

Finis[131]
July 13, 1905
2 p.m.

130. *Bonaventura*, Prologus 2; in *Acta Sanctorum Octobris* (1768), 2:741.

131. Beneath the word the circle of the Zofingia is placed (see below, 69). Next to that it says, "ὢ πωποι (two years later)."

The Centurion at Capernaum
1905

In the Winter Semester of 1905–6, Karl Barth took—among other courses, including a lecture series on "Leben Jesu" [(The) Life of Jesus] with his father—"Übungen zur synoptischen Frage" [Studies in the Synoptic question] with R. Steck. He had prepared for this exegetical work over the summer, especially by reading P. Wernle's Die synoptische Frage *(see n. 4). On August 18, 1905, while on holiday in Coffrane in the canton of Neuchâtel, he wrote to his father: "Have also begun the Synoptic question by Wernle; do not know whether I might not want to take the seminar with Steck after all, for the material seems to me at least of some importance and worth being illuminated from several sides." On August 23, he reported to his father: "I am so excited about theology that I dreamed vividly today about the Synoptic question, which—I know not how—came alive to me." By August 31 he had completely excerpted Wernle's book,[1] such that he could write to his father about his impressions and thoughts in detail. Looking back (in a letter of December 28, 1905, to his grandmother and his aunt in Basel), Barth later wrote of the investigation he had written for the New Testament seminar: "By the way, if you want to read something good about the history of the centurion at Capernaum, then I can be of service: I exposited it some weeks ago for Mr. Steck."*

The manuscript has the subtitle "(Synoptisch untersucht): Arbeit für das NTliche Seminar bei Prof. D. Steck W. S. 1905/06" [(Synoptically investigated). Term paper for the New Testament seminar with Prof. Dr. Steck, Winter Semester 1905–6] and is part of the volume "Excerpts II." In this volume, along with notes on "Bibelkunde des A. T." [Bible Knowledge of the Old Testament] and excerpts from Ueberweg's "Geschichte der Philosophie" [History of Philosophy], Barth had bound the term papers "Der Hauptmann zu Kapernaum" [The Centurion at Capernaum] and "Zwinglis 67 Schlussreden" [Zwingli's 67 Articles] and the "Aufsatz für den akadem. theol. Verein" [essay for the Academic Theological Association] titled "Die ursprüngliche Gestalt des Unser Vaters" [The Original Form of the Lord's Prayer]. A page "Präparation. Nach Wilke, Clavis NT'i" [Preparation. according to Wilke, Key to NT introduction] (a translation of some Greek vocabulary into Latin) is prefixed to the text of the term paper on the "Centurion at Capernaum."

---

1. These excerpts are in "Excerpts I" (see the editorial introduction to "The Character of the Religion of Ancient India").

Introduction

In the Synoptic tradition, the pericope of the centurion at Capernaum is preserved for only us in Matthew 8:5–13 and Luke 7:1–10, in which connection
Luke 13:28–30 is also to be considered.

If the *two-source theory* concerning the formation of the Synoptic Gospels
is proved correct—[a theory] that ascribes everything common to Matthew
and Luke beyond Mark to a common, lost source, behind which people have
searched[2] for the well-known *Logia* (Sayings) of Papias[3]—then our passage
must necessarily be assigned to that latter source, since it is missing in Mark.

I see this conclusion drawn, for example, by Wernle in *Die synoptische Frage*
(1899), 64f.,[4] who proceeds from the rule: "*Everywhere that Matthew and Luke
coincide word-for-word, the text of the collection of sayings is present*" (p. 80)—
always leaving aside the texts in Mark, of course.

Yet against this arise significant *difficulties*:

a. The very premise of that thesis is contestable, as *word-for-word* coincidence
between Matthew and Luke beyond Mark is relatively rare (cf. the Sermon on
the Mount or discourse about John the Baptist); rather, in the case of congruent
content, the greatest variation in detail prevails. Things stand similarly with the
elements of dialogue in our passage.

b. As a rather large narrative section, our text would sit almost completely
isolated in the collection of sayings, as even Wernle concedes.[5]

c. The historical setting of the words of Jesus in our passage is so different
in Luke and Matthew that if a common source is assumed, a capricious change
by the evangelist would need to be assumed, the motives for which, however,
are scarcely apparent.

Both accounts much more give me the impression that they come from different sources; this is still to be substantiated in detail.

I have taken the *critical-exegetical material* for my work principally from the
following handbooks:

H. A. W. Meyer, *Krit.-exeget. Handbuch über d. Evg. Mt* (Göttingen 1858).[6]

H. A. W. Meyer, *Krit.-exeget. Handbuch über d. Evg. Mr u. Lc* (Göttingen 1860).[7]

---

2. Here Barth is alluding to a decision of Friedrich Schleiermacher that had a notable impact upon
exegetical research, on understanding the statement about the λόγια [sayings] of Christ in a sentence
from Papias handed down by Eusebius (*Hist. eccl.* 3.39.16): Ματθαῖος μὲν οὖν ἑβραιδι διαλέκτῳ τὰ
λόγια συνεγράψατο, ἡρμήνευσε δ' αὐτὰ ὡς ἠδύνατο ἕκαστος [So then Matthew wrote the sayings in the
Hebrew language, and everyone interpreted them as he was able]) to mean "that the apostle Matthew
had composed a compilation of discourses and sayings of Christ in a Palestinian dialect, on which
many others thereafter worked, each in their own way"; to this, Schleiermacher connected the conjecture that "our Gospel of Matthew is based on the collection of discourses of the apostle Matthew, our
Gospel of Mark is based on the collection of stories of the interpreter Mark, and the names of both arise
from these relationships" ("Ueber die Zeugnisse des Papias von unsern beiden ersten Evangelien"
[Concerning the testimonies of Papias to our first two Gospels], in F. Schleiermacher, *Sämmtliche Werke*
[Collected Works], Sec. I (Berlin 1836), 2:361–92, esp. 372, 391).
3. Cf. *Antilegomena. Die Reste der ausserkanonischen Evangelien und urchristlichen Ueberlieferungen*
[Antilegomena], ed. and trans. E. Preusche (Gießen 1901), 54–63, 145–52.
4. P. Wernle, *Die synoptische Frage* [The Synoptic question] (Freiburg i. B./Leipzig/Tübingen:
J. C. B. Mohr [Paul Siebeck], 1899), 61–80, esp. 64–65.
5. Cf. Wernle, *Synoptische Frage*, 224–25.
6. H. A. W. Meyer, *Kritisch exegetisches Handbuch über das Evangelium des Matthäus*, KEK, sec. 1, 1st
half, 4th ed. (Göttingen: Vandenhoeck & Ruprecht, 1858).
7. H. A. W. Meyer, *Kritisch exegetisches Handbuch über die Evangelien des Markus und Lukas*, KEK, sec.
1, 2nd half, 4th ed. (Göttingen: Vandenhoeck & Ruprecht, 1860).

F. Godet, *Commentaire sur l'Evangile de Saint Luc* (Neuchâtel 1888).[8]

Meyer's *Handb. üb. Mt*, newly edited by B. Weiss (Göttingen 1890).[9]

Meyer's *Handb. üb. Mr u. Lc*, newly edited by B. Weiss (Göttingen: Vandenhoeck & Ruprecht, 1885).[10]

Holtzmann, *Hand Commentary on the NT*, vol. 1, Synoptic Gospels and Acts (Freiburg i. B: Mohr, 1892).[11]

We first give a short *analysis* of the two accounts, then proceed to a *comparison*, from which the *results* regarding the priority and the relation of the accounts to one another will arise naturally.

I. Matthew 8:5–13

a. The context. According to Matthew, the story of the centurion at Capernaum occurred after Jesus' return to Capernaum from [preaching] the Sermon on the Mount. In the interim (8:1–4), according to Matthew, there takes place the *healing of the leper*, which Luke locates at a different point: 5:12–14, *before* the Sermon on the Mount. In Matthew the *healing of the mother-in-law of Peter* and others then follows our story.

b. The content. On his entry into Capernaum, Jesus is received by a centurion with the news that his son is ill, evidently with the unspoken plea that Jesus heal him. By ἑκατοντάρχης [centurion], according to the agreed view of the exegetes, we have to think of a *military official in the service of Herod Antipas*, according to verse 10 a Gentile—scarcely, as *Godet* assumes, a "proselyte of the gate."[12] The meaning of παῖς, which can mean "son" and "servant," is difficult. There are certainly more examples of the latter sense in the New Testament, including the understanding of Luke; then again, however, the reference of *Holtzmann* to verse 9,[13] where Matthew has δοῦλος [slave] for servant—as well as to the Johannine parallel, which is still to be addressed[14] and explicitly gives υἱός [son]—seems to me to be decisive for "*son*." His illness, which Matthew describes as follows, βέβληται παραλυτικός, δεινῶς βασανιζόμενος [lying at home paralyzed, in terrible distress], is probably rightly conceived by *Godet* as "acute rheumatism. In befalling certain organs, the heart, for example, this illness can become fatal."[15] That the latter was the case is demonstrated by the urgency of the centurion, as well as by the explicit statement in Luke and John.

Jesus answers with the simple *promise*: "*I* will come and heal him!" (with emphasis on ἐγώ [I]). *Meyer* rightly rejects as "unnecessarily sought"[16] the view

8. Fr. Godet, *Commentaire sur l'Évangile de Saint Luc*, vol. 1, 3rd ed. (Neuchâtel: Jules Sandoz, 1888).

9. B. Weiss, *Das Matthäus-Evangelium*, KEK, sec. 1, 1st half, 8th ed. (Göttingen: Vandenhoeck & Ruprecht, 1890).

10. B. Weiss, *Kritisch exegetisches Handbuch über die Evangelien des Markus und Lukas* [Critical Exegetical Handbook of the Gospels of Mark and Luke], KEK, part 1, 2nd half, 7th ed. (Göttingen: Vandenhoeck & Ruprecht, 1885).

11. H. J. Holtzmann, *Die Synoptiker. Die Apostelgeschichte* [The Synoptics. The Acts of the Apostles], HC 1, 2nd ed. (Freiburg i. B.: Herder, 1892).

12. Cf. Godet, *Saint Luc* (1888), 1:463.

13. Holtzmann, *Die Synoptiker*, 128.

14. See below, 42–43.

15. Godet, *Saint Luc* (1888), 1:463.

16. Meyer, *Evangelium des Matthäus*, 201.

of *Fritzsche*, who wants to deduce a question: "Shall I come and heal him?"[17] Incidentally, this view has recently been taken up again by *Zahn*.[18] "Lord, . . . I am not worthy to have you come under my roof," replies the modest centurion in verse 8a. In facing the appearance of Jesus, he feels deeply his unworthiness—or, as the Jesuit *Maldonatus* expresses it, "He said not by superstition but by faith that he was unworthy" [*non superstitione sed fide dixit, se indignum esse*].[19] Indeed, he declares his faith (8:8b–9) that Christ need only *command* (μόνον εἰπὲ λόγῳ), and his son will recover. In this connection he adduces *relations in military service* as a comparison: As he, the centurion, has himself to obey his superiors, and as his soldiers and slaves obey him in turn, so diseases must obey Jesus [and] are ὑπὸ ἐξουσίαν [under authority] to him: he can bid them come and go. It is difficult to think here with *Ewald* of *demons*,[20] or with *Olshausen*[21] and *Hahn* of *angels*.[22]

Jesus is *astonished* by this, in which reaction *Holtzmann* sees a first indication "of the way corresponding to his experience by which Jesus arrives at the expansion of his messianic program beyond nationally conditioned boundaries"[23] and speaks words that are momentous for the future of Christianity: "*Not even in Israel have I found such faith!*"—or, as another version has it (παρ' οὐδενί statt οὐδέ) ["in no one" instead of "not even"]: "in no one in Israel." And further: the Gentiles from east and west will come and sit at the table with the patriarchs; the "heirs of the kingdom," however, will be banished εἰς τὸ σκότος τὸ ἐξώτερον [to the outer darkness], where weeping and gnashing of teeth prevail.

The whole eschatological description in verses 11–12 strongly evinces *Jewish coloration*. πολλοὶ ἀπὸ ἀνατολῶν καὶ δυσμῶν [many from east and west] is reminiscent of Isa. 45:6 (the LXX has the same terms!). Table fellowship with the heroes of Judaism, the patriarchs, belonged particularly to the expected blessedness of the kingdom of the Messiah (cf. also "poor Lazarus," who sits (Luke 16:23) ἐν τοῖς κόλποις [by the side] of Abraham), from which the Gentiles are naturally excluded. Even in the Midrash *Tanchuma* (on the Pentateuch) from the ninth century CE it states (as cited according to *Meyer*): "In mundo futuro, (dixit Deus) mensam ingentem vobis sternam, *quod gentiles videbunt et pudefient*" [in the future world, (God said) I will spread a great table for you, *which the Gentiles will see and be ashamed*].[24] Jesus *destroys* this hope here: it will be the other way round—the Gentiles will come into the company of Abraham, Isaac, and Jacob; the υἱοὶ τῆς βασιλείας [sons of the kingdom] will, however, stand outside. The Jews are "sons of the kingdom" insofar as they, as the historical "people

17. *Quatuor N. T. Evangelia recensuit et cum commentariis perpetuis edidit C. Fr. A. Fritzsche* [Four New Testament Gospels examined and published with continuous commentary, by C. Fr. A. Fritzsche], vol. 1, *Evangelium Matthaei* (Leipzig, 1826), 311.
18. T. Zahn, *Das Evangelium des Matthäus*, KNT 1 (Leipzig: Werner Scholl, 1903), 336.
19. J. Maldonatus, *Commentarii in Quatuor Evangelistas* [Commentaries on the four evangelists], curavit C. Martin, vol. 1, *Qui complectitur Evangelium Matthaei et Marci integrum* [Which includes the whole of the Gospel of Matthew and of Mark], 2nd ed. (Mainz 1853), 121.
20. H. Ewald, *Geschichte des Volkes Israel bis Christus*, vol. 5, *Geschichte Christus und seiner Zeit* (Göttingen: Dieterschen Buchhandlung, 1855), 242.
21. H. Olshausen, *Biblischer Commentar über sämmtliche Schriften des Neuen Testaments, zunächst für Prediger und Studirende*, vol. 1, *Die drei ersten Evangelien bis zur Leidensgeschichte enthaltend*, 2nd ed. (Reutlingen, 1834), 269.
22. G. L. Hahn, *Die Theologie des Neuen Testaments*, vol. 1 (Leipzig, 1854), 310.
23. Holtzmann, *Die Synoptiker*, 129.
24. Meyer, *Evangelium des Matthäus*, 202.

of God," would really have the next claim to the kingdom of the Messiah. *Holtzmann* regards the whole text of verses 11–12 as an *insertion from the collection of sayings* (in Luke at 13:28–30), the beginning of which (i.e., Luke 13:26–27) Matthew had already inserted in the Sermon on the Mount, Matthew 7:21–23.[25] Without desiring to allow myself a final judgment, I do not understand why the state of affairs could not just as well be *the other way round*, given that the words about the narrow gate, the false confessors (etc.) in Luke 13 do *not necessarily* have to precede those concerning the condemnation of the Jews and the acceptance of the Gentiles, while the latter would in turn fit very well in the context of our story. In this case, verses 11 and 12 would then stand in the correct place.

The repetition of εἶπεν ὁ Ἰησοῦς [Jesus said] in verse 13, which would look strange with the deletion of 11 and 12, allows one to conclude that something longer preceded it.

"'Go; let it be done for you according to your faith.' And the servant was healed in that hour." With these words the remarkable account closes. By the power working at a distance that resides in Jesus, the ill man is healed. If the two-source hypothesis is proven correct also in our case, then the addition ἐν τῇ ὥρᾳ ἐκείνῃ [in that hour] in 8:13b may, as *Holtzmann* assumes,[26] originate *from the evangelist*.

II. Luke 7:1–10, 13, 28–30

a. The context here is a little different insofar as our story clearly follows the *Sermon on the* Mount—or rather, *Plain* (Luke 6:20–49)—*immediately*, while the healing of the leper, as mentioned above, is already recounted in Luke 5:12–14, between the calling of the fishermen as apostles and the healing of the paralyzed man. The account of the centurion at Capernaum is then followed in Luke 7:11–17 by that of the *young man at Nain*.

b. The content. The immediate transition from the Sermon on the Plain to our text is marked by the words ἐπειδὴ ἐπλήρωσεν πάντα τὰ ῥήματα αὐτοῦ [after Jesus had finished all his sayings]. As in Matthew, Jesus enters Capernaum, but now the situation has changed: in Luke 7:2, the evangelist himself tells of the *ill man in the house of the centurion*, and here he is explicitly named δοῦλος [slave]. The centurion hears of the presence of Jesus; obviously the latter is thus already *in the town*, albeit not yet arrived at his usual accommodation, the house of Peter—this is shown by verse 9, where *the people are following Jesus*. However, instead of now seeking out Jesus himself, as in Matthew, he sends πρεσβυτέρους τῶν Ἰουδαίων [some Jewish elders] to him. In the earlier editions of his commentary on Luke, *Godet* understood by this term *leaders of the synagogue* (ἀρχισυνάγωγοι),[27] which has much in its favor. However, he then abandoned that view and arrived at the meaning *elders of the people*, "magistrats urbains,"[28] as he phrased it, as also did *Meyer*,[29] *Holtzmann*,[30] and *Weiss*.[31]

25. Holtzmann, *Die Synoptiker*, 129.
26. Holtzmann, *Die Synoptiker*, 129.
27. Fr. Godet, *Commentaire sur l'Évangile de Saint Luc* (Neuchâtel, 1871), 1:357.
28. Godet, *Saint Luc* (1888), 1:463.
29. Meyer, *Evangelien des Markus und Lukas*, 338.
30. Holtzmann, *Die Synoptiker*, 128.
31. Weiss, *Handbuch über die Evangelien des Markus und Lukas*, 386.

They are supposed to ask Jesus on his behalf ὅπως ἐλθὼν διασώσῃ τὸν δοῦλον αὐτοῦ [to come and heal his slave]. One might observe the vivid διασώσῃ [heal], which might correspond approximately to our "to get someone through." To reinforce the request assigned to them, the elders add of their own accord: "*He is worthy that you would grant him this. For he loves our people and built the synagogue for us.*" Apparently from this latter information, *Godet* has drawn the conclusion cited above,[32] that the centurion was a "proselyte of the gate," a גֵּר שַׁעַר. According to *Schürer's Gesch. d. jüd. Volkes* [History of the Jewish people],[33] these were non-Jews who permanently lived in the land of Israel and as a result submitted to the most essential laws of the same. Yet, as *Schürer* explains, this was an unfruitful theory, "about which the Palestinian Greeks and Romans scarcely bothered much."[34]

One might observe that *the point of our account is abandoned if the centurion is made half-Jewish.* It would still be possible to regard him as one of the φοβούμενοι τὸν θεόν [those who fear God] from the Gentile world—who, according to *Schürer*, are fundamentally different from the גֵּרֵי הַשַּׁעַר,[35] such as we find portrayed, for example, in the centurion Cornelius in Acts 10:1–2. Yet against this, in turn, is to be objected that under this designation were understood those followers who were "God-fearing" Gentiles, who attached themselves *to the Jewish communities in the Diaspora*. Gentile Caesarea in Acts 10 may be counted among the latter, but not Capernaum. Therefore, it still seems to me simplest to think of the centurion as a normal, uncircumcised *Gentile*, as does *Zahn*,[36] by which a friendly relationship with Judaism is certainly not excluded. If it were otherwise, then some trace of his disposition would have had to have been preserved in the texts. This, however, is *not* the case.

In verse 6 Jesus immediately accepts the request and follows them to the house of the centurion. On the way they encounter the latter's second delegation, this time consisting of *friends* of his, who report to Jesus on his behalf the reservation that, in Matthew, the centurion himself expresses: "Lord, I am not worthy to have you come under my roof," with the preceding clause μὴ σκύλλου [do not trouble yourself] and the parenthetical clause in verse 7a: "*therefore I did not consider myself worthy to come to you.*" Verses 8 and 9 demonstrate almost complete agreement with Matthew, apart from two explanatory additions: Luke adds ὑπὸ ἐξουσίαν [under authority] and τασσόμενος [set] to verse 8a, and to verse 9a the "illuminating" (Holtzmann)[37] στραφείς [turning] and the explicit reference that ἀκολουθοῦντες [followers] refers to the *people*, while the ἀμήν [truly] of Matthew before the words of Jesus is suppressed.

The *eschatological verses 11 and 12*, which here follow in Matthew, are missing from the text of Luke; the latter concludes instead, after the brief saying of

---

32. See above at n. 11.
33. E. Schürer, *Geschichte des jüdischen Volkes im Zeitalter Jesu Christi*, part 2, *Die inneren Zustände Palästina's und des jüdischen Volkes im Zeitalter Jesu Christi*, 2nd ed. (Leipzig, 1886), 564–75, esp. 569. ET: *A History of the Jewish People in the Time of Jesus Christ*, division 2, vol. 2, *The Internal Conditions of Palestine, and of the Jewish People, in the Time of Jesus Christ*, trans. Sophia Taylor and Rev. Peter Christie (Edinburgh, 1885), 311–27, esp. 319.
34. Schürer, *Geschichte des jüdischen Volkes*, 2:569.
35. Schürer, *Geschichte des jüdischen Volkes*, 2:567.
36. Zahn, *Evangelium des Matthäus*, 334–35.
37. Holtzmann, *Die Synoptiker*, 129.

Jesus in verse 9b, with the report that the friends go back into the house of the centurion and find the *servant healthy*. In his synopsis, however, *Huck* rightly inserts *between verses 9 and 10* the sayings from Luke 13:28–30 that have already been mentioned several times.[38]

It is even more obvious than in Matthew that these may very well be in their original place *here* [in Luke 7], especially when we consider that the verses in Luke are given in reversed order, so that it is to be assumed that Luke 13:30 (the last, who will be first, etc.) stood at the apex of the whole passage. It fits at least as well here as at the end of the address to the disciples, where Matthew 19:30 has it. Here it provides a simple transition from verse 9b [in Luke 7] to the following, that is, Luke 13:29, which follows 13:28 and the end of the pericope in Luke 7:10.

III. Comparison of the Synoptic Accounts and Results of the Same

We have now looked at both texts in detail and have already established the most essential *differences*; it still remains to recap them concisely in context and from this to form a view concerning the two passages' *relations of origin*.

a. The *location* of the story in Matthew is the same throughout: the first part and the second part of the event take place *at the entrance* to the town of Capernaum (εἰσελθόντος αὐτοῦ εἰς Κ.) [as he entered Capernaum; 8:5]. It is open to question in Luke, where we need to conceive of the first request—we have assumed from the note ἀκούσας δὲ περὶ τοῦ Ἰησοῦ [when he heard about Jesus; 7:3]—as [meaning that Jesus is] already *in* the town. The second request is certainly near the house of the centurion, thus likewise *in* the town.

b. In Matthew the *characters* are these: Jesus, the centurion, and the ἀκολουθοῦντες [those who followed]; and in Luke by contrast, the curious people: Jesus, the town magistrates, the friends of the centurion, and again ὁ ἀκολουθῶν ὄχλος [the following crowd; 7:9], while the centurion himself does not appear in the picture at all.

c. I do not wish to repeat the *textual differences*; I merely recall once again the most significant one: the elision of the [Matt. 8:11] short eschatological speech in Luke, between verses 9 and 10.

That these differences—especially those mentioned under *a* and *b* [above]—are *not* to be *harmonized*, or only so in a highly *artificial* manner, is obvious without further ado. At the time when the theory of verbal inspiration was dominant, two different stories had to be assumed for this reason, like it or not.

Today, things are more simple for us. Let us first seek to reach, if not to the bottom of the *"Whence?"* of our passage, then at least closer to it. The practicable view concerning this question is the one that we stated immediately in the introduction:

The centurion at Capernaum, together with the other extant pieces of dialogue that are present in Matthew and Luke but not in Mark, originates from the lost collection of

---

38. *Synopse der drei ersten Evangelien*, ed. A. Huck, 2nd ed. (Freiburg i. B./Leipzig/Tübingen: J. C. B. Mohr, 1898), 49.

sayings—apostolic source, logia, or whatever one may call it. So, for example, *Holtzmann*[39] and *Weiss*.[40]

Indeed this has much in its favor, above all the consistent placement of our passage in the course of the Gospels—*in Matthew and Luke immediately after the Sermon on the Mount*, whereas the story of the leper in Matthew, which is taken from Mark 1:40–44 and falls between the Sermon on the Mount and our text, proves nothing (contra *Godet*).[41] Must one not conclude that *the Sermon on the Mount and the centurion at Capernaum formed a connected whole within that source*? It is noteworthy, in the first place, that the same scholars who—as we saw above[42]—strike the section Matthew 8:10–12 from our text, now want to assign the latter to the collection of sayings; but if our text were indeed in that collection, it would only have the right to be there on the basis of that section!! Let us look more closely at this view. It leads to the necessary conclusion, which *Holtzmann* also draws,[43] that one or other or both of the evangelists have *altered* the *material* available to them, for no one would claim that the two texts were compatible without such an assumption. The assumption of such an alteration of the text would be possible, but there would need to be *reasons* for it.

The most obvious reason is to think of one of the well-known *dogmatic tendencies* that particularly the first and third evangelists undoubtedly pursue. We expect emphasis and underlining of this narrative, which is so favorable to Paulinism in *Luke*, but reticence and perhaps even obliteration of the facts in *Matthew*. But if we now examine the texts, we find to our astonishment almost the *opposite*: *in his account Matthew provides not only as many features that are Pauline, but instead an increase in features supportive of mission to the Gentiles*: although in Luke the Gentile centurion only communicates with Jesus through the mouthpiece of the Jews, in Matthew we see him personally approaching Jesus; although Luke breaks off the words of Jesus with verse 9b, Matthew 8:11 and 12 offer us that eschatological speech about judgment of the Jews. *Does that speak for the use and reworking of a common source?* In light of this state of affairs, all other possible variations of the *relationship of the accounts to one another* are now to be considered.

First there would be the conjecture that *the pericope is a double reworking of a piece of Ur-Mark*. Here the same difficulty arises as before: whence do the historical differences come, if there is no dogmatic reason for them? And why would Mark have dropped such a valuable text later? There would also be the conjecture that *Matthew had reworked Luke or Luke had reworked Matthew*. Godet rightly retorts here: "But how would Luke have embroidered upon the canvas of Matthew in this way, or the latter trimmed the picture of Luke? Our evangelists are believing and serious people" [*Mais comment Luc eût-il ainsi brodé sur le canevas de Matthieu, ou celui-ci taillé dans le tableau de Luc? Nos* évangélistes *sont des hommes croyants et sérieux.*][44] *It seems to me that we should completely refrain from the idea of a reworking of the same material in this case.*

---

39. Cf. Holtzmann, *Die Synoptiker*, 10–12 and 128–30.
40. Weiss, *Das Matthäus-Evangelium*, 165.
41. Godet, *Saint Luc* (1888), 1:461–62.
42. See above, 37.
43. Holtzmann, *Die Synoptiker*, 128–30.
44. Godet, *Saint Luc* (1888), 1:464–65.

That leads us necessarily to the conjecture that *different sources for our text were available to the evangelists*. In this case, we again have the choice between two possibilities:

1. *Both evangelists are drawing on the same source—the one from an older and the other from a newer version.* In and of itself, this view is not impossible; however, what speaks against it is its complexity, which emerges when one attempts to use our text to reconstruct the existence of both texts.

2. There remains only one further conjecture, and I have finally decided in favor of this: *Both evangelists are drawing on two completely different sources.* Thus also claim *Meyer*[45] and *Godet*.[46]

It is unnecessary to note that nothing is being said thereby against the *Synoptic two-sources theory* in general. But no rule is without exceptions. One might observe that even consistent supporters of that hypothesis such as *Wernle*[47] do not manage without such exceptions, for in Matthew and Luke are numerous passages not present in any other Gospel, and thus come neither from the Mark-source nor from the source of sayings. This is the so-called *Matthean and Lukan special material*, of which especially the latter is of greatest value (I mention only parables, such as those of the Good Samaritan, of the Prodigal Son, of the Rich Man and Poor Lazarus, of the Pharisee and the Tax Collector, the story of the road to Emmaus, and many others, all texts that we would not like to miss in the Gospel!).

If, then, there are texts that one can derive neither from Mark nor from the collection of sayings, simply because only one evangelist, Matthew *or* Luke has them, then I do not understand why, for once, *a text that is present in Matthew and Luke cannot come from somewhere else than one of those principal sources*—all the more so, if the two accounts exhibit such historical differences as in our case.

Precisely from the existence of that special material, it is to be concluded that the Gospel tradition was very diverse. One might observe, for example, in the prologue of Luke at 1:1, the text ἐπειδήπερ πολλοὶ ἐπεχείρησαν [since many have undertaken]. There are reasons for assuming that some of the texts from the special material of Matthew and Luke were originally handed down separately; the same is true even of a text that has been taken up by all three Synoptic Gospels, such as the short apocalypse in Mark 13, which *Wernle* regards as an eschatological pamphlet from the earliest time.[48]

Must we not assume something similar of the centurion of Capernaum? Or would ultimately a purely *oral tradition* need to be conceived? It is self-evident that the latter formed the basis of both the accounts available to the evangelists. In contrast, it is hardly to be supposed that Matthew and Luke drew directly on this oral tradition, as *Godet* believes;[49] instead, we need to think of *two written records*. The *speech of the centurion* in Matthew 8:8 and 9 = Luke 7:6b, 7, and 8; and the *answer of Jesus* to it in Matthew 8:10–12 = Luke 7:9b + 13, 30, 29, 28; these formed the center of both. Yet the historical frame around these parallel sections then turned out differently in both sources, as we have seen: after

45. Cf. Weiss, *Handbuch über die Evangelien des Markus und Lukas*, 386.
46. Godet, *Saint Luc* (1888), 1:461–62.
47. Wernle, *Die synoptische Frage*, 91–108, 188–95.
48. Wernle, *Die synoptische Frage*, 213.
49. Godet, *Saint Luc* (1888), 1:465.

fifty years [from Jesus' life], why should such details not have shifted in the memory? *In any case, none of the essential differences originates from the one or the other of the evangelists,* except perhaps in Matthew the relocation of the text of Luke 13:30 to Matthew 19:30, and in Luke the shifting of the eschatological discourse to chapter 13; however, these are still not differences in the proper sense. Precisely the fact that the Judaistic Matthew mentions the latter here [at 8:11–12] seems to me evidence that it belongs here.

The answer to the *question of priority* in respect to our text will be related to whether one ascribes certain "illuminating"[50] features in Luke to the evangelist himself or to his source. In analogy with other texts, the former is to be assumed. One might observe texts such as Luke 7:2, ὃς ἦν αὐτῷ ἔντιμος [whom he valued highly]; 7:6, μὴ σκύλλου [do not trouble yourself]; 7:7, διὸ οὐδὲ ἐμαυτὸν ἠξίωσα πρὸς σὲ ἐλθεῖν [therefore I did not presume to come to you]; 7:8, the τασσόμενος [set] after ἐξουσία [authority]; 7:9, στραφείς [turning]; 13:28, πάντας προφήτας [all the prophets] added to the patriarchs; 7:29, north and south added to east and west, and so on.

All these details in Luke suggest the greater age of the Matthew account, whereby, however, nothing is stated in respect to historical fidelity. Indeed, the *accuracy of the historical information in detail can be distributed across both evangelists,* as, in my opinion, the first part of the account according to Luke and the second part according to Matthew are historical. However, we here get into the area of conjectures.

Our Synoptic investigation is thereby at an end. I had originally undertaken to go into the *Johannine account of the "royal official at Capernaum"* (John 4:46–54) more deeply as well, and I have also looked over the relevant sections of the commentaries on this. A lack of time now prevents me from giving an extensive presentation of the problems that come into view (the most difficult one is John 4:48!), as would belong to the completeness of my study. May it suffice that I have come to the view (with *Holtzmann*[51] and *Weiss,*[52] contra *Meyer*[53] and *Godet*[54]) that *the Synoptic account of the centurion at Capernaum is identical with the Johannine account of the royal official at Capernaum* (cf. especially the explanations of B. Weiss in his commentary on John).[55]

Godet reckons of this hypothesis, which, incidentally, Irenaeus had already established:[56] "In truth, if these two accounts were reporting on the same fact, the details of the evangelical narratives would no longer merit the least credence" [En vérité, si ces deux récits se rapportaient au même fait, les détails des narrations évangéliques ne mériteraient plus la moindre créance].[57] I do *not* believe the matter to be so dangerous; however, a detailed justification of that

---

50. See above at n. 37.

51. H. J. Holtzmann, *Evangelium, Briefe und Offenbarung des Johannes,* HC 4, 2nd ed. (Freiburg i. B./ Leipzig: J. C. B. Mohr, 1893), 87.

52. B. Weiss, *Kritisch exegetisches Handbuch über das Evangelium des Johannes,* KEK, sec. 2, 7th ed. (Göttingen: Vandenhoeck & Ruprecht, 1886), 215–16.

53. H. A. W. Meyer, *Kritisch exegetisches Handbuch über das Evangelium des Johannes,* KEK, sec. 2, 5th ed. (Göttingen: Vandenhoeck & Ruprecht, 1869), 214–15.

54. Godet, *Saint Luc* (1888), 1:466.

55. Weiss, *Handbuch über das Evangelium des Johannes,* 215–16.

56. Godet, *Saint Luc* (1888), 1:466.

57. Irenaeus, *Contra haereses* [*Against heresies*] 2.22.3; *Sancti Irenaei episcopi Lugdunensis quae supersunt omnia* [Complete works of Saint Irenaeus, Bishop of Lyon], ed. by A. Stieren, vol. 1 (Leipzig, 1853), 357.

would require going into the material itself. I have mentioned the proposition only to show that far-reaching differences exist on the question, whose consideration would lead too far for today.

However, the *more original form of our material is in any case preserved not in the Johannine* (contra *Weizsäcker*[58] and others) *but in the Synoptic form,* again without the presence of a tendentious distortion on the side of the author of the Gospel of John, whether that be the apostle John himself or one of the teachers of the Christian congregation from John's sphere of influence in Asia Minor.

The differences between the Johannine and the Synoptic accounts are, similarly to those of the latter between each other, to be explained by shifts in the memory of the author—or rather of his written or oral originals.

Regarding the thought content, however, as *Weiss* explains well,[59] this is the same here as there, even if in somewhat different form.

29.XI.05

---

58. Cf. Weiss (*Handbuch über das Evangelium des Johannes*, 216), whose comment regarding this matter could have come from a formulation that was open to misunderstanding in H. A. W. Meyer (*Evangelium des Johannes*, 215). On Weizsäcker's own thesis, compare C. Weizsäcker, *Untersuchungen über die evangelische Geschichte, ihre Quellen und den Gang ihrer Entwicklung* (Gotha: R. Besser, 1864), 270–89, esp. 274 and 277.
59. Weiss, *Handbuch über das Evangelium des Johannes*, 215–16.

Zofingia and the Social Question
1906

Just as his father before him and his brothers with and after him, Karl Barth belonged to the student association Zofingia. Shortly after his matriculation on October 22, 1904, he handed in his "membership application"; on November 8, 1904, he was then—with the student cap (Cerevis) and with the alias "Sprenzel" ("lightweight" in the sense of "wispy," "slim")—accepted into the Bernese section of the "Swiss Zofingia Association"; on December 9, 1905, he was "fraternized"[1] (burschifiziert), and on October 31, 1908, he was declared a Zofingia-Alumnus (Alt-Zofinger).

In 1819 the Swiss Zofingia resulted from an initial gathering of students from Zurich and Bern who met halfway between the two cities in Zofingen, hence the name. In the subsequent annual festivals, students from other Swiss universities and academies joined them. Originally, the association understood itself as "a patriotic fraternity" that hoped for "a Switzerland, courageous toward abroad and unified within," "uniting the entire studying youth in a union and thus to prepare the spiritual unity of Switzerland."[2] In the following years, the eventful and in part tense history of the Zofingia was determined, on the one hand, by disputes about the concrete political decisions on the way toward this common goal and, on the other hand, by discussions brought up by the—initially deliberately rejected—adoption of certain elements of the German students' codes of conduct [= Comments]; to put it briefly, this was about the question whether the Zofingia should understand itself first as a "fraternity" (Verbindung) or primarily as an "association" (Verein).

Karl Barth's position on the Zofingia is characterized by these two problems as well. Having only recently been officially accepted, he considered the "dominant tone" in the Bernese section already "a bit too strongly emphasizing the coziness of gathering around beer (biergemütlich)."[3] His critical concerns about the "truly inexhaustible topic 'The position of the Zofinger thought in the Zofingia Bern'" intensify in a letter dated May 17/18, 1905, to the former fellow pupil and now fellow student and co-Zofingia member Otto Lauterburg, then based in Neuchâtel, who apparently had written to him expressing similar reservations. Barth's reply is rather extensive: seven pages of small octave paper, interrupted on page 5 (in the middle of the sentence, even in the middle of the word "Zofingergeist" [spirit of the Zofingia]!) by adding, "Meanwhile, I have been to the drinking night [Kneipabend]. Now it is 12:30 a.m., thus 18 May." He offers, in a way, a preliminary study of the thoughts that he set before his association in the next semester.

1. On the difference between foxes (*Füchse*, i.e., *Couleur* students [wearing colored headgear] in their first two semesters) and fraternity brothers [*Burschen*], see below, n. 95.
2. Ch. Gillard, "Zofingia," in *HBLS* 7:673.
3. Letter to W. Spoendlin, dated November 28, 1904.

Barth concedes to Lauterburg without further ado ("Do you think that I am becoming too Bernese, huh?"): "The conditions in our section, . . . especially in its financial aspects, do presently not only directly violate the central statutes, but also—what is even more important—to the gravest extent go against the ideal purposes of our association." Already in this letter as well, Barth's critique is based on the "Report of the first central discussion" of 1904–5.[4] From that point of view, he is delighted "to a huge extent that Robert wants to come here who, based on his contribution to the central discussion, certainly recognized what is rotten in the state of Denmark."[5] A point of discontent for Barth is, most of all, the association's high spending, an item that plays an especially important role in this article on "Zofingia and the Social Question" as well: "If we reach the point that one no longer gets active because of vexatious Mammon, we are in a bad state."[6] At least, "the monthly contribution was reduced to 10 Swiss francs"—"albeit still way too high,"[7] but nonetheless an "example," for "a new management has taken charge," "from which I expect the best, even if it is still tainted with all kinds of residue from a rotten bourgeois period." For "in no section does tradition have such an influence as it currently has with us. 'It has always been like that; therefore, it is good!' That is the great wisdom of the Bernese!" That is why the help from Zofingia members from outside—"the 14 days that I spent with Zofingia members from Basel during the vacation are a fond memory to me"—is so important. "If it counts anywhere not [only] to speak of Zofingia ideals, but to act and fight for them, it is the case in Bern." For him, it was "already more about leaving than about remaining; however, as I am put into this role, I want to manage it as well and consequently as possible, even though it is no great joy to always have to represent the opposition! If, however, members from chapters notoriously ruled by the true spirit of the Zofingia are coming to Bern now, should it not simply be their duty to join in and to seek to plant this spirit here as well?" Toward the end, Barth urges his friend: "When I get seriously annoyed about nonsense, waste of time and money in the Bern chapter, the thought of the 'national association' [Gesamtverein] strengthens and lifts me immensely; that

---

4. See below 54, 60.

5. See below, nn. 70 and 90.

6. This is an old topic: "For a long time, the Bern chapter has been in disrepute because of its high budget, because of the excessive financial burdens that it inflicts on its members despite the central statutes," concedes the Bernese *Centralblatt* correspondent in the report on SS [Summer Semester] 1906 (*Centralblatt* of the Swiss Zofingia Association 47 [1906–7]: 246), yet just to dismiss the "often-mentioned laying of financial claims" right away again, as criticized by Central President H. Däniker in his report on the Association Year 1906–7 (*Centralblatt* 48 [1907–8]: 87–88). After demonstrating extensively "that Bern is in no way worse off than Basel and Zurich," the Bernese reporter assures in the end: "Any upright fraternity brother who was really keen to become a Zofingia member never has been sent away by us because of financial difficulties" (*Centralblatt* 47 [1906–7]: 246–47). The protocols of the Bernese Zofingia (in the Staatsarchiv Bern) show that the topic was discussed heatedly again and again in the chapter as well (during the time of concern here, e.g., on February 18, 1905; on May 6, 1905; on October 29, 1905; on May 5, 1906 [with suggestions for cuts by Barth]; on November 3, 1906). In discussing the central topic of discussion, "Conditions for entry into the Zofingia," on June 9, 1906, Barth brought back memories of his position on the "vexed point of finance," but according to the protocol he caused "great amusement" with the suggestion not to forgo the celebratory *Commers* in memory of the Battle of Laupen (1339), but still to "drop the ball and business with young ladies" (*Ball und Besenbummel*). ("*Besen*" was the student expression for "young ladies"; "*Commers*" was the term for a special celebratory meeting of a student fraternity.)

7. Already in this letter, Barth complains: "It is . . . just *one* thing making our dealings so expensive: and that is these d. [dopey?] ladies. Ball and *Besenbummel* might be very nice things (?), yet at the least the cost should be distributed equally among the *participants*, instead of the cashbox covering it all." A similar disenchantment is expressed in a letter to his father, dated August 31, 1905: Perhaps in the Zofingia "this winter, a little different melody might be played, but now, the black ghosts of the *Tanzeten* [dance soirees] already arise, which are appearing to me more stupid than ever."

group represents an idea that is better than great, in spite of it all, standing out among the different groups to the left and to the right! May you learn to say as well: Nevertheless! [Trans. note: Barth uses the word "einewäg," from the Bernese dialect.]

The complaint in Barth's letter to his father, dated August 31, 1905, runs along the same lines: "I regret it deeply that the Bernese Zofingia offers me so little, apart from contact with my Basel and Neuchâtel friends and the abstract joyous awareness to be a Zofingia member at all. You probably had it better back in the days in Basel."

Karl Barth's critique is thus mostly caused by peculiarities of the Bernese Zofingia, where, of the three elements of the Zofingia motto "Patriae, amicitae, litteris!" [For the fatherland, for friendship, for the sciences!], friendship was cultivated the most, and where one was proud of the "honorary title 'friendship section'" (Yearbook 1907–8, similarly 1906–7; Staatsarchiv Bern).[8] Probably for that reason, the Yearbook 1908–9 notes, slightly mockingly, that "for several semesters" "the slogans have been taken down and freshly dusted again and again. Particularly the 'Patria' seems to have been sidelined, according to some, and thus they mainly ask to become more active socially and politically." Yet the majority of "positive motions . . . had proven mostly to be unfeasible and unworkable," so that the interest had waned. The fact that Karl Barth, who belonged to those critically mentioned here, felt much closer affinity to the Basel kind of Zofingia was expressed remarkably clearly when the Bernese section decided on July 7, 1906, to allow also the wearing of so-called "Storm Caps" (Stürmer: a hat common in a number of associations in Germany in those days). The report remarks after the vote: "Barth theol: advises that he wants to wear a Basel cap for gatherings in the future." In this context, it is also noteworthy that Karl Barth—maybe because of his father?—added to his signature the old Basel Zofingia circle, although since 1884 officially a slightly different form had been introduced.

The background for Fritz Barth's perception of being a member of the Zofingia in Basel—he was a member of that chapter from May 1874 to May 1879[9]—as "the longer, the dearer," and for his son's evident expectations of the chapter in Bern, can be captured most clearly in a lecture that Fritz Barth gave—"as the excited Zofingia member that I have always been"—at the Zofingia Alumni Association in Bern in 1902 on the topic "Idealism and Materialism at the University and in the Philisterium [the group of Alumni]."[10] In an exposition of the Zofingia slogan, Fritz Barth conjures the "Zofingia spirit," "which our fatherland needs," the "idealism of love of the fatherland and of appreciation of neighbor."[11] Proper idealism would, however, be possible only there, "where personalities are present" and "where love reigns," both of which are needed especially in light of the "social deficits"; this idealism would "only remain for our people if their faith remained as well."[12]

---

8. According to the semester report of WS [Winter Semester] 1903–4 in the *Centralblatt* 44 [1903–4]: 433), the Bernese Zofingia owes this title to the Central President: "Bern has always been the 'cup chapter' of the Zofingia. . . . Even our C. P. [Central President], the strict guardian of student virtue and morality, . . . could not escape the beneficial 'influence' of the foaming goblet on the exchange of the members among each other: he himself sang a hymn of praise to enthusiastic binge drinking [*Bechern*] and called Bern the 'friendship chapter.'" In the same volume of the *Centralblatt* (692), one can find a photo of the "draught room of the Bern chapter."

9. *Centralblatt* 52 (1911–12): 578 (cf. 478).

10. *Centralblatt* 42 (1901–2): 528–35, esp. 529, 535 (reprinted in F. Barth, *Christus unsere Hoffnung: Sammlung von religiösen Reden und Vorträgen* [Christ, our hope: Collection of religious speeches and presentations] (Bern: A. Franke, 1913), 140–49; here on 141, 149).

11. *Centralblatt* 42 (1901–2): 529–30, 535 (F. Barth, *Christus unsere Hoffnung*, 141–42, 149).

12. *Centralblatt* 42 (1901–2): 533–34 (F. Barth, *Christus unsere Hoffnung*, 145–47).

The section lecture held by Karl Barth is also determined by this emphasis on the "ideals" that the Zofingia "has given . . . to us."[13] In his deliberations, the critique of an exaggerated Couleur ruling[14] links up with the critique of an insufficient political ("liberal"-conservative) position on the "social question." Accordingly, the presentation—as probably already the corresponding presentation by Fritz Barth[15]—is to be understood as an element in the debates, resurfacing again and again, between those Zofingia members who cherished the association's life according to the traditional student codes of conduct, and those who wanted to reform the Zofingia, "on the one hand, in the spirit of a return to our founders' ideals and, on the other hand, in the spirit of the questions of our time."[16] During the time of interest here, the contrast seems to have developed particularly visibly in Zurich (where the two groups received their names "Ideal Zofingia members" [IZ] and—according to their preferred seat at the lower member-table [Burschen-Tisch]—"Ubetonen").[17] Yet one reads in the semester report of the winter semester 1907–8, which made public the dispute of direction in the Zurich association: "We afford ourselves . . . a 'classic' and a 'modern' direction, just as the fine arts, criminal law, the Bern chapter, the national economy, or Catholicism."[18] Without a doubt, the presentation by Karl Barth is a document of the early stages of the "modern direction" in the Basel chapter and thus also of the so-called "Ideal Zofingia Members," as they later were called. The demands of the latter were again and again the cause of heated disputes in the chapters and the association as a whole that led the IZ, or rather some of their leading figures, to socialist-revolutionary positions.[19]

13. *Centralblatt* 42 (1901–2): 529 (F. Barth, *Christus unsere Hoffnung*, 141).

14. The semester report WS 1903–4 complains: "We have too large a number of members for whom it seems much more important to answer the question whether or not one should smack a drunk fellow citizen who bumps into you in *Couleur* in the street than any literary or economical task. Indeed, some people among us are assailed by a noble unease on hearing the actually harmless little word 'social'" (*Centralblatt* 44 [1903–4]: 432). The year report 1908–9 (Staatsarchiv Bern) states, by the way, "that a total revision of the *Comment* was requested and resolved," since the *Comment*, "already for some time, . . . had often been a bone of contention."

15. Also compare, e.g., *Centralblatt* 37 (1896–97): 71–72; 48 (1907–8): 597 (Report from the Bern chapter on the winter semester 1907–8: "A Lecture by Zofingia-Alumnus Prof. Barth on the tasks of the Zofingia . . . raised social questions repeatedly in discussion during the winter").

16. This wording can be found in a summarizing memorandum from May 1910, whose signatories include, among others, Karl Barth's brothers Heinrich and Peter and his friend Eduard Thurneysen (see W. Kundert and U. Im Hof, *Geschichte des Schweizerischen Zofingervereins im Überblick*, in M. Burckhardt et al., *Der Schweizerische Zofingerverein, 1819–1969: Eine Darstellung*, ed. Swiss *Zofingerverein* and the Swiss *Altzofingerverein* [Bern: Kommission Wyss Erben, 1969], 90); see also A. Lindt, *Zofingerideale, christliches Bewusstsein und reformierte Theologie, 1819–1918* [Bern, 1969], 208–9).

17. Kundert and Im Hof, *Geschichte des Schweizerischen Zofingervereins*, 83–84; cf. Dietrich Barth, M. Burckhard, and O. Gigon, *Der Schweizerische Zofingerverein, 1819–1935* (Basel: Kommissionsverlag von Helbing & Lichtenhahn, 1935), 97–99; for information about this volume, see *Centralblatt* 76 (1935–36): 749–60 (review) and 761–62 (response).

18. *Centralblatt* 48 (1907–8): 486. The Bernese Year Report 1907–8 (Staatsarchiv Bern), too, mentions "that in Bern we distinguish two parties, the modern one and the traditional one." Admittedly, the writer does not want to accept "such a separation."

19. Kundert and Im Hof, *Geschichte des Schweizerischen Zofingervereins*, 81–108. D. Barth, Burckhardt, Gigon, *Der Schweizerische Zofingerverein*, 115–17. Aside from this, G. Strasser saw himself being led already to warn, in the stanzas dedicated to "the fatherland," against the "temptation" to seek the "progress" to which the Zofingia no doubt felt obligated (see *Centralblatt* 42 [1901–2]: 214–15; also below, nn. 46 and 91) about and with the Social Democrats ("Today, one calls to us: 'Hey! / Social democratic, Zofingia! / . . . / Away with the cross on the Swiss crest! / May our flag only be Red!"); F. Staehlin, *Bericht über das 75. Jubiläum des Zofinger-Vereins 1.-3. August 1893* (Basel: Buchdruckerei Emil Birkhäuser, zum guten Hof, 1894), 63–64.

In contrast to his brothers,[20] *Karl Barth does not seem to have immediately influenced these decisions anymore. The programmatic presentation from January 20, 1906*[21]—*on which, according to a letter to the grandmother and the aunt in Basel, he "worked hard" already on December 28, 1905—was not followed by any further advancements: one is almost tempted to say, "Quite the contrary." Karl Barth, together with three other theologians, was elected to the "Commission" (leadership) of the Bern chapter for the summer semester 1907, indeed as their "President." The vote took place during the first ordinary meeting of the semester on April 27, 1907. Barth won in the sixth ballot with a one-vote majority.*[22] *After the correspondent of the Centralblatt had given a noticeable sigh of relief that "the Bern chapter . . . had come into quieter waters again last winter [winter semester 1906–7], after a few more unsettled semesters,"*[23] *the election at first gave reason for curious and expectant expressions, to be followed by comments of relief: "When a devout spirit notes that the Bernese have filled three-quarters of their needed allotment of commission members, and all of their "fox majors" with more or less hopeful theologians, then he will fold his hands across his Philistine stomach and say: 'Yes, here, finally, a den of murderers has become a house of prayer!'" After an ironic correction of the "disdainful expression" "den of murderers" [versus] "proper people . . . speak here of dashing Couleur students"—these hopes and fears are dissipated with assurances such as "For one, those theologians all are Swiss," and "as true Swiss, always inclined to compromise. Further, all four are among those shepherds who light a small, smoldering fire, not always smelling of incense, outside the door of their future pure life; of course, they are only doing so to obtain, that way, the dark filter needed for this better period of life and a few beer pots for the tasteful decoration of their future final dwelling. Finally, however, and most of all, 'We' are still there as well."*[24] *A little later, one can read, in a report comparing the events and festivals of the Bernese chapter with different Swiss mountains: "Further to the West, who pushes the clouds around and sweeps the fields of snow bare? Right, it's our four soon-to-be world-famous theologians, in the form of angels this time, though, with red-and-white wings as well as tummies. . . . Unfortunately, I do not yet quite see what kind of mountain they want to deck out."*[25] *The yearly report 1906–7 relativized the importance of the change in the commission by speaking mockingly of the "happy natures," "who can immediately turn all kinds of small issues into major and stately affairs. These people understand it, for example, to demonstrate clearly how incredibly important it was that the commission was formed in winter by Hans and Cie, and in summer by Heiri and Gen; that Hans was meek and a former model recruit; Heiri, by contrast, not that much; [to understand] how, only for that reason, the winter was quieter than the summer, and so on." The tone of the summarizing review of the semester is similar, discussing the role of the "President" in particular: "The semester began with major fears and high hopes. The elections brought a surprise. A heretic had become pope. The fellow heretics rejoiced, the orthodox were full*

---

20. See above, n. 16.

21. In the semester report WS 1905–6, it is, by the way, mentioned as one of the presentations, "out of which, otherwise unheard of in Bern, a lively and, by some members, well-prepared, discussion" (*Centralblatt* 46 [1905–6]: 428).

22. As *Präses* [President] Barth had to represent, by the way, two motions of his chapter at the Zofingia *Centralfest* on July 23, 1907, as documented in the *Centralblatt* (48 [1907–8]: 135).

23. *Centralblatt* 47 (1906–7): 513.

24. *Centralblatt* 47 (1906–7): 517–18.

25. *Centralblatt* 47 (1906–7): 611.

of distress. Yet hopes and fears . . . were not fulfilled. The new prince of the church hardly tried to break with ancient sacred traditions. Soon he acted fully orthodox, fully according to the code of conduct. And he did well in doing so. . . . A defiance-filled, premature revolting would have only brought commotion and hate, would have only robbed us of our straightforward calmness for which perhaps, at times, we might be grateful still. In its peaceful intentions the presidency was supported by the rest of the commission and in fact by the majority of the members."[26]

Yet it was not only a peaceable disposition that came into play here. The prophecy uttered during the discussion of his presentation—Barth received it with quite some skepticism—seems much rather to have been fulfilled to a certain extent. Barth truly thought a little differently of the Couleur students[27] during this semester and spent his days in the summer 1907, as he put it himself in his old age, "with a collegiate sense of glory."[28] It would be another few years until Barth perceived the "social question" in a different, new way, until he himself indeed became "president of a temperance association."[29]

In the following years, Barth certainly came to new evaluations in relations to the Zofingia and its world. A preliminary summary can be found in the letter from May 19, 1934, in which he tells his son Markus, "I am . . . ready to gladly give you my consent to the entry into the Zofingia (and even with a certain sense of affectionate fatherly pride). When I heard that you are also considering the Zähringer, I wondered, with a little sigh, whether it was really necessary for you to step in front of me with this strange blue hat on your head. It is now supposed to be, and it will be, a white one. Grandma will tell you how many generations in our family have already worn it with honor, and you will plan to worthily continue that line. The fact that it is a step associated with all kinds of problems—particularly, if we are dealing with the Bernese Zofingia—is not unknown to you. . . . I don't know what the Bernese Zofingia members are like at the moment. But as is well known, tradition is so strong there that, I can well imagine, the basic outlines of the picture are still the same. . . . There has always existed in the Zofingia another, let's call it an "idealistic," tradition that nobody, during my time or the time before that, wanted to know much about. Its value and its importance have indeed their limits. Today I know it better than I did back then. All the same: once a Zofingia member, one can do no other but to stand on this leg and to stand up, no matter what may come, for the belief that amicitia in the Zofingia is reasonable and legitimate only within the framework of patria and scientia and cannot be an end in itself."*

Here again we notice, as the central archivist Andreas Staehlin put it in his obituary in 1969,[30] "that the relationship between Barth and the Zofingia association . . . was

---

26. *Centralblatt* 48 (1907–8): 279–80. Similarly, H. Dänike's *Bericht des Zentralpräsidenten über das Vereinsjahr 1906–7:* "Four theologians in a Bernese Commission was an astounding novelty for the fellow chapters. Nobody claims that this leadership brought with it a lasting redesign of chapter life. In Bern, one is not supportive of sudden changes, and especially in Zofingia life one has conservative leanings; . . . the cost of time and energy demanded by the Bernese chapter from its members corresponds also to what it offers: the comfortable feeling of a close togetherness of all *Weissmützen* (White Caps [i.e., Zofingia members]; see below, n. 69; and *Centralblatt* 48 [1907–8]: 86–87).

27. See below, 70, 71.

28. K. Barth, *Letzte Zeugnisse* (Zurich: EVZ Verlag), 1969, 18 [*Final Testimonies* (Grand Rapids: Eerdmans, 1977), 23].

29. See below, 65. In October 1911, Karl Barth joined the Safenwil Blue Cross; in January 1912, he was elected as its president.

30. *Centralblatt* 109 (1968–69): 152.

a special matter." *It shows even more during the years and decades after 1935, after Barth's return to Switzerland, when he "was uncomfortable with the extensive agreement between the Zofingia association and 'official' politics," and, in reverse, his "political leanings were frowned upon by . . . numerous Zofingia members and Alumni," so that "a real dispute" between Barth and parts of the Basel chapter occurred.*[31] *Be that as it may, Barth seems to have kept his active time in good memory, despite all changes in his relationship to the Zofingia. A nice example can be found in the "Considerations for Christmas" for the Centralblatt in 1935,*[32] *where he reminds the "festive Zofingia" that there is "also something like a Zofingia Christmas," which was "befittingly celebrated with drums drumming and pipes piping and all kinds of pleasantries and solemn ceremony (in Bern, for example, with the 'Christmas donkey,' unforgettable for everyone who has ever been there)."*[33]

The manuscript of the presentation "Zofingia and the Social Question" notes after the title: "Presented in the Bern Chapter on 20 January 1906." It is part of the volume "Excerpts III," in which Barth also had bound his notes on "Harnack, Seminar on Acts" and his excerpts from "Herrmann, Ethics" (3rd ed., 1904) prepared in winter 1906–7, besides many preparatory notes on Old Testament texts and other material.

Jacta alea esto![34]
The die is cast!

I.

Last Winter semester (1904–5) in the Bernese Zofingia, we had a discussion about the question of how the scientific portion of our sessions could be made more useful and stimulating. It was not entirely unjust to complain that, with the best of intentions, there was too much "talking shop" in our lectures. One contribution to that debate has remained especially impressive to me: the advice of an older participant that the postulated *free discussion*—which is often missed in the so-called scientific discussions, especially among younger members—should be much more prominent than the area of *fraternity affairs*: this would be the suitable playground for the discussion of various ideas in more formal and material terms. Without agreeing with this point of view in principle, I have taken this advice to heart in deciding my theme for today, not so much because I feared that I would find little interest in a subject from my academic discipline, but rather because the problem about which I would like to speak to you today is one that has occupied me since my entry into Zofingia, and has indeed become a matter of heartfelt concern to me.

31. See *Centralblatt* 109 (1968–69): 152; 82 (1941–42): 266–68, 472; also 100 (1959–60): 46, 303; yet also 90 (1949–50): 421–24.

32. *Centralblatt* 76 (1935–36): 126–34 (reprinted without the Zofingia allusions in *Evangelische Theologie* 3 [1936]: 457–62).

33. *Centralblatt* 76 (1935–36): 127–28. On this, cf. the report on the Bernese Christmas *Commens* 1907, where Barth participated as a student from Tübingen: *Centralblatt* 48 (1907–8): 292–94.

34. Literal translation of the saying by Menander that Caesar quoted upon the decision to cross the Rubicon: cf. G. Büchmann, *Geflügelte Worte: Der Zitatenschatz des deutschen Volkes*, 32nd ed., completely redesigned by G. Haupt and W. Hofmann (Berlin: Haude & Spener, 1972), 620, 143.

"*Zofingia and the Social Question!*"

An exhausted question, some might think, for as a glance at older volumes of our *Centralblatt* shows, it is *not the first time* that our subject will be addressed in Zofingia.[35]

However, precisely because more than one generation has worked on the solution to this question, it has always been considered important and relevant, and thus it appears to me to be a problem intimately related to the whole broad question of the *work and significance of the Zofingia Association*. This is why every good member of Zofingia should and must have taken a position in one way or another.

Moreover, because in our Zofingia state—in our "little Switzerland," as we have already been called[36]—the situation is such that our citizenry is completely different every five or six years, I do not see why occasionally subjects that "a wise man has considered before us"[37] should not be allowed to be broached again, even more so since we cannot strive enough for clarity on the fundamental questions of our fraternity life.

After these introductory remarks concerning my choice of theme, we can now confront it directly. Theoretical controversy about what we understand by the *"social question"* is likely superfluous in this circle. Anyone who has open eyes is confronted by it *in concreto* on a daily basis in a hundredfold form, even when strikes, elections, and the like are not the order of the day. Go through any report from an association of the poor or sick, of temperance or morality, from a hospital or psychiatric hospital, even from the columns of any daily newspaper, and, between the lines, the social problem emerges as a specter of frightening reality.

Social Democracy, which many consider to be the most significant aspect of the social question, is only an epiphenomenon of the great process, and yet what lies within this term! It belongs to the essence of the so-called "social danger" that it never stands still, but rather takes on a more threatening form from decade to decade. To illustrate this, I want to remind you of well-known things, for example, when I cite some of the results of the German *Reichstag elections* of 1903:[38] in 1903, in the Kingdom of Saxony, 22 of the 23 elected deputies were Social Democrats, of which 18 were elected in the first ballot. The Hanseatic cities of Lübeck, Bremen, and Hamburg elected exclusively Social Democrats: out of about 220,000 votes cast, 136,000 were for Social Democrats. Five of the six deputies elected by the capital city of Berlin were "*Sozis*"! Cities such as Munich, Stuttgart, Karlsruhe, Weimar, Brunswick, Speyer, Nuremberg, Mannheim, Darmstadt, Mainz, Esslingen, and the like—as well as, characteristically, several of the small Thuringian principalities—consistently voted for the Social Democratic proposal.

---

35. Cf., e.g., L. Christ, "Bericht über die erste Centraldiskussion: Wie erfüllt der Zofingerverein heute seine nationale Aufgabe?," in *Centralblatt* 45 (1904–5): 375–85, esp. 382–84; L. de Vallière, J. Gonin, and H. Poudret, "Le comité central aux sections," in *Centralblatt* 33 (1891–93): 1–3. See also the essays mentioned in footnotes 48 and 50, below.

36. Cf. Christ, "Bericht," 382, with opinion from P. G. Rüfenacht, theologian from Thun, student in Basel.

37. J. W. von Goethe, *Faust* 1.5.572 (night).

38. Cf. *Vierteljahrshefte zur Statistik des Deutschen Reichs: Ergänzungsheft zu 1903*, vol. 4:45–47, 58–59, 12, 39, 48, 51, 55, 56, 41–43, 51, 53, 48, 57–58.

These are numbers and names, but I think they speak a clear language! Will somebody want to reply to me: with us in *Switzerland* it is rather different, and better? He would be right, insofar as we have neither a system of Tsarism and the Cossack's lash, as in Russia; nor a Byzantine system of princes connected with an unbearable military system, as in Germany. So far, our elections have produced no such results as those just cited,[39] and an open social revolution, as we currently have before us in the great Eastern Empire,[40] might even more be a long time coming. However, we should be careful not to give ourselves up to a false optimism about this:

"It is also your concern, when your neighbor's wall is ablaze!"

What is not now the case[41] could one day become a reality for us. Everyone knows the sounds uttered in our midst on the occasion of elections and strikes. That anarchist tendencies are gradually beginning to spread (such as the recent anti-military propaganda in the bosom of our Swiss Social Democrats)[42] also seems to imply little good. I cannot refrain from quoting here some words from a sermon given by the Rev. Mr. *Ragaz* on the Day of Prayer and Repentance in Basel in autumn 1905. He says:

> Across the board, social conflict has flared up. It has assumed an unprecedented vehemence. In the most recent time, to our national shame, it has led to a violent disruption of civic order. A deep acrimony has seized the spirits. Our people threaten to separate themselves into two combative battle camps, exactly like in the worst times of our history, and once the military, furnished with live ammunition, pulls through the streets of our towns, the specter of a bloody civil war is already before us. On both sides, the struggle produces phenomena that do us harm and prophesy nothing good. Increasingly, the whole of society is being affected by the movement. Many individuals see themselves as being threatened externally; others suffer from the internal conflict that this situation entails.[43]

This sounds pessimistic, but who would claim that it is not *true*?! No: whoever wants to see, must see it, that even in our country conditions are becoming more and more acute, that the rift between capital and labor, between *Mammonism* and *Pauperism*, in short between the *rich* and the *poor*, whether or not it is idle chatter in the mouths of Social Democratic agitators, is actually becoming ever greater.

39. Cf. Election of the Swiss National Council, 1848–1919 (*Les élections au Conseil national Suisse, 1848–1919*). See *Wahlrecht, Wahlsystem, Wahlbeteiligung, Verhalten von Wählern und Parteien, Wahlthemen und Wahlkämpfe*, Collection by E. Gruner et al., vol. 1/II, in *Helvetia Politica*, Series A, vol. VI/1B (Bern 1978), esp. 762–68; in the same series also vol. 3, *Tabellen, Grafiken, Karten*, in *Helvetia Politica*, Series A, vol. VI/3 (Bern 1978).

40. After the so-called Bloody Sunday (*Blutiger Sonntag*, January 22, 1905), the strike movements in the entire Tsarist Empire turned into revolutionary riots. L. Ragaz also addresses these events in the Sermon of September 17, 1905, cited below in note 43: *Busse und Glauben* (Basel, 1905), 6.

41. The heading translates *Tunc tua res agitur, paries cum proximus ardet*, cited from Q. Horatius Flaccus, *Epistulae* 1.18.84.

42. Cf. *Die Wahlen in den Schweizerischen Nationalrat, 1848–1919*, vol. I/2:762–63; with it a note in vol. 2, in *Helvetia Politica*, Series A, vol. VI/2 (Bern, 1978), 198.

43. L. Ragaz, *Busse und Glauben* [Prayer and repentance day sermon, held on September 17, 1905, in the Basel Münster] (Basel, 1905), 7–9.

With this we have considered the social question from only one side, which is, I would like to say, from the perspective of the petit bourgeois, who has been jolted from his peace. Admittedly, it is at the same time the point of view among the widest strata of the so-called good society, whose motives for participating in social works are, consciously or unconsciously, largely *prophylactic* and defensive. One wants to build dams against the threatening flood; one wants to secure the "social order" against the revolution, and so on.

I was spontaneously reminded of this outlook when I visited a large menagerie a few weeks ago. It was just the time for feeding the predators. One had to see and hear these lions and tigers, how they all jumped up and down madly in their cages, rattled the lattice, roared, and generally gave signs of their animal hunger. Now the keeper came, threw to each one its piece of meat, and with it came sudden peace and silence, broken by nothing but the gnashing of teeth! This is how many people imagine the solution of the social question: "Throw something to them so they will be quiet." This perspective is fundamentally wrong: the social question does not coincide with the problem of an empty stomach, even if it sometimes appears to be so. Humans are simply not predators. Then, to stay with my allegory, the silence in the menagerie will last only a few hours before the hunger returns and the beasts will roar at you worse than before.

The aspirations of the *Christian Social Party* of Germany, for example, as congenial as the idealism of Stöcker might strike us, belong to this category.[44] Social effectiveness with the secondary aim of preserving "throne and altar" is and remains an absurdity. It means "stitching new cloth onto an old garment" or "pouring new wine into old wineskins" (Matt. 9:16–17).

The modern social question is more than a danger. Anyone who goes a little deeper sees in it a link in the evolution of a problem—or, better, *the* problem—of humanity with which Jesus confronted the ancient world, and which found its religious solution in the *Reformation* and its political solution in the *Revolution*, the task that Jesus formulated as "You shall love your God with all your heart and your neighbor as yourself" (Matt. 22:37, 39). In other words, this shows the problem of the *dual responsibility of the individual person: on the one hand to the Godhead, and on the other hand to humanity.* Mark my words, the opinion is not that the solution to the social question would bring the end of that development, or putting it religiously, would bring about the "kingdom of God," as one so often hears it said today. I think of this solution, in common with those brought by Reformation and Revolution, only as *necessary premises* for achieving that goal, but exactly necessary ones, and its development shall not and will not be stopped by a feeble prophylaxis.

From this point of view, then, we consider the social question and, as an integral element of the development of the human problem, it changes immediately from a general question into a *patriotic one of the first order.* It is a patriotic question, not only because—as we have shown earlier—circumstances are becoming more acute, perhaps even catastrophic, but also because, as Swiss, we justly claim to stand in the forefront of such developments. Zwingli, Oecolampadius,

---

44. Cf. K. Kupisch, "Stoecker, Adolf," in *RGG*³ 4: col. 387; E. Wolf, "Christlich-sozial," in *RGG*³ 1:1740–43, esp. 1741–42.

and Calvin belonged to us: long before the French Revolution, the principle of the equality of all citizens before the state was known in Swiss city republics like Basel and Zurich.[45]

If the social question is a *patriotic* question, then it is, eo ipso, a *Zofingian* question. We are then led into the center of our topic: *"How does Zofingia face up to the social question?"*

II.

Since it does not belong here, I leave unmentioned the necessary precondition, the sine qua non of my formulation of the question, namely, *that the Zofingia Association still has an ideal task,* although I know very well that this is by far not self-evident to everybody. One who sees Zofingia as nothing more than a "sturdy student fraternity" with distinctive colors, whose essential national (!) task consists in the passing on of the venerable old student traditions to posterity as intact as possible, will have little or no appreciation of its position on the social question. I do *not* need to concern myself with such a person here. Equally, it is clear to me from our history, our principles, and the wording of §1 of the Central Statutes,[46] as well as from the general considerations just mentioned, that *from the outset we somehow assume a positive position with regard to the social question.* In my opinion, both presuppositions are simply indisputable if one does not want to relinquish the most fundamental tenets of our association.

However, the question must now be treated in detail: *"How should this positive position be shaped?"*

From the various chapters of the association, one would receive a whole gamut of different responses. To classify the postulated responses, which could be expressed openly, I accept the distinction that was made in the central discussion of the winter semester of 1904–5 concerning [different] views about the national task of the Zofingia Association {cf. *Centralblatt* 45, no. 6 (1904–5): 375–77}:[47] the distinction between direct and indirect action (*action extérieure et action intérieure*). To these two basic attitudes, it is possible to subordinate all the possible positions that can be taken in relation to the positive orientation of Zofingia to the social question.

First, let us see what we are to count as immediate social action (*action extérieure*). A classic definition of this position can be found in volume 32 (1892–93)

45. Cf. L. von Muralt, "Renaissance und Reformation," in *Handbuch der Schweizer Geschichte* (Zurich: Berichthaus, 1972), 1:410–12 (which also presents—and relativizes—the corresponding and famous judgment of N. Macchiavelli).

46. For "Central Statutes of the Zofingia Association," see *Statuts centraux de la Société de Zofingue* (Lausanne, 1910), 2 [A]: "Article 1. The Zofingia Association has as its goal the development of a truly patriotic attitude among its members, based on the idea of the Swiss National Character. Being free and independent of any political party, it seeks, on the basis of democratic principles, to develop its members as capable citizens aspiring to make progress in every area of political and social life." (In this same work, cf. art. 2: "In order to achieve its purpose, the Zofingia Association ties bonds of friendship between students of every Canton and directs its activity primarily toward such questions as relate to the history and the social and political life of our nation.") Also cf. W. Buchmann, "Übersicht über die Fassungen der Artikel 1 und 2 der Centralstatuten," in M. Burckhardt et al., *Der Schweizerische Zofingerverein* (Bern: Kommissionsverlag Erben, 1819–1969), 341–50.

47. Christ, "Bericht," esp. 378.

of our *Centralblatt*, in an article by *Benoît*, a member of the Lausanne chapter, titled *"The Role of Zofingia regarding the Social Question."*[48] In order not to take up too much time, I omit here a detailed précis and highlight only the results to which Benoît's deliberations lead: Zofingia should "draw closer to the people, getting in touch with the working class, showing them that we do not despise them, show these people that they are our brothers [and sisters], that we consider them as such and that we are all children of the same country." It is consequently demanded that "each member of Zofingia must heartily work individually in this way."[49] These idealistic words were not in vain, especially in the French-speaking chapters. Although individual experiments in this direction had previously been made in Lausanne, in the course of the next decade in Lausanne and Geneva formal "social groups" were formed, which were, in part, directly aimed at implementing the above-mentioned ideas; and in part, yet also through active social labors, were concerned with the social formation of their members.[50] Convivial associations for young workers were founded (somewhat like the local "Philadelphia" society)[51]—or already existing societies of this sort were joined—musical and theatrical evenings were organized for families, workers' festivals were attended, delegates took part in the annual celebration of the oath of Rütli.[52] Finally, the yearly concerts of our three French-speaking chapters were—and still are—repeated as *"Séances populaires,"* at a reduced price for working-class audiences.[53] You see that there is no shortage of varied activity. The participation of the Lausanne chapter in the charitable work of the *"Maison du people"*[54] deserves special mention, as does the Genevan chapter's participation in the inquiry into charitable funds in 1903 (cf. *Centralblatt* 44:290–92).[55] I know nothing about whether a German

48. L. Benoît, "Le rôle de Zofingue dans la question sociale," *Centralblatt* 33 (1892–93): 103–11.

49. *Centralblatt* 33 (1892–93): 106–7.

50. Cf. Kundert and Im Hof, *Geschichte des Schweizerischen Zofingervereins*, 81–82; Ch. Gilliard, *La Société de Zofingue, 1819–1919: Cent ans d'histoire nationale* (Lausanne: G. Bridel, 1919), 163–64; J. Debrit, "Rapport présenté à la section genevoise sur l'activité du Groupe social zofingien pendant l'année 1902–1903," *Centralblatt* 44 (1903–4): 290–99, esp. 291–93.

51. Founded in 1885 in Bern, the "Philadelphia" was intended to serve the "formation of the moral character and strengthening" of its members. From 1887 onward, they saw in the "mixing of all the social classes" "a very special value for their society's life." According to its statutes, the association was supposed to "stimulate the members to cooperate in the solution of social tasks and to cultivate patriotism." In this sense, for a period of time it organized social evenings for workers and a Christmas celebration in the poorhouse in Frienisberg. Cf. O. Lauterburg, "Die Philadelphia während 25 Jahren," in *Philadelphia Bern: Festschrift zur Erinnerung an die Feier des 25 jährigen Bestehens, 1885–1910* (Bern o. J., 1910), 1–69, esp. 4–5, 7, 46, 65.

52. Benoît, "Le rôle de Zofingue," 107–8. Annual "Grütlicommerse" celebrations were organized in all chapters of Zofingia on November 17, to commemorate the oath of Rütli. ("Grütli" is an older variant spelling of "Rütli.") [Trans. note: The story of the Rütli oath forms a constitutive part of the foundational legend of the Old Swiss Confederacy. According to the standard account of the legend, which reached a stable form in the late fifteenth century, representatives of the Cantons of Uri, Schwyz, and Unterwalden met on the meadow of Rütli, above Lake Lucerne, to make an oath of solidarity against the tyranny of the Habsburgs. The Rütli oath features prominently in F. Schiller's *William Tell*, and it is commemorated annually in the whole of Switzerland on August 1. The first such celebration as National day took place in 1891, in Barth's own lifetime, and became an annual fixture in 1899; in 1994 it was appointed as a federal holiday.]

53. Benoît, "Le rôle de Zofingue," 107; Kundert and Im Hof, *Geschichte des Schweizerischen Zofingervereins*, 81.

54. Kundert and Im Hof, *Geschichte des Schweizerischen Zofingervereins*, 81–82; Gilliard, *La Société de Zofingue*, 162; cf. Christ, "Bericht," 384.

55. Debrit, "Rapport présenté à la section genevoise," esp. 293–98; see also Kundert and Im Hof, *Geschichte des Schweizerischen Zofingervereins*, 82; Gilliard, *La Société de Zofingue*, 163–64.

section emulated something of all this. If it did happen, it was probably very sporadic.

Very unfairly, some people have grown accustomed to, at the most, mocking these efforts. Scorn is truly the last thing that such attempts deserve. However, this does not prevent us from testing the *inner foundation* of this *"action extérieure"* and thereby coming to the conclusion that it is to be *rejected*. Despite the refreshing idealism that blows through the matter as it has been realized in Geneva and Lausanne, it rests on a misunderstanding of the purpose of student associations generally, and that of Zofingia in particular. At all times, the prevailing tendency of Zofingia has been to bring its ideals to embodiment and realization first and foremost *in its members*, and only secondarily to carry those ideals into public life *through the individual members*, as they leave university.

They were not happy times when it was done differently, when Zofingia chapters as such actively intervened in public life, whether it be in a conservative sense (as in the 1830s, when the Neuchâtel and Basel chapters, with an armed hand, crusaded against liberalism),[56] or whether it be as radical party associations (as the Bernese and Zurich chapters had become in the 1870s and 1880s[57] and, unfortunately, as Lucerne still is today).[58]

I repeat: *Zofingia's purposes are primarily ordered toward the internal side*, and this before all else, because we are a *student fraternity*. *Students*, however, are learners, people who still have much to learn, who should first *receive* before they can think of *giving* or teaching. The work for the lower social strata will be one *goal*, among others, of our academic studies. Why should we step prematurely outside the sphere of work that is proper to our current state into another, which needs mature men, not novices?!

I do not want to allow myself a conclusive judgment since I know too little about the chapters in Lausanne and Geneva. Nonetheless, it seems to me very probable that a neglect of the *internal life* of a chapter necessarily follows from an all-too-intense *action exterieure*, and that incomparably more is lost than has been gained.

Necessarily, then, we are shown to have an indirect social task, which indicates an *action intérieure* that is more appropriate to our character as students. Briefly summarized, the purpose of this *action intérieure* would be *to educate socially the individual member of Zofingia, both theoretically and practically*. Many different routes can be taken to this goal. From the outset, of course, the French-speaking chapters—whose *action extérieure* could replace everything else—have an advantage. How can one study the laborers' question better than by looking at the workers themselves? Seen in this light, all these efforts appear somewhat more significant.

Again, it stands to reason that discussing the social question, with all of its subproblems, *in the first acts of our meetings*,[59] and at least here the Swiss-

---

56. Kundert and Im Hof, *Geschichte des Schweizerischen Zofingervereins*, 42.

57. Kundert and Im Hof, *Geschichte des Schweizerischen Zofingervereins*, 64–66.

58. Kundert and Im Hof, *Geschichte des Schweizerischen Zofingervereins*, 88–89; cf. also D. Barth, Burckhardt, and Gigon, *Der Schweizerische Zofingerverein*, 104–14.

59. The "Ordinary Sessions" that took place weekly during term were constituted of two "acts": in the first part, the discussion of a political or academic or other topic of more general interest, for example, based on a paper like this one (another example is offered by the work read in the Bern chapter at the end of 1907: E. A. Schläfli, "Wesen und Ursprung der Religion," in *Centralblatt* 58 [1907–8]:

German chapters are in no way inferior to the French-speaking chapters—this is, strictly speaking, the only way we can presently take a positive stance on the social question. I consciously disregard the fact that some individual chapters are members of specific charitable societies in their cities, which lies somewhere between *action extérieure* and *action intérieure*.

That would all be well and good. However, do we not have the feeling that in the French-speaking chapters there is a lot that is manufactured and artificial, besides that which is authentic and original? Yes, and what is the point of our continual social theorizing? What is said by a sum of money that is occasionally thrown out for this or that charitable purpose? Does not all that belong to the feeble prophylaxis that I spoke about in the first part of my work? I would like to suggest a new point of view. I believe:

If the ideals of Zofingia demand from us a positive response to the social question, then what is meant is something quite different from what we have stated until now, certainly a much more demanding response: neither foundations, nor lectures, nor mild contributions to this and that, but rather *the cultivation of a social ethos and the transference of the same into the active life of Zofingia*, in other words: *Awakening and strengthening the sense of social responsibility in the individual.*

In particular, I would like to emphasize the term "responsibility." Since we students carry a heavy social responsibility, we cannot be sufficiently conscious of it. Hundreds and thousands of our contemporaries need to earn their livelihood through often laborious work, day in and day out, in the workshop, at the machinery of factories, at the dusty desk of the bureau, or in the field or forest. Meanwhile, we enjoy the high privilege of devoting ourselves for years to the free study of the highest and most beautiful things that the human heart has thought, being allowed to spend many pleasant hours in a circle of friends and in the realm of art! I do not believe that there is anyone among us who has not already at least hesitated, when, for example, he went to some party wearing his cap audaciously and then, at the door of the house, met a young worker, a postman, or whatever, [and then wondered:] *He* has his damn duties and obligations to fulfill,[60] today as on every day—*I*, however, have nothing to do today except amuse myself? What have I done to deserve this? What privilege do I have before him? This is one of the riddles that life gives to us. But one thing is certain: *"To whom much is given, from them much will be required"* (Luke 12:48).

Conditions have given us, in some respects, a great advantage over most of our people, and we have the right to rejoice over that. But woe to us if we only rejoice and are not also invariably conscious that we owe a great debt to these people, that we must give an account of that which we, more than others, receive.

434–47, 498–512); the time thereafter was reserved for the resolution of pending association matters and lasted two to three hours. The following second "act"—with songs and productions—was dedicated to the cultivation of friendship and sociability, i.e., free entertainment structured significantly by the conduct of drinking [*Trinkcomment*]. Cf. also *Die Hochschule Bern in den Jahren 1834–1884: Festschrift zur fünfzigsten Jahresfeier ihrer Stiftung* (Bern, 1884), 201–4.

60. Otto von Bismarck used the phrase "duties and obligations" [*Pflicht und Schuldigkeit*] on June 12, 1882, in the German Parliament. Cf. Büchmann, *Geflügelte Worte*, 692. [Trans. note: Perhaps more notably, the phrase appears in the early poetry of J. W. Goethe.]

On the other hand, if we not only feel this *social responsibility* but also deter-mine to seriously draw out its consequences and shape our daily lives accord-ingly, then a solid foundation is laid for our later *social activity*, from which, in my assessment, we as students rightly can still refrain, provided such a *social ethos* is there.

I ask you from the outset not to think of this social ethos as mere theory. We already have too many theories in Zofingia. What I suggest is *action*, through-and-through action; even if it is not action going outward, it is still an action of Zofingia on itself and its members.

Now I want to look in detail at a few *practical points* that show what I have in mind when I call for the "*cultivation of social ethos and the transference of the same into our fraternity's life.*" Of course, I do not claim that these points are complete, but they have already given me much to think about.

With this we come to the third part of my work.

III.

I would like to begin by saying that when it comes to the following consid-erations, I am thinking most of all about the circumstances of *Bern's Zofingia chapter*, and that I will make mention of the national association and the other chapters only in passing, at the most. This is the case, first of all, because I am not familiar enough with the conditions in other cities, yet also and especially in order to be as remote as possible from mere theory and to remain as close as possible to practical life.

Of all the various subproblems contained in the social question, there is one that in my view has become especially important for Zofingia: *the class problem.*

In ceremonial speeches, central discussions, and so on, we are very proud of the fact, and rightly so, that the Zofingia Association is able in its midst to reconcile the most seemingly impossible contradictions. "Is it not so that one man stands with the Centrists, the other with the Federalists? The one with the Conservatives or the Liberals, the other with the Radicals? The one with the ecclesial Orthodox, the other with the Reformers, and a third one in a spot where he sees the other two and can only shrug his shoulders? This one stands with the magnates of finance, with the banks and the railroads, and the other fights with his words and writings for the downtrodden and disenfran-chised?" Such were the words of the current [Bernese national] councilman *E. v. Steiger*[61] at the Zofingia Alumni Festival in 1880 (*Centralblatt* 21, no. 1 [1880–81]: 2–3),[62] and the list of contradictions mentioned by him could eas-ily be extended today. Indeed, that is something quite significant in which we surpass every other fraternity, without exception. Helvetia, Concordia,

---

61. Edmund von Steiger (1836–1908), theological student and Zofingia member in Basel and Bern; initially pastor in rural communities; 1878–1908 councilman in the Canton of Bern; member of the Swiss Federal Parliament [*Nationalrat*] 1888–90 and 1891–1908. "For Steiger, the Zofingia Association was . . . much more than a mere fraternity." Based on the Zofingia concept, he would have "liked to have realized the ideal of a selfless 'Party of the Fatherland'" (*Centralblatt* 48 [1907–8]: 463).

62. E. von Steiger, "Festrede, gehalten am letzten Alt-Zofingerfest, den 26. Juli in Zofingen," *Central-blatt* 21 (1880–81): 2–8, esp. 3.

Burgundia, Zähringia,[63] or whomever else one might mention—these are and continue to be more or less and by their own admission *cliques*, to refrain from using a familiar student term for such things;[64] they are fraternities that, with prompt exclusivity, constitute themselves with people from particular groups with common interests, careers, or philosophical dispositions, if it is not crudest opportunism that unites them, such as the Freemasonry system of "keeping positions occupied" until fraternity brothers, in their later bourgeois life, can fill them.[65] Vis-à-vis this model, Zofingia desires to be, and always has been at all times, a *"free school of free convictions,"*[66] a place where the most diverse opinions and points of view meet together in common sentiment for the fatherland.

This enormous advantage vis-à-vis all of our competitors is bestowed upon us for all time, yet only if we *know how to preserve it*. Therefore, we are not entitled to remain idle and simply take pleasure in this advantage. If Zofingia desires to continue being a living salt among the student body, it must submit its posture, its institutions, and everything to perpetual *self-criticism*, to see whether it is still in harmony with that ideal; or, in the end, are we on our way to deteriorating *into a clique ourselves*, albeit into a differently structured one?!

In my opinion, it is the latter danger that we here in Bern must confront directly. Whoever poses this question to himself sincerely, and most of all *selflessly*, must admit that, concerning the composition of our chapter, things are not as they should be. Of course, we do have conservatives and liberals, some from the positive and some from the Reformers' side, people from the city and the country, students from all departments (which is not at all a given in other fraternities). Yet do we have among us those who are also of *socially*, meaning in our case *financially*, high (or more precisely, good) and low standing? Regarding the latter, I am not thinking of the proletarian students at our university who, since they are foreigners, are not taken into consideration here.[67] I am thinking instead of numerous Swiss students from the lower or middle classes, whose

---

63. Brief information about each of these fraternities can be found in M. Vasalli, "Das Farbenstudentum in der Schweiz," *Civitas* 13 (1957–58): 480–509, esp. 492–93.

64. "Groups" (see above, 46).

65. While the other fraternities were not unjustly characterized as a kind of "nursery" or "greenhouse" for specific occupations, parties, and tendencies, the members of Zofingia, as a whole, were not committed to a particular occupation or political party. For example, both "positive" *and* "liberal" pastors emerged from Zofingia, whereas Helvetia more or less produced those of the one [stripe], Zähringia those of the other tendency.

66. The phrase was a part of Art. 2 of the Central Statutes from 1855 to 1870: "As a free school of free convictions, it [the Zofingia Association] receives into itself all opinions and abstains as an association from directly influencing practical politics" (in 1848, the phrase was "as a school of free convictions"); cf. Buchmann, "Übersicht," 342–44. For a report of the tensions that arose in connection with this characterization, see D. Barth, Burckhardt, and Gigon, *Der Schweizerische Zofingerverein*, 44–48, 58–59, 63. The phrase was omitted in the 1870 revision of the article; cf. the official text of 1906 (valid until 1934), above in n. 46. Cf. as well the allusion by Steiger, "Festrede," 4, *"a free school of free conviction."*

67. Here Barth is thinking of the many Russian male and—especially remarkable for that time— female students who studied in Bern at the beginning of the century, principally in the medical department, thanks to the xenophile institutional policies of the superintendent A. Gobat. Cf. Ulrich Im Hof, *Hochschulgeschichte Berns, 1528–1984: Zur 150-Jahr-Feier an der Universität Bern, 1984* (Bern: Bern University Press, 1984), 70, 424.

numbers in our membership are not too large.[68] And yet it would be a worthy task for Zofingia—other chapters would know to follow the lead—to aim to bridge the social divide precisely through its inner composition. Excluding a few exceptions, we must admit that, on the whole, we are on our way to becoming the *fraternity for "high society,"* which, as I know all too well, is maintained by some of us as an ideal. From the social and thus from the basic Zofingian perspective, we can only regret that in the city and canton of Bern, it is considered bon ton to wear the white cap.[69] Yet with that state of affairs, we will irretrievably become a clique, yea, something more: Zähringia can, for example, still attain certain social goals, even though it is a clique in other respects; yet if Zofingia becomes a clique, indeed a clique for "high society," then internal social action—that is, a social schooling of its members in the aforementioned sense—will be endangered right from the start, if not entirely paralyzed, because it will have become a faction within the social struggle.

And it will become especially shameful for us if people one day find out that the Shibboleth [Judg. 12:6] of this "high society" is neither intellectual nor ethical aristocracy, but rather the quite banal standard of one's moneybag. Zofingia as well has not been spared the bad fortune that this question is often one of the first directed at new members. It is then no wonder that someone who would be in agreement with our principles but comes from more humble circumstances, instead of from "high society," has to refrain from joining us right from the outset. One speaker at the aforementioned *Central* discussion last winter addressed this point quite legitimately by saying: "We earnestly demand that by the financial burdens . . . which we impose on our members, we do not exclude from Zofingia students of mean fortune, for whom this material question constitutes the sole obstacle to entry into our association and who are too proud to accept for themselves the humiliating position of being exceptional in this regard. If this were the case, and I believe that it is so in certain chapters, I would not hesitate to say that *we will have failed at our duty, which is to open the door of our association to all Swiss students, regardless of any distinction of fortune."*[70]

By the way, §31, section 3 of the C. St.[71] is relevant here, yet I can only declare that it seems to be nonexistent for the Bernese chapter.

As a first consequence of a Zofingia social ethos, I will thus postulate once more: *the official and unofficial financial burden for members must be reduced at any cost.*[72] I know right away what will be shouted at me now from all sides,

68. The Zofingia was considered the most distinguished association, at least in Geneva, Lausanne, Bern, and Basel. This is reflected by comments in the annual report of the Bern chapter (Staatsarchiv Bern), 1903–4: "We have a standing within the student body of Bern as well as in our society such that no other student association might presume to be better than us. . . ." Or in 1906–7: Zofingia "established itself as the prime or one of the prime associations of our university." The reporter adds forebodingly that it will be quite difficult to depart from such high self-esteem: "Whoever has long worn a sumptuous robe will not simply exchange it for a monk's habit at another person's insistence."
69. The cap of the Zofingia Assoication is white; see *Couleurstudenten in der Schweiz*, Schweizerisches Museum für Volkskunde Basel, Exhibition 1979–80 [Catalog], 87.
70. Cf. Christ, "Bericht," 383 (statement by [L.] Robert [cand. jur., from Peseux, student in Neuenburg studying for a degree, candidate of law]; italics added by Barth).
71. *Centralstatuten*, 10, art. 31, sec. 3 states: "The chapters ought to strive to construe the financial burden in such a way that no student is prevented from joining Zofingia simply because of said burden."
72. Approved for the winter semester 1905–6: a monthly tax of 14 Swiss Francs as well as a supplementary tax determined by additional or unforeseen costs. In addition, there were expenses for special social events.

namely, that this would cost us our so-called "social standing." That is why I said on purpose: at any cost! This is the crux of the problem, and thus we come to our second point:

If we did not pretend to be the fraternity of "high society," then we would have no obligations vis-à-vis this "high society"; if we did not have such obligations, then our whole enterprise would be significantly cheaper; and then, if we were also to limit ourselves on a few other points, every Swiss student, whether rich or poor, could join us, and one of the most important premises for Zofingia's social action would be in place!

As it is, however, we annually offer incredibly vast sums to the Moloch of "social standing" *without seeing even the meanest modicum of a return for the actual goals of Zofingia!* On the contrary and irrespective of the financial damages caused by this issue, it has led people to speak of the "matchmaking-bureau Zofingia," and seeing the way things are, this is not without reason! As a second consequence, it necessarily follows:

A certain class of festivities that are held only for the honor of "high society" must be eliminated from the list of official social events. Such social events may continue to be held in the future—unofficially, organized by individuals, primarily financed by the private means of the individual, and obviously obligatory for no one. Yet *that* state of affairs is intolerable where people who do not care one iota for such events must continue to fork over the money for them and persons of low means are therefore prevented from joining the ranks of Zofingia.[73]

I know that, by saying this, I am getting "a little too touchy" for some![74] I would like to request of all such people, in disregard of all egoistical motives, simply to ask yourselves: What is better: the *benefit* that Zofingia obtains when the individual members of Zofingia obtain wives (to put it briefly), indeed wives from "high society," or the *damage* inflicted on the fraternity by its members due to the fact that the current expensive system either drives students to the other fraternities or leaves them wild?![75] The answer seems to be immediately obvious, as is its consequence: here it would be high time to speak of a *sacrifice* that would have to be offered up to Zofingia. But enough of this business!

I know that the majority of the chapter thinks differently about this, or rather does not think about it at all, instead going along with it "because it has always been done this way." I had to speak of it here in this context because it is fitting and proper (not for the first time and probably not for the last time!).

Now, let us move to a second point, which is also connected to the class problem.

According to §1 of the Central Statutes, the Zofingia Association has the goal of developing a "truly patriotic attitude, based on the idea of the *Swiss National Character*"[76] in its members. Untenable vis-à-vis the latter concept and untenable vis-à-vis Zofingia's social ethos is the persistent semiofficial view

---

73. Here Barth is probably thinking of the Zofingia Ball and the various "*Besen*-Events" (see above, n. 6).

74. [Trans. note: Barth uses here the phrase "ans Läbige recken," a Swiss-German idiom.] Roughly, "to hit a sensitive spot"; cf. *Schweizerisches Idiotikon: Wörterbuch der schweizerdeutschen Sprache*, s.v. rĕcken, vol. 6 (Frauenfeld: Huber, 1909), col. 807.

75. That is, they do not join any association; cf. *Couleurstudenten in der Schweiz*, 102.

76. Cf. n. 46 above.

concerning the meaning of our colors, the so-called *"Color Viewpoint," which is in dire need of revision.*

As things are now, this viewpoint rests on a rather undemocratic and unsocial foundation, namely, on the antiquated view that the student as such is a member of a *caste* somehow absolutely elevated above the rest of the so-called philistine world,[77] the distinguishing mark of this caste being the colored cap. What logically proceeds from this is that very cult of color, which necessarily culminates in the institution of the student duel.[78] This point of view might have had a poetic character once upon a time; for a modern university, for a modern student organization, and especially for Zofingia, it is a relic that one ought to do away with as quickly as possible. It is through an aristocracy of thought that the student should be superior to his nonacademic fellow citizen; it would indeed be odd if this were not so, but to derive from it the external airs of belonging to a specific estate, which comes across as being medieval, is simply wrong.

A significant step toward improvement in this area has indeed already taken place, insofar as fencing has entirely disappeared from Zofingia.[79] And yet our Color Viewpoint is nothing else than a remnant of the duel system. The former makes no sense when divorced from the latter, and it is about time to progress to a more liberal point of view, just as our francophone compatriots have long since done, yet without the circumstance of advocating for any and every laxity which they, over there, permit themselves for the sake of mere convenience. I do not want to cite any examples from the laughable codex about "color-acceptable" and "non-color-acceptable" actions, localities, persons,[80] and the like: "One already knows the whole melody by the initials!"[81]

---

77. On "philistine" as a "designation for the nonstudent or the adversary of cheerful student life," cf. Büchmann, *Geflügelte Worte,* 22.

78. On the emergence of fencing and duels in Switzerland and the subsequent debates in Zofingia concerning the issue, cf. D. Barth, Burckhardt, and Gigon, *Der Schweizerische Zofingerverein,* 83–92; Kundert and Im Hof, *Geschichte des Schweizerischen Zofingervereins,* 48–49, 66–70, 78–80.

79. Duals and fencing were prohibited for the entire association in 1865; a regulation that had granted an exemption to Zurich in 1887 was abolished in 1903 following fierce controversy; cf. D. Barth, Burckhardt, and Gigon, *Der Schweizerische Zofingerverein,* 83–92; Kundert and Im Hof, *Geschichte des Schweizerischen Zofingervereins,* 69, 78–80.

80. Already in 1893–94, the semester report of the Bernese chapter warned against "measuring the flourishing of Zofingia according to the degree to which the *Comment* [code of conduct] is handled. Whoever transgresses the *Comment* does not sin against his association; he simply infringes upon the grammar of student customs." It is also by no means "an anti-*Comment* movement" when the "obligation of the Sunday pre-lunch drink" is brought into question (*Centralblatt* 34 [1893–94]: 447). The controversies concerning the *Comment,* however, continued. Thus it was discussed in the *Centralblatt* 47 (1906–7) whether a "Central *Comment*" might be called for in order to counteract a "pansification of Color custom": "something like a fundamental lesson about manners for the Zofingian wearing colors." They discussed the question whether an infringement on the *Comment,* meaning the policy regarding customs and traditions written in the conventional student fashion (appropriate to the "*Comment*") was entailed if a Zofingian "in colors" (i.e., wearing the cap [and sash] of the association) were to occupy the standing-room section of the highest tier of the theater or were to use an umbrella or carry a shopping basket or a packet; in order that "the audience not mistake the Zofingian cap for a porter's cap," then one ought "for the moment . . . to content oneself with plain, civilian headwear" (*Centralblatt* 47 [1906–7]: 430–33, citing 432–33, 495–98, 578–81; see also *Centralblatt* 48 [1907–8]: 614–16; for a later critical echo, see *Centralblatt* 52 [1911–12]: 50–51; see also Kundert and Im Hof, *Geschichte des Schweizerischen Zofingervereins,* 83–84).

81. J. V. von Scheffel, *Die Maulbronner Fuge* (6th stanza), in *Liederbuch für die schweizerische Studentenverbindung Zofingia (Deutsche Sektionen),* 4th ed. (Zurich: Zürcher & Furrer, 1891), part 2:132–33; also in J. V. von Scheffel, *Gesammelte Werke,* vol. 6 (Stuttgart: Adolf Bonz [1907]), 195–98.

We Zofingians of all people ought to help pave the way for a more modern and especially more social view of things rather than to aid the view that exists now on a legal basis and only contributes to a widening of the social divide among our people. Or does anyone believe that it improves the dignity of our colors, which are the colors of our fatherland,[82] when the common man learns that a student finds a felt cap to be good enough when the student wishes to associate with him?![83]

If we summarize what we have said about our *position on the class question*, then we have a twofold postulate, wherein the first part addresses our *inner* posture, the second part our *external* social posture:

1. Internal: establishment of the possibility of a greater social diversity in the composition of our chapter
2. External: the eradication of an antiquated emphasis on the external marks of class difference vis-à-vis the lower levels of society.

I am, however, not so optimistic as to believe that, if we were to create change in these two points, the goal concerning our social posture would then be achieved. That is where the real work would have to begin. Allow me here and now to indicate two special points that I have in mind, two areas of considerable interest for the social question and also relevant for our life in Zofingia.

There is, first of all, the *alcohol question*. I hope that no one would call me a philistine if I do not intend to proceed like a certain speaker from the previous summer semester: during the discussion of a problem in this area, which also related to the social sphere, he went no further than to explain that he would not like to make any statement on the issue, "for he would be laughed at."[84] Such a case is typical for how the issue is dealt with not only among us, but also among wide circles [in all student associations]. This approach is in good keeping with the Ovidian formula:

I see and approve the better things,
I follow the lesser.[85]

Or we could be like an ostrich, which ducks its head in the sand to avoid seeing the hunter.

However, another manner of handling the issue might be conceived, and this is what I would like to attempt here.

I begin again with the actual goal of Zofingia: "to develop its members as capable citizens aspiring to make *progress* in every area of political and social life."[86] I want to highlight the word *"progress"*; our position in this matter is already fixed without further ado. I do not need to go into the details: whoever is somewhat honest and has not lost his sense of logic will readily admit to me

---

82. The colors of Zofingia are red-white-red; see *Couleurstudenten in der Schweiz*, 87.
83. Cf. n. 80 above.
84. The reference is likely to O. König, a medical student, who on May 20, 1905, delivered a presentation on "The Causes and Curbing of Mental Deficiency."
85. P. Ovidius Naso [Ovid], *Metamorphoses* 7.20–21.
86. *Centralstatuten*, Art. I; cf. n. 46 above.

that the relation of the reality to the ideal is not what it should be. It may certainly be the case that, in comparison to earlier times, much has been changed for the better, yet it cannot be denied that there is still too much of a "good" thing taking place in this department. I know what some of you will say to me: boozing, indeed, rather heavy boozing simply belongs to the "ol' glory of fraternity brothers" [*alte Burschenherrlichkeit*].[87] I concede that this viewpoint might have once had a poetic character, yet "that is quite a long time ago,"[88] indeed, back when we were not as aware of the destructive effects of alcohol on the life of our people as we now are, or at least should be, for it makes quite perfect sense that someone does *not* become aware of the issue when he puts on those aforementioned horse blinders! I declare: *for the present day, our position on alcohol is still nonsense*: and if we do not change things, then we will betray a good portion of our principles; people in the wider society who have in the meantime come to a better view of these things will not be in the wrong when they speak of the institutions of Zofingia as troglodytic and antiquated.

Here, in a twofold sense, we have the duty, most of all *socially*, to set an example for the rest of the student body in terms of a more modern viewpoint.

More than once now, I have mentioned the concept of *"responsibility"* as the leitmotif for my entire point of view. What I would like now is that this idea be understood not merely theoretically and indirectly, but rather *directly*, especially as it pertains to our case.

Thanks to a well-informed source, I know that it happens in certain social associations, consisting largely of people from the lower classes, that the *student drinking [codes of] conduct* are imitated; everyone can imagine what kinds of misunderstandings and excesses this might entail, which perhaps the majority of us know how to avoid, yet the uneducated and the half-educated do not, precisely those who do believe in good faith that whatever a student is allowed to do, he is allowed and able to do as well. Let us not deceive ourselves: every young worker who ruins himself physically or morally as a consequence of imitating *our* customs lies to a good extent on *our* conscience. *He* does not know better, but *we* do know better, and the example we provide should be set accordingly. The prophetic word of the Old Testament applies especially to us academics: "Mortal, I have made you a *watchman* for the house of Israel!" [Ezek. 3:17; 33:7]. Or would we like to erect some kind of double morality? Would we like to claim: whatever is moral for the student is immoral for the worker?! Let us take care that another biblical word not be said of us: "Woe to the one through whom the stumbling block comes!" [Matt. 18:7].

And now for a second point of view. Is it not the case that when we emerge into public life, it should be our task to become the *leaders of our people* by virtue of the higher insight gained at the university and therefore to effect good and fight against evil among our fellow citizens, regardless of whether that occurs in the pulpit, in the infirmary, in the schools, or in the courts? Will we be able to accept this task *with a good conscience* if, when the time comes to transition from

87. The beginning of the song "Rückblick," by E. Höfling, in *Liederbuch für die schweizerische Studentenverbindung Zofingia*, part 2:22–23: "O alte Burschenherrlichkeit." Cf. Büchmann, *Geflügelte Worte*, 333.
88. Albert Lortzing, *Zar und Zimmermann* [Tsar and carpenter, a comic opera] or *Die beiden Peter* [The two Peters], act 3, no. 13 and no. 16 (finale).

the academic life to civilian life, we have need of an abrupt change of direction in our lifestyle, especially in our position on alcohol?

Nothing is more laughable and pathetic at the same time than, for example, a theologian who arrives at that point of transition, is suddenly posted on a new front, and must hide himself in priestly robes and *play* the honorable man (for it is certainly not authentic) and then perhaps even become the president of a temperance society! And I think that what goes for us goes for the other academic departments as well! Yes, and as it is for many others, the change of direction is not successful: something always remains!![89]

To put it briefly: *if we are to assume a leading social position later in life, then our current practical behavior in respect to the alcohol question must be of such a character that we will not need to be ashamed of it later in life.*

And this would now be the point at which the association could do something positive; this is where the celebrated "education of members"[90] could begin, about which everyone can *talk* quite a lot, but that too often leads to the exact opposite.

Let no one misunderstand me: I am neither postulating the abolition of the beer-conduct [*Biercomment*][91] nor the introduction of morals in the spirit of Zähringia.[92] In my opinion, both options would be neither fitting for students nor necessary. Yet there is a *middle way* between such stances and the status quo, one that could be found easily with some goodwill. It would consist, on the one hand, in a *modification of the drinking conduct* [*Trinkcomment*],[93] primarily in

---

89. Cf. Büchmann, *Geflügelte Worte*, 598 [*semper aliquid haeret* = something always sticks].

90. This formulation of the task could connect well to art. I of the Central Statutes (see above, n. 46). In roughly this sense, L. Robert terms "the education of young people for the homeland" "the essential task of Zofingia, which will subsist in spite of the changes" (Christ, "Bericht," 378). One often saw the space provided for such "education" above all in the relationship between "Foxes" (see below, n. 95) and [the] "Fox Major," or between the "Junior Fox" and the "Senior Fraternity Brother" (cf. A. Vernet, *Burschen et Füchse: Droits et devoirs réciproques*, in *Centralblatt* 37 [1896–97]: 374–84). In the following clause, when Barth laments that such education "too often leads to its exact opposite," he is likely also thinking about the excesses and abuses that occurred in this context (cf. *Centralblatt* 52 [1911–12]: 51). The question "What are the pedagogical tasks of Zofingia vis-à-vis its members?" was discussed thoroughly in the first Central meeting of 1893–94 (cf. the report in *Centralblatt* 34 [1893–94]: 360–79, 407–20; for the discussion in Bern in particular, see 445).

91. *Biercomment der Zofingia Bern* (Bern: Stämpfli & Cie, 1900), 3: "§§1–10. This Beer-Conduct has the noble aim of regulating the legal conditions relating to beer for Zofingia members. It deals with a beer state and aims to preserve peace and order in it, just as laws in any ordered state are necessary to this end. It therefore deserves the same deep respect and honor just as every genuine citizen is accustomed to showing respect to [state] laws." "§12. This Beer-Conduct is valid in every place in which Bernese Zofingia members (at least three) imbibe together a drink in accordance with the *Comment*." Barth's copy of the Beer-Conduct has been preserved (Karl Barth Archiv, Basel). It is furnished with markings and notes for memory, particularly in the section titled "Criminal Law," which were supposed to aid Barth in keeping an overview of punishments and grounds for punishment when he himself became president of the Bernese Zofingia and thus eo ipso also had to "function as the Beer-Chairman" (§43) at "tavern outings" (see below, n. 99).

92. "Motivations in the founding" of "Zähringia" (on November 3, 1888) "were [to have] a student association with a Christian spirit and to combat the deplorable customs of students" (Vasalli, "Farbenstudententum," 493). The alcohol problem was also discussed in Zofingia, ever since A. Bertholet ("Die Alkoholfrage," in *Centralblatt* 32 [1891–92]: 151–61, 187–99) dealt particularly with the social significance of the question and (successfully) demanded that "teetotalers" also be accepted into Zofingia. Nevertheless, there was still fierce controversy in 1911–12 in the Bern chapter regarding the rejection of a candidate for Zofingia at the hands of "old-school Comment champions and anti-abstinence fanatics" (*Centralblatt* 52 [1911–12]: 192–95, 291, 811–12; citation on 193).

93. As one example (by which one must, of course, be aware of the peculiar mixture of playfulness and seriousness with which the *Comment* was generally carried on): *Biercomment*, 22: according to §87, "[he] is sentenced to drink two Wholes who: (a) drinks his gut" (i.e., does not drink according to the

the sense of a reduction of all punitive measures and all other such quotas that present, in their current form, a mockery of all the results of modern research into alcohol. The *Comment* would achieve its goal of bringing some "pep" into the second act of our meetings, to exactly the same extent if half, or preferably two-thirds, of all the "Wholes" would be dropped.

My second postulate in this issue is the *curtailing of the more or less obligatory visit to the tavern.*[94] I am calling a spade a spade, even though those who love it would like to wrap it up in fine, pleasant words. Let it be understood that I have no wish to lead a principled fight against drinking, for I know that it has a relative significance for the nurturing of friendships, especially for encountering students from other academic departments. Yet we should dispose of the idea that the be-all and end-all of life in a fraternity is such that one could measure the quality of a Zofingian by the number of his weekly tavern visits, just as the weather is measured by a barometer, and thus classify him accordingly as a "good Zofingian," a "Model Fox,"[95] and so on, or as a "bad Zofingian, pansy, quitter," and so on. Really, it is well-nigh common knowledge, or at least it should be, that the taverns are in some places the bane of entire regions. Really, how will we be able to stand up against it with a good conscience if we ourselves spent a good portion of our student years in the tavern—and even if it were the Zofingia bar?! And yet again, it is that very awareness of our social responsibility that should prevent us from hunkering down idly at a tavern table every day for hours, indeed even during the best hours of the day, while the so-called "common man" is hard at work. Here, too, we must say: "*Less would be more!*"[96] And I would like to see the man who would try to tell me that true Zofingian friendship would be the worse off for it!

I had to vent in somewhat more detail concerning this point because it is exactly here that old prejudices have the deepest roots. Yet now we move on to a second point, which is just as significant for the social question: namely, the *Sunday question.*

I would like to mention, by the way, that the significance of this question for the fraternities, as well as the significance of the fraternities for it, has been impressed upon me many times by one of our academic teachers, and I would like to introduce his impulses into our ranks here.[97]

What Sunday means for societal conditions is surely a matter in which we all are in agreement, even if we disregard what it means for us as Christians. Yet what stands in total contradiction to the social significance of Sunday is the fact that *Saturday evening* is all too commonly used, above all among us students, for holding club meetings. There is really no reason to object to this practice per

---

order of pre- and post-drinking (§52)] "and refuses to drink a Whole to the benefit of the crowd as a consequence."

94. In addition to the "ordinary sessions," there were also "Early-," "Evening-," and "Night-Pints" as well as "Night-Drinking" [*Kneipabend*] in the tavern.

95. "Fox" ([German: "Fuchs"] or alternatively, "Fux") was the label for members of a fraternity during the first two semesters, prior to their promotion to the rank of Fraternity Brothers ("fraternization") (cf. the *Biercomment*, 6 [§25], further 7 [§28]: "According to their inherent character, they are called 'crazy foxes' in the first semester and 'fire foxes' in the second."

96. Cf. Büchmann, *Geflügelte Worte*, 172.

97. The text of a footnote designated for this point in the text, which was put at the bottom of the page, was lost as the "Excerpta" were cut for binding.

se, yet as we all know, these meetings run long past midnight: they last until the wee hours of Sunday morning and are regularly prolonged ad infinitum by individual members. Each one of us knows what Sunday morning then tends to look like: whoever has no specific reason to get up simply sleeps until the morning pint. What a grand overture for honoring Sunday, especially when one sees the familiar morning-pint-physiognomies! We should consider that we provide a disastrous example for the masses by doing so; yet there's more: we do not rob only ourselves of the best portion of our Sundays, we also rob some of the tavern staff of the same thing, and they need their rest just as much as we do! Is that what it means to think and act socially? Furthermore, how can we theologians of all people be representatives of Sunday later on when we ourselves during our student years could barely conceive of a Sunday morning without a mild hangover or without being somewhat tired?!

This is yet another instance where we Zofingians as a patriotic and thus socially minded fraternity should take the lead and pave the way for a new praxis, just as our sister chapters in Geneva, Neuenburg, Lucerne, and St. Gallen are already doing, by the way, by holding their meetings on Tuesday, Wednesday, or Thursday. I know that this could present difficulties, especially for the medical students, yet it would provide a natural ending for the extension of our second act into the wee hours of the morning, and there is no reason to think that the latter alone could present an objection to my proposal (even if it were only an attempt): *we should move the meeting either to Friday*[98] *or Wednesday and then either retain the evening-night drinking*[99] *on Wednesday or move it to Friday or Saturday* (because naturally it tends to conclude more quickly than the meeting!!). What works in other places ought to work for us as well. Other fraternities would surely follow our lead, and we would have the merit of having given the impetus for a useful social movement.

These are a few ways of charting the course (as I said before, the list is not exhaustive) that I envision when I think of translating into praxis what I have called *Zofingian social ethos*.

In comparison with the "action extérieure" of our francophone compatriots, my theses are simultaneously a demand for something *more* and something *less*. For *less*, to the extent that I am disregarding all of those special "activities" beyond the confines of our present daily life as a fraternity and am demanding for our usual daily life in Zofingia only social ethos and the consequences that would arise from it. A demand for *more*, in that, as I well know, the act of following these consequences would entail a significantly greater effort, indeed a much greater sacrifice, on the part of the fraternity and its individual members than the operation of an "action extérieure," which itself can be completely disconnected from the rest of the association's life.

Will the Bernese Zofingia be interested in such a demand for something *more*?

98. "The prospective rescheduling of the meeting to Friday" was discussed once again in the winter semester of 1907–8 but in the end was rejected (Annual Report [Staatsarchiv Bern]).

99. A regular (weekly) meeting in the (fraternity-)pub [*Kneipe*] as stipulated by the Drinking-Conduct, for singing, "pubbing" [*Kneipen*], and for the discussion of any pending agenda items; cf. *Couleurstudenten in der Schweiz*, 101.

For many of you, the one thing from my presentation that is likely to have made an impression is that I offered a radical critique against all those kinds of things that for you seem to belong to the "bare necessities" of life in the Bernese Zofingia. To all of you who might find yourselves in this situation, I would once again like to make two requests:

1. That those who have already made an evaluation of my remarks in silence might for one moment *dismiss* all, and I really do mean all, *egoistical motives* and only after that point tell me what remains of your evaluation.
2. I ask you to consider this remainder of your evaluation (or perhaps condemnation) once again and bear in mind the question of whether it does not perhaps derive from a pure *conservatism*, a certain yet vague preference for what is old, because it is old, and an equally vague aversion to that which is new simply because it is new?!

It is only on this basis that a fruitful discussion will be possible.

I am not delighted by the thought of wrangling with members whose opposition, I must assume, at bottom stems only from a certain contentment with the current state of affairs *for their own person* and now feel themselves startled in their peace and quiet, or with those who contest my views simply because they have already reached a prior conclusion that they would like to live out their Zofingian life in the worn-out paths of a twenty-to-thirty-year-old tradition, along the lines of the Hegelian dictum

that which exists is rational,[100]

or even better, according to the dragon's principle in Wagner's *Siegfried*:

> I lie in possession:
> Let me slumber![101]

Other opponents—and these are the ones I'll take seriously—will come at me with the following objection: "What you've said in principle about a social ethos in Zofingia is noble and good, yet you are *only making negative proposals*: you are telling us what we *shouldn't* do, what should change, without giving us a guarantee for that which should then take its place. In brief: your critique is destructive without also being constructive."

I mention this objection because I already have the feeling that it will rear its head in some form, if it hasn't already. And yet the difficulty is only a seeming one; the solution is quite simple:

The outer forms of our life as a fraternity would remain, as I emphasized multiple times, entirely the same as heretofore except for a few modifications,

100. G. W. F. Hegel, *Grundlinien der Philosophie des Rechts oder Naturrecht und Staatswissenschaft im Grundrisse* (Vorrede), in *Sämtliche Werke: Jubiläumsausgabe in zwanzig Bänden* (Stuttgart: Frommann, 1928), 7:33. [Trans. note: Barth does not cite Hegel directly but instead paraphrases a famous statement from Hegel in the preface to the *Philosophy of Right*.]

101. Richard Wagner, *Siegfried*, trans. H. L. Corder and Fredrick Corder (London: Schott [B. Schotte Soehne], 1900), act 2, scene 1.

yet these forms would be filled with a new spirit, the spirit of a *social responsibility vis-à-vis the lower social classes and above all vis-à-vis ourselves.*

The individual Zofingian would live in the steadfast conviction that the aims of Zofingia do not find their culmination in him and in his amusement but rather in the wide and far-reaching realm of public and patriotic life, indeed, that it is there that they first come to fulfillment and maturity. This life, however, demands men who know what they want, in order that they may also want what they know. In order for this to be the case with regard to the social question, it is indispensable that these men go forth from a fraternity in which they *have learned to live socially*, not merely in theory, but also in *practice*. Zofingia desires to be such a fraternity, and we all have the task of helping to purify it of those accidents that impede and stand in the way of its purpose, for our own sake and for the sake of all those who will wear the red-white-red sash after us. Then, during our transition into civilian life, we will be able to look back at our academic and Zofingian careers without regret as a time of cheerful production and becoming, in order then to embark upon our work among and with our people with a pure conscience and wholesome consciousness.

I would gladly have given my thoughts a more articulate expression. If I have, however, succeeded in making the one or the other among us aware once again of this aspect of the noble task of Zofingia, then my presentation has served its purpose.

Karl Barth, stud. theol.
14 January MDCCCCVI [1906]

Discussion

[Records were made of the meeting.][102]

Motto: They could not get together;
the water was way too deep.[103]

Amsler:[104] Regrets that Barth spends his time making useless corrections of the Zofingia structure. He is fighting an enemy that does not exist. The working people have *no prejudices* against us and sympathize with us as we are. Barth's view of "*Zofingia and good company*" is very much in need of correction. This is linked up with the arguments regarding the *financial point*. Whoever has not been a member of the commission[105] cannot judge. We have to contend with

---

102. Barth himself first recorded the course of the discussion in pencil, and later, with a few modifications, retraced his notes with ink and added the résumé of his own "final statement." In addition, the official minutes of the entire meeting are available (in the Staatsarchiv Bern), recorded by the actuary Otto King, a student in the faculty of medicine. It can supplement Barth's rendering at specific points.

103. From the famous song "Edelkönigs-Kinder" (first stanza), in the collection of songs and poems *Des Knaben Wunderhorn: Alte deutsche Lieder*, edited by L. Achim von Arnim and Clemens Brentano.

104. Hermann Amsler (1883–1926), theology, president of the Bernese chapter, winter semester 1905–6.

105. The circle of office holders of the chapter (including presidency [chairman], treasurer, actuary, assessor, senior mentor).

competition like no other chapter (except Zurich). There are many reasons for an *official ball*. Finally, the *point of view on colors*. A fraternity that wears caps must engage in intense activity (drinking!).

As with officers, an especially good performance is demanded of us. Especially regarding the beer conduct, Barth is fighting an imaginary opponent. [Compare the] Zähringer and others(!). Amsler knows nothing about drinking according to conduct among workers. *Drinking sessions* are something very essential to fraternity life. A *different approach to the sessions* is extremely difficult.

Schläfli[106] expresses his thanks, and so on. If Barth goes further, then it is to be explained by the behavior of the Bernese Zofingia members toward Barth. (Interjections from the right.)[107] It would be the duty of the older members to be more accepting of the younger ones.

Against Amsler: the enemy that Barth is fighting is not as ephemeral as Amsler contends. There exist real contradictions precisely regarding the *social question*. Amsler adheres to the traditional standpoint, especially in relation to the *color issue*. Certainly, Barth does not want to suppress the Zofinger joyfulness, even though he rarely "shows up." Very stale jokes often arise during the drinking sessions. In relation to the *financial question*, there are difficulties, as the treasurer is aware. Individual members could do much. It is true that no one is obliged to drink a lot, but still "abominable intoxications" occur as a result of the *Comment* [conduct]. In fact, student drinking habits are passing over to the lower social strata. The transition from academic beer culture to civic life is very difficult; it should not be necessary. In addition, displeasure among peasants, workers, and the like really occurs.

Steck:[108] The subject actually belongs in the closed session.[109] What Barth presented is *nothing new*. For the time being, nothing needs to be abolished. These are experiences that everyone makes and Barth too in the next two years or so. The topic is a *smokescreen*. Barth's real point is: *he sees the others as malicious or ignorant*.[110]

Lauterburg[111] welcomes the opportunity to express his views of the Bernese Zofingia. Certain basic principles can be grasped without drinking. Steck has an ideal view, but in fact the matter is different. The financial question is weighty. Some Zofingia Alumni no longer allow their sons to join. Lauterburg regrets that he is not a dancer, but certainly the *dance events* do not play an essential role for the Zofingers' goals. Especially the traditional standpoint is reprehensible, here as in all areas. Too much value is really given to the *color issue* ([involving]

---

106. Emanuel Arthur Schläfli (1884–1961), theology.

107. Apparently there were various tables in Bern (as later in Zurich and also in Basel) around which gathered, on the one hand, adherents of the "classical" concept of fraternities and, on the other hand, adherents of the "modern" ideas for reform (see above, 47).

108. Johann Rudolf Gerhard Steck-von Erlach (1879–1952), law.

109. This is *commonly* the name of the session or part of a session to which guests were not admitted. According to the chapter minutes, however, Barth made his presentation in this kind of "closed meeting." Thus, Steck probably uses the term in the *specific* sense, in which it described the part of the agenda that was usually inserted as the conclusion of the first act, between the lecture part of the evening and the second act, as guests made their "exit." Steck's criticism then (also) implies: Barth's remarks were actually not a lecture, but only offered as a detailed, well-founded agenda item.

110. The actuary records: "Barth considers anyone who does not honor his ideas as inferior. A true Zofinger, however, must come to the point of assuming the general principle: a person is not worse if he does not honor my ideals."

111. Otto Lauterburg (1886–1975), theology. Cf. above, 44–45.

heckling). Influence of the beer-conduct on high school clubs . . . Details from it: I declare that I do not submit to it! (Heckling from the right.)

Ed. von Steiger[112] (Zofingia Alumnus) also lived in a Francophone chapter. Barth deals with the great difficulties of the 1830s.[113]

Ethical thought by the Bernese chapter,[114] which Barth as conservative Baseler does not understand: a color-brother wants to spend time with the others, hence the many events, which are bequeathed with many problems, and so on. In other chapters you have the strongest opposites. We do not want mere amusements, but rather *common events*. Cheapest and best is to gather in the "beer house." The Bernese Zofinger is socially absorbed by his fraternity. Individuality must not harm *solidarity*.

Closing Statement of the Speaker: I thank the discussants for their loyal and open words. The opposite views had to be talked through for once and will likely continue to be discussed. I must reject the charge of *intolerance* (Steck); likely that can be found more on the other side. My *individual postulates* have been attacked but not refuted. Therefore, I do not need to repeat the remarks of my paper. Effective opposition should have been directed against my *principal position*, but that did not happen. As for the *pint sessions*, I admit that one can be of different opinion, that is, regard them favorably. For me personally, thus far they have offered too little to recognize them as essential. My opposition does not stem, as Amsler opines, from idle pleasure in criticizing. I have sensed certain harms to the life of our chapter from the beginning and considered it my *ethical duty* to express my reservations, because I do not want to belong to those who say "Peace, Peace!" when there is no peace (Jer. 6:14; 8:11). Whether I will think differently in two years from now, I know no more than Steck, but daresay I doubt it.

Ris:[115] It is typical that B[arth] and Lauterburg are so astonished to find that there are such "ideal spirits" as Steck and von Steiger among the Bernese.[116] The opposition to the *Biercomment* shows that some people have not yet grasped the spirit of the fraternity (Bernese section). One should first get to know the topic before wanting to reform it.

Lauterburg replies.

Amsler closes with thanks for the presentation and discussion.

---

112. Eduard von Steiger (1880–1962), law; 1914–1939, member of the Grand Council of the Canton of Bern; 1939, member of the Executive Council of the Canton of Bern; 1940–51, member of the Swiss Federal Council; cf. *Biography*, 29:314.

113. Cf. above, 56, n. 56. In the "crisis of 1833," which had lasting effects, the key issue was whether Zofingia as a whole should and could be committed to the *political* liberalism of the day (cf. Kundert and Im Hof, *Geschichte des Schweizerischen Zofingervereins*, 40–44).

114. Eduard von Steiger alludes to the traditional emphasis of *amicitia* (friendship) in the Bernese chapter (see above, 46).

115. Fritz Ris (1880–1938), medicine.

116. The actuary summarizes Ris's comments as follows: "I only noticed the surprised faces of Barth and Lauterburg as they heard Steck and Steiger speak in this manner, . . . when they became aware how even old boozers like us optimally understand and represent our cause." The "ideal Zofinger" were easily of the opinion that only they could negotiate the Zofinger questions in principle and from reasonable points of view. In contrast, Ris wants to emphasize that even the more strict supporters of the *Comment* are not just sociable beer drinkers but are quite determined by "ideals."

Zwingli's Sixty-Seven Articles of the First Disputation on Religion at Zurich, 1523
1906

In the winter semester 1905–6, Karl Barth enrolled again—as he had already done in the summer semester 1905—in the "Church History Seminar" with his father, Fritz Barth. The present text, "Seminar Work about a Writing of Zwingli," was probably written for these seminars. Barth mentioned it on December 28, 1905, in a letter to his grandmother and aunt in Basel—"presently very busy" with the Zofingia Lecture (see the preceding chapter)—as a task that "also still" was waiting threateningly for him. Further biographical documents do not exist for us. Barth appears to have crafted his material chiefly from the monograph about Zwingli by R. Staehelin mentioned in footnote 1.

The text is one of the bound pieces in "Excerpts II." Under the heading stands the notation: "Church History Seminar, W. S. 1905–6."

[Trans.: In the following, the text of Zwingli's writings that would have been available to Barth in 1905–6 is cited first in the footnotes. If there are English translations of these sources, they will be cited after the German of Zwingli's Werke. The critical edition of Zwingli's Werke in the Corpus Reformatorum was probably not in Barth's hands for use in this paper; however, the date of publication for the CR is 1905, so it is conceivable. We will cite Huldreich Zwingli's Werke (1828–32) since this was most probably the source Barth used. However, if there is no English translation of a work of Zwingli, we will include the CR information as well. References for all the CR citations can be found in the original German edition of this volume.]

I.

On December 15, 1522, the Swiss confederate states made the weighty decision that in each place "such new sermons" are to be suppressed, "for there is reason to be concerned that if such courageous resistance were not undertaken, great unrest and harm would arise."[1]

The situation was tense. In the cities of Basel, Bern, and Zurich, the battle cries of the Wittenberg Reformers had found joyful reverberations; in the East and West of Switzerland, the foundations of the old church appeared to begin to sway. On the other hand, the Waldstätte with Luzern still formed the solid refuge of all those who would not like to part from the faith of the fathers, that is, from Rome. With growing reluctance, the latter realized that Zurich

---

1. Cited in Rudolf Staehelin, *Huldreich Zwingli: Sein Leben und Wirken, nach den Quellen dargestellt,* vol. 1, *Die reformatorische Grundlegung* (Basel: Benno Schwabe, 1895), 259.

in particular, although for the time being still without a principled statement, turned more and more to the Reformation cause.[2] Events pressed for a decision, as both sides recognized, and probably nobody more clearly than the head of the Reformation movement in Switzerland, *Ulrich Zwingli*, the contentious "canon and preacher at the great cathedral of Zurich."[3] He probably recognized already then that one day it had to come to a warlike staging of the point at issue between the two factions, although no means should be left unused for bringing about a peaceful settlement, if still possible. A *public disputation*, arranged and conducted by the secular authorities—who were quite competent in theological and ecclesiastical matters, according to the views at that time— seemed to be the most suitable. To that end, Zwingli probably was pressed already by the constant attacks on his person from the Catholic camp, where they regarded him as the author of all evil. Already in his writing, *Archeteles* (1522), he had therefore claimed: "You must deal with me by means of the Holy Scriptures bestowed upon us by God (and do not forget that point), and they must not be twisted. You must not use things devised by the vanity of man, and you must come to close quarters and not fight by laying mines."[4] In the Augustinian church in Zurich, there arose, nearly to the point of violence,[5] a controversy between a preaching monk and *Leo Jud*, and this public nuisance, bound up with the entirely intolerable provisional situation and the express request of Zwingli, finally moved the Zurich City Council to the decisive writ issued on January 3, 1523, *Ausschreiben des Rates an sämtliche Geistliche der Stadt und Landschaft Zürich* (*Public Announcement of the Council to All Ministers of the City and Region of Zurich*). On January 29, all were supposed to present themselves in the town hall, and in the same place "before the gathered council, shall explain and defend their view with the help of truly divine Scripture in the German language and receive, for their further behavior, the advice of the council."[6] ["When we, with the careful assistance of certain scholars, have paid careful attention to the matters, as seems best to us, and after investigations are made with the help of the Holy Scriptures and the truth, we will send each one home

2. Cf. Staehelin, *Zwingli*, 166–77, 231, 247–49, etc.

3. With these titles Zwingli is named in the report of the disputation by E. Hegenwald, in *Handlung der versammlung in der löblichen statt Zürich uf den XXIX: Tag jenners von wegen des heiligen Evangelii zwischen der eersamen treffenlichen botschaft von Costenz und Huldrychen Zwingli, prediger des Evangelii Christi, sammt gemeiner priesterschaft des ganzen gebiets der eegenannten statt Zürich, vor gesessnem rat beschehen im MDXXIII jar*, in *Huldreich Zwingli's Werke*, ed. Melchior Schuler and Johannes Schulthess, vol. 1 (Zurich: Friedrich Schulthess, 1828), 18:105, 114–68, esp. 153. ET: *Acts of the Convention Held in the Praiseworthy City of Zurich on the 29th Day of January, on account of the Holy Gospel—Being a Disputation between the Dignified and Honorable Representative from Constance and Huldrych Zwingli, Preacher of the Gospel of Christ, Together with the Common Clergy of the Whole Territory of the Aforesaid City of Zurich, Held before the Assembled Council in the Year 1523*, in *Selected Works of Huldreich Zwingli (1484–1531), The Reformer of German Switzerland*, ed. Samuel Macauley Jackson, trans. Lawrence A. McLouth (Philadelphia: University of Pennsylvania Press, 1901), 40–117, here 111. [Hereafter, *Acts of the Convention*.]

4. H. Zwingli, *Apologeticus Archeteles adpellatus quo respondetur paraenesi a rev. domino Constantiensi (quorundam procaci factone ad id persuaso) ad senatum praepositurae Tigurinae quem capitulum vocant missae*, in *Werke*, ed. Schuler and Schulthess (1832), 3:26, 27–76, 74–75. ET: *Defense Called Archeteles in Which Answer Is Made to an Admonition that the Most Reverend Lord Bishop of Constance (Being Persuaded thereto by the Behavior of Certain Wanton Factious Persons) Sent to the Council of the Great Minster at Zurich Called the Chapter*, in *The Latin Works and the Correspondence of Huldreich Zwingli: Together with Selections from His German Works*, vol. 1 (1510–22), ed. Samuel Macauley Jackson, trans. Henry Preble (New York: G. P. Putnam's Sons, 1912), 291. Cf. also Staehelin, *Zwingli*, 236.

5. Staehelin, *Zwingli*, 259.

6. Staehelin, *Zwingli*, 260.

with a command either to continue or to desist."[7]] The appropriate spiritual authority, the Bishop of Constance, was invited to be represented at the hearing by delegates; nevertheless, the role intended for them was expressly more that of *bystanders*, which had been coordinated by the competence of the council, than of decisive *judges*, as ought to have been the case, given the nature of the matter.[8] Indeed, more than that: by its firm commitment to the exclusive validity of the authority of Scripture, the council from the start positioned itself, as *Stähelin* [= Staehelin] has rightly remarked, on Zwingli's side.[9]

With what calm and confidence *Zwingli* awaited the events, we learn, among other things, from one of his letters to Oecolampadius, where he stated, "A rumor is being spread that the substitute for [the Bishop of] Constance will be absent. May God grant that he may be delayed so that either Rome or Constance may be deprived of accustomed triumphs, that is, those triumphs that they usually reported until now."[10]

In order to give a basis and starting point to the disputation on religion to be held, and in order to deliver clearly once and for all his relationship to the gospel in contrast to friend and foe, he wrote his *67 Articles* soon after the mandate of the announcement.[11] The *67 Articles* summarize his teaching and his reformation program, which is even more worthy of close inspection, since it gives us a picture, in the most desirable brevity and conciseness, of the entire theological and ecclesial position of the Zurich reformer. They clearly demark views to the left and to the right, as opposed to *the papacy* and alongside the parallel German reformation movement, as it is embodied especially by *Luther*.

Here we refrain from a presentation of *the disputation* itself (well known as the "First Zurich Disputation"), although it offers the greatest interest for the understanding of the situation. It focused almost exclusively on one point—easily understandable given the vastness of the problem: the relationship of divine and human authority, that is, specifically of Scripture and churchdom [*Kirchentum*].

Rather, let us now turn to a brief overview of the contents of those *67 Theses*, in order to make a few general remarks about them at the conclusion.

II.

The *67 Theses* can be divided into *two groups*: (a) a *theoretical-dogmatic* group (1–16) and (b) a *practical-ecclesial* group (17–67).

Quantitatively, the second group naturally takes up the larger space by far. To a certain extent, if the first part gives us the religious *foundation* of Zwingli's

---

7. *Handlung der versammlung*, in *Zwingli's Werke*, 18:115–16; ET: *Acts of the Convention*, 44 [rev. and expanded; Trans.].

8. Cf. Staehelin, *Zwingli*, 260.

9. Staehelin, *Zwingli*, 260.

10. *Huldrichus Zuinglius Io. Oecolampadio* (Epistolae MDXXIII, I. January 14, 1523), in *Zwingli's Werke*, ed. Schuler and Schulthess (1830), 7:261 [ET by Trans.].

11. *Die 67 Artikel Zwinglis*, in *Werke*, 1:153–57 [hereafter: *Artikel Zwinglis*]. ET: *Zwingli: Selected Works of Huldreich Zwingli (1484–1531)*, ed. Samuel Macauley Jackson, trans. Lawrence A. McLouth, Henry Preble, and George W. Gillmore (Philadelphia: University of Pennsylvania Press, 1901), 111–17 [hereafter, *Zwingli: Selected Works* (Jackson)].

system of doctrine, then in the second part we have his practical *extension*, the consequences, which emerge before us from those basic views of ecclesial and civil life.

Let us take them up point by point!

a. The *theoretical-dogmatic part* begins with a negation, especially—something very characteristic for Zwingli—with the *challenge to the necessity of the "confirmation of the church" [bewährnuss der kilchen] for the interpretation and utilization of the gospel.*[12] As a counterpart to this, Thesis 2 is called the "Sum of the Gospel," *"that our Lord Christ Jesus, God's true Son, has made known to us the will of his heavenly Father, and with his innocence has redeemed us from death and has reconciled us with God."*[13] As a result, he is the only way to blessedness (3), the "guide and leader" *[wegführer und hauptmann]* of the human race (6).[14]

The *Christian church* is made up of those who believe in him, the body of Christ, as it were, a body of which he is the head. Whoever dwells in it is also a child of God: "This is the church or communion of saints, the bride of Christ, the catholic [universal] church." Just as without the head the members can do nothing, so too without Christ the church can do nothing (7–10).[15]

Hence, it arises that the *ecclesial* (therefore human) *statutes*, which are added to the gospel, are the reason for all error (11–12).[16] It is worthwhile to listen to Christ and his Spirit; the salvation of humans stands on faith in him, not on human doctrine (13–16).[17]

With that, the foundational first part is already at an end. If I previously have called this the dogmatic part of Zwingli's confession, this is not to be understood as if the confession gave a systematic representation of the complete creed of Zwingli, similar to the first part of the Augsburg Confession[18] for Luther and Melanchthon. Here is no mention of the nature of God, the Trinity, original sin, and so forth; rather, the text with greatest sharpness picks out a *point of controversy*, around which, according to Zwingli's perspective, the entire argument revolved: the *contrast between divine and human authority*, which, as I already have mentioned, had then become the subject of public disputation. We could summarize the contents of these first sixteen propositions suitably in modern words: *"Let's depart from Rome! Back to the gospel!"*[19] In contrast to a churchdom that has usurped the mediation between God and humans and, as "the

---

12. *Artikel Zwinglis*, 153; ET: *Zwingli: Selected Works* (Jackson), 111.
13. *Artikel Zwinglis*, 153; ET: *Zwingli: Selected Works* (Jackson), 111.
14. *Artikel Zwinglis*, 153; ET: *Zwingli: Selected Works* (Jackson), 111.
15. *Artikel Zwinglis*, 153–54; ET: *Zwingli: Selected Works* (Jackson), 111–12.
16. *Artikel Zwinglis*, 154; ET: *Zwingli: Selected Works* (Jackson), 112.
17. *Artikel Zwinglis*, 154; ET: *Zwingli: Selected Works* (Jackson), 112.
18. *The Augsburg Confession*, Art. 1–21, in *The Book of Concord: The Confessions of the Evangelical Lutheran Church*, ed. Robert Kolb and Timothy J. Wengert, trans. Charles Arand, Eric Gritsch, et al. (Minneapolis: Fortress Press, 2000), 36–59.
19. Concerning the "religious movement" developed in Austria against Ultramontanism in 1897–1899, which has been called the "Let's depart from Rome–Movement" but which one, "Praise God," "appropriately could call 'On to the Gospel-Movement,'" cf. Robert Aeschbacher, *Los von Rom! Die evangelische Bewegung in Oesterreich; Mit Berücksichtigung anderer Länder* [Let's depart from Rome! The Protestant movement in Austria; with consideration of other countries], 2nd ed. (Zurich: Zürcher & Furrer, 1902), esp. 2 and 9 (regarding Robert Aeschbacher, Karl Barth's confirmation director, see below, 85); also see A. Fürer, *Hin zum Evangelium! Überblick über die evangelische Bewegung in Österreich und verwandte Bewegungen in aller Welt* [Back to the gospel! An overview concerning the Protestant Movement in Austria and related movements in all the world], 2nd ed. (Karlsruhe: J. J. Reif, 1902), 332 n. 1.

only-true-saving-church"[20] [*alleinseligmachende*], closes the doors of the kingdom of heaven for anyone who does not subject themselves, Zwingli wants to lead the community of Christ back to a simple, joyous message of their founder, "who has made known to us the will of his heavenly Father and with his innocence has redeemed us from death."[21] The true catholic church exists consequently not in the obedient members of an external institution, but rather in all those who have made Christ the "guide and leader" of their lives:

> He the head, we his members
> He the light and we the glow,
> He the master, we the brothers,
> He is ours, and we are his.[22]

If this is the case, however, then the *views of the visible earthly church* will necessarily undergo a significant alteration, and Zwingli speaks of this in the second part.

b. Practical-ecclesial part of his "Articles." Since Christ is the true high priest, *the papacy* is eliminated as a human presumption (17).[23] Since Christ has offered himself up once for us, we can celebrate the *mass* not as a sacrifice and mediatorial act but only as a "remembrance" of the same (18–19).[24] Since Christ's righteousness has redeemed us, from this point onward we need neither the *intercession of the saints* nor our own *good works* (20–22).[25] Since Christ brought us freedom, all commandments about *food, holy days, pilgrimages, clothing,* and so forth are unchristian (24–26).[26]

Since in Christ all humans are brothers, it does not do to establish a special status of Christians through *monastic orders, celibate priesthood,* and so forth (27–30).[27] The *huge amount of earthly possessions of the clergy* is abominable (23),[28] especially if they come about through *conscription of unlawful goods* (33).[29] The authority for declaring *excommunication* must be restricted (31–32).[30]

Worldly power falls to the *worldly authority* alone. The latter is appointed by God in order to protect the law. Consequently, Christians are obligated to offer their obedience, as long as the authorities "rule with God alone." "But if they

---

20. The catechisms of the Counter-Reformation talk about the "only-true-saving Catholic religion," respectively, the "only-true-saving doctrine," or the "true alone-making-sanctified Catholic faith" (cf. Franz Xaver Thalhofer, *Entwicklung des katholischen Katechismus in Deutschland von Canisius bis Deharbe: Historisch kritisch dargelegt* [Freiburg i. Br.: Herder, 1899], 28 n. 1; 50 n. 2; 52 nn. 1, 3). Evidently the attribute has later been transferred to the *church,* at least since the beginning of the nineteenth century. Cf. J. S. Drey, *Ueber den Satz von der alleinseligmachenden Kirche,* part 1, in *Der Apologet des Katholicismus: Eine Zeitschrift* (1822), 5:39–85 (published again in *Geist des Christentums und des Katholizismus: Ausgewählte Schriften katholischer Theologie im Zeitalter des deutschen Idealismus und der Romantik,* ed. J. R. Geiselmann, Deutsche Klassiker der katholischen Theologie aus neuerer Zeit 5 [Mainz: Matthias Grünewald Verlag, 1940], 333–57).

21. *Artikel Zwinglis,* 153; ET: *Zwingli: Selected Works* (Jackson), 111.

22. From N. L. Graf von Zinzendorf's hymn, "Herz und Herz vereint zusammen" (Heart and heart together united), arranged by Chr. Gregor, *GERS* 161 (*EKG* 217), verse 1.

23. *Die 67 Artikel Zwinglis,* 154; ET: *Zwingli: Selected Works* (Jackson), 112.

24. *Artikel Zwinglis,* 154; ET: *Zwingli: Selected Works* (Jackson), 112–13.

25. *Artikel Zwinglis,* 154; ET: *Zwingli: Selected Works* (Jackson), 113.

26. *Artikel Zwinglis,* 155; ET: *Zwingli: Selected Works* (Jackson), 113.

27. *Artikel Zwinglis,* 155; ET: *Zwingli: Selected Works* (Jackson), 114.

28. *Artikel Zwinglis,* 154–55; ET: *Zwingli: Selected Works* (Jackson), 113.

29. *Artikel Zwinglis,* 155; ET: *Zwingli: Selected Works* (Jackson), 114.

30. *Artikel Zwinglis,* 155; ET: *Zwingli: Selected Works* (Jackson), 114.

are unfaithful and transgress the laws of Christ, they may be deposed in God's name" (34–43).[31]

True *prayer* happens "in the Spirit: . . . truly, all externals, church singing or shouting," are therefore abominable (44–46).[32] Moreover, it has to be a primary goal of Reformation preaching to liberate Christians from *"offense,"* that is, to liberate from the temptation to sin caused by unauthorized prohibitions, under which the celibacy of the priesthood stands up front as the status quo (47–49).[33]

God alone can *forgive sins* through Jesus Christ, but not humans among themselves through imposed external works of penance or even financial contribution (50–56)![34] Scripture knows nothing of a *purgatory*; in general, only God knows about things after death. Therefore, if not [having] the prayers for the departed souls, then still all the special definitions and agreements in this area are abominable (57–60).[35] The essential part of the priesthood does not consist in the inherent *character indelebilis* [indelible character] attached to it through ordination, but rather in the proclamation of the Word of God (61–63).[36] The last four theses call categorically once more for "The Cessation of Misusages." At the same time, coercion and force should not be applied by any side,[37] but the *spiritual authorities* "shall at once settle down and with unanimity set up the cross of Christ, not the money chests, or they will perish, for I tell you the axe is raised against the tree."[38] And then the resolute *conclusion* reads: "Let no one undertake here to argue with sophistry or human foolishness, but come to the Scriptures to accept them as the judge (for the Scriptures breathe the Spirit of God), so that the truth either may be found, or if found, as I hope, retained. Amen. Thus may God rule."[39]

Across the board, we see a frank renunciation of the former churchdom. Here is no trace of the peaceful tendency of a Melanchthon. Zwingli was not a mediator. The "church" is sick from head to toe, sick from the error, which penetrated it for centuries, that Christ's message of redemption can be put into one binding formula, into a formula that is made by humans and yet is supposed to be authoritative for humans. With a jolt, Zwingli here blows up this whole structure. Away with all faith in authority! Back to the personal perspective and experience of God, as it is made possible for us in the gospel *of Jesus*! Get rid of all external holiness of works and get back to a stable life in faith and love, as *Jesus* has lived it as an example for us! Get rid of the bondage through dogmas and laws invented and handed down by humans and go back to the "marvelous freedom of the children of God" (Rom. 8:21), which *Jesus* offers to humans!

---

31. *Artikel Zwinglis*, 155–56, esp. 156; ET: *Zwingli: Selected Works* (Jackson), 114–15, esp. 115. [Translation modified. Trans.]

32. *Artikel Zwinglis*, 156; ET: *Zwingli: Selected Works* (Jackson), 115. [Here I have translated the quote from Zwingli's article myself. Jackson's translation has "church song and outcry with devotion." Trans.]

33. *Artikel Zwinglis*, 156; ET: *Zwingli: Selected Works* (Jackson), 115–16.

34. *Artikel Zwinglis*, 156; ET: *Zwingli: Selected Works* (Jackson), 116.

35. *Artikel Zwinglis*, 156; ET: *Zwingli: Selected Works* (Jackson), 116–17.

36. *Artikel Zwinglis*, 157; ET: *Zwingli: Selected Works* (Jackson), 117.

37. *Artikel Zwinglis*, 157; ET: *Zwingli: Selected Works* (Jackson), 117.

38. *Artikel Zwinglis*, 157; ET: *Zwingli: Selected Works* (Jackson), 117.

39. *Artikel Zwinglis*, 157; ET: *Zwingli: Selected Works* (Jackson), 117.

That's what Zwingli's concluding articles shouted to his contemporaries with a powerful voice. These were the carefully considered words of a man who, like Luther, though in a different way, had learned for himself what bondage to faith and conscience means, and thus he was allowed to point to the gospel of freedom with even more joyful assurance.

It may be left open whether we, along with *Stähelin*, want to call the *67 Articles* virtually "the model of a Protestant confession";[40] perhaps they are a bit too one-sidedly negative-polemical, but this much is certain, that in their powerful definition and demarcation of what the gospel is, what Christianity is, what is imperishable, what the human word is, what the church is, and what is transient, they have enduring significance, for the present and also the future, even if we perhaps drew the boundaries with this and that point a little differently or even were content with a question mark.

I would like to follow up here with a few observations concerning these relations between Zwingli's expressed standpoint in the 67 Articles and our current ecclesial-theological life.

III.

As we have seen, the great contrast, which Zwingli sets up throughout his theses, is the difference between *divine* and *human* authority, between *evangelical* and *ecclesiastical* doctrine. He had before him the human, ecclesiastical dimension in the [Roman] Catholic churchdom; here there can be no ambiguity. But where did he find the *divine authority* to which he appealed? His answer, like that of all the Reformers, ran thus: *in the Holy Scriptures, the Old and New Testaments.* One has called this the *formal principle of the Reformation proclamation*,[41] in contrast to the material principle of the doctrine of justification; especially with Zwingli it comes to the fore more than with any one of the other Reformers. "Whoever wants to teach a dogma," he said in a writing that appeared later, *Auslegung und Begründung der Schlussreden* [*Interpretation and Foundation of the Articles*],[42] "that is, an opinion that relates to divine wisdom and truth, there helps no holiness, no trick, no hot air when you cannot prove it with the Holy Scriptures."[43]

The question is not that easy for us anymore. Especially in the present, the controversy concerning the authoritative validity of the Holy Scriptures has become very acute. Two extreme points of view lie before us: (1) the *orthodox view*, where the Holy Scriptures in their verbal expression are binding upon Christianity and the church for all times; and (2) the (ultra-) *history of religions view*, where the Bible is like other works of writing from antiquity, a historical

---

40. Staehelin, *Zwingli*, 263.

41. For this usage of language, which emerged at the beginning of the nineteenth century, cf. C. Beck, "Das Princip des Protestantismus: Anfrage in einem Schreiben an D. Ullmann," *Theologische Studien und Kritische* 24 (1851): 408–11; A. Ritschl, "Über die beiden Principien des Protestantismus: Antwort auf eine 25 Jahre alte Frage," *ZKG* 1 (1877): 397–413; C. Stange, "A. Ritschls Urteil über die beiden Prinzipien des Protestantismus," ThStKr 70 (1897): 599–621.

42. H. Zwingli, *Uslegen und gründ der schlussreden oder artikel durch Huldrychen Zwingli Zürich uf den XIX tag jenners im MDXXIII jar usgagen*, in *Huldreich Zwinglis Werke*, ed. Schuler and Schulthess (1828), 1:169–424; also in *Huldreich Zwinglis Sämtliche Werke*, ed. E. Egli and G. Finsler, vol. 2, Corpus Reformatorum 89 (Leipzig: Heinsius, 1908), 1.14–457.

43. Zwingli, *Uslegen und gründ*, 295; CR 89:212, l.11–14. Cf. R. Staehelin, *Zwingli*, 281.

entity, and therefore has only historical, that is, finite significance and binding force. Would Zwingli stand over here or over there today? From his writings, especially from the theses, neither the one nor the other emerges, even if it might seem, especially through the repeated citation of the well-known place, 2 Timothy 3:16,[44] as if there were a clear statement for the *theory of "inspiration."* But that is just the semblance! Let's not forget that this theory is a *post-Reformation* product,[45] so it could be even less available for Zwingli than the results of biblical-criticism research of recent times. Therefore, if the Scripture is for him on the one side divinely given, θεόπνευστος [God-breathed],[46] he still had in mind, as Stähelin correctly emphasizes, "not the Scripture as external teaching of the law, but rather in its summary as the gospel and in its living verification through the indwelling Spirit."[47] The further question, which now immediately strikes the modern and historically minded theologian, is this: *How does "the self-authenticating word of God differ from Scripture as such?"*[48] Zwingli could not and did not need to ask this question so sharply, but it has become indispensable for us. "Consequently, his position toward Scripture—as that of all the Reformers—suffers from an inner lack of clarity, which soon leads him to place the inner instruction by the Spirit over against the external instruction by Scripture and, then again, leads him to attribute the validity of a divine revelation to statements of Scripture, solely on the basis of their external affiliation to Scripture."[49] In fact, both Zwingli and Luther occasionally search the Scriptures for the proof texts for their just-represented opinion, often in a manner that has for us a Scholastic whiff; this exegetical method, which was amply applied, especially in the post-Reformation period, once prompted *Werenfels,* the Basel Antistes [head of the church], to write the nasty distich:

> *Hic liber est in quo quisque sua dogmata quaerit,*
> *Invenit et iterum dogmata quisque sua.*
> This is a book in which whoever seeks his own dogmatics,
> finds his own dogmatics again.[50]

---

44. *Artikel Zwinglis,* 153; ET: *Zwingli: Selected Works* (Jackson), 111; Zwingli, *Uslegen und gründ,* 424; CR 89:457, lines 11–12.

45. The concept of the inspiration of Scripture had first been processed in Lutheran orthodoxy into a doctrine of inspiration. Cf. "The First Commonplace: *De Scriptura Sacra,*" in Johann Gerhard's *Theological Commonplaces: Exegesis, or More Copious Explanation of Certain Articles of the Christian Religion (1625),* vol. 1, ed. Benjamin T. G. Mayes, trans. Richard J. Dinda (Saint Louis: Concordia Publishing House, 2009), esp. chap. 2: *"de causa efficiente scripturae sacrae"* [On the efficient cause of Scripture], 40–57. Also H. Vollmer, "Inspiration der Schrift, dogmengeschichtlich," in *RGG*[1] 3:552–61; also *RGG*[2] and *RGG*[3] under "Inspiration."

46. The manuscript reads: θεόπνευθστα; it is corrected here according to the marked note of the seminar leader, Prof. Fritz Barth.

47. Staehelin, *Zwingli,* 281.

48. Staehelin, *Zwingli,* 281.

49. Staehelin, *Zwingli,* 281.

50. Cf. S. Werenfels, *Fasciculus Epigrammatum,* 60: S. Scripturae abusus:

Hic liber est, in quo sua quaerit dogmata quisque;
  Invenit et partier dogmata quisque sua.
[This is a book in which whoever seeks their own dogmatics,
  finds their own dogmatics again. Trans.]

In Werenfels, *Opuscula theologica, philosophica et philologica,* Editio altera, Tom. 2 (Lausanne/Geneva: Joh. le Mair and H. A. de Chalmot, 1739), 509. The differing form, which Barth cites here (and also elsewhere), probably goes back to the imprecise reporting by K. R. Hagenbach, *Die theologische Schule Basels und ihre Lehrer von Stiftung der Hochschule 1460 bis zu deWette's Tod 1849* (Basel: Schweighauser, 1860), 39.

Still, this unclear position of the Reformers toward Scripture ("unclear" when viewed from our contemporary standpoint!) has its good reason. What is more, in certain respects it is virtually a strength; Luther, Zwingli, and all the other Reformers (except perhaps Melanchthon) were *men of the present and future*, not of the past. Their view was forward and not directed toward what was behind them [cf. Phil. 3:13]. Opposite them stood the historically grown weight of the Roman church and papacy, from whose pressure Christendom was to be liberated. The study of the Holy Scriptures had led them to this insight, and therefore it became the foundation of the new preaching, to which they appealed over and over again. Do we want to take offense at the fact that, for them, the *Holy Scriptures* were in their own way a historical entity? In [Roman] Catholicism, they saw the "Word of God" overgrown with human institutions. The elimination of the latter gave them enough work to do. No wonder, then, that it never occurred to them that the *book of the Bible was written and compiled by human beings*!

It is not acceptable for one or the other of the current trends to claim the Reformers for themselves, simply because for them the current burning question did not exist at all. To state how Luther and Zwingli today would position themselves about this is to express nothing more than *suppositions*. True, they also had a criterion for what was divine and human in the Scriptures, even though it was not scientific. Zwingli says it like this in the *Auslegung* [interpretation] of his first article: *"All human doctrines, ordinances, and judgments now rub against this gold-testing stone, Christ. If something shows the color of Christ, then it stems from the Spirit of God (and does not need the names of church fathers, councils, customs, and customary law)."*[51] And similarly Luther calls the Scriptures divine *"in the way they put forward Christ or not."*[52] I think that this good Protestant criterion will retain its enduring value for us as well, even if, in doing so, it does not yet signal the theological goal of the question.

Viewed from this angle, even the most far-reaching results and statements of modern historical criticism of the Bible, like the ones of the Baur school or the Wellhausen school, must lose their odium, which still adheres to them in some believers' circles. This much is certain: both Zwingli and Luther would have been significantly less upset about the so-called modern theology than some of those who call themselves by their names today! The history of Israel may have proceeded according to this or that *Schema*; the Gospel of John[53] and some

51. Zwingli, *Uslegen und gründ*, 178; CR 88:26, lines 7–9.

52. Cf. Martin Luther, *Vorrede auf die Episteln S. Jakobi und Judä* (1522), WA DB 7:384, lines 26–28. ET: Luther, "Preface to the Epistles of Saint James and Saint Jude 1545 (1522)," in *Works of Martin Luther, with Introductions and Notes*, Philadelphia Edition, vol. 6, ed. Henry Eyster Jacobs and Adolf Spaths, trans. C. M. Jacobs (Philadelphia: Muhlenberg Press, 1932), 478 [Translation modified. The English quotation "lays emphasis on" is the marginal reading for *"so sie Christum treibet"* in this passage; it replaces "whether they *deal with* Christ or not." Trans.]

53. The representative thesis that John's Gospel may have been authored in the second century was offered at first by Karl Gottlieb Bretschneider [*Probabilia de evangelii et epistolarum Joannis, Apostoli, indole et origine eruditorum judiciis modeste subjecit Carolus Theoph. Bretschneider* (Leipzig: J. Ambrose Barthii, 1820), esp. §21: *Genesis evangelii, quae probabilis videtur*, 115–99]. It was elaborated and given comprehensive grounding by Ferdinand Christian von Baur, "Über die Composition und den Charakter des johanneïschen Evangeliums," *Theologische Jahrbücher*, ed. E. Zeller (Tübingen, 1844), 3:1–191, 297–475, and 615–700, esp. 631–700. Also in Baur, *Kritische Untersuchungen über die kanonischen Evangelien, ihr Verhältniss zu einander, ihren Charakter und Ursprung* (Tübingen: L. F. Fues, 1847), 84–389, esp. 311–89. See further, e.g., Adolf Jülicher, *An Introduction to the New Testament*, trans. Janet Penrose Ward (London: Smith, Elder, & Co., 1904), 402–7.

or even all of Paul's letters may come from the second century[54]—after all, we will need to be content with the words of Zwingli: "In sum, all who correctly recognize Jesus Christ in this way, are taught by God, not by humans; in hearing and learning they are enlightened and drawn by the Father in their inner being and hearts."[55]

In a somewhat briefer fashion, I would still like to point out a few further points worth mentioning.

The *67 Theses* throw an interesting light on *Zwingli's conception of the sacraments*, almost more through what they do not say than through what they do say. One should note that generally nothing is said about *baptism*, about *the Lord's Supper*, except the brief mention in Thesis 18: the mass should "not be a sacrifice, but rather should be a *remembrance* of the sacrifice, an *assurance of the redemption* that Christ has demonstrated for us."[56] Here we have in nuce already the position that later led to the fateful quarrel with Luther. There is no mention of the dogmatic question of transubstantiation, the response to which—for example, in the Augsburg Confession—coincides with the definition of the concept of the Lord's Supper in general.[57] The Lord's Supper is above all a *memorial celebration*, with the death of Christ in mind; the remembrance of the latter guarantees for us "assurance of redemption." That baptism is not mentioned may be related to the fact that Zwingli, on the whole, puts forward only contentious points, but it also has a deeper reason. He generally wants to have *sacramental aspects pushed into the background*. The sober Eastern Swiss character may play a role here; nevertheless his viewpoint certainly has a deep truth, precisely in opposition to a catholicizing Lutheranism. Even here Zwingli's basic principle emerges: the eternal truths of the gospel are not to be grasped in external forms, but always to be understood spiritually. If we nevertheless retain such forms, they are nothing more than symbols of a spiritual reality.

From this we understand why Zwingli later, during the eucharistic controversy, stuck to his point of view as strongly as Luther. He later could not accept the conception of the Augsburg Confession "that the body and blood of Christ are truly present and distributed."[58] His "*significat*"[59] [signifies] has a solid basis in his entire theological position. Especially with regard to this point, a few things should be said, even in the present, even in the Reformed church. Contrary to the still widespread conception of the Lord's Supper as a *mysterium*

---

54. This assertion was also made, after and beside others, by R. Steck, who had been professor in Bern since 1881: *Der Galaterbrief, nach seiner Echtheit untersucht, nebst kritischen Bemerkungen zu den paulinischen Hauptbriefen* (Berlin: Reimer, 1888); cf., among others, Albert Schweitzer, *Paul and His Interpreters: A Critical History*, trans. William Montgomery (New York: Macmillan Co., 1951), 117–50.

55. Zwingli, *Uslegen und gründ*, in *Zwingli's Werke*, 177; CR 88:24, lines 14–17.

56. *Artikel Zwinglis*, 154; ET: *Zwingli: Selected Works* (Jackson), 112.

57. Cf. *The Augsburg Confession*, art. 10, "Concerning the Supper of the Lord" (Latin Text), in *Book of Concord*, 45.

58. *The Augsburg Confession*, art. 10, "Concerning the Supper of the Lord" (Latin Text), 45. Also see *Die Bekenntnisschriften der evangelisch-lutherischen Kirche*, 9th ed. (Göttingen: Vandenhoeck & Ruprecht, 1982), 64, lines 1–2. The Latin reads "*quod corpus et sanguis Christi vere adsint et distribuantur*" [that the body and blood of Christ are truly present and are distributed].

59. Cf. chiefly H. Zwingli, *De vera et falsa religione commentarius*, in *Zwingli's Werke*, 3:145, 147–325, esp. here 255–60. ET: *Zwingli: Commentary on True and False Religion*, in *The Latin Works and the Correspondence of Huldreich Zwingli*, ed. Clarence Nevin Heller, trans. Henry Preble (Philadelphia: Heidelberg Press, 1929), 43–340, here 224–26.

tremendum[60] caused by the unfortunate inclusion of 1 Corinthians 11 in all liturgies, something of Zwingli's sobriety may be in order.

Yet Zwingli goes somewhat too far for us when in Thesis 46, where the topic is prayer, meaning the *worship service*, he brands all musical embellishment of it simply as "temple chanting and shouting."[61] The consequence of this was a radical iconoclasm, especially in Zürichbiet,[62] to which also all organs fell victim.[63] That is certainly an extreme example, but even here Zwingli still gives us an important hint. Still today there exists again a tendency toward "religious art," which, if it is not firmly and deliberately kept within its bounds, may fall off the rails, as lampooned by *Gottfried Keller* in the novel *Verlorene Lachen* (Lost smile).[64] Be on guard with all the attempts at "liturgical worship services," in which recently even violin solos and the like are accepted, so that religion gets lost in the art, and art gets lost in religion! Otherwise, Zwingli could be correct even here, when he says, "Hypocrites do their work so that they may be seen by men; . . . without piety and for reward, they are seeking either fame before men or gain."[65]

Finally, one last thing: it is characteristic of the politician Zwingli that of his 67 propositions, he dedicates a total of 9 theses to the definition of an ideal *Christian authority*.[66] In reading through these, one easily finds the image of the theocratic democracy of *Zurich* in the background, as it then developed over the next few years under the purposeful spiritual leadership of Zwingli. Especially noteworthy is the passage about the behavior of the Christian citizen over against a potentially *bad* authority. Here it becomes especially clear that a republican guides the pen. "But if they are unfaithful and transgress the laws of Christ, *they may be deposed in the name of God*."[67] Luther would have hardly written it in this way; for in many—actually, in most—cases, this "being deposed in the name of God" amounts to violent *revolution*, as Zwingli himself admits in the *"Auslegung."*[68] The significance of this statement for the modern history of the state is certainly illuminating!

60. In relation to baptism, the term *mysterium tremendum* occurs in Adolf von Harnack, *Die Mission und Ausbreitung des Christentums in den ersten drei Jahrhunderten*, 2nd ed. (Leipzig: J. C. Hinrichs, 1906), 326–27; 3rd ed. (1915), 373–74; ET: Harnack, *The Mission and Expansion of Christianity in the First Three Centuries*, trans. and ed. James Moffatt, 2nd ed. (New York: G. P. Putnam's Sons, 1908), 1:391. It is to be understood in the context of analyzing the influence of the mysteries of the Christian faith, which had been strongly encouraged by G. Anrich, *Das antike Mysterienwesen in seinem Einfluss auf das Christentum* (Göttingen: Vandenhoeck & Ruprecht, 1884). Anrich writes on the *Lord's Supper*, alluding to corresponding phrases especially in John Chrysostom: "The celebration itself had become a mystery, and its designation as a dreadful and fear-causing mystery shows that this change, precisely in the sphere of religious feeling, made itself felt significantly" (198; cf. 156–57, 171, 220).
61. *Artikel Zwinglis*, 156; ET: *Zwingli: Selected Works* (Jackson), 115 [trans. rev.].
62. Territory under the jurisdiction of the city of Zurich.
63. Cf. Staehelin, *Zwingli*, 446.
64. "Das verlorene Lachen" [The lost smile] is the final story from the second half of the collection of novels, *Die Leute von Seldwyla* [The people of Seldwyla]; cf. Gottfried Keller, *Die Leute von Seldwyla: Erzählungen*, 2nd ed. (Stuttgart: Göschen'sche Verlagshandlung, 1874), 4:103–258, esp. 171–74, where the reintroduction of church art, undertaken with amateurish means, is satirized. ET: *Stories: Gottfried Keller*, trans. and ed. Frank G. Ryder (London: Continuum, 1982), 190–270, esp. 225–26.
65. Articles 45 and 46 in *Artikel Zwinglis*, 156; ET: *Zwingli: Selected Works* (Jackson), 115 [translation modified].
66. Articles 34–43, where art. 43 is described as "the sum." *Artikel Zwinglis*, 155–56; ET: *Zwingli: Selected Works* (Jackson), 114–15.
67. Article 42 in *Artikel Zwinglis*, 156; ET: *Zwingli: Selected Works* (Jackson), 115. [See above, n. 31. TR.]
68. Zwingli, *Uslegen und gründ*, in *Zwingli's Werke*, 369–71, esp. 370–71; cf. CR 88:342–46, esp. p. 344, line 17–p. 346, line 13.

There would probably be several more such points of contact between Zwingli's program of reform from 1523 and contemporary life. Let us settle now for the ones we mentioned.

The *67 Articles* give a peculiar cross-section through the whole view of life as well as the theology of the great Zurich Reformer. It is possible that he appears to be offensive here and there, due to the realistic prose of his position. But I do not think that we are supposed to let ourselves be put off definitively by this rather external side of his personality; a good kernel is inserted into a frequently hard shell; for this reason, upon closer inspection, Zwingli must become dear especially to modern humankind. In light of the current struggles about theology and church, we will do well, at any rate, to listen to his voice.

28. I. 06

The Tenth Christian Students'
Conference in Aarau
1906

The Christian Students' Conferences in Aarau were formed as the result of sugges-
tions from the International Movement of Student Missions, in particular, from the
first student conference in French-speaking Switzerland, in St. Croix in 1895, and the
First International Students' Missions Conference in Liverpool in 1896. On March 23
and 24, a planning committee issued an invitation by means of a circular sent to all
students in Swiss-German universities to a first conference in Aarau, which would be
"an opportunity for all students who take to heart the cause of the kingdom of God to
meet and to establish contact with their like-minded teachers. We want, seriously and
soberly, to address the questions that occupy the hearts and minds of young students,
above all."[1] At this first conference Professor Fritz Barth gave a lecture on "Hindernisse
des Glaubens" [Obstacles to Faith].[2] He continued to be associated with the Aarau
Christian Students' Conference, serving on the Senior Members' Committee and deliv-
ering papers in 1898, 1900, 1902, and 1910.[3] Karl Barth frequently participated in
these conferences: as a student, during his vicariate in Geneva, and as a pastor in Safen-
wil. It is not known at whose behest he wrote the following report, which appeared in
the Berner Tagblatt in 1906 under the byline K. B., or how this first published piece by
Karl Barth originated. Later, he also contributed frequently to the conference: a 1916
sermon on Genesis 15:6 ("Das Eine Notwendige" [The One Thing Necessary]) and
major papers in 1920 and 1927 ("Biblische Fragen, Einsichten und Ausblicke" [Bibli-
cal Questions, Insights, and Vistas] [2010] and "Das Halten der Gebote" [Keeping the
Commandments]). During this time, the following persons also had their say in Aarau:
not only his brother Heinrich, but also his friends and companions E. Thurneysen, E.
Brunner, and Fr. Gogarten, among others.[4]

[I]

For the tenth year, the annual Christian Students' Conference for German-
speaking Switzerland is currently taking place in Aarau (March 15–17).[5] An
impressive number of students from all the academic departments from *Bern,*

1. Cited in P. Gruner, *Menschenwege und Gotteswege im Studentenleben: Persönliche Erinnerungen aus der christlichen Studentenbewegung* (Bern: BEG-Verlag, 1942), 156; for the history of the student confe-rences, see esp. 154–193; further references, 453–56.
2. Gruner, *Studentenleben*, 157 and 431.
3. Gruner, *Studentenleben*, 172, 184–85, and 431–32.
4. Gruner, *Studentenleben*, 433–34.
5. Cf. "Einleitender Bericht," in *Die X. Christliche Studentenkonferenz: Aarau 1906* (Bern, 1906), 3–8 [hereafter: *Die X. Christliche Studentenkonferenz*].

Basel, and Zurich have come together again this year, eagerly received by the hospitable citizens of the up-and-coming cultural center of Aarau.

The proceedings began with a Bible study by Cand. theol. *Karl Buxtorf* from Basel on Luke 10:21. After completing organizational elections, we proceeded to the first main item of the conference, a lecture by esteemed Privatdozent Dr. phil. *Fr. v. Huene* on *"Naturanschauung und wahrer Christenglaube"* [The View of Nature and the True Faith of Christians].[6] Natural science and Christianity today often appear to be in irreconcilable contradiction to each other: mistrust prevails on both sides. But it doesn't have to be that way: natural science should always be aware that its specific inductive research certainly has objective validity, but the same does not hold for its generalizations, that is, the metaphysical ramifications that it draws from the former. The aesthetic and even more the scientific consideration of nature in its perfection and expediency opens the believers' eyes to the creative workings of a most high God; indeed, only the Christian faith provides the key to a joyful and integrated worldview. In the animated *discussion*[7] that followed the lecture, we debated especially how to confront the problem that arises when the concerns of revealed religion intersect with those of scientific knowledge. An even clearer demarcation of boundaries than was expressed in the lecture is required.

Still, it was correctly noted at the conclusion that, in the final analysis, our religious position is not dependent on theoretical considerations about nature, but rather on the ethical decision that must be fulfilled in each individual person.

After lunch together at the *Saalbau*, we reconvened to hear a lecture by Cand. theol. *O. Schmitz* from Basel on *"Die Studentenzeit als Krisis"* [Student Life as a Time of Crisis].[8] The situation of modern students is extremely difficult and complicated. They, more than others, stand on the battleground over competing worldviews even as they struggle to create their personalities. The speaker knew how to give numerous practical suggestions and advice, speaking as an experienced older friend and, even more important, as student to students. There was no *discussion*.

At 8:00 p.m. there was a service in the town church, including a sermon by Rev. *Aeschbacher* from Bern on Matthew 5:14, which treated the text in a manner that was both substantive and relevant.[9]

---

6. Not included in the conference report. Photocopy and transcription of the manuscript of the lecture are held in the library of the Evangelical-Theological Seminary of the University of Tübingen, Institute of Hermeneutics.

7. Cf. "Einleitender Bericht," in *Die X. Christliche Studentenkonferenz*, 4f.

8. Published in *Die X. Christliche Studentenkonferenz*, 23–50. Otto Schmitz (1883–1957) subsequently became a New Testament scholar and Barth's faculty colleague at Münster.

9. Published under the title "Ihr seid das Licht der Welt" [You are the light of the world] in *Die X. Christliche Studentenkonferenz*, 65–73. In a letter to his grandson, J. Jaggi, on August 1, 1951, Karl Barth writes about pastor Robert Aeschbacher (1869–1910): "He was . . . a student and later close friend of my father, and I then became one of Aeschbacher's many grateful confirmands." He credited confirmation instruction with Aeschbacher as "not merely one motivation but *the* motivation for taking up theological studies." "I can still picture the scene, on the night of my confirmation, when I revealed this to my father! At that point, my intention, however, was scarcely if at all directed toward the pastorate, but rather at how to find out more, in breadth and depth, about the extraordinary truths that I had heard!! Obviously, the path from Pastor Aeschbacher's rigorous teachings to the *Church Dogmatics* has been straight as an arrow."

[II]

The second day of the Aarau Conference began with a Bible study by Prof. D. [Fritz] *Barth* from Bern on Luke 22:24.[10] It was followed by the interesting and comprehensive presentation by *Missionsinspektor* D. Th. *Oehler* from Basel on *"Moderne geistige Strömungen in der heidnischen Welt und ihre Bedeutung für die Mission"* [Modern Intellectual Currents in the Pagan World and Their Significance for Mission].[11] The contact with European-Christian civilization has led to original *cultural, national,* and *religious* movements in pagan lands. In India, China, and Japan today, educated people are seeking new paths; even in Africa, European culture is slowly but surely penetrating. There is a related upsurge of national and racial consciousness, in contrast to European self-understanding, aided and abetted especially by Japan's victory over Russia, with consequences throughout Asia.[12] In Southern Africa, the so-called Ethiopian Movement raises the cry "Africa for Africans!"[13] In this context, certain religious currents confront Christianity and its mission. In India, convinced adherents of Hinduism work with consistency and energy for its strengthening and renewal. Especially significant, however, is the advance of Islam in India and Africa. These three spiritual currents do not present an insuperable hindrance to Christianity; indeed, in many cases they are based on its impulses and in turn converge with its aims. We believe in the divine power of the gospel, which still overcomes the world today. In the lively discussion[14] following the lecture, it was emphasized that the Christian missionary needs a strong ethical character and firm faith to proclaim the message of Christ effectively. In the subsequent *business session,* the conference formally agreed to join the World Federation of Christian Students.[15] A specific report on this matter will follow.[16]

In the afternoon, conference participants went on a leisurely *stroll to Entfelden.*[17] Cand. theol. *Ecuyer* from Geneva conveyed greetings from French-speaking Switzerland. In the evening we had a "social evening" with our gracious hosts in the *"Kettenbrücke"* brewery, where heartfelt speeches from both sides attested to the bonhomie between the citizens of Aarau and the students over the course of these many years.

[III]

The third and final day of our conference this year was opened with a Bible study by Dr. *Gust. Senn* from Basel related to Matthew 6:5–8.[18] It was followed

---

10. Cf. "Einleitender Bericht," in *Die X. Christliche Studentenkonferenz,* 5.

11. Published with a slightly altered title in *Die X. Christliche Studentenkonferenz,* 51–64.

12. After the Russo-Japanese war of 1904–5, Russia was forced, among other things, to withdraw from Manchuria and to recognize Japan's hegemony in Korea.

13. On the "Ethiopian Movement" and its pan-African ideology, cf., e.g., B. Sundkler, "Sektenwesen in den jungen Kirchen" [Sectarianism in the Young Churches] in: *RGG*[3].

14. Cf. "Einleitender Bericht," in *Die X. Christliche Studentenkonferenz.*

15. Cf. "Einleitender Bericht," in *Die X. Christliche Studentenkonferenz,* 7–8.

16. Apparently no subsequent report appeared in print. On further developments of the matter, cf. Gruner, *Studentenleben,* 184–89.

17. An excursion destination south of Aarau.

18. Cf. "Einleitender Bericht," in *Die X. Christliche Studentenkonferenz,* 6.

by the high point of the conference, a penetrating presentation by *Prof. D. Schlatter* from Tübingen on *"Paulus und das Griechentum"* [Paul and Hellenism].[19] The authorities on Paul, particularly on Pauline literature, seem to fail in their treatment of this antithesis. The antithesis, however, can be observed everywhere, though it seldom appears on the surface. The Greek emphasis on personality (the principle of the self) and the accent on virtue ethics (the virtue principle) tacitly recede in Paul. The Hellenic ethic conceives of the human creature as a unitary, autonomous figure; Paul, by contrast, says that none of us lives from himself or for himself [cf. Rom. 14:7]. For the Hellenes, the emphasis is on the prowess to think, on methodological rationalism; Paul says that God has "made foolish the wisdom of the world" [1 Cor. 1:20]. The Greeks exalted and cultivated the human body; Paul calls it "the flesh," not on aesthetic or metaphysical grounds but based on the facts. On one side, the concept of the earthly "state," so important to the Hellenes; on the other, a "citizenship" [cf. Phil. 3:20] that lies beyond space and time. The final and central point is that Paul relocates the center of human religious life in God. This contrast continues into the present. To a greater or lesser degree, each of us must decide between Paul and the Greeks.

In the *discussion*,[20] some in the gathering proposed the not entirely new argument that there must be a synthesis between Paulinism and Hellenism for the Christianity of the future. This far-reaching assertion could be supported only by means of an appeal to the familiar argument from church history: the assertion that Socrates and Plato were Christians.[21]

In the second business session that followed, spokespersons for various local committees reported on the activities of the previous year, and elections were held for the upcoming term. It should be noted that Cand[idatus] Ing[enieuer] Traugott *Bohnenblust* will head the Zurich central committee and Cand. Theol. Ed. *Schätti* [will head the] the Bern committee. After lunch together in the *"Saalbau,"* there was a final meeting in the *"Evangelische Kapelle,"* during which *Prof. Dr. Fr. Gruner* from Bern gave the final address.[22]

This year again, the attendance at the conference was gratifying. The only possible regret is that the theological element was overly dominant: of the 77 students who were present, 49 were from the theology departments, 5 from law, 7 from medicine, 13 from philosophy, and 3 were technicians. In total, there were again more than 100 participants this year, including speakers and registered guests.

Finally, it goes without saying that we are sincerely grateful to the citizens of Aarau for their hospitable welcome during the three days of the conference. The hours of serious spiritual support and student happiness will be remembered by all participants. Good-bye, and see you again next year!

---

19. Published in *Die X. Christliche Studentenkonferenz*, 9–22; with minor changes, published in A. Schlatter, *Jesus und Paulus: Eine Vorlesung und einige Aufsätze; Mit einem Geleitwort von P. Althaus*, 3rd ed., Kleinere Schriften von Adolf Schlatter, newly edited by Th. Schlatter (Stuttgart: Calwer Verlag, 1961), 2:127–41.

20. Cf. "Einleitender Bericht," in *Die X. Christliche Studentenkonferenz*, 6.

21. Cf., e.g., Fr. Loofs, *Leitfaden zum Studium der Dogmengeschichte*, 4th ed. (Halle a. S., 1906), 116f., 124, 800. In 1910, Barth himself placed Socrates and Plato at the beginning of his "Lebensbilder aus der Geschichte der christlichen Religion," in his *Vorträge und kleinere Arbeiten, 1909–1914* (Zurich: Theologischer Verlag, 1993), 73–81.

22. Cf. "Einleitender Bericht," in *Die X. Christliche Studentenkonferenz*, 6.

The Original Form of the Lord's Prayer
1906

With regard to the specific circumstances around the development of this lecture for the Bern Academic Evangelical-Theological Society we have only one indirect reference, albeit a noteworthy one. On December 13, 1906, Karl Barth wrote to his father: "I am not going to see the famous Salome by Strauss, although it is supposed to be interesting, but I cannot at this time listen to such exciting stuff, otherwise I would again become sick with fever and babble on in a dream about textual criticism as was the case with the Lord's Prayer this summer."

The "Academic Evangelical-Theological Society"[1] at the University of Bern was founded in November 1879. Its purpose was "the encouragement of scholarly theological aspirations and a close amicable fellowship among those who are studying at the Theological Faculty." In a self-description authored by the Faculty for the University Festschrift of 1884, we read further that the feeling "spread among us the more and more we journeyed together" that "we theologians must have an unmatched higher interest in a closer connection, in a more intimate cooperation, unlike what would be the case in other departments. This last thought owes its origin mainly to a look at the fractured state of our churches, from which emerged the idea of the practical usefulness, of the prospective fruitfulness of a closer relationship among those studying theology, for the upcoming generation of theologians." Therefore, the Society has "a peaceable, mediating role, in the best sense of the word. Naturally, this is not to be understood as though there would be the demand to produce dull and pointless dogmatic formulations, as though each one with his own conviction should give up a theological position acquired in serious study and accept in place of it a quite shallow, thin, and generally accepted viewpoint; everyone should be much rather as clear as possible about where he stands and defend the conviction he has gained very decisively; therein lies the mediating role of our Society, that each member should be concerned, from the perspective that he himself represents, about being also prepared to discuss the perspective of others, even though he stands furthest away from being able to share it, and to acknowledge it as a legitimate view. So then the motto of our Society is in no way 'all the same' but much rather 'unity in diversity.'"[2]

In view of this programmatic setting of the goal, the lecture—apparently the only one that Barth gave in the Evangelical-Theological Society—and especially its concluding section, gain a special significance. Barth appears here, precisely in the way

---

1. For the history and character of such academic theological clubs, cf. L. Cordier's article "Studentenverbände, christliche" [ET: "Student Associations: Christian"] in *RGG*[2] 5: column 860.

2. E. Müller, *Die Hochschule Bern in den Jahren 1834–1884: Festschrift zur fünfzigsten Jahresfeier ihrer Stiftung* [ET: The College of Bern in the years 1834–1884: Essays in honor of the fiftieth year of its founding] (Bern: K. J. Wyss, 1884), 195–96.

he proceeds theologically, to define the "point of view" by which he wanted to present himself in this circle and over against other points of view.

The manuscript is a section of the volume "Excerpta II" (see "The Centurion at Capernaum" above). The comment below the title reads: "(Work for the Academic Evangelical-Theological Society) Karl Barth, student of theology."

[Trans.: Since this essay presents Barth as a young text-critical scholar of the Bible, the biblical languages are extensively cited. In this essay we cite the original languages with English translations (in brackets).]

Introduction

The "Our Father" (*oratio dominica*, Lord's Prayer) is handed down to us in the New Testament in two forms: Matthew 6:9–13 and Luke 11:2–4.

Apart from the considerable differences that exist among the various manuscripts for both Gospel documents, it also emerges from the encounter with the evangelists themselves that the tradition has here brought about a change in the condition of the original prayer so that, in other words, *an older and an earlier form of the same material* is present. If one does not want to decide for the hypothesis of some older theologians, which is unlikely if one considers the analogously used treatment of the other sayings (*Tholuck*,[3] *Keil*,[4] *Achelis*,[5] earlier *Meyer*[6]), according to which Christ gave the disciples this teaching on *two* occasions, then the issues align themselves for our paper in this way:

1. Which are the authentic texts in Matthew and Luke?
2. What is the historical occasion of the Lord's Prayer?
3. Which text has priority?

Before we attempt to answer this threefold question, it is useful, at first, to examine the versions in detail.

I.

a. Matthew 6:9–13

1. The context. The Lord's Prayer in Matthew is found in the context of the Sermon on the Mount. While in chapter 5 Jesus set the evangelical ethic regarding one's convictions (*morality*) over against the Jewish ethic of following the law (*legality*), in chapter 6 (vv. 1–18) specific activities of religiosity in the narrower sense—such as giving alms, *prayer*, and fasting—are illuminated and put on the basis of the βασιλεία τοῦ θεοῦ [kingdom of God] proclaimed by Christ.

---

3. A. Tholuck, *Die Bergrede Christi* (Gotha: Perthes, 1872, 2nd printing), 9–11.

4. C. F. Keil, *Commentar über das Evangelium des Matthäus* (Leipzig: Dörffling & Franke, 1877), 182–84.

5. E. Achelis, *Die Bergpredigt nach Matthaeus und Lucas, exegetisch und kritisch untersucht* (Bielefeld/ Leipzig: Velhagen & Klasing, 1877), 294–300.

6. Cf. H. A. W. Meyer, *Kritisch exegetisches Handbuch über das Evangelium des Matthäus*, 2nd ed. (Göttingen: Vandenhoeck & Ruprecht, 1844), 153–55.

For the prayer of a disciple of Christ, there are two requirements to be ful-filled: it must *not* be done *publicly* (vv. 5–6) and there is to be *no babbling* (vv. 7–8): μὴ βατταλογήσητε ὥσπερ οἱ ἐθνικοί [do not heap up empty phrases as the Gentiles do], who believe ἐν τῇ πολυλογίᾳ [in their many words] they ensure the results of prayer. As a contrast to this unworthy way of conversing with God, according to Matthew 6:9–13, Christ now gives our so-called Lord's Prayer in six or—if I may say so—seven petitions: οὕτως οὖν προσεύχεσθε ὑμεῖς [you pray then in this way]. Rightly, *Bengel* explains this οὕτως (in this way) in contrast to the Roman Catholic practice of prayer as *"in hoc sensu . . . neque non in his verbis"* [in this sense . . . and not in these words].[7] The old style βατταλογία [heaping up of many words] is not simply replaced with a new kind of babbling.

At the end of the prayer, Matthew adds verses 14 and 15 as an explanation to the fifth petition; and verses 16 to 18, the teaching about fasting; while verses 19 to 34 bring a new thought, namely, the stance of the disciples of Jesus toward the world and its goods.

2. *The Text.* I cite it fully according to Tischendorf VIII[a] now:[8]

v. 9   . . . πάτερ ἡμῶν ὁ ἐν τοῖς οὐρανοῖς
             ἁγιασθήτω τὸ ὄνομά σου (I)
v. 10   ελθάτω ἡ βασιλεία σου (II)
             γενηθήτω τὸ θέλημά σου ὡς ἐν οὐρανῷ καὶ ἐπὶ γῆς (III)
v. 11   τὸν ἄρτον ἡμῶν τὸν ἐπιούσιον δὸς ἡμῖν σήμερον (IV)
v. 12   καὶ ἄφες ἡμῖν τὰ ὀφειλήματα ἡμῶν,
             ὡς καὶ ἡμεῖς ἀφήκαμεν τοῖς ὀφειλέταις ἡμῶν (V)
v. 13   καὶ μὴ εἰσενέγκῃς ἡμᾶς εἰς πειρασμόν, (VIa)
             ἀλλὰ ῥῦσαι ἡμᾶς ἀπὸ τοῦ πονηροῦ (VIb)

[v. 9 . . . Our Father in heaven,
             hallowed be your name. (I)
v. 10   Your kingdom come, (II)
             Your will be done, on earth as it is in heaven. (III)
v. 11   Give us this day our daily bread. (IV)
v. 12   And forgive us our debts,
             as we also have forgiven our debtors. (V)
v. 13   And do not bring us to the time of trial, (VIa)
             but rescue us from the evil one. (VIb)]

In this study the formulation of our theme cannot imply an exegetical treat-ment of this piece of Scripture, which occupies the largest space in most com-mentaries, although the problems there are of the highest interest. For this, I

---

7. Cf. J. A. Bengel, *Gnomon Novi Testamenti, in quo ex nativa verborum vi simplicitas, profunditas, con-cinnitas, salubritas sensum coelestium indicator* [ET: Gnomon of the New Testament, in which from the natural force of the words, the simplicity, depth, consistency, and saving power of the divine revela-tion therein contained is indicated], 8th ed. (Stuttgart: Steinkopf, 1887), 48.

8. Cf. K. Tischendorf, *Novum Testamentum Graece: Ad antiquissimos testes denuo recensuit, apparatum criticum omni studio perfectum apposuit, commentationem isagogicam praetexuit Constantinus Tischendorf,* Editio octava critica maior [ET: The Greek New Testament: With a textual commentary regarding the most ancient witnesses newly enumerated and a critical apparatus added by Constantine Tischendorf, 8th critical ed.] (Leipzig, 1869), 1:25.

refer especially to *Bengel*[9] and *Schlatter*.[10] Our study here will confine itself to what is common between the two accounts.

At first we state the most important variants for the Matthean text (passing over the purely grammatical issues).

Didache 8.2, which, by the way, is one of the most important witnesses to the Lord's Prayer, is mostly dependent upon Matthew. For this reason we include references to it here: it reads ἐν τῷ οὐρανῷ [in heaven] for ἐν τοῖς ουρανοῖς [in the heavens, v. 9].

Especially numerous are the variants for verse 11,[11] that is, for the difficult word ἐπιούσιον [daily]. As far as we can see, the variants organize themselves into four groups:

a. Sah[hidic]: *venientem* [coming]; Cop[tic]: *crastinum* [tomorrow]; Heb[rew]: *mahar*, which means bread for tomorrow, the coming day.

b. Chr[ysostom]: ἐφήμερον [for the day], It[alic = Latin], Tert[ullian], Cyp[rian], Aug[ustine], among others: *cottidianum* [every day]—that is, following the Lutheran translation, "our daily bread"

c. *syr*[p] [Syriac Peshitta]: *necessarium* [necessary], *syr*[sch] [Schaaff's Syriac]: *indigentiae nostrae* [our needed]—that is, the bread needed to live; cf. *supersubstantialem* [besides material nourishment]

d. *Hier* [Jerome]: *egregium* [excellent]; Symm[achus]: ἐξαίρετον [chosen], that is, the excellent bread

What immediately appears is that these are not actual variants as much as attempts at interpretation, which precisely, by being placed alongside each other, can only confirm the otherwise unusual ἐπιούσιον of Matthew's text, which Origen[12] already saw.

For ὀφειλήματα [debts] (v. 12), the Didache gives the noteworthy variant τὴν ὀφειλήν [debt].

In verse 13 we have one of the best-known variants in the New Testament.[13] While the older codices end with πονηροῦ [the evil one], Elzevir (and with him Luther!), following E G K L M S U V Δ Π (al pler [many others]) f g[1] q syr[utr] et[cu] et[hr] aeth arm go sl etc., offers the so-called doxology, namely: ὅτι σοῦ ἐστιν ἡ βασιλεία καὶ ἡ δύναμις και ἡ δόξα εἰς τοὺς αἰῶνας. ἀμήν [for the kingdom and the power and the glory are yours forever. Amen]. This doxology, in a less complete form, is also found in the Didache (which omits ἡ βασιλεία, ἀμήν [the kingdom, amen]) Const[2, 18] (omits καὶ ἡ δύναμις καὶ δόξα [the power and glory]) sah ("quoniam tuum est robur et potential in aevum aevi amen" [for your strength and power is forever amen]) k ("quoniam est tibi virtus in saecula saeculorum" [for virtue is yours in eternity].

9. Bengel, *Gnomon Novi Testamenti*, 48–51, 258.

10. A. Schlatter, *Das Evangelium des Matthäus, ausgelegt für Bibelleser* [ET: The Gospel of Matthew interpreted for its readers], *Erläuterungen zum Neuen Testament*, vol. 5 (Calwer/Stuttgart: Verlag der Vereinsbuchhandlung, 1895), 97–104; Schlatter, *Die Evangelien des Markus und Lukas, ausgelegt für Bibelleser* [ET: The Gospels of Mark and Luke explained for Bible readers], *Erläuterungen zum Neuen Testament*, vol. 7 (Calwer/Stuttgart: Verlag der Vereinsbuchhandlung, 1900), 255–56.

11. Cf. the apparatus for this passage in Tischendorf, *Novum Testamentum Graece*, 25.

12. Cf. Origen, *Or.* [Prayer] 27.7; in GCS 5, *Origenes*, vol. 2: p. 366, line 33–p. 367, line 2.

13. Cf. the apparatus in Tischendorf, *Novum Testamentum Graece*, 26. (Tischendorf's reference to the Apostolic Constitutions 2.18 should be corrected to 3.18.)

Today the view is fairly widespread that the words are to be considered a *liturgical addition* from the time when the Christian community was establishing itself (Bengel,[14] Schlatter,[15] Zahn[16]). For this reason the words are missing in the newer Greek editions (Blass,[17] Westcott-Hort,[18] Nestle[19]) and translations (Weizsäcker,[20] Stage[21]) of the New Testament.

From our discussion up to this point, it would appear that there are no serious differences in the tradition. Yet alongside the Matthean text we have the Lukan version, which diverges significantly from Matthew and to which we must now give our attention.

b. Luke 11:2–4

1. Here the context presents significant diversions from Matthew: Christ is found with his disciples ἐν τόπῳ τινί [in a certain place, 11:1], which is not named, and prays. As he finishes, one of them asks him: "Lord, teach us to pray, as John taught his disciples to pray." Christ answers (vv. 2–4): ὅταν προσεύχησθε λέγετε [when you pray, say], then follows the Lukan text of the Lord's Prayer. The variant, which D inserts before this—μὴ βατταλογήσητε ὡς οἱ λοιποί, δοκοῦσιν γὰρ ὅτι ἐν τῇ πολυλογίᾳ αὐτῶν εἰσακουσθήσονται [do not use empty words as the others do, for they think that they will be heard in their use of many words]—probably is clearly to be dismissed as an accommodation to Matthew (against Blass).[22]

After the Lord's Prayer, Luke adds further comments about prayer: the parable of The Friend at Midnight and the sayings about stones and scorpions.

2. The text of the Lord's Prayer according to Luke reads in Tischendorf[23] as follows:

(v. 2)   ... πάτερ
          ἁγιασθήτω τὸ ὄνομά σου (I)
          ἐλθάτω ἡ βασιλεία σου (II)

(v. 3)   τὸν ἄρτον ἡμῶν τὸν ἐπιούσιον δίδου ἡμῖν
          τὸ καθ' ἡμέραν (IV)

14. Cf. Tischendorf, *Novum Testamentum Graece*, 50.

15. Cf. Schlatter, *Evangelium des Matthäus*, 103; Schlatter, *Evangelien des Markus und Lukas*, 255.

16. T. Zahn, *Das Evangelium des Matthäus* [ET: The Gospel of Matthew], KNT 1 (Leipzig: Deichert, 1903), 284.

17. F. Blass, *Euangelium secundum Matthaeum cum variae lectionis delectu* [The Gospel according to Matthew with selected variants] (Leipzig: Teubner, 1901).

18. B. F. Westcott and F. J. A. Hort, *The New Testament in the Original Greek Text* (Cambridge/London: Macmillan, 1881); see also in the same work, "Introduction" and "Appendix" (1882), 8–10.

19. Manuscript: "Nestlé"; in *Novum Testamentum Graece cum apparatu critico ex editionibus et libris manu scriptis collecto curavit E. Nestle*, 5th ed. (Stuttgart: Württembergische Bibelanstalt, 1904).

20. C. Weizsäcker, *Das Neue Testament, übersetzt von Carl Weizsäcker* [ET: The New Testament, trans. Carl Weizsäcker], 2nd ed. (Freiburg i. B./Tübingen: Wächter, 1882).

21. C. Stage, *Das Neue Testament, übersetzt in die Sprache der Gegenwart von Curt Stage* [ET: The New Testament, translated into today's language by Curt Stage], Reclams Universal-Bibliothek (Leipzig: Philipp Reclam Verlag, 1897).

22. Cf. F. Blass, *Euangelium secundum Lucan sive Lucae ad Theophilum liber prior: Secundum formam quae videtur Romanam* [The Gospel according to Luke, or Luke's first book to Theophilus: According to the format considered as Roman] (Leipzig: Teubner, 1897), 51, lines 7–9; and xli–xlii.

23. Cf. Tischendorf, *Novum Testamentum Graece*, 562–63.

(v. 4) καὶ ἄφες ἡμῖν τὰς ἁμαρτίας ἡμῶν, καὶ γὰρ αὐτοὶ ἀφίομεν παντὶ
         ὀφείλοντι ἡμῖν (V)
         καὶ μὴ εἰσενέγκῃς ἡμᾶς εἰς πειρασμόν (VIa)

[v. 2]   . . . Father,
         hallowed be your name; (I)
         your kingdom come; (II)
[v. 3]   give us each day our daily bread, (IV)
[v. 4]   and forgive us our sins, for we ourselves forgive everyone
             indebted to us, (V)
         and do not bring us to the time of trial. (VIa)]

This text, which at first glance deviates considerably from Matthew's version, by itself led interpreters to assume that the variants primarily indicate attempts to conform to Matthew's text.

Accordingly, the textual witnesses A C D P X Γ Δ Λ [[unc[9] (al pler) a b c e ff[2] l q perus, harl* sax cop syr[cur] et[utr] aeth (and Elzevir, who follows them) add to πάτερ [Father]: ἡμῶν ὁ ἐν τοῖς οὐρανοῖς [our . . . in heaven].[24]

For an unknown reason, D adds to τὸ ὄνομά σου [your name]: ἐφ᾽ ἡμᾶς [upon us].[25] The most important variant in the whole passage is the one for petition II. Two ancient witnesses, Gregory of Nyssa (1:737) and Maxim[us the] Confess[or] (1:350), in addition to Min. Cod. 700 al. 604 and Cod. Vatic. olim Barb. IV 31, instead of ἐλθάτω ἡ βασιλεία σου [may your kingdom come] had the petition: ἐλθέτω σου τὸ πνεῦμα τὸ ἅγιον καὶ καθαρισάτω ἡμᾶς[26] [may your Holy Spirit come and cleanse us]. A similar text appears to have been read by Marcion, as recounted by Tertullian, *Adv[ersus] Marc[ion]* 4.26. It is also possible for this text—in fact, probable—that the Gospel of Marcion had *both petitions together* while petition I was possibly missing. {"A quo *spiritum sanctum postulem?* . . . *Eius regnum optabo venire* quem nunquam regem gloriae audivi, an in cuius manu etiam corda sunt regum?"}[27*] [of whom can I ask the Holy Spirit? . . . Whose kingdom can I ask to come—his, of whom I never heard as the king of glory; or—his, in whose hand are even the hearts of kings?].[28]

---

24. Cf. the apparatus for the passage in Tischendorf, *Novum Testamentum Graece*, 561.
25. Cf. the apparatus for the passage in Tischendorf, *Novum Testamentum Graece*, 562.
26. Cf. the apparatus for the passage in Tischendorf, *Novum Testamentum Graece*, 562; and A. Harnack, "Über einige Worte Jesu, die nicht in den kanonischen Evangelien stehen, nebst einem Anhang über die ursprüngliche Gestalt des Vater-Unsers," in *SPAW* 1904 (Berlin, 1904), 170–208 (Appendix: 195–208), esp. 196–97. (The whole essay is reprinted in A. Harnack, *Kleine Schriften zur alten Kirche*, vol. 1, *Berliner Akademieschriften, 1890–1907* [Leipzig: Zentralantiquariat der DDR, 1980], 663–701; the "Appendix" is revised and included in an essay by A. Harnack, "Der ursprüngliche Text des Vater-Unsers und seine älteste Geschichte," in his *Erforschtes und Erlebtes, Reden und Aufsätze*, Neue Folge, vol. 4 [Giessen: Töpelmann, 1923], 24–35).
27.* Trans. note: A comment by Barth in Latin in the margin (see Editors' Preface above, XI). It is a quotation from Tertullian, *Against Marcion* 4.26. ET: *The Ante-Nicene Church Library Translation of the Writings of the Fathers down to A.D. 325* (Edinburgh: T&T Clark, 1878), 7:289.
28. Cf. the apparatus for the passage in Tischendorf, *Novum Testamentum Graece*, 562; also in Harnack, "Über einige Worte Jesu," 197.

This variant is indirectly attested by the Acts of Thomas (chap. 27 Bonnet) and Liturg[y of] Constantinop[le] (p. 109, Swainson).[29] We will return to the reading afterward in the larger context.

The missing petition III is supplemented, following Matthew, with: γενηθήτω τὸ θέλημά σου ὡς ἐν οὐρανῷ καὶ ἐπὶ γῆς [may your will be done, as in heaven so on earth] by ℵ A C D P X Γ Δ Λ Π unc⁹ (al pler) b c e f i l q perus tol sax syr^sch et^P cop aeth.[30]

In verse 3, Syr. Sin. omits the ἡμῶν [our] after ἄρτον[31] [bread].

In verse 4, D reads with b c ff² instead of ἁμαρτίας [sins] and following Matthew: ὀφειλήματα [debts]; likewise mm and cop read instead of παντὶ τῷ ὀφείλοντι ἡμῖν [each one who is indebted to us]: τοῖς ὀφειλέταις ἡμῶν [our debtors]; ℵ^c A C D R X Γ Δ Γ Λ unc⁹ (al pler) b c f ff² i l q cop syr^cur et^P aeth add as petition VIb: ἀλλὰ (καὶ) ῥῦσαι ἡμᾶς ἀπὸ τοῦ πονηροῦ[32] [but (also) redeem us from the evil one].

From the fact that more of these variants, which conform to the Matthew text, are represented in very old manuscripts, such as ℵ A C D among others, one may not simply draw the conclusion that they represent the original Lukan text. The tendency to harmonize *must* have set in early, especially with a piece of text such as this one, which found *liturgical use*. These variants may serve as proof for the latter fact, but not for the fact that Luke has the original text.

In the discussion so far, we have examined the two forms of the Lord's Prayer and their *separate* versions. Our next task will be to clarify their relationship *to each other*, in order to draw conclusions about which of the two versions may provide the *original form* of the Lord's Prayer.

II.

Before we embark on the comparison of the Lord's Prayer texts themselves, we must discuss, as a preliminary question, the problem of what the probable *historical occasion* for the Lord's Prayer may have been.

Incidentally, I must note that for this and the following sections of my essay, I take as my starting point the two following writings:

> Ad. Harnack, "Die ursprüngliche Gestalt des Vater Unsers" [ET: The original form of the Lord's Prayer], published in "Sitzungsberichte d. kgl. Preuss. Akademie d. Wissensch." [ET: The sessional reports of the Royal Prussian Academy of Science], V (January 21, 1904), Phil. Hist. Klasse)[33] and

> G. Klein, "Die ursprüngliche Gestalt d. Vater Unsers" [ET: The original form of the Lord's Prayer], published in ZNW, 1906, Heft 1).[34]

---

29. Cf. Harnack, "Über einige Worte Jesu," 197; Acts of Thomas 27, in *Acta apostolorum apocrypha*, ed. R. A. Lipsius and M. Bonnet, part 2 (Leipzig: Herrmann Mendelssohn, 1903), 2:143, lines 2–3; Ch. A. Swainson, ed., *The Greek Liturgies: Chiefly from Original Authorities* (Cambridge: Cambridge University Press, 1884), 109.

30. Cf. the apparatus for the passage in Tischendorf, *Novum Testamentum Graece*, 562.

31. Cf. Harnack, "Über einige Worte Jesu," 197.

32. Cf. the apparatus for the passage in Tischendorf, *Novum Testamentum Graece*, 563.

33. See above, n. 26.

34. G. Klein, "Die ursprüngliche Gestalt des Vaterunsers," in ZNW 7 (1906): 34–50. (As a "Supplement," published again in Klein, *Der älteste christliche Katechismus und die jüdische Propaganda-Literatur* [Berlin: G. Reimer, 1909], 256–73.)

Yet I have also consulted the following commentaries on these two passages: Meyer,[35] Weiss,[36] Holtzmann,[37] Zahn,[38] Wellhausen,[39] and Wernle,[40] among others; they will only occasionally be drawn into the discussion, whereas the two authors mentioned above [Harnack and Klein] must be of special interest to us as representatives of two radically opposing points of view.

As far as the context of the Lord's Prayer in Matthew is concerned, the critics are in strong agreement that it is to be considered as unhistorical. The reasons for this are many:

B. Weiss[41] says this:

> If Christ taught the prayer to his disciples already in the Sermon on the Mount, then the question posed by the disciple in Luke 11:1 is not historical. If the latter is historical, then the Lord's Prayer could not have been known among the disciples from the [Sermon on the] Mount. Further to this, the historical occasion narrated by Luke does not raise any doubt about a possible invention by the evangelist; whereas it is very conceivable, that *in the redaction of our Matthew, where the Sermon on the Mount speaks about the proper way to pray, the model prayer had already been placed in the mouth of the Lord.*

Harnack[42] and Klein[43] refer correctly to the contradiction that emerges when Christ admonishes in Matthew 6:6: "When you pray, go into your room, shut the door, and pray to your Father in secret," while the Lord's Prayer obviously implies a multitude of those who pray (ἡμεῖς! [we]).

Although most critics maintain the historicity of Luke 11:1, Harnack goes one step farther and explains: not only in Matthew but also in *Luke*, the described occasion for the Lord's Prayer is *unhistorical*. His proof for this claim is quite extensive.[44] He proceeds from the text-critical assumption that the variant for petition II in the Lukan text—ἐλθέτω σου τὸ πνεῦμα τὸ ἅγιον καὶ καθαρισάτω ἡμᾶς—is original, that is, Lukan, and that petition I is an ancient conformation by Luke to Matthew. The original Lukan Lord's Prayer then would begin *with the petition for the Holy Spirit* (see below). Harnack then combines this fact—perhaps more creatively than accurately—with the story of *the disciples of John in Ephesus* in Acts 19:1–7, where Paul asks them, "Did you receive the Holy Spirit when you became believers?" They answer, *"We have not even heard that there is a Holy Spirit."* Paul then teaches them, "John baptized with a baptism of repentance, telling the people to believe in the one who is to come after him, that is, in Jesus." Hearing this, the disciples of John are baptized, and Paul laid his hands on them. And *"the Holy Spirit came upon them,"* and so on (v. 6).

35. Meyer, *Evangelium des Matthäus*; H. A. W. Meyer, *Kritisch exegetisches Handbuch über die Evangelien des Markus und Lukas*, 2nd ed., KEK 1, part 2 (Göttingen: Vandenhoeck & Ruprecht, 1846).
36. B. Weiss, *Das Matthäus-Evangelium*, 9th ed., KEK 1, part 1, first half (Göttingen: Vandenhoeck & Ruprecht, 1898); B. Weiss and J. Weiss, *Die Evangelien des Markus und Lukas*, 8th ed., KEK 1, part 2, second half (Göttingen: Vandenhoeck & Ruprecht, 1892).
37. H. J. Holtzmann, *Die Synoptiker. Die Apostelgeschichte*, HC 1 (Freiburg i. B.: Mohr, 1892).
38. Zahn, *Das Evangelium des Matthäus*.
39. J. Wellhausen, *Das Evangelium Matthaei, übersetzt und erklärt* (Berlin: G. Reimer, 1904); Wellhausen, *Das Evangelium Lucae, übersetzt und erklärt* (Berlin: Reimer, 1904).
40. P. Wernle, *Die synoptische Frage* (Freiburg i. B./Leipzig/Tübingen: Mohr-Siebeck, 1899).
41. Weiss, *Das Matthäus-Evangelium*, 131.
42. Cf. Harnack, "*Über* einige Worte Jesu," 204.
43. Klein, "Gestalt des Vaterunsers," 48.
44. Harnack, "*Über* einige Worte Jesu," esp. 205–6.

Hence, Harnack reasons: in Luke 11:1 the disciples ask Christ to teach them to pray, as John teaches his disciples. Luke 11:2 means that they ask Christ above all else for the Holy Spirit, although from Acts 19 it is clear that the disciples of John did not know about the Holy Spirit. Therefore, the petition for the Holy Spirit in Luke 11:2 as well as the occasion for it in Luke 11:1 is an antithesis to the disciples of John created by Luke the evangelist, and thus *unhistorical*. I cannot follow him in this complicated assumption. It assumes a creative combination by the storyteller, which he could hardly have done, and in addition it is text-critically insufficiently founded, as we will show below.

The description in Luke 11:1 appears to me in its simplicity and naturalness still *probable* and can be safely accepted, as long as more convincing reasons against this are not presented.

III.

We now come to the main section of our study, which will concern itself with the comparison and critique of the Lord's Prayer text itself. Let us summarize once again the findings resulting from a simple comparison of the Matthew and the Luke texts.

The additions by Matthew compared to Luke are the following:

1. Addition of ἡμῶν ὁ ἐν τοῖς οὐρανοῖς [our who is in heaven] to πάτερ [Father]
2. Possible petition II ἐλθάτω ἡ βασιλεία σου [may your kingdom come]
3. Petition III γενηθήτω τὸ θέλημά σου ὡς ἐν οὐρανῷ καὶ ἐπὶ γῆς [may your will be done on earth as in heaven]
4. Petition VIb: ἀλλὰ ῥῦσαι ἡμᾶς ἀπὸ τοῦ πονηροῦ [but redeem us from the evil one]

In addition, Luke shows the following deviations from Matthew:

1. Petition IV δίδου [give, present imperative] instead of δός [give, aorist imperative] and καθ' ἡμέραν [daily] instead of σήμερον [today].
2. Petition V . . . τὰς ἁμαρτίας ἡμῶν, καὶ γὰρ αὐτοὶ ἀφίομεν παντὶ ὀφείλοντι . . . [our sins, for we ourselves forgive all who are indebted to us] instead of τὰ ὀφειλήματα ἡμῶν ὡς καὶ ἡμεῖς ἀφήκαμεν τοῖς ὀφειλέταις ἡμῶν [our debts, as we have also forgiven those who are indebted to us].

In addition, Luke has eventually more than Matthew:

3. Petition II ἐλθέτω σου τὸ πνεῦμα τὸ ἅγιον καὶ καθαρισάτω ἡμᾶς [May your Holy Spirit come upon us and cleanse us].

In recent criticism the view prevails that the significantly shorter text of Luke is also the *original* one. *Wernle* thus comments: "The deliberation has to decide in favor of Luke, since the shortening of a prayer attributed to Jesus and frequently spoken by the community is much more difficult to conceive than the extensions that easily emerge, partly as an explanation of what precedes (your kingdom come), partly as a positive complement to the negative (lead us not into temptation)."[45]

Yet the matter is not so quickly finished. *Wernle* overlooks the variant, already mentioned several times, for petition II in Luke, which certainly does not fit into his canon, and he gives it short shrift as being "too poorly witnessed."[46] *Harnack* rightly demands that the witnesses should not be merely counted but also weighed, and to this end the minuscule codices, according to him, have not yet been examined in regard to this variant, so that the number of witnesses could easily be much more than those cited.[47]

In my opinion, the petition for the Holy Spirit is truly Lukan, as *Harnack* also assumes,[48] and this fact should throw a significant light on the whole issue of priority, or authenticity.

Our attention, therefore, focuses on that variant for Luke 11:2: Gregory of Nyssa, Maximus Confessor, and the two mentioned minuscules, as we have mentioned, offer the "petition for the Holy Spirit," instead of the usual petition II, and Marcion possibly instead of petition I: ἐλθέτω σου τὸ πνεῦμα τὸ ἅγιον καὶ καθαρισάτω ἡμᾶς. I have reached the conclusion that *this reading in the place of* ἐλθέτω ἡ βασιλεία σου [may your kingdom come] *represents Luke's original text.* Of the newer publications Blass has, therefore, rightly included it in his text.[49] Petition II, as it is usually given, cannot be anything other than an early adaptation to Matthew. "Where would a later reader," asks *Harnack*, "when he read the Lord's Prayer in Luke in the same form as in Matthew, have found the courage to correct this form and replace it with something completely new? . . . Conversely, however, how tempting was it to conform the Lukan text here again to Matthew, especially since the form presented by Matthew had prevailed in the worship services![50]

The English scholar F. H. Chase (*The Lord's Prayer in the Early Church*;[51] cf. G. Dalman's review of the book)[52] rightfully refers to passages such as Romans 8:15 and Galatians 4:6, where the prayer for the Holy Spirit is of prime importance, to show what significance it has in the early Christian communities.[53]

Harnack continues to bring several striking parallels to our variant from Acts 1:8; 11:15; and especially however, 15:8–9: . . . θεός . . . δοὺς τὸ πνεῦμα τὸ ἅγιον καθὼς καὶ ἡμῖν . . . τῇ πίστει καθαρίσας τὰς καρδίας αὐτῶν[54] [God . . . having given the Holy Spirit just as to us . . . having cleansed their hearts by faith]. The correctness of the variant appears to me to be completely evident and proven by the passage Luke 11:13, which is only a few verses away from the Lord's Prayer, where Luke makes Jesus say as a conclusion to his explanation

---

45. Wernle, *Die synoptische Frage*, 68.
46. Wernle, *Die synoptische Frage*, 68.
47. Harnack, "Über einige Worte Jesu," 199.
48. Harnack, "Über einige Worte Jesu," 202, 205.
49. Blass, *Euangelium secundum Lucam*, 51, lines 10–11; and xlii–xliii.
50. Harnack, "Über einige Worte Jesu," 199.
51. F. H. Chase, *The Lord's Prayer in the Early Church*, TaS 1.3 (Cambridge: Cambridge: University Press, 1891).
52. G. Dalman, review of *The Lord's Prayer in the Early Church*, by F. H. Chase, in *TLZ* 16 (1891): cols. 619–21, esp. col. 619.
53. Chase, *Lord's Prayer*, 23–24.
54. Harnack, "Über einige Worte Jesu," 199–200.

of the prayer: εἰ οὖν ὑμεῖς πονηροὶ ὑπάρχοντες οἴδατε δόματα ἀγαθὰ διδόναι τοῖς τέκνοις ὑμῶν, πόσῳ μᾶλλον ὁ πατὴρ ὁ ἐξ οὐρανοῦ δώσει πνεῦμα ἅγιον τοῖς αἰτοῦσιν αὐτόν [if you then who are evil know how to give good gifts to your children, how much more will the heavenly Father give the Holy Spirit to those who ask him].

This is truly understandable only if the petition for the Holy Spirit had already been given before, which is nowhere else possible except in the Lord's Prayer itself, that is, in our passage. Compare this to the otherwise almost identical parallels in Matthew 7:11, which instead of πνεῦμα ἅγιον shows the more general ἀγαθά.[55]

Since the Lucan version here, as well as in the Lord's Prayer itself, can hardly be the original one from which Matthew's version would have emerged, everything leads to the assumption that *Luke has reshaped the text available to him (that is, the text from the sayings source).*

Now the same thing can be demonstrated in a parallel way from the remaining pieces of the Lord's Prayer.

Luke was a follower of Paul and addressed primarily *a Gentile Christian audience.* In this regard he shows the *tendency to shorten* the texts that include speeches and sayings. From these three factors, his variations in contrast to Matthew's Lord's Prayer are to be explained:

1. The omission of Matthew's attribute to πατήρ [Father] is a mere abridgement.
2. Instead of the concept of βασιλεία, which is less common among Gentile Christians, he uses the more meaningful petition, especially in the Pauline communities: "Your Holy Spirit come upon us!"
3. The petition "Your will be done" . . . would seem superfluous to him, indeed almost offensive from the point of view of the Pauline conception of God.[56] In petition IV the δός ["give," aorist] is transformed into the more correct δίδου ["give," present]; καθ' ἡμέραν [daily] as opposite to σήμερον [today] betrays a deviation from Matthew's difficult word "ἐπιούσιον" [for the coming day].
4. In petition V the Pauline ἁμαρτίας [sins] takes the place of ὀφειλήματα [debts]; instead of ἀφήκαμεν [we have forgiven] we read the more precise ἀφίομεν [we are forgiving].
5. The petition VIb has been deleted for the sake of brevity.

The meaning of a few small textual changes must remain obscure to us, but that does not change the recognition that the Lukan Lord's Prayer is nothing more than a reworking of the same template that Matthew also used (but probably staying truer to it). Here Wernle interjects that such a transformation is unlikely in the case of a prayer transmitted from the mouth of Jesus and regularly spoken by the community.[57] To this it can be objected: the words of Jesus still did

---

55. Harnack, "Über einige Worte Jesu," 199–200.
56. At this point in the manuscript there is a question mark written in pencil—by another hand (Barth's father?) or from Barth himself?
57. Wernle, *Die synoptische Frage,* 68.

not have canonical status at the end of the first century,[58] in the sense that their wording was not allowed to be changed as the situation demanded. The proof of this is the variegated form of the transmission of Jesus' sayings, of all things.

Whether and in what form the Lord's Prayer was prayed in the churches at that time (that is, at the time of the first drafting of our Gospels), we can only guess. Nothing justifies our assumption that the Matthean form would have been the official usage everywhere. Probably it was widely accepted quickly, as the Didache shows. By no later than about 150 CE, we can accept it as being the only version used in worship settings. From this time onward, when the contrasts of Jewish and Gentile Christian understandings mingled, the numerous conformations, that is, re-conformations, to which the Lucan text and its variants testify, might stem.

But now back to *Harnack*! We agreed with him when we recognized the "petition for the Holy Spirit" as being from Luke. But while we were content to regard it as the Lukan transformation of the petition for God's kingdom, he goes one big step farther.

His starting point is again the petition for the Holy Spirit. We have already suggested that the Tertullian passage probably generates a sub-variant for the Marcion gospel. Harnack then constructs the Marcion text in the following way: Πάτερ, ἐλθέτω τὸ ἅγιον πνεῦμα σου (ἐφ᾽ ἡμᾶς) καὶ καθαρισάτω ἡμᾶς, ἐλθέτω ἡ βασιλεία σου . . . [Father, let your Holy Spirit come (upon us) and cleanse us; may your kingdom come . . .].

In contrast to Gregory of Nyssa [and] Maximus Confessor [are] two minuscules: Πάτερ, ἁγιασθήτω τὸ ὄνομά σου, ἐλθέτω τὸ πνεῦμα σου τὸ ἅγιον (ἐφ᾽ ἡμᾶς) καὶ καθαρισάτω ἡμᾶς [Father, may your name be holy; let your Holy Spirit come (upon us) and cleanse us].

It follows that Marcion lacks the petition for sanctification of the name, and the remaining four witnesses lack the petition for the kingdom. From this, *Harnack* concludes that either Marcion or the rest were already influenced by the Matthew text. He can explain neither the one nor the other elimination and concludes from it *that the original Luke text contained neither the first nor the second petition at all, but rather after the salutation immediately began with the petition for the Holy Spirit.*[59] He supports this assertion by the other claim that the Lucan Lord's Prayer was an *initiation prayer*, that is, a prayer by which the stance of the Christian shall be established in general.[60]

So *Harnack* finally arrives at an original Lord's Prayer containing merely three petitions, since, of course, the petition for the Spirit (as originating from Luke or from his circles) and petition III of Matthew's Lord's Prayer are also dropped, and the ἡμῶν in petition IV is deleted, according to Syr. Sin:

Father, give us the bread for the coming day,
and forgive us our debts, as we forgive our debtors,
and do not lead us into temptation.[61]

58. A handwritten note by Barth in the margin of the manuscript beside 3 to 4 lines says "toothache" (see the facsimile among the pictures in this volume. [This note refers to pictures in the German edition of this book. This translation omits the pictures and the handwritten note.]).
59. Harnack, "Über einige Worte Jesu," 200.
60. Harnack, "Über einige Worte Jesu," 201, fn. 1; 205
61. Harnack, "Über einige Worte Jesu," 208.

We reply to this the following:

1. It seems methodologically inadmissible, in support of such a far-reaching deletion hypothesis, to be satisfied with the testimony of one single authority, namely, Marcion's, which, moreover, is only indirectly preserved. Even if you weigh the witnesses and do not just count them, the names Gregory of Nyssa and Maximus Confessor will, at least, inspire more confidence than the gnostic Marcion.[62]

2. From our previous investigations, it appears that Harnack himself has partly compiled the material for our counterclaim (naturally without wishing to do so): the petition for the Holy Spirit appeared in Luke instead of in Matthew's (and the preexisting version's) petition for the kingdom. After the discussion above, the "eradication," as it is found in the witnesses of the variants other than Marcion, is no longer inexplicable to us. Similarly, as already mentioned, in Blass's version of Luke, the petition for the kingdom is replaced by the petition for the Holy Spirit. In any case, this train of thought is more simple and more natural than the forceful elimination of the petition for sanctifying the name due to the somewhat obscure source of Marcion.

3. That *"the Lord's Prayer in Luke's form is an initiation prayer"*[63] has yet to be *proven.* Harnack remains short on the proof of this claim. Initiation requests are, for example, those Pauline passages quoted by Chase: a petition for initiation is the petition for the Holy Spirit (considered by itself), as evidenced by the parallels in Acts cited by Harnack. He believes that in an initiation prayer, the petition for the Holy Spirit should come first, so the petition for the sanctification of the name should be deleted.[64] The first point may be correct, but the proof is not provided that the Lukan Lord's Prayer as a whole is an initiation prayer. Consequently, the elimination of petition I is based on a kind of circular conclusion, which we do not feel compelled to condone.

4. It should be pointed out once again that, in view of this fact, Harnack's hypothesis, claiming the *unhistorical nature of the historical occasion narrated by Luke with respect to the Lord's Prayer, becomes doubtful.* Like his whole position, it rests on the Marcion passage and on the presupposition that the Lucan Lord's Prayer represents an initiation prayer.

The *situation* thus is briefly, to recapitulate, the following:

1. The evangelist Luke used the text of the Lord's Prayer, which existed beforehand in the sayings source available to him, and he edited it for his own literary purposes.
2. Later, after the text transmitted by Matthew had succeeded in being accepted for worship-related usage, Luke's texts were adapted in varying degrees to it.
3. There are no compelling reasons to believe that Matthew contains merely a version of Luke that was extended later.

---

62. From the [first comma] on to the end of this sentence, wavy lines are marked on the margin of the manuscript; if from K. Barth himself, they would be a sign of later self-criticism.

63. Harnack, "Über einige Worte Jesu," 206.

64. Harnack, "Über einige Worte Jesu," 201–2 n. 1.

But we cannot finish our investigation before we consider a very recent hypothesis about the Lord's Prayer, which must be of interest for the view we have developed, though I cannot accept it: the hypothesis of the aforementioned Stockholm theologian *G. Klein*, who appears to have dealt specifically with the Talmudic literature and the like.

Klein's thesis is the following: *We have the original form of the Lord's Prayer in Matthew (with doxology!) because only in this form does it meet the expectations of a Jewish prayer.*[65]

First we follow his argument. According to Psalm 119:164, Jewish prayer was, until the destruction of the temple, Birkath Sheba, "sevenfold prayer." It began with a glorification of God (שֶׁבַח) followed by individual prayer (תְּפִלָּה), while concluding with a doxology (הוֹדִיה).

The Lord's Prayer follows these expectations in this way:

Petitions I–III	=	שבח
Petitions IV–VIab	=	תפלה
Doxology	=	הודיה

The following statement is supported by parallels in Jewish prayers: *the Lord's Prayer could not begin with an individual petition.* Particularly noteworthy in this respect is the so-called Kaddish prayer.[66]

Further reference is made to the passage Matthew 6:32–34, in which Klein sees "at the same time an explanation and a more detailed justification" of the first four petitions of the Lord's Prayer. The parallels he sets up are the following:

πατὴρ ὑμῶν ὁ οὐράνιος	=	πάτερ ἡμῶν ὁ ἐν τοῖς οὐρανοῖς
ζητεῖτε (בקשו)	=	προσεύχεσθε
πρῶτον τὴν βασιλείαν	=	ἐλθάτω ἡ βασιλεία σου
καὶ τὴν δικαιοσύνην αὐτοῦ	=	γενηθήτω τὸ θέλημά σου
μὴ οὖν μεριμνήσητε εἰς	=	τὸν ἄρτον ἡμῶν τὸν ἐπιούσιον
τὴν αὔριον		δὸς ἡμῖν σήμερον

[our heavenly Father	=	Our Father who is in heaven
seek	=	pray
first the kingdom	=	may your kingdom come
and his righteousness	=	may your will be done
do not worry about	=	our daily bread
tomorrow		give us this day]

In the parallel verse, Luke 12:31, δικαιοσύνη [righteousness] is missing, therefore [the same is true] also [for] petition III in Luke 11:2.[67]

From Matthew 6:34, which also has parallels among the rabbis, it is evident that in petition IV the σήμερον [today] of Matthew, over against the καθ' ἡμέραν

---

65. Klein, "Gestalt des Vaterunsers," 35.
66. Klein, "Gestalt des Vaterunsers," 35–36.
67. Klein, "Gestalt des Vaterunsers," 36 with n. 2.

[daily] of Luke, is appropriate;[68] likewise it is evident from Matthew 6:14–16; Mark 11:25; and Matthew 5:23 that in petition V the ἀφήκαμεν [we have forgiven] of Matthew is appropriate over against the ἀφίομεν [we are forgiving] of Luke.[69] Similarly, the authenticity of petition VI (in the wording of Matthew) is substantiated by Jewish and New Testament parallels.[70]

Klein believes that the *doxology* is genuine because, according to "Jewish thinking and feeling,"[71] Christ could not conclude with anything bad, but only בְּדָבָר טוֹב, with something good. And since the pattern of Jewish prayer is followed until the sixth petition of the Lord's Prayer, "Jesus would have concluded the prayer according to the Jewish pattern with a הוֹדָיָה, a doxology," which is borrowed from 1 Chronicles 29:10. Thus the Lord's Prayer becomes a complete "sevenfold prayer."[72]

Klein, in the following way, deals with the oft-mentioned variant of petition II in Luke: Jesus could not have spoken the petition for the Holy Spirit, because he was already in possession of it; it comes rather from *John the Baptist*, whose sermon is summarized in this petition.[73] And as John's sermon, according to Klein, follows Ezekiel 36,[74] so does the Lord's Prayer, which he wants to show petition by petition (Ezek. 36:23–31).

36:23: And I will sanctify my great name.	Hallowed be your name.
36:24: And I will take you from all nations and will gather you from all the lands. . . .	Your kingdom come.
36:25–27: And I will sprinkle over you	[May] your Holy Spirit come upon us
pure water that you will become clean, . . . and I will give you a new heart and a new spirit. . . .	and cleanse us.
36:26b: And I will remove the stony heart from your flesh. . . .	Rescue us from evil.
36:28: And you will be my people and I your God.	Your will be done, as in heaven, so also on earth.
36:29b–30: And I will summon the grain and lay no famine upon you. . . .[75]	Give us this day our daily bread.

As Messiah, Jesus then would have excluded the (now unnecessary) petition for the Holy Spirit from his prayer, and "it was replaced by the doxology of 1 Chronicles 29:10."[76] In later Christian circles, the petition for the Holy Spirit would have been appropriated as the baptismal prayer and attached to the Lord's Prayer. The essential concern of Klein's essay is thus outlined.

---

68. Klein, "Gestalt des Vaterunsers," 36–38.
69. Klein, "Gestalt des Vaterunsers," 38.
70. Klein, "Gestalt des Vaterunsers," 39.
71. Klein, "Gestalt des Vaterunsers," 39.
72. Klein, "Gestalt des Vaterunsers," 39.
73. Klein, "Gestalt des Vaterunsers," 44.
74. Klein, "Gestalt des Vaterunsers," 44.
75. Klein, "Gestalt des Vaterunsers," 45.
76. Klein, "Gestalt des Vaterunsers," 46 with n. 1.

How shall we now assess this new phase in the Lord's Prayer criticism?

The first impression will be one of surprise. Here we suddenly see doubts over against the "results" of critical research that had long been regarded as established. Thus, the doxology, which appears in the later manuscripts of Matthew, is described as coming from Christ himself; and the same is said of petitions III and VIb, which were deleted by most critics, since they are not present in Luke.

We have already sketched our position on these various problems, and they are not shaken in any respect by *Klein*'s statements.

As far as the results are concerned and apart from the question of the doxology, we arrive at the same results as Klein:

The Lord's Prayer is to be considered authentic in the form offered by Matthew, but the method he uses to reach this conclusion is such that we cannot help but add a word or two.

The refutation of Harnack, which Klein attempts, does not appear to me to succeed.

To emphasize first what has satisfied me in the presentations of Klein, and what seems to me to be effective in keeping the three first petitions rejected by Harnack: I would like to mention the reference to the passage Matthew 6:33 = Luke 12:31. Indeed! Here we have from Jesus' own mouth—and in both evangelists—the classic summary of what a disciple of Jesus would pray, since the ζητεῖτε [seek, strive] is correctly placed in parallel with the Hebrew בַּקְּשׁוּ: "Seek first the kingdom of God!"[77] From consideration of this saying alone, a Lord's Prayer in Harnack's version, which begins with the petition for daily bread, seems to me to be excluded. Yet if Klein, in the further pursuit of his investigation, sets the δικαιοσύνη [righteousness] in Matthew 6:33 in parallel with the petition γενηθήτω τὸ θέλημά σου [May your will be done], then this is one of those artificialities that abound in his essay.

Its basic mistake seems to me to lie in the wrong method, not seldom used in such historical investigations, by which consciously or unconsciously a proposition—of whose truth only the author is convinced, without giving reasons for it—is made to support a second proposition that still needs to be proved, whereby the author's thesis becomes a *synthetic judgment* a priori, whereas historical propositions can never be anything more than a posteriori judgments.[78]

Klein's premise here is this proposition: *the Lord's Prayer has the form of a Jewish prayer*. With the help of this proposition, he successively proves the authenticity of all controversial petitions in the Lord's Prayer up to and including the final doxology. Of course, I do not want to touch upon Klein's clearly extensive erudition in the field of ancient Jewish literature, but how does he know that the Lord's Prayer *must* have the form he claims it should have?

Let's consider the doxology question. Since in Jewish prayers a הודיה (provides the conclusion, the Lord's Prayer must conclude with Matthew's doxology, "according to the Jewish pattern."[79] But with respect to this pattern, Klein should have reason to be concerned simply by the fact that Matthew's doxology is text-critically unsustainable! Even the thesis that it is borrowed from 1 Chronicles 29:10 is doubtful, in my opinion, since in the doxology of this verse, according to

---

77. Klein, "Gestalt des Vaterunsers," 36.

78. To this use of Kantian concepts, cf. esp. I. Kant, *Critique of Pure Reason*, Introduction, IV–VI, B 10–24.

79. Klein, "Gestalt des Vaterunsers," 40.

the Septuagint, the important term βασιλεία is missing! Klein's hypothesis—that the doxology came into the "sevenfold prayer" instead of the petition for the Holy Spirit, after Jesus "excluded" the latter—is impossible.[80] How does Klein imagine this process? He himself says somewhere, and we agree on this point, that the Lord's Prayer is "a child of the moment, out of the messianic mood."[81] How does he rhyme this point with the idea that Jesus subsequently improved, in the described way, on the prayer taught to the disciples!?

The reason for the claim that the *petition for the Holy Spirit stems from John the Baptist* is not yet clear to me. The way by which it would have come from him into the Lukan text of the Lord's Prayer is still unclear in Klein's deliberations.

Likewise, in my opinion, the mysterious connection between the Lord's Prayer and John the Baptist by way of *Ezekiel 36* is no more than a presumption: at least the way *Klein* sets up the parallel between Ezekiel 36 and the Lord's Prayer, which we already reproduced, gives the impression of great artificiality. In this way parallels to the Lord's Prayer could be found eventually in every psalm.

Let's summarize in Klein's own words: Jesus certainly did not think of creating a prayer formulary for a cultic community; the Lord's Prayer rather is a "child of the moment," a "cry of the soul to God."[82] But this also refutes the claim that Jesus positively constructed the Lord's Prayer according to a Jewish model, including quotations from Jewish prayers. It is very possible that he may well have relied upon this or that petition in the thought and prayer world of his own people, but the content that he gave the petitions was completely new, as different in its content as the gospel itself is from the law of the scribes.

To illustrate this point, I give only one of the passages quoted from Jewish prayers in *Klein*: in the treatise Soferim 14.22 it says: "Exalted and praised and *sanctified . . . be the name of the King of all kings . . .* in the worlds which he created *. . . according to his will and the will of all his people Israel. May his kingdom appear and reveal itself!*"[83]

The form of the thought here may be similar, but Jesus gave a very different content to these, here still narrowly national, ideas of the *will of God* and of his *kingdom*!

We have today taken a look into the workshop of historical criticism, which, rightly so, cannot stop at the highest and most sacred place, a prayer handed down from the mouth of Jesus himself. Our investigation on the whole has decided in favor of the form contained in Matthew. But, as Harnack admits, the really valuable thing about such a piece of evangelical tradition can neither be given to us nor taken from us by historical criticism.[84]

"Your kingdom come!"—or, as the other evangelist expresses it, "Your Holy Spirit come upon us and purify us"—will always be and remain the first prayer of a disciple of Jesus.

26 April 1906

---

80. Klein, "Gestalt des Vaterunsers," 46 with n. 1.
81. Klein, "Gestalt des Vaterunsers," 48.
82. Klein, "Gestalt des Vaterunsers," 48.
83. Klein, "Gestalt des Vaterunsers," 35.
84. Cf. Harnack, "Über einige Worte Jesu," 205, 207.

Paul's Missionary Activity according to
Its Portrayal in the Acts of the Apostles
1907

After Barth had sat for the written and oral examinations of the "Propaedeuticum" in the summer and fall of 1906 and had passed this so-called "first examination for service in the Evangelical-Reformed Church of the Canton of Bern" with the [best] grade of 1, he "strove to go to Marburg," as he noted in retrospect in 1927,[1] "whereas my father would have rather seen me moving to Halle or Greifswald. The result was that I went to the allegedly neutral Berlin, where I heard . . . Harnack . . . with such enthusiasm that I nearly completely missed the opportunity to make use of the manifold excitements of the foreign metropolis due to a paper for his church history seminar." A few years later, in a letter to A[gnes] von Zahn-Harnack on December 23, 1935, Barth remembered, "Among the Swiss who were there with me at the time, there was no one who was as enthusiastic for the personality and teaching style of your esteemed father as I. It went so far that, due to a paper I had to do for his seminar and with which I was busy for several months nearly day and night, I almost completely missed out on the opportunity to take notice of the Kaiser-Friedrich Museum [now called Bode Museum] and Berlin's other beautiful sights and at the end had really seen and heard very little, apart from your esteemed father, whom I can say I had seen and heard very thoroughly." As for the 1906–7 Winter Semester in Berlin, and especially Barth's paper for Harnack's seminar, we are informed directly by the letters that Barth wrote from Berlin to his parents, relatives, and friends.

"Coming from the arid heath of theological skepticism onto a green pasture," after six weeks Barth already felt "like another man": "behind me in unsubstantial appearance orthodoxy and that plague of pretending reformers [Reformlerei]. The study of Kant "last summer with labor keen"[2] had provided the foundations. He therefore came "armed" to Berlin, where he was especially impressed by (1) Kaftan with his dogmatics, (2) Harnack the incomparable historian with his history of doctrine, and (3) Herrmann (by reading his Ethik [Ethics], which I went through for the second time).[3] This three-fold influence was, of course, neither equal nor equally important. Letters to his family, in an intensely vivid manner, portray how Barth could look back on his time in Berlin the following summer and speak simply of his "Harnack semester"[4] and how he later introduced himself on occasion not without pride as a "student of Harnack."[5]*

---

1. Autobiographical sketch for the *Album der Evangelisch-theologischen Fakultät Münster* (1927), in *Bw. B.*, 304.

2.* "With labor keen" is an allusion to the opening monologue of Goethe's *Faust*. Trans.

3. Letter from November 30, 1906, to Otto Lauterburg. Letter from November 22, 1906, to his father: "A picture of Harnack and Kaftan is hanging above my bed; they will worthily adorn my parsonage at some point—even more hopefully their spirit, which I really want to be able to understand better and more completely."

4. Letter from June 3, 1907, to Otto Lauterburg.

5. For example: A postcard to the pastor P. Walter postmarked November 5, 1909.

On October 26, 1906, he reported to his father, that, "thanks to my exam (!!)," he had just been admitted to Harnack's "Exercises in Theol. Seminar" (Dept. of Church History). On October 28, 1906, he wrote to his grandmother that he had gotten into Harnack's famous seminar, in which "the Acts of the Apostles is to be searched through and through exhaustively for the umpteenth time"—"now this means getting down to work." In this regard, he had already asked his father on October 26 for the relevant literature by Blass, Jülicher, Overbeck, Zeller, and Hadorn, and for his father's notes on Steck's introductory lecture. On November 1, he repeated and supplemented his request: "Could you procure Zeller's [analysis of] Acts from the library in Bern for me? I want to get to know the Tübingen standpoint for once thoroughly and authentically. . . . Further, I forgot my notes on your Paul [transcript of Fritz Barth's lecture on 'The Life and Writings of Paul,' which Karl Barth had heard in the summer term of 1906] and Harnack's 'Mission and Expansion of Christianity,' but it's not pressing. I am going to go about it with composure and on the broadest basis, so that it may become a 'book.'" Barth discusses what this book is about in the previously mentioned letter from October 26: "I have to deal with the following topic on the 14th of February: 'How does the Acts of the Apostles portray Paul as a missionary? (Planting and nurture of the communities.) What significance does the author give Paul in the whole of his historical trajectory?' Quite a multilayered complex, don't you think? Formally a qualifying thesis!! I want to get down to it as quickly and energetically as possible, but I have the far-reaching preliminary work to do, on top of which comes the weekly preparations for the Thursday sessions." Barth signed the letter as "The newest biographer-to-be of Paul!"

Barth writes again to his father about the Thursday sessions in a letter dated November 1: "Harnack's seminar is very interesting. He usually attends to three things. First, he indicates what's going on within the entire field of church history in terms of excavations, manuscripts, and so on; then he deals with the respective Acts text from a text-critical standpoint and with especially affectionate polemic against the D-hypothesis [based on Codex Bezae] from Blass; finally the same with respect to the content of Acts, with a constant preference for the sense offered by Luke the physician. You can imagine how fine this all is. One notices, especially on the last point, just how important the matter is to him. . . . At any rate, he becomes very fiery and enthralls everyone." "The seminar itself looks like a church assembly. The beginning is intended to be especially dignified, as the double-door house spits out two leopards at once, namely, Harnack and his amanuensis, a very slick and clever gentleman [Heinrich Scholz!] who is also senior of the seminar, who carries the books of his master like a poodle with a stick. Then all rise to their feet and sit back down in just as dignified a manner; the council is opened." On November 8, he writes to his father: "The whole thing is very much like a council, the minutes are taken and are read out at the beginning of every 'session' [Sitzung] (this is what it's called officially). . . . Harnack is masterful in detecting the tiny and tiniest clues in the text for his purposes—something that I have not at all had a sense for up to this point."

On November 15, Barth tells his parents about an approximately fifteen-minute Privatissimum [private academic audience] about his paper with the great Harnack in the royal library. "I now know more or less what's going on, and he spoke great and significant words, which I treasured in my heart. Afterward, for my personal pleasure, he showed me the famous Codex D in person, which he personally guarded like Alberich *did the treasure of the Nibelungs. I put forth the utmost effort to make the most appreciative of faces possible. Then I toddled off with the greatest of intentions"—which were subsequently expressed in a request for "the Acts commentary of Holtzmann and the (revised) Meyer." Before long he was able to report to his parents: "I have never lived with such regularity as here." He wanted "to make headway on his paper for Harnack"; so he sat "almost every day from noon until 7:30 p.m. at home" and studied "first [Herrmann's] Ethik and then Acts." "The term paper is well under way; I've at least written a very good-natured introduction and am well into the first chapter (there are four). The decision about the disposition and the like was the most difficult; now things are happily moving forward" (December 6). On December 13 he wrote to his father: "The past week stood under the sign of Luke the Physician. The paper is growing every day, in fact only too much; soon I will already have filled up two notebooks (of 40 pages apiece, but with a wide margin), and I'm still in the first section of the first chapter. . . . It is threatening to grow into a history of the apostolic age or nearly into a biography of Paul, . . . but I can't help it: the different aspects are hopelessly entangled with one another, and I want to take care of them either in a thoroughgoing manner or not at all. There's absolutely no other way of getting at the gigantic edifice of the Tübingen School other than with meticulous fine-tuning, in any case not with [just] phrases. But Harnack and his famulus [assistant] will be plenty busy for half a day, if they want to read all of that. Q.F.F.F.Q.S.[6] In any case, I will reap the profit from this in that I will for once get to know the material and the one thousand problems at the most basic level. And another thing that will remain with me for the rest of my life is the way Harnack teaches us to handle the text, namely, that in the first instance one has to relentlessly ask everywhere of the text: What does the author mean? [That is] actually a rather banal matter, but it is not at all a matter of course everywhere, at least among those [who claim to work] with "no presuppositions," not to mention the dogmaticians on the right and on the left! When such a method has become one's flesh and blood (which I am attempting to achieve), then everything else is actually . . . less important." Toward the end of this letter, Barth writes that he "now still wants to do a little Act-ing [apostelgeschichteln]," and after signing the letter, he appends "stud. act."[7]*

Due to his research, Barth even modified his travel plans for the Christmas holidays: "I want to be here again after the New Year and do more Act-ing [apostelgeschichteln]." He was "now working the entire day, so to speak. It won't be my fault if in the future someone has something to complain about the author writing 'to Theophilus.' I am defending this good man (if he only knew it!) thoroughly and against everyone." The "Tübingen School and their successors" are guilty of "a thoroughgoing misconstruction." "One cannot thank Harnack enough that he freed the discipline from this blight, if it only works! The matter has far-reaching consequences: the entire apostolic age moves into a new light.

I now have written already around 140 pages and have happily finished my first chapter, "The Missionary Method." . . . After the New Year comes chapter 2, "Missionary Preaching." . . . Then the third, "The Missionary Communities." . . . Then I am going to need to copy out this mountain—it really will be a popular tome in the history of religions; I'm already dreading it; and then the review of all the citations,

---

6.[*] = *Quod bonum, faustum, felix fortunatumque sit* (May the outcome be good, lucky, propitious, and successful). A "B." is missing between the first Q. and the first F. Trans.

7.[*] Barth is mocking his own intensity in writing his term paper. Trans.

whew!" (from a letter to his parents and siblings dated December 21). On January 2, 1907, Barth wrote his parents: "I've been working on Paul again since this morning, and the pages are piling up in the usual way." Again, writing to his parents on January 10: "Think about it, I've been sitting here a long five days without swaying once, always writing, writing. . . . During the evenings, at least, I went a few times to the theater. . . . My job's Leviathan is growing tremendously and striking with its tail. Today I finished the second chapter, which makes in total 240 pages octavo. Tomorrow I'll go on to the third. . . . On the one hand, I'll really be happy once the monumental work is over, though provisionally I can't yet see the other shore. Up to this point I've had my hands full in dealing with Holtzmann and Jülicher, in the third chapter. . . . It's Weizsäcker's turn, hey, all three of them are lying on their stomachs, 'because I know how to throw bombs. . . .' However, joking aside, isn't all this Tübingen stuff and their entourage really something bad? To me it appears more and more that way. Certainly, a year ago when I was sitting there and listening to Steck and how the Pauline letters were being done in with those old-fashioned templates (and was thinking, 'Yes, Sir'), it never would have entered my mind that 365 days later I'd be sitting behind such a behemoth, in which various parts or the whole thing comes out completely different." On January 17, to his father: "Now the third and final chapter of the behemoth is finished; mind you, it only has fifty pages. Tomorrow comes a clanging final symphony for the whole thing, where I want to put in some antics and other clowning around, and then I'll have to take this pile of thick notebooks lying before me, copy it all out, and work over it in part to some degree."

On January 31, Barth was able to write his father and say: "The work is now finished, bound by the bookbinder, and looks stately from the outside. Tomorrow I'll carry it to Harnack. I am quite afraid, because the papers that have been turned in up to this point were from 20 to 60 small pages, and I have 160 in quarto. If he complains, then I'll tell him that in Bern one never does less than 150. . . . Fourteen days from today will be my Dies irae, dies illa [Day of wrath, that day], for which I am more afraid than I was of the Propaedeuticum [preparatory instruction]. I can already see coming what's going to happen to me [and what Harnack will say]: "A strange fellow, this young bird, a strrrrange fellow," and so on. My paper contains egregiously harmless things, [I tell myself] as I think about the fact that tomorrow at this time it'll be lying on the desktop of Adolf Harnack, theol." Barth wrote his father again on February 7 in the same anxious tone: "Today in 8 days my Jena[8]* in the seminar will be over; then I'll be able to use my term paper to wrap my socks for the journey home! I am facing the whole thing with a kind of pessimistic-optimism, or an optimistic-pessimism; it could be dismal." But on February 14 (in a letter to his parents), Barth expressed himself in a tone of relieved and modest pride:

> *The Battle went forward,*
> *the enemy was struck down,*
> *and I sat on the baggage cart!*

"Now I've endured it, and again I can look worry free (or at least relatively worry free) into the future. There were great moments. The people laughed quite heartily when the great man began: 'The paper by Mister Barth is a small volume: he wrote 160 pages altogether; I'm only wondering how you found time to do all that in Berlin!' With

8.* Referring to Napoleon's defeating the Prussian Army at Jena on October 14, 1806.

respect to the content, I received some pertinent criticism, but also some rather nice ornate epithets in the final comments at the end of the paper, several times a 'good' and 'right' on the margin, in one place sure enough also a two-page-long wavy line precisely where I thought I was especially astute!! . . . The oral critique, by the way, proceeded in a much friendlier manner than the written one, and luckily the first student speaker had committed the same sins as I, and on this Harnack himself said that he can well understand it, because there is no way we could have known about the remaining contemporary literature.

"You can be provisionally happy about the tome that is already underway. . . . By the way, tomorrow we'll be celebrating the slaying of the dragon (the event was announced as either a celebration or a funeral) with a group of seven friends, here in our room with sandwiches and some beer."

On February 21 Barth could already thank his father for having provided a basically affirmative assessment of the term paper (letter from February 20), which was nonetheless critical on specific points:[9] *"When I came rattling back home after the seminar on the obligatory automobile, I found your letter and am thankful many times over for the comments on the head, rump, and members of the Leviathan; the animal has been completed with much daily and nightly perspiration and now is happy when the sun shines! I overcame the temptation to put down a short treatise, or rather a few of them, on mythical and non-mythical earthquakes, on Paul's conversion, and so on, since that can happen orally in a few weeks anyway."* Today one can rue the fact that Barth put off stating his own position on his father's critiques until a later conversation.[10]

We only know that a discussion between Barth and his father about his term paper for Harnack's seminar was planned. Nonetheless, this fact in itself is worth mentioning; on December 6, 1908, Karl Barth, who in the meantime had become editorial assistant for *Die Christliche Welt* in Marburg, asked his parents: *"Would you look under the lid of the coffin bearing my personal effects in the suitcase closet to see if my paper for Harnack is easy to reach? If so, would you send it as quickly as possible? Tutor Bultmann is vehemently demanding to see it. But only if it's easy to reach."*

The manuscript is exactly in the form described by Barth: 158 pages in quarto format, bound by a bookbinder with cardboard covers. The complete text of the title page runs thus:

The Missionary Activity of Paul according to Its
Portrayal in the Acts of the Apostles.
Examined for the Seminar in Church History of Prof. Dr. Harnack
(Session on 14. Feb. 1907).

Berlin S.W.   *Karl Barth*
Hallesche Strasse 18[111]   *cand. theol.*

She had suffered much under many physicians!
Mark 5:26

---

9. On the passage at the bottom of p. 120 below: "What is mythical about an earthquake?" On Harnack's mark on the bottom of p. 157 (see n. 169 below): "I am marking with him."

10. In the aforementioned letter of February 14, 1907, Barth had already announced: "We'll have to hammer out the details during a stroll at Wittighofen." (Wittighofen was a destination for day trips to the east of Bern.)

Table of Contents

Introduction

The history of the modern [historical] criticism of the Acts of the Apostles—"a pitiful history," as it has recently been called[11]—begins with adopting the following thesis: The author writing "to Theophilus" is pursuing a *specific goal that is to be understood historically,* and he arrives at the selection and ordering of his material accordingly. This way of looking at the matter can be found clearly first in 1841 with the Bernese theologian *Schneckenburger,* who set out to find

---

11. A. Harnack, *Luke the Physician: The Author of the Third Gospel and the Acts of the Apostles,* trans. J. R. Wilkinson, ed. W. D. Morrison, New Testament Studies I (New York: G. P. Putnam's Sons, 1908), 12.

a Pauline-apologetic goal.[12] He was, however, overtaken by the researchers of the *Tübingen School*, for whom the Acts of the Apostles by contrast became the work of a *conciliator*, a thesis based on the historical construction arising from the critical examination of the Pauline Letters.[13] Thus, *Zeller* calls it (citation in Overbeck)[14] the "draft of a proposal for peace presented to the Judaists by the Pauline party, . . . which was intended to purchase the recognition of the Gentile Christians by the Jewish Christians via concessions to Judaism, and designed to act upon both parties in this sense."[15] *Baur*,[16] *Schwegler*,[17] *Hilgenfeld*,[18] and others assess the matter in this way or similarly.

A divergent standpoint, even if on the whole it ensued from the positions of the Tübingen school, was maintained by F. Overbeck in Basel (in his 1870 reworking of the commentary by De Wette).[19] According to him, the Acts of the Apostles is "the attempt of a Gentile Christianity, which already has been strongly influenced by early Christian Judaism, to come to terms with the past, especially with its own emergence and its founder Paul." In this, however, "Acts has given up the essential features of Paulinism with the single exception being its universalism."[20] *Hausrath*[21] and *Pfeiderer*[22] are similar.

Holtzmann summarizes the results of this phase as follows: "Those points where the author did not want to apply the Tübingen critique were the points where he was unable to see anything at all, according to the new reading," since he "mostly no longer" had "any sympathy for early Christian antitheses, in particular for the questions vital to Paulinism. . . . The fact that the leading perspectives, according to which the actual history suffers a shift that affects the whole of its content and presentation, have not been derived from the author's systematic reflection but, on the contrary, imposed themselves on him is now assumed even by the most resolute critique."[23] On the whole the newer critics keep to this

---

12. M. Schneckenburger, *Ueber den Zweck der Apostelgeschichte: Zugleich eine Ergänzung der neueren Commentare* (Bern: Chr. Fischer, 1841), esp. 151–52, 217–18; cf. [Fr. Overbeck,] *Kurze Erklärung der Apostelgeschichte*, von W. M. L. De Wette, 4th ed., bearbeitet und stark erweitert von Fr. Overbeck, *Kurzgefasstes exegetisches Handbuch zum Neuen Testament* (Leipzig: S. Hirzel, 1870), I/4: xxviii.

13. Cf. Fr. Overbeck, *Erklärung der Apostelgeschichte*, xxvii.

14. Overbeck, *Erklärung der Apostelgeschichte*, xxix.

15. Fr. Overbeck, "Introduction to the Acts of the Apostles," 18, reprinted in *The Contents and Origins of the Acts of the Apostles, Critically Investigated*, by E. Zeller, trans. Joseph Dare (London: Williams & Norgate, 1871).

16. F. Chr. Baur, *Paul, The Apostle of Jesus Christ: His Life and Work, His Epistles and Doctrine. A Contribution to the Critical History of Primitive Christianity* (London: Williams & Norgate, 1876), 1:11–13; Baur, *Ueber den Ursprung des Episcopats in der christlichen Kirche: Prüfung der neuestens von Hrn. Dr. Rothe aufgestellten Ansicht* (Tübingen: Baum, 1838), 142.

17. A. Schwegler, *Das nachapostolische Zeitalter in den Hauptmomenten seiner Entwicklung* (Tübingen: L. F. Fues, 1846), 2:73–123.

18. A. Hilgenfeld, *Historisch-Kritische Einleitung in das Neue Testament* (Leipzig: Fues, 1875), 574–608, esp. 593–602.

19. Overbeck, *Erklärung der Apostelgeschichte*.

20. Overbeck, "Introduction," 22, reprinted in Zeller, *Origins of the Acts*; cf. Zeller, *Origins of the Acts*, 149–50.

21. A. Hausrath, *Der Apostel Paulus*, 2nd ed. (Heidelberg: Bassermann, 1872), 2–3; Hausrath, *A History of the New Testament Times: The Time of the Apostles*, vol. 3, trans. L. Huxley (London: Williams & Norgate, 1895), 146 n. 2.

22. O. Pfleiderer, *Das Urchristenthum, seine Schriften und Lehren, in geschichtlichem Zusammenhang* (Berlin: Reimer, 1887), 544–47; Pfleiderer, *Der Paulinismus: Ein Beitrag zur Geschichte der urchristlichen Theologie* (Leipzig: Fues, 1873), 500–504.

23. H. J. Holtzmann, *Die Synoptiker. Die Apostelgeschichte*, 2nd ed., HC 1 (Freiburg i. B.: Akademische Verlagsbuchhandlung, 1892), 308–9.

framework, which *Holtzmann* (xvi) brings under the rubric of "Tübingen and related positions." In *Apostolischer Zeitalter*,[24] *Weizsäcker* comes to the conclusion that is now put down as apodictic knowledge: "The author of the Acts, as those indications also show, was so remote from the events he relates that he cannot be accepted as a witness of the first rank," although he certainly makes a sharply pointed exception with respect to his predecessors in relation to the so-called "We-source."[25] *Jülicher* also means, as far as this tendency is concerned, "that one erroneously presents the author's intentions, where, in fact, knowledge is lacking."[26] With respect to the value of the book as a source, he comes to the conclusion, as does Weizsäcker, that "in Act[s] materials of impeccable quality are strangely mixed with what is nearly unusable,"[27] but at least with the qualification that the author "did not seek to hide his non-knowledge with bold fictions."[28]

Holtzmann recapitulates as follows: "If Luke is the painter, according to the self-proclaimed church tradition, then he decisively belongs among the old masters whose presence can be recognized in the garb in which the persons of the holy history appear in their work. In this regard the Acts of the Apostles differs from the group of actual history books and puts itself among that class of portrayals, so richly represented in antiquity, whose content lies only partly in the past and to a large extent in the immediate present of its respective author. *One is writing from the times and for the times.*"[29] This passage is typical for all critical standpoints.

The theses given above are at the same time the major premise: The author writing "to Theophilus" is an unknown person from the end of the first century or beginning of the second century, writing for his time while using older sources. The self-evident minor premise follows from this: His historical reliability can only be very relative (i.e., it corresponds to the reliability of the historical sources he uses) while its bona fide position is contentious.

Apart from the scholarship on the right (called "Apologetic," which since Overbeck is decisively disreputable!),[30] under which authors such as *Meyer*,[31] *Wendt*,[32] *B. Weiss*,[33] and *Klostermann*,[34] among others, rank the entirety of NT

---

24. C. Weizsäcker, *The Apostolic Age of the Christian Church*, vol. 1, trans. James Millar, from 2nd and rev. ed. (London: Williams & Norgate, 1907), 240.

25. Weizsäcker, *Apostolic Age*, 240–45.

26. A. Jülicher, *Einleitung in das Neue Testament*, 3rd and 4th ed., GThW 3.1 (Tübingen/Leipzig: J. C. B. Mohr, 1901), 346.

27. Jülicher, *Einleitung*, 350.

28. Jülicher, *Einleitung*, 346–47, 351.

29. Holtzmann, *Die Apostelgeschichte*, 322.

30. Cf. Jülicher, *Einleitung*, esp. xviii.

31. H. A. W. Meyer, *Das Neue Testament Griechisch: Nach den besten Hülfsmitteln kritisch revidiert mit einer neuen Deutschen Übersetzung und einem kritischen und exegetischen Kommentar*, part 2, *Kritisch exegetischer Kommentar über das Neue Testament*, KEK, part 3 (Göttingen: Vandenhoeck & Ruprecht, 1835), esp. 1–9. Also cf. the "*Zweite, verbesserte und vermehrte Auflage*" (Göttingen: Vandenhoeck & Ruprecht, 1854), 1–13; and the 3rd and 4th eds., under the title *Kritisch exegetisches Handbuch über die Apostelgeschichte*, 3rd ed., KEK 3 (Göttingen: Vandenhoeck & Ruprecht, 1861), 1–15; or 4th ed. (1870), 1–16.

32. H. H. Wendt, *Kritisch exegetisches Handbuch über die Apostelgeschichte*, von H. A. W. Meyer, 5. Aufl. neu bearbeitet von H. H. Wendt, KEK 3 (Göttingen: Vandenhoeck & Ruprecht, 1880), 1–24. Barth's quotations in the following are taken from this edition. Cf. also the "Sechste, resp. siebente Auflage" (Göttingen: Vandenhoeck & Ruprecht, 1888), 1–32; and the 8th ed., under the title *Die Apostelgeschichte*, KEK 3 (Göttingen: Vandenhoeck & Ruprecht, 1899), 4–34.

33. B. Weiss, *Lehrbuch der Einleitung in das Neue Testament*, 3rd ed. (Berlin: Verlag W. Herz, 1897), 541–60.

34. A. Klostermann, *Vindiciae Lucanae seu de itinerarii in libro Actorum asservati auctore* (Göttingen, 1866), esp. 46, 61–63, 68, 70–71.

scholarship approved of these theses up to summer 1906. On the other hand, *Holtzmann* could quite rightly say that "more than with others among the disputed books, an understanding appears possible and imminent with respect to Acts."[35]

Yet it was not to be!

In May 1906, Harnack's *Luke the Physician*[36] was published, wherein it was proven primarily through lexical-statistical and style-critical studies that not only the author of the "We-source" and the other parts was *one person*—a view Jülicher had named "adventurous,"[37] despite its honorable age—but also that there was no one to find behind this unitary author other than the physician and companion of Paul, as had been accepted by the tradition.

We can provisionally leave the question of the accuracy of this assumption aside. One thing is for sure: with respect to the abundance of materials recently made available for scholarly research on Acts, there will have to be *a careful revision of all previous material and literary-critical results.*

The following work is intended to be an attempt in this direction.

The figure of *Paul* stands at the center of our interest in the apostolic age from time immemorial. He is the one who, according to the unanimous and undoubtable witness of the tradition, led nascent Christianity out of its national-Jewish parochialism and into the cultural world of the Greco-Roman spirit and who at the same time gave it a form that was designed to enable this rather heterogeneous world to take up Christianity into itself.

The singular significance of this man is also suggested to us in a purely external manner by the fact that the sources about him flow in a disproportionately abundant manner in comparison to the sources regarding the other apostles. One of these sources is precisely our *Acts of the Apostles*, and there is therefore no reason to wonder that, with the controversy about Acts we have just briefly sketched, his person and the role intended for it in the stories formed one or the primary object of the discussions.

The *entire* critique was unanimous in the fact that in Acts *we do not have the historical Paul before us but rather a version of him that had been intentionally or unintentionally and in one way or another distorted.*

The *Tübingen School* found this Paul to have been "peterized" in line with harmonizing designs (whereas Peter, in turn, had been "paulinized").[38]

This was also the opinion of *Overbeck*, but without accepting the *dolus*.[39]* Jülicher, on the contrary, held that Paul, like Peter, has been "lukanized, that is, catholicized."[40] These judgments were made on the basis of the critical comparison of data from Acts with the authentic Paul in his letters and the consideration emerging from them *that the existing differences between both are explainable only as either being intentional or the result of the ignorance of a writer who describes what lies thirty to forty years behind him, in the past.*

---

35. Klostermann, *Vindiciae Lucanae*, 309.
36. Cf. Harnack, *Luke the Physician*.
37. Jülicher, *Einleitung*, 253.
38. Cf. Baur, *Ursprung des Episcopats*, 142; Zeller, *Origins of the Acts*, esp. 149–50, 154.
39.* *Dolus eventualis* = conditional intent; in this case, that the author was willing to accept the risk of producing a misleading portrait of Paul. Trans.
40. Jülicher, *Einleitung*, 347.

I cannot render a systematic comparison of the data from Acts and the [Pauline] Letters here since this would take us too far and moreover is not essential for the proposed approach. It really is not the goal to demonstrate, by means of comparison, what happened but rather [to answer]:

"What is the author's standpoint?"

"How much does he know, or respectively, invent?"

"Does his writing have an agenda?"

"If so, then which one?"

But even within the material given in Acts, I also have to work with a constraint, which appeared necessary to me in setting the topic: I will not tread on the related controversy arising at this point about the *parallelism between Paul and Peter.*

> This is found in another book
> And is a wondrous chapter.[41]

Likewise, I will not take into account the difficult and complicated question of *Paul's relationship to Judaism,* to *the law* and to *the earliest Christian community in Jerusalem.*

Finally, I have also avoided, perhaps unjustly, all investigations into the *chronology* since I think this needs to be done on a much broader basis than is possible for me here.

On the contrary, I will confine my investigation strictly to what Acts reports about the missionary work of Paul in the Diaspora but hoping at the same time to obtain enough material to possibly arrive at some observations of a more general scope.

Chapter I: The Missionary Method

The questions to be discussed here are necessarily of a somewhat disparate nature. We are dealing with the external aspects of Pauline propaganda, that is, everything related to *personal questions, travel routes, kinds of connections,* and the like, to the extent that it is important for our theme, thus more about peripheral matters. All the same, there are a few aspects to be attained here which can have an influence on the assessment of the whole.

A. Historical Overview

First we will simply follow the accounts given in the Acts of the Apostles by critically engaging the questions under consideration and at the same time collecting the material, from point to point, that we will need later for a more general consideration.

We will begin at the point where Paul emerges onstage as a future missionary.

In Acts 9:30 we hear that *Saul* was brought by the "brothers" from Jerusalem to Caesarea, and from there to his home city of Tarsus, to protect him from the

---

41. J. W. von Goethe, *Faust* 51.2349–50 (witch's kitchen).

pursuit of the Hellenists. The follow-up to this is given in 11:25–26:[42] *Barnabas*, who as "a good man, full of the Holy Spirit and faith," was sent by those in Jerusalem to the newly arisen and flourishing [Christian] community of *Antioch in Syria*, fetching Saul of Tarsus to have his support. Together they developed what appears to have been a beneficial activity: they "taught a great many people." Under the influence of "prophets [who] came down from Jerusalem" (11:27–30), the Antiochenes decided on a charity tax for the mother congregation, which was threatened by hunger, and Barnabas and Saul were charged with delivering it. This thread, after having been interrupted by other stories, will be picked up again in 12:24–13:1.[43] Already in 11:27 we hear that in the Antiochene community the prophetic-charismatic moment played a preeminent role, indeed intervening decisively in its resolutions. Now we hear something more. Barnabas and Saul (who in 12:25 returned from Jerusalem with John Mark) join in a meeting of prayer and fasting (13:1) with Simon Niger, Lucius of Cyrene, and Manaen (as "prophets and teachers," a self-evident combination!). Here they are commanded by direct address of the Holy Spirit: "Set apart for me Barnabas and Saul." The command is immediately obeyed: After further prayer and fasting, those who were called then receive the laying on of hands, this time, it seems, before the assembled congregation, and so they are sent out in this way before God and humanity for proclamation of the gospel, ordained "for the work to which I have called them," and are dismissed (13:2, 3). *The mission to the Gentiles thus begins, according to the author, under the intensive working of the Holy Spirit*, that is, in fulfilling the specific will of God. Formally, we must note: *Among the missionaries who have been sent out, it is Barnabas who is initially of preeminent significance* (cf. 11:30; 12:25; 13:2). From the comments after the fact in 13:5b (cf. 12:12, 25), we hear in addition that the two were accompanied by this John Mark as one "to assist them."

The "First Missionary Journey"

The "ones set apart" make their way from the Syrian port city of Seleucia first to *Cyprus*, which 4:36 says was the home of Barnabas and where, according to 11:19 and 21:16, there were already Jewish Christians. They cross "the whole island" [13:6] from Salamis to Paphos, *preaching* everywhere in the synagogues *to the Jews. There is no word here of an attempt to make contact with the Gentiles*, even if it is not excluded on principle, as it was by the missionaries after the persecution of Stephen in 11:19, and it then happens by chance, though independently from the synagogue, through the receptivity of the proconsul Sergius Paulus.

From this point onward, the *priority* is given to Saul, who according to 13:9 is also called *Paul*: 13:13 already has it written as "Paul and his companions."

From Paphos the journey goes by sea to Perga in Pamphylia. There, likely due to a lack of courage according to 15:38, John Mark separates from them; they go on to *Antioch in Pisidia* (13:14), "and on the Sabbath day they went into the synagogue." After the "reading" of the law, "the presbyters" (cf. Mark

---

42. The manuscript was corrected at this point, presumably by Harnack, to read "11:25–27."
43. Harnack [?] corrected this as follows: "12:25; 13.1ff."

5:22; Acts 18:8, 17; etc.) entreat the strangers to offer an "edifying address" after they had likely made themselves known as rabbis.[44] Paul immediately stands up, beckons with his hand, and then makes a long speech (13:16–41), in which it is notable that "those who fear God" are also being addressed, which points to the fact that the audience consisted partially of the "proselytes of righteousness." When he has finished, they are asked to come again on the following Sabbath. That occurs in 13:44, and since additional circles have evidently become aware of these happenings, "the whole city," as it says, came to hear the word of God. Now, however, there occurs a sudden reversal in the mindset of the *Jews*: "They were filled with jealousy," so they *contradict* and slander Paul. Subsequently he turns away from them and, calling on Isaiah 49:6, turns to the Gentiles (13:46–47), who rejoice and begin to believe, "as many as had been destined for eternal life."

Driven out by the persecutions erupting in Antioch [of Pisidia], the missionaries move on to *Iconium* (14:1–8), where everything proceeds nearly the same way as before: Here things also begin with a *sermon in the synagogue* . . . "in such a way that a great number of Jews and Greeks became believers" (14:1). It is evidently the presupposition here as well that there were "God-fearers" or "God-respecters" from among the Gentiles in the synagogue community, and it was likely they, especially from among the non-Jews, who accepted Paul's proclamation. According to 14:2, 5, the Jews who remained "unbelieving" were able to win Gentiles to be against the apostles. But again, apart from these "Greeks" who are friendly toward the Jews, other circles also were apparently drawn into the movement: the populace divided itself into *two parties*, one of which held to the Jews, the other to the apostles. The first gained the upper hand, making it necessary for Paul and Barnabas to flee, turning southeast to the "cities of Lycaonia: *Lystra, Derbe*, and the surrounding area" (14:6–7).

"And there they continued proclaiming the good news." *We do not hear anything about making contact with the synagogue here, as we do in the first three cases;* on the contrary, we can conclude from 14:19 that no Jews were there. From what occurred after the healing of the lame in Lystra, it is allowable to draw the conclusion that the verb "proclaiming the good news," despite 14:9, is not to be understood as street preaching before a large audience, because this would then make the scenes in 14:11–12 inexplicable. Instead, we will have to think about an activity in a smaller circle, and yet the miraculous deed first attracted larger amounts of people. But then the Jews from Antioch and Iconium came, and it was necessary for Paul to withdraw from here as well.

Paul then goes with Barnabas to *Derbe*, but here again: . . . "they had proclaimed the good news to that city and made many disciples" [14:21]. Once more, no [mention of] contact with the Jews!

From here begins the return via Lystra, Iconium, and Antioch in Pisidia. They stop in Perga, which was barely touched on the outward journey (13:13), where "they had spoken the word" (14:25), and from there they travel through [sail beside, 14:26] Anatolia to the starting point, Antioch in Syria, "where they were commended to the grace of God for the work that they had completed" [14:26].

---

44. Wendt, *Handbuch über die Apostelgeschichte*, 282.

The "Second Missionary Journey"

In 15:1–34 comes the story of the controversy over circumcision and its settlement at the "Apostolic Council" in Jerusalem. Then 15:35–41 conveys the continuing history of mission: After their return from Jerusalem, Paul and Barnabas
stop in Antioch [of Syria] and preach for a few days "with many others." Then
they are gripped by a new thirst for action, first Paul, who then directs the
request to Barnabas: we shall go back again and look after the brothers, to see
how things are with them. *The initial goal of this journey is thus not in the first
instance the evangelization of new areas, but rather the preservation and consolida-
tion of the communities that had been established up until that point.* One could be
tempted to see this limitation as related to the prior conflict.

Along with Paul, Barnabas, and the delegation from Jerusalem, consisting of
Judas Barsabbas and *Silas* (15:22), plus *John Mark*—the·nephew of Barnabas (Col.
4:10), who in 13:13 returned to Jerusalem—evidently also came back to Antioch.
Barnabas wants to take him along on the new journey, but Paul refuses (15:38),
indicating his "falling away" in Pamphylia. This results in a serious quarrel
between them (the verse even speaks of a "sharp disagreement"!), and the end
result is that the two go their separate ways: Barnabas heads toward Cyprus for
the second time with his nephew; Paul takes *Silas*, the one who in 15:32 is designated a "prophet" along with Judas, as his companion and strikes out overland
to the north [and west]. *Holtzmann*[45] sees the passage 15:35–41 as an attempt to
blur what is recounted in Galatians 2:11–12.[46] However, apart from the fact that
substantial reasons speak against interpolating the Antiochene conflict between
Paul and Peter already here, before the second journey, it is not clear why such
a crass construction must be imputed to the author precisely at this point. The
report and the motivation for the separation read very naturally, and the whole
affair—an expression of human nature, as also it could have manifested itself
in the apostolic age—appears to speak for rather than against the veracity of
the one making the report, regardless of his position in relation to the events,
whatever it may have been.

At first, this new undertaking has the character of a journey for the purpose of visitation. [Acts] 16:4 [reports], "As they went from town to town,"
[they visited] the congregations that came into being on the first journey, now
in reverse order: *Derbe, Lystra, Iconium.* According to 16:4, the activity of Paul
and Silas, who in 16:3 were joined by the half-Israelite *Timothy*, consisted in the
communication of the results of the Jerusalem Council. It would be very misguided
to wish to see a proof, in this passage, for the tendency of the author to want
to situate Paul as being especially accommodating to Jewish Christianity. The
point of the journey in 15:36 is very clearly stated; likewise the later passage in
16:5 clearly shows where the author's interest is concentrated, namely, not on
the fight about the law and circumcision, but on the activity and success of the
great apostle in the work of the mission to the Gentiles.

---

45. Holtzmann, *Die Synoptiker*, 386.
46. Barth's manuscript reads: Gal. 15:35–41; corrected by Harnack (?) to 2:11–12; Holtzmann (*Die
Synoptiker*, 386) writes 2:11–14.

The following section, 16:6–8, forms a crux for the exegetes, due to the extreme brevity of the information provided. *Holtzmann* (following Zeller[47] and Overbeck)[48] again presumes intention: "The fleeting brevity of this itinerary has its ultimate purpose in the author's tendency to lead the apostle toward Europe."[49] The only thing not explained in this case is the strange route of the journey. If the author had only had this in mind, then he could have reached his goal more simply and plausibly.

The author's outlook is evidently the following: Paul's plan was to turn west from Iconium (Antioch in Pisidia?), that is, to the heavily populated southwest of Asia Minor, where large cities attracted him, like those that would become so important in the later development, such as Laodicea, Philadelphia, Ephesus, [and] Smyrna, among others; this area, according to the author's usage in 2:9 and 6:9, is called *Asia*.[50] However, this plan fell through: . . . "having been forbidden by the Holy Spirit to speak the Word in Asia" (16:6)—that is, again, as with the first journey, a direct intervention of divine factors in the outward action of the apostle. *Holtzmann's* question "Where on this journey are the prophets that are part of it?"[51] would have appeared strange to the author under any circumstances. Neither he nor early Christianity thought so mechanically about the communication of the Holy Spirit, as if the latter were bound to specific kinds of media. With regard to Paul, the notion of such a limitation seems to me to be out of place (cf., by the way, 13:1!). Here we are dealing with a bit of the eternally irrational, which has always belonged to the essence of genuine religion.

The "Holy Spirit" does not approve of a journey to the west, and so the journey goes "through the region of *Phrygia* and *Galatia*." This is where the great controversy about the location of the latter area arises. It is certain that this passage (16:6) is *not* referring to what is sometimes called South Galatia. It is from there (that is, from Lystra, Iconium, etc.) that Paul comes, or, at least, Phyrgia would be mentioned second.[52] What is rather meant here is the actual northern Celtic Galatia. This is where, in passing, the congregations made known by the Epistle to the Galatians were founded. Having reached the middle point between Mysia and *Bithynia*, they "attempted" to visit Bithynia, but once again the intervention of the mysterious working of the Spirit occurs: "The Spirit of Jesus did not allow them" (16:7); they "passed by" both lands on their right and turned—there was no longer any other option, between Asia on the one hand and the northern lands on the other—toward the west coast in the direction of *Troas*. The author's striking brevity is explainable by the fact that his written or oral sources flowed meagerly, and—we might add, if *Harnack* is proved right—because he saw the moment coming where he himself would be active in the narrative and in a psychologically explicable manner headed for this destination at a somewhat quicker tempo. (At 20:1–4 we also notice a similar urgency in the account, and in 20:5 the "We-Source" begins again.)

47. Zeller, *Origins of the Acts*, 180–81.
48. F. Overbeck, *Handbuch zum Neuen Testament*, 252–53.
49. Holtzmann, *Die Synoptiker*, 386–87: "The brevity of this itinerary resulted from the author's haste in wanting to lead the apostle into Europe."
50. Wendt, *Handbuch über die Apostelgeschichte*, 342.
51. Holtzmann, *Die Synoptiker*, 386.
52. Artificial excuses are given in Weizsäcker, *Apostolic Age*, 230.

In Troas (16:9) there was once again (within a few verses the third!) an occurrence of the work of the Spirit: During the night Paul had a "vision," namely: "There stood a man of Macedonia pleading with him and saying . . . " The content of his request is "Come over to Macedonia and help us." Immediately, in 16:10, the highly disputed "We" appears for the first time: "We immediately tried" . . . ! Harnack expressed the conjecture (in his seminar) that there could have been a very intimate relationship between this "man of Macedonia" from[53] Troas and the highly significant unknown person who came to the same place, who later revealed precisely so much specific interest in and knowledge of Macedonia. A reader who does not allow oneself to be deterred by the somewhat rationalistic coloring of the notion would find that it has a great deal to speak for it. Be that as it may, the perspective of the author in any case is this: *The new phase of the missionary activity will again be started under special divine guidance* (16:10). This notion would not be disturbing, according to early Christian sensibility, even if we wanted to accept a human medium for revelation, for which precisely the book in question shows many examples (cf. 9:17; 21:11; etc.). The passage would then be a new proof that the one speaking here, in all modesty, sees himself as independent and co-called to this great work (16:10; 28:10).

The departure thus takes place by ship. In the seaside town of *Neapolis*, on the Thracian mainland, *the proclamation of the gospel arrives upon European soil.*

They turn toward *Philippi.* The expression "a leading city of the district of Macedonia" (16:12) should be understood with Wendt as "most respected colonial city."[54] Thus respected,[55] according to the view of the author, because in and of itself the city, apart from the *Jus Italicum* awarded by Augustus in 42 BCE, had no claim to any kind of exceptional position.

Contact is established, similar to the first journey, via *Judaism and its religious cult.* There was no synagogue there, as the newcomers correctly surmise; instead there was a "place of prayer," which on account of the necessary cultic washings was "by the river." They go there on the Sabbath in 16:13 (but not at the hour of the worship service) and come upon a few "women who had gathered there." (*Holtzmann*[56] points out, for purposes of comparison, the corresponding Catholic custom.) Again, "a worshiper of God," Lydia, the dealer in purple cloth from Thyatira, is the one who, according to 16:15, was of considerable means and opened her heart up for Paul's proclamation; indeed, she "prevailed upon" the missionaries to accept her hospitality. To understand what happens next, we need to read between the lines to some extent because of what the author forgets to mention (because his attention is concentrated on the miracle stories to come): *over the next few days they preach publicly in the city.* This comes afterward from the mouth of the girl who was possessed, according to 16:17: "These men are slaves of the Most High God {τοῦ θεοῦ τοῦ ὑψίστου is an allusion to the secret cult of the Hypsistarians, disseminated throughout this region}, who proclaim to you a way of salvation" and similarly in the formulation of the complaint before the Praetors in 16:20–21: "These men are disturbing our city . . . and are advocating customs that are not lawful for us." From this

---

53. Harnack (?) wrote "in" above the preposition as either a correction or variant.
54. Wendt, *Handbuch über die Apostelgeschichte*, 344–45.
55. Holtzmann, *Die Synoptiker*, 387; Harnack in seminar.
56. Holtzmann, *Die Synoptiker*, 387.

it comes to light that *the apostles have turned their attention directly to the Gentiles without any additional segue.* The life of that Jewish community evidently only pulsated very weakly, had never produced a synagogue, and as a result Paul had found it better (without breaking with the Jews, as he was staying with one of their number!) to make a direct approach to the Gentiles themselves. (We shall pay attention to this case for the overall evaluation of the question at hand.)

At this point two partially miraculous stories take place: the driving out of the spirit of divination and the freeing of Paul and Silas from prison, which we will not be considering here. But one specific element of the last story is valuable for our purposes: the conversion of the jailer (16:29–30). Even though there are grounds to largely omit the story as mythical, we nonetheless have a case before us where, according to the author writing to Theophilus, Paul *directly addresses the Gentiles.* At least we can say that the narrator had found, if not this one, other similar events in his personal memory or at least encountered it in the tradition and used it here without regard to his otherwise pragmatic manner of doing things. This suffices for emphasizing the special importance of 16:32[–33].

In 17:1–10 Paul is in *Thessalonica*, to which he has traveled via Amphipolis und Apollonia after having been freed from captivity in Philippi. The "We" has once again disappeared, and where Timothy has remained from 16:19–17:14 is not clear either. They go into the *synagogue of the Jews* (17:2) {i.e., the synagogue in this district. According to all the evidence, the Jews in this area were few and far between, with the result that the "district synagogue" satisfied the needs. According to C, along with Harnack (Seminar) and against א A B D Tischendorf,[57] Nestle,[58] and Holtzmann,[59] one should read "the synagogue" [ἡ συναγωγή] instead of merely "synagogue" [συναγωγή], in which the latter variant is understandable from the former, but not the former from the latter. The matter shows that the speaker has knowledge of the area}; "as was his custom," Paul went in and "argued with them from the Scriptures. . . ." Paul's making recourse to the Old Testament shows that the audience consisted primarily of *pure Jews*, whereas the success of his speech shows that a significant number of "devout Greeks" were also present.

Believers are won from both categories, which arouses envy from among the remaining Jews, who attract "some ruffians in the marketplace (Weizsäcker:[60] "a few bad subjects, hanging out on the street") and form a mob (17:5–10), all of which ends with Paul and Silas having to leave the city.

In 17:10–15 we find both in *Beroea*, where they have been transported overnight by the brothers. Here too, immediately upon their arrival, they go to the

---

57. [K. Tischendorf,] *Novum Testamentum Graece: Ad antiquissimos testes denuo recensuit, apparatum criticum omni studio perfectum apposuit, commentationem isagogicum praetextuit Constantinus Tischendorf*, Edito Octava critica maior (Leipzig, 1872), 2:148. (In his reproduction of the Greek text, Barth occasionally adopts the orthographic peculiarities of Tischendorf.)

58. "Nestle" in manuscript, which Harnack (?) corrected to [the spelling in French] Nestlé, *Novum Testamentum Graece cum apparatu critico ex editionibus et libris manu scriptus collecto curavit E. Nestle*, 5th ed. (Stuttgart: Privilegierte Württembergische Bibelanstalt, 1904), 352.

59. Nestle, *Novum Testamentum Graecum*, 389.

60. *Das Neue Testament, übersetzt von Carl Weizsäcker*, 2nd ed. (Freiburg: Akademische Verlagsbuchhandlung, 1882), 242.

synagogue. Apart from that, the circumstances are different: the Jews are willing to speak with them, indeed, they "welcomed the message very eagerly and examined the Scriptures every day to see whether these things were so" (17:11). Here are also *"Greeks"* in attendance, especially women, but also men, though Paul nonetheless still had greater success among those who were born Jewish. As it becomes known in the area, these extremists from Thessalonica follow the same tactic as their comrades from Antioch in Pisidia in 14:19: they come over and stir up the crowds so that the missionaries also need to withdraw from this place. They are brought to the coast, where Paul boards a ship and is led to *Athens* by those who conduct him. The *personal details* given at this point leave a few things unclear: according to 17:14, Timothy, who in Philippi was nowhere to be seen, is now with Paul again, but then remains with Silas "there," meaning[61] in Beroea; from Athens, Paul then summons Silas and Timothy, sending his request via those conducting him (who was that?), to come to him "as soon as possible." The author's information is not the best at this point. What is certain is that the statement about Timothy is to be corrected according to 1 Thessalonians 3. A critical argument cannot be made out of this lapse. Something like this is not impossible even for one who stood temporally closer to his object than, we assume, our own author.

We now come to the interesting section 17:16–34: Paul in *Athens.*

The historical tenability of the account in detail is questionable, as *Harnack* emphasized (in his seminar). If anywhere in the whole book, it is here that the assumption of an *ideal construction* suggests itself, externally at least, because Paul is here for the first time without one of his traveling companions, whose report of the events could be taken into account. At a later point it will be shown to what extent the centerpiece of the section, the so-called speech on the Areopagus, is nevertheless thoroughly valuable. The same thing, however, also applies to the main features of the account about the external events, which is also proven by the detail given at this point, especially 17:34, which certainly could not have simply been made up.

According to the account in 17:17, Paul once again spoke in the synagogue, and indeed, "with the Jews and the devout persons." Nothing counts against the veracity of this entry—apart from the established critical general hypothesis, as always, and the same holds for the following: Paul preached furthermore . . . "also *in the marketplace* every day *with those who happened to be there.*" I only provisionally point out the fact that there is *no connection* between these two dates (Harnack in his seminar). What follows is more problematic: With this sermon in the street or marketplace, "some Epicurean and Stoic philosophers debated with him." They concluded by taking hold of him and leading him to the Areopagus and very politely asking him for information about his teaching (17:19–20). Paul responds to this with his speech. Why is the most important of philosophical tendencies in Athens, the *Platonic,*[62] not mentioned? There can be only one answer: because the author did not wish to see Paul in conflict with them, which also becomes apparent in the speech itself. But if this is especially unlikely, then it is *questionable* whether Paul had debated with the

---

61. Wendt, *Handbuch über die Apostelgeschichte,* 362.
62. Manuscript: "the most important"; "the" was struck out by Harnack (?).

philosophers at all, to the extent that what is meant, as is evidently the case here, are the *heads of the [philosophical] schools*. Only to these could the use of the Areopagus, which formed the central point of public and cultural life, have been available for such a purpose, without further ado.

But apart from these academic philosophers, it was known that there had always been an alleged or actual *philosophy of the streets*, which was directed, unlike the former, not to the educated, but rather to the general public. Paul had already learned by listening to them how one was to behave (17:17b), and a clash with this group is what we most likely have as the historical basis of our account. This is also better suited to the character of the Athenian public, wherein 17:21 applied to the "professors" of the philosophical schools would sound decidedly harsh. The manner in which the existing account could have come about is very simple and explicable without assuming a *dolus*:[63*] the author heard an oral report from Paul about a conflict with Athenian teachers of wisdom. As a Greek who knew the area and in an easy-to-understand idealizing embellishment, he then added the Areopagus, the Stoics, and the Epicureans. The notice at the end about the conversion of the Areopagite (i.e., a member of the court of the Areopagus)[64] is no proof against it, since this is more likely to have been precisely what led the author to specifying this location.

In 18:1–17 we find Paul in Corinth, where he now (18:11) remains *one and a half years*. On this Holtzmann says: "It is essential not merely to show how the mission to the Gentiles was motivated by the stubborn demeanor of the Jews, but rather also how the Gentile authorities on this occasion once again took a position that was beneficial to Paul."[65]

Let us look at this more closely! According to 18:2, Paul finds the Jewish married couple *Aquila* and *Priscilla*, who were driven out of Rome by the edict of Claudius:[66] "Since the Jews constantly made disturbances at the instigation of Chrestus, he expelled them from Rome." It turned out that he "was of the same trade" as they (according to the prevailing rabbinic custom, Paul also had to learn a trade along with his studies), so he took up residence with them as a "tentmaker."[67] Paul thus lived one and a half years with someone who was a Jew by birth, although the author actually forgets to mention that the latter was baptized, which can first be derived from 18:18. Is that an anti-Jewish tendency? Further, in 18:4: Paul spoke every Sabbath in the synagogue "to convince Jews and Greeks"; indeed, in 18:8 even "Crispus, the official of the synagogue, became a believer in the Lord, along with all his household." Yet in between, at 18:6, we hear that here too, heavy opposition arose from the midst of the Jewish community: "They opposed and reviled him." Indeed, Paul got caught up in a previously unfamiliar kind of commotion: "He shook the dust from his clothes" and said: "Your blood be on your own heads! I am innocent. From now on I will go to the Gentiles." That in fact sounds sharp and appears at first glance to justify the accuracy of the Tübingen assessment as few other parallels do. However, the authenticity of the account is one thing, when the

63.* Cf. the translator's footnote above, at n. 39.
64. Holtzmann, *Die Synoptiker*, 393.
65. Holtzmann, *Die Synoptiker*, 394.
66. Suetonius, *Divus Claudius* 25.4.
67. Wendt, *Handbuch über die Apostelgeschichte*, 383.

propounded "motivation for the mission to the Gentiles by the stubbornness of the Jews"[68] is simply a construction of the author's, and another thing when it is given with the matter itself. If it is the first, what then of the Jews who in 18:4 are placed before the Greeks? What, especially, of the synagogue official who converted in 18:8? That certainly does not speak for a general Jewish stubbornness, but on the other hand the fact that the majority of European Jewish community was in fact hostile to Christianity, which is shown by the entire history of the apostolic age (Justin!)[69] and is doubted by no one. The objection to this account ultimately and simply goes back to the thesis that Paul's missionary activity did not begin at all with the synagogue. More on that later. After this break with official Judaism, Paul left the synagogue and went to the house of the "worshiper of God" *Titius Justus*. The meaning of the author is obvious: in order to assemble there with his supporters (*Harnack*[70] assumes a complete relocation, though to me 18:18 seems to speak against this). There Crispus and a number of Corinthians convert. The following night Paul has a *vision* (18:9–10). The Lord appears and encourages him to continue his activities: "For there are many in this city who are my people." In this passage I find nothing of a tendentious antithesis to Judaism. Moreover, what follows does not stand in connection with this quarrelsome appearance in the synagogue: 18:12–17. The Jews use the appointment of a new proconsul in Achaia, *Gallio*; "make a united attack" against Paul; and "brought," that is, ordered him before the tribunal. The Roman, however, rejects having competence[71] in "a matter of words and names and your own laws"; indeed, their leader Sosthenes (identical with the one named in 1 Cor. 1:1?) is beaten up (by the mob or by the Jews themselves?).

"But Gallio paid no attention to any of these things." It is not within the scope of my task to decide whether the report on the scene is, as the Tübinger and others say,[72] political and apologetic. At least, the contemptible response of the proconsul hardly seems to speak for this.

After all this, Paul remains there a little while longer; then he departs, setting out for *Syria*, taking Aquila and Priscilla with him. (In Cenchreae he received the famous haircut, also a *"Rocher de Bronze"* of the critical system,[73] yet with which I cannot impede myself here.) In 18:19 he leaves his companions in *Ephesus*, speaks *in the synagogue* to the Jews, finding (18:20–21) approval and supporters. Then he goes to *Caesarea* (perhaps because the ship traffic did not allow a direct return home to Antioch in Syria? or did he receive bad news from Jerusalem while in Caesarea and therefore make the unexplainable curve?). He goes by land (*he went up*, 18:22, not toward Jerusalem, contra *Wendt, Weizsäcker,*

---

68. Cf. Holtzmann, *Die Synoptiker*, 394: It is necessary at the point to show "how the mission to the Gentiles once more was motivated by the stubborn behavior of the Jews."

69. Harnack, *Die Mission und Ausbreitung des Christentums im den ersten drei Jahrhunderten* (Leipzig: J. C. Hinrichs, 1902), 40–41 n. 3.

70. Barth likely reproduces a view that Harnack propounded in the seminar: Harnack had likely first publicly expressed this interpretation of Acts 18:7 in his *Beiträge zur Einleitung in das Neue Testament*, vol. 3, *Die Apostelgeschichte* (Leipzig: J. C. Hinrichs, 1908), 95–96 n. 1, where he specifies a more general claim made in *Luke the Physician*, 36 n. 1.

71. (Here the German editor notes a textual variant appearing in Nestle, *Novum Testamentum Graece*, 357. Trans.)

72. Cf. Zeller, *Origins of the Acts*, 161–65; cf. also Overbeck, *Handbuch zum Neuen Testament*, 294; Holtzmann, *Die Synoptiker*, 394.

73. Holtzmann, *Die Synoptiker*, 395–96. *Rocher de Bronze* means "something hard to shake."

and *Holtzmann*),[74] greets the community there [in Caesarea] (cf. 21:8–14!), and then journeys by land down toward *Antioch in Syria*. {What is recounted in Gal. 2:11–12 occurs at this point. Why doesn't the author say anything about that? Either he is not in possession of information about it (he is indeed in Macedonia), or, what I consider to be more likely, he doesn't discuss it because it is not germane to his topic (not his tendency!)}

The "Third Missionary Journey"

In 18:23, the book Acts of the Apostles leads us immediately onward. After Paul "spent some time" in *Antioch in Syria*, he sets out anew, and indeed first with the intention of "strengthening the disciples." In 18:23 we see him first in *Galatia* and *Phrygia*, then in 19:1–20 in *Ephesus*. We will have to deal with these accounts later; the foundational missionary activity, which was to be done here, was already taken care of both here and there. But there is already one thing to be mentioned. The point of the Acts of the Apostles should not be misunderstood as if it were supposed to render a chronicle-like enumeration of all the important events in the history of the Christian world. Whoever attempts to treat it as a historical source in this sense will always come up against all sorts of conspicuous gaps and irregularities. This is precisely the case with chapter 19, which receives an especially bad mark from *Weizsäcker*.[75] As a matter of fact and by means of inference, we need to attain a number of things that are important to us.

Here the following point is important: according to 19:10, Paul stays in *Ephesus* for *two years*. According to 19:10b, we need to accommodate this timing without any specific statements being made. From there he generally undertook mission to *southwest Asia Minor*, to catch up on what he had to leave due to the work of the Spirit in 16:6. This is illuminated by 19:22 as well: "while he himself stayed for some time longer in Asia," even if, according to *Holtzmann*,[76] it might have only been a matter of a few days; the emphasis is on a general description of the area. Even clearer, however, is the same fact from 19:26. There, the great accusation of the silversmith Demetrius against Paul runs: "Not only in Ephesus but in almost the whole of Asia this Paul has . . . drawn away a considerable number of people." Understanding "Asia" here to mean the "interior regions" mentioned in 19:1 (according to 18:23, Galatia and Phrygia) does not conform to the already mentioned use of language in Acts. Moreover, according to 14:11–13, there the worship of Artemis was less prominent than other pagan cults, so that it [the interior regions] did not come into question as a trading area for Ephesian industry (19:25–27). "Now after these things had been accomplished" . . . (19:21)—thus, according to 19:20, after the proclamation of the gospel in Ephesus had gained a foothold on the entire west coast—Paul makes the decision to go to Jerusalem via a detour to the Macedonian and Achaean congregations. (I will forgo an investigation into the motive at this point.) In 20:1 he is in *Macedonia* (i.e., likely Philippi); in 20:2 in *Achaia/Greece* (i.e., Corinth), where he remained for three months; and then, because of a plot by the Jews, he was

---

74. Wendt, *Handbuch über die Apostelgeschichte*, 392; Weizsäcker, *Apostolic Age*, 240–45; Holtzmann, *Die Synoptiker*, 395.

75. Weizsäcker, *Apostolic Age*, 328–30, 389–91.

76. Holtzmann, *Die Synoptiker*, 399.

prevented from a voyage at sea and turned around. In *Philippi* he rejoined at 20:5 the subject of the "We"—who in 16:17, precisely at the same location, had become invisible—after the friends listed in 20:4 had joined him (it is unknown where). In 20:7–16 he is in Troas, takes leave in 20:17–38 of the church leaders of Ephesus, who were ordered to come to *Miletus*; and finally in 21:1–16 he reaches Jerusalem via *Tyre* and *Caesarea*.

The Trial

This part of the book does not come directly into consideration since missionary activity is no longer mentioned from chap. 21 onward. Nevertheless, we can still gain a few insights from the text that are relevant to our topic; indeed, we are compelled to do so if we want to achieve a complete picture of how the author wants to sketch Paul as a missionary.

Chapters 21–28 interest us here to the extent that over the course of the presentation of the trial against Paul, they reproduce a number of *Jewish testimonials* against him, which deal in particular with his missionary activity in the Diaspora. In contrast, there are Paul's various *defense pleas*, which we also need to consider in relation to this point. The last section of the book once again—certainly no coincidence—gives an account of an encounter between Paul and Judaism, altogether like the one previously depicted, in *Rome*.

In 21:20–21 the elders of the Jerusalem congregation tell Paul, who is just arriving, that resentment against him is predominant in the "myriad" Jewish-Christian circles in the city [who have been told] ". . . that you teach all the Jews living among the Gentiles to forsake Moses, and that you tell them not to circumcise their children or observe the customs." The statement made here about the Jewish-Christian sentiment against Paul has not been objected to by [higher] criticism! *Holtzmann*: "Full Paulinism certainly also includes the emancipation of the Jews who have become believers from the customs and traditions of Mosaic religion as such."[77] In the pronounced acrimony of the formulation, a good bit of the complaint is certainly nothing but rumor and calumny. But one thing remains: *Paul preached to the Jews in the Diaspora*. Just how precarious the position of [higher] criticism is at this point can be seen by *Holtzmann's* excuse: "Even at this point Acts makes another concession with respect to the actual history, which is dangerous for the depiction of Paul otherwise being implemented."[78]

In 21:27–28, just as Paul wants to complete his Nazirite offering in the temple, *Jews from Asia*, that is, the opponents from his primary mission field, throw the people into an uproar: "Fellow Israelites, help! This is the man who is teaching everyone everywhere against our people, our law, and this place. . . ." This is naturally referring to the proclamation of freedom from the law in the Diaspora. Once again, it is necessary to place a question mark next to the individual statements of the Zealots, for the entire matter is, as the Epistle to the Galatians shows, not plucked out of the air. But at center, this complaint really makes sense only if Paul had actually preached to the Jews in the Diaspora.

---

77. Holtzmann, *Die Synoptiker*, 406.
78. Holtzmann, *Die Synoptiker*, 318.

This becomes even more evident from the plea of the "attorney" Tertullus, who had been engaged by the high priest, Ananias, as reproduced in 24:2–9. There we hear: "We have, in fact, found this man a pestilent fellow, an agitator among all the Jews throughout the world."

I am amazed not to be able to find any close examination of these passages by the Tübingen school or their followers, which are rather more fateful for their critical position than not. Even if one wanted more or less to stipulate all the individual occasions for which this accusation was dropped as being not historical—for which the needed proof has in no way been delivered—at some point still, according to all the rules of assessing sources, this claim, which according to Acts was made from three different sides, must have been made. Otherwise we have to view the author here as the most subtle pragmatist, not just that, but the subtlest falsifier known in the history of literature. That, however, is precisely what has been rejected by the newer critics with respect to *Zeller* and others.

It seems to me that the whole Jerusalem conflict is inconceivable without the preceding mission, which was aimed precisely at the Jews of the Diaspora. Where else would this bitterness against Paul come from? It could not in any way be directed merely at his character as a Christian or as a Christian missionary to the Gentiles or—though there are many years in between—as a fallen Pharisee.

At this point I want to emphasize only two of *Paul's statements*, which are especially characteristic.

One comes in the speech before Felix in Caesarea in 24:19. Paul is complaining about his unjustified arrest in the temple in Jerusalem: "But there were some Jews from Asia—they ought to be here before you to make an accusation. . . ." What is generally present in the three passages mentioned—the Jews "among the Gentiles, everywhere, throughout the world"—is now at this point specified (with reference to 21:27). Is that once again arbitrary guessing or construction? Why does the pragmatic author, who according to the critics was so little concerned with factual information, name not Antioch in Pisidia, Macedonia, or Corinth, where the Jews, according to his account, had been so oppositional, but Asia, precisely from where he was not able to report anything of the sort?!

The issue can be illuminated from yet another side, through the passage at 26:19–20 in the speech before Agrippa: Paul reports on his conversion and its consequences: ". . . declared first to those in Damascus, then in Jerusalem and throughout the countryside of Judea, and also to the Gentiles that they should repent." I dare not decide whether this, with *Holtzmann*,[79] relates to 9:27–29 (whereby a collision with Gal. 1:17–22 looms) or with *Wendt*[80] to 11:30. The fundamental notion that always returns is obviously here as well: first to the Jews, then to the Gentiles.

Finally, I would like to call attention to one factor: The tenor of the Pauline defense pleas is manifestly the following: the gospel that I am proclaiming is not only not the destruction of the religion of Moses and the Prophets but rather its completion and fulfillment (24:14–15; 25:8; 26:6, 22–23; 28:17, 20). This, however, presupposes that a mission to the Jews came first.

---

79. Holtzmann, *Die Synoptiker*, 419.
80. Wendt, *Handbuch über die Apostelgeschichte*, 504.

At the end of this overview, there remains the section 28:17–28, which, as already indicated, was certainly not appended by the author unintentionally to the end of his work, and the story included here can count as a type for everything that has come before it.

Three days after his arrival in Rome, Paul had the "local leaders of the Jews" called together and delivered the speech before them as quoted, whose content can be summarized with his statement: "It is for the sake of the hope of Israel that I am bound with this chain" (28:20). The answer given by the Jews runs: "We have received no letters from Judea about you, and none of the brothers coming here has reported or spoken anything evil about you. *But we would like to hear from you what you think, for with regard to this sect we know that everywhere it is spoken against*" [28:21–22]. For us, this is just as diplomatic as it is puzzling. The first half is in and for itself correct: the Palestinian Jews could not possibly have already informed their fellow Jews in Rome about Paul's arrival. However, what about the rest? *Holtzmann*[81] references Tacitus,[82] where an "immense multitude" of Roman Christians is mentioned, who, as the Epistle to the Romans indicates, are at least in part composed of *born Jews*. On top of this is the passage in Suetonius,[83] already cited, which indicates that the ban by Claudius was most likely caused by the unrest within the Roman Jewish community as a result of the intrusion of the Christian mission. With respect to these dates, is it likely that a Roman Jew could have said, "No one . . . here has spoken evil about you"? (Because this is, as Wendt suggests,[84] implied in these words.)

Is it likely that these local leaders would have still wanted "to hear from you," and that they really didn't know any more about this "sect" than that "everywhere it is spoken against"? It is necessary to answer the question, along with the Tübinger and others, with a "No." The point of the statement is "to characterize the way in which the Jewish community initially related to Paul and were not inimical, but rather unbiased and accommodating at first."[85] It would nonetheless be overreaching to want to conclude from this that an historical impossibility has been proven against the author, that the entire scene is not historical (as *Holtzmann* opines).[86] The assumption that this erroneous statement (such as 17:18) also goes back to the non-presence and lack of orientation on the side of the author has nothing against it except for the generalizing historical perspective exercised by the critical position. A few are convinced by Paul, "while others," evidently the majority, "refused to believe." Then Paul applies the word from Isaiah 6:9–10 to them and opens up to them the fact that salvation has now been sent to the Gentiles.

"They will listen."

Thus, this final story consciously forms a thematic recapitulation of the external course of the Pauline mission as a whole.

---

81. Holtzmann, *Die Synoptiker*, 427.
82. Tacitus, *Annales* 15.44.
83. Suetonius, *Divus Claudius* 25.4.
84. Wendt, *Handbuch über die Apostelgeschichte*, 59.
85. Wendt, *Handbuch über die Apostelgeschichte*, 540.
86. Holtzmann, *Die Synoptiker*, 427.

B. Results

The Pneuma

The missionary activity takes place under constant pneumatic influence.

We have seen, in the detailed examination of the Pauline mission lying behind us, that according to the author writing to Theophilus, at the decisive turning points an extra-human and extra-worldly principle intervenes in the external events, especially in steering or modifying all the doings of the acting persons.

The ideas about it are always concrete, but formally they render a colorful picture of different points of view.

The Lord, *Jesus himself*, embodies this mysterious power in the story of Saul's conversion (9:3–7, 10–18, 27; 22:6–21; 26:13–19; cf. 1 Cor. 9:1; 15:8; Gal. 1:15–16) and the vision of 18:9 in Corinth.

The *Holy Spirit* speaks directly (13:1–3) to the five prophets, to Paul and Silas in the famous passage of 16:6 and as the spirit of Jesus in 16:7, and to Paul alone in 20:23. We hear about *dream visions* in 16:9–10; 18:9; 27:23–24.

Finally, the Spirit speaks through the mouth of *prophets*: 11:28 and 21:11, through Agabus; 15:32, through Judas and Silas; 19:6–7, through the disciples of John in Ephesus; 21:4, through the disciples of Tyre; 21:9, through the daughters of Philip.

It would be easy to draw parallels from the first part of Acts and the Gospel of Luke. This is a peculiar feature always noticeable in Lukan theology. Here, only the following features need to be considered:

The whole historical picture of the author writing to Theophilus is supported, even conditioned, by the various effects of Pneuma (the Spirit); notably, they occur throughout the entire book, regardless of whether the work speaks from the perspective of "we" or not.

The canon of *Holtzmann* has already been mentioned: "*One writes in time and for time.*"[87] Accepted! Does the intellectual world, in which the author obviously lives, correspond to the enthusiastic age of the seventies or eighties of the first century, which was quite receptive to all supernatural effects because of the resurrection tradition and the eschatological expectations? Or to the time of the ancient self-constituting catholic [universal] church, which is already becoming suspicious of those spiritual effects (Didache!)?[88]

Perhaps it's rather the former.

The Independence of the Pauline Mission

The effectiveness of Paul takes place independently of but in agreement with the original community in Jerusalem and with the free involvement of Jewish and Gentile Christian helpers.

The special investigation of the relevant problems falls into the domain of other studies. Still, I cannot easily ignore this part of my task since it plays an important role in the positions of the criticism.

---

87. Holtzmann, *Die Synoptiker*, 322.
88. See esp. Didache 11.7–12.

Regarding the background of the Pauline mission, Acts 9:10–30 should be consulted: under the leadership of the Damascene Christian Ananias, the final conversion of Saul, who had previously snorted threats and murder, takes place. In 9:19–25 he [proclaims Jesus in the synagogues of Damascus to hearers' amazement, but his life is threatened]. In 9:26–30 he comes to Jerusalem but is received with suspicion. This then changes through the intercession of Barnabas, and from then onward "he came in and out of their place" and even acts in the name of the Lord and contends with the local Hellenists. As a result of persecutions by the latter, he goes to Tarsus, from where, as we have seen in 11:25–26, he is brought by Barnabas to Antioch.

I cannot go into the very complicated examination of the details of Galatians 1:16–2:10, about which so much ink has already flowed. One thing is enough: the thought, clearly emphasized here and there, is this: *Paul's position* over against Cephas, James, and others is a sovereign one: the relation of the two sides to each other is neither one of dependency nor one of enmity but that of a *friendship from afar*. The same goes for the rest of the narrative of the Acts of the Apostles: in 13:2, the Jerusalemite Barnabas and Saul [from Tarsus] are sent out together [from Antioch of Syria], but in the course of the narrative, Saul, who was initially second, visibly takes center stage more and more (13:13, 16, 43, 46, 50; 14:9; etc.) indeed in 15:39 there is a separation of the two, and from that point forward the principle applies: "March separately, strike together."[89] In 15:40 Paul recruits *Silas*; in 16:2, *Timothy*; in 16:10, the *unknown of Troas*; and so forth.

From then on, *the independent position of the Pauline apostolate vis-à-vis Jerusalem* is implicitly a presupposition of the account of the Acts of the Apostles. One passage seems to make a big exception here: I mean the equally notorious section 15:1–33, which deals with the *Jerusalem Apostolic Council*, in its relation to Galatians 2:1–10. Various details remain controversial here, such as the question of whether Paul only negotiates with the acknowledged leaders (Gal. 2:2) or also with the apostles and elders (Acts 15:6), and whether only Paul and Barnabas, or also Peter and James, have represented the cause of freedom. All the accusations of the Tübingen-oriented criticism against the author of our book are finally concentrated on one point, namely, the result of the entire negotiation.

Galatians 2:6, 10   Acts 15:28–29

Galatians 2:6, 10
Those leaders contributed nothing to me. On the contrary . . . They asked only one thing, that we remember the poor.

Acts 15:28–29
It seemed good for . . . us to impose on you no further burden than these essentials: that you abstain from what has been sacrificed to idols and from blood and from what is strangled and from fornication.

---

89. For the sources of this summary of Helmuth von Moltke's strategic principles, cf. G. Büchmann, *Geflügelte Worte: Der Zitatenschatz des deutschen Volkes*, revised by G. Haupt and W. Hofmann (Berlin: Haude & Spener, 1972), 739.

At first, this much must be said: if it is, as it seems at first sight and as the critics incessantly assert, *that these texts are mutually exclusive*, giving preference to the Galatians passage, then a more than fatal light falls on the value of the Acts of the Apostles as a source. Indeed, its whole depiction of the Pauline missionary activity becomes suspicious. For it is impossible that one who personally knew Paul could have attributed to him such a rationale for his propagandistic activity and thus set himself in direct opposition to his clearly expressed standpoint.

Now, in contrast to the exaggerated estimation of the report in the Letter to the Galatians, there is *Harnack's* objection about its character: "[It] is not so much written down as flung down pell-mell; such is the vigour with which it seeks to emphasize the final result, that its abrupt sentences render the various intermediate stages either invisible or indistinct."[90]

But then it is, above all, *questionable* whether it really was a basic principle in the opinion of the author of Acts of the Apostles. The criticism asserts it, because its whole position is based on the hypothesis, and in the older generation specifically we also find the hypothesis of so-called "union Paulinism."[91]

Against that the following is to be said: If that were the case, then the rest of Acts would have to show further traces of this "basic principle."

However, this is not the case, with the sole exception of 16:4, where it has already been shown that the matter does not play an essential role. The "Apostolic Decree" was not considered either generally or by the author of Acts to be of fundamental importance for the mission, but rather as a kind of social rule of wisdom, issued from the hardship of the situation, which was soon overtaken by events even though it may have lasted longer in individual Christian circles. The fact that it was materially based on an early Christian—even Pauline— view, is ensured by Romans 14; 1 Corinthians 5; 6:12–20; 8:1–13; but neither for Paul nor for the author of Acts did the matter have more than secondary significance. In this light, I myself explain the non-mention in Galatians 2: Paul does not consider putting the decree, as a correlating legal minimum with an absolutely obligatory character, in place of the discarded rite of circumcision. Neither does the author of Acts want this; otherwise he would not have let Paul circumcise Timothy in 16:3.

In the rest of Acts, we hear nothing that resembles a dependence of Paul on the pillars in Jerusalem. (Fortunately, the tax for the Jerusalem poor is not in Acts, but in the letters; otherwise it would probably be interpreted like that!) Consciously and independently, not listening to people, only listening to the Lord's voice, we see him walking through history. More and more the focal point of interest shifts westward; from chapter 15 onward, the Jerusalem elders are no longer mentioned (except in 21:18 and there in a less praiseworthy role!). It is the lone Paul who captures the interest of the author.

Could the author of the Acts of the Apostles have proceeded like this at the beginning of the second century, if he had been a zealous, unionizing pragmatist

90. A. Harnack, *The Mission and Expansion of Christianity in the First Three Centuries*, trans. and ed. James Moffatt, 2nd ed. (London: Williams & Norgate, 1908), 1:60.

91. See, e.g., Hilgenfeld, *Einleitung*, 543–614, esp. 599–601.

(Zeller) or a good-natured but somewhat ignorant compiler (Holtzmann)? [That is] hardly believable!

The author of Acts, from the point of view of his tendency, must have had an interest in giving more precise information about what was, for him, such an important relationship to the Pauline mission, more than the information that we actually have.

This author—at least from his temporal position and as a chronicler of the apostolic age, into which Holtzmann and the critics in general have made him again and again—should not have restricted his interest in this way to Paul.

The fact that the one [account centered on Paul] is happening and the other [chronicle] is not happening seems to me to be explainable only when the author is placed closer to the events themselves, both locally and temporally, than hitherto has been the case.

From the Jews to the Gentiles

"Paul evangelizes earnestly, testifying both to the Jews and Greeks repentance and faith" (20:21).

Thus we have arrived at the recurring position of the author writing to Theophilus, which we know from the previous discussions, "that everywhere [*this sect*] *is spoken against!*" (see Acts 28:22). In addition to the parallelism between Paul and Peter, in addition to the Jerusalem Council and Decree, we have here one of the main pillars of the critical edifice before us.

It will be appropriate here, because the matter touches the core of our theme, to let the criticism speak for itself through some of its modern representatives more than has been the case so far (I disregard the older generation since their positions here are essentially contained in those of recent scholars).

Does the missionary sermon of Paul originate from the synagogue?

Weizsäcker's answer is strangely ambiguous. At first, I read: "According to narrative of the Acts of the Apostles, this is true for Paul everywhere; it has always been the regular way." But soon thereafter, it sounds different: "It cannot be denied that the habit of beginning in the synagogue and passing from there to the Gentiles has the character of a suspicious regularity, which is also tied to a dogmatic premise of the author." This suspicion is then proven by a number of Pauline passages, to which I will return shortly.[92]

Jülicher sounds much sharper: "According to the Acts of the Apostles, Paul always visited the synagogue first on his missionary travels, and only when his compatriots rejected the crucified Messiah did he think he was now justified in dedicating himself to the Gentiles; an unthinkable principle for Paul, who had so clearly recognized the work to the Gentiles as the task God had set for him."[93] I see the most unreserved and detailed explanation of the alleged unhistoricity of the account of Acts of the Apostles in *Holtzmann*: "Whoever wrote (the following texts) could not always conceive of the fundamental

---

92. Weizsäcker, *Apostolic Age*, 92–93.
93. Jülicher, *Einleitung*, 351.

question as dependent on the circumstance that the Jews must have forfeited their right again and again."[94]

Again, let's just say: If the critics are right and if the method used in the Acts of the Apostles is indeed unhistorical, then we could not help but judge the author either as a pragmatist in the bad sense or at least as a very poorly oriented writer of the late period.

However, after weighing the pros and cons for a long time, I did *not* come to this conclusion.

This will need to be justified in two ways: first by a recapitulative examination of the individual data of the Acts of the Apostles, then by comparison and criticism of the Pauline texts cited by both sides.

1. First, let us mention those passages in the Acts of the Apostles in which, according to Holtzmann, "explicit reference is made to the principle" "on which the practice in question is based":[95] Acts 13:46–47; 18:6; 28:26–27. Here in Pisidian Antioch, there in Corinth, finally in Rome, we hear Paul make the statement in the face of Jewish stubbornness: *The Jews had to be preached to first, but since they are hardened, I turn to the Gentiles with the gospel.*

In the opinion of the critics, this is the unbearable template, the schema into which the author forces the real story for the sake of his dogmatic prejudices.

In fact, according to the author writing to Theophilus, the missionary activity of Paul, in most cases, now takes place in this framework.

a. *Paul first goes to the synagogue:* Acts 13:5 in Salamis, 13:14 in Pisidian Antioch, 14:1 in Iconium, 16:13 in Philippi, 17:2 [in Thessalonica, 17:10] in Beroea, 17:17 in Athens, 18:4 in Corinth, 18:19 and 19:8 in Ephesus, and finally 28:17 in Rome, which, in the spirit of the author, is also to be consulted here.

At first, I have only to deal with the possibility of an internal motivation for the method that is indisputably present here. As *Weizsäcker* and *Holtzmann* also admit, this method cannot be denied a priori, because—I use the precise words of the latter—"this practice of always first visiting the synagogue of the Jews and using it as a base for effectiveness among the Gentiles *is the most natural approach, especially since the worshipers present offered the most favorable starting point."*[96]

To date, the critics have not put forward anything effective against the inner probability of this view. Rather, we have seen that *Weizsäcker* is half-heartedly prepared to acknowledge it.

But now the other side of the matter:

b. *Paul sooner or later encounters opposition and persecution in the synagogue:* attested at 13:45 in Pisidian Antioch, 14:2 in Iconium, 17:5 in Thessalonica, 18:6 in Corinth, 19:9 in Ephesus, and 28:21–25 in Rome. Does this position of Judaism correspond to the actual situation in those decades or not?

c. *Paul therefore turns away from the synagogue and goes directly to the Gentiles.* This is explicitly mentioned in 13:46–48 for Pisidian Antioch, in 18:6 for Corinth, in 19:9 for Ephesus, finally in 28:26–28 for Rome. Was this transition the most natural approach or not?

94. Holtzmann, *Die Synoptiker*, 317.
95. Holtzmann, *Die Synoptiker*, 317.
96. Holtzmann, *Die Synoptiker*, 316.

But now, above all, the numerous cases have to be taken into account, where the matter *proceeds differently* according to the report of the Acts of the Apostles.

a. *Paul does not evangelize in the synagogue but directly among the Gentiles*: so 14:8 in Lystra, 14:21 in Derbe, 14:25 in Perga, 15:4–6 in Phrygia and Galatia.

b. *Paul evangelizes in the synagogue and is heard among the Jews*: 17:11 in Beroea, 18:20–21 in Ephesus, and in general among more or less numerous individuals!

c. *Paul evangelizes in the synagogue and independently also among the Gentiles*: 13:7–12 in Paphos, 16:32 in Philippi, 17:17b–18 in Athens.

In view of all these discrepancies, I cannot see that there is a "scheme" here in the sense of the critics. If that were the case, the author should not have broached it in this way over and over. But what is not done for the sake of a theory? I am not at all surprised that *Hilgenfeld*[97] wanted to argue for a *special source* for those reports that deviated from the "scheme"! It could not be more clearly demonstrated that understanding history in terms of set patterns is much less present on the part of the author writing to Theophilus than on the part of his modern critics.

The view of history that the author of the Acts of the Apostles has before him is the following on this issue:

a. As a rule Paul begins his missionary activity with the Jews and only because of their recalcitrance goes from them to the Gentiles.

b. He is mostly rejected by the Jews, though often partially and often completely heard among them.

c. Where circumstances suggest it, he addresses the Gentiles directly, in some places at least independently of the synagogue, but also without contradicting it.

But now to what *Weizsäcker* calls the *"dogmatic premise"*[98] of the method. It is indisputable that the generally hostile behavior of Judaism and the consequent transition of the mission from them to the Gentiles take up the interest of the author to a high degree and that this relationship is a *main theme* of his book. Otherwise he would not keep coming back to it over and over again; otherwise he would not close with that typical passage 28:17–28. The underlying dogmatic thought is obviously the following: after the Messiah has been preached to the Jews, they have rejected him; now salvation comes to the Gentiles.

Is this thought historical? In this case, was this also the opinion of Paul?

2. We thus come to the statements of the Pauline Letters about our subject. The last question asked is not difficult to answer in view of Romans 2 and 9–11 and Galatians 3–5, and the critics will also have to affirm it. It becomes more difficult, however, when the other question arises: *Did Paul really follow the practice indicated in Acts*: "the Jews first, then the Gentiles"?

Jülicher and *Holtzmann* answer "impossible" with a certain emphasis. Their main arguments, to name only the most effective ones for the sake of brevity, are as follows: Above all, some passages of the Epistle to the Galatians:

---

97. Hilgenfeld, *Einleitung*, 584–85; see also Holtzmann, *Die Synoptiker*, 316.
98. C. Weizsäcker, *Das apostolische Zeitalter*, 93.

1:16, "It pleased God . . . to reveal His Son to me that I might preach him among the Gentiles."

2:7, ". . . having seen that I have been entrusted with the gospel for the uncircumcised"

2:8, ". . . for he who worked through Peter, . . . worked through me for the Gentiles. . . ."

2:9 ". . . right hand of fellowship given to me and Barnabas that we [should go] to the Gentiles and they however to the circumcised . . ."

Certainly, this division of labor was the important result of the Jerusalem Council. If you would like to, you can with *Holtzmann* call it a "program."[99] (If it was the author of the Acts of the Apostles, one would probably speak of a "set template"!) However, there is no point in focusing on this as much as the critics do. In my opinion, the contrast [involving the] "uncircumcised-Gentile" here is not to be understood in terms of national religion, but geographically, that is, Paul among the *Diaspora*, the original apostles in *Palestine*. In any case, Paul would not have been the man forced to accept such an imposed scheme, according to the view of the critics (if here one could speak of such a thing!), thus being robbed of the most important and often the only possible starting point for his mission to the Gentiles through such a formal convention.

The passage just referred to by *Holtzmann*, Romans 1:14, is only apparently effective here: "I am a debtor both to Greeks and to barbarians, both to the wise and to the foolish." The emphasis (Paul is addressing a predominantly Gentile Christian community) is on the contrast *educated–uneducated*. The national designation Greeks and barbarians in itself plays a quite subordinate role.

One of the most important authorities for the critical position is, finally, *1 Thessalonians 2:1–2*, about which especially Weizsäcker[100] talks in detail. There the apostle gives a report of his first appearance in Thessalonica, with which, according to Weizsäcker's opinion, Acts 17:1–10 is supposed to be incompatible, because [in 1 Thess. 2:1–2] "there is no mention of preaching to the Jews, nor of any intervention of the Jews present in Thessalonica in the course of the matter." Harnack, on the other hand, referred (in the seminar) to 1 Thessalonians 2:14. Here, however, Weizsäcker[101] seems to me to be right in asserting that ἴδιοι συμφυλέται [your own fellow citizens] are to be understood as the Gentile compatriots of the Christian Thessalonians, compared with the Ἰουδαῖοι [Jews] in Palestine, who behaved similarly in opposition to the communities there. The readers that Paul addresses in the First Letter to the Thessalonians are obviously Gentile Christians (1:9). Nevertheless, it is to be denied that the two versions are mutually exclusive. Acts 17:4 reports about a πλῆθος πολύ [great multitude] of converted Greeks. Acts 17:5–10 reports the struggles that Paul has to go through in preaching the gospel, ἐν πολλῷ ἀγῶνι [amid much conflict], according to 1 Thessalonians 2:2. Perhaps the house of Jason, who is suddenly mentioned in Acts 17:5, has formed a center of the Gentile Christian preaching to which 1 Thessalonians 2:3 is referring. But in any case, it can be

99. Holtzmann, *Die Synoptiker*, 317.
100. Weizsäcker, *Das apostolische Zeitalter*, 93. [ET: *The Apostolic Age of the Christian Church*.]
101. Weizsäcker, *Das apostolische Zeitalter*, 49, 93, 115; cf. *Das Neue Testament*, trans. C. Weizsäcker, 281.

explained from the information of Acts 17, τινες [Ἰουδαίων] ἐπείσθησαν [*some* Jews were obedient; cf. 17:4], that in the letters Paul finds no reason to consider them specifically.

I refrain from addressing the other instances, especially those compiled by Holtzmann.[102] These are Galatians 3:28; 4:21–23; Romans 2:28–29; 3:29–30; 4:11, 16; 1 Corinthians 1:24; and others. They all express the same thought: Jews and Gentiles are equal before God. But it cannot be disputed that the author of Acts shared this view! In any case, these texts do not add anything against the probability of the practice described in Acts. On the other hand, we have very specific indications that *confirm* them:

I count *Romans 9–11* especially [in this category]. The tenor of these chapters is very clear: The Jews are excluded from salvation insofar as they themselves reject it; but for Jews *and* Gentiles alike, the Messiah has died. "God has not rejected his people" (11:2). "By their wrongdoing, salvation comes to the Gentiles" (11:11). "So they are enemies for your sake according to the course of the gospel, but darlings for the sake of the fathers according to their election" (11:28; etc.). Does not the author writing to Theophilus view Judaism as corresponding to all this, from his angle of vision?

Furthermore, could the man who speaks of his people with such heart-moving fidelity in Romans 9:1–5 pass by the Jewish communities of the Diaspora without having made at least an attempt to suggest salvation in Christ to them where it was possible? Then the classic passage from *Romans 1:16*: "But I am not ashamed of the gospel, δύναμις γὰρ θεοῦ ἐστιν εἰς σωτηρίαν παντὶ τῷ πιστεύοντι, Ἰουδαίῳ τε πρῶτον καὶ Ἕλληνι [it is the power of God for salvation to everyone who has faith, to the Jew first and also to the Greek]."

Finally, on another occasion Holtzmann complains[103] of the "incessantly invoked word" of 1 Corinthians 9:20, which says the same thing with all desirable clarity: "ἐγενόμην τοῖς Ἰουδαίοις ὡς Ἰουδαῖος, ἵνα Ἰουδαίους κερδήσω. τοῖς ὑπὸ νόμον ὡς ὑπὸ νόμον, μὴ ὢν αὐτὸς ὑπὸ νόμον, ἵνα τοὺς ὑπὸ νόμον κερδήσω [To the Jews I became as a Jew, in order to win Jews. To those under the law, I became as one under the law, though I myself am not under the law, so that I might win those under the law]."

From all this, I want to forgo further arguments; I cannot draw any conclusion other than that Paul himself also considered the missionary work to the Jewish people to be part of his life's work.

His personality and activity were by no means as clear as they should have been, in the opinion of the "Tübingen and related directions" of thought.

To sum up: The important role of the propagation of the gospel among the Judaism of the Diaspora, its rejection of the gospel, and the apostle's consequent transition from it to the Gentiles—what this role plays in the *historical pragmatism* of the author writing to Theophilus is unmistakable.

On the other hand, the hypothesis of the Tübingen School and its successors, taking the portrayal by the Acts of the Apostles as no longer mere pragmatism but a tendentious *construction*, must be *rejected*, because the above-mentioned

102. Holtzmann, *Die Synoptiker*, 317.
103. Holtzmann, *Die Synoptiker*, 407.

presentation was internally consistent and also corresponded to the view of Paul himself.

But more than that. Here again it must be said: A writer of the Acts of the Apostles, as the critics imagine him, could not have described the events in this way.

The union politician of *Zeller* should not have narrated everywhere the bitter contradiction of the Jews, and above all he should not have concluded his work by rejecting the Jewish people.

The uninformed chronicler *Holtzmann* should at least have carried out his "scheme" more comprehensively and consistently than he actually did.

Both are *not* the case here either.

Chapter II: The Missionary Communities

The material under discussion here falls to a large extent in the domain of another paper ("[Government and Church] Constitution and Worship according to Acts."[104] Nevertheless, I may not bypass it since it forms an integrating component of the material needed to establish a well-rounded picture of the missionary activity of Paul, so far as it may be obtained from the book of Acts.

Nevertheless, I will apply a few constraints that, it seems to me, arise from the standpoint of my theme, "Planting and Care of the Communities." By these communities, I am referring exclusively to the *Pauline missionary communities*, according to the book of Acts. Therefore, the communities of Tyre, Caesarea, Cyprus, and, above all, Syrian Antioch and Rome are *not* under consideration, even though Paul seems to have had, in part, very intimate and interesting relationships even with them.

The missionary communities to be discussed are the following:

a. in *Eastern Asia Minor*: Iconium, Lystra, Derbe, Antioch of Pisidia, Perga, Galatia, and Phrygia
b. in *Macedonia:* Philippi, Thessalonica, Beroea
c. in *Achaia/Greece:* Corinth, Athens
d. in *Western Asia Minor:* Ephesus, Troas

{The organization corresponds entirely to *Weizäcker*'s four "Provinces."[105]}

The question that must be examined is this: What may we discern from Acts about *Paul's founding and organization of these communities*? How is *the relationship between the communities and the apostle* structured from then on?

I will then try in turn, at the very least in outline from case to case, to draw parallels to the data of the Pauline Letters and to engage with the critical problems, so far as this seems necessary to me in the context of a specialized portrayal such as this.

---

104. According to Barth's notes (Excerpt III, 418), the theme (to be dealt with at the seminar session on February 21, 1907) read in its entirety: "What may we infer from Acts about the constitution of the church and the worship practices in Jerusalem and in the Diaspora?"
105. Weizäcker, *Das apostolische Zeitalter*, 190–99, esp. 195.

A. Historical Overview

Eastern Asia Minor

The much-discussed question "What and where is Γαλατία [Galatia]?" necessarily arises right at the outset, since the order of our material must be so arranged according to the answer.

We may assume that it is the genuine region of Galatia *on the upper Halys River*, which since 280 BC was settled by Celts. Among recent scholars, this judgment is made by *Hilgenfeld*,[106] *Holsten*,[107] *Holtzmann*,[108] *Schürer*,[109] *Lipsius*,[110] *Schmiedel*,[111] and others.

Or, conversely, Galatia is *the Roman province by that name* and hence comprises, in addition to those [central] regions, the lands of southeastern Asia Minor: Lycaonia, Pisidia, and so on. *Renan*,[112] *Hausrath*,[113] *Weizsäcker*,[114] *Pfleiderer*,[115] *Wendt*,[116] *Zahn*,[117] among others, have decided for this interpretation.

If the latter is true, then we would have to speak only about Galatian congregations (in the wider sense of the term [in that province]).

I will forgo treading upon the well-known rows of arguments and counterarguments that have been addressed especially by *Holsten*[118] and *Hausrath*.[119] The problem is such that, if not even new findings or excavations can offer irrefutable testimony, it will be very difficult for one or the other view to be proven. "Enough words have been exchanged,"[120] and new points of view will no longer be produced from the sparse available data. Subjectively conditioned assumptions about probability will generally be what decides on either side for the time being.

Absent better instruction, I have decided in favor of so-called *North Galatia*. What led me to it were the details of the book of Acts, whose language usage suggests it, as even *Hausrath* admits[121] (one should take note of the sequence of locations in 16:6 and 18:23). Whoever holds fast to the South Galatia hypothesis must either reinterpret these or reject them as completely unhistorical, for

---

106. Hilgenfeld, *Einleitung*, 250–52.

107. C. Holsten, *Das Evangelium des Paulus*, vol. 1, *Die äussere Entwicklungsgeschichte des paulinischen Evangeliums*, part 1, *Der Brief an die Gemeinden Galatiens und der erste Brief an die Gemeinde in Korinth* (Berlin: G. Reimer, 1880), 35–43.

108. Holtzmann, *Die Synoptiker*, 235.

109. E. Schürer, "Was ist unter Γαλατία in der Ueberschrift des Galaterbriefes zu verstehen?," *JPTh* 18 (1892): 460–74.

110. R. A. Lipsius, *Briefe an die Galater, Römer, Philipper*, HC 2.2 (Freiburg i. B.: J. C. B. Mohr, 1891), 1–3.

111. W. Schmiedel, "Galatia. B. Galatians of the Epistle and Acts. II. Case for the North Galatian Theory," in *EBI* (1901), 2:1596–616.

112. E. Renan, *Histoire des Origines du Christianisme*, vol. 3, *Saint Paul* (Paris, 1869), 48–52. [ET: *The History of the Origins of Christianity*.]

113. Hausrath, *Neutestamentliche Zeitgeschichte*, 135 n. 2. [ET: *A History of New Testament Times: The Time of the Apostles*.]

114. Weizsäcker, *Das apostolische Zeitalter*, 196–97, 228–29.

115. Pfleiderer, *Das Urchristenthum*, 57–58.

116. Wendt, *Handbuch über die Apostelgeschichte*, 341.

117. T. Zahn, *Einleitung in das Neue Testament* (Leipzig, 1897), 1:123–38. [ET: *Introduction to the New Testament*.]

118. Holsten, *Das Evangelium des Paulus*, 35–43.

119. Hausrath, *Neutestamentliche Zeitgeschichte*, 135 n. 2. [ET: *A History of New Testament Times: The Time of the Apostles*.]

120. J. W. von Goethe, *Faust* 5.214 (prologue to the play).

121. Hausrath, *Neutestamentliche Zeitgeschichte*, 135 n. 2.

which I find no cause, despite the arguments taken from Galatians. Certainly, it seems to me weightier than *Weizsäcker*[122] wants to concede that neither in Acts is the southern countryside called Galatia, nor in Galatians are the Galatians called Lycaonians or the like. Even if we would have to assume that the book of Acts originated at the start of the second century, its details would show, at a minimum, that in those days (cf. 2 Tim. 4:10 the variant Γαλλίαν [Galatia]!) one had Celtic North Galatia in mind. Judged from the standpoint of Galatians, the observation likewise treated very contemptuously by *Weizsäcker*[123] may not be without merit, that the distinctive characteristics of the Celtic tribes—known, for instance, from Julius *Caesar*[124]—turn up again in a striking way in the depictions Paul gives of the manner of the Galatians (Gal. 1:6; 4:12–20; 5:1–7; etc.).

Here we will, therefore, initially have to deal with the communities of southern Asian Minor and then, separately, of the northern, that is, the genuinely Galatian communities.

Antioch in Pisidia. In the synagogue of Pisidia in [Acts] 13:14, Paul initially won contact with Jews and proselytes. The apostles speak to them and succeed in persuading them (ἔπειθον αὐτούς [urged them], 13:43). On the next Sabbath, σχεδὸν πᾶσα ἡ πόλις [almost the whole city] (13:44) comes to hear the apostles, which rouses the envy of the Jews, and so Paul turns to the Gentiles, who were glad and believed (13:48). Yes, δι' ὅλης τῆς χώρας [throughout the region] (13:49) the Word is carried. Apparently now a longer time passes. Then the Jews agitate the upper circle of the city, and Paul and Barnabas must escape from their region. οἵ τε μαθηταὶ ἐπληροῦντο χαρᾶς καὶ πνεύματος ἁγίου [And the disciples were filled with joy and with the Holy Spirit] (13:52). Paul and Barnabas now travel around Iconium, Lystra, and Derbe. Then they return, and are at last back in Antioch. ἐπιστηρίζοντες τὰς ψυχὰς τῶν μαθητῶν, παρακαλοῦντες ἐμμένειν τῇ πίστει. . . . χειροτονήσαντες δὲ αὐτοῖς κατ' ἐκκλησίαν πρεσβυτέρους, προσευξάμενοι μετὰ νηστειῶν παρέθεντο αὐτοὺς τῷ κυρίῳ εἰς ὃν πεπιστεύκεισαν [There they strengthened the souls of the disciples and encouraged them to continue in the faith. . . . And after they had appointed elders for them in each church, with prayer and fasting they entrusted them to the Lord, in whom they had come to believe] (14:22–23).

Already here we must point out a circumstance that stands out in all the texts under consideration: The details found in Acts regarding the missionary communities are generally, aside from the history of their founding in the narrowest sense, extremely succinct and mentioned only in passing. For the time being, a reference to the fact is sufficient, which is hardly superfluous as a memorandum in advance.

For the moment I will put together the picture that results from the portrait of Acts sketched above.

In Pisidian Antioch an ἐκκλησία [church] (14:23) formed itself from the πιστεύοντες [believers] (13:48), composed of former *Jews, proselytes* (13:43), and *Gentiles* (13:44), whose members as such are called μαθηταί [disciples] (13:52; 14:22). At its head stand the πρεσβύτεροι [elders] (14:22–23) chosen by the apostles and consecrated with prayer and fasting. According to 13:44, 48, 52, in this

122. Weizsäcker, *Das apostolische Zeitalter*, 232.
123. Weizsäcker, *Das apostolische Zeitalter*, 228.
124. Julius Caesar, *Civil War* 2.1.3–4.

community an especially *joyful enthusiasm* for the new faith had prevailed. Or would the emphasis of the last point, which does not recur in such a marked way, be rather an anticipation, in that the author wanted to imply that this is how it happened everywhere?

Iconium. In 13:52, Paul, driven out of Antioch, has arrived here. He preaches in the synagogue, and the consequence is ὥστε πιστεῦσαι Ἰουδαίων τε καὶ Ἑλλήνων πολὺ πλῆθος [a great number of both Jews and Greeks became believers] (14:1). Perhaps we may infer from 13:49 that Paul had already prepared the ground from Antioch. Despite the opposition of the Jews (14:2), they remain in Iconium, successfully engaged for a longer time. Then, however, they must go, but even here, according to 14:23, an ἐκκλησία [church] has come into being, consisting of μαθηταί [disciples] (14:22) or ἀδελφοί [brothers] (16:2) of *Jewish* and *Greek* origins (14:1). As in Antioch, at its head are the πρεσβύτεροι [elders] (14:23). Recommended (ἐμαρτυρεῖτο) by the communities at Antioch and Lystra, Timothy joins the entourage of Paul [later], in 16:2.

Lystra. Having fled from the threats of the Iconian Jews, Paul and Barnabas have now come further southeast, toward the Cilician hill country, and now live εὐαγγελιζόμενοι [proclaiming the good news] in the little villages of Lycaonia and their surroundings (14:6–7). Now that strange scene takes place in Lystra in 14:8–19 in the wake of the lame man's healing, which shows so clearly the state of religiosity at that time. Thanks to the intervention of the Antiochene and Iconian Jews, it comes to an end in that Paul must also leave here. But he achieved his goal: according to 14:23, here there is now also an ἐκκλησία [church] of μαθηταί [disciples] (14:20, 22) or ἀδελφοί [brothers, believers] (16:2), who, together with the others, will be visited again at the beginning of the second journey (16:1).

Derbe. Here the same picture again: The apostles proclaim the gospel, μαθητεύσαντες ἱκανούς [making many disciples] (14:21). Without a doubt what has been said in 14:22–23 applies to this community as well. A "Gaius from Derbe" is named in 20:4 among the entourage of the apostle.

Perga. On the return trip from Attalia to Antioch in Syria, the missionaries stop off at this place λαλήσαντες . . . τὸν λόγον [speaking the Word] (14:25–26). Is an ἐκκλησία [church] founded here as well? Apparently, because otherwise the city would scarcely have been explicitly named.

From all these communities one gets the impression that a lively Christian life has begun in them. They also do not seem to have been lacking πολλαὶ θλίψεις [many persecutions] (14:22) (esp. from the side of the Jews!), yet the encouragements of Paul (14:22; 15:41) have not missed their goal. αἱ μὲν οὖν ἐκκλησίαι ἐστερεοῦντο τῇ πίστει καὶ ἐπερίσσευον τῷ ἀριθμῷ καθ᾽ ἡμέραν [So the churches were strengthened in the faith and increased in numbers daily] (16:5). That is the gratifying last report that is made about them.

Galatia and *Phrygia.* After this second visit to the southern congregations, Paul moves northward: διῆλθον δὲ τὴν Φρυγίαν καὶ Γαλατικὴν χώραν [They went through the region of Phrygia and Galatia] (16:6).

What happened here? *Weizsäcker* calls the assumption that the first missionary work named in Galatians has taken place here "unfruitful," because there is "no talk of a stayover or a mission at all, but only of a passing through."[125]

---

125. Weizsäcker, *Das apostolische Zeitalter*, 230.

From this point of view, then, the note of 18:23 (Paul travels from Antioch in Syria διερχόμενος καθεξῆς τὴν Γαλατικὴν χώραν καὶ Φρυγίαν στηρίζων πάντας τοὺς μαθητάς [passing through the region of Galatia and Phrygia, strengthening all the disciples] (cf. 19:1) stands "completely in the air"[126] for him. Of course, this view is a consequence of his *presuppositions*. If the author of Acts wanted to be a *chronicler of the time of the apostles*, then, if he was a contemporary, it is very puzzling why he speaks so little of the Galatian communities, which for Paul were so important. But if he were an epigone, then either ignorance or a bias would be irrefutably established and 18:23 would have to be understood with *Weizsäcker* as a reference to Galatians.[127]

The question is simply whether this presupposition is correct. My observations up to now have led me to *reject* it. *Paul evangelized in 16:6 in Galatia and Phrygia.* Apart from 18:23—which, in our judgment of the *value* of Acts as a source, would be sufficient—it seems to me that, even without explicit details, it follows from the context of 16:6 that the entire trip in 16:6–8 is understandable only if Paul has preached here and there. Or is it possible to imagine the man, as if he had silently carried out this strange voyage in zigzag, listening only to the promptings of the Spirit? With the intention λαλῆσαι τὸν λόγον ἐν τῇ Ἀσίᾳ [to speak the word in Asia] (16:6), he moved on from Pisidia, and so on. Now the πνεῦμα [Spirit] steers him otherwise. Will he have, for this reason, broken off the intended missionary activity?

"But why this brevity?" someone will ask. In an earlier investigation I pieced together a few motives.[128] The primary one is this: *The author pushes forward*. The gospel is now native to Asia Minor; the course of events with the founding of the communities there has been described several times. Now he is in a hurry to come further, toward Macedonia, about which so many grand things were reported. On the other hand, it may be gathered that he had *no precise news* from the events of 16:6 in Galatia. For the south, Timothy, who was a native there, was the given informant, whereas for the north, such a person was evidently lacking.

In any case it should be noted that no incongruity exists between 16:6 and 18:23; 19:1; and that, on the other hand, both passages are confirmed by the statement in Galatians (4:13) of Paul's visiting there twice.

A parallel in the "we" passages, which confirms my view in any case, will be discussed further below.

Now, however, someone will object: *Why is there no description or mention at all of the Galatian conflict over circumcision*, which, according to Paul's letter, moved these communities so deeply? Is this not conjuring away (erasing) the sure sign that the author worked there, either being intentionally conciliatory or doing so unintentionally because of ignorance?

Hardly so. In a chronicle, of course, these events may not be left out without justifiably awakening one or the other suspicion. In itself, however, the book of Acts of the Apostles is simply no chronicle: what it intends to relay is the history of the first confrontations of Christianity with the Jewish and Gentile world,

---

126. Weizsäcker, *Das apostolische Zeitalter*, 230.
127. Weizsäcker, *Das apostolische Zeitalter*, 230.
128. See above, 118.

while little more than a few names and traces can be taken from it regarding the internal history of the communities.

So without forcing the argument, we can say: the author knows of the Galatian conflicts, but simply because they do not belong to the theme that he undertook, he has no reason to deal with them here.

Macedonia

By the vision of *Troas*, it has become clear to Paul where the πνεῦμα [spirit] intends to lead him: with Silas, Timothy, and the narrative subject of the "we," he travels from Asia Minor to the coast of Macedonia.

Philippi. We don't need to review the course of events that take place here. As for the success of the mission, let me once again point out that from 16:17, 20 one should infer from 16:15 the following: They preached to *Jews* and *Gentiles* in that place. The author was content to report a few special cases: in 16:14–15 the conversion of *Lydia* and her household; in 16:30–34 that of the jailor; for both, it is explicitly said that they were *baptized* (16:15, 33). Already in 16:40, ἀδελφοί [brothers] are mentioned, so apparently at least the kernel of a community formed there—indeed, according to 16:17[–18], Paul stayed πολλὰς ἡμέρας [many days] in the city. That is also the presupposition of 20:1–2: Paul comes from Ephesus to Macedonia and travels through the countryside παρακαλέσας αὐτοὺς λόγῳ πολλῷ [speaking many words of encouragement to them]. That the Philippians are also, perhaps primarily, to be counted among the αὐτοί [they] is rather self-evident since the author named Philippi πρώτη τῆς μέριδος Μακεδονίας [first of the district of Macedonia] (16:12).

Thessalonica. Paul preaches with success in the synagogue and here too wins ἀδελφοί τινες (17:6, 10) [some brothers] of the *Jews*—a πλῆθος πολύ [large number] who are *Gentiles*, including οὐκ ὀλίγαι [not a few] noble women (17:4). I have already attempted a discussion of 1 Thessalonians 2 above.[129] From these ἀδελφοί [brothers] a few names have been preserved for us, like *Jason* (17:5, 6, 9), in whose house (17:7) the gatherings likely occurred. Furthermore, we hear in 20:4 of the Thessalonians Aristarchus (cf. 19:29) and Secundus, who accompanied Paul on the last trip from Macedonia back to Asia Minor.

Beroea. Here the *Jews* are εὐγενέστεροι [more noble in character] than in Thessalonica; πολλοὶ ἐξ αὐτῶν [many of them] become believers and οὐκ ὀλίγοι [not a few] of the noble *Greek* women and men (17:12). So now there are ἀδελφοί [brothers] (17:14) here as well, of whom one is named in 20:4: Sopater, son of Pyrrhus.

Achaia/Greece

Athens. Here especially, the scarcity of information leaves nothing to be desired. Paul's missionary enterprise apparently failed for the most part (17:32), and he must have been glad to get away from his opponents unmolested. At least, his stay is not useless: τινὲς ἄνδρες κολληθέντες αὐτῷ ἐπίστευσσαν [But some of them joined him and became believers], among them Dionysius, the judge

129. See above, 134–35.

on the Areopagus, and a certain Damaris καὶ ἕτεροι σὺν αὐτοῖς [and others with them] (17:34). Presumably 20:2 refers as well to a visit to this small community. With great certainty Weizsäcker declares of this passage: "Everything bears the stamp of the mere appropriation of well-known things and no trace of real events."[130] "Credat Judaeus Apella" [Let Apella the Jew believe it]![131] He owes us proof for this assertion, for the fact "that Paul never spoke of it" (referring most likely to the Letters to the Corinthians) is by no means "decisive."[132]

Most likely it is a case of an insignificant beginning. However, it is not very plausible that Paul had completely missed such an important city on the way from Macedonia to Corinth or that he had received no approval there at all.

Corinth. Paul preaches in the synagogue with initial success: ἔπειθέν τε Ἰουδαίους καὶ Ἕλληνας [trying to persuade Jews] (18:4). Then there is this counterattack of the Jews who remain unbelieving, and Paul relocates his preaching to the house of *Titius Justus* (18:7). Κρίσπος δὲ ὁ ἀρχισυνάγωγος ἐπίστευσεν, . . . καὶ πολλοὶ τῶν Κορινθίων ἀκούοντες ἐπίστευον καὶ ἐβαπτίζοντο [Crispus, the official of the synagogue, became a believer, . . . and many of the Corinthians who heard Paul became believers and were baptized] (18:8). Paul remains there one year and six months (18:11) διδάσκων . . . τὸν λόγον τοῦ θεοῦ [teaching the word of God], apparently with success, which we may conclude from the promise made to him by the κύριος [Lord]: . . . λαός ἐστί μοι πολὺς ἐν τῇ πόλει ταύτῃ [There are many in this city who are my people] (18:10).

Weizsäcker's criticism here too is directed primarily against "the whole of Paul's initial and continued preaching to the Jews."[133] We have already dealt with this question at length.[134] I will just point once more to places like 1 Corinthians 1:22, 23; 9:20; and the like, that, at least in general, confirm the narrative of Acts regarding the origins of the Corinthian community: first Jews, then Greeks. It is also evident from our report in 18:8 that the latter ultimately form the majority, as implied, for instance, in 1 Corinthians 12:2. The effectiveness of the Alexandrian *Apollos* (cf. 1 Cor. 1:12; 3:4–9) is mentioned episodically in Acts 18:27–28.

Now the question might arise again: why is there no talk of the events that occupy Paul so deeply in Corinth—not even in 20:2, when Paul visited the community again—of the σχίσματα [divisions] in 1 Corinthians 1:10–17, and of the false teachers in 15:12 and 2 Corinthians 10:7–8 (etc.)? Did the author know nothing about it, or does he once again, with irenic intention, cover these things with the mantle of love?

Neither is the case. Rather, like the Galatians' conflict, these conflicts did not belong to what he wanted to relay. If his report gives the impression that there weren't such things at all, it is due to his literary aim rather than factual pragmatism.

---

130. Weizsäcker, *Das apostolische Zeitalter*, 255.
131. Q. Horatius Flaccus, *Sermones* 1.5.100; See Büchmann, *Geflügelte Worte*, 551.
132. Weizsäcker, *Das apostolische Zeitalter*, 255.
133. Weizsäcker, *Das apostolische Zeitalter*, 259.
134. See above, 128–36.

Western Asia Minor

Ephesus. In 18:19–21 Paul comes to Ephesus for the first time, but only associates temporarily with the Jews. In 19:1, then, he visits for a second time, coming from Galatia.

In 19:2–7 he succeeds initially in bringing the *"disciples of John the Baptist"* to join with the rest of the Christian community. Then he works for three months in the synagogue (19:8) and, after disagreements with the Jews (19:9), for two years in the σχολὴ Τυράννου [hall of Tyrannus] (19:9–10). Paul's person seems to have exercised δυνάμεις οὐ τὰς τυχούσας [extraordinary miracles] (19:11–12), which the author reports with obvious interest; the same goes for Paul's collision with Jewish exorcists (19:13–16), which ends with the shameful defeat of the latter and a new success within the community: Those who have become believers, who earlier practiced περίεργα [magic], bring their magic books and burn them, with a value of 50,000 drachma (19:17–19).

Οὕτως κατὰ κράτος τοῦ κυρίου ὁ λόγος ηὔξανεν καὶ ἴσχυεν [So the word of the Lord grew mightily and prevailed] (19:20).

Clearly, the Ephesian community has been especially thriving and developing, as the speech at Miletus later shows (20:17–38). The μαθηταί [disciples] (19:1, 9, 30; 20:1, 30) are made up of former *Jews* (18:19; 19:10; 20:21), *Johannine Christians* [*Johanneschristen*] (19:5), and *Gentiles* (19:10; 20:21). At their head stand the πρεσβύτεροι [elders] (20:17), among whom the specially addressed ἐπίσκοποι [overseers] (20:28) probably occupy a preeminent position. Perhaps a kind of *church discipline* has already been exercised, as these eager burners of magic books demonstrate: ἐξομολογούμενοι καὶ ἀναγγέλλοντες τὰς πράξεις αὐτῶν [confessing and disclosing their practices] (19:18). Paul taught, however, "publicly and from house to house" (20:20) and "did not cease night or day to warn everyone with tears" (20:31).

Even *outwardly*, the community seems to have been of some standing. The *Asiarchs* are called ὄντες αὐτῷ φίλοι [friends to him] (that is, to Paul; 19:31). The attitude of the town clerk (γραμματεύς, 19:35) testifies to the same fact.

Of course, on the other hand, there is no shortage of strong opposition, which once even puts Paul's life at risk because, despite the warnings of his friends, he wants to confront the fanaticized crowd in the theater (19:30–31). This is probably the event that Paul himself refers to in 1 Corinthians 15:32 as θηριομαχία [fighting with wild beasts].

In the activity of the apostle in Asia, as mentioned in 19:10, we may think of the founding of the communities of *Laodicea* and *Colossae*.

Troas. The reports about this community are highly interesting in numerous ways. First of all, in 16:9 an overnight stay by Paul himself is mentioned, but *missionary activity is not mentioned*. According to the standard by which *Weizsäcker* measures 16:6 (see above), such a thing would not have happened here either. But now we have in 20:7–13 a narrative (a piece of the so-called "we" source, reliable even according to the critical view!), which clearly presupposes an already founded community. It is irrelevant whether this founding happened in 16:6 or eventually on the return trip: in any case, its beginning is not mentioned by the author. The literary practice appearing in the parallel texts

Acts 16:6; 18:23; 19:1; and
Acts 16:9; 20:7–13,

not only shows, therefore, that the same author is at work here and there, but also enables us to make the historical conclusion *that mission and church plantings have occurred even when they are not explicitly mentioned.*

The report in 20:7–13 also gives us an illustrative account of the way we should think of the *early Christian assemblies.* The timing already is remarkable: the Christians come together ἐν τῇ μιᾷ τῶν σαββάτων [on the first day of the week] (20:7). Is this a coincidence? If not, we have here (cf. 1 Cor. 16:2; Rev. 1:10) the beginnings of our Sunday observance. The service takes place *at night,* in a ὑπερῷον [upper room], which is equipped with lamps (20:8). The next purpose is κλάσαι ἄρτον [to break bread] (20:7, 11), which, according to the straightforward presuppositions of 2:46 and 1 Corinthians 11:20–21, is part of each instance of a Christian worship service. As can be seen from 20:11, the action is framed by edifying lectures of the apostle (20:7, 9, 11), whose first half extends until midnight and the second half all the way ἄχρι αὐγῆς [until dawn].

By now we've essentially exhausted the information given in Acts concerning Paul's communities. It remains for us to comment on it, to examine how the findings relate to our other results.

B. Results

First of all, the *formal observation* that, above all, imposes itself, which has already been hinted at several times, is summarized correctly by *Holtzmann:* "The internal side, all that Paul has done as the leader and guardian of his communities, appears only in fleeting notes; and often, precisely where one would have most expected it, [it appears] almost not at all."[135] In view of this fact, must we conclude with him that "such a method seems conceivable and natural only when the memory of the meaning of the questions of the apostolic age has completely faded"?[136] Absolutely—that is, if the author of the letter "to Theophilus" wanted to write a history of the apostolic age. That this is not the case, however, is shown just as clearly by the other fact recognized by *Holtzmann,* that the author of Acts was "for the most part"—we say: *only*—interested in "the outward success of the apostolic journey, the extensive growth of the Christian cause."[137]

The fact that he, as a writer, works in a skillful and deliberate manner in composition and presentation is what most critics tell us; but why do they always demand that he should have talked of such things that did not matter at all to his literary task, which according to *Harnack,* was to show that *vexilla regis prodeunt*[138] did not matter to him at all?!

As we have seen in detail, his task was to leave to the side the internal, though still important, events in Galatia and Corinth. *Wendt* defends him as follows: "We must assume that he thinks that the events, because of their unpleasant

---

135. Holtzmann, *Die Synoptiker,* 318–19.
136. Holtzmann, *Die Synoptiker,* 318.
137. Holtzmann, *Die Synoptiker,* 318.
138. Harnack, *Lukas der Arzt,* 116 n. 1; regarding the processional hymn by Venantius Fortunatus, which begins with these words [The royal banner forward goes], see H. Lausberg, "Vexilla Regis prodeunt," in *LThK,* 2nd ed. (1957–68), 10:760. [ET for Harnack: *Luke the Physician.*]

character, should not be handed down in his account of the ideal development of the Church in its early days."[139] This is equally *inaccurate*, because elsewhere we see that he does not steer clear of events of a very unpleasant character (6:1; 13:13; 15:2, 38–39).

Acts is everywhere a history of beginnings, to which, however, these internal church disagreements no longer belong.[140]

The same applies to the scarcity of information about church constitution and worship practices. These are given only episodically and always in connection with the history of mission. Even the speech at Miletus is only seemingly an exception, since it (as *Harnack* said in the seminar) may be regarded as a solemn look back not only on the Ephesian stay, but also on the entire missionary activity of Paul.

To what extent do the forms of government, especially the church offices, presupposed in the reports of Acts correspond to historical reality? That question would have to be discussed in a broader context and does not really belong here. I am simply hinting at how I see the situation.

Weizsäcker[141] criticizes these statements, especially the installation of πρεσβύτεροι [elders] (14:23; 20:17) with reference to the [major] Pauline Epistles, where such do not occur. In fact, in Philippians 1:1, for example, only the ἐπίσκοποι καὶ διάκονοι [overseers and deacons] are addressed.

I have to object as follows. Precisely from *Weizsäcker's* remarks on the subject, it becomes clear that our precise knowledge of it is concentrated in a narrow space. Precisely in the oldest time we are dealing with here, the terms and names seem to have been, if not fluid, at least variable. It is therefore not possible to build such a canon from the meager conclusions that we can make here and there.

The most probable thing seems to me, especially in view of the data of the Pastoral Epistles, that in the earlier time the title πρεσβύτερος [elder] was *a collective name for the Christian* (administrative) *offices in general*. Thus, it would not be impossible for Paul to have addressed the individual ranks in Philippians 1:1, while the collective term "presbyter" was also used at the time for both.[142]

The information of Acts then fits into this framework, too, in that, as already mentioned, the presbyters of Ephesus in 20:28 are addressed in part as the ἐπίσκοποι of the community of the Lord, who were appointed by the Holy Spirit.

Yet another controversial point, which more concerns the *worship*, may be mentioned briefly, namely, the status and meaning of *baptism*. In 16:15, 33; 18:8; 19:5 it is mentioned that the entry into the Christian community was outwardly marked by βάπτισμα [baptism].

Weizsäcker takes exception especially to the passage in 19:2–6 (the Johannine Christians), "according to which the fulfillment of baptism involved the laying on of hands, *in which the communication of the Spirit is effected* and which is carried out by the apostles."[143] The historical Paul allegedly knew nothing of this.

---

139. Wendt, *Handbuch über die Apostelgeschichte*, 416.
140. Harnack's comment in the margin next to this paragraph: "Good!"
141. Weizsäcker, *Das apostolische Zeitalter*, 606.
142. Harnack's marginal comment next to this sentence: "Good!"
143. Weizsäcker, *Das apostolische Zeitalter*, 552.

To respond: Of the passages cited by *Weizsäcker* for his assertion, 1 Corinthians 12:13 and Galatians 3:27 (cf. 4:6) testify that the view of Paul also has a certain affinity with the ideas of Acts 19:2–6. But then it must be emphasized that, as far as Paul is concerned, this is a quite singular case, which also plays an essential role in the theology of the author writing "to Theophilus" and thus has to be understood from there.

In the other cases, no significant observation can be made as to the inner meaning of ἐβαπτίσθη [was baptized]. In any case, from this point [in history] one cannot prove that it should be clear "how far off the representation of Acts already lies."[144]

Finally, even with regard to the *personal relationship* of the apostle to the missionary communities, Acts does not give us more than a few hints. Corresponding entirely to what we know from the letters, Paul, even after their founding, remains the faithful adviser and friend of his communities (14:22; 15:36; 18:23; 20:2, 19–21; etc.) and also cares about their future (20:29–30). But his position toward them is sovereign. He does not want to be a pecuniary burden to anyone. Paul reluctantly accepts hospitality (16:15), but he generally seeks to feed himself by his own hands (18:3; 20:33–35; cf. 1 Cor. 4:12; 9:12–13; 1 Thess. 2:9).

Finally, we may now draw the further conclusion: A *writer at the beginning of the second century* or even at the time of Trajan and Hadrian, who wrote "from the times and for the times,"[145] *could not have proceeded in this way*.

He would need to have had an interest in dealing more fully with the ecclesial past than is the case here. In particular, the establishment of ecclesiastical offices, which began to consolidate and differentiate themselves so markedly in the time to which he is supposed to belong, should have received a completely different consideration.

And certainly, references to the internal story would not have gone missing—one thinks of the *false teachers* who are by now mentioned everywhere—as is the case here, except for the isolated passage 20:29–31. All this cannot be explained either by the hypothesis of ignorance or by the other hypothesis of the harmonizing tendency of the writer [*unionistische Tendenzschreiberei des Verfassers*], but only by the fact that he wanted to describe the triumphant advance of the gospel and its taking root in Asia and Europe, but not present a "history of the early days" of the Christian communities.

Chapter III: Missionary Preaching

The question that concerns us here is of the most central importance. It is this: What, according to the writer to Theophilus, was the content of the Pauline Diaspora sermon?

Before we attempt to examine the question, there is a formal *preliminary question* not to answer but merely to pose provisionally. On various occasions the book of Acts gives us shorter or longer descriptions of the content of Paul's

---

144. Weizsäcker, *Das apostolische Zeitalter*, 552.
145. Holtzmann, *Die Synoptiker*, 322.

proclamation to Jews and Gentiles. The question that must be addressed here a priori, as with all such written documents of antiquity, is *to what extent the afore- mentioned speeches and words attributed to Paul constitute an authentic historical account.* To pose the question differently: Is the missionary preaching depicted in the book of Acts the product of Paul, or is it partly or entirely the product of his historiographer?

Either way, the answer will depend on the overall assessment of the book. We will venture an answer only after completing such a detailed examination. Just a few general considerations should concern us here.

We have to *dismiss* or to approach with the greatest caution on a case-to- case basis the opinion of the older scholarship (*Meyer!*)[146] that the existing texts as a whole a priori are *authentic reproductions* of the Pauline speeches, either literally or in the main features. First, because the analogy of all ancient literature speaks against it, I need mention only the names of Thucydides, Titus Livius, Sallust, and so on. (The speeches of Jesus in the Synoptics, whose evolution was different, are the exception, as *Jülicher* correctly emphasizes.)[147] Moreover, there are also internal reasons. We have cases such as the Athens speech in Acts 17, where, according to the narrative, Paul is entirely alone. Who is supposed to have conveyed to the author the finely arranged "Are- opagus" speech? On other occasions, companions certainly were with him, in which case we cannot rule out the possibility that they made synopses of his sermons for the author. But is it believable to think of these men or even Paul himself as kind of parliamentarian reporter? The closest thing to the idea of an actual reproduction is with the speech at Miletus in Acts 20 because of its direct relationship with the "we" source. Nevertheless, following *Wendt,*[148] it too can only be understood at most as a reproduction "based on accurate reminiscences by Luke of a speech of Paul given in Miletus at the time." In any case, it is not reliable as a presentation that can be treated like a simple source and must therefore first be examined with the same caution as the other speeches.

The stance of the *critics* in this matter is quite self-evident, given their pre- suppositions. *Jülicher* assesses these speeches without further ado as "(more or less) free inventions of the author."[149] "The possibility that these speeches are authentic in the modern sense is out of the question."[150] "In a rhetorical work of art, the historian lets his main characters portray themselves and their time."[151] Apart from the points that I have already stated, his main argument for this opinion is as follows: "The Paul of these speeches has nothing more in common with the one who is well known to us in thought and expression from many letters than any believer could have in common with him."[152]

---

146. Meyer, *Kommentar über das Neue Testament* (1835), 6 (more cautiously in the 2nd ed. [1854], 10; the 3rd ed. [1861], 12; and the 4th ed. [1870], 12–13).
147. Jülicher, *Einleitung*, 352.
148. Jülicher, *Einleitung*, 423.
149. Jülicher, *Einleitung*, 351–52.
150. Jülicher, *Einleitung*, 352.
151. Jülicher, *Einleitung*, 353.
152. Jülicher, *Einleitung*, 352.

Similarly, *Holtzmann* critiques the material in question as "the product of the writer *ad Theophilum* not only formally but also materially."[153] The missionary preaching of Paul "merely contrasts . . . monotheism and the purer Jewish ethos with paganism and deals with the general themes of Jesus' messiahship and resurrection."[154]

All details will have to be examined later. Here we are only concerned with presenting the opposing points of view. According to the older (*apologetic*) writers, the book of Acts was to be regarded without hesitation as a source for the authentic Pauline teaching.

According to *Wendt*, at the least 17:22–23 and 20:18–19 would constitute "faithful traditions, as far as their central content is concerned."[155]

According to *Jülicher, Holtzmann,* and the like, the Paul of Acts would not readily be the historical Paul.

Our book includes *three major Pauline sermons,* taken from the three missionary journeys and the three most important Pauline missionary regions:

Acts 13:16–41 in Pisidian Antioch to *Jews* [and proselytes]
Acts 17:22–31 in Athens before *Gentiles*
Acts 20:18–35 in Miletus before *Christians*

This arrangement, as *Holtzmann* without any doubt correctly observes, witnesses to the "artistry of the composition" of the author, but it should be uncontroversial that art does not necessarily mean artifice, as he seems to assume.[156]

In addition to these three speeches, several further passages need to be included here as well, in order to obtain a clear picture of the author's concept, memory, or tradition of the Pauline teaching. In this regard I am thinking of the more detailed sections such as 14:15–18 (speech at Lystra) or 22:2–21; 24:10–21; 26:2–33 (trial speeches), and finally of an entire series of more or less significant incidental references and allusions.

The method of presentation must be different here, where it is a matter of speech and ideas, than in the first chapter, where it involved external events and conditions. While I could easily proceed chronologically there, here the thetic-argumentative procedure must be applied, not in the form of dogmatic loci, which would give a very scholastic quality to my work and would not be adequate to my task, because neither Paul nor the writer *ad Theophilum* was a systematic theologian! But rather [I proceed this way so] that I might pursue several essential features of the teaching ascribed to Paul, arrange various features, and thereby try to achieve a comprehensive picture of what comprises the "Pauline" type of teaching in our book. Finally, I will need, with the individual moments, to show whether and to what extent those individual pictures and finally the entire picture correspond to or contradict the authentic Pauline doctrine, so far as this is possible by implication, as is necessary here.

153. Holtzmann, *Die Apostelgeschichte,* 314.
154. Jülicher, *Die Apostelgeschichte,* 314–15.
155. Wendt, *Handbuch über die Apostelgeschichte,* 19.
156. Holtzmann, *Die Apostelgeschichte,* 315.

This procedure will also shed new light on the above-mentioned preliminary question, which perhaps will enable us to attempt to answer it differently
than previous scholars did.

A. Historical Overview

At first, something purely external: In the kind of collective designation for the
proclamation of Christ that Paul brought to Jews and Gentiles, various conceptions intersect and complement one another.

The Pauline preaching is intended above all to be λόγος τοῦ θεοῦ [word
of God]; thus 13:5, 7, 44, 46, 48, 49; 16:32; 17:13; 18:11; or βουλὴ τοῦ θεοῦ
[will of God], 20:27. As such, its content is determined by the χάρις θεοῦ
[grace of God], 13:43; 20:24; or λόγος τῆς χάριτος [word of grace], 14:3; 20:32.
Grace exists as λόγος τῆς σωτηρίας [word of salvation], 13:26; "to show" ὁδὸς
σωτηρίας [the way of salvation], 16:17; and is mediated through the person
of Jesus, thus as τὰ περὶ τοῦ κυρίου Ἰησοῦ χριστοῦ [the things concerning the
Lord Jesus Christ], 28:31; λόγος κυρίου [word of the Lord], 13:49; 15:35, 36;
19:10; διδαχὴ τοῦ κυρίου [teaching of the Lord], 13:12; or ὁδὸς τοῦ κυρίου [way
of the Lord], 18:25.

We find simply λόγος [word] in 16:6; 17:11; 19:20; 18:5; cf. 18:8; διδαχή [teach-
ing] in 17:19; and ὁδός [way] in 19:9; 22:4.

Finally, what for us is the most common expression: That which Paul offers
Ἰουδαίοις καὶ Ἕλλησιν [to Jews and to Greeks] should be "good news" for them,
εὐαγγέλιον, as in 13:32; 14:7, 15, 21; 15:[7]; 16:10; 17:18; 20:24 [cf. 15:35]; or (following the Synoptic perspective) βασιλεία τοῦ θεοῦ [kingdom of God], 19:8;
28:23, 31; or simply βασιλεία [kingdom], 20:25.

I point to this *juxtaposition*. Is this matter more easily clarified if we locate the
emergence of the book at a time when there was fluidity among these terms and
concepts and they were as yet unclarified, as is the case in the older writings of
the New Testament canon? Or at a time in the Christian church when they were
condensed into precisely delimited formulas (e.g., λόγος [word] in Johannine
circles, or ὁδός [way] in Jewish-Christian circles, as in Didache!)?

Pre-Christian Religiosity

*The religious contents of the diverse publics up to now are comprehended as the given
and necessary basis for the Christian proclamation and accordingly shape how the apostle establishes a connection.*

A. For the preaching to the Jews, this means of connecting takes the form of
scriptural proof, the classic definition of which I find to be, for example, 28:23: . . .
πείθων τε αὐτοὺς περὶ τοῦ Ἰησοῦ ἀπό τε τοῦ νόμου Μωυσέως καὶ τῶν προφητῶν [to
convince them about Jesus both from the law of Moses and from the prophets].
This same express relationship to the Old Testament or to an individual part
of it is found in 13:17–22, 27, 32–41; 17:2, 11; 24:14; 26:6–7, 22; 28:20. The fundamental idea is that there is salvation already in the Old Testament, although
only *veiled* as prophecy, but potentially everywhere and especially *prepared*
through the developing history of the people of Israel. With Jesus, the period
of *fulfillment* has now begun, and whoever recognizes the Old Testament as

authoritative must consequently also worship him as the long-promised *Messiah*, "the hope of Israel" (28:20).

According to the author writing ad Theophilum, this is how *Paul thinks* and obviously how he sees it himself, in that, as in 17:11, the Jews in Beroea are manifestly praised: "They examined the Scriptures every day to see whether these things were so." The idea here is virtually that because Christ is already prophesied, thus included in the Old Testament, his messiahship can be *deduced* through diligent study of the Old Testament codex. This entire procedure has become very strange to us. That period had no consciousness, nor could have had it, that such exegesis necessarily becomes *allegorical*. Rather, this method was readily *taken for granted*, and Paul also used it extensively and unhesitatingly in his letters (most noticeably in Gal. 4:21–30).

For our case it should be noted that this method of scriptural proof has its history; from the first writings of the New Testament, where it is common, we undoubtedly notice an increasing tendency in the direction of allegorizing, which reaches its high point in the catechetical school of Alexandria. It also seems not clear to me that the author of the book of Acts, who permits Paul to use this method, might not be closer to the Paul of the letters than to Justin or even to [the Epistle of] Barnabas, for example, in whose proximity, however, he must be placed, according to the critics! On the contrary, his use of the Old Testament is actually quite restrained, compared to Paul himself, and with a few exceptions (e.g., 13:34), natural and unforced, and mostly reminiscent of the manner in which the Synoptics treat the Old Testament.

B. Of greater interest to us is how the connection with the *Gentiles* takes place. Here, naturally, the appeal to the well-known worship book of the Jewish people would have neither appeal nor effect, except for a few of the educated, at most; the apostle had to proceed on the basis of general human ideas. As I see it, there are three [general ideas] that the author of the book of Acts attributes to Paul with this intention:

1. Heretofore, God permitted the Gentile peoples to go their own way, in contrast to Israel; but he has also *witnessed to them* about himself *in nature*, 14:17: καίτοι οὐκ ἀμάρτυρον αὐτὸν ἀφῆκεν ἀγαθουργῶν, οὐρανόθεν ὑμῖν ὑετοὺς διδοὺς καὶ καιροὺς καρποφόρους, ἐμπιπλῶν τροφῆς καὶ εὐφροσύνης τὰς καρδίας ὑμῶν [Yet he has not left himself without a witness in doing good, giving you rains from heaven and fruitful seasons, and filling you with food and your hearts with joy].

2. The Gentiles presently worship false gods, to be sure, but *inasmuch as [Gentiles] are human beings, there is placed in their soul the pull to the one true God.* This feature shows in the Athenian speech, which is correctly praised as classical by Curtius,[157] especially 17:26–28. According to the Gentile idea, from one man originate the inhabitants of the entire earth; God directs and controls them; the goal is, as the text continues—here it is impossible not to think of Spinoza and Schleiermacher—that they should ζητεῖν τὸν θεόν, εἰ ἄρα γε ψηλαφήσειαν αὐτὸν καὶ εὕροιεν, καί γε οὐ μακρὰν ἀπὸ ἑνὸς ἑκάστου ἡμῶν ὑπάρχοντα, ἐν αὐτῷ γὰρ ζῶμεν καὶ κινούμεθα καὶ ἐσμέν [search for God and perhaps grope for him

---

157. E. Curtius, *Paulus in Athen*, in *Sitzungsberichte der preussischen Akademie der Wissenschaften*, 1893, 925–38, esp. 925–28, 938; reprinted in E. Curtius, *Gesammelte Abhandlungen* (Berlin: Hertz, 1894), 2:527–43, esp. 527–31, 543.

and find him—though indeed he is not far from each one of us. For "In him we live and move and have our being"] (which *Luther* splendidly and aptly translates: "in him, we live, and move, and are"). The text continues with the quotation of the Cilician poet Aratus, τοῦ γὰρ καὶ γένος ἐσμέν [For we too are also his offspring].[158] This means that, by virtue of our capacity as human beings, there is something divine in us that points beyond us and to God, to whom we are essentially related, again entirely in the Augustinian sense of *Ad te nos creasti, Domine . . .* [We are created toward you, Lord . . .].[159]

3. *Moreover, the Gentiles have heretofore sought a relationship with God with the right notion but along a false path* [as in 17:22: κατὰ πάντα ὡς δεισιδαιμονεστέρους ὑμᾶς θεωρῶ] [I see how extremely religious you are in every way]. It is not lost on them that, above or other than the Hellenistic world of gods, there is something higher. In Athens, Paul encountered an altar with the inscription:

ΑΓΝΩΣΤΩ ΘΕΩ [To an unknown god]

{The existence of such altars ἀγνώστων θεῶν [to unknown gods] is attested by Pausanias,[160] Philostratus,[161] and Diogenes Laertius.[162] If the intention therein was, as *Holtzmann* correctly assumes,[163] "not so much monotheistic, but rather . . . notably polytheistic, it still pointed to a gap in God consciousness."}

The transition to the proclamation of the gospel occurs along all three lines of thought from the same viewpoint; it is also principally the same as we saw earlier: The preaching of Christ crucified and risen, which I, Paul, bring you, is nothing other than the fulfillment or the proof of what until now you have worshiped as divine in nature and in humanity, and which you have erroneously given the form of idols made with hands. [Thus he says in] 17:23: ὃ οὖν ἀγνοοῦντες εὐσεβεῖτε τοῦτο καταγγέλλω ὑμῖν [What therefore you worship as unknown, I proclaim to you]. It is incomprehensible to me how *Pfleiderer* arrives at the idea that "we notice, too, the interesting case that the historical Paul has here, at a stroke, been given by his biographer a Gentile aspect, whereas otherwise he gives him a Jewish aspect."[164] The previously stated belief about the pre-Christian religiosity among Jews and Gentiles was certainly also that of Paul, namely, that it too is revelation from ὁ θεὸς γὰρ αὐτοῖς ἐφανέρωσεν [because God has shown it to them] (Rom. 1:19).

However, this revelation needs to be supplemented, because Jews and Gentiles have fallen into judgment through their fall from God's commandments (Rom. 2:9). This higher complementary revelation, however, appears

158. Aratus, *Phaenomena* 4–6 [trans. G. R. Mair], in *Callimachus, Hymns and Epigrams. Lycophron. Aratus*, Loeb Classical Library 129 (London: William Heinemann, 1921).

159. Aurelius Augustine, *Confessions* 1.1.1: "Tu excitas, ut laudare te delectet, quia fecisti nos ad te et inquietum est cor nostrum, donec requiescat in te" ["Thou hast formed us for Thyself, and our hearts are restless till they find rest in Thee," in *Basic Writings of Saint Augustine*, ed. Whitney J. Oates (New York: Random House, 1948), 1:3].

160. Pausanias, *Graeciae descriptio* 1.1.4 [*Description of Greece*, trans. W. H. S. Jones and H. A. Omerod, Loeb Classical Library (Cambridge, MA: Harvard University Press, 1918)].

161. Flavius Philostratus, *Apollonii vita* 6.3 [*Flavius Philostratus in Honour of Apollonius of Tyana Vita Apollonii*, trans. J. S. Phillimore (Oxford: Clarendon Press, 1912)].

162. Diogenes Laertius, *Vitae philosophorum* 1.110 [*Lives of the Eminent Philosophers*, trans. Pamela Mensch, ed. James Miller (Oxford: Oxford University Press, 2018)].

163. Holtzmann, *Die Apostelgeschichte*, 391.

164. O. Pfleiderer, *Urchristentum* (Berlin: F. Reimer, 1902), 590.

in the person of Christ. As for the Gentiles in particular, compare Acts 14:17; 17:26–28; Romans 1:19–20: . . . τὸ γνωστὸν τοῦ θεοῦ φανερόν ἐστιν ἐν αὐτοῖς, . . . τὰ γὰρ ἀόρατα αὐτοῦ ἀπὸ κτίσεως κόσμου τοῖς ποιήμασιν νοούμενα καθορᾶται, ἥ τε ἀΐδιος αὐτοῦ δύναμις καὶ θειότης [what can be known about God is plain to them. . . . Ever since the creation of the world his eternal power and divine nature, invisible though they are, have been understood and seen through the things he has made].

Moreover, for the thought of the godlikeness of the human spirit, in Acts 17:28, it is easy to produce parallels in Paul, as in Romans 8:14; compare Galatians 3:26, where those who are filled with the Spirit of God are actually called υἱοὶ θεοῦ [sons of God]. Or even more clearly, Romans 8:16: αὐτὸ τὸ πνεῦμα συνμαρτυρεῖ τῷ πνεύματι ἡμῶν . . . [it is the very Spirit bearing witness with our spirit . . .]; compare 1 Corinthians 2:10–11! Any one of the passages cited from Acts could just as easily be in any of Paul's letters, most of all in Romans.

On this point, however, I must now move from the defense to the attack on the critical positions. That speech from Lystra and especially the one from Athens are cited again and again as "a first apology of Christianity against paganism," states *Holtzmann*.[165] This much is clear: the author intentionally included both statements in the account for possible Gentile readers of his book. The Pauline apology for Christianity shall also in his sense be effective in the present. Particularly from this perspective, it seems to me that the critics' customary dating of the book is suspect. It raises a serious *argumentum e silentio* [argument from silence], asking, *Where is the controversy with Greek philosophy that later was so important for the actual apologists?*

That the writer ad Theophilum is familiar with them is evident in 17:18, with its reference to the Epicureans and Stoics and the equally significant omission of any reference to the Platonists. An author of the second century would hardly have passed by the convenient point of contact afforded, especially by the latter reference. He does not make a single attempt for a connection in this direction and he rather limits himself to letting Paul appeal to general human consciousness in its specifically Greek expression (as Paul himself does in Rom. 1!); that fact clearly proves that he does not belong to that later period, but rather to a time when academic controversy between Christianity and paganism was of no interest yet, because the actual life-and-death conflict between the two intellectual powers had not yet begun.

These considerations have already led us to the *content* of the Pauline doctrine presented in the book of Acts.

God

The Pauline doctrine in Acts, as we have already seen externally, is first of all *doctrine of God*, λόγος τοῦ θεοῦ [word of God]. This God is the one God, the same who revealed himself (13:17–22) to the *Jews* from the time of the exodus out of Egypt until David, from the time of Moses until the prophets, and who has appeared to the *Gentiles* in nature (14:17) and in the self-reflection of the human spirit (17:26–28).

165. Holtzmann, *Die Apostelgeschichte*, 393; cf. 391.

He is the θεὸς ὁ ὕψιστος [most high God] (16:17), and therefore the task of the Gentiles is *to turn from the false gods* (14:15; 17:24–25, 29; 19:26) and of the Jews and Gentiles to turn to the good news of his *grace* (20:24), "*to turn to God*" (20:21; 26:20). This grace consists in *the sending of Christ* (13:23–41; 17:30–31; etc.), especially his *resurrection* from the dead (13:30–37; 17:31; etc.).

The God-consciousness before us undoubtedly includes the general Christian standpoint of the apostolic period and nowhere contradicts the Pauline standpoint. Nevertheless, we must consider whether, on the basis of the additional features of genuine Pauline teaching, we must conclude that we have here a late Deutero-Pauline derivation, with little similarity to the prototype.

If we compare the concept of God attributed to Paul in the book of Acts with the statements that Paul himself makes about God, most of all in Romans, a noticeable divergence—not difference!—is unmistakable. If I see it correctly, it consists in the fact that the point of view of the writer ad Theophilum is primarily *cosmological-rational* and that of Paul himself is most of all *ethical*.

The former argues that heaven and earth and sea, as well as the human race ἐπὶ παντὸς προσώπου τῆς γῆς [upon all the face of the earth] (17:26), in short, our experiential world—[all] points through its existence to a creator, who manifests himself ominously but clearly in the heart of each individual. The lacuna in pre-Christian times is that they are χρόνοι τῆς ἀγνοίας [times of ignorance] (17:30), so also the Jews are ἀγνοήσαντες [ignorant] vis-à-vis Jesus (13:27). The μετάνοια εἰς θεόν [turning to God] (20:21) is thus essentially an *intellectual acceptance* of that (metaphysically achieved) truth, and only secondarily an ethical conversion. Therefore, the gospel is preeminently *instruction* (λόγος, διδαχή) [word, teaching].

Paul himself proceeds differently: not from a theory about the cosmos, but rather from the concrete fact of the ethical incapacity of the human creature, whether Jewish or Greek, involving *sin*, which cannot exist before God. From the very beginning, Romans asserts (1:18): "For the wrath of God is revealed from heaven against all ungodliness and wickedness of those who by their wickedness suppress the truth." From this vantage point the Gentiles (despite that natural revelation, which also Paul recognizes) and the Jews (despite their law) are equally *lost* and must be *redeemed*, not physically, metaphysically, and intellectually, but rather ethically and religiously (Rom. 1–2). So, the following concept of God is evident in the remainder of the letter and is expressed throughout in Paul: above all, God *is* in relationship with the creature, who longs for freedom from the yoke of his sinful nature.

How must we assess these divergent points of view?

If we approach the matter solely with our Kantian-oriented thinking, the distinction will be unbridgeable for us: it seems to me that this is the origin of the critical stance. In that case, we simply assume the designated position of Paul himself and assert that he is correct and the writer ad Theophilum is incorrect; that is, he has misunderstood Paul or not understood him at all. I do not believe that much is gained by this approach for our understanding of the apostolic period and its intellectual thought.

Let us rather seek a genetic understanding of the relationship: The viewpoint of the writer ad Theophilum expresses throughout the *uniformly naive thinking of the ancient Greek*, which was not internally overcome even by such

a powerful movement as Platonism. The question Are a priori synthetic judgments possible?[166] did not exist for him, because the answer was obvious; hence
his cosmological-teleological concept of God. *Undoubtedly, Paul also thought the
same way*, and the fact that the latter view in Paul withdrew behind the ethical
is not because Paul's thought is principally different, but rather because of the
provenance of his concept of God: the latter originates from the *Old Testament
religion of the prophets*, and so religion is for him unthinkable if not based on
ethical consciousness.

In antiquity, the threads between these two viewpoints were not torn, as
they necessarily are for us; rather, they were consciously and unconsciously
one in the same person. The writer throughout ad Theophilum also relied on
the Old Testament and could have appealed to many a psalm to justify his perspective. He also emphasizes the ethical point, as we will see, only not as the
leading idea, that is, where it concerns the knowledge of God. Then again, he is
not a stranger to Paul's cosmological (Col. 1:15–16) and rational (Rom. 1:19–20)
speculation, yet it obviously played only a subordinate role.

This easily explains the origin of the account in the book of Acts: *The writer
ad Theophilum selected from the Pauline doctrine of God that which especially appealed
to his Greek thinking*; undoubtedly, however, he thought of doing nothing other
than reproducing it authentically. What he recorded for us can be considered
authentic—according to the main reason that indicates such, seen in context—
only we will miss the more important side; in this respect we can say that what
we have here is only half of Paul.

Yet this leads us nowhere near to the conclusion that therefore the author
must have written forty years later, using the sources.

One could simply note, for once, the great difference in the intellectual
worlds from which the Semitic Paul and the Greek Luke came! The Greek way
of thinking is deep in the blood of Luke, as we shall see below, despite his honest conviction about the truth of the Christian faith.

Even apart from that, it is certainly not unheard of in the history of more
recent theology, in which shifts in doctrine occur between master and student,
albeit in other ways, even as the younger claims to represent the genuine position of the older; it is not unlikely that "modern" criticism in two thousand years
will take similar wrong turns in its assessment as has the doctrinaire spirit of
our contemporary Tübingen-oriented [scholars] in assessing the apostolic age.

Jesus

Now we come to the subject that has at all times been the centerpiece of Christian theology, to the "good news" about Jesus, which at the time, fortunately,
was only beginning to develop into "Christology."

We begin, however, with a brief excursus about the formal but not entirely
indifferent question: How does Paul, according to our author's usage, name

---

166. According to I. Kant, "The real task of pure reason . . . is contained in the question: How are
synthetic judgements a priori possible?" I. Kant, *The Critique of Pure Reason*, trans. J. M. D. Meikle-
john (London: Bohn, 1860); Kant's works *The Critique of Pure Reason* and *Prolegomena to Any Future
Metaphysics* are primarily dedicated to the elaboration of this question.

the man (ἀνήρ, 17:31!) whom he proclaims to Jews and Gentiles as the sole salvation?

If we survey all the Pauline texts in our book [Acts], the result is a great spectrum of different forms of expression.

We have simply Ἰησοῦς [Jesus] in 13:33; 16:7; 17:3, 7, 18; 18:5; 19:5, 13, 15; 22:8; 25:19; 26:9; 26:15; 28:23; and the notable variant σωτὴρ Ἰησοῦς [Jesus the Savior] in 13:23. More typical for the author writing "to Theophilus" is the expression κύριος [Lord]: 13:2, 10–11; 14:3, 23; 15:35, 36, 40; 16:15; 18:8, 9; 19:10, 20; 20:28; 21:14; 22:8, 10, 19; 26:15; and especially the connection κύριος Ἰησοῦς [Lord Jesus] in 16:31; 19:5, 13, 17; 20:21; 24:35; 21:13. The compound Ἰησοῦς Χριστός *[Jesus Christ]* we find in 16:18; Χριστός Ἰησοῦς *[Christ Jesus]* in 24:24; (κύριος Ἰησοῦς Χριστός in 28:31 [Lord Jesus Christ]); ὁ Χριστός in 17:3; 18:5; 26:23 [the Christ].

Without putting too much weight on statistics, generally and specifically, I would like to indicate how I explain the situation before us, in other words, how I would interpret it within my overall view.

Ἰησοῦς [Jesus] is the expression used most frequently in the *Synoptics*. According to the general consensus, the author is writing "to Theophilus," whether he is called Luke or someone else; in Acts he uses Ἰησοῦς as the third most frequent name for Jesus.

The expressions κύριος, κύριος Ἰησοῦς, and so on derive from the *terminology of Paul*. The following samples may show what this means in detail (counting mistakes notwithstanding!).

In 1 Corinthians, the Messiah is called (apart from ὁ Χριστός): Jesus 1×; Jesus Christ 2×; Christ Jesus 7×; *the Lord 13×; the Lord Jesus Christ 8×.*

In the *Synoptics*, the use of κύριος is as follows:

Matthew: 79×, but *always*
  (a) related to God,
  (b) related to human authorities [*Herren*], or
  (c) related to Jesus and only used in the appellative mode (κύριε).
Mark: 18×, of which *only* 2× (2:28; 11:3) used by Jesus in direct speech.
But Luke: *104×, of which 21× used by Jesus in direct speech and as an absolute.*

Which of the three is closest to Paul?

That the usage of Paul's terminology is no mere coincidence follows from the fact that it also emerges in the first part of the book [of Acts], which I did not consider in the overview above.

A critic probably would respond to me here: precisely this proves that the author knows Paul only in a literary sense, indeed, from his letters.

But that is not the case. For if it were the case, if Paul's teaching presented here were only a clumsy excerpt from his Epistles, what would then have prevented the author from using the terminology he found there more consistently? Why does he put this terminology in Peter's mouth and, indeed, even use it in describing Jesus' life itself?

Both are only explicable by the fact that his Christian consciousness had absorbed the orally heard teaching of Paul about Christ and merged that with the historical tradition of Jesus of Nazareth that he knew, making an indivisible whole. For only in the apperception of a personally learning individual, not in the compiling work of a later copier, could the two different points of view implied in the different nomenclature have amalgamated in this way. Be that as it may, the hiatus would have to become even more visible for a later copyist, when he focuses on the subject matter itself, than is, in fact, the case.

What does the Paul of Acts know about the historical Jesus?

He comes out of the *house of David* (13:23), a native of *Nazareth* (22:8; 26:9). His activities are *prepared through John the Baptist* (13:24–25; 19:4). From this activity we learn in 20:35 an otherwise unknown saying and about his *failing with the Jews*: "The residents of Jerusalem and their leaders did not recognize him" (13:27); yes, they put him on trial: μηδεμίαν αἰτίαν θανάτου εὑρόντες ἠτήσαντο Πιλᾶτον ἀναιρεθῆναι αὐτόν [even though they found no cause for a sentence to death, they asked Pilate to have him killed] (13:28). Thus he dies the *death on the cross* (13:29; 17:3; 25:19; 26:23). God's power, though, has *raised* him from the dead (13:30; 17:3, 18, 31; 25:19; 26:23). Those who moved with him from Galilee to Jerusalem witness this: 13:31, οἵτινες νῦν εἰσιν μάρτυρες αὐτοῦ πρὸς τὸν λαόν [those who came up with him from Galilee to Jerusalem now are his witnesses to the people] (i.e., to the people of Israel in Palestine, therefore the *original apostles* [Urapostel]).

If we compare these findings with what Paul himself says in his Epistles, one thing leaps predominantly to the eye: The framework, within which the life of Jesus takes place, corresponds first of all with the framework of the Synoptics.

The extensive consideration of *John the Baptist* and his βάπτισμα μετανοίας [baptism of repentance], however, should perplex us. He would have played a certain role in the preaching of Paul, according to 13:24–25, but even if one ignores the conflict with the disciples of John the Baptist in Ephesus 19:2–7, the epistles *know nothing about that*.

This whole aspect of the theology of the author writing to Theophilus would merit a special discussion. Here I mean especially the relationship of the Johannine baptism of repentance to the reception of the πνεῦμα ἅγιον [Holy Spirit] (19:2), who plays an important role in the Third (and Fourth!) Gospel, as well as its roots in the primitive Christian kind of doctrinal consciousness and of tradition. Because I am missing the necessary expertise, I need to content myself by and large with a non liquet [an unclear situation]. However, I would like, quite within parentheses and very tentatively, to state briefly my preliminary understanding of the *place of the Baptist within the Pauline preaching*.

The history of the Baptist and his call to repentance are of special importance for the author writing to Theophilus. He is the only one among the evangelists who narrates (Luke 1:5–25, 57–80) his *pre-story* [*Vorgeschichte*] and especially extensively (3:1–20) describes his *preaching and baptizing* in the river Jordan, then finally (7:18–34) his relationship with *Jesus*, wherein the *baptism* always has a special significance (cf. Luke 7:24–34 in contrast to Matt. 11:7–19). This thread is taken up again also in Acts: In Acts 1:5 Jesus summarizes his promise to the apostles: "John baptized with water, but you will be baptized with the Holy Spirit not many days from now." This combination of thoughts entails that the character of the Baptist becomes an integral part in the Lukan *preaching of Jesus*: The σωτὴρ Ἰησοῦς [Jesus the Savior] cannot appear in another way than in the context of προκηρύξαντος Ἰωάννου . . . βάπτισμα μετανοίας [John's announcing the baptism of repentance] (10:37; 13:24); at the same time John points to the greater one who will come after him (13:25; 19:4).

John the Baptist, though, is nothing else than the Old Testament law in highest potency, which as such points beyond itself to Christ.

The following parallel is a particularly instructive sign that this thought is not simply Synoptic but also specifically Lukan:

Matthew 11:13[–15]: πάντες γὰρ οἱ προφῆται καὶ ὁ νόμος ἕως Ἰωάννου τοῦ βαπτιστοῦ[167] ἐπροφήτευσαν. καὶ εἰ θέλετε δέξασθαι, αὐτός ἐστιν Ἡλείας [Ἡλίας] ὁ μέλλων ἔρχεσθαι. ὁ ἔχων ὦτα ἀκουέτω [For all the prophets and the law prophesied until John came; and if you are willing to accept it, he is Elijah who is to come. Let anyone with ears listen!].	*Luke 16:16*: ὁ νόμος καὶ οἱ προφῆται μέχρι Ἰωάννου. ἀπὸ τότε ἡ βασιλεία τοῦ θεοῦ εὐαγγελίζεται καὶ πᾶς εἰς αὐτὴν βιάζεται [The law and the prophets were in effect until John came; since then the good news of the kingdom of God is proclaimed, and everyone tries to enter it by force].

Doubtlessly, the thought expressed in Luke is present also in the obscure and probably more original version of Matthew, at least potentially. But that Luke interprets it in this way (note also the precedence of the νόμος [law] and the more precise μέχρι [until]) is actually a highly significant process! Who does not immediately recognize in this the *disciple of Paul*? From there, however, a new light is also shed on our question: *The whole integration of John into the preaching of the gospel corresponds to a basic Pauline thought.* Whether this once happened in the way indicated in Acts 13:24–25 is not something I will insist on (the silence of the epistles is weighty). I do consider it probable: The relation fit well, especially over against a Jewish audience. But even if it were only about the expression of that problematic preference of the author writing "to Theophilus," it seems to me irrelevant in assessing the principal result: He then would let his Paul simply express a formally Lukan, but *in regard to the content, definitely genuinely Pauline* thought.

From there I would then further conclude: According to the view of the author writing "to Theophilus," τὸ πνεῦμα τὸ ἅγιον [the Holy Spirit] (Acts 19:2, 6) in the area of the βασιλεία τοῦ θεοῦ [kingdom of God] (Luke 16:16) is equivalent to the βάπτισμα μετανοίας [baptism of repentance] (Acts 13:24; 19:4) in the area of the νόμος καὶ οἱ προφῆται [the law and the prophets] (Luke 16:16). {Precisely because I regard this juxtaposition, which ultimately goes back to the Pauline doctrine of justification, as a characteristic feature of the Lukan theology, I could not agree with how *Harnack* dismissed Luke's explicit transformation of the kingdom petition of the Lord's Prayer (Luke 11:2) into a petition for the Holy Spirit.[168] Compare Luke 11:13.}[169]

---

167. In v. 13 Barth inserts τοῦ βαπτιστοῦ [of the Baptist] from vv. 11 and 12.

168. Cf. above, 92 n. 26 and 96–100.

169. A serpentine line, obviously written by Harnack, in the margin from the top of 157 down to here, and in the middle of 157 additionally a large question mark related to the sentence: "The whole integration [. . .]" See also above, n. 9.

It is, in any case, an act of violence to interpret the episode of John and his disciples with *Weizsäcker* as an allegory of Jewish Christianity.[170] I believe I was able to show that it has a specific and distinct place in the thought of the author writing to Theophilus.

Nobody has the desire to put great weight on the definition of Ἰησοῦς ὁ Ναζωραῖος [Jesus the Nazarene] (22:8; 26:9). It does not appear in Paul's own writings, but it appears in the first half of Acts (2:22; 6:14; etc.) and is therefore likely to be attributed to the author.

Now let us address the aforementioned ἄγραφον [assumedly unwritten saying by Jesus] in 20:35 (at Miletus) μακάριόν ἐστιν μᾶλλον διδόναι ἢ λαμβάνειν [It is more blessed to give than to receive], which is handed down to us similarly in Clement of Rome: . . . ἥδιον διδόντες ἢ λαμβάνοντες.[171] [More pleasant are givers than receivers.] How did it come here? "From the source," *Holtzmann* suggests, of course.[172] Still, it remains enigmatic: Why did this author writing "to Theophilus" not integrate it into the proverbs of his Gospel [Luke]? It will be hard to tell whether, in this context, it stems from the author's memory of a real speech by Paul or if it is a literal embellishment added by him (but anyway of reliable provenience). But this does matter little or nothing at all; I am more inclined toward the latter opinion.

Very important, however, is the following observation: remaining in the preaching of the Lukan Paul, after the deduction of these secondary features of Jesus' life, are his *death* and his *resurrection*. Actually, these two facts come everywhere clearly to the forefront as the point in the preaching of the gospel, as especially visible when, in 17:3 or 26:22–23, the content of the Pauline doctrine is meant to be displayed not extensively, as elsewhere, but only in one single sentence. I will come back to this issue soon. Preliminarily only this [should be said] formally: *In clear conformity with the doctrine of Christ displayed in the Pauline Epistles, death and resurrection are the facts that definitively surpass everything else in the life of Jesus in terms of importance, also according to the preaching of Paul in Luke.*

Hence, now we are standing immediately in front of the main question: *In what way is the person Jesus the center of the proclamation of the gospel to Jews and Gentiles?*

The Paul of Acts answers the question in his statements, which I organize according to their content again, as follows:

Jesus is the Christ (9:22; 17:3; 18:5; 24:24), meaning the Messiah of the old covenant announced for long (26:6), whom Israel had desired "in earnest worship day and night" (26:7). As such, he is the υἱὸς τοῦ θεοῦ [Son of God] (9:20; 13:33; cf. Rom. 1:4; 1 Cor. 1:9; 2 Cor. 1:19; Gal. 1:16; Eph. 4:13; Col. 1:13; etc.) and the βασιλεύς [king] (Acts 17:7) of those who believe in him.

What is the content of the salvation he brings? He is the φῶς [light] (cf. 2 Cor. 4:6; Eph. 5:8–9) that overcomes the darkness, that leads from Satan's night to God (Acts 26:18, 23; cf. Col. 1:13; 2 Thess. 2:7–8), the σωτήρ [Savior] for Jews and Gentiles (13:23; 16:31; cf. 2 Tim. 1:10; Titus 1:4; 2:13; 3:6) who belong to the community of those who believe in him, which means ὅσοι ἦσαν τεταγμένοι

---

170. Weizsäcker, *Das apostolische Zeitalter*, 341.
171. See 1 Clement 2.1.
172. Holtzmann, *Die Apostelgeschichte*, 405.

εἰς ζωὴν αἰώνιον [those who had been destined for eternal life] (Acts 13:48; cf. Rom. 8:28–29), ἣν περιεποιήσατο διὰ τοῦ αἵματος τοῦ ἰδίου [that he obtained with the blood of his own Son] (Acts 20:28; cf. Rom. 3:25; 5:9; Eph. 1:7), which means that through his death God made him overcome through the ἀνάστασις [resurrection] (Acts 13:30–31; 17:3, 18; etc.; cf. 1 Cor. 15; Phil. 3:10) as πρῶτος ἐξ ἀναστάσεως νεκρῶν [the first to rise from the dead] (Acts 26:23; cf. 1 Cor. 15:20) πίστιν παρασχὼν πᾶσιν [giving assurance to all] (Acts 17:31). The gift that he brings to humankind is δικαιοσύνη [justice] (Acts 24:25; cf. Rom. 3–6; 8–10), which consists in ὅτι διὰ τούτο ὑμῖν ἄφεσις ἁμαρτιῶν καταγγέλλεται, καὶ ἀπὸ πάντων ὧν οὐκ ἠδυνήθητε ἐν νόμῳ Μωϋσέως δικαιωθῆναι ἐν τούτῳ πᾶς ὁ πιστεύων δικαιοῦται [that through this man forgiveness of sins is proclaimed to you; and by this Jesus everyone who believes is set free from all those sins, from which you could not be freed by the law of Moses] (Acts 13:38–39; 26:18; cf. Gal. 2:16; Rom. 3:28; 10:4!!!). The author knows the thought here expressed, that the Mosaic law is overcome in Christ, also apart from this case as an integral part of the Pauline doctrine; this is shown by the statements he makes about the content of the Jewish charges against Paul (Acts 21:21, 28; 24:5) where Paul is downright blamed that he taught τὴν ἀποστασίαν ἀπὸ Μωϋσέως [the apostasy from Moses]!

Finally, he will be the judge of the world, because God has determined a day τοῦ κρίματος τοῦ μέλλοντος [of the coming judgment] (24:25) ἐν ᾗ μέλλει κρίνειν τὴν οἰκουμένην ἐν δικαιοσύνῃ ἐν ἀνδρὶ ᾧ ὥρισεν [on which he will have the world judged in righteousness by a man he has appointed (17:31; cf. 2 Thess. 1:7–10).

Is all this merely a *Deutero-Paulinism*, understood later, not at all, or only half, as *Pfleiderer* and *Holtzmann*[173] have it? Or is it, according to *Jülicher*,[174] only *common Christian tradition* [Gemeingut] of the first decade of the second century?

The latter seems to me out of consideration: The man who was able to write Acts 13:38–39 must have been living under the profound and at least literary influence of Paul. With regard to the first hypothesis, I do not want to waste my time with the debate about the known parallels to Paul. Some of them are evident at first glance. In other cases it might be possible, sometimes even likely, that the author writing "to Theophilus" took them not from Paul but from what *Jülicher* calls common Christian tradition.

What I would rather illumine here are the *basic themes* of the Christology and soteriology that we can see here. I summarize them in four points:

1. *Jesus is the Messiah* and as such the fulfillment of the old covenant, which at the same time is overcome in him.

2. The Jews rejected him, even crucified him (this also had to occur in this way according to prophecy). For all human beings (now the gospel became universal), this death means the forgiveness of sins.

3. *But God raised him as the "firstborn" from the dead,"* and at the end of the days he will *judge* the world.

4. *Believing in him*, both the Jews, who are not able to achieve it by their law, and the Gentiles, who are not able to achieve it on their own power, will be *justified*, which means they will participate in the forgiveness of sins.

---

173. Pfleiderer, *Urchristentum*, 581–82; cf. Holtzmann, *Synoptiker*, 315.
174. Jülicher, *Einleitung*, 352.

Next to this I place the words with which Paul in 1 Corinthians 15:3–4 summarizes his proclamation: παρέδωκα γὰρ ὑμῖν ἐν πρώτοις, ὃ καὶ παρέλαβον ὅτι Χριστὸς ἀπέθανεν ὑπὲρ τῶν ἁμαρτιῶν ἡμῶν κατὰ τὰς γραφὰς, καὶ ὅτι ἐτάφη, καὶ ὅτι ἐγήγερται τῇ ἡμέρᾳ τῇ τρίτῃ κατὰ τὰς γραφάς [I handed on to you as of first importance what I in turn had received: that Christ died for our sins in accordance with the Scripture, and that he was buried, and that he was raised on the third day in accordance with the Scriptures].

Is this now the same Christ-doctrine as the one just compiled, or not?

The congruence here actually cannot be demonstrated quite so simply, which is due to the nature of the matter. Here is a brief summary:

If you compare the image of Christ in Paul with that of the author writing "to Theophilus," one thing catches your eye: In the Lukan preaching of Paul, the *resurrection* has first significance over everything else.

In the sermon in Antioch of Pisidia, in Acts 13:16–43, verses 30–37 deal exclusively with it, while the narrative of the death is dispatched in the short passage of 13:27–28 without any further comment. The Athenian philosophers say 17:18 about Paul: "He seems to be a proclaimer of foreign δαιμόνια [divinities]." Why that? The author paraphrases: ὅτι τὸν Ἰησοῦν καὶ τὴν ἀνάστασιν εὐαγγελίζετο [he was telling about the good news about Jesus and the resurrection]. And in the following *speech on the Areopagus*, Jesus' death is not even mentioned at all but well culminates in and concludes with the message of the resurrection.

Finally 25:19: Festus reports to Agrippa on the events of the trial up to then, and there we hear: ζητήματα δέ τινα περὶ τῆς ἰδίας δεισιδαιμονίας εἶχον πρὸς αὐτὸν καὶ περί τινος Ἰησοῦ τεθνηκότος, ὃν ἔφασκεν ὁ Παῦλος ζῆν [they had certain points of disagreement with him about their own religion and about a certain Jesus, who had died, but whom Paul asserted to be alive].

We should also notice the somewhat confused relation that exists between the ἄφεσις ἁμαρτιῶν [forgiveness of sins] and Jesus' death. (Some light is shed on it only from 20:28, where, however, Christians are addressed.) On the other hand, in 13:32–33 the (typical) meaning of the resurrection is discussed and broadly elaborated. Now there is actually no doubt that Paul himself also had a central interest in this aspect, as especially 1 Corinthians 15 proves again. However, was the relation really as our author portrayed it? Certainly not! Already in Paul (1 Cor. 1!) and then in general in the early Christian doctrine, Jesus' cross, above all, moves to the forefront. This is another proof that our book cannot have originated in those [later] decades, in which, even if not the doctrine of justification, but clearly Paul's doctrine of reconciliation and of sacrifice has become common Christian tradition.

But what is then the special interest of the author in putting Jesus' death so much in the background while placing his resurrection so clearly to the foreground? I believe this: It is, once again, the *Greek* who is speaking here, who comes *positively* from the acquaintance, perhaps friendship, with Platonic ideas and for whom the ἀνάστασις νεκρῶν [resurrection of the dead] is of highest importance, in opposition to the Stoic and Epicurean schools (17:18, 32), but also to the Saducean school of thought in Judaism (note the debate 23:7–10!). This Hellenic interest in ἀφθαρσία [immortality] can actually be traced in the subsequent history of dogma. It reaches its climax in the doctrine of diviniza-tion in Athanasius.[175]

On the other hand, I would like to assume this: *negatively*, our author is con-sciously or unconsciously still rather tangibly influenced by the equally Hellenic sentiment toward the cross of Jesus, which Paul displays in 1 Corinthians 1:22–23: Ἕλληνες σοφίαν ζητοῦσιν, ἡμεῖς δὲ κηρύσσομεν Χριστὸν ἐσταυρωμένον, . . . ἔθνεσιν . . . μωρίαν [Greeks desire wisdom, but we proclaim Christ crucified, . . . foolish-ness to Gentiles]. Of course, this sentiment is overcome in principle in the author writing "to Theophilus," but it seems to me very obvious that something of it is still echoing in the noticeable brevity of his remarks regarding this matter, but also *that the whole position is not possible for a man of the second century, but only for a neophyte of earlier times.*

The relation of the christological view displayed here as Pauline to the genu-ine Pauline stance in the epistles will have to be discussed in the survey of the whole project.

The Gospel as Imperative

What does the Pauline gospel demand from the human being?

First, the answer of the author writing "to Theophilus" is the same every-where: πίστις [faith], which means the faithful acceptance of the salvation revealed by God in Christ.

This is clearly formulated in Paul's answer to the jailer of Philippi: πίστευσον ἐπὶ τὸν κύριον Ἰησοῦν καὶ σωθήσῃ [Believe in the Lord Jesus, and you will be saved] (16:31). And so it is also the most common expression for those accept-ing Paul's preaching: *they believed*, which means they became *believers* (13:12, 39, 48; 14:22, 27; 16:5; 17:34; 18:8, 27; 19:18; 20:21; 21:20, 25; 22:19).

In the context of the discussion about the concept of God, I already identi-fied of what this *faith* consisted in the eyes of the author, this "letting yourself be talked into" (ἐπείσθησαν [they were persuaded], 17:4; cf. 13:43; 28:23!): in the first place, it is simply regarding the facts of salvation preached by Paul as true. However, it would be completely wrong, therefore, to think of Paul now as being convicted of intellectualism. I repeat: The rational and the ethical moments merged in the theology of those days, and always in such a way that the ethical was thought to be more or less causally dependent on the rational. Depending on the personality of the preacher, the one or the other aspect had to become either prominent or secondary. *In the Paul of the author writing "to Theophilus," the rational element clearly dominates.* Yet indeed, the πίστις [faith] that this Paul is teaching is not thereby exhausted, as made plain enough by a series of circumstances.

In 20:27 the proclamation of the gospel is called βουλὴ θεοῦ [purpose of God] (cf. 1 Thess. 4:3); in 13:10; 18:25; 19:9; 22:4, ὁδὸς τοῦ κυρίου [way of the Lord]. In both descriptions an ethical element is at least included.

---

175. Cf. A. Harnack, *Lehrbuch der Dogmengeschichte*, vol. 2, *Die Entwickelung des kirchlichen Dogmas I*, 3rd ed., Sammlung theologischer Lehrbücher (Freiburg i. Br./Leipzig: C. B. Mohr [Paul Siebeck], 1894), 43–46.

An ethical relationship is also present in the way Paul narrates his conversion at 26:19. "After that, King Agrippa" it says οὐκ ἐγενόμην ἀπειθὴς τῇ οὐρανίῳ ὀπτασίᾳ [I was not disobedient to the heavenly vision].

Paul preaches the βασιλεία τοῦ θεοῦ [kingdom of God] (14:22; 19:8; 20:25; 28:23, 31; cf. 1 Cor. 4:20; 6:10; Gal. 5:21).

It must have been natural for the author of Luke 8:9–15 that the obedience to God's commandment must be paramount in the kingdom of God, where οἵτινες ἐν καρδίᾳ καλῇ καὶ ἀγαθῇ ἀκούσαντες τὸν λόγον κατέχουσιν καὶ καρποφοροῦσιν ἐν ὑπομονῇ [the ones who, when they hear the word, hold it fast in an honest and good heart, and bear fruit with patient endurance] are most advanced in the knowledge of the μυστήρια τῆς βασιλείας [secrets of the kingdom].

And in the same sense, the expression in Acts 20:21, ἡ εἰς θεὸν μετάνοια [repentance toward God], probably means, like 26:20, μετανοεῖν καὶ ἐπιστρέφειν ἐπὶ τὸν θεόν [that they should repent and turn to God].

But there is also no lack of direct moral demand, as, for example, in general: 17:30: . . . νῦν ἀπαγγέλλει τοῖς ἀνθρώποις πάντας πανταχοῦ μετανοεῖν [now he commands all people everywhere to repent] and 26:20: . . . ἄξια τῆς μετανοίας ἔργα πράσσοντας [do deeds consistent with repentance]—and especially 20:35: πάντα ὑπέδειξα ὑμῖν, ὅτι οὕτως κοπιῶντας δεῖ ἀντιλαμβάνεϲθαι τῶν ἀσθενούντων, μνημονεύειν τε τῶν λόγων τοῦ κυρίου Ἰησοῦ, κτλ [in all this I have given you an example that by such work we must support the weak, remembering the words of the Lord Jesus, etc.]. Finally, in the interesting passage 24:25, διαλεγομένου δὲ αὐτοῦ περὶ δικαιοσύνης καὶ ἐγκρατείας καὶ τοῦ κρίματος . . . [and as he discussed justice, self-control, and the coming judgment . . .].

All this needs to be considered as the clear effect of the ethical side of Paul's real teaching. However, also here one will have to ask: *How was it possible that this side receded?*

Once more, the primary answer has to be this: *The author writes as a Greek*, first in the sense just aforementioned: a new religion must, above all other things, bring *new knowledge*.

But then again, negatively as well: The way Paul talked about sin as something inherent to all σάρξ [flesh] from the outset (Rom. 7:14) must have appeared to be not very convincing and even repugnant for a Greek. Actually, the human body was, according to the teaching of the Greeks' greatest philosopher, nothing else than the entelechy of the soul indwelling it; the soul though, in turn, was a part or emanation of the Godhead's self.[176] How alien to this was the atmosphere [around Paul]: ταλαίπωρος ἐγὼ ἄνθρωπος. Τίς με ῥύσεται ἐκ τοῦ σώματος τοῦ θανάτου τούτου; [Wretched man that I am! Who will rescue me from this body of death?] (Rom. 7:24)!

A Greek could probably understand the superficial talk about the necessity of ἐγκράτεια [self-control]—for this also his national philosophy did offer quite a few clues; but he could not quickly reach the depth of recognizing sins and the resulting conviction of the unavoidability of a comprehensive internal separation from the αἰὼν τοῦ κόσμου τούτου [course of this world] (Eph. 2:2) and

---

176. According to Aristotle, the soul is the *entelechy of the body* (cf. *De anima* B 1.412a.27ff.). The "so-called reason of the soul" (*De anima* B 1.142a.22) is considered by him as something "divine," entering from outside (Aristotle, *De generatione animalium* B 3.736b.27–28).

from the σάρξ [flesh], as they existed in the real Paul, in spite of many years of personal struggle.

But one also may look at the whole relationship between faith and morality in the preaching of the Lukan Paul even from yet another perspective, and from there one will have to say: the author writing "to Theophilus" was clearly a disciple of Paul. For what else is the whole preponderance of πίστις [faith] but the purest Paulinism? Precisely the fact that the term appears almost as a catch-phrase indicates, as it seems to me, that the author learned from Paul, even if he evidently associates intellectualizing ideas with faith in many places.

An author of later times would be expected to make himself known, exactly here and unequivocally, through a legalistic emphasis of a new morality (cf. the catalog of virtues and vices of the Didache!).[177] This, too, is not the case for the author of Acts.

Sapienti sat [A word is enough to the wise].[178]

The Last Things

The eschatological statements of Paul in Acts are scarce.

We have the hope (ἐλπίς [hope], 23:6; 24:15) that at some time an ἀνάστασις νεκρῶν [resurrection of the dead] (17:32; 23:6; 24:21) will take place, which will be an ἀνάστασις δικαίων τε καὶ ἀδίκων [resurrection of the righteous and of the unrighteous] (24:15). That will be the day when Jesus will *judge* the οἰκουμένη [the world] in righteousness (17:31; 24:15). By this, the faithful enter into the ζωὴ αἰώνιος [eternal life] (13:46, 48) that is destined for them, the ἡγιασμένοις [sancti-fied] (20:32), as their κλῆρος [inheritance] (26:18; cf. Col. 1:12) or κληρονομία [inher-itance] (20:32; cf. Eph. 1:14). With that the state of the βασιλεία τοῦ θεοῦ [kingdom of God] (14:22; cf. 1 Cor. 15:50; 2 Thess. 1:5) has become definitively dominating.

At first glance it is indeed already very sparse in comparison with the col-orful imaginations of 1 Corinthians 15 or 1 Thessalonians 4:13–18; 5:1–11; and 2 Thessalonians 1:7–10.

However, it must be noted: Here, too, the *difference* between the Lukan Paul and the real Paul is merely *quantitative*. The essential features are here the same as there: the resurrection of the dead, Christ sits in judgment, eternal life for the faithful. But whence comes the minus of Acts? Is it again the *Greek* to whom the envisioned Semitic eschatology is unsympathetic? I am almost inclined to assume so, but I believe that I have an even better explanation for it, about which we will have to talk in the general summary.

Saul's Conversion

We still must discuss two moments that actually do not belong to the content of the Pauline preaching as such, but yet are inseparable from it: They are related to the personal connection of the apostle with his teaching.

One of those is this: Paul's missionary activity, in his view, is based on his conversion, as he repeatedly states.

---

177. Cf. Didache 1.1–6.3.
178. T. Maccius Plautus, *Persae* 5.729 (4.7.19); P. Terentius Afer [Terence], *Phormio* 5.541 (3.3.8).

Paul actually does not make this statement often—he does not waste words about it—but only when he wants to *give an account* of his actions.

In Acts, this is, for example, the case regarding the *speech at Miletus*, where Paul summarizes the experiences and the meaning of his apostolate with Jews and Gentiles. He suggests that his διακονία [ministry] (20:24) is one ἣν ἔλαβον παρὰ τοῦ κυρίου Ἰησοῦ [that I have received from the Lord Jesus]. The same relationship reappears more clearly and extensively at the various interrogations during the trial in Palestine.

The first time is in 22:1–21. Paul is standing on the outside staircase in front of the palace in Jerusalem; behind him was the Roman commander with his officers and soldiers, in front of him the fanaticized Jewish crowd. He raises his hand, it becomes quiet, and now he tells his fellow countrymen how he once, as Gamaliel's orthodox disciple, had become convinced that he should persecute [those holding] the Christian teaching. Then, though, everything had changed through the event on the way to Damascus. First through the mouth of Ananias, then soon afterward through a second vision in Jerusalem, the task had been handed to him ἐν ἐκστάσει [in trance] from Jesus: πορεύου, ὅτι ἐγὼ εἰς ἔθνη μακρὰν ἐξαποστελῶ σε [Go, I will send you far away to the Gentiles] [22:17, 21].

And the second time in 26:1–24: Paul is standing in front of Agrippa and Bernice in Caesarea. Again, he tells his life story up to the day of Damascus. This event and the calling are portrayed a little differently. Both accounts have in common that the epiphany of Christ peaks in the injunction: You shall be my ὑπερέτης καὶ μάρτυς [servant and witness] [26:16]. I, Jesus, select you from Jews and Gentiles as the one who is called to open the eyes of both [cf. 26:17–18]. Since then, Paul has acted in obedience to this command, setting out to call Jews and Gentiles to μετάνοια εἰς θεόν [to repentance toward God; cf. 26:20]. This appearance of Christ, whom he now proclaims, is at the same time the legitimization of his missionary work for all times.

One may juxtapose to this what Paul, in Galatians 1:15–16, says to *justify his apostolate beside that of the original apostles*: here as in Acts, it is the same process, the same consequences: ἀφορίσας [having been selected], καλέσας [having been called], ἀποκαλύψαι . . . ἵνα εὐαγγελίζωμαι αὐτὸν ἐν τοῖς ἔθνεσιν [to reveal . . . so that I might proclaim him among the Gentiles].

Or one should hear how he defends this apostolate against *the Corinthian heretics*, as in 1 Corinthians 9:1: οὐκ εἰμὶ ἀπόστολος; οὐχὶ Ἰησοῦν τὸν κύριον ἡμῶν ἑόρακα; [Am I not an apostle? Have I not seen Jesus our Lord?]; and in 15:8, 10: ἔσχατον δὲ πάντων ὡσπερεὶ τῷ ἐκτρώματι ὤφθη κἀμοί [Last of all, as to one untimely born, he appeared also to me]. He is clearly conscious about what this meant to him: χάριτι δὲ θεοῦ εἰμι ὅ εἰμι, καὶ ἡ χάρις αὐτοῦ ἡ εἰς ἐμὲ οὐ κενὴ ἐγενήθη . . . [But by the grace of God I am what I am, and this grace toward me has not been in vain].

But is it perhaps bothersome that the information in Acts is so disproportionately more extensive than that from Paul himself [in his letters]? I do not believe so because how the latter approaches the issue shows clearly that he expected the accounts to be known in detail in his congregations. It is not the same with the author of Acts. For him, it was important to describe the origins of the Pauline mission as extensively as possible. Therefore, he talks about it no less than three times. *Precisely this interest, though, is an additional hint that he knew Paul not only from a distance.* For even if that suspicion may be justified—if indeed the elaborateness of the author writing "to Theophilus," inconsistent in itself [i.e., some details vary], suggests that some question marks should be put to his narrative—then this only results in the very welcome insight that we have to state that we know as little as Luke does about how these things happened in detail and have to be content with the effects instead of the causes: *In any event, it is a fact that near Damascus something incomparably great occurred in and with Paul,* namely, in a way that shows the limits of all causal historical analysis, positively or negatively. And if in this religious assessment, not adverse to miracles, the fight around Saul's conversion, zealously fought on the right and the left, more or less becomes splitting hairs,[179] this also may be fine.[180] In any case, the Lukan Paul as well as the real Paul states with clarity: On my conversion rests "My Gospel."

My Gospel

This key word is the basis of the second characteristic of the Pauline preaching, closely and thoroughly connected with the first:

The gospel I am bringing is my gospel.

Acts expresses this thought predominantly through the whole external course of the narrative, as we already saw it in an earlier investigation and therefore do not need to repeat it. ἡμεῖς εἰς τὰ ἔθνη—αὐτοὶ δὲ εἰς τὴν περιτομήν [we to the Gentiles—they to the circumcised] (Gal. 2:9). The presentation of Acts actually reproduces this thought of the internal and external independence of the Pauline apostolate, although it does not turn it into an ideological program, as had to be done in Galatians. In this light, passages like Acts 15:38–40 should be noted, the conflict with Barnabas; or 19:1–16, the discussion with the disciples of John; or 20:18–36, the thrust of the speech in Miletus; finally, the meaningful passage in 17:3, . . . ὅτι οὗτός ἐστιν ὁ Χριστός, ὁ Ἰησοῦς, ὃν ἐγὼ καταγγέλλω ὑμῖν [that this is the Messiah, Jesus, whom I am proclaiming to you]. This is the same self-consciousness that makes the apostle rage in 2 Corinthians 11:4 against someone ὁ ἐρχόμενος ἄλλον Ἰησοῦν κηρύσσει, . . . ἢ πνεῦμα ἕτερον . . . ἢ εὐαγγέλιον ἕτερον [who comes and proclaims another Jesus . . . or a different spirit . . . or a different gospel]. Compare also Galatians 1:8!

B. Results

With this we now have the material in hand that enables us to answer this question: *To what extent is this the real Paul who is speaking here* [in Acts], *or not?*

The question is of importance for judging the literary position and qualification of the author writing ad Theophilum, for if Luke's Paul has "in his thoughts and expressions" "no more in common" with the historical [Paul]

---

179. Actually, Fritz Barth also had offered his views on this subject in 1905: *Die Bekehrung des Paulus,* in F. Barth, *Christus unsere Hoffnung: Sammlung von religiösen Reden und Vorträgen* (Bern: A. Francke, 1913), 180–98.

180. Manuscript: incorrect spelling of the German idiom (substantive) "Recht," corrected by the German editor to (the adj.) "recht."

"than any other believer might have had,"[181] and if this "Pauline sermon simply contrasts monotheism and the stricter Jewish customs with paganism, and circles around the general themes of Jesus' messianism and resurrection,"[182] then we will have to say with *Jülicher* and *Holtzmann*: This cannot be a direct student of the apostle, but must have been either a later vulgar Christian or at most an equally later Deutero-Paulinist.

The investigation of the individual positions above has shown, however, that such a presupposition comes with a certain superficial judgment that cannot be denied.

Let us briefly recapitulate the *negative* side of our results, that is, just the plus and minus that the Lukan teaching displays in contrast to the Letters of Paul.

The picture is the following:

1. In the *conception of God*, the rational-cosmological perspective prevails over the ethical one.

2. The *significance of Jesus* is based less on his death than on his resurrection.

3. The *gospel requires* faith first of all, and moral conversion is only second.

4. Eschatology is quantitatively less detailed.

Do these divergences justify the above-mentioned constellation of criticism? No!

In contrast, one must emphasize, above all: *Not a single one of the essential positions of historical Paulinism is missing in the salient Pauline teachings in the book of Acts.*

I believe that I have shown in detail the parallels that exist between Paul of the book of Acts and Paul of his Epistles, not only in certain striking passages to which it would be improper to give too much weight, but also in the whole way of seeing.

But even more: We have also seen that even at such points where we noted a relative departure from Paulinism proper—I recall the primacy of ἀνάστασις [resurrection] in the doctrine of Christ, or later of πίστις (faith): the reference back to Paulinism, or rather the starting from it, is unmistakable. I do not want to come back to all that once more.

Now I expect the following objection to follow immediately afterward: Do you not see that in Paul's teaching in the book of Acts, *the most authentic Paulinism plays a very subordinate role?* Why are verses like Acts 13:38–39 not much more frequent with a pupil of Paul? Why does such an important speech as the one at Athens not contain "any true Paulinism" (*Holtzmann*)?[183] The tacit assumption of such questions is the following: Of course,

Paulinism = the doctrine of justification!

In his day, Baur and the Tübingen School built their critical system upon this equation, into which, following the Hegelian schema, the history of the apostolic age had to reach its climax in Galatians 2—that is, in the struggle between Gentile Christianity freed from the law and embodied by Paul, and

---

181. A. Jülicher, *Introduction to the New Testament*, trans. Janet Penrose Ward (London: Smith, Elder & Co., 1904), 444.

182. H. J. Holtzmann, *Die Synoptiker. Die Apostelgeschichte*, 314–15.

183. Holtzmann, *Die Apostelgeschichte*, 391.

Jewish Christianity faithful to the law and embodied by Peter. As a result, the received Pauline Epistles were declared one after another not to be authored by the apostle, because they did not contain, or only vaguely, that contrast.

Modern criticism has relativized these implications, but nevertheless it appears to me that this equation still continues to play its role; otherwise it would not be possible to revile the Paul of the book of Acts, as is still the case.

The emphasis on faith alone (sola fide), as it is found in the doctrine of justification in the Epistles to the Galatians and Romans, has only come into Paulinism as an integral, that is, explicit component through the polemical confrontation with the Judaizers (cf. Wrede).[184]

Clinging to the contrary can be only the one who, in one way or another, accepts in a scholastic manner that the whole structure we call "Paulinism" had arisen in the hour of conversion before Damascus, springing from sudden revelation—like Pallas Athene from the head of Zeus![185]

But since this point of view is not universally accepted, and I cannot go any further here than I do anyway, the matter should be considered from another generally illuminating point of view.

The Pauline sermon in Acts of the Apostles is not a congregational sermon, but a missionary sermon, and as such, its distinctive form of teaching possesses for itself a high degree of probability.[186]

It would be interesting to examine how one actually thinks critically about the Pauline missionary sermon, after those recorded in Acts have been spirited away as "non-Pauline"![187]

Holtzmann: "The content of Paul's preaching is shaped without any consideration of specific and actual Paulinism."[188]

I really cannot accept it as probable that Paul would have preached, for example, to the Athenians as though he were shooting from a pistol, especially the doctrine of justification by faith, even if, from the beginning, it had been an explicit component of his theology.

How much more reasonable would it have been—just as in the case, for example, of the palpably polytheistic Lystrans—to begin, above all, with the proclamation of the one God, who created heaven and earth, and before whom the gods made by hands melt into nothingness?

From this perspective, it seems to me not only dubious, but also almost impossible, simply to refer over and over to the theology laid down in the epistles when critiquing the Pauline teaching of the book of Acts and then, measured against the former, to call the latter un-Pauline. The difference is surely obvious, that the apostle was speaking to people in whom the *foundation*, the monotheistic concept of God, had first to be won; but in his Epistles he had people to whom most of the positions of the Christian faith were readily familiar. *Within* this same framework, the task was to assert polemically quite specific ideas, to the right or to the left.

---

184. W. Wrede, *Paulus*, RV (Halle a. S., 1904), 72–73; Wrede, *Paul*, trans. E. Lummis (London: Green, 1907), esp. 122–24.
185. Cf. Wrede, *Paul*, 137.
186. Marginal note by Harnack (?) to this paragraph: "Very true!"
187. Beside this statement an exclamation mark by Harnack (?).
188. Holtzmann, *Die Apostelgeschichte*, 419.

One must not always think and speak in such an abstract and academic way; observe, for example, how our Christian missionaries in the pagan world still proceed and must proceed today. Will they come to the Negro, Hindu, or Chinese above all with sentences like these: "We are justified before God, not by works of the law, but by faith alone" [cf. Rom. 3:28]?[189] Or, "The blood of Jesus Christ cleanses us of all sin" [cf. 1 John 1:7]? No, because the person does not know the meaning of God, justification, law, faith, sin, and so on. So the missionary will start *ab ovo* [from the beginning] and will tell them above all: "I have a joyful, liberating message in the name of the one, almighty God to share with you: Believe in the Lord Jesus; then you will attain the bliss that your pagan gods could not give you!"[190]

And this is exactly how the Paul of the book of Acts speaks; do we have any reason to believe that the real [Paul] had done it differently? When we hear how he reminds the Corinthians, for example, how he preached the gospel to them for the first time, then I really cannot believe that we have any reason to do so: Κἀγώ, ἀδελφοί, οὐκ ἠδυνήθην λαλῆσαι ὑμῖν ὡς πνευματικοῖς ἀλλ' ὡς σαρκίνοις, ὡς νηπίοις ἐν χριστῷ. γάλα ὑμᾶς ἐπότισα, οὐ βρῶμα, οὔπω γὰρ ἐδύνασθε [Brothers, I could not address you as people who live by the Spirit but as people who are still worldly—mere infants in Christ. I gave you milk, not solid food, for you were not yet ready for it] (1 Cor. 3:1–2)!

By discussing the individual positions, I have tried to establish that the plus and minus with respect to Paul can be traced almost everywhere to the theological sympathies and antipathies of the author writing ad Theophilum, which grow naturally out of *Greek forms of thought*.

I adhere principally to this observation, but it still needs to be supplemented by the point of view just discussed.

In part, such relative deviations from the teaching format of the letters as noted— precisely because they are missionary sermons—have also been made by Paul himself.

1. When Paul talked about *God* before a pagan audience, he could not simply start from the idea that God is the good, to whom all sin is an abomination, because for the Greek person, as the perspective of the Homeric poems shows, the concept of deity was not eo ipso connected with that of the καλὸν κἀγαθόν (noble and good), that is, with morality, but rather initially only with that of relative power. Paul had to build on that by first showing that the power of deity is absolute, which leads directly to the idea of monotheism. Only then was it possible for the Greeks to understand the revelation of God in Jesus.

2. As far as the person of *Jesus* is concerned, there was nothing more obvious for Paul—as the book of Acts suggests—than to make a connection above all to the concept of ἀφθαρσία [incorruptibility], which is so familiar to the Greeks and frequently discussed in philosophy, by emphasizing the ἀνάστασις [resurrection]. Nonetheless, here a large question mark must be placed in the presentation of the book of Acts insofar as it emerges from 1 Corinthians 1, that, despite the previous consideration, the cross of Christ certainly played a more significant role in Paul's missionary sermon than is recognizable from Acts.

---

189. An exclamation mark in the margins by Harnack (?).
190. Marginal note by Harnack (?): "cf. 1 Thess. 1:9–10."

3. The *gospel* first and foremost *calls* for faith. This, too, is very naturally a part of the missionary sermon, though probably the demand for moral μετάνοια [repentance] was more pronounced than is evident here. The gospel was not the proclamation of a new morality, but "good news," and such requires, in the first place, πίστις [faith], that is, a trusting acceptance of what is heard.

4. Ultimately *eschatology* had to take a back seat in the missionary sermon. As little as the doctrine of justification, so too the doctrine of the *parousia* [return] of Christ could not be placed at the front for newcomers. Even mission today— unless it occurs under the sign of S. J. [Society of Jesus]—will not begin by "making hell hot" for the heathen.

It is probably unnecessary to emphasize that these modifications are no accommodations in the Catholic sense. What is present here is nothing other than an objectively justified method, applied with practical-psychological insight, in which the core of the gospel suffered no harm, especially when a personality like that of Paul was behind it.

And once again we are now in a position to turn the tables on the critics: If Paul's missionary preaching in the book of Acts were constructed according to what *Holtzmann* and *Jülicher* think should be obvious—in order to be accepted as authentic before their forum—then from the foregoing we would have to conclude with great certainty: the man who is writing there did not know the real Paul and his missionary preaching, but rather writes from his literary knowledge of him, that is, he reproduced "Paulinism."

Because this is not the case, the opposite is true: since the author writing ad Theophilum wishes to portray Paul as a missionary, the sermon he depicts is also a missionary sermon. And precisely because this is not simply "Paulinism," the author must have had personal knowledge of it [Paulinism].

We must still answer the literary-critical question posed at the outset: *To what extent are these speeches and speech fragments an authentic communication of the Pauline doctrine?* After the above discussions, that answer is easy to give.

On the whole, it would read: *According to the testimony of a contemporary and pupil, this was the Pauline missionary sermon.*

How that is to be understood is obvious: For Pauline doctrine, the book of Acts is and remains a second-rate source.[191]

This entails the following. Its statements contain the missionary sermon of Paul, but reproduced through the medium of the person of his pupil, which resulted in the modifications we have noted, insofar as these are not conditioned by their character as a missionary sermon.

One should then proceed accordingly if, for example, it was a matter of presenting Pauline teaching as such. Thus the speeches of the book of Acts should be considered more explicitly than was hitherto possible under the dominating presuppositions of literary criticism that we have opposed here; however, it is always to be done with the reservation that is a matter of course in every critical examination of a speaker who displays such strong literary peculiarities as the author writing ad Theophilum.

---

191. Harnack's marginal note: "I would say, *first rate*, although Paul appears here in the understanding of a Gentile Christian; for this Gentile Christian has grasped the essential perspectives correctly."

Should we still put up a smaller or greater fight for the measure of authenticity that should be ascribed to the relevant individual pieces, for example, the speech in Athens or Miletus? I do not think that is necessary.

In general, it will likely be the case that the author—where he thought it to be appropriate, according to his usual "art of composition,"[192] as we have already stated—composed and inserted these speeches, adhering substantially to what he himself had heard here and there from Paul himself. Whether and to what extent the very ideas of the Athenian speech in Athens are those presented in the Antiochian speech in Antioch [of Pisidia], that is simply no longer discernible for us, and all inquiries about them can, in the best case, lead to hypotheses without yielding anything objectively important.

Thus I think I can refrain from it, and therefore I think that my task is complete.

Conclusion

With this the most essential—but not all—aspects of Pauline missionary activity have been discussed. To the perhaps wrongly neglected questions, I would count, for example, the following: To what extent is Christian mission at the same time a battle against demons? (See, e.g., *Harnack*[193] et al.). Our book especially could have offered a rich yield, but I was not allowed to let this work bloat any further. Perhaps other issues I touched on too briefly, while with others I missed the opportunity to draw upon the first part of Acts. If the work as such remains a torso, I have at least achieved the personal goal of acquiring some reference points for the newly enflamed dispute about the author writing *ad Theophilum*.

It now remains for me to attempt an answer to the second question posed in my topic, drawing on the viewpoints arising from my three areas of investigations.

What significance does the author of the book of Acts give Paul in the whole of his historical course?

The title πράξεις ἀποστόλων [Acts of the Apostles] is misleading insofar as it creates the opinion—which has occurred repeatedly in the past and present, and which we have already challenged frequently here—that it is a church history of the first thirty years of Christianity, a "history of the planting and training of the Christian church by the apostles" (*Neander*).[194] This judgment is incorrect because, as we have seen many times, individual moments and entire series of incidents and developments are missing, which no chronicler—regardless of where one places him temporally—would have left unexplained. A chronicler of the earlier time—here I agree entirely with the criticism—would

---

192. Holtzmann, *Die Synoptiker. Die Apostelgeschichte*, 315.
193. Harnack, *Mission and Expansion of Christianity*, 1:152–80.
194. August Neander (1789–1850) published his *History of the Planting and Training of the Christian Church by the Apostles*, trans. J. E. Ryeland (Philadelphia: J. M. Campbell, 1844), as a history of the apostolic period.

need to offer better information on the internal currents and countercurrents flowing over all the congregations than is the case here.

A later chronicler, however, would inevitably reveal himself with reference to aspects of the Christian life at work in his time.

Specifically, the sketch of the figure of *Paul* as drawn in the book of Acts is, one way or another, unthinkable in a chronicle.

Paul is portrayed in the book of Acts only as a missionary. All other aspects of his work are absent altogether or are only hinted at. No matter how tendentious or ignorant, no church historian writes this way!

So if it is not a chronicle, then what? Should the second part of the book be understood perhaps as a *biography of Paul*? Even that cannot be the case, for the information about him has too many gaps for an earlier or a later author, for which *Weizsäcker*[195] has compiled a whole catalog of sins of omission. The conclusion of the book, too, would remain inexplicable from this perspective.

No, the observation is inescapable that, above all, the author wants to express an *idea*. Is this idea determined by inner-church partisanship? The older critical school thought so, but since *Overbeck*, everyone realizes that this cannot be the case; with equal probability the author could be put on one side or the other.[196]

Or does this idea consist—as *Overbeck* now thinks—of an argument between the Judaized Gentile Christian church with its own past and its founder, Paul?[197] The impression the book made on me is that it would be a very strange and contradictory argument.

If I am correct, then this idea is *the progression of the gospel through the* οἰκουμένη [inhabited earth],[198] from Jerusalem to Syria, then to Asia Minor, and then to Macedonia and *Hellas* [Achaia/Greece], finally culminating in the arrival of Paul in Rome. Can one object to this perspective and say with *Overbeck* that it overlooks the personal relation to the apostle Paul?[199] Probably not, since this triumphant advance as a whole actually does coincide with the effectiveness of the great apostle. The fact that the author does not treat the historical painting with a large brush is shown by the feature that, rather ill-suited to his pragmatism, the very first mission to the Gentiles does not come from Paul but from those persons scattered by the persecution [stoning] of Stephen [Acts 8:1, 4; 11:19–21]. Indeed, even at the climax, in Rome, Paul is not the first proclaimer of the gospel.

Someone later would not have proceeded in this way! Why is Paul the focus of [Luke's] interest in this way?

He is the greatest hero of Christian thought, and in no other apostle has that joyous and victorious idea been embodied as in him: "The gospel for the whole world!" [cf. Mark 16:15]. However, this knowledge could not be more directly known to anyone than to those who accompanied him on his travels, his known and unknown pupils.

A writer of the later period would certainly not have failed to provide Paul, the missionary to the Gentiles, with a distinctly colored dogmatic and

---

195. Weizsäcker, *Das apostolische Zeitalter*, 201.
196. Cf. F. Overbeck, "Introduction to the Acts of the Apostles," in *The Contents and Origins of the Acts of the Apostles, Critically Investigated*, by Edward Zeller, vol. 1, trans. Joseph Dare, 2–81 [London/Edinburgh: Wiliams & Norgate, 1875)], esp. 17–22; see also above, 111–13 [German 157–59].
197. Overbeck, "Introduction to the Acts of the Apostles," 21.
198. Harnack's marginal note: "Correct!"
199. Overbeck, "Introduction to the Acts of the Apostles," 16.

church-political coat. This is not the case here [in Acts], but in this Paul we recognize the actual historical personality—albeit in the mirror of another likewise very distinct personality—depicted exclusively as the warrior of the Christian cause moving outward. This account indicates to us that this second, reflective personality is familiar with the history of the Christian church and doctrine, but everything steps into the background for him, behind the significance of that victorious struggle for which the apostle is the first champion, but in which this [second] personality is himself, in his thought, in midstream.

And the latter observation, which runs through the whole of the second part of the book, finally justifies us in assuming that behind this personality there is none other than the one who in Acts 16:10 could say of himself:

"God has called *us* to proclaim the good news to them!"

The End[200]

---

200. Harnack's concluding comment: "The last section, 'Paul in the economy of the book of Acts,' is treated too briefly and does not do justice to the problems. Conversely, in the foregoing some things are treated too broadly, and some unnecessary things are also brought in. However, on the whole the work is very studious and very proficient. Its results have been achieved with circumspection and prudence and are tenable."

The Concept of Christ's Descent to the Underworld in Church Literature until Origen

1908

For the Winter Semester 1907–8, Barth moved to the University of Tübingen—"rather than obeying one's own instincts, paternal authority now takes hold more sharply."[1] *While otherwise thoroughly dissatisfied with the teaching offered in Tübingen, he worked there especially in preparation for his "second," systematic and practical, examinations in the State Church of Bern, which he began to plan for the Summer/Autumn of 1908.*[2] *Barth was initially "not quite sure" concerning the subject of his Accessarbeit (a required thesis as part of the examination in Bern). "First and foremost," he gathered literature; "one must just watch," he wrote to his father from Tübingen on October 24, 1907. On October 31, he declared to his parents: "Upon closer examination, my subject shifts very significantly, almost in its entirety. My mind is also not (!) capable of venturing into the Revelation of John. . . . Now I am considering another topic and urgently ask for expressions of opinion and pedagogical hints as soon as possible. It is about Christology, more precisely: the beginnings of the two-natures doctrine in the first and second centuries. . . . [The task would be to show] why the development from the New Testament . . . to the Apostolic Fathers . . . and the apologists, especially Justin, with a 'view' toward Irenaeus.*

"What do you think? For the time being, I'm studying the great Harnack, volume 1; material is there in abundance. If it becomes too much for me, I could easily limit myself to the New Testament. In any case, I would be a little more in the center here and would not need to be consumed by a thousand preliminary squabbles." On November 13, however, he had to admit to his parents: "As far as the Accessarbeit is concerned, I have realized for myself that I was going to bleed to death with that subject. Nevertheless, the completed preparatory work is not wasted. Through the reading of Gunkel's commentary on 1 Peter, another new question has opened for me, which is, however, decidedly more peripheral, but is on the other hand clearer, namely, a study of the ideas of Christ's preaching in Hades in the first and second centuries (i.e., again until about the time of Irenaeus). Already I have collected a mass of material and add something new to it daily: Old and New Testament Apocrypha, Apostolic Fathers, Talmud, and so on, plus a thousand comments 'from every dogmatic direction.' Anyway, I just want to complete this material, then one can still see. But the matter does not appear so noxious to me. I could dish out a hefty dose of Religionsgeschichte, and there are plenty of controversies contained there, but in predictable ways. Incidentally, this is a specifically Bernese subject; the old Güder wrote a book on the subject, and Professor Lauterburg wrote the

---

1. Autobiographical sketch for the album of the Protestant Theological Faculty of Münster (1927), in *Bw. B.*, 304.
2. Autobiographical sketch, 304–6.

article in the Realenzyklopädie. *However, I would be concerned only with the time before the creedal adoption [of the topic]."*

On November 20 Barth is already working intensively. He reports to his parents: *"I have experienced little. I am working almost constantly on the descensus, walking back and forth between the library and Neckargasse, and excerpting from all sorts of dusty old books. I am still not clear about the proper delimitation of the time that is to be examined; if I were to come to the third century, there would be no end in sight. Would it be possible simply to start with Tertullian and Clement of Alexandria?"* He remarks about the literature: *"I have consulted nineteen authors so far about 1 Peter 3:18–19 alone, and each one has a different opinion."* He now reported that the bibliographic work was *"quite complete, lacking only a rather important recent compilation by an American. The lemurs in the library do not want to acquire it; the topic is too remote for them. Perhaps I will get it without official permission from Berlin or Marburg, through a member of Zofingia."* For this purpose, he had the previous day already written a request to Otto Lauterburg: For his Accessarbeit he urgently needed *"the book or booklet of Huidekoper,* The Belief of the First Three Centuries concerning Christ's Mission to the Underworld *(New York, 1876),[3] which contains copious references. The doddering lemurs[4] at the local library do not have it and do not want to buy it either. Would you check and see if it is there in Marburg, and if it is, check it out in your name and send it to me illegally for a few weeks?! You would be doing me and the history of the apostolic age an extremely important service!"* Regarding *"the book of the old Güder,"* Barth expressed himself respectfully in a letter of November 20 to his parents: *"It was very erudite and judicious."* On November 25, he called Güder's book *"really shrewd"* to his father. In the same letter he described the previous Sunday, that, *"apart from the evening"* (which he probably spent, as so often, as a guest in the house of the student fraternity *"Königsgesellschaft Roigel"),* as having been *"rather Philistine":* he spent *"a nice long day"* making *"excerpts for the thesis from a fat edition of Irenaeus." "Probably I will only go to work on the thesis itself after New Year, since the procurement of material requires much running and copying out (one can only take four books home from the library at a time)."* Similarly, on December 12 to his father: *"As far as the thesis is concerned, I hope by Christmas to have all the material together, and after Christmas to proceed to writing."*

So it happened. After he spent his Christmas holiday first in Bern and then visiting Bad Boll (from December 28, 1907, until January 2, 1908), he got to work elaborating his study. On January 6, he wrote about it to his school friend Willy Spoendlin: *"Now I am sitting here again, smoking vast quantities of tobacco, and building up my Accessarbeit. My youthful happiness is buried, for the 23rd time. Day by day, I become more and more a gloomy, grumpy old-man. . . . Tübingen is a miserable nest, and the Theology Faculty is a dive."* On January 15, to his parents: *"There is not much to tell you about. I work all day long on the descensus, which has already grown to over a hundred pages and will be worthy to stand next to my folio on Paul. Often I'm going until midnight, or even half-past. I would still like to finish it in January."* On January 21, again to his parents: *"My thesis, which keeps me constantly occupied*

---

3. Frederic Huidekoper, *The Belief of the First Three Centuries concerning Christ's Mission to the Underworld* (1853), rev. ed. (New York: James Miller, 1876).
4. Trans.: Here Barth quotes from Goethe's *Faust* (2.11.515–611). Mephistopheles summons a gang of lemurs [= ghosts] to dig Faust's grave.

every day and especially every night, develops significantly. I hope to finish the manuscript soon; I only have Origen left to do, admittedly a fat mouthful. Lüdemann will hardly take a positive view of the stuff, because in all general questions I nourish myself on the chunks that fell from Harnack's tables. I also do not quite harmonize with the views of Lauterburg, especially not in relation to 1 Peter 3:18–20. Clearly Spitta has made too much of an impression on him there." In a letter on January 28, he thanked his parents for his father's newly published Introduction to the New Testament:[5] *"This morning I received the letter and book. Many thanks indeed; they come at a good time, because yesterday afternoon Leviathan II was definitively killed and is now resting with the bookbinder, so I will now have plenty of time to study the Introduction. The torment of the last weeks was great. Since the beginning of the month, I have seldom gone to bed before 12 and I have also skipped lectures quite a bit, both circumstances alike having impacted on quality as in the semester when I was president!!!"* (In the summer semester of 1907, Barth was president of the Bernese Zofingia, with the implied consequences for this study.) *"Now 190 pages are freshly written, and I pity the Pastor Gentlemen who have to read the whole thing. I can already hear in my mind the voice of Lüdemann: lopsided, wrong, and dependent on Harnack, and on your daddy: a couple of times you have wildly missed the mark."*

It is just annoying that the stuff has to sit in the drawer for three-quarters of a year, during which time I can think of many additional things, which will then annoy me. Relatedly, this Accessarbeit really isn't meant to be a confession of faith, right? From A to Z, it contains not a syllable of my own dogmatics. I even deleted the occasional forays from the draft (in a similar way to the study for Harnack) because they only disturbed the unity of an otherwise purely historical work. I also skipped a concluding dogmatic section, because without enlisting some or all of the remaining dogmatics, I would only have been able to make assertions. Certainly I am not very satisfied, because now the stuff again corresponds much too closely to the Overbeckian ideal of 'profane' church historiography. Well, I am glad that this piece of examination work is behind me."

In fact, the feared trouble over subsequently discovered omissions did not fail to materialize. On June 9, Barth wrote to his parents from Marburg, giving a melancholic outlook on the approaching exam: "It will be miserable. . . . The Accessarbeit is full of cabbage, and now it falls into Lüdemann's hands. Oh, woe is me, woe is me!" Even after he had passed the examination with the mark 2 [good], Barth was not absolutely satisfied with his performance. On December 14, 1908, he offered his judgment in a letter to his parents: "I have recognized with increasing clarity that academic work in the narrow sense is not for me. Constructing the descensus ad inferos was all well and good! After Lauterburg's death, I can take over the article in the Realenzyklopädie. But sunt certi denique fines [there are certain limits]. . . ."

The manuscript comprises 194 pages in the 23 × 18.3 cm format, with a wide margin for corrections, bound in paperback with a calico spine. The title is on a special title page with the addition: "Accessarbeit. Submitted: Tübingen, January 27, 1908. Karl Barth, cand. theol." [The page numbers in the following table of contents have been changed to correspond to the pages of this volume:]

---

5. Fritz Barth, *Einleitung in das Neue Testament* (Gütersloh: C. Bertelsmann, 1908).

Contents

Introduction

It could already be said in the eighteenth century that *"de descensu tantum ferme dissertationum est, quantum es muscarum, quum calteur maxime"* [concerning the descensus nearly as many discourses have been made as there are flies, since it is especially heated].[6] Indeed, our topic appears to have been a popular theme in the old theological schools at Helmstedt, Wittenberg, Altdorf, and others. This did not change in the nineteenth century. On account of 1 Peter 3:18–20, theologians of every observance have always returned to the descensus with particular eagerness, whether to glorify its "all-encompassing meaning"[7] or to discard it as "a myth without biblical foundation."[8] Through the well-known dispute concerning the Apostles' Creed,[9] it has gained prominence altogether,

---

6. H. Witsius, *Exercitationes sacrae in Symbolum quod Apostolorum dicitur et in Orationem Dominicam,* 3rd ed. (Amsterdam, 1697), 319. Barth obviously cites this following E. Güder, who cites the *Exercitationes* from the edition of 1730: E. Güder, *Die Lehre von der Erscheinung Jesu Christi unter den Todten: In ihrem Zusammenhange mit der Lehre von den letzten Dingen* (Bern, 1853), 257.

7. Cf. J. L. König, *Die Lehre von Christi Höllenfahrt, nach der heiligen Schrift, der ältesten Kirche, den christlichen Symbolen, und nach ihrer vielumfassenden Bedeutung* (Frankfurt am Main, 1842), see esp. 202.

8. Cf. A. Schweizer, *Hinabgefahren zur Hölle, als Mythus ohne biblische Begründung durch Auslegung der Stelle 1. Petr. 3, 17–22 nachgewiesen* (Zurich, 1868).

9. Cf. F. M. Schiele, *"Apostolikumstreit,"* in *RGG*[1] 1:601–8, esp. 605–6.

and finally the modern *religionsgeschichtliche* school has not passed over the subject without leaving its mark.

I was led to this topic by coincidental reading. Certainly, without the harsh necessity[10] of an *Accessarbeit*—which approaches every Bernese theologian once, when his hour has come [cf. John 2:4; 16:21]—I would hardly have been induced to approach such a tried and tested question, which moreover at first sight has something so fantastical and bizarre about it. However, I have felt that the study of precisely this kind of religious phenomena, as strange as they might seem to us today, has peculiar charm, provided one does not try in advance to make the work of this phenomena serve an alien, modern purpose—whether it be to "save" a piece of Christian antiquity by carrying it into dogmatics, or to signal how imaginatively and inadequately earlier generations thought "and how we have finally made magnificent advances."[11] I have, therefore, consciously left untouched the *dogmatic* question, which could only be negotiated on a much broader foundation. For similar reasons, I have refrained from discussing the *history of religion* (taken in the narrower sense!) side of the matter: I know too little about the area and would therefore depend upon authorities or upon individual conjecture.

I have limited myself, then, to the history of the exegetical-doctrinal approach to the problem and set myself the question: *Which religious and theological motives have led to the establishment of ideas about the descensus ad inferos in Christian theology and in the church?* Concluding with Origen is commended for factual reasons: the subsequent period had, perhaps, a new way of formulating the question, which brought with it a new form of the idea, but from then on, an actual expansion of the conceptual realm has not come to pass.

Before I now proceed to the matter itself, I need to lay down an account of the literature that I have used. [This bibliography is retained in its original form as in Barth's monograph. Trans.]

Specialist literature concerning the Descensus

- König, *Die Lehre von Christi Höllenfahrt* 1842[12]
- E. Güder, *Die Lehre von der Erscheinung Jesu Christi unter den Todten* 1853
- A. Schweizer, *Hinabgefahren zur Hölle* 1868
- Josephson, 'Niedergefahren zur Hölle' in 'Der Beweis des Glaubens' 1897 401–9
- Kattenbusch, 'Niedergefahren zur Hölle' in 'Die christliche Welt' 1889 Nr. 27 u. 32x
- Fr. Spitta, 'Christi Predigt an die Geister' 1890

---

10. Horatius, *Camina* 3.24.6.
11. J. W. von Goethe, *Faust* 1.5.573.
12. J. L. König, *Christi Höllenfahrt*; E. Güder, *Christi unter den Todten*; A. Schweizer, *Hinabgefahren zur Hölle*; H. Josephson, "Niedergefahren zur Hölle," *BGl*, NF, 18 (1897): 401–17; F. Kattenbusch, "Niedergefahren zur Hölle," *CW* 3, no. 27 (1889): 531–34; F. Kattenbusch, "Ein Wort über 1. Petr. 3, 19," in *CW* 3, no. 32 (1889): 627–29; F. Spitta, *Christi Predigt an die Geister (1 Petr. 3, 19–20): Ein Beitrag zur neutestamentlichen Theologie* (Göttingen: Vandenhoeck & Ruprecht, 1890); M. Lauterburg, "Höllenfahrt Christi," in *RE3* 8 (1900): 199–206; C. Clemen, *"Niedergefahren zu den Toten": Ein Beitrag zur Würdigung des Apostolikums* (Giessen: J. Ricker, 1900).

- M. Lauterburg, Art. 'Höllenfahrt Christi' in P. R. E.[3] 1900 VIII 199–200.
- C. Clemen, 'Niedergefahren zu den Toten' 1900[13]

Literature on 1 Peter 3:18–20, etc.

- Weizel, 'Die urchristl. Unsterblichkeitslehre' in 'Stud. u. Kritiken' 1836 S. 895f.[14]
- B. Weiss, Der petrinische Lehrbegriff [2]1855 S. 216f.
- G. Volkmar, 'Über die kathol. Briefe und Henoch' in Z. w. Th. 1861 S. 422f.
- Baur, 'Vorlesungen über die neutestamentl. Theologie' 1864 291–292.
- De Wette-Brückner, Kurzgefasstes exeg. Handbuch zum NT.[3] III[1] 1865 74–75.
- Sieffert, 'Die Heilsbedeutung des Leidens u. Sterbens Christi' in Jb. f. d. Th. 1875 371–373
- Hofmann, Die hl. Schrift Neuen Testamentes zusammenhängend untersucht VII 1875
- C. W. Otto in Z. f. kirchl. Wissensch. 1883 83–85.
- Usteri, Wissensch. u. prakt. Commentar über den ersten Petrusbrief 1887 140–141.
- v. Soden, in 'Handkommentar zum NT' (Holtzmann) III[2] 1890 131–133.
- Oppenrieder, in 'D. Beweis d. Glaubens' 1893 230–232.
- Burger, in 'Kurzgef. Handcommentar' (Strack u. Zöckler) B. IV 1895 171–173.
- J. T. Beck, 'Erklärung der Briefe Petri' 1896 S. 188–190.
- Kühl, im Krit.-Exeg. Kommentar über das NT (Meyer) 1897 219–220.
- Gunkel, in 'Die Schriften des NT' (Joh. Weiss) II [Lfg.] 3 1907 51–53.[15]

---

13. In an unfamiliar handwriting (correctors?), the following title is added in pencil here: J. M. Usteri, *"Hinabgefahren zur Hölle": Eine Wiedererwägung der Schriftstellen; 1. Petr. 3, 18–22 und Kap. 4, Vers 6* (Zurich: S. Höhr, 1886). In addition, two further bibliographical references are added by Barth himself in pencil, the second also with a clearly later handwriting: J. Weiss, "Höllenfahrt im NT," in *RGG*[3] 3 (1912; delivery issue, 1910): 82–88; F. Loofs, *Die Auferstehungsberichte u. ihr Wert* [booklet for *Christlichen Welt* 33 (1908): 3; see esp. 41–43, Appendix 1: "Das vere resurrexit im Lichte der ursprünglichen Vorstellungen vom descensus."

14. K. L. Weizel, "Die urchristliche Unsterblichkeitslehre," *ThStKr* 9 (1836), vol. 2:579–640, 895–981; B. Weiss, *Der petrinische Lehrbegriff: Beiträge zur biblischen Theologie, sowie zur Kritik und Exegese des ersten Briefes Petri und der petrinischen Reden*, 2nd ed. (Berlin, 1855); G. Volkmar, "Ueber die katholischen Briefe und Henoch," *ZWT* 4 (1861): 422–36; 5 (1862): 46–75; F. C. Baur, *Vorlesungen über neutestamentliche Theologie*, ed. F. F. Baur (Leipzig, 1864); W. M. L. De Wette, *Kurze Erklärung der Briefe des Petrus, Judas und Jakobus*, ed. B. Brückner, 3rd ed., vol. III/1, Kurzgefasstes exegetisches Handbuch zum Neuen Testament (Leipzig, 1865); F. E. A. Sieffert, "Die Heilsbedeutung des Leidens und Sterbens Christi nach dem ersten Briefe des Petrus," *JDTh* 20 (1875): 371–440; J. C. K. von Hofmann, *Die heilige Schrift neuen Testaments zusammenhängend untersucht*, vol. 7, *Die Briefe Petri, Judä und Jakobi*, part 1, *Der erste Brief Petri* (Nördlingen, 1875); C. W. Otto, "Auslegung von 1 Petr. 3, 17–22 in besonderer Beziehung auf 1 Petr. 3, 21," *ZKWL* 4 (1883): 83–96; J. M. Usteri, *Wissenschaftlicher und praktischer Commentar über den ersten Petrusbrief*, part 1, *Die Auslegung* (Zurich, 1887); H. von Soden, *Hebräerbrief; Briefe des Petrus, Jakobus, Judas*, HC 3.2 (Freiburg im Breisgau, 1890); A. Oppenrieder, "1 Petr. 3, 19: Von der Predigt, welche Christus nach Petri Wort den im Gefängnis befindlichen Geistern gehalten hat," *BGl*, NF, 14 (1893): 230–46; K. Burger, *Der erste Brief Petri*, in KK, B: Neues Testament, sec. 4, 2nd ed. (Munich, 1895), 153–80; J. T. Beck, *Erklärung der Briefe Petri*, ed. J. Lindenmeyer (Gütersloh, 1896); E. Kühl, *Die Briefe Petri und Judae*, 6th ed., KEK 12 (Göttingen 1897); H. Gunkel, *Der erste Brief des Petrus*, 2nd ed., SNT 2 (Göttingen, 1908), 529–71.

15. [Translator's note]: The Tübingen University Library permits only four volumes to be checked out at any time. I thus have had to proceed with the help of excerpting and ask the reader's pardon when no page number is given in the cited literature.

For the later sections, I used especially Harnack's textbook *Grundriss*[16] and my notes from the lectures on the history of dogma (Winter Semester 1906–7).[17]

Editions Used

Ignatius / Polycarp	*Hilgenfeld* 1902[18]
Shepherd of Hermas	*Harnack* Patr. Apost. III 1875
Justin	*Migne*, Patrologia graeca VI
Irenaeus	*Stieren* 1853
Tertullian	*Öhler* 1853
Hippolytus	*Lagarde* 1858
Clement of Alexandria	*Migne*, Patr. Gr. VIII, IX
Origen	*Migne*, P. Gr., XI–XIV
Eusebius	*Migne*, P. Gr., XX, XXII
Epiphanius	*Dindorf*, 1859–62
The Gospel of Peter	*Preuschen*, Antilegomena 1901
Sibylline Oracles	*Geffcken* 1902
Testament of the Twelve Patriarchs	*Migne*, P. gr., II

Chapter 1: The New Testament

Harnack (*Lehrbuch*, vol. 1) says of the concept of the descensus ad inferos: "In the first century, it remained uncertain, standing on the border of those productions of religious imagination that could not immediately find their home in the community."[19]

Let us compare this judgment with that of *Josephson*: "If we did not know about Christ's journey into hell from Holy Scripture, we would almost have

---

16. A. Harnack, *Lehrbuch der Dogmengeschichte*, vols. 1–3, 3rd ed., Sammlung theologischer Lehrbücher (Freiburg im Breisgau/Leipzig, or Freiburg im Breisgau/Leipzig/Tübingen, 1894–1897); Harnack, *Dogmengeschichte*, 4th ed., Grundriss der theologischen Wissenschaften 4.3 (Tübingen, 1905).

17. "Dogmen-Geschichte. Gehört bei Prof. D. Harnack, Berlin im W. S. 1906–7 (Mittwoch u. Samstag 9–11)" [History of Dogma, Heard from Professor D. Harnack, Berlin, in the Winter Semester of 1906–7, Wednesday and Saturday] (in the Karl Barth Archive, Basel).

18. *Ignatii Antiocheni et Polycarpi Smyrnaei epistulae et martyria*, ed. and annotated at the instruction of A. Hilgenfeld (Berlin, 1902); *Hermae Pastor graece: Addita versione latina recentiore e codice palatino, recensuerunt et illustraverunt O. de Gebhardt* and A. Harnack, *Patrum Apostolicorum Opera: Textum ad fidem codicum et graecorum et latinorum adhibitis praestantissimis editionibus recensuerunt commentario exegetico et historico illustraverunt apparatu critico versione latina passim correcta prolegomenis indicibus instruxerunt O. de Gebhardt, A. Harnack, and Th. Zahn*, Editio post Dresselianam alteram tertia, Fasciculus 3 (Leipzig, 1877); *S. P. N. Justini opera quae existant omnia*, PG 6 (Paris, 1857); *Sancti Irenaei quae supersunt omnia*, ed. A. Stieren, vols. 1–2 (Leipzig, 1853); *Quinti Septimii Florentis Tertulliani quae supersunt omnia*, ed. F. Oehler, vols. 1–3 (Leipzig, 1851–54); *Hippolyti Romani quae feruntur omnia graece*, ed. P. A. de Lagarde (Leipzig/London, 1858); *Clementis Alexandrini opera quae exstant omnia*, PG 8–9 (Paris, 1857); Origen, *Opera omnia*, PG 11–17 (Paris, 1857–60); Eusebius, *Pamphili opera omnia quae exstant*, PG 19–24 (Paris, 1857); *Epiphanii opera*, ed. G. Dindorf, vols. 1–4 (Leipzig, 1859–62); E. Preuschen, ed. and trans., *Antilegomena: Die Reste der ausserkanonischen Evangelien und urchristlichen Ueberlieferungen* (Giessen, 1901); *Die Oracula Sibyllina*, ed. J. Geffcken, GCS (Leipzig, 1902); *S. Clementis I opera omnia: Accedunt S. Barnabae Apostoli Epistola Catholica, S. Hermae Pastor, et aliae aevi apostolici reliquiae*, PG 1–2 (Paris, 1857); *S. P. N. Athanasii opera omnia quae exstant vel quae ejus nomine circumferuntur*, PG 25–28 (Paris, 1857).

19. Harnack, *Lehrbuch*, 1:194.

to postulate it."[20] It is obvious that this belongs to the dogmatic side of the theme as a *question de vie* [matter of life]. Hence, it is necessary to proceed even more cautiously if our study is to follow the evidence from the early church. A comparison of the naive and likewise extensive collection of positions in *König*[21] with the statements of *Schweizer* allows us to recognize how many of the positions go against each other here.

First, we have to clarify the question of structure of the used works. The type of approach adopted by *Güder*—who simply considers the passages in their biblical-theological order of occurrence—appears to me to be confusing: (Christ in Hades, the mode of the event, the work of Christ in hell, the triumph).[22] Even with the greatest caution, the danger of *petitio principii* [begging the question] is all too obvious. It probably does not need proving that the higgledy-piggledy structure of *König*, who simply orders the material according to the degree of the probative force of the evidence as it appears to him,[23] is not appropriate. I cannot, however, agree with *Clemen* either when, on the basis of his hypothesis concerning the history of the creed, he simply proceeds from 1 Peter 3:18–20 without further argument.[24] Even in historical questions, the old methodological principle of illuminating "dark" places with "bright" ones is not without danger.

I propose, then, to proceed here in *chronological* order, insofar as this is possible, given the uncertain specific results of New Testament scholarship.

The areas given serious consideration can be divided into three main groups:

1. *Paul*: One of the pertinent places is in the Epistle to the Ephesians. From the perspective of the Tübingen School, this would be accordingly read as "Pauline Literature." However, the question of Pauline authorship has little meaning here: whether we attribute the relevant passage to Paul himself or to a Pauline thinker is irrelevant to the consequences of this study.

2. *Matthew* and *Luke*: What is under consideration in the following sections all come from the so-called "distinctive sources" or from the Acts of the Apostles.

3. *1 Peter*: I mention this writing in last place, because it occupies a place of special prominence in our question and certainly is to be set chronologically after the Pauline corpus. The former aspect, however, is not, as already happened, to be misunderstood, as if the descensus concept here *in itself* could be used as an argument for the pseudonymity of the epistle.

We will now initially proceed purely inductively and then at the end of the chapter set out some general considerations.

§1. Paul

One of the keystones of Pauline theology is built upon here: the death of Christ is the life of the world, because it is the death of death: κατεπόθη ὁ θάνατος εἰς νῖκος [death has been swallowed up in victory] (1 Cor. 15:54). In the circle

20. Josephson, "Niedergefahren zur Hölle," 411.
21. König, *Christi Höllenfahrt*, 10–63.
22. Güder, *Christi unter den Todten*, 15–36, 36, 37–61, 61–88.
23. Cf. König, *Christi Höllenfahrt*, 12.
24. Clemen, *"Zu den Toten,"* 104.

of Pauline ideas, this is subsequently followed by a broader train of thought, which comes into question here.

That victory manifests itself in the complete dominion of Christ over the world—over the δυνάμεις, ἀρχαί, ἐξουσίαι [powers, principalities, and authorities] (1 Cor. 15:24; Col. 2:15; Eph. 1:21)—in both the future and the present. This is outwardly presented in the belief in Christ's exaltation over the heavens (Rom. 10:6; Phil. 2:9, Eph. 1:20; 4:10): Christ is ἀναβάς [raised up]. As a counterpart to this, although admittedly not equally pronounced, it is occasionally the case that the καταβάς [descent] is found to precede this. The meaning of this thought is explained by Paul in only one place unequivocally: *Romans 10:6–7*. Righteousness will be granted to everyone from Christ onward, on condition that they believe. The "achievements" of the law are superfluous, because the one achievement has been fulfilled once and for all. Who can ascend to the heavens in order to bring Christ down? ἢ τίς καταβήσεται εἰς τὴν ἄβυσσον; τοῦτ᾽ ἔστιν Χριστὸν ἐκ νεκρῶν ἀναγαγεῖν [Or who will descend into the abyss? that is, to bring Christ up from the dead]. Without further argument, it is clear from this that Paul knows of a time when Christ was in the ἄβυσσος [abyss] and therefore, as the addition shows, lingered in the kingdom of the dead.

More difficult is the parallel text from Ephesians (4:8–10), which the church fathers preferred to employ for the descensus. The multifarious gifts that are given to people are illustrated here through the various phases that their giver, Jesus Christ, has undergone, he who nonetheless always remained the same: ἀναβὰς εἰς ὕψος ᾐχμαλώτευσεν αἰχμαλωσίαν . . . τὸ δὲ ἀνέβη τί ἐστιν εἰ μὴ ὅτι καὶ κατέβη εἰς τὰ κατώτερα μέρη τῆς γῆς; ὁ καταβὰς αὐτός ἐστιν καὶ ὁ ἀναβάς [having ascended into the heights, he made captivity captive. What does "he ascended" mean, other than that he descended into the lower parts of the earth; the one who descended is the one who ascended]. . . . The question of the meaning of this passage for our present topic is ultimately concentrated on the interpretation of κατώτερα μέρη τῆς γῆς [the lower parts of the earth]. The context can be brought into play against the reference to the underworld, and in favor of the reference to the first or second coming of Christ on earth. Nonetheless, it seems advisable not to overstretch this authority, since as Romans 10:7 and 1 Peter 3:18 indicate, sometimes our subject occurs in parentheses on precisely the occasions when it is not clearly anticipated.

This is also the case in other such questions that lie on the boundary between theology and speculation, as indicated in the well-known kenosis passage, Philippians 2:6–11. When it comes to the interpretation of the descensus ad inferos, it seems to me that the expression κατώτερα μέρη τῆς γῆς [the lower parts of the earth] speaks for itself: as reference to the earth and in contrast to ὕψος [heights], it sounds somewhat unclear and artificial. It is furthermore the case that parallel texts, both older (Rom. 10:7) and younger (Shepherd of Hermas, *Similitudes* 9.16.6; etc.) characteristically present the descensus concept in terms of the contrast between ἀναβαίνειν [ascend] and καταβαίνειν [descend]. Finally and above all, it is the case that in later literature the descensus thought is well witnessed—if not for Ephesus, then for Asia Minor a short time later—and that the probability therefore increases, the later the dating of the Epistle to the Ephesians is pushed.

Certainly the exegesis of the church fathers erred on another point (although Irenaeus, *Against Heresies* 5.31.1, still avoided this mistake) when they took ἠχμαλώτευσεν αἰχμαλωσίαν [captivity captive] (Eph. 4:8) to refer to the success of the descent,[25] whereas it is especially characteristic of the Pauline conception that the victory over the δυνάμεις [powers] and the like, and even over death, is attributed to the exalted Christ, without reference to any special success of the descent. For these texts, ἵνα πληρώσῃ τὰ πάντα [in order that he might fill all things] (Eph. 4:10) and ἵνα ἐν τῷ ὀνόματι Ἰησοῦ πᾶν γόνυ κάμψῃ ἐπουρανίων καὶ ἐπιγείων καὶ καταχθονίων [so that at the name of Jesus every knee should bend, in heaven and on earth and under the earth] (Phil. 2:10), already portray the consummation of perfection.

The descensus motif is of interest in the Pauline literature as a counterpoint to the *ascensus in coelum* [ascent into heaven], as such, however, always already as part of the glory of Christ.

In the Pauline system as a whole, it plays its role (though, at the same time, being subordinate and receding), as the *completion of the christological concept*: even Hades was not left untouched by Christ. I do not overlook the fact that, at that time, statements about the person and work of Christ corresponded in a very different manner than was later the case. While separating these motifs inside this unity, one is permitted to say: the statements of Paul about the descensus (the oldest literary documents that we know on the issue) are to be explained from Christology and not from ideas about salvation.

§2. Matthew and Luke

First, we must refer here to Matthew 12:40 (ὥσπερ . . . Ἰωνᾶς ἐν τῇ κοιλίᾳ τοῦ κήτους [just as . . . Jonah in the belly of the sea monster], etc.), which also played a major role in the patristic reasoning from Irenaeus onward. The question of whether this is an authentic saying of Jesus is irrelevant in this context, since the question here is only what was understood by it in the years 70–100.

The answer will have to be this: *perhaps* merely a sojourn in the grave, but *perhaps* a sojourn in the underworld. Although, as *Güder* already emphasized,[26] ἐν τῇ καρδίᾳ τῆς γῆς [in the heart of the earth] is not to be pressed into this meaning, since the LXX (Jonah 2:4) uses ἐν καρδίᾳ θαλάσσης [in the heart of the sea] without a similar meaning. On the other hand, however, we may point out, following *Clemen*,[27] that the LXX's ἐκ κοιλίας ᾅδου [in the belly of Hades] (Jonah 2:3) would give a fitting counterpoint to κοιλία τοῦ κήτους [in the belly of the sea monster] (Matt. 12:40). Today it would hardly be possible to enter a certain judgment about how the early Christian community interpreted this, let alone about what meaning the author (possibly Jesus himself) wanted to put into these words. Nonetheless, if it were referring to the descensus ad inferos, then it would belong to the same circle of ideas that we encountered in St. Paul, namely, purely christological: the "sign of the prophet Jonah" is Christ's visit to the place of deepest darkness (self-evidently completed at the resurrection).

---

25. See below, 210–11.
26. Güder, *Christi unter den Todten*, 17–19.
27. Clemen, "Zu den Toten," 156.

In contrast, *Matthew 27:50–54*—the description of the miraculous natural events in the moment of Jesus's death—leads us into a totally different context. If we have—as has recently been supposed—a memory of historical occurrences[28] in the description of the temple curtain being torn, the earthquake, and the opening of (rock) tombs, then 27:52b–53 is certainly based on legend: πολλὰ σώματα τῶν κεκοιμημένων ἁγίων ἠγέρθησαν, καὶ ἐξελθόντες ἐκ τῶν μνημείων μετὰ τὴν ἔγερσιν αὐτοῦ εἰσῆλθον εἰς τὴν ἁγίαν πόλιν καὶ ἐνεφανίσθησαν πολλοῖς [many bodies of the saints who had fallen asleep were raised, and after his resurrection they entered the holy city and appeared to many]. As recent critics rightly suppose, μετὰ τὴν ἔγερσιν αὐτοῦ [after his resurrection] should for now be deleted as a dogmatically interested interpolation (cf. 1 Cor. 15:20; Col. 1:18; Acts 26:23).[29] Various ideas intersect in curious ways in this report. On the one hand, the state after death is clearly thought to be material: they are bodies (not like Luke 24:37, 39, πνεύματα [spirits]) and—after the presentation of certain layers of Jewish eschatology—they reside in the grave until the moment of resurrection. At the same time, they have, however, the property of invisibility, or at least partial visibility: ἐνεφανίσθησαν πολλοῖς [they appeared to many] (Matt. 27:53). In any case, the original idea of the report is this: at the moment of the death of Jesus, or in its immediate aftermath, "many bodies of the departed saints were raised to new life." Which saints? All of them? Those who belonged to the old covenant, or the recently dead? Only in the region of Jerusalem, or also elsewhere? To all of these questions, we receive no answer. This is the best proof that we are dealing not with a reflective belief, but with an immediate, almost self-evident, popular conviction. In Christ's death is the life of humanity, for the living just as for those who are already dead: one of the most certain elements of the early Christian faith, which was admittedly at that time already differentiating itself in specific details. We have before us one such area of differentiation at the popular level. Undoubtedly, it indicates one of the roots of the descensus concept. As a result of the preaching of the generally efficacious nature of Christ's death, the question must have been taken up, at the latest in the second generation: *How do things stand with the faithful who died before the coming of Christ?* The tradition had no answer to this; consequently, legends and theological speculation were given more scope. What we have before us is an attempt at such an answer. Later, we will see which consequences are drawn from it.

Turning to Luke, we need to deal above all with the word from the cross to the repentant thief, *Luke 23:43*: "Today you will be with me in paradise." Recall that παράδεισος = κόλπος Ἀβραάμ [paradise = the bosom of Abraham] (Luke 16:22) was, in late-Jewish eschatology, not a final eschatological state, but rather the stay of the righteous in the intermediate state, and thus—according to Greek terminology—a part of Hades. Therefore, we have from the mouth of Jesus himself, possibly according to the understanding of a specific Christian community in the first century, the idea expressed that Jesus after his death lingered for a certain period of time in the realm of the dead. Luke seems to have handled this idea with a certain degree of self-confidence, as is indicated

---

28. Cf., e.g., T. von Zahn, *Das Evangelium des Matthäus*, 2nd ed., KNT 1 (Leipzig, 1905), 706–14.

29. Cf. also for the following, J. Weiss, *Das Matthäus-Evangelium*, in *Die Schriften des Neuen Testaments*, ed. J. Weiss, 2nd ed. (Göttingen, 1907), 1:398.

by *Acts 2:27, 31*, where the resurrection is essentially depicted as liberation from Hades, but there is an utterly clear distinction between this liberation on the one hand, and the general resurrection on the other hand: οὔτε ἐνκατελείφθη εἰς ᾅδην οὔτε ἡ σὰρξ αὐτοῦ εἶδεν διαφθοράν [he was not abandoned to Hades, nor did his flesh undergo corruption]. *Acts 2:24*—ὅν ὁ θεὸς ἀνέστησεν λύσας τὰς ὠδῖνας τοῦ θανάτου [but God has raised him up, having freed him from the pain of death]—was understood in a similar sense, as is indicated by the parallel text from Polycarp on Philippians 1:2, where the final two words [i.e., "of death"] are rendered by τοῦ ᾅδου [Hades].

If, then, the thought of the descensus could ever actually be established in Luke, the question concerning his interest in it could easily be answered: according to Luke, as in Paul, the sojourn of Christ in Hades is the antipole of his exaltation at the right hand of the Father, but just as is the case there, it is at the same time already part of this exaltation. Here again, the motif is christological.

§3. 1 Peter

"This is as strange and obscure a text as the New Testament contains. I do not know at all what St. Peter meant"; thus *Martin Luther* occasionally commented upon 1 Peter 3:18–19.[30] In fact, if one examines the sections concerning this verse in commentaries and detailed studies, one can say that this verse has found as many interpretations as it has interpreters. It is, then, more paradoxical than perceptive when *Spitta* claims that "there can be little talk of exegetical difficulties."[31]

From the outset I would like to reject two types of "moods" that can be brought to this text. One is characterized by the saying in *Weizel* that this passage "through its artificial and clumsy words, as through the apocalyptic darkness of its doctrine and its adventurously mysterious character, easily betrays the late origin of the epistle and the idea in question."[32] The other can be found in *Burger*: "For those interpreters who deny the authenticity and inspiration of the epistle, the present difficulty is, of course, significantly reduced. . . . For our part, we must conclude our exposition with a serious question mark."[33] One is just as ahistorical as the other. But equally, *Schweizer's* appeal to the general "fundamental view of the New Testament"[34] should not be allowed to gain the decisive place. Rather, *Josephson's* consideration—if perhaps in something of a different sense—applies here: "The New Testament writings are not textbooks. Rather, they are occasional writings, in the best sense of that word, in which it more or less depended upon chance (if the expression is permitted here) whether one of the saving truths is placed more in the foreground, while the other is mentioned rarely or not at all."[35]

---

30. M. Luther, *Epistel S. Petri gepredigt und ausgelegt*, first ed. (1523), WA 12:367, 27–29; Güder, *Christi unter den Todten*, 223.

31. Spitta, *Predigt an die Geister*, 2.

32. Weizel, "Urchristliche Unsterblichkeitslehre," 923, note a.

33. Burger, *Brief Petri*, 173.

34. Schweizer, *Hinabgefahren zur Hölle*, 17.

35. Josephson, "Niedergefahren zur Hölle," 409–10.

The context of 1 Peter 3 concerns the attitude of suffering Christians, especially the sufferings of persecution. "Be ready to give an answer to anyone, . . . but in meekness and timidity! For it is truly better, if it should be in God's providence, to suffer for righteous deeds than for evil deeds" (1 Pet. 3:15–17). It is premature when *Spitta* immediately chimes in: "from the outset it is therefore probable that 1 Peter 3:19–20 somehow illustrates the misery of the suffering of the unjust in comparison to the destiny of the righteous."[36] The righteous had already been mentioned, and as 1 Peter 3:18 continues ὅτι καὶ Χριστὸς ἅπαξ περὶ ἁμαρτιῶν ἀπέθανεν, δίκαιος ὑπὲρ ἀδίκων [for Christ also died for sins once for all, righteous and unrighteous], it rather seems to me (in agreement with *Güder*,[37] *Kühl*,[38] et al.) probable that what follows is somehow intended as a parallel between the behavior of Christ and the path to be taken by the reader.

Before we enter into the details of this matter, it must first be considered in which *external circumstances* verses 19–21 relate to their context. Remembering the overall style of the letter, we can first observe with most interpreters (only *Spitta* explicitly maintains the opposite)[39] that this is a *digression* from the actual topic, insofar as the point mentioned here does not necessarily cohere with the context: with verse 18 the parallel was already clearly drawn. Three possibilities exist in relation to this digression: either it originates with the *author's* own independent composition, or the author here inserts a piece from a *christological formula*, as *Clemen* holds,[40] or the whole passage is a *gloss*, indeed from one of the hymns of the early Christian community, as (naturally!) a Dutchman, *Cramer*, has suggested![41] Without eliminating the possibility of this last solution, it would nevertheless be advisable, on account of its lack of text-historical foundation, to be somewhat cautious about dissolving exegetical difficulties into hymns and therefore to first consider the other two possibilities.

Concerning the former, which ascribes the passage to the independent context of the letter, it has the most powerful support in the hint to the already-mentioned skittishness in the thought of the author, who—precisely in the process of proof—is fond of inserting such thoughts that disrupt the flow. One would then have to choose between two views: (1) either with *Kattenbusch*,[42] *Gunkel*,[43] and others, supposing that the emphasis lies on the idea of the preaching to the spirits (as a continuation of the theme of 1 Pet. 3:17–18: ἀγαθοποιεῖν [doing good]), and 3:21 would be a further randomly symbolic sub-digression, connected to ὕδατος [water] (v. 20); (2) or with *Weiss*,[44] supposing that the author already had the flood in mind, in order to proceed from there to baptism in verse 21 (this also draws out the consequences of ἀγαθοποιεῖν [doing good]).

36. Spitta, *Predigt an die Geister*, 9.
37. Güder, *Christi unter den Todten*, 39–40.
38. Kühl, *Briefe Petri*, 209–11.
39. Spitta, *Predigt an die Geister*, 9–13; cf. 63.
40. Clemen, *"Zu den Toten,"* 113–14.
41. Cf. J. Cramer, "Exegetica et Critica II. (Het glossematisch karakter van 1 Petr. 3:19–21 en 4:6)," in *Nieuwe Bijdragen op het Gebied van Godgeleerdheid en Wijsbegeerte* 7, no. 4 (Utrecht, 1891): 221–97, 263–82; see esp. 275.
42. Kattenbusch, "Über 1. Petr. 3, 19," 629.
43. Gunkel, *Brief des Petrus*, 560–62.
44. B. Weiss, *Petrinische Lehrbegriff*, 310.

Now, *Baur*[45] has already drawn attention to the parallelism of the two
πορευθείς [he went] in verses 19 and 22; from this, he concluded that there is an
intentional emphasis on the christological moments connected with death and
resurrection. Supplementing this observation with the hypothesis of *Clemen*,[46]
it thus indeed seems to be likely that the whole section 3:18–22 is a paraphrase
of a christological formula, which would have read approximately like this:

Χριστὸς ἅπαξ περὶ ἁμαρτιῶν ἀπέθανεν
  θανατωθεὶς μὲν σαρκὶ
  ζωοποιηθεὶς δὲ πνεύματι
    ἐν ᾧ καὶ τοῖς ἐν φυλακῇ
    πνεύμασιν πορευθεὶς ἐκήρυξεν
  ὅς ἐστιν ἐν δεξιᾷ θεοῦ
    πορευθεὶς εἰς οὐρανὸν
    ὑποταγέντων αὐτῷ κτλ.

Christ died once for sin,
  Put to death in the flesh,
But made alive in the spirit,
  In which in prison
  To the spirits he went and made proclamation;
Who is at the right hand of God,
  Has gone into heaven,
  Subjected to him, etc.

Between the second and third part, it would then be necessary to consider,
following either *Gunkel* or *Weiss*, the insertion of the transition to baptism. Note
that, in this way, the peculiar position of the preaching to the spirits *after* the
ζωοποιηθείς [made alive] is explained, which led J. T. Beck[47]—perhaps, by the
way, in a sensitive understanding of original ideas—to the supposition of a
ζωοποίησις [making alive] differentiated from the ἀνάστασις [resurrection],
while it led *Gunkel*[48]—incorrectly, in any case—to place the descensus *after* the
resurrection.

So we would have before us a kind of confession in three parts, each composed by two subdivisions, forming a parallel in which the second paraphrases
the first:

1. Christ died: he was really killed in the flesh.
2. Christ is raised: he went in spirit and has preached to the Spirits in
   prison.
3. Christ sits at the right hand of God: he has indeed ascended into
   heaven, ruler of the angels, and so on.

If we recall what was said earlier, then it is immediately obvious that, here
as well, the idea of the descensus stands in the same context as it does in Paul

45. F. C. Baur, *Vorlesungen*, 292 n. 1.
46. Clemen, "*Zu den Toten*," 112–20.
47. Beck, *Briefe Petri*, 188–90.
48. Gunkel, *Brief des Petrus*, 562.

and Luke, namely, christological. But, of course, the difference is that there it remained factually indefinite, while here it is given a concrete content, for the ἐκήρυξεν [proclaimed] of verse 19 cannot be omitted from the core of the passage, the christological formula. Since *it cannot be determined, however, whether the interpretation of this ἐκήρυξεν [proclaimed] in verse 19 can be regarded as authentic*, we content ourselves with the confirmation that, in any case, the idea of a sermon in Hades goes back to a time before 1 Peter and returns to the solid ground of the text.

In any case, this hypothetical kerygma is put in a thoroughly independent context in 1 Peter 3 and significantly expanded, and the meaning of this context now remains to be determined. Above all, this concerns verses 19 and 20: ἐν ᾧ καὶ τοῖς ἐν φυλακῇ πνεύμασιν πορευθεὶς ἐκήρυξεν, ἀπειθήσασίν ποτε ὅτε ἀπεξεδέχετο ἡ τοῦ θεοῦ μακροθυμία ἐν ἡμέραις Νῶε κτλ [in which he went also and made a proclamation to the spirits in prison, who in former times did not obey, when God waited patiently in the days of Noah, etc.]

Four main conflicting *interpretations* are available:

1. The πνεύματα [spirits] are the souls of the flood generation, and the time of the ἐκήρυξεν [proclamation] is the time between death and resurrection, according to *König*,[49] *Güder*,[50] *B. Weiss*,[51] *Sieffert*,[52] *Usteri*,[53] *Kattenbusch*,[54] *von Soden*,[55] *Burger*,[56] *Josephson*,[57] *Kühl*,[58] *Clemen*.[59]

2. The πνεύματα [spirits] are the souls of the flood generation, but the time of the ἐκήρυξεν [proclamation] is the time of Noah, and the [proclaiming] subject is the preexistent Christ; so *Schweizer*,[60] *Hofmann*,[61] *Otto*,[62] and *Oppenrieder*.[63]

3. The πνεύματα [spirits] are the fallen angels (Gen. 6:1–4). The time of the ἐκήρυξεν [proclamation] is the time of the resurrection: so *Baur*,[64] *Volkmar*,[65] *Lauterburg*,[66] and *Gunkel*.[67]

4. The πνεύματα [spirits] are the angels of Gen. 6:1–4, but the time of ἐκήρυξεν [proclamation] is the time of Noah, the [proclaiming] subject being the preexistent Christ, as per *Spitta*.[68]

This four-part combination intersects with the further question of whether the object of the ἐκήρυξεν [proclamation] is the announcement of salvation or of judgment.

---

49. König, *Christi Höllenfahrt*, 17–22.
50. Güder, *Christi unter den Todten*, 43–50.
51. B. Weiss, *Petrinische Lehrbegriff*, 227–32.
52. Sieffert, *Heilsbedeutung*, 411–14; however, cf. 417–18.
53. Usteri, *Petrusbrief*, 146–48; Usteri, "Hinabgefahren zur Hölle," 22–30.
54. Kattenbusch, "Über 1. Petr. 3, 19," 628–29.
55. Von Soden, *Briefe des Petrus*, 132.
56. Burger, *Brief Petri*, 171–74, but cf. 172, 174.
57. Josephson, "Niedergefahren zur Hölle," 409–10, but cf. 410.
58. Kühl, *Briefe Petri*, 219–22.
59. Cf. Clemen, "Zu den Toten," 133–36.
60. Schweizer, *Hinabgefahren zur Hölle*, 30–33.
61. Hofmann, *Brief Petri*, 124–34, esp. 133–34.
62. Cf., however, Otto, "Auslegung von 1 Petr. 3," 89.
63. Oppenrieder, "Petri Wort," 238–40.
64. F. C. Baur, *Vorlesungen*, 291 fn. 1.
65. Volkmar, "Katholischen Briefe und Henoch," 428.
66. Lauterburg, "Höllenfahrt Christi," 201, lines 11–26.
67. Gunkel, *Brief des Petrus*, 561–62.
68. Cf. Spitta, *Predigt an die Geister*, esp. 22–32.

First, we have to decide between the four possibilities, starting with the last one.

Ad [in relation to] 4. For the *interpretation of* πνεύματα [spirits] as angelic beings, there is first a negative reason, that for "departed souls" one rather expects the word ψυχαί [souls] (cf. Acts 2:27; Rev. 6:9), and positively, that in the Greek version of 1 Enoch 15.8, the children of the angels mentioned in Genesis 6:1–4 are called πνεύματα πονηρά [evil spirits]. However, as far as the particularly important first argument is concerned, it can be seen—in Luke 8:55; 23:46; 24:37; Acts 7:59; Hebrews 12:23; and Revelation 22:6—that πνεῦμα [spirit] is sometimes also used for "soul" as the life-substance of the human person that is separated from the body in death. More illuminating is the second argument. As it happens, the tradition actually reports that those angels in Genesis 6:1–4 are tethered with huge chains to a place in the underworld (cf. 2 Pet. 2:4). However, it can already be interjected with *Usteri*[69] that the angels in the book of 1 Enoch are spoken about in such a way that any thought of salvation seems definitely excluded (2 Pet. 2:4).

Spitta,[70] however, seeks to prove in detail that the *subject of* ἐκήρυξε [proclaiming] must be *the preexistent Christ,* in the person of Enoch. The idea is, at first glance, dazzling: in the book of Enoch the angelic sacrilege is followed by the archangel's indictment and by the judging command of God. Next Enoch first preaches to Azazel and then to the others who are fallen. "As Christ can be preexistent in Noah (cf. ad 2 [above]) or in the desert rock of 1 Corinthians 10:4, so he can be preexistent in Enoch," *Spitta* argued,[71] and the proof probably is indeed given that in Jewish thought until the emergence of the Christian community, Enoch did play the role of a kind of incarnation of the divine σοφία, and he was identified not only with the Metatron but also occasionally with the "Son of Man," indeed, with the Anointed.[72]

However inviting all this might be, it seems to me to be bought at too heavy a cost, if, in order to be able to locate the ἐκήρυξεν [proclamation] in the time of the construction of the ark, one must insert a νῦν [now] before ἐν φυλακῇ [in prison] in verse 19, which is not at all indicated in the text.[73] Above all, however, the [problem of the] expression πορευθείς [he went] and the position of ποτε [times] after ἀπειθήσασιν [disobeyed] (not after ἐκήρυξε [proclaiming]) is insurmountable. In regard to the whole explanation, it is to be charged that the sentence ὅτε ἀπεξεδέχετο κτλ [when [God] awaited etc.] is too short. The sentence would be pointless, precisely with the goal of explaining the contrast between the long-suffering of God and the behavior of the ἀπειθήσαντες [unbelieving], as *Spitta* correctly emphasizes,[74] if we suddenly understand the latter as angels, whose fall has nothing to do with the construction of the ark; otherwise the sentence becomes a mere date, introduced with quite unnecessary verbosity.

Ad 3. Regarding the interpretation of πνεύματα [spirits] as the angels (Gen. 6), to whom Christ preached between death and resurrection or after

---

69. Usteri, *Petrusbrief,* 147; Usteri, *"Hinabgefahren zur Hölle,"* 23.
70. Spitta, *Predigt an die Geister,* 34–43.
71. Cf. Spitta, *Predigt an die Geister,* 36.
72. Cf. Spitta, *Predigt an die Geister,* 38–41.
73. Cf. Spitta, *Predigt an die Geister,* 28, and 28–29 fn. 2.
74. Cf. Spitta, *Predigt an die Geister,* 47–49.

the resurrection (*Gunkel*),[75] we must first refer to the last-mentioned point, but with the explicit acknowledgment that the arguments against it are less strong than against the argument from preexistence, and that they give a possible—indeed, a good—context: "Christ, by his death, led sinners to God, and then he went and preached to the spirits in prison" (*Gunkel*).[76] However, this only applies if the content of the sermon is understood as an announcement of salvation.

Ad 2. Concerning the opinion that the πνεύματα [spirits] are indeed the souls of the flood generation but that the ἐκήρυξεν [proclamation] was a deed of the preexistent Christ in the time of Noah, the arguments against point 4 are also valid here, whether they appear in the version of *Schweizer*: "In the revealed salvation by the ark, the preaching of the spiritually present Christ can be recognized":[77] whether it is understood as *Oppenrieder's* reading of πορευθείς [he went] as "turning of Jehovah toward Noah to speak with him"(!),[78] or with the opinion of others that the preexistent appears in Noah himself, so that the construction of the ark depicts the sermon [of the preexistent].[79] All these interpretations indeed "violate the simple wording of the text" (*von Soden*)[80] and do not solve the problem of the πορευθείς [he went], the position of ποτε [times], and the fact that ἐκήρυξεν [proclaimed] is not a pluperfect.

Ad 1. Finally, we return to the prevalent explanation, according to which the πνεύματα represent the generation of Noah's day that was drowned in the flood, to whom Christ preached before his resurrection. The most difficult misgiving about this version is the objection to the use of πνεύματα [spirits]. However, it appears to me to recede, when, on the other hand, verse 20 is placed onto the scales, which remains puzzling if it is said to refer to the angels.

Certainly, the idea connected with the presence of Christ ἐν πνεύματι [with the spirits] is not to be isolated in such a way that ἐκήρυξεν [proclaimed] only applies to the generation of the flood (*Usteri*).[81] *Kattenbusch*[82] has rightly pointed out the role that the latter played for the Jewish theologians of that time. It represents—with the generation of the desert wandering and the deniers of the resurrection, with Jeroboam, Ahab, and Epicurus (!)—the figure of highest rejection. "The generation of the flood has no part in the future world and is not raised to judgment" ([Mishnah] Sanhedrin 10:1–3; cf. Baba Mezi'a 4:2; Matt. 24:37–39; 2 Pet. 3:6).

Thus, the flood generation is deployed as a type for the universal salvific significance of the death of Christ: "Christ was able to preach salvation even to the worst, because he suffered, died, and was thereby made into a spirit" (*Kattenbusch*).[83] Of course, we must indicate that it is rash to draw the conclusion (with *Gunkel*) that "the idea veiling itself in half-mythological vesture is that of *apokatastasis*,"[84]

75. Gunkel, *Brief des Petrus*, 562.
76. Gunkel, *Brief des Petrus*, 562.
77. Cf. Schweizer, *Hinabgefahren zur Hölle*, 35.
78. Cf. Oppenrieder, "Petri Wort," 239.
79. Cf. Oppenrieder, "Petri Wort," 237–39.
80. Von Soden, *Briefe des Petrus*, 132.
81. Usteri, *Petrusbrief*, 147–48.
82. Kattenbusch, "Über 1. Petr. 3, 19," 628–29.
83. Kattenbusch, "Über 1. Petr. 3, 19," 629.
84. Gunkel, *Brief des Petrus*, 562.

for if, a hundred years later, Origen drew this conclusion—with undeniable consequence—it was not yet within the horizon of the New Testament writers.

First of all, however, it is yet to be determined whether ἐκήρυξεν [proclamation] actually means *salvific* proclamation. The rather bloodthirsty old Protestant dogmatics has rather read into it a *concio damnatoria* [assembly of the damned]. (Hollaz: "Christus descendit in ipsum carcerem sive πού damnatorum . . . ut de daemonibus triumphum ageret et ut homines damnatos in carcere infernali jure concludi convinceret"),[85] and some of the newer commentators have joined themselves to this [un]friendly version: *Baur*,[86] *Hofmann*,[87] *Otto*,[88] *Spitta*,[89] *Lauterburg*.[90]

Two arguments are cited chiefly against the interpretation taking this as a salvific proclamation, one exegetical and the other factual. The first is found in *Spitta* in the form of a circular argument: "The salvation of the suffering doers of good must be further defined through a comparison with the judgment of the wrongdoers. . . . What, then, is more appropriate than the presumption that the sermon given to them is one of judgment?"[91] Similarly, I could not make the opinion of Professor *Lauterburg* my own, that the acceptance of a salvific proclamation does not give a satisfactory context because the remainder of the letter emphasizes judgment.[92] Although the latter is self-evident, it is not clear why the idea of an annunciation of salvation to the pre-Christian world should thereby be ruled out, especially since a "*return of all*"[93] is *not* spoken of: "Peter wants to emphasize how something else could happen for these unfortunates, even after the loss of God's patience, but not how they received it" (*Usteri*).[94] And Clemen has rightly pointed out that the letter knows the concept of *sins of ignorance* (cf. 1 Pet. 1:14).[95] Finally, when *Schweizer* argues, "The fact that Christ directs a completely useless sermon to the spirits, who are beyond redemption, cannot be found to rhyme with the general fundamental view of the New Testament,"[96] it may be permitted to say that the Reformed dogmatician has, perhaps, more of a stake in this than the historian.

What inclines me to reject this explanation is the fact that the meaning of "announcing punishment" for κηρύττειν [proclaiming], used in an absolute sense, has yet to be proved (for *Spitta's*[97] reference to Gal. 2:2 is really a little strange), while the Gospel of Peter 41 likewise uses κηρύττειν for the same process undoubtedly in the sense of a salvific proclamation. But even in context, a proclamation of punishment after the . . . δίκαιος ὑπὲρ ἀδίκων ἵνα ὑμᾶς

85. D. Hollaz, *Examen theologicum acroamaticum universam theologiam thetico-polemicam complectens*, part 3, theol. sec. 1, chap. 3, q. 138–39 (Stargard, 1707), 2 [1]: 299; cf. Chr. E. Luthardt, *Kompendium der Dogmatik*, 4th ed. (Leipzig: Dörffling & Franke, 1873), 169.
86. F. C. Baur, *Vorlesungen*, 292 fn. 1.
87. Cf. Hofmann, *Brief Petri*, 128–29.
88. Otto, "Auslegung von 1 Petr. 3," 88–90.
89. Spitta, *Predigt an die Geister*, 18, 20–21, 27.
90. Lauterburg, "Höllenfahrt Christi," 201, lines 26–32.
91. Spitta, *Predigt an die Geister*, 18.
92. Lauterburg, "Höllenfahrt Christi," 200, lines 24–25 and 28.
93. Cf. Gunkel, *Brief des Petrus*, 562.
94. Usteri, *Petrusbrief*, 146; Usteri, "Hinabgefahren zur Hölle," 28.
95. Clemen, "Zu den Toten," 140.
96. Schweizer, *Hinabgefahren zur Hölle*, 17.
97. Spitta, *Predigt an die Geister*, 26.

προσαγάγη τῷ θεῷ [for the righteous and unrighteous, in order to bring you to God] (v. 18) would look very strange.

The passage is an elaboration of the theme "suffering evil—doing good": Christ died because of our sins, in order to lead us to God, and then he went and offered salvation even to the worst, who once missed God's patience.

The further question to be answered now is *whether and to what extent the passage 1 Peter 4:6 should be consulted.* The talk here is about the sufferings that Christians must endure from Gentiles. These are alienated since Christians no longer take part in their shameful life: hence their blasphemy (1 Pet. 4:4). Yet they must give an account to the one who stands ready to judge the living and the dead (4:5), and 4:6 continues: εἰς τοῦτο γὰρ καὶ νεκροῖς εὐηγγελίσθη, ἵνα κριθῶσι μὲν κατὰ ἀνθρώπους σαρκί, ζῶσι δὲ κατὰ θεὸν πνεύματι [for this is the reason that the gospel was proclaimed to the dead, so that though they had been judged in the flesh as everyone is judged, they might live in the spirit as God does]. First of all, once more the *external context* is to be considered, in which the verse relates to the preceding verses. *Cramer*[98] has suspected a gloss here as well, and *Kühl* is partly in agreement with him: "To a great extent, all the conditions for the acceptance of a later, interpolated, marginal note are met."[99] I do not dare to make a decision here, though it seems to me more likely to be content with *Kühl's* own suggestion that it is a "midrashic remark of the author."[100]

More important is the other question: is 4:6 connected with 3:19? It is denied by those who see in 3:19 no reference to the descensus, like *Hofmann*,[101] *Schweizer*,[102] *Spitta*,[103] and others, yet also by those who do somehow recognize the idea of descensus there, by *Usteri*,[104] *von Soden*,[105] *Burger*,[106] and *Lauterburg*.[107] This opinion occurs in two versions:

One possibility is that the νεκροί [dead] are those blasphemers mentioned in 1 Peter 4:4, as *Hofmann*[108] and *Burger* argue. Then we would have to paraphrase with the latter: "There was a proclamation of the gospel even to those who at the time of judgment were in the state of death, with the intention that the death they as human beings must suffer would become a temporary judgment, followed by eternal life, according to the Spirit by God. If this intention has not been fulfilled on account of their guilt, then Christ will hold them responsible."[109]

With *Clemen*, however,[110] it is to be countered that according to 1 Peter 3:12, the hostile behavior of the Gentiles is something new; their death may not be placed in the past, as would have to be the case with the aorist κριθῶσι [judged] of verse 6.

98. Cramer, "Exegetica et Critica II," esp. 294–96.
99. Kühl, *Briefe Petri*, 260.
100. Kühl, *Briefe Petri*, 260.
101. Hofmann, *Brief Petri*, 164–65.
102. However, cf. Schweizer, *Hinabgefahren zur Hölle*, 36–38.
103. Spitta, *Predigt an die Geister*, 63.
104. Usteri, *Petrusbrief*, 174–87; Usteri, *"Hinabgefahren zur Hölle,"* 41–53.
105. Von Soden, *Briefe des Petrus*, 134–35.
106. Burger, *Brief Petri*, 175 note f.
107. Lauterburg, "Höllenfahrt Christi," 201, line 59; 202, line 2.
108. Hofmann, *Brief Petri*, 162–64.
109. Burger, *Brief Petri*, 175 note f.
110. Clemen, *"Zu den Toten,"* 138.

Alternatively, the νεκροί [dead] are the Christians who have already died (as *Usteri*,[111] *von Soden*,[112] *Spitta*,[113] and *Lauterburg*[114] hold); then the author (in analogy to 1 Thess. 4:13 and 1 Cor. 15:17–19) wanted to counter the objection: what help does what was said in 1 Peter 4:5, the second coming of the Lord in order to judge, give to our brothers [and sisters] who have died in the intervening time? "He answers that they too have the compensatory prospect of judgment, for this is precisely why they, the dead, have received a share in the gospel, so that in spite of the judgment they experience in the body (as is appropriate to human nature), they might live in the spirit (as corresponds to the nature of God)" (*von Soden*).[115]

However, this does not fit with the context, for 4:5 speaks of the judgment of punishment, so here the idea of deceased fellow Christians could not be implied, especially not if the date of 1 Peter were not to be moved to the beginnings of early Christianity, when this concern was current, but rather to its final years.

The whole conception is already suspect, because it is compelled, here as in 1 Peter 3:19, to insert a νῦν [now] into the text before νεκροί [dead] (in 4:6), which would have to stand there if any of these meanings were intended.

These considerations lead me to assume—in the sense of *König*,[116] *Güder*,[117] *B. Weiss*,[118] *Baur*,[119] *De Wette-Brückner*,[120] *Beck*,[121] *Josephson*,[122] *Kattenbusch*,[123] *Kühl*,[124] *Clemen*,[125] and *Gunkel*[126]—that there is also here an *allusion to the preaching in Hades*. We assert, especially over against *Usteri, von Soden*, and *Burger*: "How does one imagine this to be possible, that the readers of the epistle would have had the talk of proclaiming the gospel in the underworld fresh in their memories, and now should not associate νεκροῖς εὐηγγελίσθη [preaching to the dead] with it?" (*Kühl*).[127]

Clemen has widened his hypothesis,[128] claiming that the final phrase of the christological formula paraphrased in 3:18–21 would be contained in 1 Peter 4:5 and would therefore have been read: . . . ἑτοίμως ἔχων κρῖναι ζῶντας καὶ νεκρούς [stands ready to judge the living and the dead]. In this case, the connection between the two passages would be totally clear, but this seems to be the case to me anyway, even more so, since they belong externally to the same series of thoughts, from which 1 Peter 4:6 clearly stands out. "The author asks himself: is it fair that the judgment is delivered also to the dead, who have not heard

---

111. Usteri, *Petrusbrief*, 183–86; Usteri, *"Hinabgefahren zur Hölle,"* 49–51.
112. Von Soden, *Briefe des Petrus*, 135.
113. Spitta, *Predigt an die Geister*, 63–66.
114. Lauterburg, *"Höllenfahrt Christi,"* 202, lines 2–11.
115. Von Soden, *Briefe des Petrus*, 135.
116. König, *Christi Höllenfahrt*, 36.
117. Güder, *Christi unter den Todten*, 51–60.
118. B. Weiss, *Petrinische Lehrbegriff*, 228–30.
119. F. C. Baur, *Vorlesungen*, 292–93 fn. 1.
120. De Wette, *Briefe des Petrus*, 87–88.
121. Beck, *Briefe Petri*, 203–6.
122. Josephson, *"Niedergefahren zur Hölle,"* 409–11.
123. Kattenbusch, *"Über 1. Petr. 3, 19,"* 627.
124. Kühl, *Briefe Petri*, 256, 259–60.
125. Clemen, *"Zu den Toten,"* 139–40.
126. Gunkel, *Brief des Petrus*, 564.
127. Kühl, *Briefe Petri*, 256.
128. Clemen, *"Zu den Toten,"* 104, 113.

the gospel? He answers: it has also been preached to the dead, so that they also still can come to life, despite the judgment that they underwent in their death" (*Gunkel*).[129] Thus, as *Güder*[130] has already pointed out, 3:18–21 and 4:6 are to be explained together alternately:

From 3:18–21 it can be deduced, in regard to 4:6, that the εὐαγγελιζόμενος [preaching] is nothing other than [by] Christ, descended into the φυλακή [prison] before the resurrection. It therefore is not possible here to think of the apostles, because the writer is himself an apostle, or speaks under the name of such a person.

Equally, from 4:6 it is clear for 3:18–21 that the flood generation mentioned there, as has already been shown, must not be thought of as isolated, but rather as a type, as an example of pre-Christian humanity in general.

The consequences yielded by these results are now to be considered in a wider context.

§4. Review

We have encountered two primary forms of the idea of descensus up to this point:

1. Christ lingers in the underworld after his death. He proves himself to be Christ in that he does not remain there, but rather God awakens him and raises him to heaven, where he now sits at the right hand of the Father, Lord over the angels and the powers.

We found these thoughts in Paul, in Luke, and finally in the christological formula underlying the passage in 1 Peter 3:18–20. The question is posed: What role did this play in early Christian thought? *B. Weiss*[131] and *Clemen*[132] have assumed that it formed an integral part of the Christian kerygma already in the first century. How are we to understand this? "The New Testament certainly ascribes to Christ power over death, the underworld, and the powers of darkness. The only thing [to ask] is, Does it really portray this power as gained only, and specifically, through Christ's presence in Hades?" (Güder).[133] The question formed so generally is to be decisively rejected; instead this power (cf. §1) is a predicate of the raised Christ as such. If it were different, then according to the general Christian feeling in the first century per se, the descensus ad inferos would have been included with the thought of the *sessio ad dextram* (session at the right hand), meaning that we should be able to detect completely different and clearer traces of it in the New Testament than is now the case. One certainly cannot remind oneself often enough that readers of New Testament texts during the years 80–100 in many ways read with completely different eyes than we do: they discerned and understood overtones and connections that we disregard today. Here I am thinking especially about the numerous passages (cf. 1 Cor. 15:12; Rom. 1:4; Acts 3:15; 4:10; 13:30, 34; 1 Pet. 1:3; etc.; cf. Ign. *Magn.* 9.3; and so forth) that speak about Christ being

---

129. Gunkel, *Brief des Petrus*, 564.
130. Güder, *Christi unter den Todten*, 60.
131. B. Weiss, "Petrinische Lehrbegriff," 250.
132. Clemen, *"Zu den Toten,"* 113–14.
133. Güder, *Christi unter den Todten*, 62.

raised ἐκ νεκρῶν (from the dead). The notion of descensus thus was expressed according to the eschatological notions of the time.

However, even if these and similar connections are correct, what is not yet established is that this thought as such played an independent role in religious feeling. This is because the idea of the descensus we are considering here is to be distinguished sharply from the obviously existing *self-evident* assumption that Jesus went into the realm of the dead like everyone else prior to the resurrection. This, therefore, cannot be our concern but rather only the question: *Was an emphasis generally placed on this idea* in the Christian communities of the first century? Was it, for example, considered to be so important that it generally figured in the brief creedal summaries of the common kerygma that might have been circulating? Until the opposite is proven, this is *not to be assumed*, despite 1 Peter 3:18–20, since its modest role in Paul already speaks against this. It will therefore need to remain the case that the idea of the descensus remained uncertain and had not yet become established in the Christian communities (*Harnack*).[134]

Nevertheless, it is extremely old, as can be seen not only in the passage in Paul, but also in the background of 1 Peter 3:18–20, even though their respective conceptions do not fully correspond. In any case, it has the character of a rather well-known theologumenon, of which the preacher or writer could make use or not use, which might find acceptance in this or that kerygma or not, without a serious doctrinal difference emerging as a result. It is therefore a matter of a *side current* in Christian thought, which receives its impulse from a *christological interest*, whereby it remains anyone's guess whether it was induced specifically by "reflection on the emptiness of days"[135] between death and resurrection, as *Weizel*[136] and *von Soden* have supposed, or rather by the need to underscore the thought of the *sessio ad dextram* through the marked emphasis of its opposite (Rom. 10:7!).

In any case, it first gained entry into common Christian consciousness after being combined with related soteriological thoughts, and with a particular form of the same, as it was then reflected in the theology of the second century.

2. We still have to deal briefly with the soteriological formulation of this notion. It splits apart again into two parallel lines.

a. The death of Christ also means life for the pious who have fallen asleep; thus, as a result of his death, they awaken to (earlier?) life.

We should not overlook the implications of the thought in Matthew 27:52–53, despite its crass formulation, which arises during the later development. The idea was, by all means, completely isolated within the New Testament, which does not preclude that it was widespread throughout early Christianity in this form and probably also in other forms. Could it have possibly been connected with the idea of the descensus for the first time in the context of 1 Peter 3:18–20?

b. After his death and before his resurrection, Christ went to the custody of that part of humanity that had deceased prior to Christianity and proclaimed the gospel there.

134. Adolf von Harnack, *Outlines of the History of Dogma*, trans. Edwin K. Mitchell (London: Hodder & Stoughton, 1893), 1:202–3.
135. Von Soden, *Briefe des Petrus*, 132.
136. Weizel, "Urchristliche Unsterblichkeitslehre," 928–29.

We should note first that this thought, the proclamation in Hades, necessarily presupposes the christological concept of the descensus ad inferos as such. It may have been instigated by the supplementary question about the salvation of pre-Christian humanity and the deeds of Christ in Hades. To what extent have these questions stimulated precisely this answer? This is where the examination with respect to the history of religions would have to begin: at this point I can only make suggestions, first from the standpoint of the Jewish synagogue (cf. F. Weber).[137] For a start, we encounter here the fundamental idea: "No one who is circumcised shall stay in Gehenna forever" (Midrash Tanhuma, Lech Lecha 20).[138] At the very end, the generation of the wilderness—the horde of Korah, Manasseh, and the like—will emerge from Sheol (Bamidbar [Numbers] Rabbah 16.18.19; Debarim [Deuteronomy] Rabbah 2).[139] And this course of events at the end of time was placed directly in connection to the Messiah, the Son of David, Jalkut Schim['oni]:[140] "At this time, since the future world is breaking in, Holy Israel will be redeemed from Gehenna for the sake of the circumcision" (cf. Bereshit Rabbah):[141] "Rabbi Joshua ben Levi said: . . . The Messiah, the Son of David went with me until I arrived at the gates of Gehenna. . . . But as those who were bound in Gehenna saw the light of the Messiah, they rejoiced in receiving him and said: This is the one who will lead us out of the darkness" (similarly Bereshit Rabbah on Gen. 44:8).[142] The thought we find in 1 Peter 3 may have been formed in relying on these eschatological notions of the time, while eliminating Jewish national particularism.

At this point it would be very important to ascertain the relationship of this idea to that of the "resurrection of the saints." However, due to the complete lack of additional material a *non liquet* [no applicable rule] remains in effect over the question of priority.

The *common* factor in both is the notion that the salvation of those who have already departed belongs to the effects of the death of Christ. Both here and there, the thought of salvation comes to the fore, because it is impossible to consider the ἐκήρυξεν [preaching] of 1 Peter 3 as being unsuccessful. Both here and there, a certain limitation is made, because it is just as impossible to speak of success in every case of the ἐκήρυξεν of 1 Peter 3.

---

137. See F. Weber, *Die Lehren des Talmud*, §§74 and 81; = *System der altsynagogalen palästinischen Theologie aus Targum, Midrasch und Talmud*, edited, after the author's death, by Fr. Delitzsch und G. Schnedermann (Leipzig: Dörfling & Franke, 1880), 341–44, 364–71. A new edition of this work was published under the title given above by Barth. A "second, improved edition" was later published under the title *Jüdische Theologie auf Grund des Talmud und verwandter Schriften gemeinfasslich dargestellt*, ed. Fr. Delitzsch und G. Schnedermann (Leipzig: Dörfling & Franke, 1897). The improvements relate especially to corrected citations and the marking of those references "that could not be newly validated" (2nd ed., vi).

138. Cf. Weber, *Altsynagogalen palästinischen Theologie*, 1st ed., 327; cf. 2nd ed., 342.

139. Cf. Weber, *Altsynagogalen palästinischen Theologie*, 1st ed., 328; cf. 2nd ed., 342–43.

140. In the manuscript this is followed by "on Is. 26.9," though this entry is based on an error. Cf. Weber, *Altsynagogalen palästinischen Theologie*, 1st ed., 351; cf. 2nd ed., 368.

141. In the manuscript this is followed by "on Hos. 13.14," though this entry is based on an error. Cf. Weber, *Altsynagogalen palästinischen Theologie*, 1st ed., 351; cf. 2nd ed., 368. A. Jellinek, *Bet ha-Midrasch: Sammlung kleiner Midraschim und vermischter Abhandlungen aus der älteren jüdischen Literatur*, 3rd ed. (Jerusalem: Wahrmann Books, 1967), 2:50.

142. Cf. Weber, *Altsynagogalen palästinischen Theologie*, 1st ed., 351; cf. 2nd ed., 368.

The *differences* emerge just as clearly: here [in 1 Pet. 3:18–20] salvation concerns only the "saints," that is, a decision for or against it is no longer possible; there [in 4:6] Christ turns precisely to the rejected: they are also still free to decide ἵνα κριθῶσιν μὲν κατὰ ἀνθρώπους σαρκί, ζῶσιν δὲ κατὰ θεὸν πνεύματι [so that, though they had been judged in the flesh as everyone is judged, they might live in the spirit as God does]; here the particular version of salvation, there the universal version.

Therefore, the situation at the end of the New Testament period, to summarize it briefly, would be the following:

1. From a christological standpoint, the need arises here and there to emphasize, among the "facts of salvation" in the context of Christ's death, his sojourn in the underworld.

The question of the salvation of pre-Christian humanity emerges (earlier, at the same time, or later?) from soteriology.

2. With respect to the saints, it is answered in Matthew 27:52.

3. With respect to the totality of the pre-Christian dead, it is answered in 1 Peter 3 and 4, in the latter case in combination with the idea of the descensus ad inferos [in chap. 3].

The further development is now to be pursued with these points in mind.

Chapter 2: The Early Catholic Church until Tertullian

It would also be possible here to compare the material we have to work through with a sunken pile village [houses built on stilts]. Here and there the upper end of a pile [stilt] is still visible on the surface of the lake, others are destroyed, and a third kind are covered by the moor [bog]. Whoever wants to reconstruct the situation and structure of one of the houses is reliant on conjecture and assessments of probability, for which, with respect to the details, the potential for error is greater as the house is smaller.

In the preceding we have seen, with respect to the notion of the descensus ad inferos, that we are dealing with a side current of Christian thought, which we have tried to follow back to its various sources. If we now attempt to draw out the interlinking lines further, it is necessary to make clear from the outset that we are thereby proceeding on the grounds of hypothesis. This is especially the case for the next sections, though we already have solid ground under our feet again when we come to the early catholic fathers.

For the material that comes into consideration before Irenaeus, the geographic divisions fall into place: *Asia Minor* and *Rome*, which are, when rounded off, also chronologically more or less justified. From there I arrive at the early catholic fathers: Irenaeus, Tertullian, and Hippolytus, then concluding with a few Christian *Apocrypha*. A review will again summarize the findings.

§5. Asia Minor

We are under all circumstances pointed back to the [Roman] Province of Asia when we trace the idea of the descensus ad inferos backward. The three witnesses who come into question here are Irenaeus's *"presbyter,"* Ignatius, and

Polycarp; the period of time in which we place them stretches from 100 CE to 150, with the result that, in order for us to deal with the matter here, the question of whether the *Short Recension* of the *Epistles of Ignatius* is apocryphal, as the Tübingen school alleged, or is of no importance.[143] The terminus ad quem [terminal point] that comes into consideration is under all circumstances the middle of the [second] century. Given that it is the oldest witness, we would be first and foremost interested in the text of the *presbyter*; however, since we first need to identify it as it appears within Irenaeus's train of thought, we will do well to start off with *Ignatius*.

Here we find the concept of the descensus clearly articulated, above all, in the *Epistle to the Magnesians* 9.2 in the following context: "When those who were following the older order came to new hope (namely, through Christ), how could we live without him, οὖ καὶ οἱ προφῆται μαθηταὶ ὄντες τῷ πνεύματι ὡς διδάσκαλον αὐτὸν προσεδόκων καὶ διὰ τοῦτο ὃν δικαίως ἀνέμενον παρὼν ἤγειρεν αὐτοὺς ἐκ νεκρῶν [whose disciples the prophets themselves in the Spirit did wait for him as their teacher? And therefore he whom they rightly waited for, being come, raised them from the dead].[144] Next to this we must consider the passage from the *Epistle to the Philadelphians* 9.1. In response to the questioning of those who doubt the sources of Christian proclamation, Ignatius answers: Christ, his cross, his resurrection are my sources; it is in these that I want to be justified. At the earlier (Jewish) stage of revelation, the priests served this purpose and they were good, but the high priest [Christ] was better: αὐτὸς ὢν θύρα τοῦ πατρός, δι' ἧς εἰσέρχονται Ἀβραὰμ καὶ Ἰσαὰκ καὶ Ἰακὼβ καὶ οἱ προφῆται καὶ οἱ ἀπόστολοι καὶ ἡ ἐκκλησία. πάντα ταῦτα εἰς ἑνότητα θεοῦ [He is the door of the Father, by which enter in Abraham, and Isaac and Jacob, and the prophets, and the apostles, and the church. All these have for their object the attaining to the unity of God].[145] And in the same sense altogether, we occasionally read about the prophets in the *Epistle to the Philadelphians* 5.2: ἐν ᾧ (scil. εὐαγγελίῳ) καὶ πιστεύσαντες ἐσώθησαν [in which (to wit, the gospel) also believing, they were saved],[146] whereas it appears questionable to me whether the *Epistle to the Trallians* 9.1—ἐσταυρώθη καὶ ἀπέθανεν βλεπόντων καὶ οὐρανίων καὶ ἐπιγείων καὶ καταχθονίων [He was truly crucified and truly died, in the sight of beings in heaven, and on earth, and under the earth][147]—is to be interpreted, with the author of the *Long Recension*[148] and Zahn,[149] as referring to the descensus.

In consideration are primarily the *Epistle to the Magnesians* 9.2 and the *Epistle to the Philadelphians* 9.1. To start, in regard to the latter passage, what the

---

143. Cf. F. C. Baur, *Über den Ursprung des Episcopats in der christlichen Kirche: Prüfung der neusten von Hrn. Dr. Rothe aufgestellten Ansicht* (Tübingen: Fues, 1838), 148–84; A. Schwegler, *Das nachapostolische Zeitalter in den Hauptmomenten seiner Entwicklung* (Tübingen: Fues, 1846), 2:159–61, 176, 178–79.

144. Trans.: Ignatius, *To the Magnesians* (Shorter Version), in *The Ante-Nicene Fathers*, vol. 1, *The Apostolic Fathers: Justin Martyr. Irenaeus.* (New York: Scribner's, 1899), 62.

145. Trans.: Ignatius, *To the Philadelphians* (Shorter Version), 84.

146.* Trans.: Ignatius, *To the Magnesians* (Shorter Version), 82.

147.* Trans.: Ignatius, *To the Trallians* (Shorter Version), 70.

148. Cf. *Ignatii Antiocheni et Polycarpi Smyrnaei epistulae et martyria*, ed. A. Hilgenfeld, p. 235, lines 2–7.

149. Cf. *Ignatii et Polycarpi epistulae, martyria, fragmenta*, recensuit et illustravit Th. Zahn, Patrum Apostoloricum Opera, Fasc. 2 (Leipzig, 1876), 51, commentary on the passage; cf. Clemen, *"Zu den Toten,"* 174 n. 3.

circumstances could make perplexing is the fact that the patriarchs, prophets, apostles, and the church are named in one line with one another as the subject of εἰσέρχονται [to enter in] (i.e., εἰς τὴν βασιλείαν τοῦ θεοῦ [the kingdom of God]). The final two groups could indeed have nothing to do with the descensus. At the same time, look at the concluding sentence: Ignatius wants to place the universal meaning of the person of Christ in the foreground, which—in contrast to dualizing ideas (Cerinthus?)—concerns not only Christians, but also the men of the old covenant, εἰς ἑνότητα θεοῦ [in the unity of God]. In addition, the other passage from the *Epistle to the Magnesians* 9.2 provides a peculiar supplement: To what extent is Christ the θύρα τοῦ πατρός [door to the Father] for the prophets, and so forth? They have long awaited him as their teacher in spirit, and now he has come to them and awakened them from the dead. What did Ignatius mean by this last point?

Let us provisionally view his position in general. Which thought is the basis for his expression of the descensus? This undoubtedly occurs in both of the contexts we have identified from the perspective of *the question of salvation*: We, just as little as the prophets, are not going to obtain the same thing in any other way than through Christ (*Magn.* 9.2); and, in reversing the same idea: Christ is the entryway to the Father for *everyone*, for the patriarchs and others as for us (*Phld.* 9.1). At this point we can already say: this thought could not have been uttered by Ignatius for the first time. He wields it as if it is self-evident, which excludes this possibility.

And we find this presumption confirmed when we now arrive at the *presbyter* of Irenaeus, who can be seen as being an older contemporary of Ignatius. His witness forms a part of a complicated anti-gnostic deduction by *Irenaeus*, in his work *Against Heresies* 4.21–34, whose course we need to bring to mind briefly in order to obtain a judgment about the question of credibility.

We are dealing with the great dispute about whether the Old Testament is valid for those who believe in the new covenant, or whether it is not rather the manifestation of a God who has now been overcome. "No, [it is valid,]" Irenaeus answered, and then sought to prove this by means of many side deliberations to the right and to the left: the same God speaks in both Testaments. Abraham's faith and ours is the same, Jacob is the type of Christ (4.21), patriarchs and prophets are his forerunners (4.23), Christ is the *thesaurus* [treasure], the actual object of Old Testament revelation (4.26.1). Now the author swerves with apparent suddenness: Listen to the authority of your presbyters *qui successionem habent ab apostoli* [who possess the succession from the apostles]![150] Beware of false presbyters, of false teaching! (4.26.2–4). With this the prompt is given, the necessary attention has been aroused that he needed to establish his authority: *"Quemadmodum audivi a quodam presbytero qui audierat ab his qui apostolos viderant et ab his qui didicerant"* [as I have heard from a certain presbyter, who had heard it from those who had seen the apostles and learned from them]. The communications of this presbyter are now the following: The reproach we exercise against the behavior of a number of the pious in the Old

---

150. Trans.: Irenaeus, *Against Heresies*, in: *The Ante-Nicene Fathers (ANF)*, vol 1. This and the next 5 citations of the ET are from *Against Heresies* 4.21–34 in ANF 1:497–99.

Testament like David and Solomon is superfluous, because *"sufficienter increpa-vit eum scriptura"* [the punishment declared in Scripture . . . was sufficient]—*"sicut dixit presbyter"* [as that presbyter said], Irenaeus emphasizes one more time (4.27.1). And then comes our passage (4.27.2):

> Et propter hoc Dominum in ea quae sunt sub terra descendisse, evangelizan-tem et illis adventum suum, remissione peccatorum existente his, qui credunt in eum. Crediderunt autem in eum omnes qui sperabant in eum, id est, qui adventum eius praenuntiverunt et dispositionibus eius servierunt, justi et prophetae et patriarchae, quibus similiter ut nobis remisit peccata.
>
> [It was for this reason, too, that the Lord descended to the regions beneath the earth, preaching his advent there also, and [declaring] the remission of sins received by those who believe in him. Now all those believed in him, who had hope toward him, that is, those who proclaimed his advent and sub-mitted to his dispensations, the righteous men, the prophets, and the patri-archs, to them he remitted sins in the same way as he did to us.]

Therefore, we cannot reproach them for the same sins. To warn us and make us aware that their God also judges us, their evil deeds are recounted for us. On the contrary, *"inquit ille senior"* [that presbyter remarks], we should ". . . *ipsi timere ne forte post agnitionem Christi agentes aliquid, quod non placeat Deo, remissio-nem ultra non habeamus delictorum sed excludamur a regno eius"* [ourselves . . . fear, lest perchance, after we have come to knowledge of Christ, we obtain no fur-ther forgiveness of sins, but are shut out from his kingdom]. Sure enough—Ire-naeus continues on, still citing the presbyter—the greater grace of God appears in the New and not the Old Testament—but it is the grace of the same God (4.28). God is not the author of evil (4.29) but rather always one and the same good [God] (4.30), who manifests himself in varying ways (4.32). Here ends the citation, and Irenaeus himself carries on: Whoever can acknowledge all of this is the true *"discipulus spiritualis"* [spiritual disciple], who as a result condemns Marcion, Valentinian, and the like—he alone can really be a martyr (4.33). Thus he recapitulates being self-assured of his victory: It is the same God in the old covenant and the new covenant.

What is the state of things with this citation? This much is clear: In the long section of chapters 27–32, we not only hear the presbyter speaking, but also in part hear Irenaeus himself, as chapter 29 indicates, which is only understand-able as a dispute over the doctrine of God held by the later gnostics. Neverthe-less, it also remains certain that Irenaeus is really drawing from a source, very likely from a written one, because this *"sufficienter increpavit"* [the punishment . . . was sufficient] stands out clearly as a citation over against the rest, precisely because it is partially repeated. Furthermore, it is clearly discernible that the first of the sentences that are interesting for us in 4.27.2, *"Et propter . . . credunt in eum"* [it was for this reason . . . those who believe in him], belongs to the citation beginning with *"sicut dixit presbyter"* [as that presbyter said] as the *"descendisse"* [descended, past tense] makes clear. Finally, it comes across as trustworthy that shortly after our passage there follows again the phrase *"inquit ille senior"* [that presbyter remarked]. However, what about the internal credibility? It is first and foremost the second sentence in 4.27.2, "crediderunt autem . . ." [now . . .

those who believe], which could appear suspicious. Is it not perhaps a clarifi-
catory gloss from Irenaeus? In order to make a judgment on this question, we
need to draw a comparison with the passages from Ignatius, in whose temporal
and local proximity the *presbyter* is to be placed.

We will assume that the second vulnerable sentence, where the believers
as such are described, those "qui sperabant in eum, id est, qui advendtum,
eius praenuntiaverunt et dispositionibus eius servierunt, justi et prophetae
et patriarchae" [who had hope toward him [Christ], that is, those who proclaimed his advent, and submitted to his dispensations, the righteous men,
the prophets, and the patriarchs]. Here we immediately note that all these
points are also articulated by Ignatius: To begin with, determining who is
involved, it is the patriarchs and the like; further, they await his arrival in
hope; and finally, they have lived righteously. This passage contains only one
thought beyond that of the passage by Ignatius, that of the *"remissio pecca-
torum"* [the remission of sins]. Is this to be accounted to Irenaeus? For two
reasons it is not to be:

1. If an actual quote is acknowledged here at all, then the very thought just
mentioned is necessary here, because the presbyter in 4.27.1 assumes the *"pec-
cata"* [sins] of the pious in the Old Testament.

2. The thought does not otherwise occur in Irenaeus; on the contrary he
deals with the salvific purpose of the descensus in all contexts according to a
specific scheme, which, however, is not oriented to the concept of sin.

All this induces me now to ascribe the passage indeed to the *presbyter*, and it
therefore remains only to make it understandable in its own contexts.

The witness of this presbyter shows that in Asia Minor around the turn of
the first to the second century, *the question of the ulterior salvation of the pious of
the Old Testament* had played something of a role. We've already seen from Matthew 27:52[–53] that the thought is not new among the Christian congregations.
This soteriological question *was now tied to the thought of Christ's journey into
Hades*, and, respectively, answered by it: Christ proclaimed the gospel to them
and thus freed them from their inherent imperfection.

However, and here we come back to Ignatius, this change of thought by no
means became common currency, let alone ecumenical, not even in Asia Minor;
on the contrary it was still one among others, even though it later became established. One can still find a repristination of this older notion in Ignatius: Christ
went to Hades and awoke them from the dead, even if he did not conceive of it
as solidly as the author of Matthew 27:52.

Finally, the fact that in the end the thought lived on in its purely *christological*
form, as it is present in Paul and Luke, is shown, by its merely being mentioned
in the passage found in Polycarp's *Epistle to the Philippians* 1.2, in the context of
a confession-like resume of the principal points of Christology: ὅν ἤγειρεν ὁ θεὸς
λύσας τὰς ὠδῖνας τοῦ ᾅδου [whom God raised from the dead, having loosened
the bands of the grave].[151]

In looking back at what was said at the conclusion of [my] chapter 1, we can
summarize our results as follows:

---

151. Trans.: Polycarp, *To the Philippians*, in *ANF* 1:33.

1. The purely christological thought: Christ's sojourn in Hades as a "fact of salvation" is still known in the first half of the second century in Asia Minor.

   The question of the salvation of pre-Christian humanity is condensed in the question of the salvation of the pious of the Old Testament.
2. It receives a twofold answer, both times in combination with the descensus.
   a. Christ preaches to them in Hades.
   b. He "awakens them from the dead."
3. Provisionally muted is the question of the salvation of all those who died before Christ's coming.

§6. Rome

The community in Rome appears to have formed a second geographical center for the belief in the descensus around 120 CE to 130, since we possess in the subsequent period especially many witnesses originating from it, from the church by pastor *Hermas*, from *Justin*, and from the heretics *Marcion* and *Theodotus*. Finally, the invective referring to this matter is passed along by one who stands outside the church, *Celsus*.

We begin with the witness of *Hermas*, whose "Shepherd" is to be placed in the time of Antoninus Pius, around 140.

There is Similitude 9,[152] where the grand οἰκοδομή [tower] is described, whose fundament is the preexistent Christ and whose gate is the revealed Christ (9.12.1–3). There the following process is described from 9.3.3–9.4.4. The six men (according to 9.12.8 the ἔνδοξοι ἄγγελοι [glorious angels]), command that *stones come up* from a certain "deep place" (ἐκ βυθοῦ τινος = ex profundo) *to build a tower.* "And there went up ten stones square and polished, not hewn from a quarry." They were the foundation of the tower. Following them were an additional 20 + 5, then an additional 35 and finally again 40 stones. All of them ἀνέβησαν [came up] and are used for the tower.

In order to ease our understanding, Hermas then receives a kind of co-inspired commentary to this enigmatic story, namely, in 9.16.2–7. Disastrously, however, this commentary itself is again in need of commentary, and misunderstandings are difficult to avoid. I analyze the passage as follows:

1. We shall begin with 9.16.3, where we learn for the first time that the stones are those κεκοιμημένοι [who had fallen asleep]. Apart from their bodily death they are—and this is the crucial point—spiritually νεκροί [dead], afflicted with νέκρωσις [deadness] (9.16.2–3), which consists in the fact that they do not yet have "the seal of the Son of God" (9.16.3, 7): ἡ σφραγὶς οὖν τὸ ὕδωρ ἐστίν [the seal is the water], namely, baptism (9.16.4). In this condition it is impossible for them εἰσελθεῖν εἰς τὴν βασιλείαν τοῦ θεοῦ [to enter the kingdom of God] (9.16.2); they must therefore go through the experience ζωοποίησις [of being made alive] in this sense (9.16.2).

---

152. Trans.: Shepherd of Hermas, in *The Apostolic Fathers*, ed. J. B. Lightfoot (London: MacMillan, 1912). The section numbers correspond to this edition, 468–72.

2. Now the ἀπόστολοι καὶ οἱ διδάσκαλοι [apostles and the teachers], who proclaimed the name of the Son of God during their earthly life, κοιμηθέντες [have fallen asleep], but ἐν δυνάμει καὶ πίστει [in power and faith] (9.16.5). Now what is more likely than that they ἐκήρυξαν καὶ τοῖς προκεκοιμημένοις καὶ αὐτοὶ ἔδωκαν αὐτοῖς τὴν σφραγῖδα [preached also to them that had fallen asleep before them, and themselves gave unto them the seal of the preaching] (9.16.4–5). This process is now described more closely: They climb like them [the apostles and teachers] into the water (9.16.6), ἐκεῖνοι δὲ οἱ προκεκοιμημένοι νεκροὶ κατέβησαν, ζῶντες δὲ ἀνέβησαν [whereas the others who had fallen asleep before them went down dead and came up alive] (9.16.4, 6).

3. And now all can once again ἀναβαίνειν [enter in] the οἰκοδομή [tower] together and be put to use there, first the 10 + 25 + 35, προκεκοιμημένοι [those that had fallen asleep before them], then the 40, the ἀπόστολοι καὶ διδάσκαλοι [apostles and teachers] (9.16.7).

A few details are not yet clear, such as the peculiar notion that the apostles climbed into the baptismal water with κεκοιμημένοι [those who had fallen asleep] (9.16.6); but the main idea is fairly clear: in the βυθός [water] one can discern the underworld without difficulty; and in προκεκοιμημένοι [those that had fallen asleep before them] according to 9.16.7, where it says that they ἐν δικαιοσύνῃ καὶ ἐν μεγάλῃ ἁγνείᾳ [fell asleep with righteous and great purity, only they had not this seal], we discern just as clearly the pious of the Old Testament. They are evangelized and baptized by the apostles and the like, who were in the position to do this through their bodily deaths, and [these pious of the OT] enter into the kingdom of God.

This modification of the descensus is one of the most peculiar points in its entire history. "*Unde Hermas hoc theologumenon sumpserit, nescimus*" [We do not know where Hermas picked up this theologumenon], comments *Harnack* [in Latin] on this.[153] Indeed! And for our topic this is all the more important, since it was most likely *not borrowed*, but instead is *to be attributed to speculation by Hermas himself*. One should take note that not only the ἀπόστολοι [apostles], but also the διδάσκαλοι [teachers] are already dead and that the last group implies an altogether different class of representatives of early Christianity, presumably those who learned from the apostles themselves. This is shown not only by the limited number of forty, but also their exceptional role, which is attributed to them in building the οἰκοδομή [tower]. The entire version of the idea along this line indicates one who looks back to the apostolic age as into a time already far in the past. *We are therefore standing before the fact that, around 140, a frequently read devotional work applies the notion of Christ's preaching in Hades to the apostles and their disciples.* How are we going to explain this?

The fact that this expression of the notion cannot have been a general Christian one, not even in Rome at the time, we shall see at a later point. The fact that it could, nonetheless, emerge so relatively late and exist next to the others proves—in agreement with what was said in the previous §[5]—that the entire thought was still in flux to the highest degree.

The idea from Hermas is not completely exterior to the development up to this point. It is also guided by the soteriological-eschatological question of how

153. Gebhardt and Harnack, *Hermae Pastor graece*, 232, commentary on Similitude 9.16.5.

the pre-Christian pious relate to the βασιλεία [kingdom] established by Christ. Hermas, too, answers them in a manner parallel to the adage of the presbyter from Asia Minor: The gospel was proclaimed to them in the underworld. And if he now alters the subject, inserting the apostles instead of Christ, this perhaps could have been due to christological misgivings. In any case, it shows that it was not the case that the descent of *Christ* was an integral component of the Christian kerygma at the time, much less even (*B. Weiss*,[154] *Clemen*[155]) already in the first century. As we will see at a later point, this side current found its way back into the common Christian understanding in a rather peculiar manner.

The second Roman witness for the descensus, *Justin Martyr*, also poses a conundrum for us. *Dialogue with Trypho* 72 (near the chapter's end) reproaches the Jews for spiriting away certain passages in the Old Testament in which the christological interpretation cannot be avoided: ἀπὸ τῶν λόγων τοῦ αὐτοῦ Ἰερεμίου ὁμοίως ταῦτα περιέκοψαν. ἐμνήσθη δὲ ὁ κύριος ὁ θεὸς ἀπὸ Ἰσραὴλ τῶν νεκρῶν αὐτοῦ τῶν κεκοιμημένων εἰς γῆν χώματος καὶ κατέβη πρὸς αὐτοὺς ἀναγγελίσασθαι αὐτοῖς τὸ σωτήριον αὐτοῦ [And again, from the sayings of the same Jeremiah, these have been cut out: "The Lord God remembered his dead people of Israel who lay in graves; and he descended to preach to them his own salvation"].[156] Since this citation does not come from Jeremiah, the question then is, where does it come from?

Irenaeus cites this saying no less than five times, once without giving the source in *Against Heresies* 4.33.1, once as Isaiah at 3.20.4, once as Jeremiah at 4.22.1, and twice as the word of the prophets in general at 4.33.12 and 5.31.1. This includes every time Irenaeus comes to speak of the descensus, apart from the passage citing the presbyter at 4.27.1.2–3, which, as we have already said, can create a favorable bias for the descensus.

There are three possibilities for the provenance of this saying:

Either Justin outright invented it;
Or it is found in a Jewish *apocryphon* that had been "edited" by Christians (so *Stieren*,[157] *Kattenbusch*,[158] et al.);
Or Justin's reproach is turned directly on its head, and an eager Christian reader of the Bible "*supplemented*" in this way the *manuscript* of Jeremiah that Justin had before him.

We are, under all circumstances, dealing with a *pia fraus* [pious fraud] at this point, and we only have yet to decide which one [of the three possibilities]. The first one [Justin as inventor] might fall out of consideration as too plump and easy to refute. The question then remains: Is it an *apocryphon* or an intentional *falsification of the text*? It is not altogether irrelevant to the extent that accepting the apocryphon option would possibly lead us back to the first century, which is excluded with the latter option, since this kind of reading was even less usual

---

154. Gebhardt and Harnack, *Hermae Pastor graece*, 230.
155. Gebhardt and Harnack, *Hermae Pastor graece*, 113–14.
156. Trans.: Justin Martyr, *Dialogue with Trypho, a Jew*, in *ANF* 1:235.
157. Stieren, *Sancti Irenaei*, 1:530 n. 10.
158. Kattenbusch, "Über 1 Petr. 3.19," col. 628.

in the first century. Strictly speaking, the question cannot be answered; yet I believe it is more likely that we are dealing with an intentional *falsification of the text*. This is because, on the one hand, it is precisely in a polemical writing that it would have been in Justin's own interest not to make the mistake of misappropriating biblical passages; and on the other hand, the entire manner in which he introduces the passage seems to me to speak for the fact that he is acting in good faith. We shall therefore not place too much emphasis on the citations in Irenaeus that we have mentioned because it is not impossible but rather likely that he got the passage from Justin; one could otherwise claim his constantly returning to the passage as a prophetic saying in support for the expressed opinion.

A few words will suffice about the passage itself. As a falsification, it is not ineptly redacted, to the extent that the subject of the proceedings is not called the Messiah, but instead Jahweh Elohim, ὁ κύριος ὁ θεός [the Lord God]. Also, the designation of the netherworld as γῆ χώματος [graves] corresponds to Israelite thinking (cf. Isa. 14:15; Ezek. 32:23). Finally, the entire event is not in fact without parallel, not in the Israelite [texts] but rather in the ancient Jewish religious conceptual sphere (cf. §4.2.b, above). Nonetheless, the entire wording of the passage dispels any doubt that we have Christian thinking before us. Speaking for this are three features: (1) the designation "those who had fallen asleep," which already in the first century (cf. 1 Thess. 4:14; 1 Cor. 15:6, 18, 51; etc.) had virtually become the technical term for Christians who had died; (2) the phrase ἀναγγελίσασθαι αὐτοῖς τὸ σωτήριον αὐτοῦ [to preach to them his own salvation]; and finally, (3) the earlier and contemporary Christian parallels to which, in respect to content, it is much closer than to the Jewish ones. Materially, the word brings out nothing new beyond what was found in the presbyter from Asia Minor, but it is apparent in any case—this would also apply if we were dealing with an apocryphon—that precisely this version that we encountered in the presbyter was also known in Rome around 140: *Christ went to Hades and preached his salvation to the pious of the Old Testament.*

This notion was certainly not singularly prevalent in the time in which we are now standing, but it was undoubtedly on the way to this point. In support, we can draw on *Marcion* as an additional witness, who with photographic accuracy—though only as a negative—allows us to recognize the ordinary state of the belief of the Christian community. In Irenaeus, *Against Heresies* 1.27.3, after some introductory invectives, we find the following presentation of the Marcionite notion of the descensus:

> dicens . . . : *Cain et eos qui similes sunt ei, et Sodomitas et Aegyptios et similes eis et omnes omnio gentes, quae in omni permixtione malignitatis ambulaverunt, salvatas esse a Domino, quum descendisset ad infernos et accucurrisset ei, et in suum assumisse regnum; Abel autem et Enoch et Noë, et reliquous justos et eos qui sunt erga Abraham Patriarcham, cum omnibus prophetis et his, qui placuerunt Deo, non participasse salutem*
>
> [*saying . . . that Cain, and those like him, and the Sodomites, and the Egyptians, and others like them, and indeed, all the nations who walked in all sorts of abominations, were saved by the Lord, on his descending into Hades, and on their running unto him, and that they welcomed him into their kingdom; . . . Abel, and Enoch, and*

> *Noah, and those other righteous men, who sprang from the patriarch Abraham, with*
> *all the prophets and those who were pleasing to God, did not partake in salvation].*[159]

To this Irenaeus appended, in a friendly manner, "qui in Marcione fuit ser-
pens praeconavit" [but the serpent that was in Marcion declared]: ". . . Scie-
bant, inquit, Deum suum semper tentatem eos; et tunc tentare eos suspicati non
accucurrerunt Iesu" [they knew that their God was constantly tempting them,
so now they suspected that he was tempting them and did not run to Jesus],[160]
giving this as a reason for the exclusion of the pious of the Old Testament. Marcion's view is easy to reconstruct over against the official ecclesial notion: Christ
saved the righteous of the old covenant in Hades and gave them entrance into
the kingdom—an understanding identical with what is in Justin and the other
sources we have encountered.

An independent role is *not* to be assigned to Marcion in the development
of the idea. It would be rather preposterous to suppose a resumption of the
universal idea of salvation from 1 Peter 3 and 4, although the material tan-
gency is unmistakable. Marcion, in his way, is tuned in just as particularistic
a manner as his catholic opponents, because, what in regard to "omnes omnio
gentes, quae in omni permixtione malignitatis ambulaverunt" [all the nations
who walked in all sorts of abominations], his own opinion without a doubt is
formulated more precisely in Epiphanius, *Refutation of All Heresies* 42.4, where
the discussion is, on the contrary, about πάντα τὰ ἔθνη τὰ μὴ ἐγνωκότα τὸν θεὸν
τῶν Ἰουδαίων [all the Gentiles who had not known the God of the Jews].[161] If
he therefore also relates the redemption in Hades respectively and exclusively
to the non-Israelite pre-Christian humanity, then this occurs in the interest of
his dogma of the "invisible God" of the gospel in contrast to the "Maker and
Creator" of the Old Testament.

The matter is similar with *Theodotus*, whose view on the descensus comes
down through *Clement of Alexandria* in *Excerpts from Theodotus 18*. Also here it
is possible to distinguish clearly between the Christian common content and
the theology of Theodotus himself. Essential is the following: Καὶ τῷ Ἀβραὰμ
καὶ τοῖς λοιποῖς δικαίοις . . . ὤφθη . . . εὐηγγελίσατο . . . καὶ μετέστησεν αὐτοὺς
καὶ μετέθηκε καὶ πάντες ἐν τῇ σκιᾷ αὐτοῦ ζήσονται [But he was also seen by
Abraham and the other righteous men . . . preached the good tidings to the
righteous who are in paradise, and moved them and translated them and they
shall all live under his shadow].[162] His christological presuppositions explain
the fact that he describes the deed as occurring *after* the resurrection: The just
are thus already ἐν τῇ ἀναπαύσει ἐν τοῖς δεξιοῖς [in paradise on his right hand].
Abraham was joyous as he saw the day of Christ (John 8:56), namely, τὴν ἐν
σαρκὶ παρουσίαν [the advent in the flesh]. First when this is over: ὅθεν ἀναστάς

---

159. Trans.: Irenaeus, *Against Heresies*, ANF 1:352.
160. Trans.: Irenaeus, *Against Heresies*, ANF 1:352.
161. Trans.: *The Panarion of Epiphanius of Salamis, Book 1 (Sects. 1–46)*, trans. Frank Williams, 2nd ed.,
Nag Hamadi and Manichaean Studies 63 (Leiden: Brill, 2009), 297.
162. Trans.: Robert Pierce Casey, *The Excerpta ex Theodoto of Clement of Alexandria*, Studies and Documents 1 (London: Christophers, 1934).

[= upon having arisen], the proclamation of the gospel to him [Abraham] and the other righteous occurs.

The *Celsus* passage in *Origen* causes greater problems; in *Against Celsus* 2.43, Celsus directs the polemical question to Christians: Οὐ δήπου φήσετε περὶ αὐτοῦ ὅτι μὴ πείσας τοὺς ὧδε ὄντας ἐστέλλετο εἰς ἅδου πείσων τοὺς ἐκεῖ [You will not, I suppose, say of him that, after failing to gain over those who were in this world, he went to Hades to gain over those who were there].[163] Origen answers: "Christ already converted many here once before, as many, namely, as were longing for him. This is how it also stands with the souls to which he preached in Hades." To determine the concept against which Celsus was polemicizing, we are not to begin with Origen's response because this emerges in the context of the latter's understanding and accordingly does not correspond to the situation in which Celsus was writing.

We are therefore directed to the single sentence of Celsus. The salient point here is the expression πείσων [to gain over]. If the latter truthfully reproduced the state of the concept around 177–80 in Rome, then we are standing before a great riddle. For our results up to this point, for the second century in Asia Minor as well as in Rome, had consistently conceived of the righteous prior to Christ, the object of the sermon in Hades, as longing and from the outset accommodating, lacking nothing other than εὐαγγελιζόμενος [the preaching of the gospel]. The nerve of the whole thought would be touched if the latter were turned into a πείσων [gaining over] in Celsus's sense, that is, if the inhabitants of Hades, to whom the sermon was addressed, had still been in need of persuasion and conversion. There appear to me to be only two remaining possibilities: Either, and I hold this to be more likely, it is an intentional *caricaturizing* of what was passable as the descensus at the time, a possibility to which the μὴ πείσας τοὺς ὧδε ὄντας [gaining over those who were in this world] indeed points. It would not be difficult to separate the notion of the descensus from this caricature.

Or rather, it is not even precluded that Celsus knew 1 Peter 3:18–20 and took his use of πείθειν [to gain over] from there, which with goodwill or in case of only a cursory reading is quite possible.

In any case, he did an injustice to his Christian contemporaries with his reproach, because precisely this latter passage, apart from its incorrect interpretation, did not a play a role in the formation of the concept of the descensus at the time.

If we summarize things again, we come to the following results:

1. The christological significance of the notion of the descensus ad inferos has receded.

2. It is expressed in the second century in Rome in increasing measure as a notion of Christ's preaching in Hades to the righteous of the old covenant.

3. Completely missing (apart from Marcion) is finally the memory of there being a goal and accomplishment of the descensus outside the ambit of the pious of the Old Testament.

---

163. Trans.: Origen, *Against Celsus*, in *The Writings of Origen*, vol. 2, *Origen contra Celsum*, trans. Frederick Crombie (Edinburgh: T&T Clark, 1872), 45.

§7. Irenaeus

There are essentially two trains of thought in Irenaeus wherein the concept of the descensus of Christ appears, though not without elements of one making itself evident in the other.

The one can be summarized in this way: Christ is the only salvation for his disciples, meaning for those who long for him; among them also belong the pious of the pre-Christian era, which is why he redeemed them by means of his descent.

The primary passage is in Irenaeus, *Against Heresies* 4.22.1–2. We can recall this from the context we sketched during the discussion of the presbyter from Asia Minor. It concerns the identity of revelation in the Old Testament and New Testament, which was contested by the gnostics and Marcion. The sending of Christ concerns everyone; this is what 4.22 was to have shown—that is, also the believers, meaning the pious of Israel. This last thought is to be proven, first in a series of symbolic interpretations of the gospel story:

"Qui pedes lavit discipulorum *totum* sanctificavit *corpus* . . . recumbentibus eis ministrabat escam, *significans eos qui in terra recumbebant, quibus venit ministrare vitam.*" [For he who washed the feet of the disciples sanctified the entire body and rendered it clean. . . . He administered food to them in a recumbent posture, indicating that those who were lying in the earth were they to whom he came to impart life.][164] Then comes this pseudo-Jeremiah saying, which in its lengthiest version by Irenaeus runs: "*Recommemoratus est Dominus sanctus Israël mortuorum suorum qui praedormierunt in terra defossionis et descendit ad eos, uti evangelizaret eis salutare suum ad salvandum eos.*" [The holy Lord remembers his dead Israel, who slept in the land of sepulture; and he descended to them to make known to them his salvation, that they might be saved.] In Matthew 26:40–46, Jesus finds the disciples sleeping in the garden of Gethsemane: "primo quidem dimisit, significans patientiam Dei in dormitione hominum; secondo vero veniens excitavit eos . . . *significans quoniam passio ejus expergefactio est dormientium discipulorum propter quos et descendit in inferiora terrae*" [and when, in the first instance, the Lord found them sleeping, he let it pass, . . . thus indicating the patience of God regarding the state of slumber in which men lay; but coming the second time, he aroused them and made them stand up, in token that his passion is the arousing of his sleeping disciples, on whose account "he also descended into the lower parts of the earth"].

He then draws the conclusion from these biblical deliberations:

> *Non propter eos solos, qui temporibus Tiberii Caesaris crediderunt ei, venit Christus; nec propter eos solos qui nunc sunt homines, providentiam fecit pater; sed propter omnes omnino homines qui ab initio propter virtutem suam in sua generatione et timuerunt et dilexerunt Deum et juste et pie conversati sunt erga proximos et concupierunt videre Christum et audire vocam eius.* Quapropter omnes huiusmodi in secundo adventu primo de somno excitabit et eriget. . . .
>
> [For it was not merely for those who believed in him in the time of Tiberius Caesar that Christ came, nor did the Father exercise his providence for the men only who are now alive, but for all men altogether, who from the

---

164. Trans.: This and the further citations of Irenaeus, *Against Heresies* 4.22.12, in this section are taken from *ANF* 1:493–94.

beginning, according to their capacity, in their generation have both feared and loved God, and practiced justice and piety toward their neighbors, and have earnestly desired to see Christ, and to hear his voice. Wherefore he shall, at his second coming, first rouse from their sleep all persons of this description, and shall raise them up, as well as the rest who shall be judged, and give them a place in his kingdom. . . .]

Essentially the same notion returns again in 4.33.1: here is also the distinction of *both adventus Christi* [comings of Christ]. Here again the *descensus* belongs temporally to the first coming, materially to the second coming, in that the descending Christ proclaims salvation "mortuis suis" [to his dead], that is, prepares them for the second coming.

What is striking about this first cohesive portrayal of the *descensus* is, first, the way the thought of *the resurrection of the saints*, which more or less featured prominently in the tradition, is refurbished in a theologically correct manner through precisely this citation of the second coming. Any weakening of the primary thought is just as happily avoided by this; also avoided is the earlier unclarity: Those who are redeemed in Hades are now in the same situation as the Christians who have died: they have forgiveness of sins (cf. 4.27.2), they know Christ, and like them they hope for the day of his return; he will wake them from the dead and will lead them into the kingdom of fulfillment.

Who is the *object of the preaching of salvation?* First, in any case (cf. 4.22.1, "Dominus sanctus Israel" [The holy Lord remembers . . . Israel]; and 4.27.2), as usual, *the pious of the Old Testament*. Was Irenaeus thinking only about them? If one reads the expression from 4.22.2, where the discussion concerns "omnes omnio homines qui timuerunt et dilexerunt Deum et juste et pie conversati sunt erga proximos" [all men altogether who have both feared and loved God, and practiced justice and piety toward their neighbors], then the supposition suggests itself that Irenaeus did not consider the *possibility* to be ruled out immediately that *the righteous outside of Israel also* could attain salvation. However, we then have to emphasize immediately that this did not have *any influence on his theology* because it would have been a dangerous concession to Marcion. In any case, his theory of the *descensus* does not form a turning point in the history of the dogma, just as little as that of Marcion does. And there is one more point that must not be overlooked here: in *Against Heresies* 3.20.3–4 we read "*quoniam non solum homo* erat, qui moriebatur pro nobis, Esajas ait: Et commemorates" . . . [that it was *not a mere man* who died for us, Isaiah says: "And the holy Lord remembered His dead Israel"][165] . . . [3.20.4]. Not every person could have done in Hades what Christ did. As only he could die for us, the God-man was necessary to bring salvation to the pre-Christian world.

Against Heresies 5.31.1–2 leads us into a completely different context. The passage concerns, as later with Tertullian, the question of our current condition. Irenaeus answers it with ψυχαὶ ἀπέρχονται εἰς τὸν τόπον . . . {invisibilem} τὸν ὡρισμένον αὐταῖς ἀπὸ τοῦ θεοῦ κἀκεῖ μέχρι τῆς ἀναστάσεως φοιτῶσι . . . ἔπειτα ἀπολαβοῦσαι τὰ σώματα καὶ ὁλοκλήρως ἀναστᾶσαι . . . [souls . . . shall go away to the {invisible} place allotted to them by God, and there remain until the

---

165. Trans.: Irenaeus, *Against Heresies*, ANF 1:451.

resurrection, . . . then receiving their bodies, and rising in their eternity . . .].[166] Why does it have to happen like this? "Quum enim *Dominus in medio umbrae mortis abierit ubi animae mortuorum erant, post deinde corporaliter resurrexit*" [For as the Lord went away in the midst of the shadow of death, where the souls of the dead were, yet afterward he arose in the body] [5.31.2]. The opponents who maintain something else do not know the *"ordo resurrectionis"* [order of the resurrection] of Christ; according to their understanding, after dying on the cross, he had to go directly to heaven, leaving his body behind. "Nunc autem tribus deibus conversatus est ubi erant mortui; quemadmodum propheta ait de eo Commemoratus est . . . ; et ipse Dominus: Quemadmodum, ait, Ionas . . ." [But the case was, that for three days he dwelt in the place where the dead were, as the prophet said concerning him . . . ; and the Lord himself says, "as Jonas . . ."], followed by Matthew 12:40; "sed et apostolus ait: Ascendit autem, quid est . . ." [then also the apostle says, when he ascended, what is it . . .] followed by Ephesians 4:9; "hoc et David in eum prophetans dixit: Er eripuisti animam meam . . ." [This, too, David says when prophesying of Him . . .], followed by Psalm 86:3 [*Haer.* 5.31.1].

Again here, we are unmistakably put into the midst of the old *christological notion*: the descensus as a necessary link in the series of salvific facts that relate to Christ's exaltation, or, as Irenaeus expresses it, of the *"ordo resurrectionis."* He gave it, however, a further nuance along the same lines: the passage continues as follows: "Si ergo *Dominus legem mortuorum servavit, ut fieret primogenitus a mortuis et commoratus usque in tertiam diem in inferioribus terrae . . .* quomodo non confundatur? . . ." [If, then, *the Lord observed the law of the dead, that he might become the first from the dead, and tarried until the third day, "in the lowest parts of the earth,"* . . . how must these men not be put to confusion?] [*Cels.* 5.31.2]. Thus it belongs to the completeness of the work of the God-man that he also experienced the fate of the dead himself in order to be able to be "the first from the dead."

One should note, however—as already in the last turn, but above all in the pseudo-Jeremiah saying, which again is not missing here—how the soteriological thought once more comes through, despite the different context. It is from this standpoint that Irenaeus's conception is oriented, that the Holy One "thought of his dead"; this is the motive that always brings him back to the descensus!

§8. Tertullian

Tertullian's doctrine of the descent should be understood in closest connection with *Irenaeus's* doctrine, since Tertullian simply repeats various ideas of the latter and builds on them. Therein lies its significance.

The main passage is *A Treatise on the Soul* 55.[167] Tertullian wants to point out (cf. Irenaeus, *Against Heresies* 5.31) that the souls of Christians after death enter the underworld rather than paradise. Proof: Even Christ fared no differently. It is noteworthy, above all, how Tertullian combines the various versions of the descent concept, each of which in Irenaeus still required a specific thought

---

166. Trans.: The remaining citations in this section are from Irenaeus, *Against Heresies*, ANF 1:560.
167. Trans.: Translation for this and the Tertullian passages that follow are from *A Treatise on the Soul*, trans. Peter Holmes, in *Ante-Nicene Fathers* (*ANF*), vol. 3, via Christian Classics Ethereal Library.

process, and simply places them next to each other. A single sentence from the passage [by Tertullian] thus reveals Irenaeus's main ideas.

With the same law of His being [Christ] fully complied, by remaining in Hades in the form and condition of a dead man; nor did He ascend into the heights of heaven before descending into the lower parts of the earth, that He might there make the patriarchs and prophets partakers of Himself.[168]	Christus . . . huic quoque legi satisfecit forma humanae mortis apud inferos functus ned ante ascendit in sublimiora caelorum quam descendit in inferiora terrarum ut illic partriarchas et prophetas compotes sui facerit.

That he is aware of the emphasis on the last point in Irenaeus is shown by the passage in *The Soul* 7, which speaks of the *"corporalitas"* [corporeality] and of the spatiality of the separated souls: "[If you ask,] *Ad quod et Christus moriendo descendit? Puto ad animas patriarcharum*" [to whom Christ also, on dying, descended? I imagine it is the souls of the patriarchs]. Thus with Tertullian, too, this moment is decisive.

Finally, in his portrayal, too, the thought of a resurrection *before* the [last judgment] is excluded. To be sure, Christians are *"in sinu Abrahae"* [in Abraham's bosom], the heathen *"in carcere"* [in prison]; but in both cases:*"Nulli patet caelum terra adhuc salva, ne dixerim clausa"* [To no one is heaven opened; the earth is still safe for him, I would not say it is shut against him]. There is only one exception to this rule: *"Tota paradisi clavis tuus sanguis est"* [The sole key to unlock paradise is your own life's blood], that is, become a Christian martyr, and heaven is already open for you! (*The Soul* 55).

§9. Hippolytus

First, Hippolytus expressly affirms for us the observation already made with regard to Irenaeus and Tertullian. The thought of the resurrection of the saints when Christ descends is theologically completed but spiritualized. Although he still describes σωτῆρα [the Savior] as λυτρούμενον τὰς ἁγίων ψυχὰς ἐκ χειρὸς θανάτου [the one who would descend to ransom the souls of the saints from the hand of death] (*Treatise on the Antichrist* 45),[169] this is no longer to be misunderstood: ἐπειδὴ ἀπαρχὴ ἀναστάσεως πάντων τῶν ἀνθρώπων ἦν ὁ σωτήρ, ἔδει τὸν κύριον μόνον ἀνίστασθαι ἐκ νεκρῶν [since the Savior was the beginning of the resurrection of all men, it was meet that the Lord alone should rise from the dead] (*The Antichrist*, 46).

Two other points are of more specific interest in that they show how [the view of] Hippolytus points both forward and backward in the history of the concept.

1. The *Treatise on the Antichrist* 26 describes the descent as follows: καὶ ἐν νεκροῖς κατελογίσθη εὐαγγελιζόμενος τὰς τῶν ἁγίων ψυχὰς διὰ θανάτου τὸν

---

168. Tertullian, *A Treatise on the Soul*, 55.
169. Trans.: Translation for the citations from Hippolytus are by Peter Kirby, www.earlychristian writings.com.

θάνατον νικῶν [And he was also reckoned among the dead, preaching the gospel to the souls of the saints, (and) by death overcoming death]. We have encountered the latter thought in close connection with the descent conception in Paul. Yet we have also seen that it does not necessarily imply the latter but is rather an element in the thought of the resurrection and the exaltation, respectively. Accordingly, in the literature of the descent concept discussed so far, the victory over death was *not* incorporated. It appears here for the first time, albeit reasonably circumscribed, presumably based on inaccurate exegesis of Ephesians 4:8–10 or 1 Corinthians 15:55. As we will see in what follows, this way of conceiving the matter has been frequently followed.

2. In a completely different way, Hippolytus developed the descent concept found in the Shepherd of Hermas. In that work, there is no mention of Christ's descent. Instead, the deceased apostles fulfilled this function instead. Such variations have become no longer possible by the second half of the second century. But the question that had given rise to the concept remained: What role do the others who are "great in the kingdom of God"[170] play in the hereafter? Was it not only natural that they, too, should pursue their earthly activity there, as did Christ? These questions are answered in later theology, sufficiently and dogmatically. Hippolytus begins the process when he says of John the Baptist (*The Antichrist* 45): οὗτος προέφθασε καὶ τοῖς ἐν ᾅδῃ εὐαγγελίσασθαι, ἀναιρεθεὶς ὑπὸ Ἡρώδου πρόδρομος γενόμενος ἐκεῖ σημαίνων μέλλειν κἀκεῖσε κατελεύσεσθαι τὸν σωτῆρα . . . [He also first preached to those in Hades, becoming a forerunner there when he was put to death by Herod, that there too he might intimate that the Savior would descend . . .].

§10. Second-Century Christian Apocrypha

This literary genre is of particular interest because in the questions less central to ecclesiastical interests, it offers to some extent greater insight into the perception of the congregation than does the dialectic of the theologians.

Let us therefore, finally, try to gather a sampling from the period of the common Christian view [of the descent] as it may have appeared in the second half of the second century.

The Gospel of Peter may have originated in about 150 in Syria. The passage to be considered in the history of the descent comes in the context of the well-known resurrection report. The observers see three men emerge from the grave, two supporting the third, and a cross following them. The heads of the first two are directed toward heaven; the head of the one being led out by them, however, is directed beyond the heavens; (v. 41:) καὶ φωνῆς ἤκουον ἐκ τῶν οὐρανῶν λεγούσης. Ἐκήρυξας τοῖς κοιμωμένοις; (v. 42:) Καὶ ὑπακοὴ ἠκούετο ἀπὸ τοῦ σταυροῦ ὅτι "Ναί" [And they were hearing a voice from the heavens saying, "Have you made proclamation to those fallen asleep?" (v. 42) And an obeisance was heard from the cross, "Yes"].[171]

---

170. Cf., e.g., Matt. 5:19; 11:11; 18:1–4.
171. Trans.: Translated by Raymond Brown, http://www.earlychristianwritings.com/text/gospelpeter-brown.html.

To cite further, book 8 of the Sibylline Oracles comes from about 180 CE (according to *Hennecke*).[172] In a "prophetic" description of the main facts of Jesus' life, we find the following passage, verses 310–13:

> ἥξει δ' εἰς Ἀίδην ἀγγέλλων ἐλπίδα πᾶσιν
> τοῖς ἁγίοις τέλος αἰώνων καὶ ἔσχατον ἦμαρ
> καὶ θανάτου μοῖραν τελέσει τρίτον ἦμαρ ὑπνώσας
> καὶ τότ' ἀπὸ φθιμένων ἀναλύσας εἰς φάος ἥξει.

> [And into Hades shall he come announcing
> Hope unto all the saints, the end of ages
> And the last day, and having fallen asleep
> The third day he shall end the lot of death.][173]

And finally a passage from the Testaments of the Twelve Patriarchs (around 200) certainly deserves consideration. In 12.9 (= T. Benj. 9), there is a recapitulation of the main christological matters: ἀνελθὼν ἐκ τοῦ ᾅδου ἔσται ἀναβαίνων ἀπὸ γῆς εἰς οὐρανόν [And he shall ascend from Hades and shall pass from earth into heaven].[174] On the other hand, along with Clement,[175] I tend to doubt whether 7.5 (T. Dan 5) of the same book points to the descent: ἀνατελεῖ ὑμῖν ἐκ τῆς Ἰούδα καὶ Λευὶ τὸ σωτήριον Κυρίου. καὶ αὐτὸς ποιήσει πρὸς τὸν Βελιὰρ πόλεμον καὶ τὴν ἐκδίκησιν τοῦ νίκους δώσει πέρασιν ὑμῶν. καὶ τὴν αἰχμαλωσίαν λάβῃ ἀπὸ τοῦ Βελιὰρ ψυχὰς ἁγίων, καὶ ἐπιστρέψει καρδίας ἀπειθεῖς πρὸς Κύριον καὶ δώσει τοῖς ἐπικαλουμένοις αὐτὸν εἰρήνην αἰώνιον . . . [And there shall arise unto you from the tribe of (Judah and of) Levi the salvation of the Lord. And he shall make war against Beliar and execute an everlasting vengeance on our enemies. And the captivity shall he take from Beliar (the souls of the saints), and turn disobedient hearts unto the Lord, and give to them that call upon him eternal peace].[176]

It seems to me far more likely that here is meant the activity of Jesus in Galilee (Dan!)—think, for example, of the demon exorcisms—or his soteriological work in general. To conclude otherwise, we would need to have before us already the universalist form of the thought as we will meet it in Clement of Alexandria—which cannot be ruled out temporally—joined with the idea that by his descending, Christ has overcome death and the devil (cf. Hippolytus and particularly Origen, above).

A comparison of the three aforementioned passages is instructive:

- The Gospel of Peter 41–42 has the familiar conception of Christ as the one who entered Hades to preach to the dead.

172. J. Geffcken, "[Einleitung zu] christliche Sibyllinen," *Handbuch zu den neutestamentlichen Apokryphen*, ed. H. Hennecke (Tübingen/Leipzig: Mohr, 1904), 321.

173. Trans.: Milton S. Terry, trans., *The Sibylline Oracles*, translated from Greek into English blank verse ([New York: Hunt & Eaton, 1890], repr., American Theological Library Association Historical Monographs] (1899) [ET labels this line 410].

174. Trans.: Translation of "The Testaments of the Twelve Patriarchs," from *The Apocrypha and Pseudepigrapha of the Old Testament*, by R. H. Charles, vol. 2 (Oxford: Oxford University Press, 1913), http://www.earlychristianwritings.com/text/patriarchs-charles.html.

175. Geffcken, "Christliche Sibyllinen," 178.

176. Trans.: Translation by R. H. Charles, *Apocrypha and Pseudepigrapha*, 295.

- The Sibylline Oracles 8.310–12 exhibits the concept in a form similar to that of Irenaeus: the keynote is soteriological, but the christological motif is added: θανάτου μοῖραν τελέσει [he shall end the lot of death].[177]
- The Testaments of the Twelve Patriarchs 12.9 shows, finally, that despite its attenuation, even the purely christological motif in the Pauline-Lukan version is not lost. The descent is the beginning of the ascent to heaven.

Hence, these passages confirm the outlines of the situation as indicated above.

§11. Review

We have charted a small part in the development of the early church's teaching doctrine, unimportant when compared to the great questions of the time. We have been content to establish the facts as a whole. Now an attempt will be made, at least suggestively, to show the connections with the main data of the concurrent dogmatic history of the period.

So let us once again recall the most important stages that the conception has undergone in this period.

From the New Testament period, the descent to the dead was adopted as a christological moment: Christ was in Hades, but God freed and exalted him. That is how we still saw it in *Polycarp*. We noted a marked decline of this motif, however, in other literature, until it resurfaced in a renewed form in *Irenaeus*.

How do we explain this change? Perhaps, to some extent, because the process was of no interest to the apologists' philosophically and rationalistically oriented Christology, but chiefly because the questions of the time and the controversies in the second century kept the attention focused exclusively on the soteriological moment. This situation changed during the period of the early catholic fathers. The significance of Irenaeus is that he combined apologetic rationalism with the *salvation history* [*Heilsgeschichte*] of the New Testament and that he identified the Logos-God with Jesus Christ of the Gospels. "This salvation is accomplished, not through the Logos in itself, but solely through Jesus Christ, and indeed through Jesus Christ insofar as he was God and became man" (Harnack).[178] But if this was the case, then necessarily each individual moment of the history of salvation, that is, of the manifestation of the God-become-man, obtains a new and independent significance. "Since Christ became what we are, he as God-man likewise passed through and suffered what we should have suffered."[179] In the case of the *descent* idea received from the tradition, the necessity of the doctrine as a component of the *ordo resurrectionis* [order of the resurrection] arose from the view that it was a *completed* act; at the same time, in contrast to docetic Gnosticism, its necessity arose from the *lex mortuorum* [law of death].

2. Of greater impact during the entire second century was another train of thought, which related the descent of Christ more to the *redemption of the Old Testament pious*. The New Testament offered only one statement about this: at the moment of Christ's death, there was an awakening of the saints. The second

---

177. Trans.: See https://trisagionseraph.tripod.com/Texts/Sibyl8.html
178. Harnack, *History of Dogma*, 1:132.
179. Harnack, *History of Dogma*, 1:142.

century (*Ignatius*) first combined this with the thought of the descent: Christ goes to Hades and there "awakens" them. But even earlier (Irenaeus's presbyter) and in the same period, we find the other version: Christ preaches the gospel to them. The early catholic fathers adopt this idea eagerly and spiritualize it, that is, simultaneously conjuring away the originating idea, the resurrection of the saints.

The process is fairly transparent in the history of dogma. The battle with Gnosticism, which dominated the second century, became more sharply focused on the battle concerning the Old Testament, that is, concerning the *continuity and identity of all true revelation*. In various degrees, the gnostics taught that the God of the Old Testament is a secondary aeon and concluded, with *Marcion*, that he is an evil principle, unlike the God of the Gospels. By contrast, the post-apostolic age and the apologists emphasized that in both instances, the same God speaks—because the Old Testament is a *Christian book*, and so the pious of the Old Testament were *unconscious Christians*, "who lacked only the Spirit" (Shepherd of Hermas, Similitude 9.16.7). On this basis, nothing seemed more natural than to conclude that Christ has raised them from the dead, that is, that they *now already* have access to his kingdom! (*Ignatius* and Shepherd of Hermas).

The early catholic fathers drew back from this extreme, as from every extreme. The doctrine of *two Testaments* arose in part as a response to Gnosticism: the Old Testament is the *precursor* of Christ and of the New Testament. But if those pious are still at a preliminary stage, they need the preaching of the gospel just as much as those who are still alive. It is the descending Christ who brings it to them. This thought must have been all the more valuable to the church's theology in that a "historical" observation of the Old Testament was fully acknowledged while proving what needed to be proved: the very identity of all revelation.

The teaching of the Shepherd of Hermas about the apostolic preaching is a theological diversion, without importance for the history of dogma. We have seen the need from which it originated and how it was corrected in later theology.

3. The New Testament, however, offered the thought of the descent in yet a third form, not as a mere appendage, but in a very developed form: Christ entered into the realm of the dead to offer salvation to *the entire pre-Christian world*: 1 Peter 3:18–19; 4:6. As for the development of this concept, *the second century ignored it*. This was possible, because even though First Peter generally appeared in the canon, the main sources that formed the basis for the church's doctrine, besides the Old Testament, were "the Gospel and the Apostle,"[180] under which all other sources were subsumed. And the *actual* grounds for this disregard [in the second century] are, in any case, fairly clear. Despite all the hellenizing of thought, it would have posed a danger to the foundations if the non-Israelite world of the past had been included in Christian salvation. If this conclusion had been reached on the basis of 1 Peter 3 and 4, it would have courted the gnostic contempt for the Old Testament with a vengeance. This

---

180. Cf. Adolf von Harnack, *History of Dogma*, trans. of 3rd ed. by Neil Buchanan (Eugene, OR: Wipf & Stock), 2:43–46.

explains why the passage in the New Testament that contained the most developed form of the concept of the descent "in no way served as the basis for the development of the church's teaching" (*Lautenburg*).[181]

Moreover, what *Harnack* says at one point about the Pauline doctrine of justification is, mutatis mutandis, also applicable to the conception of the descent into hell in this passage: "In the second century, no one understood it better than Marcion—and he misunderstood it."[182]

Chapter III: The Alexandrians

§12. Clement

Here we find ourselves in an entirely new theological atmosphere; it will be important at the outset to keep in mind the difference between this situation and that of Irenaeus and the like. Ultimately, the difference can be attributed to the different relationship between faith and knowledge in the respective situations.

For the *early catholic fathers*, these concepts constitute a unity, in contrast to heretical Gnosticism. "A correct statement of theology is also a correct statement of faith" (*Harnack*).[183] To be sure, academic speculation played no small role in this theology. However, for Irenaeus and Tertullian, speculation was never an end in itself; "speculation was mistrusted and still was not yet discarded."[184]

The *Alexandrians* were different. For them, academic concerns belonged to the essence of the matter. The true Christian is the true gnostic, who fortuitously transforms the truth of history into the eternally valid truth of reason.[185] In this way, the Alexandrian also approaches salvation history. Certainly, individual statements of "the ancients," such as Plato, are a secondary source of revelation, in which knowledge presupposes faith. But the overall Hellenic perspective ultimately turns Christian theology into a philosophy of religion, "warmed by the gospel,"[186] though it does not do so to Christianity itself, since γνῶσις [knowledge] and πίστις [faith] are now clearly distinguished. Thus the highest religion is Christianity, because it is the only religion whose myth, meaning its inherent "contingent truth of history," is at the same time "truth" in the gnostic sense and thus eternal truth.

This is the perspective for understanding the development of the descent motif in Clement and Origen.

The main passage to consider from *Clement of Alexandria* is *Miscellanies* 6.6. The context is the universal significance of the gospel. Chapters 3–4 declare that the Greeks certainly receive their best from the Jews and Egyptians.

---

181. Lauterburg, "Höllenfahrt Christi," 202, lines 12–14.
182. Cf. Harnack, *History of Dogma*.
183. From the lecture transcript, Winter Semester 1906–7 (see n. 17 above).
184. Harnack, *History of Dogma*, 131.
185. Trans.: In Barth's transcript of Harnack's lecture, 217, we read on Clement of Alexandria: "The spirit does not live in history, but from the idea, thus [there is] always the transformation of the contingencies of historical truth into the eternity of rational truth. *Miscellanies* 4.22, an odd contact with Lessing!"
186. From Harnack's lecture transcript, 218: "The theology of Clement is Greek philosophy of religion (Plato!) warmed by the gospel."

Nevertheless, according to chapter 5, they do not entirely lack an accurate knowledge of God. Chapter 6 claims that, therefore, *the gospel is proclaimed to the Gentiles in the underworld no less than to the Jews who are also there and to the Gentiles who are still alive.*

This idea is so new, given the developments described above, that we will do well to follow Clement's train of thought in detail.

Jews *and* Greeks have a certain measure of the divine gift, for which they were prepared *before* Christ and *by* Christ: ἐδόθη νόμος μὲν καὶ προφῆται βαρβάροις (!), φιλοσοφία δὲ Ἕλλησι τὰς ἀκοὰς ἐθίζουσα πρὸς τὸ κήρυγμα [The Law and the Prophets (were) given to the barbarians (!), and philosophy to the Greeks, to fit their ears for the gospel].[187] Now, according to Isaiah 49:9, the Jews are nevertheless δέσμιοι [captives]; the Hellenes are clearly οἱ ἐν σκότει [in darkness], οἱ ἐν τῇ εἰδωλολατρείᾳ κατορωρυγμένον ἔχοντες τὸ ἡγεμονικόν [who have the ruling faculty of the soul buried in idolatry]. *Both* need salvation. Διόπερ ὁ Κύριος εὐηγγελίσατο καὶ τοῖς ἐν ᾅδου [*Wherefore the Lord preached the Gospel to those in Hades*]. According to Job 28:22, Hades said: φωνὴν αὐτοῦ ἠκούσαμε [We have heard his voice]. However οὐχ ὁ τόπος δήπου φωνὴν λαβών [It is not plainly the place, which, the words above say, heard the voice]. Rather it is οἱ ἐν ᾅδου καταταγέντες [those who have been put in Hades] about whom it is said: Αὐτοὶ τοίνυν εἰσὶν οἱ ἐπακούσαντες τῆς θείας δυνάμεώς τε καὶ φωνῆς [They, then, are those that hear the divine power and voice]. Now comes the decisive passage: It is known that εὐηγγελίσθαι τὸν κύριον τοῖς τε ἀπολωλόσιν ἐν τῷ κατακλυσμῷ μᾶλλον δὲ πεπεδημένοις καὶ τοῖς ἐν φυλακῇ τε καὶ φρουρᾷ συνεχομένοις [The Lord preached the gospel to those who perished in the flood, or rather had been chained, and to those kept "in ward and guard"]. For what follows, it is important to observe that for Clement the flood generation clearly pertains to Israel. He reminds us (in a backward glance at a passage in *Miscellanies* 2.9; see below) of the apostles, who also have preached the gospel in Hades: ἐχρῆν γὰρ οἶμαι, ὥσπερ κἀνταῦθα οὕτω δὲ κἀκεῖσε τοὺς ἀρίστους τῶν μαθητῶν μιμητὰς γενέσθαι τοῦ διδασκάλου, ἵν' ὁ μὲν τοὺς ἐξ Ἑβραίων, οἱ δὲ τὰ ἔθνη εἰς ἐπιστροφὴν ἀγάγωσι [For it was requisite, in my opinion, that as here, so also there, the best of the disciples should be imitators of the Master; so that he should bring to repentance those belonging to the Hebrews, and they the Gentiles; that is, those who had lived in righteousness]. What qualities does he assume belong to those who are brought to repentance? It is those[188] οἱ ἐν δικαιοσύνῃ τῇ κατὰ νόμον καὶ κατὰ φιλοσοφίαν βεβιωκότας μέν, οὐ τελείως δέ, ἀλλ' ἁμαρτητικῶς διαπερανάμενους τὸν βίον. τουτὶ γὰρ ἔπρεπε τῇ θείᾳ οἰκονομίᾳ τοὺς ἀξίαν μᾶλλον ἐσχηκότας ἐν δικαιοσύνῃ καὶ προηγουμένως βεβιωκότας, ἐπί τε τοῖς πλημμεληθεῖσι μετανενοηκότας, κἂν ἐν ἄλλῳ τόπῳ τύχωσιν, ἐξομολογουμένως ἐν τοῖς τοῦ θεοῦ ὄντας τοῦ παντοκράτορος, κατὰ τὴν οἰκείαν ἑκάστου γνῶσιν σωθῆναι [who had lived in righteousness according to the law and philosophy, who had ended life not perfectly, but sinfully. For it was suitable to the divine administration, that those possessed of greater worth in righteousness, and whose life had been pre-eminent, on repenting of their transgressions, though found in another place,

---

187. Trans.: Translation for the citations from *Miscellanies* (in *ANF* 2) is from http://www .earlychristianwritings.com/text/clement-stromata-book6.html.

188. Barth evidently altered the syntax of the source to accommodate his sentence construction.

yet being confessedly of the number of the people of God Almighty, should be saved, each one according to his individual knowledge].[189]

Already in the earthly life of Christ, τὸ σώζειν ἔργον αὐτοῦ [his work to save] concerned all those whom he had called according to his proclamation: ἑλκύσας εἰς σωτηρίαν [those called to salvation]. He went to Hades for the same purpose. When he preached there to Israel, it was the case that δῆλόν που ὡς ἄρα ἀπροσωπολήπτου ὄντος τοῦ θεοῦ καὶ οἱ ἀπόστολοι . . . ἐπιτηδείους εἰς ἐπιστροφὴν εὐηγγελίσαντο [God is no respecter of persons, the apostles also, as here, so they preached the gospel to those of the heathen who were ready for conversion]. So, by virtue of an act of recapitulation, Γέγονεν ἄρα τις καθολικὴ κίνησις καὶ μετάθεσις κατὰ τὴν οἰκονομίαν τοῦ Σωτῆρος [*there took place, then, a universal movement and translation through the economy of the Savior*].

These ideas are supported by the following general considerations. The attribute of righteousness does not depend upon Israelite or Greek nationality. God is Lord over all people, προσεχέστερον δὲ τῶν ἐγνωκότων πατήρ [and more nearly the Father of those who know him]. Those who καλῶς βιοῦν [live well] and those who νομίμως βιοῦν [live according to the law] are identical before him. If, however, those who observed the law δίκαιοι ἐκρίθησαν [lived rightly], then it is clear that also those outside the law ὀρθῶς βεβιωκότας, εἰ καὶ ἐν ᾅδου ἔτυχον ὄντες καὶ ἐν φρουρᾷ, ἐπακούσαντας τῆς τοῦ Κυρίου φωνῆς εἴτε τῆς αὐθεντικῆς εἴτε καὶ τῆς διὰ τῶν ἀποστόλων ἐνεργούσης . . . ἐπιστραφῆναί τε καὶ πιστεῦσαι [having lived rightly, in consequence of the peculiar nature of the voice, though they are in Hades and in ward, on hearing the voice of the Lord, whether that of his own person or his voice acting through his apostles, with all speed turned and believed].

A further consideration: the gospel is to be proclaimed to all upon the earth; no one is free of guilt. τί οὖν; οὐχὶ καὶ ἐν ᾅδου ἡ αὐτὴ γέγονεν οἰκονομία, ἵνα κἀκεῖ πᾶσαι αἱ ψυχαὶ ἀκούσασαι τοῦ κηρύγματος, ἢ τὴν μετάνοιαν ἐνδείξωνται, ἢ τὴν κόλασιν δικαίαν εἶναι . . . ὁμολογήσωσιν; [What then? Did not the same dispensation obtain in Hades, so that even there, all the souls, on hearing the proclamation, might either exhibit repentance, or confess that their punishment was just?] It would be πλεονεξίας οὐ τῆς τυχούσης ἔργον [the exercise of no ordinary arbitrariness] to those who died before Christ and were unable to make such a decision, in contrast to those who came later. God forgives the sins committed in ignorance when God sees repentance. Christ has commanded that the gospel be taken to the Gentiles: εἰ τοίνυν τοὺς ἐν σαρκὶ διὰ τοῦτο εὐηγγελίσατο, ἵνα μὴ καταδικασθῶσιν ἀδίκως, πῶς οὐ καὶ τοὺς προεξεληλυθότας τῆς παρουσίας αὐτοῦ διὰ τὴν αὐτὴν εὐηγγελίσατο αἰτίαν; [If, then, he preached the gospel to those in the flesh that they might not be condemned unjustly, how is it conceivable that he did not for the same cause preach the gospel to those who had departed this life before his advent?].

Here we have a unified conception of the descent [into Hades] that we do not encounter again in the entire ancient history of the idea, including even that of Origen. Thus, it will be of interest to engage in a more precise analysis. For this specific purpose, above all, the *frame of reference* of each of the respective sources, which can be recognized in the presentation, needs to be investigated.

---

189. Trans.: All of the following *Miscellanies* quotations are from the same ET: http://earlychristian writings.com/text/clement-stromata.

1. Immediately recognizable and explicitly mentioned is the Shepherd of Hermas, with its apostolic preaching in the underworld. This passage is already referenced in *Miscellanies* 2.9 in a more detailed way and is completely analogous to *Miscellanies* 6.6: the apostles preached to Jews *and* Gentiles not only on earth but also in the underworld. In the main passage in *Miscellanies* 6.6, this is now modified, insofar as the sermon to the pagans is explicitly attributed to the apostles. Likewise, the latter passage from Clement does not relate the text from the Shepherd of Hermas to Christ (contra *Clemen*).[190]

2. The detail with which Clement proceeds indicates that he is not stating the obvious. Rather, he is clearly conscious that even if he does not oppose an alternate view, he must revise it. If we follow these leads, we notice that, given our preceding considerations, this is the *descent concept of the second century*, which undergoes a *correction*, without any observable polemics. The law, the righteousness of God, demands that the offer of salvation not be limited to the pious of Israel and must include pre-Christian humanity as such.

3. And finally, if we ask about the starting point of his own account, apart from Clement's own rationality, we are undoubtedly confronted, for the first time in the development of the doctrines, with *1 Peter 3 and 4*. We once encountered the thought in the beginning, since in the reference to "those who perished in the flood and those in prison," we will easily recognize "the spirits in prison" in 1 Peter 3:19. And again, the passage concludes with the reference to the flood as instruction and chastisement, which does not eliminate the salvific will of God to save those who repent. Likewise in the details about the dispensation of the divine justice, one can hear echoes of the phrase "that they might not be judged unjustly," and so on, in 1 Peter 4:6.

Clement's perspective first must be understood as an extension of the old doctrine of the descent based on Hermas, on the one hand, and on 1 Peter, on the other.

Undoubtedly, there are also *material* reasons why this combination turned out as it did rather than differently.

In this respect the apostolic motif, which has no independent significance in the thought of the descent, is not a factor. According to Clement, it is a matter of indifference for the object of the preaching "whether it occurs authentically or whether according to the apostles"; either way, it is "the voice of the Lord." The entire consideration of the apostles merely supports the great significance that "the Shepherd" of *Hermas* must have had within the tradition known by Clement.

Moreover, it is not objectionable that the object of Christ's own preaching, according to *1 Peter 3:18–20, is Israel alone.* This should not be seen as a step backward toward the point of view of the second century, since the latter (with the possible exception of Irenaeus, *Against Heresies* 4.22.2) always envisioned only the patriarchs, prophets, and the [people] of Israel. *If we have to understand the preaching of Christ and of the apostles as a whole*, in accordance with what has been said, then it seems inevitable to me (against *Clement*)[191] that Clement did in fact think of an "absolutely *general* offer of salvation." Of course, it is a matter of the *offer* of salvation, and Clement expressly allows for the *possibility of its rejection.*

---

190. Clemen, *"Zu den Toten,"* 175.
191. Clemen, *"Zu den Toten,"* 179.

If, in the earlier period, it was a matter of the fully righteous who lacked nothing but baptism and the preaching of the gospel, here clear distinctions are made among the listeners. They are saved according to their own innate knowledge (of God) ("according to the measure of the knowledge of each"). Although it is openly admitted that they had lived ἁμαρτητικῶς [as sinners], it is also emphasized that they were not ἀπολωλότες [had not perished] but μᾶλλον πεπεδημένοι [rather were bound]. For Clement, the μετάθεσις [transposition] is καθολική [universal], and it is no coincidence that he cites Matthew 27:52 (understood spiritually, of course) about the ἀνάστασις [resurrection] of κεκοιμημένοι [those who have fallen asleep] and omits the word ἅγιοι [the saints].

Jews and Gentiles are equal before God, endowed with the same gifts, equally in need of the Savior. This Savior appears among the Jews, but his mission and his work equally affect the Gentiles. If God's righteousness requires that he also remembers those who died before Christ, it follows that the Gentiles cannot occupy a lesser place in relation to the Jews, for philosophy has prepared them just as well for him as the law prepared the Jews. Thus, they too face a decision once again.

This, in short, is Clement's view. Its themes are quite obvious. If we recall what was said at the outset, we understand how it was clear to him that the fact of Christ's appearing specifically in Israel was, in and of itself, an indifferent matter.

The γνῶσις [knowledge] that guarantees salvation was therefore not dependent on the affiliation with this people.

The redemption of only the Old Testament righteous in Hades would have offered little or no interest to the gnostic, who would have regarded it as one among many myths. But because it was not a myth, or rather, because it was a myth of the Christian church's tradition, it also had to be in the form of a general truth, which means, according to the above-mentioned principle, that *all* who possessed a partial amount of that γνῶσις [knowledge] had to be included, even non-Israelites.

And finally, this conclusion may be confirmed by the Alexandrians' obvious practical question about the eternal fate of the great ones of the Hellenic past, analogous to earlier events regarding the prophets, and so on.

§13. Origen

The passages relevant to the descent motif by this well-known odyssey among the early theologians are so numerous, in this case presumably not even fully complete, that I must refrain from explaining in detail their connections (for the most part irrelevant, incidentally). I am therefore content to classify their essential content according to a few synoptic perspectives, which should not be understood as dogmatic schemata, because fundamentally there are as many perspectives as there are passages.

Analogous to the development of the concept until the end of the second century, I see two main lines in Origen's thought. First, we meet the concept in its fundamental *soteriological* basic form, but then the *christological* motif, which is not used by Clement, is also resumed and reconstituted.

We start with the *question of salvation. Why was Christ's journey to Hades neces-sary?* Origen answers: ἦλθεν ὁ σωτὴρ ζητῆσαι καὶ σῶσαι τὸ ἀπολωλός [The Savior came to seek and to save the lost] [Luke 19:10]. What could be more natural than that ἦλθε τοὺς κάτω καὶ πολιτογραφηθέντας ἐν τοῖς κάτω μεταστῆσαι ἐπὶ τὰ ἄνω [he came to transfer those who are below, and who have been enrolled as citizens among the things that are below, to the things that are above] (*Commentaries on John* 19.5).[192] This coincides with another view, which we have met already in *Hippolytus,* that Christ is the lion of Judah, who fights *"leo ille contrarius"* [the lion who opposes] *"in somno suo leo fuit vincens omnia et debel-lans et destruxit eum qui habebat mortis imperium"* [in his own person prevailed and vanquished all and has destroyed him who has the power of death], thus *"ascendens in altum captivam duxit captivitatem"* [When he ascended on high, he made captivity itself a captive"] (Eph. 4:8! *Homilies on Genesis* 17.5; cf. *Commen-taries on Romans* 55.1).[193] The salvation of those who are in Hades is partially viewed from the perspective of the victory and the reign of Christ. Previously, they were under the reign of death: ἐν τῷ ᾅδῃ τίς ἐξομολογήσεταί σοι; [Who shall confess you in Hades?] (Ps. 6:5). However, ἐνώπιον τοῦ Χριστοῦ προπεσοῦνται μὲν πάντες οἱ καταβαίνοντες [All those who descended fell into the presence of Christ] ([cf.] Ps. 22:29) (*Commentaries on John* 19.5).[194] He must (Rom. 14:9) rule over the dead and the living. (*Commentaries on John* 6.28). Not only Ephesians 4:9 but also Philippians 2:10 are explicitly related to the descent. And the cul-mination of this victory is that ἔσχατος ἐχθρὸς καταργεῖται ὁ θάνατος [the last enemy, death, is destroyed] (1 Cor. 15:26) (*Commentaries on John* 19.5).[195]

How does this process take place? Here we come to the distinctively great development that occurred in the doctrine of the apostolic preaching with Origen (cf. Shepherd of Hermas, *Hippolytus,* and *Clement*): Christ's descent to Hades is now only the culmination and perfection of a work that has already been undertaken before him. What were Samuel, Isaiah, and others after their deaths but Christ's forerunners among the dead, the ἰατροί [healers] who preached in advance of Christ, the ἀρχιατρός [chief healer]! Christ came, and his natural activity was εἰς τοὺς τόπους τῶν καμνόντων στρατιωτῶν εἰσίτωσαν ὅπου αἱ δυσωδίαι τῶν τραυμάτων αὐτῶν. Τοῦτο ὑποβάλλει ἡ ἰατρικὴ φιλανθρωπία [to places of afflicted soldiers and where the foul smells of their wounds have been. Healing beneficence sets this aside].[196] So here we find the mere passivity of expectation, as previously attributed to the great persons of the Old Testa-ment, but transformed into activity, though provisional in character. The last and greatest forerunner of Christ in Hades is John the Baptist: ὁ τὸν ἄνθρωπον ὑποδησάμενος καὶ τὸν νεκρὸν ὑπεδήσατο [the one who put on man, also put on death].[197] So the history of salvation on earth corresponds to a history of

192. Trans.: Origen, *Commentary on the Gospel according to John, Books 13–32,* trans. Ronald E. Heine, Fathers of the Church Patristic Series (Washington, DC: Catholic University of America Press, 1993), 198.

193. Trans.: Origen, *Commentary on the Gospel according to John, Books 1–10,* trans. Ronald E. Heine, Fathers of the Church Patristic Series (Washington, DC: Catholic University of America Press, 1989), 155.

194. Trans.: Origen, *John, Books 13–32,* trans. Heine, 199.

195. Trans.: Origen, *John, Books 13–32,* trans. Heine, 200.

196. Trans.: Origen, *Homilies on Jeremiah: Homily on 1 Kings 28,* trans. John Clark Smith (Washington, DC: Catholic University of American Press, 1998), 330.

197. Trans.: Origen, *John, Books 13–32,* trans. Heine, 218, par. 77.

salvation in the underworld, crowned through the ἐπιδημία τοῦ Κυρίου [sojourn of the Lord] (in the homily on 1 Sam. 28 and *Commentaries on John* 6.18; cf. 2.30).[198] The concept of a *preaching* in Hades does not occur again in Origen, with the exception of a reference to 1 Peter 3:18 (*Commentaries on John* 6.18). For him, this mythical process was unnecessary; the ἐπιδημία [coming] in itself was sufficient ἵν' οὕτως τὴν ὁδὸν ἀνοίξῃ [that he might open up the *way*] (In Homily on 1 Kings 28, i.e., on 1 Sam. 28).[199]

What is the effect of the process? Christ brings ἀπὸ θανάτου ἐλευθερία [freedom from death] (*Commentaries on John* 2.30), he wrests the dead from death (Matt. 27:52, in *Commentaries on Romans* 55.1); he is the ὁδοποιῶν . . . τὴν φέρουσαν ὁδὸν ἐπὶ τὰ ὑπεράνω πάντων τῶν οὐρανῶν τουτέστι[ν] ἐπὶ τὰ ἔξω σωμάτων [he who prepared a way . . . that leads to the things that are above all the heavens, that is, to the things that are incorporeal] (*Commentaries on John* 19.5).[200] "Ibi nos invenit devoratos et sedentes in umbra mortis; et inde educens non jam locum terrae, ut iterum devoraremur, sed locum praeparat nobis regni caelorum" [And there he found us devoured and "sitting under the shadow of death." And leading us hence, he does not now prepare a place on earth for us, lest we be devoured again, but a place in the kingdom of the heavens] (in *Homilies on Exodus* 6.6).[201]

And now finally the particularly important question: Who is the object of the whole process?

"Revocabo te inde in finem" (Gen. 46:4) "hoc est arbitror . . . quod in fine saeculorum unigenitus Filius Dei pro salute *mundi* usque ad inferna descendit et inde *protoplastum* revocavit" [and I will recall you from there in the end] (Gen. 46:4). [I think this means, as we said above, that at the end of the ages his only begotten Son descended even into the nether regions for the salvation of the world and recalled "the first-formed man] [in *Homilies on Genesis* 15.5].[202] These general statements are frequently countered and qualified. In precisely the passage that was cited, Luke 23:43, Origen concludes that it is not only the thief who is referred to "sed et omnibus sanctis intellige, pro quibus in inferna descenderat" [but all of the known saints who will have descended into Hades].[203] There is a parallel passage in *Against Celsus* 2:43 about Jesus converting the souls τὰς βουλομένας πρὸς αὐτὸν ἢ ἃς ἑώρα δι' οὕς ᾔδει αὐτὸς λόγους, ἐπιτηδειοτέρας [of them as were willing to himself, or those whom he saw, for reasons known to him alone, to be better adapted to such a course];[204] or in *Commentaries on Romans* at 5:1, ". . . eos qui inibi non tam praevaricationis crimine quam moriendi conditione habebantur" [those who in that place had the conditions of death not so much from a charge of collusion].[205] Indeed, in *Selections in Psalms*, on 9:17, a category of such persons is expressly mentioned, those in the underworld who

198. Trans.: Origen, *Homilies on Jeremiah: Homily on 1 Kings 28*, trans. Smith, 331; Origen, *John, Books 1–10*, trans. Heine, 190.

199. Trans.: Origen, *Homilies on Jeremiah: Homily on 1 Kings 28*, trans. Smith, 332. In the Septuagint, the designation "I Kings" refers to 1 and 2 Samuel, and "II Kings" refers to 1 and 2 Kings.

200. Trans.: Origen, *John, Books 13–32*, trans. Heine, 198.

201. Trans.: Origen, *Homilies on Genesis and Exodus*, trans. Ronald E. Heine, Fathers of the Church 71 (Washington DC: Catholic University of America Press, 1982), 292.

202. Trans.: Origen, *Genesis and Exodus*, trans. Heine, 211–12.

203. Trans.: Origen, *Genesis and Exodus*, trans. Heine, 212.

204. Trans.: Origen, *Contra Celsum*, trans. Crombie, 2:45.

205. Trans.: Ronald E. Heine, *The Commentaries of Origen and Jerome on St. Paul's Epistle to the Ephesians* (New York: Oxford University Press, 2002).

have received no share in salvation: ἀποκλεισθήτωσαν . . . ὅπως μὴ ἴδωσιν Ἰησοῦ ψυχὴν καταβαίνουσαν καὶ ἀναβαίνουσαν ἔνδον ἀπεστραμμένοι [those shut up in prison, not beholding the soul of Jesus descended and ascended]; whereas the justified ὡσπερεὶ ἔξω ἔβλεπον, . . . πρῶτον μὲν οἱ προφῆται, ἔπειτα οἱ λοιποὶ πάντες δίκαιοι [as if they saw without, . . . first prophets, then all the remaining justified].[206] But I do not believe that this limitation is to be understood as absolute, because Origen juxtaposes it with the other interpretation: ἢ πρῶτον μὲν οἱ ἐν ἡμῖν ἁμαρτωλοί, εἶτα τὰ ἔθνη [first, those among them who are sinners, then the Gentiles], in which the difference between them is merely gradual and temporal, because προπεσοῦνται πάντες οἱ καταβαίνοντες . . . τινὲς μὲν πρότερον, τινὲς δὲ ὕστερον [all who have descended will go forward, . . . some first, some last] (*Commentaries on John* 19.5).[207] Origen's actual view, which characteristically he does not offer at every point, we read in *Homilies on Exodus* 6.6: Extendit dexteram suam et devoravit illos terra. . . . Nec tamen penitus desperandum est. Possibile namque est, ut, si forte resipiscat qui devoratus est, rursum possit evomi, sicut Jonas. Sed et *omnes nos* puto, quod aliquando terra devoratos in inferni penetralibus retinebat et propterea Dominus noster descendit non solum usque ad terras sed usque ad inferiora terrae [You stretched out your right hand; the earth devoured them (Korah's crew). One need not, however, despair completely. For it is possible that if, by chance, he who has been devoured recover his senses, he can again be vomited forth like Jonah. But I also think that at some time the earth retained in the innermost parts of its depths *all of us* who were devoured, and for this reason our Lord descended not only to the earth but also to the "lower parts of the earth"].[208]

The soteriological motif of the descent conception is doubtlessly complete with this doctrine of Origen. A more extensive and precise comprehensive account that avoided heresy was not possible, and in fact we see that all the subsequent attempts to repristinate the concept until the modern period (cf. *Güder*[209] and *Clemen*,[210] e.g.) hew to Origen's approach in the soteriological area. There we find the concept extended, considered from the goal of the descent: not only the salvation of the dead but also the defeat of death.

The doctrine of the apostolic preaching is widened: the entire prophetic witness is incorporated into the process. The estimate of the achievement is broadened: the descent ushers the dead to immediate entrance into the kingdom of heaven.

Finally, and this is the salient point: *through introducing the idea of a gradation, the possibility of the conversion of all is envisaged.* Here the soteriological theme beginning with 1 Peter 3:18–19 and 4:6 converges with a second eschatological theme, which Origen presents in the form of the doctrine of ἀποκατάστασις [restoration; cf. Acts 3:21]. This is indisputably not the result of the New Testament thought itself; it is the consequence of how Clement deploys it in his philosophically informed religion. And if the later age no longer dared to follow Origen, that speaks not against the logical consistency of the deduction

---

206. Trans.: *Selecta, Psalm 9:18* [9:17]. Translation of the Greek supplied by translator.
207. Trans.: Origen, *John, Books 13–32*, trans. Heine, 19.5 on pages 199–200.
208. Trans.: Origen, *Genesis and Exodus*, trans. Heine, 291–92.
209. Güder, *Christi unter den Todten*, 360–81.
210. Clemen, *"Zu den Toten,"* 182–232.

of the latter, but rather of its own incapacity to incorporate unreservedly the results of the Ἑλληνικὴ παιδεία [Hellenic teaching] into dogmatics. Hence, in the final analysis, it speaks for the impossibility of adequately combining Neoplatonic ideas and New Testament religion.

If Origen's account signifies a completion in the soteriological area, so does his *christological* treatment of the descent concept, which is significant as the beginning of the development that follows. It is of secondary significance, and not to be confused with Theodotus's [later] account[211] of Origen positing that Christ first went to paradise, then to Hades, since both are understood as simply two parts of the underworld. The essential meaning of Christ in Hades is that he ὡς ἐν νεκροῖς ἐλεύθερος "was free among the dead";[212] that κατελήλυθεν . . . οὐχ ὡς δοῦλος τῶν ἐκεῖ, ἀλλ᾽ ὡς δεσπότης παλαίσων [he went down to those regions not as a servant but as a master].[213]

Origen's teaching that the descent is an aspect of Christ's glory is a resumption of earlier accounts (Paul!) as well as foreshadowing the later orthodox development *"Descende cogitatione in abyssos et videbis eum etiam illuc descendisse. . . . Considera virtutem Domini quod impleverit mundum"* [Descend in your imagination into the abyss, and you will see him also there to have descended. . . . Consider the virtue of the Lord, who filled the world] (in *Homilies on Luke* 6, on Luke 1:32).[214] Οὕτως Χριστὸς ἦν καὶ κάτω ὤν, ἵνα οὕτως εἴπω, ἐν τῷ κάτω τόπῳ ὤν, προαιρέσει ἄνω ἦν [So, Christ was Christ even when he was below, that is to say, while he was in the place below, he was above in purpose] (Homilies on 1 Kings, in the homily on 1 Sam. 28).[215]

Most important, however, for the later development was Origen's assertion about the mode of the christological event. The subject who descends is, according to *Selections on Psalms*, on Ps. 9:17, ψυχὴ Ἰησοῦ [Jesus's soul];[216] and, according to *Contra Celsus* 2.43, the ψυχὴ γυμνὴ σώματος [naked soul of the body].[217] We recall another christological idea of Origen: the divine Logos joined himself to a human soul excelling in ethical worthiness, which along with the body constitutes true humanity in the person of the Savior. If this is the case, the ψυχή [soul] (meaning σὺν τῷ λόγῳ [with the logos]), must be the subject who descends to Hades, as is the case with human beings.

This aspect of Origen's account of the descent idea still lacks an internal exigency, as the passage *Against Celsus* 2.43 demonstrates especially clearly. The emphasis of the christological thought rather lies on the motif of glory and victory. Because the subsequent development places the emphasis not on the latter, but on the inner divine relationship in the one who was descending, the doctrine of Origen constitutes a completion and turning point in the christological area.

211. See the section on Theodotus, above, page 205 above.

212. Trans.: *The Commentary of Origen on the Gospel of Matthew*, vol. 1, trans. Ronald E. Heine (Oxford: Oxford University Press, 2018), 92. Origen, *Commentaries on Matthew* 12.3.

213. Trans.: *Homilies on Jeremiah; Homily on 1 Kings 28*, 330. Origen, *Homily on 1 Kings 28*, trans. Smith.

214. Trans.: Origen, *Homilies on Luke and Fragments on Luke*, trans. Joseph T. Lienhard (Washington, DC: Catholic University of America Press, 1996), 27.

215. Trans.: *Homilies on Jeremiah; Homily on 1 Kings 28*, 330.

216. Trans.: *Selecta in Psalmos*, at Ps. 9:18 [9:17]. Translation by translator.

217. Trans.: Origen, *Contra Celsum* 2.43, 100.

§14. Prospect

In order to correctly assess the position of the Alexandrian school, we finally must consider, at least suggestively, the development of the dogma, since from the isolated concept and over the centuries, a dogma arose in the church's theology in the Orient, which stood under the influence of Origen.

We can only give some samples rather than a coherent presentation. I choose two theologians from the third and fourth centuries who seem to me to be suitable representatives for this purpose: *Eusebius of Caesarea* and *Epiphanius*.

In *Clement* and *Origen*, we have traced the formation and the completion of the soteriological motif in the thought of the descent. We find these taken up again in *Eusebius*, predominantly through reproduction of ideas that come from Origen: οἱ τῆς φιλανθρωπίας αὐτὸν ἐκάλουν νόμοι ὡς ἂν καὶ τῶν πάλαι τεθνεώτων τὰς ψυχὰς ἀνακαλέσοιτο [Now the laws of love summoned him Him even as far as Death and the dead themselves, so that He might summon the souls of those who were long time dead].[218] The battle and victory over the powers of Hades move increasingly into the foreground and are depicted dramatically and graphically: τὰς ἐπανισταμένας αὐτῷ δυνάμεις, ἃς εἰκὸς κατ᾽ ἀρχὰς μὲν κοινὸν ἄνθρωπον, καὶ τοῖς πολλοῖς ὅμοιον αὐτὸν ὑπειληφέναι ... ἐπεὶ δὲ ἔγνωσαν κρείττονα ἢ κατ᾽ ἄνθρωπον καὶ θειοτέραν φύσιν, τραπῆναι καὶ τὰ νῶτα παραχωρῆσαι αὐτῷ [the powers arrayed against Him, which perhaps at first conceived that He was an ordinary man and like all men, and so encircled Him and attacked him as they would anyone else, but when they know that He was superhuman and divine, they turned their backs and fled from Him].[219] Typical for Eusebius is the concept that Christ destroyed ἐξ αἰῶνος πύλας τῶν σκοτίων μυχῶν [eternally the gates of innermost darkness][220] the φραγμὸν τὸν ἐξ αἰῶνος μὴ σχισθέντα [the barrier which had not been broken from the beginning of the world][221] and (Origen!) freed the prisoners there ἐπὶ τὴν ζωὴν ἀνόδου τὴν πορείαν [and made a road of return back again to life].[222] Indeed, in the rendering of the Legend of Abgar (the passage refers back, if not in in the wording then certainly in the essential integral parts, to the second century), we read: συνήγειρε νεκροὺς τοὺς ἀπ᾽ αἰώνων κεκοιμημένους, so that he κατέβη μόνος, ἀνέβη δὲ μετὰ πολλοῦ ὄχλου πρὸς τὸν πατέρα αὐτοῦ [raised the dead ... from the beginning of the world], so that he [descended alone and with a great multitude ascended to His Father].[223] However, even though Eusebius sounds these ideas so strongly that he can even speak of [salvation of all for ages past].[224] it should not be overlooked that in the same connection he practically limits again the resurrection to the πολλὰ σώματα τῶν κεκοιμημένων ἁγίων [many bodies of the sleeping saints] [Matt. 27:52],[225] so that despite everything, he does

---

218. Trans.: Eusebius of Caesarea, *The Proof of the Gospel* 4.12, trans. W. J. Ferrar (Society for Promoting Christian Knowledge (New York: Macmillan, 1920), 186.
219. Trans.: *The Proof of the Gospel* 8.1, p. 111;-cf. 4.12, p. 186.
220. Trans.: *The Proof of the Gospel* 4.12, p. 186.
221. Trans.: *Ecclesiastical History Books 1–5*, trans. Roy J. Deferrari (Washington, DC: Catholic University of America Press, 1953), 81.
222. Trans.: *The Proof of the Gospel*, 186, 4.12.
223. *Ecclesiastical History Books 1–5*, 81.1.12.
224. Trans.: *The Proof of the Gospel*, 186.4.12.
225. Trans.: *The Proof of the Gospel*, 186.

not go beyond the position of Clement: a general *offer* of salvation, while the ramifications of Origen are here carefully obviated.

Increasingly, the *Logos Christology* became a central church dogma, and the history of our dogma also reveals the traces of this development. It would incidentally be a theme by itself to present the dogma's role in the developing controversies.

Already in *Eusebius* the interest in the *christological motif* is at least as strong as the rest: καὶ ταῦτα πάλιν ἀναμὶξ ὑπῄει τὴν οἰκονομίαν ὡς μὲν ἄνθρωπος τὸ σῶμα τῇ συνήθει παραχωρῶν ταφῇ, ἀναχωρῶν δὲ αὐτοῦ ὡς θεός [here again he underwent the dispensation in His mingled Natures: as Man, he left His Body to the usual burial, while as God He departed from it][226] and even more precisely: τὸ πνεῦμα παραδοὺς τῷ πατρὶ, ἄσαρκος καὶ γυμνὸς οὗ ἀνειλήφει σώματος . . . κατῄει [when yielding up His spirit to the Father, disembodied and stripped of that flesh, which He had assumed].[227]

Under the influence of *Arianism*, the dogma was, for the first time, included in the church's symbols (Councils of Sirmium [357–58], Nikä [Nicaea, 325], and Constantinople, 359–60 CE).[228] It was believed to be an effective way to demonstrate the subordinate relationship of the Logos to God the Father. However, now the earlier christological tendencies in the concept (Origen!) became effective. *Athanasius* could answer: Christ went to Hades μήτε τῆς θεότητος τοῦ σώματος ἐν τῷ τάφῳ ἀπολιμπανομένης μήτε τῆς ψυχῆς ἐν τῷ ἅδῃ χωριζομένης [without either the removal of the divinity of the body in the grave nor separation of the soul in Hades].[229]

In *Epiphanius* we meet the result of this controversy. The work of salvation is in the physical-metaphysical communication of the ἀφθαρσία [incorruption] to humankind, accomplished through the combination of the true divinity with the true humanity in the person of Christ. All the "facts of salvation" are now seen in this context. The mystery of the death of Christ is the juxtaposition of the σωτήριον πάθος [suffering of the Savior] (of the human Jesus) with the ἀπάθεια τῆς θεότητος [impassibility of the divinity] (of divine Christ) (cf. "Anakephalaiōsis" in *Dindorf*) [cf. Eph. 1:22; 2:14–16].[230] However, the work of the God-man is not yet thereby fulfilled: ἤμελλε γὰρ ἡ θεότης τελειοῦν τὰ πάντα τὰ κατὰ τὸ μυστήριον τοῦ πάθους καὶ σὺν τῇ ψυχῇ κατελθεῖν ἐπὶ τὰ καταχθόνια [For the divine nature was about to accomplish all that the mystery of the passion involved and descend to the underworld with his soul].[231] A consequence of the Athanasian idea is that the emphasis lies on the phrase τῇ ψυχῇ [with the soul]. Because with the soul alone, emphatically without body, the divinity reaches the underworld. So that—Epiphanius further construes—ὁ ἄρχων ὁ Ἅιδης καὶ ὁ θάνατος χειρώσασθαι ἄνθρωπον θελήσας κατὰ ἄγνοιαν ἀγνοῶν τὴν ἐν τῇ ψυχῇ τῇ ἁγίᾳ θεότητα καὶ μᾶλλον αὐτὸν τὸν Ἅιδην χειρωθῆναι καὶ τὸν θάνατον καταλυθῆναι [though the archon Hades and Death intended to

---

226. Trans.: *The Proof of the Gospel*, 186.4.12.
227. Trans.: *The Proof of the Gospel*, 111.8.1.
228. *BSGR*, 3rd ed., §§163, 164, 167.
229. Trans.: *De incarnatione* [*Domini nostri Jesu Christi contra Appollinarium*, I.II] c. 14. Greek translation by the translator. 1.2.14.
230. Trans.: Dindorf, *Epiphanii opera*, 1:239; *The Panarion of Epiphanius of Salamis Books II and III. De Fide*, 2nd edition; trans. Frank Williams (Leiden: Brill, 2013), 369.69.42.
231. Trans.: *The Panarion of Epiphanius*, 393.69.65.

subdue the man, he would unknowingly <seize> the <holy> Godhead <concealed> in the soul and Hades himself would be subdued].[232] The significance of the entire process, there, because δέδεικται πᾶσιν ὅτι μὴ τὸ σῶμα ἦν ὁ λόγος ἀλλὰ σῶμα ἦν τοῦ λόγου [it has been shown to all that the body was not the Word but the Word's body].[233]

Besides the metaphysical play of these factors θεότης, ψυχή, σῶμα, Ἅιδης, θάνατος [divinity, soul, body, Hades, death], the soteriological element completely recedes. Certainly Epiphanius faithfully takes it from the available tradition, but it is typical enough that in the sole occasion where he does this with his own words, he uses it to reduce the προκεκοιμημένοι [those who had previously fallen asleep] to the ἅγιοι πατριάρχαι [holy patriarchs]![234] Apart from that, he remains content with the citation of the usual biblical passages: Ephesians 4:8; Acts 2:27; and other such. The use of 1 Peter 3:18–20 is also characteristic. What attracts him here is what is so splendidly suitable to his scheme: those θανατωθεὶς μὲν σαρκί, ζωοποιηθεὶς δὲ πνεύματι [who died in the flesh, yet were made alive again in the Spirit]. Then for the same reason, [he cites] the phrase ἐκήρυξε πνεύμασιν· ὅ μάλιστα δείκνυσι τὴν ἄνοιαν τῶν λεγόντων εἰς ὀστέα καὶ σάρκα τετράφθαι τὸν λόγον [proclaimed by the spirit to show more than anything the ignorance of those who turn the logos into flesh and bones], whereas he no longer knows what to make of the ἐκήρυξεν [proclaimed], in and of itself, and makes nothing at all of the ἀπειθήσαντες [sufferers], which he intentionally disregards anyway.[235]

Thus the descensus ad inferos [doctrine] definitively became a part of the scheme naming christological "facts of salvation," and as such it soon found its way into the Western symbols (first in [the Council of] Aquileia around 400 [381 CE]).[236] "It was only an even stronger emphasis of the idea that Christ {that is, the divine-human Logos} had undergone the complete death of a human being, such a death as presents itself according to its nature and its laws, that is, without preferential treatment, if one added to the statement 'buried' the phrase 'descended into the underworld'" (*Kattenbusch*).[237]

As a part of the *status exaltationis* [exalted state], the Descent appears from then onward in the confessions and in dogmatics until the time of Protestant Orthodoxy; yet it is significant that there has been no final verdict about its use from the perspective of the *munus regium* [kingly office].

232. Trans.: *The Panarion of Epiphanius*, 393.69.65.
233. Trans.: *The Panarion of Epiphanius*, 588.77.7–8.
234. Trans.: *The Panarion of Epiphanius*, 393.69.65.
235. *The Panarion of Epiphanius*, 369.69.42.
236. *BSGR*, 3rd ed., §36.
237. Kattenbusch, "Niedergefahren zur Hölle," 534.

Introduction to the Reviews

In October 1908, after passing his "candidate examination" [Kandidatenprüfung], the "second examination for ministry in the Reformed Church of the Canton of Bern," with the mark 2 ["good"], Karl Barth felt very fortunate to be able to return once again, as Martin Rade's editorial assistant at Die christliche Welt, *to Marburg—or, as he occasionally called the place in his letters, "Holy Marburg," "Marburg-Zion," or even just "Zion."*

At first, it was fortunate simply in an external sense: Apart from his father's agreement to the plan, which could not be readily presumed, and from his father's great confidence in Rade,[1] who after all was oriented quite differently theologically, Karl Barth owed this possibility to his friend Otto Lauterburg and his "friendly disposition, which drove you to give me the Rade post after your refusal" (Letter to O. Lauterburg, August 9, 1908). As a matter of fact, there was, at first, another candidate who stood between Barth and the "position of assistant editor of the Christliche Welt."[2] But, "Deus ex machina, the mother of the other candidate vetoed it because she was orthodox, and I moved into first place with a bang" (Letter to O. Lauterburg, August 9, 1908). And so, Barth could sign a letter dated August 11, 1908, to his school friend Willy Spoendlin, as not only "candidate of theology and half of a minister" but also "newspaper laborer in spe [in hope]."

A retrospective published almost forty years later testifies to the fact that the "adjunct"[3] found "the socage in the Rade House" also to be "cheerful and light" and that he regarded himself as fortunate for the time spent from November 1908 until August 1909 "as something like a coxswain" on Die christliche Welt. *In this retrospective, Barth could finally also describe it in a deeper sense as "the good will of Providence," in view of his path in theology then and later, that he was able to be so completely absorbed by "the magic of* Die christliche Welt" *at this time.[4] Concerning his work Barth reported: "The chief task consisted of reading the many incoming manuscripts, forming a preliminary judgment about them, presenting this in an appropriate manner to Martin Rade, and finally getting the material he selected ready for the printer. . . . Since the system of reviews played an important role in this flood of paper, a full year's production of liberal, or as we said at that time, 'modern' theology, passed through my hands one way or another. . . . With time, I was even permitted to burst on the scene myself in a few small reviews—I thought they were masterpieces."[5] In Barth's*

---

1. See Bw.R., 59–65.
2. Bw.R., 62.
3. Bw.R., 66.
4. Letter to Dr. J. Rathje, April 27, 1947, in: K. Barth, *Offene Briefe 1945–1968*, ed. D. Koch, *Gesamtausgabe* 15 (Zurich: TVZ, 1984), 119–20.
5. Letter to Dr. J. Rathje, April 27, 1947, 119–120.

letters to his parents we find many glances of this aspect of his work. Already on December 6, 1908, he can report: "By the way, I have already written some reviews, which will appear at a time yet to be determined." Barth makes a subtle joke with a slightly varying allusion to Eugen Höflings "Rückblick eines alten Burschen" [Retrospective of an old Frat Brother] ("Da schreibt mit finsterm Amtsgesicht / der eine Relationen, / der andre seufzt beim Unterricht, / und der macht Rezensionen . . ." [The one writes mathematical relations with a grim official scowl, the other sighs during class and produces reviews]). Barth writes, "yes, yes, quite like this song says:

> *Da schreibt mit finsterm Amtsgesicht*
> *der eine Rezensionen . . .*
> *O quae mutatio rerum*
> *[The one writes reviews with a grim official scowl . . . O how things have*
>   *changed]!"*

On December 8, he tells of work on three reviews: "And imagine how excited all these people are to hear what Die christliche Welt *will say about them (consider: the world and then even Christian!). To be sure, whether Rade will print my pronouncements is another question, perhaps I have the honor of personally burying it in Box II [the rejection box]!" On January 11, 1909: "Recently, for half a day and half a night, the pencil shavings were flying as I did nothing but review. . . . By the way, I do not know yet if Rade will print any of it. In any case it is a good exercise in style and thought." Yet on January 22, 1909, Barth can report to Bern: "Rade has praised and accepted seven of my smaller and larger reviews all at once; five of them will be sent a tempo to the printers, such that you should be able to be edified by my pronouncements in the next few issues."*

In any case, four of the five reviews that were immediately sent to the publisher indeed appeared soon: The first (Mix) on January 28, 1909, in Volume 23.5 the second (von Broecker) on February 18, 1909, in 23.8; the third (Mezger) and fourth (Voigt) on March 4, 1909, in 23.10. The review of Jahnke appeared on May 13, 1909, in 23.20. Is it the last of the five pieces? If so, it would have been published quite late. Still, one other, the Pfister review, which Barth completed together with the Jahnke review (letter of January 11, 1909) had to wait even longer. It did not appear until April 27, 1911, in Volume 25.17. But even with this we only have six of the seven of the works by Barth which were accepted "all at once." For indeed, still another of Barth's reviews appeared on December 9, 1909, in Volume 23.50 (on Elias Schrenk, Seelsorgerliche Briefe für allerlei Leute). *But the correspondence between Barth and Rade shows that Barth only received this book for review from Rade after he was in Geneva—"I thought this book would interest you especially now"—and that Barth had sent the review from Geneva to Marburg on November 29.[6] So we have to assume that one of the seven mentioned reviews subsequently fell into some "sort of theological wolf's glen" in which papers considered "of less significance" vanished "for a more or less extended or even permanent waiting period."[7]*

In any case, it can be assumed that the missing review was of Richard Ernst's Wie ich ein moderner Theologe wurde [*"How I became a modern theologian"*]. *For Barth probably refers to this work in his letter of December 8, 1908: "I am also pleased that*

---

6. Bw.R., 71–72.
7. K. Barth, *Offene Briefe 1945–1968*, 119. [Translator's note: The reference to a "wolf's glen" is an allusion to Carl Maria von Weber's opera, *Der Freischütz* (The Marksman), much of which is set in a lonely, isolated, and forsaken "Wolf's Glen."]

Dad approves of the booklet on the modern theologians to an extent. My review hardly praises it at all, but only gives a report and says this is how things stand, although no development is like another." Possibly, Rade had accepted Barth's review (and perhaps already given it to the printer with the other four), but then subsequently replaced it with a review by Paul Drews (sent to him in the meantime?), which was published on March 4, 1909, in 23.10. Drews was able to write about these "self-confessions" with knowledge about the real identity of the pseudonymous author; Martin Schian was the author of this account of the development of a theologian from an orthodox home, who, after struggles and doubts, "finds the ground beneath his feet" when he comes to Herrmann. And Drews does not merely give a report, unlike Barth, who apparently had only wanted to cautiously comment on this path that was not entirely unfamiliar to himself. Instead, Drews praises the "little book" as "a very effective defense of the much maligned 'modern' theology."[8] If the assumption is correct that Drews's review subsequently replaced Barth's, then Barth's text was the fifth in the series of seven reviews, which concludes with the reviews of Jahnke and Pfister.

In any case, the review of Ernst or Schian belongs among the "series of reviews" which are missing and which we know of only from Barth's letters.[9] Only two unpublished reviews have been preserved in manuscript form. The first is a critical review of the first two issues of Zeitschrift für wissenschaftliche Theologie, *Vol. 51, which Barth, in a letter to his parents dated March 21, considering the length of his reviews written in "these days," simply calls "an extended review of an essay by Troeltsch." The other—which exists only as a fragment—is a broad review of* La cure d'âme moderne et ses bases religieuses et scientifiques *["Modern Pastoral Care and Its Religious and Scientific Foundations"] published in 1910 by the Genevan pastor and theology professor Ch. Durand-Pallot (see VukA 2, 227–229). It is not mentioned in the letters, as far as we can see, perhaps because Barth began writing it on his own, but soon abandoned it when there ujappeared to be no way that he could fruitfully complete the chosen task. The "Troeltsch Review" however (written in ink on seven octave pages) is referred to in the aforementioned letter of March 21, 1909; "Rade and Stephan" had "approved" it and "formally also Bornhausen." "Perhaps it will not be published in the* Christliche Welt, *but in the* Zeitschrift für Theologie und Kirche *somewhat revised into so-called 'antitheses.' It all depends on whether Rade thinks it expedient to provoke Troeltsch in this way." It would seem Rade didn't think such a provocation was a good idea after all. The review did not appear in either the* Zeitschrift für Theologie und Kirche *or the* Christliche Welt. *Nor were the other "venomous or friendly" reviews, which Barth wrote at this time, published (letter of March 21, 1909). The reasons were—as Rade's letters show[10]—by no means due to a lack of interest or esteem on Rade's part. He just had "a tremendous amount of material" for the* Christliche Welt.[11] *The more likely reason is that Barth's criticisms were "too long" and "too sharp"—"You see the standard by which I am measured is very clear to me at this moment in time," Barth added when he sent Rade a review of which he "was convinced from the outset" that Rade would "hardly let it see the light of day" because of the reasons mentioned.[12]*

---

8. *CW* 23 (1909): 235–236.
9. See, Bw.R., 70.
10. See only Bw.R., 82 and 86.
11. Bw.R., 82.
12. Bw.R., 74.

Review of Gustav Mix,
Zur Reform des theologischen Studiums
[Toward the Reform of Theological Study]
1909

G. Mix, Zur Reform des theologischen Studiums: Ein Alarmruf *(Munich: Leh-mann, 1908).* [Toward the Reform of Theological Study: A Call for Alarm*]*

The relationship between university study and practice, which is relatively simple and self-evident in the other academic disciplines, has been a problem for the theologian since Schleiermacher.[1] The ideals of science do not correspond with the demands of the pastorate. The overcoming of this hiatus is a task that arises enormously before everyone who wants to cross over from one to the other. And it is undoubtedly and urgently necessary, precisely in light of the present situation of theology, that the church, and above all those closest to it—academic teachers, students, and the young clergy—look at this problem seriously.

But whoever sounds the alarm, in order to get the attention of the public and the ecclesiastical authorities, would have to overlook the problem from a higher vantage point than the author of this little piece, to which unfortunately once again the word of Lessing applies: The good he brings is not new and the new is not good.[2] "Theological education should impart a precise knowledge of Christianity and its history, especially of the religious and moral forces living in it."[3] The author would not deny that the very ideal of the academic teaching up until now has been the same. Academic study should further introduce students "to the intellectual life of the present with its various currents, . . . examine the ecclesiastical, social, and cultural relationships of our people, and . . . guide them to their own research in this field."[4] As far as the intellectual currents of the present are concerned, there is no doubt that every student, who has the goodwill to do so, will have ample opportunity to become acquainted with these currents during their university years; who is it then, who calls them to limit their study to the parameters of their academic department? The postulates of

---

1. See "Introduction to the Reviews," 227–29.
2. Here X. (= Johann Heinrich Voss), "Auf mehrere Bücher: Nach Lessing," in *Musen-Almanach für 1792,* ed. J. H. Voss (Hamburg: G. E. Bohn, 1792), 71 [= J. H. Voss, *Sämtliche Gedichte,* part 6, "Oden und Lieder," in vol. 7, *Vermischte Gedichte, Fabeln und Epigramme* (Königsberg, 1802), 292]:

    Your loquacious book teaches many things that are new and true.
    O that the true things were new! O that the new things were true!

    See Gotthold Ephraim Lessing, "Briefe, die neueste Literatur betreffend," part 6, "Letter 111," in Lessing, *Werke,* ed. Herbert G. Göpfert (Munich: C. Hanser, 1973), 5:306.
3. G. Mix, *Zur Reform des theologischen Studiums: Ein Alarmruf* (Munich: Lehmann, 1908), 15.
4. Mix, *Reform,* 15: Theological studies should "(2) introduce the student to the intellectual life of the present with its various currents, subject the present state of ecclesial life and the social and cultural conditions of our people to a thorough examination, and above all give guidance for independent research especially into this area."

ecclesiastical and religious folklore also have long been established and even partially realized, especially in the modern direction within practical theology, which is not foreign to the author.[5]

The third thesis is evidently the core element of the desired reform. Theological education ought specifically "to teach students how to theoretically and practically bring together both of these given variables, Christianity and empirical reality, effectively . . . and in such a way that an answer can be given to these questions: (1) How do I reach the soul of the people? (2) How should I utilize the existing vitality of the gospel, in order to . . . accomplish the result desired?[6] The "exercise on the object," modeled on the example of the medical profession,[7] should be the center of focused academic instruction.

What are we actually doing when we study dogmatics and ethics other than precisely "bringing together" Christianity and empirical reality? The author must either deny or ignore this, because for him Christianity is a "given entity," a complex of thoughts, ideas, and motivations. It is thus easy enough to see why, among the equipment that the study of theology gives to the candidate, he misses the technique for "bringing together" this complex with the other, that of empirical reality! For Christianity is not a given entity, but an individual certainty. Its relationship to the past is a question of the study of history; its engagement with the empirical reality of contemporary life is a question involving the doctrine of faith and ethics. This, however, makes the author's idea of science as a "purposeful" collection of material[8]—which, strangely enough, shall later be thrown overboard after all[9]—to be impossible, and Haupt's proposition that "purposefulness" consists in the method remains valid.[10]

Yet then the problem mentioned at the beginning cannot be defined with the author: How do I "effectively" unite the two complexes of thought and reality? Instead, it should be defined: How do I practically convey a personal certainty, whose peculiar grounding in history and whose relationship to present reality has become theoretically clear to me, to another person? And I have no doubt that there is no scientific answer to this question, no universal prescription. Apart from its historical elements, so-called practical theology can offer nothing other than a more or less farsighted casuistry. The student and aspiring clergyperson must himself make sense of things when he gets to the pastorate. The most regrettable aspect of the author's presentation, it seems to me, is that he has not recognized how the hiatus between theory and practice corresponds to the essence of the subject matter and can therefore never be completely eliminated, and so he calls for scientific methods to be devised that would, when one follows their instructions, "effectively" awaken faith. Certainly, the advice of practical theology will always need to be improved and adapted to the basic features of modern life. Certain imponderables on the part of the individual persons involved remain more important. I think that a student who has attended the school of historical and systematic theology with enthusiasm and

5. Mix, *Reform,* 29–30 (and the works mentioned there).
6. Mix, *Reform,* 15.
7. Mix, *Reform,* 20–24, "Medical Studies as a Model."
8. Mix, *Reform,* 19: "In any case, a little more purposefulness could not harm university studies."
9. Mix, *Reform,* 7.
10. Mix, *Reform,* 19 and 6; see E. Haupt, "Prinzipielles zur Professorenfrage," in *Deutsch-evangelische Blätter* 33 (1908): 283–90, esp. 283, 286–87.

love and not merely for the sake of passing examinations—such a student will not go to work in the church without some guidelines to build upon. And vice versa: the historical and systematic work of a teacher who is in touch with the life of the church and knows the latter's needs not only from a distance—such a teacher will, without confusing scholarship with "edification," provide students with the liveliness and the skills required for their future tasks.

Review of A. Von Broecker,
Protestantische Gemeinde-Flugblätter
[Pamphlets for the Protestant Community]
1909

A. von Broecker, Protestantische Gemeinde-Flugblätter: *No. 1*, Deines Kindes Zukunft: Ein Wort zur Taufe. *No. 2*, Der Konfirmation—dem Leben entgegen! *No. 3*, Auf der Lebenshöhe—ein Gruss zum Hochzeitstage. *No. 4*, Stille Samm-lung vor dem Abendmahl. *No. 5*, Krankentrost. *No. 6*, Mut an Gräbern! *No. 7*, Es blühe die Gemeinde! *(Göttingen: Vandenhoeck & Ruprecht, 1901–6).*

[*A. Von Broecker, Pamphlets for the Protestant community: No. 1, Your child's future: A word about baptism. No. 2, Toward confirmation—Toward life! No. 3, At the height of life—A greeting on the wedding day. No. 4, Silent reflection before the Lord's Supper. No. 5, The consolation of the sick. No. 6, Courage at gravesides! No. 7, The congregation shall flourish! . . .*]

The author is already widely known from his *Flugblätter für männliches Christentum* [Pamphlets for a masculine Christianity][1] in which he addresses "those who are on the outside" [cf. 1 Cor. 5:12; Col. 4:5; 1 Thess. 4:12; 1 Tim. 3:7], especially the modern working class. The pamphlets under review are addressed to those who think of themselves, whether by conviction or by rou-tine, as being part of the Christian community. They aim to show the Christian what he [or she] can have in one's Christianity, not only in Christianity but also in the Christian Church, when a Christian learns to participate of one's own accord in the life of the church. All of them express a strong and free religiosity. Their intellectual and linguistic stance recommends them to be used especially among an urban population.

---

1. See "Introduction to the Reviews," 228. *Moderne Flugblätter für männliches Christentum*, nos. 1–10 (Göttingen: Vandenhoeck & Ruprecht, 1901–6); New Series, nos. 1/2 and 3 (1906).

Review of P. Mezger, *Eigenart und innere Lebensbedingungen einer protestantischen Volkskirche* *[The particularity and inner life of a Protestant people's church]* Address of the Rector, 1909

P. Mezger, Eigenart und innere Lebensbedingungen einer protestantischen Volkskirche. *Basler Rektoratsrede, Basel, 1909.* [The particularity and inner life of a Protestant people's church, *Address of the Rector, 1909*]

It is well known that the [Reformed] Church in Basel is currently in the process of organizing itself as a public corporation with the rights of self-governance vis-à-vis the state.[1] This provides an external occasion to say something about its foundations, "to examine it in regard to its ultimate purpose,"[2] thus about its character as a people's church without adherence to a confession, built on a democratic basis.[3] In contrast to the "highest church-ideal"[4] of a visible community of faith and love,[5] which surfaces time and again, Mezger wants to understand the church as "an essentially pedagogical institution that serves the interests for the formation of Christian piety."[6] The prerequisite for such an institution is a people who are somehow already bound together by Christian motives.[7] Likewise, it is necessary that in this institution diverse convictions have full freedom for action side by side.[8] For Christian knowledge of God is not absolute knowledge but instead is connected to personal and ethical conditions; it is thus of infinite diversity on an individual basis, and the value of a confession of faith depends on its truthfulness.[9] Different convictions are nothing but different expressions of the same experience.[10] Even a doctrinal confession taken in the most latitudinarian manner possible is forbidden in view of the Protestant understanding of the essence of Christianity, which we understand as a solemn task, not as a secure possession;[11] the latter is also true

---

1. See "Introduction to the Reviews," 228. Here see Ulrich Lampert, *Kirche und Staat in der Schweiz* (Freiburg: Universitätsbuchhandlung Rütschi & Egloff, 1938), 2:117–36, esp. 125–36.
2. Paul Mezger, *Eigenart und innere Lebensbedingungen einer protestantischen Volkskirche* (Basel: Helbing & Lichtenhahn, 1909), 5 (emphasized there).
3. Mezger, *Volkskirche*, 5.
4. Mezger, *Volkskirche*, 10, 12 (emphasized on both pages there)
5. Mezger, *Volkskirche*, 13.
6. Mezger, *Volkskirche*, 15 (partially emphasized there).
7. Mezger, *Volkskirche*, 16–17.
8. Mezger, *Volkskirche*, 18, 21.
9. Mezger, *Volkskirche*, 19.
10. Mezger, *Volkskirche*, 20.
11. Mezger, *Volkskirche*, 22–25.

for the religious individuality of the preacher[12] and also for the true interest of the church, which can only exist in the free air of truth and truthfulness.[13] The foundation of the faith and unity of the church is instead the great historical fact of revelation.[14] Only a church that, standing on this ground and serious about freedom and truth, will be able to meet the demands of the present.[15]

The non-theologian would perhaps have been grateful for an explicit description of what Mezger means by "gospel" and "revelation."[16] We wish that his fine remarks will be heard above all on this side of the Rhine, too.[17]

12. Mezger, *Volkskirche*, 25–26.
13. Mezger, *Volkskirche*, 26–27.
14. Mezger, *Volkskirche*, 29.
15. Mezger, *Volkskirche*, 30.
16. Mezger, *Volkskirche*, 6, 7–9, and throughout.
17. Addition of the editor of *Die christliche Welt*, Martin Rade: "[See above col. 225ff. The Editor.]" This refers to the article by F. Kattenbusch, "Volkskirche und Katechismus," in *CW* 23 (1909): 225–28, which contains a "Rector's Speech" by P. Mezger and also discusses the treatise by H. Matthes, "Neue Bahnen für den Unterricht in Luthers Katechismus," *MPTh* 5 (1909): 103–24.

Review of Fr. A. Voigt, *Was sollen wir tun?*
[*What should we do?*]
1909

Fr. A. Voigt, Was sollen wir tun? Ein Laienvotum zur gegenwärtigen Krisis in der evangelischen Kirche *(Leipzig: M. Költz, 1908).*[1] *[What should we do? A lay vote on the current crisis in the Protestant Church.]*

This is a spirited polemical pamphlet against "modern" theology[2] from the camp of the *Gemeinschaftschristen!*[3] Above all, the reader should not be put off by the fact that "an under-current of coarseness pervades the whole," as *Scheffel's* Ekkehard so nicely puts it.[4] I have read it with enjoyment and believe that it has something to say to us, precisely because it does not come from a pacesetter of the theological right, but from a person who is ecclesiastically nonpartisan, who is spirited in his own way and well versed in the literature of the opposition, whose attitude, moreover, demonstrates some sympathy toward the opposition.

Not that he hasn't thoroughly misunderstood his opponents. We hear from *Troeltsch, Bousset,* and *Wernle* (!) that, in contrast to *Harnack,*[5] they attempt to construct the historical basis of theology, the source of revelation, in the manner

---

1. See "Introduction to the Reviews," 228. The title reviewed here was initially published anonymously in 1908 by the publisher M. Költz of Leipzig, as stated. In 1909, the title was issued under the name of the author and published by Vereinsbuchhandlung G. Ihlhoff & Co. of Neumünster. The cover, title page, and foreword were apparently reprinted for this edition, which appears to have remained unchanged. In his foreword, signed "Leipzig, August 1909," the author—the philologist Dr. Friedrich Adolf Voigt (1857–1939), a member of the Moravian Church—explains: "For personal reasons, a first edition of this publication was issued anonymously. . . ." Barth had this first edition available for his review.
In a letter to Karl Barth dated February 14, 1924, Voigt says, "I simply had had the brochure from 1908 printed at my expense." He thanks his reviewer, "somewhat very retrospectively," "that you heard the voice from another camp and listened more to the What than to the How. I am even more pleased that your judgment on Reformation and modern theology—on 'Paulinism' and the real, old Paul—is now as you expressed it in your commentary to the Romans." In a later publication, Voigt comes back again to his writing of 1908–9 and to the review by Karl Barth. With reference to the critical treatment of Schleiermacher in his "Layman's Opinion" and with regard to Barth's criticism of Schleiermacher in the 1922 *Epistle to the Romans,* he notes: "Since my reviewer is the same as the commentator of the *Epistle to the Romans,* it is clear that Barth has come close to my judgment of Schleiermacher and the conception of modern Protestantism that goes with it." Friedrich Adolf Voigt, *Sören Kierkegaard im Kampfe mit der Romantik, der Theologie und der Kirche: Zur Selbstprüfung unserer Gegenwart anbefohlen* (Berlin: Furche-Verlag, 1928), 425; see 362–63.
2. Friedrich Adolf Voigt, *Was sollen wir tun?,* 2–6, 77, and throughout.
3. See Voigt, *Was sollen wir tun?,* 27, 48, 64–65, 66–67, 70–71. [Trans. note: the term *Gemeinschaftschristen* [Community-Christians] refers to a Pietist movement, a sort of great awakening, that affected a number of Protestant churches in Germany and Switzerland in the second half of the nineteenth century. In many places, this awakening led to the creation of community circles that later developed into independent ecclesial communities still existing alongside the mainstream Protestant churches.]
4. Joseph Victor von Scheffel, *Ekkehard: A Tale of the Tenth Century* (New York: W. S. Gottsberger & Co., 1890), 2:89.
5. Voigt, *Was sollen wir tun?,* 7–9.

of proof *e consensu gentium* [from truth by consensus], by "circumnavigating the world" of the totality of religions.[6] *Troeltsch* in particular comes off poorly: he declares faith in a God who has worked and still works for a supra-naturalism that is scientifically finished.[7] The times are over when *Herrmann* protested against *Pfleiderer's* world religion of the future.[8] Until that point, rather much everything is judged wrongly. The starting point of "modern" theology is correctly recognized in Schleiermacher's speeches,[9] but the interpretation of the latter has been completely unsuccessful: he wanted to fathom the essence of religion by speculation,[10] found it in the Spinozist universe,[11] and at first identified natural monistic religion with Christianity.[12] Starting with *Schleiermacher*, "modern" theology created a "pedagogical religion [*Bildungsreligion*]" (*Troeltsch!*);[13] its content was "drawn from the depths of modern self-consciousness,"[14] the essence of which is the reduction of religious earnestness to the level of average morality,[15] the "alleviation of humanity from the belief in redemption,"[16] and the lack of criticism of cultural deteriorations.[17] The crisis of the Protestant Church, the author tells us, is that this theology prevails in so many cathedrals and pulpits:[18] yet despite his erudition, he has not understood it.

However, those who expect a robust orthodoxy or at least biblicism from the author in his positive presentation of his own standpoint will be mistaken. Rather, in a surprising manner he demonstrates how close he basically is to the opponents he fights so hard against. For him, the basic problem is not that there are too many "liberal" theologians, but that in fact there are too few Christians[19] and that the church has often become an end in itself rather than a means,[20] a caste institute.[21] The foundation of the truth of religion has falsely been left to church doctrine and book learning,[22] while it is only possible by pointing to its origin, which lies beyond human subjectivity and yet can be experienced subjectively.[23] For faith is not a worldview,[24] but the human

---

6. Voigt, *Was sollen wir tun?*, 9–19 and esp. 16 and 19, "Circumnavigation of the Religions of the World."

7. Voigt, *Was sollen wir tun?*, 10–11.

8. Voigt, *Was sollen wir tun?*, 9–10. See Wilhelm Herrmann, *Die Religion im Verhältniss zum Welterkennen und zur Sittlichkeit: Eine Grundlegung der systematischen Theologie* (Halle: Max Niemeyer, 1879); and Herrmann, review of (1) Johannes Claravallensis, *Die falschmünzerische Theologie Albrecht Ritschls und die christliche Wahrheit: Allen Christgläubigen gewidment* (Gütersloh: Bertelsmann, 1891); and of (2) Otto Pfleiderer, *Die Ritschl'sche Theologie, kritisch beleuet* (Braunschweig: C. A. Schwetschke & Sohn, 1891), in *TLZ* 17 (1892): 382–87.

9. Voigt, *Was sollen wir tun?*, 21, 27, 28, 32.

10. Voigt, *Was sollen wir tun?*, 22.

11. Voigt, *Was sollen wir tun?*, 22–23.

12. Voigt, *Was sollen wir tun?*, 24–26, 28.

13. Voigt, *Was sollen wir tun?*, 32–33, 38–39. See Ernst Troeltsch, *Protestantisches Christentum und Kirche in der Neuzeit (1906/1909/1922),* ed. Volker Drehsen, *Ernst Troeltsch: Kritische Gesamtausgabe,* vol. 7 (Berlin: de Gruyter, 2004), 425–51.

14. Voigt, *Was sollen wir tun?*, 54.

15. See Voigt, *Was sollen wir tun?*, 37.

16. See Voigt, *Was sollen wir tun?*, 48.

17. Voigt, *Was sollen wir tun?*, 33–38, esp. 33, 35–36, 38.

18. Voigt, *Was sollen wir tun?*, 29, 46.

19. Voigt, *Was sollen wir tun?*, 3–4.

20. Voigt, *Was sollen wir tun?*, 67.

21. Voigt, *Was sollen wir tun?*, 38–39.

22. Voigt, *Was sollen wir tun?*, 46.

23. Voigt, *Was sollen wir tun?*, 16.

24. Voigt, *Was sollen wir tun?*, 26–27.

being ruled by God;[25] its criterion of truth is the "emergency case," "the hot struggle of God-seeking hearts, frightened and anxious consciences, not the cool, balanced mind."[26] Its foundation is Jesus Christ, "faith in whom is very much taught and very easily and mistakenly called the dogma of the divinity of Christ."[27] But where the love of God has been made effective by Jesus in the individual and in the community, there faith becomes a declaration of war against the corruption of a dull world;[28] it is not a mood that accompanies life, but a disposition that transforms life.[29]

The antithetical character of these statements, which mainly results from a misunderstanding, does not put us off from sincerely enjoying the broad religious consensus. We will also accept the often somewhat mechanically handled notion of conversion and the un-Protestant concept of the holiness of the church and the pastoral office,[30] but this means that we let rest the answer to the question "What should we do?" given in the last two paragraphs of this document.[31] For it comes down to the friendly advice, "Is not the whole land before thee? Separate thyself, I pray, from me!" (Gen. 13:9),[32] and a positive challenge to the laity to devote themselves more zealously and independently to evangelization and works of charity[33] and thus to support the "professor and pastor's church,"[34] potentially replacing it.[35]

The gap between our academic theology and the educated laity, treated in the first edition of this volume among other issues,[36] is frighteningly illustrated in this document. Is the guilt only on the side of the latter, when one can see here and there nothing in the former or wants to see it only as radical historical criticism ("gospel problems instead of the gospel," says our author)[37] and a mitigation and a leveling of current religious problems? It is precisely this misunderstanding, as though the intention is to present the "historical-critical Jesus"[38] as Savior to the congregation, that is widespread even in theological circles, and this is certainly not only due to the *readers* of the *Religionsgeschichtliche Volksbücher*.[39] Misconceptions about terminology—among which I count the fatal expression "educational religion," for example—also help to widen the gap. But the real error must lie deeper. What should *we* do? If I may allow myself a wish for the sake of the supporters of "modern" theology, it would be this: more personal contact and concern with the problems and tasks in the practice of proclaiming the gospel, a task for which academic theology usually

25. See Voigt, *Was sollen wir tun?*, 44.
26. Voigt, *Was sollen wir tun?*, 47.
27. Voigt, *Was sollen wir tun?*, 47.
28. Voigt, *Was sollen wir tun?*, 42–43.
29. Voigt, *Was sollen wir tun?*, 43, 55.
30. Voigt, *Was sollen wir tun?*, 61–64, 84–85, and throughout.
31. Voigt, *Was sollen wir tun?*, chap. 4: "What Should We Do?," 49–76; and Appendix: "Stay in Your Professions! Or New Professions!?," 77–87.
32. Voigt, *Was sollen wir tun?*, 31.
33. Voigt, *Was sollen wir tun?*, 65–76, 77–78, 85, and throughout.
34. See Voigt, *Was sollen wir tun?*, 79.
35. See Voigt, *Was sollen wir tun?*, 82–87.
36. Martin Rade, "Vergeblich?," in *CW* 23 (1909): 3–7.
37. See Voigt, *Was sollen wir tun?*, 51.
38. Rade, "Vergeblich?," 3, 5.
39. Voigt, *Was sollen wir tun?*, 4, 9, 30, 35, and throughout. For more about the *Religionsgeschichtliche Volksbücher für die deutsche christliche Gegenwart*, edited by Fr. M. Schiele (Halle, later Tübingen, 1904–21), see Fr. M. Schiele, "Volksbücher, religionsgeschichtliche," in *RGG*[1] 5:1721–25.

wants to be the preparation. I do not think I am the only one who, on the boundary between the university and the parish, feels pain with the difficulty of leaving theology and yet approaching the thinking and feelings of others through theology. From the same difficulty, however, those unfortunate misunderstandings of our theological literature have arisen. Is that postulated preoccupation with practice really just a waste of time for the work of our academics, or is it rather an integral part of this work?

Review of R. Jahnke,
Aus der Mappe eines Glücklichen
[From the portfolio of a lucky person]
1909

Richard Jahnke, Aus der Mappe eines Glücklichen, 2nd ed. (Leipzig: B. G. Teubner, 1908). *[From the portfolio of a lucky person.]*

"The Cyrenian worldview is a jovial philosophy that knows how to get the best out of everything, does not desire the impossible, and cannot be disturbed as it merrily enjoys existence"; so we read in Karl Vorländer.[1] This also describes the strength and weakness of this book. It contains several friendly instructions for people who seek happiness. "The author wants to show them that it is in their power to become happy."[2] "He does not surmise that he has found the Philosopher's Stone."[3] No one has found it yet; but why then does he roll up problems such as "optimism and pessimism,"[4] "the goodness of fate,"[5] and "the mystery of death and of God"[6] in order to deal with them in this comfortable way?

It is worth noting that it was necessary to print a second edition after a little more than a year.[7] This is proof enough as to how the roots of such an ethic still extend, despite Nietzsche and Schopenhauer. After reading this book, I advise, as an antidote, to read something like Vischer's *Auch Einer*.[8]

---

1. Karl Vorländer, *Geschichte der Philosophie*, vol. 1, *Philosophie des Altertums und des Mittelalters* (Leipzig: Dürr'sche Buchhandlung, 1903), 78. See "Introduction to the Reviews," 228–29.
2. See Jahnke, *Mappe eines Glücklichen*, 119.
3. See Jahnke, *Mappe eines Glücklichen*, 119.
4. Jahnke, *Mappe eines Glücklichen*, 12–17.
5. Jahnke, *Mappe eines Glücklichen*, 106–12.
6. Jahnke, *Mappe eines Glücklichen*, 113–16.
7. A review of the first edition (Leipzig : B. G. Teubner, 1908) was written by M. Schian in *CW* 22, no. 23 (1908): 572.
8. Friedrich Theodor Vischer, *Auch Einer: Eine Reisebekanntschaft* (Stuttgart/Leipzig: Deutsche Verlagsanstalt, 1904). Barth may have suggested this novel-like narrative work as a suitable "antidote" because the main character is depicted as in a constant struggle with internal and external adversities, among other things, the now proverbial concept of *die Tücke des Objekts* (the malice of things).

Review of O. Pfister,
Religionspädagogisches Neuland
[The unknown territory of religious pedagogy]
1909

Oskar Robert Pfister, Religionspädagogisches Neuland: Eine Untersuchung über das Erlebnis- und Arbeitsprinzip im Religionsunterricht *(Zurich: Schulthess, 1909). [The unknown territory of religious pedagogy: An investigation of the principles of experience and work in religious instruction.]*

Teaching as education for a powerful, self-contained, and yet free individual—here is the ideal for the teacher of today, who has eyes for the seeking and finding of our times. This is nothing new; Pestalozzi already said it;[1] and yet there is no denying that a great step forward has been made, especially in the last few decades. I need only mention the name of *Friedrich W. Forester.*[2] And this movement in the field of education crosses with another, the religious, of which the so-called modern theology is but only an especially loud echo; religion as a liberation from the limitations of the impersonal, as obedience and trust in the God who reveals himself to us in individual experience. In the field of religious education, these two lines intersect. But the task of education in personal religion is more easily set than solved.

In this sense, Pfister's short work is intended to inspire; anyone interested in the question, who comes to it from one side or the other, will put it down with thankfulness. The goal he sets for the religion teacher and catechist is to awaken the self-expression of the individual according to a person's peculiar character and thereby to tutor the reader for free, religious experience, for individual acts of faith.[3] The primary prerequisite for this is always the personal emotion of the teacher about the inner need of the people and the power of the gospel.[4] And the primary means for instruction in this spirit will always be the spoken word.[5] But it cannot be only this. From his practical work, the author describes the "attempts" that are intended to guide the child to the person's own intuition and activity in the field of religion.[6] The main thing is that the readers feel encouraged to grapple with the basic thesis: Let them live [*erleben*]; thereby you create life [*Leben*]. Let them work; thereby you create workers![7]

---

1. See O. Pfister, *Religionspädagogisches Neuland*, 4, also 3, 6, 11–12. See "Introduction to the Reviews," 228–29.
2. For more on the philosopher and pedagogue Friedrich Wilhelm Foerster (1869–1966), see articles dedicated to him in the three earliest editions of the *RGG*.
3. See Pfister, *Religionspädagogisches Neuland*, 13.
4. See Pfister, *Religionspädagogisches Neuland*, 12.
5. See Pfister, *Religionspädagogisches Neuland*, 12.
6. Pfister, *Religionspädagogisches Neuland*, 13–36.
7. Pfister, *Religionspädagogisches Neuland*, 37 (there emphasized).

The Belgian Mission Church
1909

On February 10, 1909, Barth wrote to his parents from Marburg: "This evening, Rev. Gautier from Jemappes (Belgium) is giving a lecture here. I am on informal terms with him since a fraternity meeting and will glorify him in the liberal local paper." This comment brought to light a previously unknown Barth text, which was published on February 13 in the "local review" column in the Hessische Landeszeitung: Liberales Volksblatt *für Stadt und Land. Aloys Gautier (1879–1944)—with whom Barth, as he says in his letter, agreed to call each other by the first name at a Zofinger fraternity meeting—had been a member of Zofingia since 1898. From 1919 to 1927 he served as Secretary General of the Belgian Missionary Church.*

Rev. Aloys *Gautier* from Jemappes spoke about this subject last Wednesday evening with a genuine French temperament. The number of attendants was deplorable: the matter deserved far more attention.

The work of evangelism among Catholics often suffers, and even in Protestant circles, from the preconception that it represents an unnecessary disturbance of confessional peace. This is not true concerning Belgium, where the peace of local Catholicism is the peace of the churchyard. The consequence of this is that radical liberal thinking and reactionary clericalism divide the intellectual life of the people and all too often replace one another. The Belgian mission church, which was born from the humblest beginnings,[1] wants to counter this need, not so much by means of proselytization as by a living defense of the gospel. Their primary means is the distribution of Bibles; secondarily, and only where the people who are involved spontaneously demand it, they found congregations, which for the most part are recruited from among the miners. The constitution of the larger church is modeled on that of the Free Churches of French-speaking Switzerland,[2] with complete independence from the state and a synod with lay majority; the executive body of the administrative council is in Brussels, but there is no allegiance to a confession and merely an obligation of

1. See "Introduction to the Reviews" above. The *Église chrétienne missionaire belge* [Christian Missionary Church of Belgium] emerged in 1901 from the *Société évangelique belge* [Protestant Society of Belgium], which was founded in 1837. See Georg Fritze, *Die Evangelisationsarbeit der belgischen Missionskirche*, Studien zur praktischen Theologie II/3 (Giessen: Alfred Töpelmann, 1908), 3–4; see also Georg Fritze, *Los von Rom und Hin zum Evangelium in Belgien*, Berichte über den Progress der Los von Rom-Bewegung, Second Series 5 (Munich: J. F. Lehmann, 1904), 42–48.
2. For more on the free churches, which were formed in the eighteenth and nineteenth centuries in French-speaking Switzerland from a "pursuit for independence from the state and sharper dogmatic limitation and expression," see Friedrich Meyer, "Switzerland," *RE3* 18: 62–63.

the pastoral candidates to adhere to the practical fundamentals of the church.[3] In addition to the religious work, which is the central task, the elevation of the intellectual, moral, and social conditions is also intended. Anyone interested in the work of evangelism only as a superficial and cheap clamor against Rome and the Roman Catholic essence—such a person will not be satisfied with this type of church. On the other hand, whoever is convinced that the powers of Catholicism, which are rooted in very specific human faculties, can be overcome only by positive forces from the inside—such persons will rejoice in this work in Belgium and grant it their sympathy.

In the *Studien zur praktischen Theologie* published by Töpelmann in Giessen, a booklet from P. Georg *Fritze* of Nordhausen appeared, titled *Die Evangelisationsarbeit der belgischen Missionskirche*, available for the price of 1.60 marks; this clear and thorough introduction is highly recommended.

---

3. See Fritze, *Die Evangelisationsarbeit*, 2–3.

Modern Theology and Work
for the Kingdom of God
1909

In 1907, the Marburg professors Wilhelm Herrmann and Martin Rade had taken over the editorship of the Zeitschrift für Theologie und Kirche *[Journal for theology and church]. Barth heard Herrmann again as his preferred academic teacher during his second Marburg stay (November 1908–August 1909). Barth came and went in Rade's house as he pleased in his role as editorial assistant of* Die Christliche Welt, *whose editor was Rade, as well. The* Zeitschrift für Theologie und Kirche *brought in the fourth issue of 1909, published in July, under the regular concluding section "Theses and Antitheses," a short essay by the then twenty-three-year-old Karl Barth: "Modern Theology and Work for the Kingdom of God." It was deemed as such a challenge that the aged Marburg Chair for Practical Theology Ernst Christian Achelis (1838–1912) wrote a reply, which was published in the September issue, the fifth of the year, in the same section. Subsequently, it also led the practical theologian Paul Drews (1858–1912) from Halle, who was one of Martin Rade's student friends and cofounder of* Die Christliche Welt, *to speak up. Drews's reply was published, together with a reply from Barth to both of his critics as well as a concluding reflection from Rade, in the "Theses and Antitheses" of the sixth issue in November 1909. These five connected pieces are published here together—defying the strict chronological order of this volume.*

The transcript of Barth's contribution that opened up the discussion is dated three months earlier than the lecture on the cosmological proof of God (according to an entry in his pocket calendar, this took place on February 11 and 12, 1909) and seems to have happened, contrary to this lecture, spontaneously. On February 15, 1909, Barth reports to his father that he had "produced two items" in the preceding week, namely, before a sermon for the following Sunday: first of all "an article on 'Modern Theology and Work for the Kingdom of God,' where I tried to show the reasons why there is no zeal with the students and candidates on our side for mission, but also for parish ministry more generally, compared to those who are coming, for example, from Tübingen or Halle. . . . Rade is reading the work today on the train (!), so I don't know as yet whether he wants it."

It was only three months later that he knew the answer. On May 22, he reported to his father that his "little essay" [Aufsätzli] had been accepted for the Zeitschrift für Theologie und Kirche, *and he glosses this message: "I am now sitting like a boy at the source who does not only want to drink, but is also allowed to throw stones, soil, and frogs in there, just like an adult." Then on June 9, he announced that he was sending over a galley proof: "I am curious about what you think of this. It was written already in January or February. There is nothing new in there, but I think I have said some things a little bit more in an unvarnished way than the older Ritschlians (not Herrmann!) are generally used to doing, and that is always a good deed."*

244

A good thing—that was, of course, not what the father thought of the son's essay, and he did not think of the son himself as an "adult." With the objection that Fritz Barth (letter dated June 7, 1909) raises, a severe dispute begins between father and son, accompanying the soon-to-start public debate for months. The father's letter from June 17 says: "I take it [i.e., your article] mainly as a public declaration of a state of emergency felt by yourself, and in that regard, I welcome it; for every public confession has its blessing. I am only surprised that the article was accepted for the J. f. Th. u. K. *rather than for* Die Chr. W. *I would not have recommended you to print it, for again you put yourself here on the side of the 'Moderns' with a vehemence that has a mere personal, but in no way a scientifically justifying, character. You might not approve of this fervor yourself anymore in a few years, just as I consider now some of my statements during the Aargau Synod against the Reformers and mediators as too rash. What is in print, however, binds a lot more strongly for the subsequent time; the development should happen at your age much more inwardly and not in the public square like that. And it is precisely such fundamental considerations like this one that a person should keep for the time of greater maturity. Why start precisely with the most difficult?" And this was followed by a page-long critique of the central terms "individualism" and "relativism."*

Karl Barth answered immediately, on June 18, with a twenty-page-long "very saddened" letter: "The purpose of the essay is in no way that of a subjective confession, namely, a saddened confession from me. I think that I have spoken in the name of a large group of young theologians. That is how Rade understood it and that is why he accepted it for the J. f. Th. u. K., *for there surely is an interest in the church for such an intervention. Thus, first, it is not a confession; and second, not a saddened confession. I wanted to sketch what our strength and weakness is, but explicitly without joyful or regretful flavoring. There was nothing to regret there, and there was nothing to prove, but it was simply to make a point. . . . I stated explicitly, after all, that I feel to the same extent mature with my understanding of religion for religious work, since it is not just theology for me but a living experience. Is that a state of emergency? A reason for sadness on my part? Or the most serious and simultaneously the most hopeful starting point for someone who is about to start pastoral ministry? My remark about the equality of orthodox colleagues should, after all, not be understood as if I envy such bigwigs (very often, that is what they are), who very often have the urge, already in university, to continuously 'give witness.' Faith is not measured by the ability to talk about it. And is not that theology the best one if it most quickly places in your hands the tools to do it??*

"And now the question of the article's opportunity for me: Certainly, if I were to publish articles on 'faith and knowledge' or the like, that would be immature and a public stunt, yet I did not want to prove anything but much rather delineate a scientific cross-section. A German theologian of my age would not be allowed to do that, for that would make him unacceptable with his church administration. And regarding the Swiss church parties, I care even less when this or that person left or right without any knowledge thinks that I am 'bound.' The main thing is that I do not consider myself as bound by a printed piece of paper, should I later ever come around at a later point, which is not impossible a priori, although rather improbable."

Barth found solace in a very different reaction from Berne: from the pastor Robert Aeschbacher, who was friends with his parents and who had confirmed him seven years earlier and who wrote to him now (on July 15, 1909): "Many thanks for graciously sending over the article, which I have read with great interest as the situation is sketched out, in my opinion, in a clear, correct, and friendly way." Barth told his parents about that twice, the second time with the underlined addition: "in which I persist." In the same letter (July 27, 1909), the first sign of the public debate is found: "In the next issue (September) of the J. f. Th. u. K., there is presumably a sequel. A certain Someone, whom Herrmann does not want to name to me, did supposedly come to him and protest strongly. He demanded that he write against me. I would then be allowed to reply with my argument. In a discussion forum such as the J. f. Th. u. K., such a declaration of conscience does not seem to me to be all that pointless."

A week later, on August 2, the secret is disclosed: "Just think: the certain Someone who will respond to me is no less than the Consistorial Counselor Professor Achelis (who also comes to Äschi!!)." In Aeschi, close to Spiez on Lake Thun, Barth's parents— as well as the Achelis couple—spent their summer holidays. On August 17, Karl Barth joined them and also met Achelis there, whose homiletics seminar he had attended in summer 1908. In Aeschi, it came about, as it becomes clear from a later letter from the father (October 2, 1909), that there were animated verbal debates between father and son "that made the walls shake." The aforementioned letter of August 2, 1909, to the parents continues: "I have already read his article but can, of course, not retreat an inch, yet will not reply right away, maybe not even at all, because a direct dialogue between E. Chr. Achelis and Karl Barth could easily be perceived by the public as laughable and, if regarding me, could be taken as tactless. Oddly, I have also heard of disapproving reactions from Jülicher and Heitmüller. It is not clear to me what it is that they do not like. Yes, even Herrmann said that I was right although only after a few explanations. He had concerns about relativism. That is, of course, an ironic thing for me, but it is at least a satisfying attestation that my theological position is not a mere poor copy of the typical Marburg position."

The intervention by Drews announced itself in a no less mysterious a way than that of Achelis. On September 4, 1909, Barth wrote from Bern to his friend Wilhelm Loew: "My J. f. Th. u. K. article is met with far-reaching rejection. Both my father as well as Wernle[1] have given me a piece of their minds; today, a pastor from here will do the same. In the J. f. Th. u. K., there are two counter articles: apart from the one by Achelis, another one from someone called D.: Bornhausen wrote me only this initial. Maybe Deissmann?" Barth learned that he had been wrong in guessing the Berlin New Testament Professor Adolf Deissmann, and [in guessing] how the second attack was shaped, at the very latest from Rade's letter of September 21, 1909.[2] A prompt from Rade[3] and the tone of Drews's attack moved Barth now to a response after all—the more so because the text from Drews was in front of him in a first draft, which was toned down for print: ". . . He is considerably more hostile [i.e., than Achelis], 'flouts' twice such a 'theology,' also accuses me of subjectivism, yes, even ignorance of the difference between science and religion, and speaks very disgruntledly of 'this Mister Barth'" (September 23, 1909, to his father).

Barth's intention to answer publicly is met again with rejection from the father: he was "somewhat annoyed" about Rade, "that he even drives you to a reply. Especially Achelis's article, which contains a lot of right things, shows me that your thoughts had not been ready for publication yet, and I just cannot see what would be gained from a reply. Send me Drews's article as well, though, and in case you reply to him, which God

---

1. Paul Wernle (1872–1939), professor for church history in Basel. Barth had, according to an entry in his pocket calendar, visited him together with Eduard Thurneysen on August 29, 1909.
2. In *Bw. R.*, 66–67.
3. In *Bw. R.*, 66–67.

forbid! (quod Deus avertat), be polite to him and safeguard yourself against the spirits of theological madness (rabies theologica)" (September 25, 1909). On September 28, 1909, the one admonished in that way wrote back to his parents: "I think that when you have seen Drews, you will understand that it would have been curious if I had stayed silent, as had been my intention toward Achelis alone. I have, as far as possible, suppressed the theological anger (rabies theologorum), and I do have the sense in any case to have spoken as matter-of-factly as possible. Whether Rade had expected that, I do not know, of course, even less what he himself wants to write on the subject. In any case, however, due to me being fairly public, I owed it to the name Barth and my theological upbringing to show that I am not the naively roaring Storm-er and Stress-er I appear to be in the articles of the two. If I have been successful in showing them theologically-historically: "Sir, that's my house, not yours!" (Minheer, dat is min Pard und nicht das Eurige!), then the purpose has been met. Now, on Sunday, the induction[4] took place. I had already written the sermon last Monday-Tuesday and had it memorized by Friday. That way, I was strangely enough no longer busy with that on Saturday but instead worked on the composition of that opusculum (little work)." [The text for Barth's induction sermon was Philippians 3:12–15—the same to which he makes reference in his reply to Achelis and Drews.]

Barth did not get his father's approval this time either. Aside from his contradicting the content, Fritz Barth took offense at his son's language: "Is that supposed to be newest method of systematic theology, bringing to light such monsters of agonized sentences while at the same time 'swearing by the Master's voice'? [Trans. comment: The quote is an allusion to Goethe's Faust 1.6]. I understand very well what you want to say; but what nonsense is it, to drag a young theologian into the arena before his thoughts clear themselves and are able to become independent! . . . Is the congregation supposed to stay in suspense (in suspenso) about the content of the gospel until you have resolved your preliminary questions? Do not take offense at what I say, but also do not just dismiss it. I explicitly regret as well that this 'German theology' [deutsche Theologey] has come across your way just in the days of your induction sermon; that surely was not the right thing to do to spend the day before your induction in thoughts of Marburg rather than Geneva. Be sure to send us your sermon; that one will surely bring greater joy to us than the reply to your article. You will not need dilution in the future so much as deepening, but not most of all in Kant and Schleiermacher, whom you exploit in a very one-sided way, but in Scripture, from which you still have a lot, yes, even everything, to gain" (Letter from September 24, 1909).

Immediately (September 30), the son wrote a reply, saying that his father's letter left him at a loss. He felt drawn to the time of the middle of the nineteenth century, "when . . . in theology and otherwise, one faced up to the problems of thinking, when theologians had the confidence in themselves to be scientists like all the others yet in their own particular way, and therefore did not shy away from speaking in their own language, which had to be different from the one in the pulpit. . . . Might be that I am limping along behind world history by fifty years; in any case, the intellectual community where I feel at home is there, and from that point, you will understand that the accusations and objections that you raise against me and how you do it, do hurt me physically, as they 'interfere' with my whole theological being, instead of complementing and helping with understanding, for which I keep myself open."

---

4. Barth's induction in Geneva, September 26, 1909.

When Rade judged the reply as "excellent,"[5] Barth passes this assessment on to his mother and adds the remark: ". . . Now that an expert tells me that it is not just empty straw, I think it is a pity all the more when people talk so much past one another." If the rejection were to come from a friend, he would shake it off. However, with one's own parents, "I just cannot get over the story. Enough, enough, that is the dark point of my past weeks, remaining dark however I might want to turn it" (October 12, 1909).

The family dispute only becomes silent when the father, after having read the galley proof of the reply once more, adopts a somewhat milder tone: "I am glad about any attention that these articles gain for you in Germany; it is not I who has to make your way in life, but God has to do it, and he has led you with kindness up to this point in spite of many things that I do not understand yet. Yet one thing I want to say to you again: as for me, write as much as you want; but do not get it printed right away, even if all the Rades and Stephens of the German intellectuals' heaven ask you to do it! You are not supposed to become a journalist; store your cigars for a little while before offering them; your life will hopefully still last long for you. Ceterum censeo. [Trans. comment: Adopted from Cato the Elder's practice of a formulaic ending of every speech, no matter the topic, with ceterum censeo, meaning "furthermore, I propose."]

A reconciliatory epilogue to the debate was written by one of the discussants, Achelis, in a letter to Fritz Barth on December 6:

"Allow me, my highly esteemed colleague, to pour out my unhappy heart to you as a way to express my apology or justification. The negotiation with your son in the Zeitschrift für Theologie und Kirche was concluded in the last issue in such a way that really lives up to the name of the sensation-seeking journalist Rade. My little essay, which I published because of your dear son's outpouring of his heart, had the mere purpose to avert misunderstandings and to prevent undesirable consequences for our theology students' joy. Immediately, Rade gave the situation a very different appearance by following it with a second essay, the one by Prof. Drews, regarding the same matter. Now the situation looks as follows: Two full professors of theological faculties unsheathe their lances in order to savage a harmless and conscientious young theologian, two against one, not a knightly fight, but in the spirit of robber knights and, in analogy to Don Quixote and Sancho Panza, who fought against a windmill, with the only difference being that the opponent is not a windmill but a student of theology (Cand. theol.). It goes without saying that there is not a hint of blame to be raised against your son that he responds to Rade's challenge to stand up for himself and speaks his mind to the two un-knight-like cavaliers. But Rade crowned the affair by sitting down on the judge's seat and distributing the prizes and recording the wounds.

"I told my colleague Herrmann about my opinion and have received his approval. I remain silent toward Mr. Rade; he is too much of a journalist that I could expect understanding about the dishonorable situation in which he put myself and also Prof. Drews. If, in your son's eyes and mind, any aura of credibility should pale that he credited us with, I would mourn it, but also find it very much understandable. I only wanted to present to you as father my point of view and my non-involvement in Rade's actions so that at least in your eyes my honor suffers no damage."

Vertical lines in the text show the original pagination from the Zeitschrift für Theologie und Kirche of 1909.

---

5. Letter of October 10, 1909, in *Bw. R.*, 69.

Modern Theology and Work for the Kingdom of God

Some time ago, a group of students in a university town with a "modern" theological faculty were asked what the reasons might be for so noticeably few students turning toward missionary work after finished studies. There was a variety of responses, but finally the deepest reason for this was found in certain difficulties that arise from our scientific understanding of religion in history and the present. It was good that this was said openly, for what is valid for this special area is valid for the practical theological work at large: it is incomparably more difficult to move on to an occupation in the pulpit, at the bedside, or in the clubhouse—to move from the auditoriums of Marburg or Heidelberg than it is from those of Halle or Greifswald.[6] And the opponents know this quite well: even the most understanding one among them will explain to us: "By their fruits you shall recognize them" [Matt. 7:16, 20].

Can you give witness of the faith that is in you [cf. 1 Pet. 3:15], as we can do it? Both the accusation implied here, as well as a certain embarrassment on the side of "modern" theology that tends to arise then, are nothing new. Not for the sake of "apologetics to the right," but for the sake of one's own clarity and deeper knowledge, it is for the latter a question of life, so that one might become aware of the reasons and consequences of the entire phenomenon.

The character of "modern" theology is that of *religious individualism*. Strictly individual character is, in the modern opinion, already part of the presupposition of religion, involving morality. Morality is not obedience to norms that approach the human being from outside, but the reflection and direction of the will toward a truth or authority that reveals itself within the human being.

The awakening of religion, as we understand it, is individually conditioned. When a person comes to the knowledge that it is factually impossible for him [or anyone] to put the moral commandment that has been recognized as good into practice, then he can experience that he meets, in the tradition of the Christian church or in its present life, a power to which he must surrender completely in obedience and trust. But when does he come to the knowledge of this break in his moral willing? And what side of the Christian tradition, what manifestations of contemporary religion, become for him the revelation that sets him free and subjects him? These are all questions that each individual can answer only for oneself; there is no universally valid *ordo salutis* (order of salvation), but also no universally valid source of revelation, which one could demonstrate to another.

Finally, the life of religion that is based on revelation is individual. The Christian who succumbs to that power overcomes the world [cf. 1 John 5.4]. With increasing clarity, of course in constant struggle, the new takes over in his inner life, in his will and thought; the new touches him in this experience, his

6. The theological faculties of Marburg and Heidelberg counted as strongholds of "modern" theology, those of Halle and Greifswald as centers of "positive" theology. In Marburg, where Barth wrote this essay, professors teaching in 1909, among others, were Ernst Christian Achelis (practical theology), Karl Bornhäuser (practical theology), Wilhelm Heitmüller (New Testament), Wilhelm Herrmann (systematic theology), Adolf Jülicher (New Testament), Martin Rade (systematic theology), Horst Stephan (systematic theology); Heidelberg was dominated by Ernst Troeltsch (systematic theology); Halle by Martin Kähler (systematic theology, since 1879) and Friedrich Loofs (church history); the theological faculty of Greifswald was under the lasting influence of Hermann Cremer (died 1903).

acting follows the divine norms, and his world becomes a world of God that serves those best who love God [cf. Rom. 8.28]. But the standards for this overcoming of the world must come from his own faith: no one else can give them to him. Christian morality does not know any normative singular commandments, and there is no normative Christian worldview. (The concept of religious individualism represented here follows *Herrmann*. In its broad strokes, "with only a few other words,"[7] it should be that of "modern" theology in general in its individual nuances.)

The other characteristic of "modern" theology is *historical relativism*. This is not an essential feature of this theology, as opponents—and even friends in the heat of the battle—often argue, but only an externally highly perceivable moment of the individually understood assertion and renewal of the life of religion. Because this religion stands upon a personal and not a universally valid grounding, it interprets religion not only as self-harm, but also as a command of moral truthfulness to examine the source of revelation, which is the occasion of its emergence and its continuation, using the means of generally valid science. This examination corresponds to a vital religious interest not only as a step of "overcoming the world," but also because it is suitable, again and again, to give the present life new challenge and advancement. "The truth will set you free" [John 8:32]. As soon as this task is properly grasped, historical relativism is also a given, since for science, insofar as it is science, there is no absolute entity in nature and the intellectual world. The same theologian, who owes the power and peace of his inner life to the New Testament, which lifts him above the world to God—that same theologian sees in the New Testament a collection of religious writings like any other, in the Christian religion a religious phenomenon like others, in Jesus the founder of a religion like any other, and he treats the emergence and the history of these writings while using the same method with which he treats the Avesta and Zoroaster.

Religious individualism and historical relativism—this is the content of the school satchel that the student of "modern" theology takes from systematic and historical studies into life; that means for the student, however, that this is what is given him for the religious work with others. The two are, first of all, in harsh opposition to each other. Religion knows only individual values; history knows only universally valid facts.

The difficulties of religious work that has been preceded by this school are very obvious. One as well as the other one of Moses' tablets has slid from our grip; in these tablets, our ancestors saw the essence of religion and morality. What is left to us? The more or less precise knowledge of the Christian past, about whose scientific relativity we are clear, and—our own religious life. Yes, if we have one! Somewhere Gottfried Keller makes fun of theologians "who sit on the farthest branch of the tree, from where they will one day fall down with great clamor."[8] We have become aware now that we are not sitting on the

7. See below 289 n. 50.
8. G. Keller, *Das verlorene Lachen* [The lost smile], in *Die Leute von Seldwyla: Erzählungen* [The people of Seldwyla: Stories], 2nd exp. ed. (Stuttgart: Göschen, 1874), 4:167–68. A translation of this story is in *Stories: Gottfried Keller*, trans. Frank G. Ryder (London: Bloomsbury 1982).

New philosophers, who flipped their buzzwords like old hats from one nail to the other, disseminated evil rash phrases, and a great coercion in hear-say opinions and sayings occurred.

branch of a Christianly tinted pantheism, as it is satirized there, but it is good if we make clear to ourselves that we are indeed any moment in danger of falling down "with great clamor" when the individual religion that we want to preach is to us a theologumenon like others, without a personal, living reality. Whoever holds to "modern" theology must be willing to hear that "to be or not to be" is the question.[9] For through science, taken from a person is the whole historical apparatus of ideas and terms that belonged to the past "motive and calmative" of one's life of faith; he is ruthlessly forced to take a stand himself, that is, to confront the question if and how far they are an expression of his own faith as well. In this task lies the difficulty for the "modern" theologian who wants to give witness to others about one's faith. It is for him a lifelong task because a position on the thoughts of the past cannot be dealt with in a few semesters, but only by drawing on multifaceted practical experience, just as these thoughts are also the products of multifaceted experience. For him, this task is not theoretical; it is practically shoved into his conscience since it can only be solved in the most inward relatedness to his own moral-personal development.

There is a way for the "modern" theologian to withdraw from this task and this difficulty, a way in which one can quickly become a "usable" worker, and quite a few have taken this way. It goes like this:

> As centaurs, they walked through poetic forests once,
> but the wild race has converted them quickly.[10]

One throws the whole modern school satchel overboard (following the recipe of one of today's many reformers of theological study);[11] one adapts to the milieu in which one has to work, and one defends the whole thing by doing incredible mischief with the word "reality."

I think whoever was not just a schoolboy when he filled his lecture note booklets under Herrmann or Harnack—that student will have no desire to

---

Whoever was quieter and more modest amongst the priests thought a certain measure of the more or less ambiguous would not be the decisive factor and acted cleverly in a peaceful way on the gained position, disputatious only against former enemies and suppressors. Others, by contrast, did under no circumstance want to give the impression as if they were left behind on some issue, were not in the know about everything and were not at the forefront of the issues. Those armed themselves with heavy armory and sat on the farthest branches of the tree, from where they would one day be falling with great clamor.

[Trans. note: The quote is found in vol. I/1, chap. 7, in the German ed.]

9. Cf. W. Shakespeare, *Hamlet*, 3.1: "To be or not to be, that is the question."

10. Fr. Von Schiller and J. W. Goethe, *Die Xenien*, no. 99: "Das Brüderpaar" [The brothers] (aimed at the brothers Christian and Friedrich Leopold Grafen zu Stolberg).

11. G. Mix, *Zur Reform des theologischen Studiums: Ein Alarmruf* [On the reform of theological study: A clarion call] (Munich: Lehmann, 1908), 7:

> The first thing to be done by the young pastor entering into ministry in the current situation is to throw overboard as soon as possible the unnecessary weight of the satchel of his university teaching, so that it does not restrict his freedom of movement or even drag him down into the deeps. The faster he forgets what he gathered together in university with intensive effort for the examinations, the more productively will his activity unfold. And the firmer he holds onto the ideals of his time at university, the more he will be alienated from his actual work until he will eventually have lost all ground under his feet.

On this, cf. Barth's review in *Die Christliche Welt* 23 (1909), column 116 (above, 230–32).

walk this way of "flight into praxis."[12] Science does not become content for him, but method; and this method is nothing but a concrete case of applying his moral steadfastness; with that, his personality stands and falls.

And now it stands as follows: a theologian who overcomes this temptation, who nonetheless wants to speak of his strictly individually experienced and experience-able religion to others, will feel much less "mature" to do so than the other one for whom, in honest conviction, a whole range of normative terms and ideas is available. The "usefulness" and the "effectiveness" of the Roman Catholic concept of priesthood offers a large counterexample. The one who wants to speak to the others only about that which has become the cause or the effect of faith in his own life—that one will always be accompanied by the Scylla of priesthood, which offers more than it has, as well as the Charybdis of agnosticism, which does not offer anything at all. Both, however, stand in an especially threatening way before us disciples, and it is to this fact that I ascribe our "immaturity," our noticeably low drive to religious activity, which, next to the zeal for evangelization of pietistically influenced circles, is often almost embarrassing. Yet only almost so, for the feeling disperses as soon as we remember the reasons for this relationship. This is not the sense in which we wanted to consider ourselves. Because of our understanding of religion in the spirit of the gnostics, we wanted to be in a higher category of Christianity than those who manage to speak faster and louder and more massively of their faith. We consider this understanding to be the best, because truest, but we apply historical relativism to our own religion as well and consider it, when comparing ourselves to others, as one manifestation of the gospel next to others. Just as we acknowledge in orthodoxy, pietism, rationalism, yet also in the Catholic Church with the charismas as their unique ways of prosecuting their faith, it will probably also be with us. We are not Christianity κατ' ἐξοχήν (par excellence), but we seek to energetically give expression to the immeasurable powers of the Christian religion in the areas that have become especially important to us. Religion is, to us, strictly individually grasped experience, and we consider it a duty to engage clearly and positively with the general human cultural conscience according to its scientific side. If we want to pursue "work for the kingdom of God" in the narrower sense, this is, for us, simultaneously our strength, in which we delight, as well as our weakness, which we acknowledge, but not regret, since we can do no other.

Once Again: Modern Theology and Work for the Kingdom of God

[Response] by Ernst Christian Achelis

It is not my intention to polemically reply to the remarks by *Karl Barth* on the same topic in the fourth volume of the current issue of this journal (pp. 317–21). I have too much respect for the author's open articulation of his theological and

---

12. Cf., e.g., E. Troeltsch, *Protestantisches Christentum und Kirche in der Neuzeit* [Protestant Christianity and church in modernity], in *Die Kultur der Gegenwart* [The culture of the present], ed. P. Hinneberg, part 1, sec. 4, first half (Berlin/Leipzig, 1906), 450 (on contemporary theology in the UK and USA): "The flight into practical matters is the means to escape from the infiltrating modern ideas, while one feels exalted over the unfruitful theorizing of German theologians."

church-related distresses, so I would not try to tone them down in any way. My concern is to understand B., perhaps to clarify his thoughts that do suffer from an exaggerated honesty, in order to avert misunderstandings as well that could possibly lead him and others into a wrong direction. Anyone, while still standing outside practical church work and testing the instruments that he considers to be at his disposal in order to do justice to his future work, will easily be led away from the correct estimation of these tasks and of his abilities. We find the same mood with some of our young friends shortly before the exam: *timidi saepe sunt optimi* [often the best are timid], and the mark "good" seems unbelievable to them. Perhaps the author would have benefited from inquiring with pastors who have stayed faithful to their "modern" (what is "*modern* theology"? The term is *not* unambiguous!) theological faculty so that it would have brought him the encouragement that he painfully misses due to his own ideas.

Individualism and historic relativism are, according to B., the characteristics of "modern" theology and the sources of the reduced suitability of its disciples for practical church work. First, *individualism*—shouldn't "subjectivism" be the more proper expression? Barth finds the individualism of "modern" theology in terms of morality in the fact that this morality is not obedience to norms that (only?) approach human beings from outside, but rather in reflection on and direction of will toward a truth and an authority that expresses itself within himself. In other words, it is the autonomy of the moral will that he describes with the term. However, is it supposed to be a characteristic of "modern" theology alone? Is there any Protestant theology at all that denies the autonomy of the moral will, thus demanding obedience to the moral command without the individual will making it its own? This "individualism," however, is misleading if one portrays, as B. seems to have in view, the moral command as *product* of individual autonomy. The moral community would thereby be abolished, and the existence of the solely normative divine will would be disavowed. If, however, the autonomy of the individual will is not determined with regard to content by theonomy because it opens up thereby the depth of one's own being, it is, in my opinion, morally valueless.

The issue is similar with the individual conditionality of the awakening of religion, "as we understand it." I heartily agree that the completed salvific faith develops when the human being, in his moral plight toward the moral command considered as good, is encountered in the tradition of the Christian church or in its current life by a power to which he must submit wholly in obedience and trust. Yet here B. is mistaken in ignoring the *developing* faith, demanding in *one* step to obtain the completed salvific faith. In the case of every Christian, it is "from faith to faith" [Rom. 1:17]. "For the youth," *Gottschick* writes (in this journal),[13] "having grown up in the atmosphere of the spirit of Christ, the intensive feeling of the need to be saved is not natural; for them, it is the first form in which they experience the *assurance of salvation*, the joyful devotion to the Christian ideal as a delightful one; included therein is the *personal*

---

13. J. Gottschick, "Erklärung gegen D. Walther in Rostock" [Declaration against Dr. Walther in Rostock], *ZTK* 14 (1904): 462: "The second case is that of the youth who does not have any worries and for whom the intense feeling of the need for redemption is not natural, especially when they have not grown up under the pressure of the law, but in the atmosphere of the spirit of Christ. For them, the first form . . ." The remainder of the quote is correct. Emphases by Achelis.

certainty of God's grace." Let us have patience with ourselves and our emerging salvific faith; after all, God also has patience with us!

My concern becomes more serious with B.'s question: "Which page of Christian tradition, which aspect of contemporary religious life, becomes for him the revelation that liberates and subjugates him? All of these are questions that the individual can only answer for himself; there is . . . no universally valid source of revelation that one can demonstrate to another." Indeed, the source of revelation is not *demonstrable*; however, for B., that does not seem to be emphasized either. Am I wrong that B. wants to leave to each person what the individual wants to recognize as liberating revelation in the Christian tradition or in the life expressions of contemporary religion? Is there an innumerable number of possibilities of the liberating revelation that subjugates us? For Protestant theology and piety, there is only *one* revelation worthy of its name, where "God has poured God's heart into us,"[14] and this revelation is called Jesus Christ. Only *these* pages of Christian tradition and only *these* life expressions of contemporary religion can help us toward faith and strengthen us in faith where *this* revelation encounters us. Christ alone is the source of revelation valid for us all; our faith is bound only to him and to the God revealed through him and in him; and the power that meets us and to which we must surrender in obedience and trust is Jesus Christ and only [Jesus Christ]. Certainly all of us, individually for ourselves, need to look to Christ with our individual eyes, need to listen to him with our individual ears; the individual experiences of faith will therefore be very different. But only that which articulates itself as obedience and trust toward the Lord Jesus Christ is counted in "modern" theology as faith (or also as "religion"). Yet is this the case only in "modern" theology? It is surely right that, from the disciples of the theological faculties where particular weight is laid upon correct delivery of so-called church teaching, the agreement (*assensus*) to the teachings handed down *can be regarded* as the faith of the church. They are then, *under certain conditions*, capable of covering up their own individual lack of faith with the cloak of accepted teaching, of understanding their poverty as wealth, and of considering themselves quite qualified for service in the church. That, however, is impossible for the disciples of "modern" theology. The faith (the "religion") is invoked here completely in its full Protestant determination, and this self-deception does not find room. Through this, the path to usability in the church is certainly made more difficult: it leads through a few serious discussions between God and the individual soul, through many battles of self-reflection and self-denial; the result alone is incomparably more valuable. If you want to ask "modern" theological faculties why so noticeably few turn, after completed studies, to the work in foreign mission, at least *one* answer is obvious. Our young theologians take a serious path. The awareness of not being done yet, of still being on the road to completed salvific faith, wondering whether they are captured by Christ—this awareness pervades them, often in a discouraging way. The joyfulness of becoming a missionary to the heathens overcomes this only where the internal divine vocation (*vocatio Dei*

---

14. Maybe an allusion to M. Luther, *Large Catechism*, trans. John Nicholas Lenker (Minneapolis, MN: Luther Press, 1908), 117, Explanation of art. 2 (*BSLK* 65.1.10–15): "Here we learn to know the second person of the Godhead. . . . He has poured out himself upon us, bestowing all and withholding nothing."

interna) overcomes it inescapably, and this vocation is God's business, which one isn't allowed to claim for oneself by force.

Apart from religious individualism, according to B., *historical relativism* is "the content of the satchel that the student of 'modern' theology receives from systematic and historical classroom studies to take with him into his religious work with others, and the two are irreconcilable with each other." B.'s opinion is surely not going to be that what the systematic and historical classrooms are offering represents the religious tools for the religious work with the other. Against such a misunderstanding, W. Herrmann has certainly protected him. What is the situation, however, with historical relativism? No doubt it is insepa-rably linked with all purely historical research. On a purely historical path, I can easily substantiate that Christianity, among all historical forms of religion, is *up to this point* the most complete one. The fact that it is *the* religion, the *absolute* religion, stands outside of purely historical proof because that is a *religious value judgment*.[15] Faith rests not on historical relativism, but rather on the religious value judgment of the specific religious life. It is characteristic of comparative religious history that it levels the religions: this fact has the consequence, for the religiously uneducated person who is attempting to base his religious life on such historical relativism, that he loses all religion, perhaps finding it impos-sible to arrive at the religious life. The same phenomena brought to light by today's religious research have to a certain degree been known for a very long time; but it is also for a very long time that, in the Christian community, the religious value judgment has engaged the *interpretation* of these phenomena. Let me call to mind the fact that, in the area of *morality* since the apologists of the second century, [the task] was [interpreting] the *lex naturalis* (natural law); yet, in the area of *religion*, it was the doctrine of the *Logos spermatikos* (semi-nal word)[16] in which the religious value judgment made itself known; what appeared to lead to the leveling of Christianity sufficed to glorify Christianity. In this or that way, the religious value judgment always proceeds, for faith tol-erates neither leveling nor relativity, but rather the absoluteness of its object is its life. From another side, it is of high value for investigating the historical reality of the life of Jesus to report on what can be ascertained from the literary resources for this historical reality.

It is a mistake that Protestant piety had to acknowledge the image of Christ that shines forth toward it from the crucible of historical-critical fire, recogniz-ing the image of the Savior who redeems souls and leads them to completion, who is also the Redeemer of the world. No scientific "life of Jesus" will reli-giously completely satisfy the Protestant Christian. Imponderable aspects exist

---

15. On the "theological value judgment," a key term in the cognitive theory of Albrecht Ritschl, cf., e.g., A. Ritschl, *Die christliche Lehre von der Rechtfertigung und Versöhnung* [The Christian doctrine of justification and reconciliation], 4th ed. (Bonn: Marcus, 1895), 3:197 and 202; ET: trans. and ed. H. R. Mackintosh and A. B. Macaulay (Clifton, NJ: Reference Book Publishers, Inc., 1966): "In Christianity, religious knowledge consists in independent value-judgments, inasmuch as it deals with the relation between the blessedness which is assured by God and sought by man, and the whole of the world which God has created and rules in harmony with His final end" (207); "Knowledge of God can be demonstrated as religious knowledge only when He is conceived as securing to the believer such a position in the world as more than counterbalances its restrictions. Apart from this value-judgment of faith, there exists no knowledge of God worthy of this content" (212).

16. Cf., e.g., A. Harnack, *Lehrbuch der Dogmengeschichte* [History of dogma], 4th ed. (Tübingen: J. C. B. Mohr, 1909), 1:507–25. ET: trans. Neil Buchanan (New York: Russell & Russell, 1958), 2:325–45.

that may not be proven by historical research, but which the religious person can experience anew and indeed does experience anew. It is for that strange experience, for example, that the Fourth Gospel, although not a literal historical source in the narrow sense, is nonetheless recognized as historicizing utterance of true religious experiences of the world, overcoming sin and death in the Christian community, and throughout the centuries is judged to be "the agreed-upon, tender, true, main gospel, to be by far preferred to the other three and to be elevated higher," to speak with *Luther*.[17] There as well, it is the religious value judgment that exposes truths long hidden to historical relativism; the experiences of faith of the present Christian community confirm as well the validity of the religious value judgment.

Religious individualism, rightly understood, is not only recognized in "modern" theology; it also is recognized in all of Protestant theology as the form of all true religious life. Historical relativism can pose neither inhibition nor hindrance to the development nor the completion of the religious life, as long as a religious capacity is not expected of it that it is incapable of sustaining.

For the Third Time: Modern Theology and Work for the Kingdom of God

[Further Response] by Paul Drews

If the "theses" of this journal have the objective to articulate contradiction so as to come to a clarification of a matter, the "thesis" by Karl Barth under the above heading in the fourth issue of this volume surely fulfills this purpose. Whether my "antithesis" contributes to the clarification, I am, of course, not able to say.

As characteristic of "modern theology," Barth, first of all, names "religious individualism." I'll leave it for discussion whether other currents of the Christian kind in the modern era can, in the same way and with the same right, claim "individualism" for themselves as well. Granted, dogmatics and ethics in so-called "modern theology" have an individualistic form, and a valuable moment of truth is contained therein. Most of all this: the precondition of complete, unconditional truthfulness in terms of religion,[a] not only in one's own religious life, but also in terms of proclamation. We welcome it with a sense of satisfaction and as a sign of healthy spirituality that the "modern theology" does not have much regard for mere "parroting" and "empathizing," which leads to the gravest error of religion, that of hypocrisy. This deplorable practice has had devastating effects in our church life. Whoever declares war against it will surely have in me a combatant at his side.

I'll take another step. Insofar as the thesis about "religious individualism" contains the sentence that everybody needs |476| to design Christianity for oneself, according to one's own mode of spirit and mind, I am also with them. For it is an error that we are all capable of becoming and being faithful in the same way. We are, in point of fact, not able to do that. The further the individualism

17. EA 63:115 = WA DB 6:10.25–27.
[a] I understand "religion" in the following, of course, only as the *Christian* religion, not an abstract understanding of religion.

of modern spirituality continues to develop, the more it will fight for its right in the religious realm as well. There will always be mystics and rationalists, always those believing in authority and skeptics, always pietists and moralists. But none of them represents Christianity truly completely and entirely. Each one of us experiences only a part of the whole, and each surely does so with multiple turbidities. Of this, every serious Christian needs to remain conscious, in order not to assault Christians of a different kind. The more serious, the truer, the more that individuals personally experience Christianity in themselves, the more valuable their contribution will be for the whole religious life of the community.

The only thing is that this religious individualism has its limits. If it is still to be regarded as Christian, it needs to identify as being bound to Jesus and to the values given to us by Jesus. Christian individualism, the more serious it is, knows itself to be bound to an ideal, to a norm, to an authority that is binding for the believer. How else would Christian piety even be possible? Apart from this, it is certainly possible as a process of letting oneself drift along with feelings and moods, as a twilight condition, a life of pleasure. But with that, true Christian religion is dissolved. Whoever is pious knows oneself to be claimed directly by God, the Father of Jesus Christ. One senses a large feeling of should-ness above himself. He painfully feels the limits of his capability and his being. He knows that, with God, a goal has been marked out for him to which, in the end, all must submit.

In that way religious individualism, insofar as one takes it seriously, leads beyond itself and arrives at a generally valid normative. It is the opposite to an aimless and limitless subjectivism.

This individualism also leads beyond the "historical relativism" that Barth posits as the second characteristic of "modern theology." I will concede for now that he was right about that. How is it, however, that he does not bring to aware-ness the very simple fact that *science* |477| must always remain in the relative and the conditional, whereas *religion* is essentially different in that its realm is the absolute? Barth himself correctly says that "for science, insofar as it is science, there is in nature and the intellectual world no absolute entity." But there is for religion. If one is serious about "religious individualism," and thus about personal Christian piety, then one is elevated above and beyond the relativism of all science. Thus it is unacceptable to speak with the same breath of "religious indi-vidualism" and of "historical relativism" and to see in both of them the hallmarks of "modern theology." Either/or! "Both stand initially in harsh contrast to each other," explains Barth. But why only *"initially"*? The fact that science and religion are two essentially different things is something we should know by now.

But what then constitutes the essence of theology? It is precisely this, that in theology, religion and science connect with each other in such a way that for once the Christian religion becomes the object of scientific knowing, again in such a way that in the personality of the theologian as scientist, the abso-lute knowledge of values of the Christian religion is presupposed. A person can also occupy oneself with religion scientifically, without being convinced of the absoluteness of the Christian religion, without being pious oneself. But the question arises whether a recognition of the Christian religion of a truly scientific merit is possible in that case. Even in the history of Christendom, as soon as one approaches its major thinkers, a mere "sense" for religion, a mere "empathy," does not suffice for understanding and for personally proper judgment. Personal piety is ultimately the actual key for understanding piety in history. Yet the theologian, as a scientific person, needs to be ready for the sake of truth—thus ultimately also for the sake of religion—to relinquish former points of view that have linked up with piety because of the facts contradicting them. Theology ultimately emerges not least out of a tension between science and religion, and yet it is their synthesis.

The aforementioned is valid not just for "modern theology" alone, but also for all theology today. |478| The modern theology, however, is more willing to relinquish points of view inherited from tradition. Why? Because it has faith in the eternal value of the gospel, which is impossible to destroy or to support by means of any kind of human thoughts. If "historical relativism" were really a special characteristic of "modern theology," it would, from my point of view, lose any value. For by doing so, it would surrender itself: it would become a science of religion without power or life, but it would no longer have any significance for our religious life.

Now to the question in which Mr. Barth's "thesis" culminates! Modern theology supposedly renders one incapable of praxis. If he were right about that, it would—I am repeating myself—be of no value. I openly confess that this thought profoundly surprised me. In any case, our mood with which we entered praxis, based on the "modern" theology of *Ritschl*, was a completely opposite one. We were sure of the fact that—especially because we had become aware of the difference between religion and theology (and science altogether)—we were better equipped by far for the practical office than our colleagues who were taught and rooted in orthodox dogmatics. Asserting that it made one incapable of comfort at the beds of those sick and dying was an accusation from the opponents of the theology represented by Ritschl. We could only laugh at this judgment as defamation. *Uhlhorn* himself acknowledged once that the finest pastors in the Church of Hanover came out of Ritschl's school.[18] Yet this is only as an aside, to capture the difference in mood back then and today. But to return to Mister Thesis-Poser, I cannot understand him completely. When he, rightly, emphasizes religious individualism so strongly, it does not by default follow that the young preacher of the modern kind is only supposed to preach himself, only his already achieved experience of faith. Certainly, that as well. But whoever lives religiously at all—we said it above—knows that he is challenged with a goal, that he acknowledges ideals, that he stretches out toward a higher stance of life. Should that be so, however, a vast, rich, fertile area opens up for the sermon. They have to speak, not as complete people, "having a whole range of normative terms and ideas without further ado at their disposal," but as people striving together with fellow strivers, |479| as the one in whom the Christian religion has somehow, be it ever so weakly, taken root, and yet who wants to grow into those who desire this as well. Why a "modern" theologian should, by his theology, be made unsuitable for practical action, is thus not understandable. Just as immaturity and inactivity are unhealthy in the pulpit and thus highly unpleasant, an exaggerated reserve is something *unhealthy* as well. I do not want to, nor can I, advocate a "flight into praxis," but rather I can advocate serious

---

18. This cannot be proven.

work in the practice of ministry, using the degree of knowledge, experience, and strength that one has, so that the power might develop further and knowledge and experience might deepen. Whoever wants to wait until he is "ready" will need to wait till the end. As important as theorizing is for religious develop- ment, without practical action it will be overtaken by the sand.

I deny that the mood described by Barth—he calls it a "charisma," a "power"—should be of any more serious importance for the religious commu- nity or for our church life. We do not need resignation, reservations, personal self-protection, but surely what we need is friendly optimism, "faith" that is active and wants to be active. "Where there is no joy of sharing, there is also no religion at all," *Paul Wernle* said once.[19]

Let me remark at the end that what is said above is, of course, not applicable to the theology student. For him come, first of all, concentration on theology and as far as possible distance from practical activity.

Reply to Dr. Achelis and Dr. Drews
Karl Barth

When I had read the reply by *Dr. Achelis* in number 5, I was determined to refrain from a reply as he moved toward my perspective, in the spirit of Psalm 141:5, to such an extent that I had to consider an examination of the points of difference in the public forum of this journal as unnecessary. This situation has changed since I have become aware of the heavy artillery of *Dr. Drews*.

Following my essay, *Dr. Achelis* came to the point of noting that a young theologian of "modern" direction walks a "serious path" in transitioning to the office, indeed, to a |480| higher degree than the average of his conservative colleagues, as, in any case, they lack the "mantle of accepted teaching" that enables them to regard their poverty as wealth. Anything more than positing this historical situation was not the intention of my essay. Yet *D. Drews* rejects this characterization of the situation and calls the feeling of this difference in the internal disposition an "exaggerated reserved-ness." This judgment hits the core of what I intended, and thus I can be silent no longer. A short descrip- tion of my position is all the more important to me, since I have learned from both articles and am to a great extent also in agreement with both of them.

My essay defined the essence of "modern" theology as *religious individualism*. I understood that as applying the *principium individuationis*—first represented powerfully in Romanticism in the more recent history of thought, not that it doesn't have its analogous, older streams (Renaissance, Descartes, Leibniz)—to Christian dogmatics and ethics as the associative presentations of ideals for the two pillars of Christian pious consciousness.[20] I thought of *Schleiermacher's* discovery that there were no examplars, but only individuals of religion.[21] And

---

19. P. Wernle, *Einführung in das theologische Studium* [Introduction to theological studies] (Tübingen: J. C. B. Mohr, 1908), 18 (= 2nd ed. [1911], 17).

20. The second part of the sentence (after the parenthesis) is marked in Barth's handwritten manu- script. In the margin, written by himself, "Oh!"

21. Cf. F. D. Schleiermacher, *On Religion: Speeches to Its Cultured Despisers*, Cambridge Texts in the History of Philosophy (Cambridge: Cambridge University Press, 1986), ???.

it means, as the basic presupposition of systematic theology, "that everything belonging to religion is only given in that a spiritually alive creature awakens to its full life" (*Herrmann*, in *Kultur der Gegenwart*).[22] Dr. Achelis and Dr. Drews accuse me that this or something similar might be the basic precondition of *all* Protestant theology. I can admit that, insofar as *Luther* already showed a tendency toward a related rewriting of the knowledge ground of Christian truth.[23] And in the nineteenth century, *J. Chr. K. Hofmann* even went beyond Schleiermacher by explicitly elevating the isolated Christian *individual*-consciousness to the principle of knowledge.[24] But apart from that, the history of more recent theology before and alongside *Albrecht Ritschl* is a history of turning away from this fundamental insight of Schleiermacher. Those to the right and those to the left were, as is well known, equally involved. Indeed, even within the Ritschl school, *Kattenbusch* sought to find the importance of that theologian most of all in his argument so "that he broke with Schleiermacher's method more completely and more happily than anyone else,"[25] and so that he does not take his starting point in the "pious consciousness" but in the "gospel."[26] If I envision this fact, I only have to remind myself of the others—we live in a time in which one of the noisiest theologians, *R. Grützmacher*, has explicitly recommended the return to scholasticism[27]—in order to assess the present situation of theology a little bit less optimistically than D. Achelis and D. Drews.

22. W. Herrmann, *Christlich-protestantische Dogmatik* [Christian-Protestant dogmatics], in *Die Kultur der Gegenwart*, ed. P. Hinneberg, I/4, 2nd part (Berlin/Leipzig: Teubner, 1906), 593–94; reprinted in W. Herrmann, *Schriften zur Grundlegung der Theologie* [Writings on the basics of theology], ed. P. Fischer-Appelt, part 1, ThB 36/1 (Munich: Chr. Kaiser, 1966), 311 (considering Schleiermacher):

> If science and morality are about becoming fully aware of the universally valid or provable, then religion is about becoming fully aware of the individual or that which can be experienced. Whoever becomes inwardly so alive that he gains a perspective from the pondering of his own eternal existence has obtained therewith religion. . . . He [Schleiermacher] does not only mean that we possess all that belongs to religion only religiously by applying it to ourselves. All that belongs to religion is only supposed to be given when a spiritually living creature awakens to its complete life.

23. Cf., e.g., the Luther presentation in W. Herrmann, *Der Verkehr des Christen mit Gott: Im Anschluss an Luther dargestellt* [The Christian's interaction with God: Presented following Luther], 4th ed. (Stuttgart/Berlin: J. Cotta'sche Buchhandlung, 1903), 132–37.

24. Cf., e.g., the well-known programmatic statement in J. Chr. K. Hofmann, *Der Schriftbeweis: Ein theologischer Versuch* [Scriptural proof. A theological attempt] (Nördlingen: C. H. Beck, 1852), 1:10: "Theology is only a free science if that which makes the Christian a Christian, his independent relationship to God, in scientific self-knowledge and self-declaration makes the theologian a theologian, when I, the Christian, am the theologian's very own scientific material." In the theological-historical assessment of Hofmann, Barth follows W. Herrmann, *Verkehr des Christen*, 604 [ET, 323–24]: "Yet not Schleiermacher himself, but one of his most important students, the Erlangen-based Lutheran J. Chr. K. Hofmann, has developed from this thought [i.e., to view doctrines as the expression of Christian pietistic frames of mind] the right task of systematic theology of Protestantism." Cf. also W. Herrmann, *Verkehr des Christen*, 607 [ET, 327–28].

25. F. Kattenbusch, *Von Schleiermacher zu Ritschl: Zur Orientierung über die Dogmatik des neunzehnten Jahrhunderts* [From Schleiermacher to Ritschl: For orientation on dogmatics of the nineteenth century], 3rd ed. (Giessen: de Gruyter, 1903), 55.

26. Kattenbusch, *Schleiermacher zu Ritschl*, 59; cf. J. Kaftan, *Dogmatik* [*Dogmatics*], 3rd and 4th eds. (Tübingen/Leipzig: J. C. B. Mohr, 1901), 97, §10.3: "It is to *Ritschl's* credit to have gone back to and picked up again *Schleiermacher's* basic tendency. He did this in such a way that he sought to avoid *Schleiermacher's* mistakes, while validating the character of the knowledge of faith as true knowledge as well as its foundation on revelation."

27. Barth might possibly have thought of R. H. Grützmacher, *Modern-positive Vorträge* [Modern-positivist lectures] (Leipzig: Deichert, 1906), 164: "[There] . . . arises . . . the problem . . . whether, in addition to the means of grace of the word, other special actions of grace have to come indispensably. Here as well, our ancestors have already found the correct answer following after Scholasticism."

By the way, it will shortly be shown that the explicit and strongly worded support for the individualistic method of systematic theology as especially expressed by D. Drews (page 476) is not the same as what I have in view. For me, the old theologian's sword of "aimless and limitless subjectivism" is already a meaningful sign. Schleiermacher and Ritschl had to endure its attack against themselves:[28] wouldn't it be time to leave this double-edged yet nonetheless rusty weaponry in its sheath, even over against lesser thinkers?

But let's turn to the subject itself. I had spoken in my essay, first of all, of the individualism of *morality* as the presupposition of religion. D. Achelis confirms me in regard to the autonomy of the moral will, yet he wants its content to be determined by theonomy. But this last term has "an unavoidable tendency to turn in circles and to secretly posit the morality it is supposed to explain as a presupposition";[29] compare also the beginning of the preamble to the first edition of the "religion within."[30] If a rational ethic, of which I was thinking there, is supposed to avoid positing God as the object of the will, then it does not thereby surrender the thought of moral community; indeed, the community is

28. The accusation of subjectivism in Schleiermacher can be found, e.g., in M. Kähler, *Die Wissenschaft der christlichen Lehre von dem evangelischen Grundartikel aus im Abriss dargestellt* [The science of Christian teaching sketched out based on the Protestant basic article], 3rd ed. (Leipzig: Deichert, 1905); reprint (Neukirchen: Neukirchener Verl. d. Erziehungsvereins, 1966), 221. Kähler speaks there of Schleiermacher's "subjectivist phenomenology of consciousness" and "one-sided individualism." See a corresponding accusation of Ritschl in O. Pfleiderer, "Die Ritschl'sche Theologie nach ihrer erkenntnistheoretischen Grundlage kritisch beleuchtet" [The Ritschlian theology examined critically according to its knowledge-theoretical basis], in *Jahrbücher für protestantische Theologie* (Freiburg: J. C. B. Mohr, 1889), 15:186: "Accordingly, the presentation of the third edition [i.e., Ritschl's "The Christian dogma of justification and reconciliation"] draws the consequence, already found in the second edition, of the subjectivist concept of religion for scientific knowledge of religion as well as for theology: theology is not allowed to enter the realm of value judgments, i.e., that of mere subjective truth. . . ." Compare also I. Lemme, *Die Prinzipien der Ritschl'schen Theologie und ihr Werth* [The principles of Ritschlian theology and their worth] (Bonn: Weber, 1891), 15.

29. I. Kant, *Grundlegung zur Metaphysik der Sitten* [Groundwork of the metaphysics of morals], ed. K. Vorländer, PhB 41 (Leipzig: Dürr, 1906), 70–71; I. Kant, *Kant's gesammelte Schriften* [Kant's collected works], ed. Königlich Preussische Akademie der Wissenschaften, vol. 4 (Berlin: Reimer, 1903), 443; ET, trans. and ed. Mary Gregor (Cambridge: Cambridge University Press, 1997), 49:

> Among the *rational* grounds of morality or those based on reason, the ontological concept of *perfection* (however empty, however indeterminate and hence useless it is for finding, in the immeasurable field of possible reality, the greater sum appropriate to us; and however much, in trying to distinguish specifically the reality here in question from every other, it has an unavoidable propensity to get involved in a circle and cannot avoid covertly presupposing the morality which it is supposed to explain) is nevertheless better than the theological concept, which derives morality from a divine, all-perfect will; it is better not merely because we cannot intuit the perfection of this will but can only derive it from our concepts, among which that of morality is foremost, but because if we do not do this (and to do it would be a grossly circular explanation), the concept of his will still left to us, made up of the attributes of desire for glory and dominion combined with dreadful representations of power and vengefulness, would have to be the foundation for a system of morals that would be directly opposed to morality.

30. I. Kant, *Die Religion innerhalb der Grenzen der blossen Vernunft* [Religion within the boundary of pure reason], ed. K. Vorländer, PhB 45 (Leipzig: Dürr, 1903), 1; *Kant's gesammelte Schriften* [Kant's collected works] (Berlin: Reimer, 1907), 6:3: ET, trans. J. W. Semple (Edinburgh: Thomas Clark, 1838):

> Ethic, in so far as founded on the Idea of Humanity as a free Agent, binding himself, by virtue of that very Freedom, to an unconditionate Law of Reason, is by itself complete and entire; so that mankind neither requires the idea of any Superior Person to enable him to investigate his duty, nor does he need any incentive or spring to its execution other than the law itself. At least it must be his own fault if there exist any such want or need; a defect, however, quite without remedy from any foreign sources; since, whatsoever is not originated by himself from his own freedom, cannot supply or make up the want of his own morality. A System of Ethics, therefore, needs no Religion. . . .

nothing other than precisely the content of the moral law. And as synthesizing, practical statement a priori, the moral law is not the product of autonomy but is its transcendental[31] principle, its *ratio cognoscendi*. If moral autonomy, on the one hand, is rooted in the universally valid, on the other hand—and in this sense, Kant's ethic is to be deepened in the sense of *Schleiermacher*—its carriers are precisely not exemplars, but individuals. "Certainly, there will also be cases, where virtually all will have to act in the same way, but the difference will never disappear entirely. . . . Thus the general, in human action and absolutely separate from all individuality, does not exist, and the individual cannot be captured in formulas. . . . To the extent that an action has its grounding in the individuality of the human being, to that extent it cannot be adjusted by anyone but the individual. But each person is his own judge in that regard, not his own teacher."[32]

Analogically, yes, intensified, the situation returns in the religious area. Dr. Achelis and Dr. Drews want me to keep in mind that individualism finds its limit there, that it, insofar as it is Christian individualism, is bound to Jesus Christ as its norm and authority. I am pleased that I am in agreement with them; but all the more I want to object that this common position is not suitable to silence me, as attempted by Dr. Drews on page 476. May I call to mind *Schleiermacher's* words from the well-known letter to Sack: "The word of John 1:14: We saw his glory etc. is the seed of all dogma, and gives itself for nothing [other] than the affection transferred in speech. Yes, even what Christ says of himself would not have become a Christian truth if it had been proven immediately by this affection. *So, this is and remains for me what is the original in Christianity, and all the rest is only derived from it.* The effective, that is, in a certain way affecting appearance of Christ, is the true revelation and the objective."[33] And even more precise is that which matters here expressed in a different remark by the very same theologian: "Finally, it needs to be remembered that the unchangeable in Christian teaching can in no way be separated mechanically, but also in no way organically; for *everywhere, the emergence in thoughts and word is already the changeable*; the innermost lying behind thoughts and word is, of course, that which is in agreement, the identical, but that can never be communicated outwardly as such."[34] The energetic concentration on the individual "affection" as the only normative thing, over against which everything that occurs in thoughts and words is secondary, is therefore the operative point of the question. It is not about religious life and experience itself, but about |483| the conceptual communication and articulation of the inner factuality. For that, older theology somehow possessed norms valid among Christians, whereas we

---

31. Concerning this orthography, compare M. Rade's letter to Barth, dated February 17, 1914, and Barth's reply dated February 19, 1914, in *Bw. R.*, 87–88.

32. Fr. D. E. Schleiermacher, *Die christliche Sitte nach den Grundsätzen der evangelischen Kirche im Zusammenhang dargestellt* [Christian morality described in context following the basic tenets of the Protestant Church], from Schleiermacher's handwritten bequest, and transcribed lectures, ed. I. Jonas, 32nd ed. (Berlin: G. Reimer, 1843), 65.

33. "Aus Schleiermacher's Leben," in *Briefen* ["From Schleiermacher's life," in *Letters*], vol. 4, ed. W. Dilthey (Berlin, 1863), 335. Letter of April 9, 1825, to K. H. Sack, with emphasis by Barth; "other" omitted by Barth.

34. Schleiermacher, *Christliche Sitte*, 11. Trans. note: The original note here highlights that Schleiermacher orders the words differently. The difference is not noticeable in either German or English.

see ourselves confronted with the task of generating such norms, both producing and reproducing them.

Here, I certainly also suspect that there is a decisive disagreement especially
with Dr. Drews. For if I am not supposed to understand his presentation about
the normativity of the revelation in Jesus Christ as an *obliteration* of the question
I have just discussed and which I laid out in my essay, then I can only suppose
that he also finds the significance of *A. Ritschl* in the fact that his dogmatic,
in contrast to that of Schleiermacher, "specifies, according to the revelation of
God in Jesus Christ, what the obedience of faith has to refer to," or "it shows
to the individual how he must be oriented in order *to be called* a church-based,
Protestant, Lutheran Christian."[35] He understands Christ, then, as the normative authority with which he confronts me, *a somehow restricted transmission of
the historical person of Jesus*. Then, I might be able to understand his description.
Otherwise, as said, only as an obliteration. *Tertium non datur* [a third option
does not exist].

And now, in close proximity to what has just been said, a few more comments on *historical relativism*. Dr. Achelis and Dr. Drews confirm the necessity of a strict application of this methodical principle. Yet, they continue, this
relativism is overcome by the absolutizing value judgment of the living religion that interprets history. This understanding of the relationship of science
and religion is mine also. *First*, in the abstract sense apart from the synthetic
individuality of the living religious person, the purely historical and the purely
valuing interpretation are in harsh opposition to each other. (*Not* irreconcilable: Dr. Achelis reiterates my statement disapprovingly on [the article's] page 409;
and *not* remaining irreconcilable, as Dr. Drews on p. 477 above wants to correct
me!) The coexistence of both becomes possible and true through identifying
the subject of such necessarily relativizing scientific analysis of history with
the living individual of religion. Out of the stream of history, the individual
lifts the absolute norm, which becomes |484| for his life both liberation and
overcoming, even more: this norm grasps, liberates, overcomes the individual.
But only in the "affection" of this inner experience lies the normative, objective,
eternal. All that enters into thoughts and words belongs in itself already to the
relativizing stream of history and is, as something ephemeral, only a parable.[36]

Speaketh the soul, the *soul*, oh, speaketh no more;[37] and (even if in a different
understanding than in Schiller):

What never and nowhere happened,
That is the only thing that never ages.[38]

---

35. Kattenbusch, *Schleiermacher zu Ritschl*, 60, with emphases by Kattenbusch.
36. Cf. J. W. von Goethe, *Faust* 2.5.12103–4: "All of the transient is parable only. . . ."
37. The distich "Language" in the collection "Votive Tablets," by Fr. von Schiller:

   Warum kann der lebendige Geist dem Geist nicht erscheinen?
        Spricht die Seele, so spricht, ach! schon die Seele nicht mehr.
   [Why can the living spirit not appear to the spirit?
        Speaks the soul, so speaks, oh, the soul does speak no more.]

38. Closing verses of the poem "An die Freunde" [To the friends], by Fr. von Schiller (1802).

By a different way we have reached the same destination as earlier: here, I will have to suspect, in Dr. Drews, the view that would make the gulf between us deep, as if a somehow noticeable *thoughtful* objective norm might be taken from the value judgment made absolute, which "shows the individual what one might live by."[39] Against this, my opinion is that all religious thought formation—dogmatics and sermon in the same way!—can only be a *confession* of faith to faith (Herrmann,[40] Kähler[41]), but not "proof and as complete as possible deployment of the *norm* of all piety in the Christian church";[42] compare Kaftan in *Dogmatik*,[43] on the character of the Christian religion[44] and on the truth of the Christian religion.[45] This is because I can find the character of Protestant piety in nothing other than in the absolutely inward act of faith, unapproachable to all adequate conceptual formation; yet from this opposing view, I will have to fear, with Herrmann, that it is not difficult from there "to find the way back to the orthodox dictum that the Christian faith might come into being with the willing acceptance of a doctrine."[46]

After what we have addressed thus far, it will become obvious that I cannot strike out any of the content of my thesis. The mistake in my essay was that in my thoughts I had drawn the circle of what I called "modern theology" much too large. Similarly, I am more than ready to cash in the label "modern," since, after all, the publication of the *Reden über die Religion* was 110 years ago, surely not without the reminder that the one [Schleiermacher] who wrote them

39. Compare above at note 34.

40. Cf., e.g., Herrmann, *Christlich-protestantische Dogmatik*, in Hinneberg, *Die Kultur der Gegenwart*, part 1, sec. 4.2, 617; reprinted in Herrmann, *Grundlegung der Theologie*, part 1, 340, and translated here:

> It is, of course, correct that we can only comprehend those thoughts with hearty faith that do not merely penetrate to us from outside but rather grow out of our own faith. But for that very reason, can these thoughts that resound in the faith confessions of the individual never be formulated as the thoughts normative for the Christian community, as the modern dogmatics of Protestantism does? For the Christian community consists of singular people of individual kinds. If these become alive religiously, then that does not mean that their spiritual uniqueness is leveled, but rather that it blossoms in each. Religious thoughts develop in each out of the special experiences that are the most important for him and make for the unique way of his inner life. If he allows a dogmatic to force normative thoughts upon him, then he is alienated exactly from the only thing from which he can gain the leading thought, the fountain of his religious life, which is always rushing in the experiences given solely to him.

41. Here Barth probably has M. Kähler's summarizing presentation in Kattenbusch in view: Kattenbusch, *Schleiermacher zu Ritschl*, 54:

> Based on the personal religious "experience" of the "justification of the sinner," he pursues his overview. Yet if all dogmatics is somehow a *confession* to him, then all of our Protestant confession is for him only the echo of the confession of the apostles, somehow traced in all ages of church history, now heard again and fully understood in the Reformation. It is unique to Kähler to understand the Bible, first of all the New Testament, as "confession," namely, of having experienced salvation in Jesus Christ.

42. Kattenbusch, *Schleiermacher zu Ritschl*, 60: "Dogmatics is for him [Ritschl] not the description or interpretation of a *fact* of piety within the Christian community, but proof. . . ."

43. Cf. Kaftan, *Dogmatik*, 98: "This improvement [i.e., Ritschl compared to Schleiermacher] is visible in the proof that faith itself is a distinctive and in itself complete knowing, and that it gains this importance precisely with regard to revelation."

44. J. Kaftan, *Das Wesen der christlichen Religion* [The character of the Christian religion] (Basel: C. Detloff's Buchhandlung, 1881), 106–7.

45. J. Kaftan, *Die Wahrheit der christlichen Religion* [The truth of the Christian religion] (Basel: C. Detloff, 1888), 569–70.

46. Herrmann, *Christlich-protestantische Dogmatik*, in Hinneberg, *Die Kultur der Gegenwart*, 615; reprinted in Herrmann, *Grundlegung der Theologie*, part 1, 337: "From this view of Ritschl, in any case, the return route is not difficult. . . ."

once, is even in the current generation still "a stranger, a prophetic citizen of a *later* world."[47]

But *for those concerned*, I have to take back nothing. For all of them, the following is valid:

No other advocate intercedes for him,
He stands for himself entirely alone.[48]

No other than God, and God not as some kind of outside norm, but as the individual, inner certainty and authority that in Christ, as he walks through the history of peoples and human beings and becomes revelation for them. Therefore, the task of religious *thought* formation in church office becomes a problem for him in a quite different way than for his conservative colleague, but, of course, also—I have shown why this is the case—different than for the theologian of the older Ritschlian direction. I repeat: It will be made a matter of conscience for such a theologian. For one should not forget that this theological individualism contains a very serious nerve (which forms simultaneously its *inner* corrective against the danger of deterioration toward "subjectivism"), determining *all* Christian teaching, *all* emergence of pious consciousness in thought and word, "both in its scientific and common form" (thus as dogmatics and ethics as well as sermon), to "completely found itself on and refer itself to the Christian church; a presentation only is useful if it contains what is valid in the Christian church, or why one is convinced that it should apply in the Christian church, which is in itself only derived from the idea of the Christian church."[49]

As soon as a person takes the thought of church seriously, as soon as one sees in the church a living whole undergoing a living development, that person is grasped by the church and recognizes oneself as a part thereof. I cannot imagine a stronger religious-moralistic stimulus than this heuristic, *regulative* mode of thinking of the supra-individual and objective in religious articulation and proclamation. James 3:1 becomes very relevant there.

Suppose someone wants to tell me, on the other hand, that this task is somehow pushed into the conscience of every theologian from every camp of the Protestant church. I will answer then: Surely, insofar as the issue for every serious theologian, whatever his theology may be, is the same. Yet for us, the issue has evolved from a latently religious |486| problem (cf. Isa. 6:5) to an openly theological one.

I wanted to highlight the difficulty and seriousness of the situation after becoming aware, in myself and others, of the dangers of a somewhat harmless

47. Fr. D. E. Schleiermacher, *Monologen* [Monologues] (1800), ed. Fr. M. Schiele, new ed. (Darmstadt: Wissenschaftliche Buchgesellschaft, 1953), 41. "Thus, I am a foreigner to the way of thinking and life of the current generation, a prophetic citizen of a world to come, drawn to it by living fantasy and strong faith, belonging to it in every deed and thought."

48. Closing of the first stanza of Fr. von Schiller's "Reiterlied" (also to be found in Schiller, *Wallenstein's Lager*, scene 11).

49. Fr. D. E. Schleiermacher, *Die christliche Sitte nach den Grundsätzen der evangelischen Kirche im Zusammenhang dargestellt* [Christian morality described in context following the basic tenets of the Protestant Church], from Schleiermacher's handwritten bequest and transcribed lectures, ed. I. Jonas (Berlin: G. Reimer, 1843), 3–4: "*Of what kind is that to which we refer as Christian teaching?* From the way the Christian teaching has come into being, both in its scientific as well as its popular form, it emerges *that it is founded on and refers completely to the Christian church, and a presentation of the same is only useful if it contains this. . . .*"

dogmatizing that a person enters easily upon seeing oneself liberated by the followers of Ritschl from the tentacles of metaphysics and their conflicts with science.

I am happy to be told by Dr. Achelis that there exists a *developing* salvific faith, and by Dr. Drews that this applies to the theologian as well. In awareness of Philippians 3:12–15, I have meanwhile entered a church office. But because of that fact to "beat chamade"[50] in relation to the sensing and articulation of that difficulty, I cannot regard this as well done. It is not about some kind of irrelevant, personal mood, but about a serious, intellectual situation with which we who are concerned need to contend.

I wanted to point out a difficulty. I could have spoken of the developed importance and magnitude of the task. I have not spoken of resignation or an incapacitating mood or ineligibility, and that is not my opinion. But it is my opinion that an inwardly living theology can cope with issues and even demand engagement with and discussion of its problems.

Editorial Closing Comment

by Martin Rade

The topic "Modern Theology and Work for the Kingdom of God," initially raised in the July edition, has occupied us through three editions. Maybe that in itself is already proof that it is not an easy quarrel to pick. We do not want to close the debate, however, without adding a word from the side of the editorial team.

The sufficient reason for accepting the first piece was simply the insight that in the short article we were dealing with a "human document"[51] that, with gracious honesty, allowed us to look into the soul of a valiant theologian about to finish his studies and turn to praxis. One deals a lot nowadays with religious psychology and regards it highly: how should "the fledgling pastor" not |487| profit from this interest? How should he not be a very noble subject of this art?

Since we now reached out with warm sympathy for the essay offered to us, we could not be disturbed by the shadow that its content apparently cast on the theology we represent. For if we were pleased by the openness of what was said, it could not lose value or the right to be published because of what it unashamedly exemplified for us. On the contrary: had the accusation resting in the confession confronted "Halle or Greifswald" instead of "Marburg or Heidelberg," the document would have been far less interesting to us, and we would have been hard pressed to accept it. But by *not being able to do otherwise* in "Marburg or Heidelberg," and our young friend's knowing that we were not able to do otherwise, indeed, not even wanting to be able to do otherwise—his need became our common need, which could not be alleviated through silence. But perhaps through good suasion and friendly disagreement? Certainly, we are very grateful to Mister Achelis and Mister Drews for their engaging so

---

50. Chamade: a drum roll showing the intention to capitulate, to surrender = to cave in.

51. Edmond de Goncourt used the expression *document humain* as the parole (watchword) of literary naturalism in France, in the preface to *Quelque créatures de ce temps* [Some creatures of this time] (Paris, 1876), a book coauthored with his brother, Jules de Goncourt.

seriously and helpfully with Barth's concerns. We were even aware of the fact that such voices would answer him, and if we had been mistaken in that, we would have taken a stand ourselves. Meanwhile *Barth* has supplemented what he wrote back then in the most serendipitous way.

But I, for my part, do not want the matter to be over with that.

For me, a sting remains in the *first* statements by *Barth*. Not that they were new to me. Quite the opposite, I suffer under the reality that he took as point of departure that our young theologians with honest piety and intensive study do not enter their office with a very different joyfulness. Or, in case this cannot be controlled so clearly in the office at home, that they do not eagerly seek free positions open to them in the diaspora or in mission—which are available with the ease of today's exchange in the world and the interest with which we children of today engage in the unfamiliar and the distant and build completely new bridges. I am well aware that the disciples of an explicitly conservative theology do not *push* for such work either; but enough of that. A deficiency in our ranks is obvious.

That I do not acknowledge his justification *in principle*, I have stated in my lecture on mission to the heathens[52] and also in other places. What continues to concern me with growing urgency is the need for the reform of theological study. What *Frühauf*[53] and *Mix*[54] have said publicly on this matter, I have rejected on these pages as not constructive.[55] But I wholeheartedly agree with the urgent demand for it. I also believe that men of *all* theological camps in Germany share this concern. On the other hand, the hour might not have come yet. At our universities, the constitution and usages of inherited structures are extremely resistant to change. It contrasts remarkably with our spiritual and scientific mobility. And if I wanted to make some suggestions for reform now, they would soon be destroyed by the general criticisms. In light of that, it remains to be hoped that the conviction that the formation of our pastors is in need of reform will, given the seriousness of the situation, find more and more supporters. Publications like that of Mr. *Barth* will help in this regard.

52. M. Rade, *Heidenmission die Antwort des Glaubens auf die Religionsgeschichte* [Mission to the heathens as the answer of faith to religious history], in M. Rade's *Das religiöse Wunder und anderes: Drei Vorträge* [Religious wonder and others: Three lectures], SgV 56 (Tübingen: Mohr, 1909), 28–70, esp. 49–50.

53. W. Frühauf, *Praktische Theologie! (Kritiken und Anregungen)* [Practical theology! (Criticisms and suggestions)] (Dresden: Pierson, 1906).

54. See above n. 11.

55. M. Rade, review of W. Frühauf, *Praktische Theologie! (Kritiken und Anregungen)* [Practical theology! (Criticisms and suggestions)] (Dresden: Pierson, 1906), in *ZTK* 17 (1907): 67–69; M. Rade, "Reform des theologischen Studiums?" [Reformation of theological study?], in *ZTK* 19 (1909): 76–77.

Review of
Zeitschrift für Wissenschaftliche Theologie
Volume 51, Numbers 1–2
1909

Zeitschrift für wissenschaftliche Theologie. Founded by *Adolf Hilgenfeld.* Volume 51 (1908–9), issue 1 (September 25, 1908) and issue 2 (December 28, 1908). Frankfurt am Main: Moritz Diesterweg. Annual subscription: 15 Marks.

The Hilgenfeldian Journal aims to serve all the theological disciplines, primarily by focusing on those "central and core questions,"[1] which, from the perspective of a single discipline, are also of programmatic or methodological significance for the other disciplines.

In the first issue, *H. H. Wendt* talks about the relationship of Christianity to modern natural science.[2] *W. Staerk* comments (in critical dialogue with Sellin) on the *'ebed Yahweh* songs [songs of the suffering servant of Yahweh] in Isaiah 40–43.[3] *Johannes Dräseke* speaks, on the basis of Geffcken's commentary, about the Greek apologists Aristides and Athenagoras.[4] The issue concludes with a literary review of Old Testament publications by the late *Bruno Baentsch*[5] and of the New Testament by *W. Staerk.*[6]

The second issue contains a treatise by *E. Wendling* on the more recent literature on the Synoptics and the Acts of the Apostles,[7] a continuation of *Baentsch's* Old Testament literary review,[8] and a literary review of church history publications by *Hermelink, Lietzmann,* and *Loeschke.*[9]

---

1. This phrase is from the notice "An unsere Leser," inserted without pagination at the end of the fourth issue of vol. 50 ([1907/]1908). It is signed by the coeditor, Heinrich Hilgenfeld, who was the sole "Editor in charge" of the journal from 1909 onward. Also, see the last paragraphs of the Translators' Preface, above.

2. Hans Hinrich Wendt, "Das Verhältnis des Christentums zur modernen Naturwissenschaft," in *ZWT* 51 (1908): 1–28.

3. Willy Staerk, "Bemerkungen zu den 'Ebed-Jahwe-Liedern in Jes. 40ff.," in *ZWT* 51 (1908): 28–56. Staerk refers to Ernst Sellin, *Serubbabel: Ein Beitrag zur Geschichte der messianischen Erwartung und der Entstehung des Judentums* (Leipzig: A. Deichert, 1898); Sellin, *Studien zur Entstehungsgeschichte der jüdischen Gemeinde nach dem babylonischen Exil,* vol. 1, *Der Knecht Gottes bei Deuterojesaja* (Leipzig: A. Deichert, 1901); and especially, Sellin, *Das Rätsel des deuterojesajanischen Buches* (Leipzig: A. Deichert, 1908).

4. Johannes Dräseke, "Zwei griechische Apologeten," in *ZWT* 51 (1908): 57–68. Dräseke refers to Johannes Geffcken, *Zwei griechisehe Apologeten,* Sammlung wissenschaftlicher Kommentare zu griechischen und römischen Schriftstellern (Leipzig/Berlin: B. G. Teubner, 1907).

5. Bruno Baentsch, "Literarische Rundschau: Altes Testament, [Parts] I and II," in *ZWT* 51 (1908): 68–86.

6. According to the table of contents (iv), the "Literarische Rundschau: Neues Testament," *ZWT* 51 (1908): 89–95, was not edited by Staerk but rather by Erich Klostermann and Hans Windisch.

7. Emil Wendling, "Neuere Schriften zu den synoptischen Evangelien und zur Apostelgeschichte," in *ZWT* 51 (1908): 135–68.

8. Bruno Baentsch, "Literarische Rundschau: Altes Testament, [Part] III," in *ZWT* 51 (1908): 169–72.

9. Heinrich Hermelink, Hans Lietzmann, and Gerhard Loeschcke, "Literarische Rundschau über Kirchengeschichte," in *ZWT* 51 (1908): 172–92.

The pièce de résistance, for interested readers of the narrower circle of *Die Christliche Welt*, is *Ernst Troeltsch's* "Half a Century of Theology: A Review," which is found in the second issue.[10] With sharply defined strokes, the master of intellectual-historical empathy presents the picture that emerges for him from the overall development of modern theology. This development is positioned between two poles: history and present-day religion. For the sharp grasp of the characteristics of these two poles is the product of a specifically modern way of thinking; theology is under the influence of this modern way as one progressive member among others of the *universitas litterarum* [world of literature], just like any other science. The intimate historical conditionality of the present-day religion means that the science of religion initially finds its object entirely in the history of religion; it is an objectifying, but not normative science.[11] The "uselessness"[12] of such a science for praxis, more precisely for the dogmatic presentation of religion, leads to the necessity of a reversal on this side.

Dogmatics is compelled to withdraw from the proof of universal truth to subjective confession and (here lies the root of all conflicts!) to harmonize the content and form of this confession with the tradition of the church. Dogmatics becomes *mediation*.[13] "What thus came about as a result of the situation itself was naturally made a matter of principle and theory."[14] And this theory is dogmatic *agnosticism*, which consists of the renunciation of proper knowledge in the area of religion, of the foundation of religious truth in a practical-confessional feeling way, a truth that can be expressed as necessary only in an inadequately symbolic manner.[15] At two points, this theory has intervened in an epoch-making manner in history: the first time (against rationalism and supernaturalism) in the formulations of *Kant and Schleiermacher*,[16] the other time (against the Tübingen School and the revival of orthodoxy) in the theology of *Ritschl* and his school, which differs from that older agnosticism not in principle but only through the energetic, christocentric basis of pious experience.[17] This is put into practice classically by [*Wilhelm*] *Herrmann*.[18] However, it is precisely with this christocentric basis that the principle of mediation is resumed and the problem of history arises with renewed sharpness. The reason for this is because, in the meantime, historical theology has increasingly and intentionally put the Christian religion into the stream of the rest of religious and secular history.[19] At two central points, the relativism that follows from this principle has asserted itself especially and awkwardly concerning the recognizability of the person of

10. Ernst Troeltsch, "Rückblick auf ein halbes Jahrhundert der theologischen Wissenschaft," in *ZWT* 51 (1908): 97–135. Reprinted with slight changes in Troeltsch, *Gesammelte Schriften*, vol. 2, *Zur religiösen Lage, Religionsphilosophie und Ethik*, 2nd ed. (Tübingen: Mohr Siebeck, 1992), 193–226. ET: "Half Century of Theology: A Review," in *Ernst Troeltsch: Writings on Theology and Religion*, ed. and trans. Robert Morgan and Michael Pye (1977; Louisville: Westminster John Knox, 1990), 53–81.
11. See Troeltsch, "Half Century of Theology," 55–56.
12. This term does not appear in Troeltsch's essay; but for the idea, see "Half Century of Theology," 56–57.
13. Troeltsch, "Half Century of Theology," 58.
14. Troeltsch, "Half Century of Theology," 58.
15. Troeltsch, "Half Century of Theology," 58–59.
16. Troeltsch, "Half Century of Theology," 59–61.
17. Troeltsch, "Half Century of Theology," 62–65.
18. Troeltsch, "Half Century of Theology," 65–66.
19. Troeltsch, "Half Century of Theology," 68–69.

Jesus and concerning the absoluteness of Christianity.[20] With increasing precision, *Herrmann* seemingly founded and put into practice agnostic theory and religious-ethical autonomy, but in his opinion, it is still the case that "all questions are cut off rather than satisfied."[21] The science of history and the science of present-day religion still stand facing each other basically as foes. What can be done? A remedy can only be expected from a historical theology that deals with the question of the recognizability of Jesus in a positive sense—and this must happen—yet on the other hand from a *philosophy of religion* that is superordinate to history and dogmatics, which on the broadest basis demonstrates the worth of Christianity by means of psychology and epistemology, and which simply takes seriously *Schleiermacher's* encyclopaedic program.[22]

So much for *Troeltsch's* astute construction. To me, the contradiction seems to begin with his view of the development of historical theology. According to Troeltsch, it appears as if this development was straightforward, as if its method from the outset was the same "presuppositionless" one, for example, "no longer liberal, but scientific,"[23] as if it were to be regarded as a methodologically uniform structure over against the systematic theology it was encountering. Thus Troeltsch comes to celebrate *D. F. Strauss* and the Tübingen school as luminaries of a "presuppositionless" historiography.[24] Certainly they were, according to the terms of their agenda. But this agenda, at highly essential points, was still based on dogmatic-metaphysical presuppositions. The implementation of a truly presuppositionless historical science was only created through *Ritschl's* dogmatic regress to the Kantian-Schleiermacherian "agnosticism," as little as he as a historian was able to carry this out himself. Since, in *principle*, he places the religious individual in relation to history completely on one's own feet, he gives to the religious person the possibility of gaining a scientific relationship to history that is independent of religious norms.

The typically modern theological historians are still oriented toward Ritschl's position, in opposition to the pre-Ritschlian science—not only Harnack, but also the so-called "left-wing Ritschlians," *Bousset, Wernle*, and others—not least *Troeltsch* himself. Hence, particularly with this decisive turn from *Baur* to the modern history of religion, one cannot say that the theory has adapted to match the circumstances. On the contrary, it is the other way around: *Ritschl's* "agnostic" position contained the embryonic elements that gave the "religious historians" the clear conscience—*si vales valeo* [if you are well, I am well]—to engage in truly scientific and presuppositionless historical work that abstains from religious norms and influences. And on the other hand, *Herrmann's* ethical-religious autonomism is not so much a dogmatic refuge, as one often hears, but the consistent, *internally* necessary implementation of the strictly individualistic understanding of religion initiated by Schleiermacher and *Ritschl*.

Who would dispute that for the student, and for the individual theologian in general, the conflict between historical and systematic theology, as indicated

20. Troeltsch, "Half Century of Theology," 69–76.
21. Troeltsch, "Half Century of Theology," 74, revised in ET; see 73–75.
22. Troeltsch, "Half Century of Theology," 76–81.
23. See Troeltsch, "Half Century of Theology," 54–58, and esp. 56.
24. Troeltsch, "Half Century of Theology," 61.

by Troeltsch, exists in full and definitely increasing acuteness? The only question is whether or not this conflict is a *proper* one, whether it can be the task of theology to resolve the conflict in religion between the historical and the present-day times for the individual. But this then brings before us the well-known controversy between *Troeltsch* and *Herrmann* about the question of whether there is a religion in general that can be the object of scientific analysis, or rather only the religion of the individual, which cannot be verified by any psychology nor justified by any epistemology.[25] Depending on the answer, the question would then have to be decided as to whether *Troeltsch's* postulates of "certainty" about the historical life of Jesus and of a philosophy of religion that proves the objective value of Christianity have the significance of being an advance.[26] Formally, they represent a repristination of analogous positions of the older liberalism. And the conflict does not hang between Herrmann the dogmatician and Troeltsch the *historian*, but between Herrmann the "agnostic" individualist and Troeltsch the *metaphysician*.

---

25. See, e.g., Wilhelm Herrmann, "Die Lage und Aufgabe der evangelischen Dogmatik in der Gegenwart," *ZTK* 17 (1907): 1–33, 172–201, 315–51; reprinted in Herrmann, *Gesammelte Aufsätze*, ed. Fr. W. Schmidt (Tübingen: J. C. B. Mohr, 1923), 95–188; and in Herrmann, *Schriften zur Grundlegung der Theologie*, ed. Peter Fischer-Appelt, Theologische Bücherei 36 (Munich: Kaiser, 1967), 2:1–87; see esp. 1–8 (= 1–7 and, respectively, 95–102) and 175–86 (= 32–42 and, respectively, 128–39) and Troeltsch's publications discussed there by Herrmann.
26. See Troeltsch, "Half Century of Theology," 70, 74, 77.

The Cosmological Proof for the Existence of God
1909

On April 4, 1909, Barth received (as he reported to his parents two days later) a three-hour visit from a medical student, Freiherr von Seld, whom he had known only casually until then. According to Barth's depiction, von Seld lived more for his spiritual and religious interests than for dedication to his studies. He was a disciple of the Marburg professor of Semitic philosophy Peter Jensen (1861–1936), who was known for his hostility toward theology. Jensen had attracted attention with his thesis that world literature and particularly the Old and the New Testaments had been fundamentally influenced by the Babylonian Gilgamesh epic. Von Seld belonged to a student circle of like-minded thinkers and other colleagues whose common basis apparently consisted in admiration for the ideas of the religious writer and orator Johannes Müller (1864–1949), the publisher of Blätter zur Pflege persönlichen Lebens *[Gazette for the care of personal life]. (On April 28, 1909, Barth wrote about the group to his friend Otto Lauterburg: "Such people have become orthodox in their obscurity. But Allah is great and Johannes Müller is his Prophet.") The organization of this circle cannot be precisely discerned from Barth's letters. He refers to it alternately as the Free Students and as the Society for Personal Life.*

Freiherr von Seld invited Barth, during his visit with him, to hold a Bible study in this circle on the subject of 2 Corinthians 3:4–6. Neither the letters Barth retained nor his calendar indicates whether the Bible study took place. However, he attended a meeting of the Free Students on April 28, during which a member of that circle named Husemann delivered an opening lecture titled "On an Exceedingly Simple Question: What Is Truth?" (as Barth wrote to O. Lauterburg on April 28, 1909). He attended another meeting on May 5, during which von Seld led a Bible discussion about the Gethsemane pericope. In response to his critical intervention, Barth unexpectedly received the assignment of delivering a lecture on the cosmological proof for the existence of God. When von Seld had concluded his talk, Barth explained to those present, "If you wish to discuss the matter, you would do better provisionally to lay aside the devotional attire and then take up the fundamental questions wholly secularly and specially. A Catholic insidiously suggested the theoretical proofs of God, and I equally insidiously accepted the offer to lecture in reproach, limiting myself, however, to the existing problem under discussion [i.e., to the cosmological proof], in order to say something suitable about it." Afterward, he continued to speak for a long time with this Catholic student, summarizing the impression he gained as follows: "The entire way of thought seems somewhat adventurous and remarkable, and the results are interestingly squarely the antitheses of my own. What great powers are Aristotle and Thomas in this world, whom we for the most part hardly know. Perhaps the same person will give a lecture alongside me, and then the confusion will be complete, as it was already the last time when I had to defend myself simultaneously against Gilgamesh, the pseudo-Enlightenment, and Catholic Dogma" (letter to his parents on May 7, 1909). Barth experienced his need to prepare for this assignment both as a welcome challenge and a disruption of his ongoing reading, in which he had "just arrived at the most interesting point, namely, Kant's religious philosophy" (May 7, 1909).

In the following weeks, he busied himself mainly with drafting the lecture, without, so it seems, attending subsequent meetings of the Free Students. On May 16, he wrote to his grandmother, Johanna Maria Sartorius, "Up to now I am enjoying this work, since I can put a lot into it that I have just put into myself once again during the last few months. However, I do not know if it will please the 'personalities' who themselves prefer to chatter rather than to listen because inwardly they believe that one becomes personal by shouting and arguing."

Four days before the lecture took place on May 26, Barth announced to his parents that he was sending them the manuscript: "For those overseeing the topic, it must be a peculiar spectacle to see how I worked together the codices of Kant, Schleiermacher, Herrmann, Cohen, and Natorp. The primary thing for me is that I have brought about a detailed and, even if it coincides with Herrmann's findings, still independently grounded philosophical credo. Whether they can deal with it as anything other than a ponderous lecture is a different question. The 'knowledgeable' among my friends declare it to be too difficult for a lecture. In case of emergency, you can turn it over to the baby boy for censuring" (May 22, 1909). "Baby Boy" was the family's nickname for Barth's four-year-younger brother, Heinrich, who later became a philosopher and who was then a student in his second semester. No reports are preserved about the reception of the lecture that evening. At his home in Bern, Barth's brother did indeed take up the argument. His "critical annotations" have been reprinted here at the end of the lecture. Although no response to his brother's criticisms can be located, a response to his father does exist. His father had written him on June 6, ". . . I have read with delight your essay together with Heiner's keen-witted marginal glosses; I believe he is right that the criticism in it is grounded better than the positive views at the conclusion. I also detect in it a certain 'salto mortale' ['dangerous leap'] as with your teacher, Herrmann. But let us simply agree in the sentiment of your closing verses and grow in it still more deeply; for then the joy of a simple word of Scripture will again come to you. Everything is thine, whether it be Kant or Schleiermacher, whether it be Herrmann or Die Christliche Welt, *but you belong to Christ, whom neither you nor I have first to make, but from whose objective fullness we may draw and who supports and surrounds us with his spiritual effects like the sunlight and the morning breeze." In response, Barth answered on June 9, "With reference to your remark about the 'positive views in the conclusion' of the last section: 'Cosmology and Faith in God,' I am actually rather in agreement if you sense a leap there. For I believe it was also a leap for the apostle Paul, and I am against all slick theology that just develops what every clever person thinks. Whether he takes it from his enlightened reason or from revelation passed down by tradition makes no difference; it's all the same: the clever fellow is the one who thinks. Yet religious certainty is a consciousness of something that does not come about by itself in any human heart and that therefore always stands in relation to culture analogously to a leap, a 'mortal' one if you will. Greater spirits than me, thank God, were the target of the hue and cry of dualism."*

The manuscript was composed on sixty-one pages in octavo format with broad margins, which Barth subsequently had bound together. Heinrich Barth's critical remarks are written on both sides of four loose pieces of paper of the same size. The indication of authorship appears at the bottom of the title page: "Karl Barth, V.D.M." (= Verbi Divini Minister, that is, the title of a theologian in Switzerland who has passed the exams but has not yet been employed as pastor); later written in pencil underneath: "Marburg June 1909." Apart from the reproduced pages, the roman and arabic numbers provided in curly brackets indicate the passages of the text to which Heinrich Barth's "annotations" refer under the same numbers respectively.

Introduction

Cultural Significance of the Problem, the Formulation of the Question, and the Line of Argument

By the cosmological proof for the existence of God, considered apart from any divine revelation, we understand the deduction by natural reason, [arguing] from the existence of the world to the existence of God, that is, from finite causes to an infinite ultimate cause, from the accidental to an absolutely necessary, to which we are entitled to attribute the divine predicates.

This proof has been a fundamental postulate of Roman Catholic theology and philosophy since Thomas Aquinas[1] and of Catholic scholarship in general, insofar as it does not bear the seeds of heresy within itself. Such a proof finds its expression in one of the theses of the Vatican Council of 1870:

> If anyone says that the one and true God, our Creator and Lord, by way of the created world of appearances, cannot be assuredly recognized by the natural light of reason, let him be condemned. (Session III c. I.)[2]

That came to expression in Leo XIII's encyclical *Aeterni Patris*, of August 4, 1879,[3] which, certainly with deep understanding for the nature of the specifically Catholic conception of the relations between religion and culture, commanded a general return of theology and philosophy to Thomas as their foundation, over against which every other modern grounding of theology, as had been sought here and there in the nineteenth century, was regarded as a deviation from the essence of Catholicism. On September 8, 1899, the aforementioned pope issued a letter to French clergy that, with the sharpest expressions, warned about the "groundless skepticism"

> that sacrifices all proofs that traditional metaphysics provided . . . as necessary and unshakable foundations for the demonstration of the existence of God.[4]

---

1. See Thomas Aquinas, *Summa theologiae* I q.2 a.3.

2. Vatican Council I, Session III, Constitutio dogmatica *Dei Filius*, Canones 2, De Revolutione, n. 1 (in DS 3026): "*Si quis dixerit, Deum unum et verum, creatorem et Dominum nostrum, per ea, quae facta sunt, naturali rationis humanae lumine certo cognosci non posse: anathema sit.*"

3. See DS 3135–40, esp. 3139–40.

4. See *Acta Sanctae Sedis* XXXXII (Rome, 1899–1900), 199: Leo XIII, to the French clergy:

> We reprove those doctrines that possess nothing of the true philosophy but the name and that, shaking the foundation of human knowledge itself, lead logically to universal skepticism and to irreligion. For it is profoundly sad for us to learn that, for several years, some Catholics have believed it possible to put themselves under the sway of a philosophy that, under the specious subtext of liberating human reason of every preconceived idea and of every illusion, denies to

And finally, the most recent communication of the Vatican, the encyclical *Pascendi* of September 8, 1907, names so-called agnosticism as the foundation of the modern philosophy of religion and [the modern] theology condemned with it, indicating as its most serious consequence the fact that, through it, God can in no way be the straightforward object of knowledge.[5] If you recall this repeated emphasizing of the theses for the provability of God, over against what there is termed "skepticism," which in reality is the express or implicit presupposition of all nonecclesial scholarship; and if I, by way of anticipation, make you aware that this provability of God, at least in Thomas Aquinas, stands and falls with the cosmological argument that we briefly summarized at the beginning, you will therefore join me in understanding the extraordinary cultural and religious importance of our topic. What we are discussing here is not a special problem of theology, but the question of the relationship between science and religion in general.

For the *world [related to] God*, knowledge and faith are the two factors that the cosmological argument seeks organically to connect by means of natural reason's reflection on causality. If we initially isolate this beginning and that end point of our thoughts, we gain a twofold concept of the problem:

Suppose, specifically, we put the question as follows: *Can we causally infer a divine author from the existence of the world?* Then without question we essentially have a problem of culture, more precisely, of natural science before us, since the question of causation, and potentially about *the* cause of the cosmos, is—and here we agree with the presuppositions of the proof—the central task of "natural reason," which bases itself on perception. In this case, we need to research—and that will become our primary task—the extent to which the idea of this proof is reconcilable or not with a natural scientific method anchored in philosophy, that is, in the critical insight into the capacity of "natural reason." We thus need to show whether, via pure reason, it is possible and desirable to infer from the empirical existence of a causal sequence to a final causality, which itself is no longer caused, thus to a highest cause.

If we start from the end point of the idea, that is, from God, then the problem is a problem of religion and may now be formulated, *Might we find God in the causality of worldly existence?* Then we need to consider the extent to which the belief in final causality plays a role in the life of religion and, potentially, how this conviction is related to the dispute between the philosophy of science and the proof of God.

Only at the conclusion will I come back to this twofold way of asking the question, which is, if you will, already an anticipation of my answer. In what follows, we will turn our attention to the proof itself, which is a unity in the sense of its most important advocate, in order then, in a critique of that presupposition and of the proof itself, to gain the justification for the dissolution,

---

reason the right to affirm anything beyond its own operation, thus sacrificing to a radical subjectivism all the certitudes that traditional metaphysics, consecrated by the authority of the most vigorous spirits, gave as necessary and unshakable foundations for the demonstration of the existence of God, of spirituality, and of the immortality of the soul, and of the objective reality of the external world.

5. Encyclical from Pius X, *Pascendi dominici gregis* (September 8, 1907), in DS 3475: "*Philosophiae religiosae fundamentum in doctrina illa modernistae ponunt, quam vulgo agnosticismum vocant. . . . Hinc infertur, Deum scientiae obiectum directe nullatenus esse posse. . . .*

suggested above, of its rational-supernatural inflected unity into its original components. After having developed the question in this twofold form, it will then, at the same time, be possible to give a positive evaluation of both sides.

I. The Proof, Its Presuppositions, and Consequences

A. The Proof

Natural and Supernatural Theology—The Scope of the Proof—The Proof

Thomism, and thus the current Catholic doctrine of principles, distinguishes between *theologia naturalis* and *theologia supranaturalis*. It therefore expressly establishes a *duplex veritas* [double truth] in reference to God.

The truth of natural theology is, as the name suggests, that *"ad quae ratio naturalis pertingere potest"*[6] [to which natural reason can come], that is, the experiential knowledge of the macrocosm of the world and the microcosm of human nature. Its inner principle is that natural light of reason.

The truth of supernatural theology is, as the name suggests, such *"quae omnem facultatem humanae rationis excedit"* [that it exceeds the entire range of human reason].[7] Its source is the doctrinal revelation of God in Scripture and tradition. Its interpretive principle is the continuity of church-sanctioned theological doctrine arising from the decisions of the pope and the [church] councils, respectively.

This *duplex veritas* cannot therefore contain within itself any contradiction because both of its parts come equally from God.

The proofs of God are thus *propositions of natural theology*. Let us first understand them in the sense of the aforementioned distinction in Catholic doctrine about the *scope* of the proposition that the world proves the existence of God.

The renowned Catholic apologist *Hettinger* starts by establishing the following:

> The finite mind cannot perceive the essence of God, as he is in himself, for here on earth it is bound in essential unity with the body. Therefore, our knowledge corresponds only to that which appears in sensibly perceptible objects and is gained by abstraction. God is certainly knowable in higher ways because he is the truth itself. But to see him as he is, that exceeds the natural capacity for knowledge of even our highest intelligence. Only an infinite being may perceive the Infinite.[8]

By this restriction of the natural knowledge of God, Catholic doctrine does *not* mean that the divine being is wholly unknowable. The "seeing" mentioned in the above-cited passage is only quantitatively, not qualitatively, distinguished

6. Vatican Council I, Session III, cap. 4 (DS 3015): ". . . *praeter ea, ad quae naturalis ratio pertingere potest, credenda nobis proponuntur mysteria in Deo abscondita. . . .*" See also note 7.

7. Thomas of Aquinas, *Summa contra gentiles*, L.I c.3: "*Est autem in his, quae de Deo confitemur, duplex veritatis modus. Quaedam namque vera sunt de Deo, quae omnem facultatem humanae rationis excedunt, ut Deum esse trinum et unum. Quaedam vero sunt, ad quae etiam ratio naturalis pertingere potest, sicut est Deum esse, Deum esse unum et alia huiusmodi. . . .*"

8. Fr. Hettinger, *Timotheus: Briefe an einen jungen Theologen*, 3rd ed. (Freiburg i. Br., 1909), 199–200.

from knowledge. *Hettinger* approvingly cites Aristotle's comments about the night birds that cannot see the clear daylight without becoming blinded.[9] So knowledge is blinded over against God, but yet not blind as we may interpret it. Thus natural reason is denied only the adequate, perfect knowledge of God, and it is (as another Catholic theologian, *Becker*, puts it) capable of proving the being [*Wesen*] of God as *relatively evident*.[10] {I.1}

The natural knowledge of God is not only restricted by the limits of our power of reason in comparison with the intellect of the angels and by the intuitive perception of God himself, but also equally by the facts of special, supernatural revelation. Hence, the Trinity of the Godhead, for example, is inaccessible to natural knowledge.

What remains left after this characteristic subtraction is indeed still sufficient. The object of the natural knowledge of God and the absolutely manifest proof is not just the existence of God alone but also his existence as a thinking and willing Being, that is, his personality.

According to the presentation of Catholic theology, it is nothing other than a more subtly trenchant knowledge of our common sense. *Becker* opines, for instance, "The natural knowledge of God is so simple that it urges itself upon rational thought involuntarily and can only be held back by forcible disregard of the simplest laws of thought."[11]

How does this "simple" knowledge come about? According to its object and the aforementioned limitation, not immediately but *mediately*, discursively, that is, by rising through concepts from the *causae secundae* [secondary causes] of the given experience to a *causa prima* [primary cause]. Let us follow the argument in its details.

In a form that, by the way, underlies most other forms, the proof starts from the empirical fact of *movement*. Like everything in experience, the thing moved must have its cause and, since space and time are infinite but an infinite regression is impermissible since it would contradict the natural need of human reason to ascribe causes, a *primum movens* [first moving] is finally reached, which must be thought of as unmoved and immovable, as singular, perfect,

---

9. Aristotle, *Metaphysics* 993b9–11: "ὥσπερ γὰρ τὰ τῶν νυκτερίδων ὄμματα πρὸς τὸ φέγγος ἔχει τὸ μεθ᾽ ἡμέραν, οὕτω καὶ τῆς ἡμετέρας ψυχῆς ὁ νοῦς πρὸς τὰ τῇ φύσει φανερώτατα πάντων." See Hettinger, *Timotheus*, 200.

10. See J. A. Becker, "Gott," in *Wetzer und Welte's Kirchenlexikon oder Encyklopädie der katholischen Theologie und ihrer Hilfswissenschaften*, 2nd ed., vol. 5. (Freiburg i. Br., 1888), col. 865:

> The existence of God is evident to human understanding and metaphysically certain, although not immediately, but mediately, since from evident grounds it follows with logical necessity. Therefore, the essential elementary concept of the divine being is also evident in this knowledge, while the further development of that concept may be brought to a full certainty, though not to absolute evidence. For that reason, according to historical witnesses, human reason gives itself over to many false perceptions of the being itself when ascertaining conviction of the existence of God. The difficulty of relatively complete and errorless knowledge of God for the human being left to his own devices motivates the moral or relative necessity of supernatural revelation as being absolutely essential for the supernatural final end.

11. J. A. Becker, "Gott," col. 882: "A supernatural revelation would also be absolutely, not simply relatively, necessary for the merely natural order, but humans could not grasp and recognize it as a divine work if a natural knowledge of God were not possible. The latter is moreover so simple...."

immaterial, and thus a rational being.[12] In the same way, Aristotle had already proved the "νοῦς" [mind] as "πρῶτον κινοῦν" [first set in motion].[13] {I.2} Analogously, Thomas infers—and for our interpretation, this category is the center of the proof—from the empirical fact of many caused *causes* to a *"causa efficiens prima"* [efficient first cause], which is not itself caused and cannot be caused according to its very concept.[14] Moreover, from *contingency*—that is, from the existence of objects of experience that are not necessary in themselves, but always conditional—follows the assumption of an absolutely unconditional and necessary, which is "per se *necessarium*," that is, which has its necessity in its very concept.[15] And from the limited, finite *perfection* of individual things finally follows the presupposition of an absolute, infinite perfection, which already by virtue of its very concept is *"maxime ens"* [maximal Being].[16] Scholars seek to isolate Thomas's fifth argument, which infers from the existence of rational *natural ends* in the world to the existence of a rational author, as the teleological,[17] but it only apparently does not fit with the schema of "cause-effect" within which the others operate. We remain fully within the framework of Thomistic thought if we consider it only as another offshoot of the cosmological proof. {It should nevertheless be mentioned here that thought of a final end as a *problem* for modern natural scientific thought might be discussed independently, and we pass over it here only due to the fact that it, as a *proof of God*, can indeed be taken care of with the presentation and criticism of the cosmological proof.}

Those among you who are knowledgeable about the topic will have long since recalled to mind that, in the background of the cosmological proof and the arguments associated with it, lies another idea of an entirely different nature— none other than the *ontological*, the inference *from* the presence of a maximal concept as that of a highest perfection, highest necessity, highest causality, and so forth, in our consciousness, and *to* the existence of a correlated fact in reality. But the citation of this fundamental argument would already be subject to critique since Thomas did not allow it to be regarded as an independent argument.[18] Admittedly, we will soon need to investigate whether his version of the cosmological argument developed without secret recourse to the ontological [argument].

12. The argument from movement is the first of Thomas Aquinas's "five ways," that is, proofs of God. See *Summa theologiae* I q.2 a.3 i.c.: *"Ergo necesse est devenire ad aliquod primum movens, quod a nullo movetur: et hoc omnes intelligunt Deum."*

13. Aristotle, *Metaphyics* 1073a 26–27: "ἐπεὶ δὲ τὸ κινούμενον ἀνάγκη ὑπό τινος κινεῖσθαι, καὶ τὸ πρῶτον κινοῦν ἀκίνητον εἶναι καθ᾿ αὑτό." On νοῦς, see Aristotle, *Metaphyics* 1074b 15–1075a 11. Barth apparently drew on the presentation of K. Vorländer, *Geschichte der Philosophie*, PhB 105 (Leipzig, 1908), 1:130.

14. Thomas's second "way"; see *Summa theologiae* I q.2 a.3 i.c.: *"Ergo est necesse ponere aliquam causam efficientem primam: quam omnes Deum nominant."*

15. Thomas's third "way"; see *Summa theologiae* I q.2 a.3 i.c.: *"Ergo necesse est ponere aliquid quod sit per se necessarium, non habens causam necessitatis aliunde, sed quod est causa necessitatis aliis; quod omnes dicunt Deum."*

16. Thomas's fourth "way"; see *Summa theologiae* I q.2 a.3 i.c.: *"Est igitur aliquid quod est verissimum, et optimum, et nobilissimum, et per consequens maxime ens. . . . Ergo est aliquid quod omnibus entibus est causa esse, et bonitatis, et cuiuslibet perfectionis; et hoc dicimus Deum."*

17. See Thomas, *Summa theologiae* I q.2 a.3 i.c.: *"Ergo est aliquid intelligens, a quo omnes res naturales ordinantur ad finem; et hoc dicimus Deum."*

18. For example, Thomas Aquinas, *Summa theologiae* I q.2 a.1, ad 2; Thomas, *Summa contra gentiles* L.I, c.10S.

B. The Presupposed Concept of the World and Human Knowledge

"Veritas est adaequatio rei et intellectus" [truth is the equation of a thing and the intellect], the Syllogism, the Idea.

If we wish to rightly understand the cultural and religious significance of this Thomistic theologoumenon, we must try to provide information about its origins in the Aristotelian-Scholastic doctrine of principles and its consequences for the concept of God founded on it. Only on the basis of a critique of these consequences and those presuppositions will it then be possible to subject the proof itself to a thoroughgoing critique.

The concept of knowledge presupposed in Thomas's proof can be popularly defined by saying that reason believes in order to get to the ground of things. *"Veritas est adaequatio rei et intellectus."*[19] Ἡ ψυχὴ τὰ ὄντα πώς ἐστι πάντα [the soul is, in a way, all existing things].[20] This is the program of [all] science. Science is the knowledge of the *"quidditas,"*[21] the essence of things.[22] Aristotle had already rejected Plato's view that ultimate real existence can be found in pure thought but also admittedly kept himself from Democratus's opposed view that the material atom is the ultimate substance. Plato and the medieval scholastics with him chose an apparently pragmatic middle way: *The true being subsists in an individual to the degree that it is determined by a universal.* That is to say, knowledge begins with sensible experience. We perceive the *individual* by our sense organs and a *shape*, a *"phantasma"* of the object, arises within us, marked by all the accidental qualities of the individual thing, and therefore does have the character of necessity and hence of real being. We do not move beyond this πρότερον καθ' ἡμᾶς,[23] as Aristotle calls this shape, without the *intellectus agens*, which transforms it by abstraction[24] from what is accidental into a πρότερον τῇ φύσει.[25] This activity of the intellect is the syllogism or the deduction and is the foundation of all knowledge. Thus the object of the knowledge of the intellects is intelligible, universal, necessary, the essence of the thing, which exists intellectually in the individual thing, but is veiled itself by the accidents of the individual. By the syllogism, the intellect subjects the individual to the universal and, via abstraction, gains the *idea*, which is not the essence of the thing itself that subsists in the individual thing, but a mirror image, the generic concept, which is obtained by abstracting from the accidents of the individual thing. This is the principle of knowledge. The principle of the *world* is nothing other than its converse:

---

19. Barth penciled in the margin of the manuscript: "Truth consists in the equation of thing and thought." This well-known definition of truth (according to Thomas Aquinas in, e.g., *De veritate* q.I a.I, i.e., with reference to Isaak Israeli; Thomas, *Summa theologiae* I q.16 a.1 i.c.) does not appear in the literature, according to *RGG*³ 6: col. 1520, before Albert the Great and Thomas.

20. Aristotle, *De anima* Γ 8, 431b 20–21: Νῦν δὲ περὶ ψυχῆς τὰ λεχθέντα συγκεφαλαιώσαντες, εἴπωμεν πάλιν ὅτι ἡ ψυχὴ τὰ ὄντα πώς ἐστι πάντα. Cited according to Hettinger, *Timotheus*, 192 n. 1. The manuscript incorrectly has Ἡ ψυχὴ τὰ πάντα. . . . Barth's penciled note in the margin of the manuscript reads, "We know all things as they *are*."

21. See, e.g., Thomas Aquinas, *De ente et essentia* I, 2: *"Et quia illud per quod res constituitur in proprio genere vel specie, est quod significamus per definitionem indicantem quid est res; inde est quod nomen essentia a philosophis in nomen quidditatis mutatur."*

22. Barth formulates the following sentences in a close approximation to Vorländer, *Geschichte der Philosophie*, 123.

23. Barth's penciled note in the margin of the manuscript reads: "Thing in representation."

24. See, for instance, Thomas Aquinas, *Summa theologiae* I q. 79 a.3s; q.84 a.6. On Aristotle, see Vorländer, *Geschichte der Philosophie*, 128.

25. Barth's penciled note in the margin of the manuscript reads: "Thing in itself."

The universal concepts or ideas are contained in physical, sensible things not yet *realiter* but potentially, as much as their respective individually different forms stand in internal relation to thought. The intellectualizing energy of reason, the *"intellectus agens,"* seizes the shape of the individual thing presented through the sense organs and through the latter generates the universal concept.

Knowledge begins with experience, but it does not stop with experience. For once the *veritas* is found in a generically intelligible form as *adequatio rei et intellectus*; what prevents the syllogistic method from continuing on, that is, successively stripping away everything accidental in individual generic concepts and rising to a highest necessary being? Because it begins with experience, this knowledge of the highest idea always remains indirect—as every cognition is just cognition of its mirror image. That is why it provides only relative evidence of the knowledge of God's being [*Wesen*]. But precisely because it arises from experience, at least an inadequate knowledge is evident, providing proof of God's existence with absolute evidence.

C. The Concept of God and Its Dialectic

Actus Purus, The "Pantheism" of Thomas, Its Avoidance by Recourse to the Ontological Inference

The concept of God gained on the basis of this principle with help of the cosmological proof, through its internal dialectic and the way in which Thomas and his disciples seek to avoid it, offers us the point of departure from which we can turn from presentation to critical evaluation.

God is the Πρῶτον κινοῦν, Aristotle tells us, the νόησις νοήσεως insofar as he is the highest idea, the idea of ideas.[26] And now we hear from Thomas that the *"essentia Dei est actus purus et perfectus,"*[27] pure actuality without corporeality, and we know from the deduction of the proof that God is to be more precisely understood as the *"primum movens immobile,"* as *"causa efficiens prima,"* as a *"necessarium per se necessarium,"* as an *"ens nobilissimum."* In addition, we know that all individual movements, causes, necessities, perfections, and so forth are only these to the extent that they participate in that one immaterial *"actus purus"* of the highest Being.

The venerable ecclesiastic's [Thomas's] notes of this metaphysics sound a very different and more lively melody in my ears at the beginning of the twentieth century: At the basis of all becoming lies the being of absolute substance; all finite causality is only a particle of this substance. The observing and thinking rationality rises from individual sense perception to the final synthesis of the cosmos. You know from what quarters such a promising message sounds today, from a camp that is completely *unindebted* to Thomism, namely, the circle of the philosophizing natural scientists.[28] Let us suppose that Thomistic theology is

---

26. Aristotle, *Metaphysics* 1074b.33–35: αὐτὸν ἄρα νοεῖ, εἴπερ ἐστὶ τὸ κράτιστον, καὶ ἔστιν ἡ νόησις νοήσεως νόησις; See Vorländer, *Geschichte der Philosophie*, 130–31.

27. Thomas Aquinas, *Summa theologiae* I q.87 a.1 i.c.: *"Essentia igitur Dei, quae est actus purus et perfectus, est simpliciter et perfecte secundum seipsam intelligibilis."*

28. Barth may have been thinking about the biologist Ernst Häckel (1834–1919) and his followers. He had Haeckel's influential work *The Riddle of the Universe: Popular Studies on Monistic Philosophy* (1899) in his possession since the winter of 1906–7. The "law of substance" plays a central role in Haeckel; see,

the scientific representative of the interests of religion. Do we not then stand here before the much-desired bridge between faith and knowledge? *Hettinger* assures us with a clear allusion to *Haeckel* "that precisely the most competent masters of natural religion do not find satisfaction in the findings of rigorously exact research and thus have made the attempt from the 'physical description of the world' to push on to a metaphysical explanation of the universe in order to solve the 'holy riddles of the cosmos.'"[29]

We thus see that Pilate and Herod became good friends (see Luke 23:12) on the day when they, abstracting from the purely empirical, undertook to rise up to general concepts and, from there, to an absolute ground of the world. {I.3} But how can that be? Those natural philosophers infer a *pantheistic* worldview from their absolute concept of substance. Saint Thomas a pantheist? Impossible! Indeed, anyone who knows his theology knows that he explicitly rejected the inference of pantheism. The only question is how this rejection is grounded in his system. Earlier we have already noted that he attributes the character of *personality* to the *actus purus* of the Godhead, which stands at the peak of his syllogism, and that this character should definitely be known by natural reason. The absolutely perfect, root cause, and necessary being is a personality. Yes, how do we know that? How do we come to this assertion? The pantheist who, like Thomas, syllogistically infers an absolute substance, would object: the concept of personality contains a delimitation within itself. A delimitation is, however, always a limitation, a negation. But the absolutely perfect being tolerates no limitation in itself. Thus, God is not personal. Thomas did indeed acknowledge similar objections and, if we consider his concept of personality, we must admit to ourselves that he is actually *not* caught by that criticism from the side of the pantheists. He lays down, namely, *"cum omne illud, quod est perfectionis, Deo sit attribuendum, eo quod eius essentia continet in se omnen perfectionem, conveniens est, ut hoc nomen persona de Deo dicatur."*[30] The pantheistic objection is thus undoubtedly rejected, since personality is simply made equivalent in this formula to the concept of the highest perfection. A *determinatio* is definitely not ascribed to it. But precisely here the Thomistic concept of God moves into suspicious proximity to pantheism. The intimate relation of its *"perfectissimum in tota natura, scil[icet] subsistens in rationali natura,"*[31] with the concept of being and substance of the old and new pantheists, appears very apparent, a relationship that, over against which the *"nomen persona"* that Thomas purports to want to have attributed to it, appears more like an ecclesial emblem. The fact that precisely the newer Catholic theology has considered it necessary to eagerly cleanse its master [Thomas] from the

---

for instance, *The Riddle of the Universe*, translated by J. McCabe (New York: Harper & Brothers, 1905), chap. 1, subhead, "Cosmological Perspective" (13); and chap. 12, "The Law of Substance," 211–32, among others. See also Haeckel's *Monism as Connecting Religion and Science* (1892), 5th ed. (Bonn, 1893).

29. Hettinger, *Timotheus*, 239.

30. Thomas Aquinas, *Summa theologiae* I q.29 a.3 i.c.; Barth's penciled note in the margin of the manuscript gives an imprecise translation: "Since all perfection shall be attributed to God, to the one, who in his essence already contains all perfection, it is easy to also call him a personality."

31. Thomas, *Summa theologiae* 1 c.: ". . . *persona significat id quod est perfectissimum in tota natura, scilicet subsistens in rationali natura."*

suspicion of pantheism shows that this is not such a strained interpretation.[32] And this defense takes place for a reason, insofar as Thomas definitely saw that pantheism was not warded off by the sheer hypostatization of the final abstraction of individual things in the *"noman persona."* Hettinger interprets his position as follows:

> {I.4} [Thomas] distinguishes between *universal* being and *divine* being. The first is nothing other than the product of our final abstraction from individual things, but without any determination of the content, apart from the negation of nonbeing, and which thus exists only in the idea and belongs to everything that has being. The divine being, by contrast, is not an ideal that exists purely in the intellect of existing beings, but the most real being of all.[33]

This leads to the following: the syllogistic path, submitting the empirical individual thing to general concepts, simply does not lead reason to a final real and, thus, *supernatural* being, but only to the idea of the latter, to a being about which nothing can be said except, on the one hand, that it is the negation of nonbeing and, on the other hand, that this Being is absolutely prior to everything finite; according to its construction and concept, it remains completely *innerworldly*. From that perspective, the equation "God = World" is entirely understandable. At any rate, pure being in the sense of Thomistic theism is not reached as long as the ontological argument for the most real Being and thus the supernatural, understood theistically, is not added to the abstracted universal being. That is, *the cosmological argument argues for the existence of God only insofar as it purports to enclose the existence of this most perfect Being in its concept of the highest perfection, which it is able to reach.* The saying of Mephistopheles about theology is fulfilled here, that "even where concepts"—that is, additional syllogisms—*"fail,* a *word* arrives at the right moment."[34] This word is *"ens realissimum"* [most real Being].[35] And we have thereby reached the point where we may begin with our critique.

II. The Critical Resolution of the Proof and the Scientific Theory of Experience

A. The Ontological Argument

As we saw, Thomas rejected the ontological proof, which Anselm of Canterbury introduced into theology as such. As we have also seen, however, precisely

---

32. See, e.g., Hettinger, *Timotheus*, 201ff.
33. Hettinger, *Timotheus*, 204–5.
34. J. W. von Goethe, *Faust* 1.5.1995 (study room).
35. This expression does not appear in the works of Thomas Aquinas. The interpreter of Thomas, Franz Hettinger, on whom Barth relied, used a corresponding German concept when referring to *Summa theologiae* I. q.3 a.4, in order to show how the followers of Thomas warded off pantheism: ". . . The divine being is, by contrast, not an ideal whose being *subsists* merely in intellect, but the most real being of all; it is not at all a sheer hypostatization of the *universally abstract*, undetermined being of pantheism" (Hettinger, *Timotheus*, 205). One also finds the superlative of the "real" in Immanuel Kant's doctrine of God: ". . . But did [the proof] of God from the concept of a most real being (from the contingency of the changeable and the necessity of a first mover), once it left the schools and eventually landed among the public, have the slightest bit of influence?" *Critique of Pure Reason*, Preface, B XXXII.

according to the interpretation of Catholic theologians, his cosmological proof is unavoidably grounded, in the final instance, on the ontological argument: *The concept of a highest perfect being includes in itself the existence [of such a being]; otherwise it would stand in contradiction to itself.*

{II.1} In this argument, it is correct that, following formal logic, the predicate of existence is given with the epistemic concept of a thing. In this case, however, the proposition *"God is"* remains purely analytic; that is, the existence of God to be proved is already presupposed in advance by its epistemic concept. What is achieved is not a proof but only a tautological elucidation of this concept.

Insofar as our concept of an object contains so much as "may be," it still remains empty, that is, a tautology, if the objective reality of the synthesis, from which it came about, is not furnished. Indeed, one hundred imaginary Thaler admittedly contain nothing less than one hundred real Thaler, but one hundred Thaler are not made real by being really and completely conceived,[36] but only because a complete intuition, for example, of one hundred Thalers here in front of me on the table corresponds to the perfect concept.[37] {II.2}

The ontological argument, to which the cosmological proof tacitly has recourse, turns out to be purely *elucidatory* of an epistemic concept; consequently, it is an analytical proposition that depends on the proposition of noncontradiction, but it does not provide an *extension* of the epistemic concept, that is, a synthetic proposition through which alone the previously indicated empty highest concept of the cosmological proof would gain content.

B. The Cosmological Antinomy

The Typical Significance of the Contradiction between Theism and Pantheism, the Antinomy, the Way toward the Resolution of the Antinomy

I have just said that the objective reality of a synthesis can only be verified by the correlation with its subject, that is, by the *concept* at its basis with an object in *intuition*. One or another of you may have thought that I asserted that point rather dogmatically. Before I attempt to clarify the principles of possible experience to you, I would like to return once more to the syllogistic structure of the cosmological argument, and so on, calling your attention to the characteristic inner dialectic of the cosmological idea as *Kant* first discovered and presented it in the section "Antithetic of Pure Reason" in his central work.[38]

The parallelism between Thomistic deism and pantheism has already been discussed. Both have in common the ascent from the connection of the sensible given to general concepts, from general concepts to a total synthesis of objects of the sensible world in the idea of an ultimate ground. The difference

36. Marginal comment by Barth's father, Fritz Barth: "Too bad!" (see the facsimile page reproduced in this volume).
37. See Kant, *Critique of Pure Reason* B 627.
38. See Kant, *Critique of Pure Reason* B 448–53.

consists only in their definition of the ultimate ground. For theism, it is a real cause existing-for-itself, while for pantheism it is the sheer *actus purus* of the all-encompassing substance. In the former, the ultimate ground is freedom; in the latter, it is nature itself. Both can call on claims of pure reason for their assertions, for it is just as impossible for reason to conceive of an uncaused final cause in the Thomistic sense as it is to let go of the idea of a free cause existing-for-itself as such and to imagine an *actus purus* without being a cause of movement.

In the antithesis of theism and pantheism, we have nothing other before us than the "scandal of pure reason" in general, as *Kant* called it,[39] which consists in the fact that, on the basis of the syllogistic [thought] that extends beyond the limits of empirical knowledge, two series of "sophistical theorems" are conceivable and, in fact, also postulated, "which may neither hope for confirmation in experience nor fear refutation by it; and each of them is not only without contradiction in itself but even meets with conditions of its necessity in the nature of reason itself, only unfortunately the opposite has on its side equally valid and necessary grounds for its assertion."[40]

For our subject, primarily Kant's third and fourth antinomies come under consideration, which concern the problem of a *free* causality of the world existing in-itself and a being in the world that is *necessary* in-itself.

(1) [41]*We have standing over againt one another:*

Thesis: *For the explanation of the world, the acceptance of a final free causality is necessary.*	Antithesis: *There is no free causality; everything takes place according to laws.*
Proof: With the sheer concept of natural lawfulness, no complete series of interdependent causes is reached, thus leaving unsolved the question about unrestricted general causality.	Proof: The concept of causality can only be completed if we presuppose a situation of not-yet-operative causes. This, however, is not the case with a free, that is, uncaused causality; consequently, uncaused causality as such is an empty conceptual product.

39. The expression "scandal of pure reason" is not found in the passage that Barth cited from Kant (*Critique of Pure Reason* B 449). Barth appears to have conflated a similar formulation by Kant from the preface to the 2nd ed. (B) of the *Critique of Pure Reason*, which is directed against the psychological idealism of René Descartes (B 34) and the critical discussion of "sophistical theorems" (B 449). On the "refutation of [Cartesian] psychological idealism," which puts into question the reality of things other than the self, Kant comments in the Preface: "No matter how innocent idealism may be held to be as regards the essential ends of metaphysics (though in fact it is not so innocent), it always remains a scandal of philosophy and universal human reason that the existence of things outside us (from which we, after all, get the whole matter for our cognitions, even for our inner sense) should have to be assumed merely *on faith*, and that if it occurs to anyone to doubt it, we should be unable to answer him with a satisfactory proof." See I. Kant, *Critique of Pure Reason*, trans. and ed. Paul Guyer and Allen W. Wood (Cambridge: Cambridge University Press, 1998), B 39, p. 121.
40. Kant, *Critique of Pure Reason*, B 449, p. 467.
41. See Kant, *Critique of Pure Reason*, B 472ff.

(2) The 4th Antinomy runs in parallel:[42]

Thesis: *Some absolute necessity belongs to the world.*	Antithesis: *There is no absolute necessity either inside or outside the world.*
Proof: The fact of changes in the sensible world, which come about necessarily under temporally antecedent conditions, allows the inference to an absolutely necessary being, which is the condition of all change inside the sensible world.	Proof: The selfsame fact of changes in the sensible world, which come about under temporally antecedent conditions, precludes the acceptance of an absolutely necessary being in time. An absolute, that is, uncaused necessary being in time, is, again, an empty concept.

The demonstration of this "most remarkable phenomenon of human reason" (by Kant) does not have the goal of arousing a sensation of groundless skepticism. But, correctly understood, it is the wake-up call that awakens us from our "dogmatic slumber" and calls us to the way of *critique*.[43]

Methodologically, I may well presuppose unanimity among us as I go on to remark initially in judgment of these theses and antitheses: *Two propositions that contradict one another can both be right, if their underlying concept allows for a different understanding.* For instance, I can say, "All paper is valuable to the extent that paper as paper possesses a certain value," and can say, "All paper is worthless insofar as all virtue or theory, to the extent that it simply exists on paper, does not have the slightest value." Both propositions are contradictorily opposed and yet both are correct if in the thesis I understand by "paper" something different than I do in the antithesis. Now the concept presupposed in the antinomy is *the world as actual thing.* {II.3} The dispute revolves around the causality of the *world*, around necessity in the *world*. We have thus to ascertain for ourselves whether this concept might not possibly be equivocal. Are we thinking the same thing in the thesis and the antithesis with the word "world"? The best historical proof that that is actually *not* the case is the recourse we already discussed from Thomas's syllogistic thinking, which allegedly draws only from natural reason [yet applies it] to the ontological argument. He reaches a final and free cause of the world, and a necessity internal to the world, only because he posits and explains to us that he is thereby dealing with an "*ens per se necessarium*," that is, in the language of modern philosophy, a *thing-in-itself*. In other words, he expands his concept of the world that he obtained through his syllogism with a synthesis, which shall be valid in itself, without his (or medieval Catholic thinking in general) becoming suspicious of the yawning gap between the rationalism of the foundation and the supernaturalism of the capstone.

42. See Kant, *Critique of Pure Reason*, B 480ff., pp. 490ff.
43. See I. Kant, *Prolegomena to Any Future Metaphysics That Will Be Able to Come Forward as Science*, trans. and ed. Gary Hatfield, rev. ed. (Cambridge: Cambridge University Press, 2004), 9: "This product of pure reason in its transcendent use [that is, the cosmological ideas] is its most remarkable phenomenon, and it works the most strongly of all to awaken philosophy from its dogmatic slumber, and to prompt it toward the difficult business of the critique of reason itself."

We just found ourselves confronted by the fatal fact that reason is inclined, on equally strong grounds, *to posit* and *to reject* a final free causality of the world and an absolute necessity in the world. What that tells us, we can clarify for ourselves with the best and most important example, the help of a representation of the *beginning of a human action*. On the one hand, we can think of no action without a cause in time and, again, this cause is not without determination of its condition before it becomes causal, that is, without its own cause. In the same way, we must picture every action as coming about through a causal nexus or, from the standpoint of its subject, as not absolutely necessary, but as conditioned, as accidental. But, on the other hand, we must ascribe freedom to our human actions or those of others, to the extent that we regard them as proceeding from the choice or judgment of reason, that is, from a causality that is not bound to time. In the first case, we judge ourselves on an empirical basis; in the second, from the basis of pure practical reason. In the first case, we think of human beings as members of a lawfully ordered nature; in the second, as citizens of an intelligible kingdom of freedom. How do we make sense of this double viewpoint, which we all feel ourselves— every day, continually, knowingly or unknowingly—irresistibly drawn to apply when evaluating not only human actions and relations but, doubtlessly, also organic and inorganic nature?

Two worlds next to one another? A *mundus intelligibilis* next to a *mundus sensibilis*?[44] You know the indissoluble conflicts in which this supposition would trip up our thinking even in its first steps. Before we decide to accept this supposition, it needs to be shown whether the reality of both[45] "actual worlds" that we have encountered can be defended in the forum of critical philosophy. {II.4}

C. The Constitutive Principles of Experience

Space and Time—The Concepts

The Aristotelian-Scholastic theory of knowledge starts from individual things as real and given objects of experience. From the idea of a continuity in the changing states of the individual thing and by way of syllogism, it gains the general concepts, which, though indirect, still are held to present actual knowledge of actual things.

If we examine the concept "object of experience" more closely, we quickly discover that we have every motivation not to rush to "actuality" and the "givenness" of things, potentially leaving them entirely on their own. At any rate, we should consider as given, not the "things-in-themselves" straightaway, but rather the empirically knowable changing states.

By "object," we understand, following *Natorp's* distinction, *either* the X of the intended object given to us for determination in the forms of sensibility *or* the thing as already determined by the concepts of the understanding, the known object. Knowledge of an object thus comes about to the extent that it is given to

---

44. On the concepts, see I. Kant, *Critique of Pure Reason* B 312.
45. [Editorial annotation deleted.]

us for determination in the forms of sensibility and to the extent that it can be thought in concepts.[46]

We become conscious of the multiplicity of the given objects through the forms of sensibility, that is, in space and time. Neither are determinations of the thing-in-itself, but nothing other than the characteristic determinations of our consciousness, insofar as it is receptive of the intended object. *Negatively*, it can indeed be demonstrated that space and time cannot originate from experience since experience is absolutely impossible without space and time. You can verify that if you take an object and try to abstract away from it all content of intuition; but you will not manage to abstract away intuition itself, that is, the spatial-temporal determination. And, *positively*, the fact of the possibility of pure mathematics shows that this spatial-temporal determination is, in fact, an a priori, which precedes all experience: the propositions of *geometry* have apodictic validity, in contrast to all propositions of empirical experience, because they are not created from any individual intuition, but from pure intuition. We are convinced that the sum of the angles of a triangle must always add up to 180°, even if we could not check it even once with a goniometer, simply because we can be certain of it a priori by constructing it in space, even if only conceptually. And the same holds for the pure *arithmetic* in which *time* is the form of intuition a priori, as all concepts of number only come into being through the successive composition of units in the time-series. {II.5} By its spatial a priori, the perceiving [*anschauende*] consciousness orders objects *next to one another*; and by its temporal a priori, *after one another*.

From that follows a twofold conclusion:

1. Those objects that affect our powers of perception in the forms of space and time are objects of our intuition, but *only* these; that is, objects that transcend space and time conceptually do not come into consideration, not only relatively but also absolutely.

2. We ascribe reality to the objects affecting, in the forms of space and time, our perceptual powers only with reference to their spatial-temporal state and not in the sense of objective objectivity. But that means (and here we stand before the signpost that divides the minds): What we perceive is an appearance, not the thing-in-itself. We take note of its empirical actuality without having the capacity to make any proposition about its "real" state.

The formal factor of knowledge given in receptivity is indispensable if experience is to come about, but it is not able to constitute experience by itself.

Experience comes about only when the self-activity (spontaneity) of the understanding combines the multiplicity of a given intuition into a necessary unity.

Aristotle, the Scholastics, and the vox populi among contemporary natural scientists think that a scientific synthesis arises simply from the comparison of the largest possible series of cases of perception, which are combined into one concept. For, if from A follows B in one thousand cases, they believe themselves warranted to assume that it so occurs also in the 1001st and 1002nd cases and declare the perception that from A follows B to be "scientific" knowledge. As a

46. See Paul Natorp, *Philosophische Propädeutik (Allgemeine Einleitung in der Philosophie und Anfangs-gründe der Logik, Ethik und Psychologie) in Leitsätzen zu akademischen Vorlesungen*, 3rd ed. (Marburg: N. G. Elwert, 1905), 24–25.

matter of fact, this synthesis would be valid only relatively; it would remain a purely perceptual judgment if it were not grounded on an unassailable *concept* of *understanding*, which in no way originates from perception, but by which it first becomes possible to obtain objectively valid experiential propositions from individual perceptions. These a priori concepts or categories *are therefore only applicable to objects of spatial-temporal intuition* because receptivity and spontaneity of knowledge are not given to us except as correlates, in other words, *because intuition and concept mutually depend on one another by the original synthetic unity of logical consciousness.* You will find confirmation that this is no criticist dogma but the result of the simplest insight into the workings of [our] consciousness if you pay attention to the fact that you are completely incapable of applying a concept in any other way than applying it to an intuition. If you think in terms of "quantity," you cannot get by without space. For instance, to recognize a line, you must draw it, at least mentally, in space. If you think of "cause," you cannot do so without thereby conceiving a temporal series in which the effect is given. For instance, the barometer rises *after* the air has begun to expand and exert pressure on the quicksilver.

The two forms of a priori knowledge known to us—that of receptivity in space and time and that of spontaneity in concepts—are thus to be combined if experience in the scientific sense is to come about. What results from this combination are different schemata, or *fundamental propositions*, analogously to the various classes of concepts. Its system is simultaneously the system of nature, which—insofar as, for the knowing subject, whether he is aware of it or not—precedes all empirical knowledge of nature; even more, it makes the empirical knowledge of nature possible at all.

D.[47] The Natural Scientific Laws of Relation

Substance—Causality—Dynamic Association

Since it is not our task here to provide an introduction to the critical system, we have only to focus our attention on the third of the Kantian fundamental propositions. It arises from applying the category of "relation" to the intuition of space and time and reads: *"Experience is possible only through the representation of a necessary connection of perceptions."*[48]

But precisely here the critical decision must be taken about the question of the scientific license for the cosmological proof of God, which indeed claims to rest on a necessary connection of perceptions.

The three "analogies of experience" that *Kant* deduces from the fundamental proposition of the necessary connection of perceptions are nothing other than case-by-case applications of this fundamental proposition, respectively, to the concept of the object connected in perception, to the relation between the connecting subject and the connected object, and to the being-mutually-connected. The critical consequences for the cosmological argument can be established for each analogy.

---

47. [Editorial annotation deleted.]
48. Kant, *Critique of Pure Reason*, B 218, p. 295.

1. In regard to a series of perceptions in time, we think necessarily of change on the one hand, and on the other hand of something permanent within the change: *"The substance persists with every change of appearances."*[49] We found something almost exactly analogous asserted in the Scholastic doctrine of principles, "only with a few other words":[50] everything accidental; changing points to something necessary, permanent. Yes, but! This continuity of substance results from the change of accidents only insofar as this change takes place in a temporal series. *Apart from time*, the series of [399] accidents could not come about at all, for a sequence is only conceivable in time; consequently, the persistence of a substance outside of time could not only not be known, but even the object of knowledge itself would be veiled in impenetrable darkness, that is, unknowableness. A substance persistent by itself *in time* is, however, an empty concept since time itself has only empirical reality. In no way would we reach a substance that exists in itself and is on the one hand cognizable, and on the other hand thinkable. Rather, from the empirically understood law of substance follows the *concept of development* (understood as a principle, hence not, without further qualification, in the sense of its special manifestation, for example, in Darwinism), which lies at the basis of modern science. {II.6} For in time, we can think of all change only as change regarding an identical substance, that is, as a kind of existing that follows upon another kind of existing of the same object, but not as an absolute arising and perishing.[51]

2. All change is alteration, as we just saw. But in the law of substance, we perceive only the temporal sequence of the two states without perceiving the objective necessity of this sequence. The latter is achieved only by the concept of *causality*, which, like the concept of substance, we correlate to the objects of experience, and which is dictated to us by the second analogy: *"All alterations occur in accordance with the law of the connection of cause and effect."*[52] Only with this knowledge, order is brought to the temporal sequence of our perceptions and, to that extent, the concept of causality can be called the basic concept of all science.

Is it thus a *primum movens* existing in itself, in the sense of Thomas Aquinas?[53] Not at all, since causality, *apart from the temporal series*, is once again unknowable, insofar as causality cannot be made understandable except as the connection of a series of perceptions in time. An initial causality *in time, however,* or some other such thing that enters initially from a state of being-in-itself into the temporal series, contradicts its own concept, inasmuch as every state in time presupposes a preceding one and, even disregarding that, it would always have only phenomenal significance in time and would deserve the appellation "absolute causality" as little as the previously discussed persisting substance in time

---

49. See Kant, *Critique of Pure Reason*, B 224, p. 299: "In all change of appearances substance persists, and its quantum is neither increased nor diminished in nature."

50. See J. W. von Goethe, *Faust* 1.5.3460–61 (Martha's garden): "The pastor says approximately the same, only with a few other words."

51. See Kant, *Critique of Pure Reason*, B 230, p. 302: "Arising and perishing are not alterations of that which arises or perishes. Alteration is a way of existing that succeeds another way of existing of the very same object."

52. See Kant, *Critique of Pure Reason*, B 232, p. 304.

53. See note 12 above.

merits being called *"ens per se necessarium."*[54] Rather, from the concept of cause applied to the world of appearances follows the *law of causality, which initially determines* the concept of development (previously mentioned), to the extent that the concept of cause leads back, through the concept of action, to that of power and, through that, to the concept of substance,[55] the alterations of which are, once again, determined by causality.

3. The unity of experience peaks in the a priori necessity expressed in the third Kantian analogy: *All substances must be thought of as in thoroughgoing mutual dependence on one another.*[56] We can conceive of two appearances or series of appearances existing next to one another in time under the objective unity of a scientific synthesis only by applying the concept of *dynamic community*[57] or reciprocity. That is, we always think of both cause and effect as determined by each other. Thus the unity of empirical experience—that is, the unity of the total object of our experience or, to speak with the Kantian school, still more clearly, the unity of nature[58]—is thereby made possible methodologically.

More recently, from the side of Protestants regrettably, the attempt has been made, on the basis of this concept of necessary reciprocity, to revitalize the cosmological proof of God, if only in a coy way. The conjecture of a comprehensive Universal Being, standing behind the entire complex of reciprocal effects, is supposed to explain why the latter cohere and mesh together. The philosopher *Lotze* wanted to assert such a conjecture as at least a plausible postulate by positing an *intellectual inner dimension* of individual atoms, through which they stood in *intellectual relations.*[59] It's only that all closer determination of this assertion leads in supra-empirical usage into the darkness of the absolutely unknowable and in empirical usage either to an empty concept or does not advance one step further in its concept of substance and of causality than the critical theory of experience: that is, it invariably leads to phenomenally valid knowledge only. And if Lotze believes himself entitled to draw justification for asserting the relationship of the ego to its sensations,[60] by doing so he just shifts the discussion to another field, that of rational psychology, which is as equally contested on entirely parallel grounds as the field of rational cosmology.

The modern theology of *Wobbermin* moves along an entirely similar train of thought, though I think it seems to be much more naive. He posits an analogy

---

54. See note 15 above.

55. See Kant, *Critique of Pure Reason*, B 249, p. 313: "This causality leads to the concept of action, this to the concept of force, and thereby to the concept of substance."

56. See Kant, *Critique of Pure Reason*, B 256, p. 316: "All substances, insofar as they can be perceived in space as simultaneous, are in thoroughgoing interaction."

57. See Kant, *Critique of Pure Reason*, B 260, p. 318: "The word 'community' is ambiguous in our language and can mean either *communio* [communion] or *commercium* [commerce]. We use it here in the latter sense, as a dynamical community, without which even the local community (*communio spatii*) could never be empirically recognized."

58. See Kant, *Critique of Pure Reason*, B 263, p. 320: "Our analogies therefore really exhibit the unity of nature in the combination of all appearances under certain exponents, which express nothing other than the relations of time (insofar as it comprehends all existence in itself) to the unity of apperception, which can only obtain in synthesis in accordance with rules."

59. H. Lotze, *Grundzüge der Religionsphilosophie: Diktate aus den Vorlesungen*, 3rd ed. (Leipzig, 1894), esp. 23–39; thus 39: "But insofar as the powers of matter produce *spatial movements*, it may be asserted that the existence of such powers from *intellectual relations* that take place between the *intellectual inner dimension* of the individual atoms is not inconceivable."

60. See Lotze, *Grundzüge der Religionsphilosophie*, 41.

from the concept of reciprocity to the mathematical *concept of a function,*[61] without mentioning that precisely the concept of a function can find application
only in relation to *numbers,* thus in *time,* and that it is thus quite fitting to clarify
the concept of dynamic community in the empirical realm, but not to demonstrate, or even only to portray as "highly probable,"[62] the objectivity of an
idea that may be aloof from space and time, just like the Christian concept of
God. Everything else that Wobbermin says about the necessity of positing an
objective ground in natural events is, compared to Thomas and his followers,
nothing new and may be dispatched as soon as we turn to speak about the
regulative use of the idea.

E. Result of the Critique

Let us summarize the result of our critical investigation.

We have become familiar with the cosmological argument as a syllogism,
which purports to grasp the totality of things synthetically within itself and
then ascribes to the maximal concept so achieved the character of the absolute,
of being-in-itself. Then we saw, however, that this concept only becomes that of
the maximal concept through its hypostatization in the ontological argument.
This ontological argument, on closer inspection, proved to be the mere elucidation of an already previously conceived concept and, to that extent, not suitable
to give independent validity to the steps of the syllogism for the cosmological
argument. Nothing of the cosmological argument remained, apart from a syllogistic series that takes its point of departure in the individual "given" thing
and then transcends the limits of experience, climaxing in the *idea* of a final free
cause of the world, a necessity in the world. Yet from the fact of the antinomy of
pure reason, we extrapolated that reason is just as inclined to posit and to can-
cel out such a free cause and final necessity. A solution to this antinomy seemed
at hand in the assumption that possibly entirely different concepts of the world
and thus of knowledge might be presupposed in thesis and antithesis. Taking our point of departure in the critical dissolution of the supposedly "given"
object resting at the basis of the cosmological argument, we developed the basic
contours of the theory of an experience, which gains apodictic certainty from
the relation of the a priori concept to a perception set in the a priori forms of
intuition, but which, with this apodictic certainty, also is aware of the strictly
phenomenal character of its cognitions. In the characteristic application of this
theory of experience to the connection of perceptions, we discovered the three
mutually complementary and distinctive relational laws of natural science: the
law of substance, the law of causality, and the law of dynamic community—
and we could then demonstrate the dissolution of the cosmological proof in its
different forms.

61. Wobbermin, *Der christliche Gottesglaube in seinem Verhältnis zur heutigen Philosophie und Naturwissenschaft,* 2nd ed. (Berlin, 1907), 51.
62. See Wobbermin, *Christliche Gottesglaube,* 59: "But is the ruling out of atheism in the strong
sense the only thing that we can achieve by way of the cosmological argument? It is the only result
that counts here as definite and explicit. Considerations of probability point, however, in a farther
direction. That we should think of that unitary ground of the world more precisely as a kind of
mathematical-logical intelligence should, according to our arguments, undoubtedly be termed the
next closest conclusion by far."

The concept of the world that came about in the process then appeared to align itself in the internal conflict of pure reason entirely with the side of the antithesis, insofar as it cancels out the concept of a *free* cause, a *final* necessity, and replaces the latter with the unrestrictedly valid dynamic community, that is, with natural lawfulness. But this presumption collapses as soon as we bring the phenomenality of this concept of the world into consideration. So that dissolution only affects the connection of perceptions in space and time, and those indeed without reservation, but not the causality and necessity of things-in-themselves, about which *nothing* is determined in the theory of experience.

And now it seems reasonable to relate the thesis of the antinomy to those things-in-themselves that are inaccessible to the conceptual-intuitional cognition. In the last part of our considerations, we will see how consciousness wins back its unity, which is apparently lost and frequently bemoaned as forsaken: on the one hand, with general validity for the regulative use of the idea and, on the other, just as certainly (though not with general validity) in the Christian belief in God, as it has become for many people the root of their personality and of their cultural existence.

III. The Problem of the Final Ground in Science and Religion

A. The Regulative Use of the Idea

I may have convinced some of you that the critical grounding of experience permanently rules out a constitutive use of the idea, that is, that any expansion of or addition to empirical knowledge by way of purported knowledge of absolutely final data from pure reason is *unscientific*.

Nevertheless, it remains the case that our reason has the intrinsic need to expand its individual cognitions into a total synthesis and to seek an epitome of all necessity and causality. The *idea* exists precisely in this irrefutable need, in this orientation of reason toward a goal that lies beyond the limits of constitutive experience—thus in line with the *philosophia perennis* in which Plato and Kant join hands over the millennia between them—that goal to which reason looks *out* without ever thereby being bothered that it does not see *into* it. If, by contrast, the idea is hypostasized and made into a specific being existing-for-itself, an *ens realissimum*, a transcendental object that would serve to extend our knowledge, then the dialectic of pure reason, for which Kant raised a cautionary funerary monument in his antinomy, is always again inevitable.

Our *knowing* remains thus contained within the limits of experience as constituted by intuition and concept, but our *thinking* inevitably strives to move beyond them. Might we satisfy ourselves with the contingency of appearances? Do not the appearances have to be appearances of *something*? Indeed. But we will take care, cautioned by the critique of reason, never to *posit* that something as knowable: either as an allegedly empirical datum, for then we end up at an empty concept; or as a datum of supra-empirical intuition, for by so doing we would abolish the scientific character of knowledge and end up in the realm of myth.[63]

---

63. See notes 38–43 above

The idea has, for us, rather the character of a *problem*, which is given to us, but not given with a solution—the character of a *"focus imaginarius,"*[64] to which our empirical cognition is *oriented*. It is nothing other than sophistical sentimentality when one hears complaints over and over again, even from clear-eyed people, that thereby the question mark, which is called knowledge, is merely extended into infinity. "Knowledge" comes from the verb "to know," meaning that it is an *activity*, according to its own concept, and this concept would be abolished by the positing of an absolute given. Kant calls a reason that lightens its labor through such posits *Ignava* or even *perversa ratio*,[65] and the conditions, which Faust set for himself in his contract with the devil, also apply to science:

When on an idler's bed I stretch myself in quiet,
there let, at once, my record end! . . .
When thus I hail the Moment flying:
"Ah, still delay—thou art so fair!"
Then bind me in thy bonds undying.
My final ruin then declare![66]

Reason, fully clear about itself, finds its entirely satisfying inner conclusion in the Idea, which offers it a *viewpoint*, in the direction of which it strives in its endeavor for knowledge.

The idea is a *limit concept*,[67] insofar as it cautions reason about sensible-conceptual thinking encroaching into the territory of being-in-itself, but also positively, insofar as it gives sensible-conceptual thinking the guidance and orientation toward the goal of an absolute totality of all experience.

And, with that last meaning, we understand the *regulative*, direction-giving, *heuristic* use of the idea in contrast to its attempted constitutive use, which seeks to ground experience and always becomes dialectical.

Applied to the problem of the cosmological proof, the regulative character of the idea means the following:

Science operates *as if* a correlate in reality corresponds to the a priori known dynamic community of substances in appearance. Its tendency leads in the direction of ever more establishing a knowledge of this unity of the totality of experience or this "unity of nature."[68] However, science, in the face of all possible progress in that direction, must *guard against positing, even hypothetically*, a ground of the world, an *"actus purus"* existing in itself, whether conceived of materialistically or theistically, since doing so would already constitute, in principle, a break with the fundamental laws of experience.

In the place of the cosmological proof of God, science therefore includes the regulative idea of a final unity of the lawful connection of perceptions or *the fundamental proposition of the dynamic community of substances conceived of as a regulative idea.*

---

64. See Kant, *Critique of Pure Reason*, B 672, p. 591.
65. See Kant, *Critique of Pure Reason*, B 717–20, pp. 631–34.
66. J. W. Goethe, *Faust: A Tragedy*, trans. Bayard Taylor (London: Ward, Locke & Co., 1889), 1.5.1692–93, 1699–1702 (study room), p. 48.
67. See Kant, *Critique of Pure Reason*, B 310–11, pp. 362–63.
68. See note 58 above.

B. Cosmology and the Christian Concept of God

Our overview of the problem would not be complete if we did not also attempt to give at least a few indications of its significance in the life of religion.

Thomas Aquinas admittedly only succeeded in proving an *"ens realissimum,"* that is, the concept of it. We have seen how he sought to set it in close proximity to the Christian concept of God by giving it a *nomen persona.*[69] This *"ens realissimum"* can gain a religious significance in his system only insofar as he equates it with the concept of God in the church tradition. I would digress too much here if I sought to establish the extent to which the Christian concept of God, as it is reflected in the expressions of Jesus's *self-consciousness,* is altered by this identification in favor of a naturalistic idea of the absolute. In the best case, and also according to the Catholic view, the cosmological proof is a technique (to use *Herrmann's* terminology)[70] to prime religion in people. *We* will actually contest its capacity to do even that: first, because its technique is false; and second because, even if true, it could not lead people to what we understand by religion but only at most to an intellectual belief in a scientific concept. We hold that Christian religion is found where a human being becomes certain of the gravity and also the love of a *supernatural* God in the most individual way. This certainty does not come about through the work of "natural reason," yet also not through a *sacrificium* of this reason when confronted by supernatural doctrinal revelation, but by the combined active and passive openness of the most individual being of the human in face of a power that cannot be exhausted by any claims or expressive forms of cultural consciousness.[71] For, to the one who is grasped by it, it becomes the kernel and the polestar of his individual cultural consciousness; it impacts him as the bearer of his *personality* in every branch of culture and gives to the latter—*not* new forms, but a personal inner value for individuals that[72] they would never have in themselves.

This power is *God*, and if we have felt something of it, we owe it all in some way to the aftereffects, no, to the effects of the person of *Jesus* in *history*. For our characters and personalities develop in the stream of history, in the ramifications of which we all stand, in contrast to the objects of nature, which owe their existence to the empirical causal nexus. And at no point in history has that power, by which a Christian first consciously knows oneself as called to be fully human, so purely and completely become manifest as in those days among the forlorn people of Galilee.

---

69. See note 30 above.

70. Barth bases his argument here on his transcript (preserved in the Karl Barth Archive in Basel) of W. Herrmann's lectures "Dogmatics I," which he attended during the summer semester of 1908 in Marburg. In §5, "The Attempt to Come to Religion through the Proofs for the Existence of God," one finds the following passage in the context of a critique of the cosmological proof: "But it conceals also a *religious error*, namely, that of Catholicism: It is a technique to produce religion."

71. Barth presumably adopted the term "cultural consciousness" from Hermann Cohen, *Religion und Sittlichkeit: Eine Betrachtung zur Grundlegung der Religionsphilosophie* (Berlin, 1907), 29; Cohen, *Ethik des reinen Willens* (Berlin, 1904), 603; see also Paul Natorp, *Religion innerhalb der Grenzen der Humanität: Ein Kapitel zur Grundlegung der Sozialpädagogik,* 2nd ed. (Tübingen, 1908), 98. In the defense against the limitation of religion to the "claims . . . of cultural consciousness" by way of the "individual," Barth accords with his teacher, Wilhelm Herrmann. See W. Herrmann, *Die Auffassung der Religion in Cohen und Natorps Ethik* (1909), in Herrmann, *Schriften zur Grundlegung der Theologie,* ed. P. Fischer-Appelt, part 2, ThB 36/2 (Munich: Kaiser, 1967), 206–32.

72. [Editorial annotation deleted.]

Christian belief in God is present where a human being seeks to pursue the certainty of God once that certainty has arisen for him in his limited or broad cultural existence. That takes place, above all, in the direction of *ethical* willing, which does not gain a new form but only a new intensity and power through religion. And what about knowing through *thinking*? Should science through personal religious certainty receive those supplements to its constitutive knowledge, which many of you believe science must be lacking? No. For then religion would make itself guilty of a violation of the limits of humanity[73] and forfeit its interiority, in which its strength resides. The religious perspective on the world stands, rather, in the closest analogy to the regulative use of the Idea in science. In the events of the empirical world, the religious person (according to *Schleiermacher's* saying) sees the acts of God.[74] He lives from the certainty that, to those who love God, all things must serve the best (Rom. 8:28). However, that actually means that religion gives him the capacity to understand the empirical world in which he finds himself placed and in connection with his most individual personal life; religion helps him to understand the world as absolutely dependent on supernatural power, to whom he knows himself to be completely subject in his personal life. Religion frees us from the pressure of the causal nexus of empirical things insofar as it shows us that this causal nexus is no power existing unto itself, but only a tool in the hand of the God whom we call Father. Religion shows us the will of God *with us* in the context of the things of the world of experience, and we therefore in no way think of God as a *"primum movens"* [First Mover] in a series of moving things, but as the one who *created* all things, created them from nothing.

But let us not forget: This worldview of Christian belief in God is *never* a finished, absolute given, but—and here lies the most significant parallel with the regulative use of the idea in science—is always a task, that is, a gift, the possession of which we need *to assert* in continuous struggle. Even religion and the religious perspective on the world never *is*, but only *becomes*. The religious life of individual human beings with respect to willing *and* knowing always stands under the sign of movement, forward—or backward. "For God is not a God of the dead, but of the living" (Matt. 22:32).

Lessing paraphrased the concept of truth in *science* most adequately when he said in the famous passage during the controversy with Goeze: "If God came before me and held all truth in his right hand and the striving after truth in his left and said to me, 'Choose!' I would fall humbly before his left hand and say, 'Father, give me the left; the right is only for you alone!'"[75]

---

73. See Natorp, *Religion innerhalb der Grenzen*, e.g., 49: "Religion, or whatever up to now concealed itself under that name, should be retained precisely to the extent that it remains enclosed *within the limits of humanity* and, conversely, no longer to the extent that the immeasurable force of feeling tempts it to break through these limits and to deny obedience to their eternal laws." See also 54: "Nothing should any longer be authorized on account of religious feeling if it does not pass the criticism of human reason, whether theoretical, practical or even aesthetic. . . ."

74. Schleiermacher, *On Religion: Speeches* (1799), trans. and ed. Richard Crouter, 2nd ed. (Cambridge, 1996), 25: "To present all events in the world as the actions of a god is religion."

75. G. E. Lessing, "A Rejoinder," in *Lessing: Philosophical and Theological Writings*, trans. and ed. H. B. Nisbet (Cambridge: Cambridge University Press, 2005), 98: "If God held fast in his right hand the whole of truth and in his left hand only the ever-active quest for truth, albeit with the proviso that I should constantly and eternally err, and said to me: 'Choose!', I would fall upon his left hand and say: 'Father, give! For pure truth is for you alone!'"

This concept of truth finds its characteristic deepening and supplementing in the worldview of Christian belief in God. In the experience of religion, the most personal kernel of the human being is being taken hold of by the *task* of understanding the world as the world of God. And this understanding is not idle reflection, but *act*. But those who are engaged in this task know enough to say that the *gift* is contained in the task, that they run and do not become faint, walk and yet do not become weary (see Isa. 40:31).

We cannot render the essence of the Christian-religious worldview better than by confessing with the poet:

> I am satisfied
> that I have *seen* the city;
> and without fatigue
> I will *go closer* to it
> and not lose sight of its bright golden gates
> for the remainder of my life.[76]

Critical Annotations

By Heinrich Barth

{I.1} "and it is capable of proving the being [*Wesen*] of God as *relatively evident*" (according to Becker). This expression ("relatively evident") does not correspond to the flow of the argument; the being of God can be proved to be absolutely evident, but what is proved is not adequate to reality, is quantitatively not congruent. The expression is repeated on page 15, where, however, it is corrected by the following sentence.

{I.2} "In the same way, Aristotle had already proved the "νοῦς" as "πρῶτον κινοῦν" (First Mover). The phrase "in the same way" is objectionable. For a wide gap does exist between the mechanical *primum movens* and the highest intellectual-teleological principle of Aristotle. On the whole, the mechanical-causal elements are amalgamated in unjustified ways with the presentation of the Thomistic proofs, as Proof 5 shows. After all, the greatest possible philosophical contradictions are enclosed in these points of view.

{I.3} The underestimation of the contradiction between the "modern" worldview and the Aristotelean-Scholastic worldview also follows from that. Kantians will simply line them up too closely and reject them together as "uncriticial." Drawing a connection to Fichte or Schelling perhaps would have been more appropriate.

{I.4} Hettinger's distinction between general and divine, corresponding to ideal and real being, is not Thomistic. He reads it into Thomas for apologetic motives. It thus may not be drawn on when continuing to develop Thomistic ideas, as it happens on p. 22.

{I.5} From the point forward (as well as in the presentation as a whole), the role of the ontological proof is not specified entirely correctly. It should have

---

76. Strophe 5 of the song, "Ich hab' von ferne, Herr, deinen Thron erblickt," by J. T. Hermes (1738–1821), in *GERS* 352.

already been highlighted on p. 10 that proof number 4 is actually the ontological proof: the highest perfection (but not, however, per 11, highest necessity, highest causality, etc.) is ontologically utilizable. For (and thereby indicating the valid core of the ontological way of thinking): The value of the perfection of an object, the truth of a proposition, the moral goodness of an action, and the beauty of an object presupposes, for instance, not just the superlative concepts on the scale of comparison but also the ideas of absolute perfection, truth, goodness, and beauty. This stands in distinction, however, to all relative determinations: A big object, a red object, and so forth, already permit the construction of maximal concepts but do not presuppose them, let alone as absolute ideas (in the Platonic sense). Concepts such as "necessary" and "causal" cannot be increased at all. Thus, the ontological proof from the concept of perfection evidently does not play the same role for Thomas as it is accorded here, following Hettinger's interpretation. Thomas's "five ways" deduce God (cosmologically) (1) as first mover, (2) as final cause, (3) as absolutely necessary, (ontologically) (4) as the most perfect, and (teleologically) (5) as the purpose-setting power. The most perfect is then made equivalent to the personal. The ontological proof thus stands in a line with the others; it does not bring the result of the other proofs to actualization, as per the presentation, although the concept of personality is tied to it, thus first bringing about the theistic concept of God. For the rest, however, the other proofs remain independent of it. For that reason, the citation of Faust is made quite wrongly used here.

{II.1} "In this argument, it is correct that . . . " If this is conceded, the ontological proof must also be acknowledged. (See my theory of the concept of being and existence, and so on; a solution to this question appears possible to me only from that perspective. Of course, it would have been partially expressed in somewhat different form today.)

{II.2} "but only because a complete intuition . . . corresponds." The "complete intuition" as the condition of "reality" stands in conflict with epistemology. The Thaler do not have to be seen at all in order to be real. The point here really has nothing to do with the conditions of the reality of an object, but it is only noting that in our thinking an object is posited as either hypothetical or real. It seems self-evident that a hypothetical fact never becomes a real one by way of an analytical judgment.

{II.3} The point of departure for the discussion of the antinomies as well as the examples selected as illustrations are not well chosen. According to the principle of noncontradiction, no contradictory and opposed expressions can be made about the same *concept*. That such a thing can be the case for a *word* (for instance, "paper") is simply a matter (or lack) of language and style. The word *"world"* denotes an absolutely univocal concept, namely, the totality of all realities.

{II.4} (Unfortunately, I do not have the *Critique of Pure Reason* at hand; I take it that the antinomies are accurately represented.) In the presentation, the third antinomy of pure reason is used as if it solely concerns the problem of freedom within causality in general, as the exposition on page 31 clearly shows. This, however, is not the case. The thesis reads, "For the explanation of the world, the acceptance of a *final* free casualty is necessary." It thus deals simply with the problem of ultimate origin. The supposition of a final, free cause would likely be connected with an absolutely causal lawfulness. Antinomy 4 is rather unclear; the reader does not know if it has to do with an a priori necessity or the necessity of a natural law (as already is the case in Thomas). Both antinomies have been combined with one another at the cost of clarity.

{II.5} The correspondence of the temporal a priori with arithmetic is not acceptable, even if Kant himself expressly supposes it. The mathematical series of concepts does not play out either in space or time; that an arithmetic development can be conceived in thought only temporally is due to the overall nature of thinking and equally affects a geometrical series.

{II.6} The concept of the self-renewing substance does not in any sense contain in itself the idea of development. The latter presupposes the application of a scale of value to nature. Development signifies a change in the direction of perfection. There is no talk of that here. Compare the Heraclitean system, which stands rather remote from the idea of development.

{II.7} This attempt at introducing religion into the philosophical worldview principally falls completely outside the bounds of Kantian thinking. A telltale sign is the sudden disregard of theoretical knowledge in favor of a "most individual certainty" about a supernatural God. Rather than at least connecting to practical reason, with its ideal generality and unity, that which is valued as the highest being is ascribed to the psychologically conditioned contingent condition of the individual: an orientation to Thomas Aquinas rather than to Kant. Transcendental philosophy suddenly turns into a cult of personality. The "flow of history" as such is certainly not character forming. It does not constitute an opposition to the empirical process of nature, as the expression already indicates. Character and personality arise where the latent ethical-intellectual, which is everywhere present, comes to the fore, in opposition to the causal processes of the psychological-contingent.

The so-called "analogy" of the religious perspective on the world with the regulative ideas should be proved. In our view, the regulative ideas are only those that form a final point for ideal human striving in thought, will, and action; they are of a kind with the already-mentioned absolute ontological concepts. The idea of God in and for itself, however, does not belong to this realm. The position of religious thoughts as epistemic functions or in relation to epistemic functions is not made clear, nor is their content (p. 59) epistemologically justified, at least as a possibility. Once more, "religion" can never be a regulative idea. To the extent that religion is a worldview, the regulative idea for religious seeking is the *truth*; to the degree that religion is ethical demand, the regulative idea for ethical striving is the *good*. Religion cannot be at the same time both final point (as regulative idea) and the thing that is being moved in the striving after it. Practically, it could hardly be conceded, from a religious perspective, that the elements of the religious worldview, such as "acts of God in the events of the world," "creation of the world from nothing," and so on, are only transitory theories of religious development. Religious striving as such exists only empirically, not ideally; the empirical can be dissolved in the striving after truth (Lessing) and after ethical perfection.

May 30, 1909
Pentecost

Brief Communique
1909

The short lines initialed "K.B." in No. 14 of Die Christliche Welt, *August 19, 1909, in the section marked "Brief Communiques," have a somewhat longer prehistory.*

As early as 1892 (no. 6, cols. 161–69), 1893 (no. 7, cols. 815–18) and 1899 (no. 13, cols. 153–55, 177–82, 202–6), Die Christliche Welt *had drawn attention to the North Schleswig question, that is, to the situation of the Danes in what, since 1866, had been Prussian or German North Schleswig. Martin Rade's critical stance toward German policies on this question was unambiguous,[1] as it was later unmistakably expressed in the publication of a "Grenzmarken-Korrespondenz" [Borderlands correspondence] and in preparations to found a "Society for the Protection of German Honor in the German Nordmark" [northern borderlands].[2] And so Rade did not hesitate to take up the inquiry about the matter submitted by Valdemar Ammundsen, professor of church history at the University of Copenhagen. For his part, Ammundsen connected the matter with a controversy in which Rade—shortly after the* Daily Telegraph *affair—had demanded, especially with regard to the British nation, that every means be used "to understand foreign folk culture in order to avoid misunderstandings" (CW 22 [1908]: col. 1139).*

Rade himself reports looking back (CW 23 [1909]: cols. 832–33): "Dr. Ammundsen challenged the editor in an open letter regarding the North Schleswig question. 'How can the German folk, how can Christians in Germany be silent regarding the injustice that the Prussians constantly do to the Danes in North Schleswig?' [CW 23 [1909]: cols. 159–61]. I have responded as well as I could [CW 23 [1909]: cols. 161–62]; Dr. Ammundsen has continued to make his accusation with new arguments in support of it [CW 23 [1909]: cols. 438–40], and I have responded again [CW 23 [1909]: cols 440–42]."

There was a good reason for Rade to get involved with the problem presented to him: "The distressing situation in North Schleswig has been a matter of strong concern for me for many years. To the extent that is possible for an outsider, I know it very well. But for that very reason it was certainly not my intention at the current time to introduce a discussion of this difficult theme in Die Christliche Welt. *Now, however, since without my agreement the initiative to do so came from outside, I have not for one moment hesitated to address the situation."*

---

1. "An offense for many friends" of *Die Christliche Welt*, reports J. Rathje in *Die Welt des freien Protestantismus: Ein Beitrag zur deutsch-evangelischen Geistesgeschichte; Dargestellt an Leben und Werk von Martin Rade* (Stuttgart: Klotz Verlag, 1952), 158 [The World of Free Protestantism: A contribution to German Protestant intellectual history; Illustrated by the life and work of Martin Rade].

2. See J.-P. Leppien, *Martin Rade und die deutsch-dänischen Beziehungen, 1909–1929: Ein Beitrag zur historischen Friedensforschung und zur Problematik des Nationalismus*, Quellen und Forschungen zur Geschichte Schleswig-Holsteins 77 (Kiel, 1979), 40–66 [Martin Rade and German-Danish relations, 1909–1929: A contribution to historical peace studies and the problematic of nationalism].

"In the process it was granted to me," Rade further wrote, "to loosen the man's tongue," who then was supposed to treat "the situation in North Schleswig" in three numbers of Die Christliche Welt (23 [1909]: cols 578–88, 603–14, 697–714; see 642–44, 739–40). The author, who here as well was introduced anonymously, signed his articles simply as "a" or "the North Schleswigian." Rade addresses this circumstance himself in the introduction to the expanded special issue of the articles,[3] where he looks back: "There were objections to his not revealing his name. But it was necessary to do so for the time being. We had to force the people to deal solely with the matter itself, without glancing right or left at any specific person. To the extent that strong attacks by the anonymous author ensued, . . . I personally and expressly take responsibility for that. Not only pro forma. I am indeed delighted with the author. To be sure, he may see this or that incorrectly and here or there err in his judgment: his temperament and attitude are genuine. And that is certainly the main thing." The report was written by the pastor's son Johannes Tiedje (1879–1946). As a result of his time as a student in Marburg, he was known to Rade "personally and very well."[4] Tiedje, by the way, later became Barth's successor as editorial assistant at Die Christliche Welt. His series of articles, precisely because their authorship remained nameless for the time being, initiated an influential movement that later was called "Tiedjebevaegelsen" in Danish historical writing.[5]

Rade published his introduction (dated July 17, 1909) to the separate piece under the title "A Preface That Has Become Superfluous?" in Die Christliche Welt 23, no. 35 (August 26, 1909): cols. 832–33); he attached to it the lightly shortened document "in which the author of our North Schleswig article gave his name" (see cols. 833–34). Thus thereby, Rade's introduction, which had been originally intended to intercede on behalf of the anonymous author, appeared to have become dispensable. The piece appeared "in German and Danish" in Modersmaalet, no. 180, August 5, 1909. In this text the "North Schleswigian" surfaced with his name; to this text initially referred the "Brief Communique," which Karl Barth inserted at the end of no. 34, August 19, under the rubric "Miscellany" (following three book reviews from the pen of Rudolf Bultmann).

This edition was the second of the two numbers that Barth—"my self-confidence swelled to the extreme"—"was allowed to edit and on which he could responsibly sign off . . . because the Rades went on holiday [from August 3 to 16, 1909]."[6] Already on May 7, 1909, he had announced to his parents, "For a few weeks in August I will manage the journal and will be allowed to formulate the brief communiques, and until then I will be ruminating about a few oracular utterances that I want to unload there!! He wrote to them on July 13, 1909, about this time as "sole Christian world ruler" and reported to them on August 2, 1909, "Rades . . . are going on holiday, . . . and for the remainder of my time here, I am even supposed to move into their house as a kind of night watchman, in preparation for which they solemnly presented me today with a dagger and a cudgel. Isn't that marvelous?! In exchange, in the [two numbers] I'm in charge of, I may only publish things that delight me." And on August 9, 1909, [he wrote] to his parents and siblings, "The responsibility is no small pressure. As proud as a Spaniard, I walk among the secretaries and printing apprentices who are all focused

---

3. J. Tiedje, *Die Zustände in Nord-Schleswig* (Marburg: Schünemann, 1909).
4. In *CW* 23 (1909): col. 855; see Leppien, *Martin Rade*, 35.
5. Leppien, *Martin Rade*, 35.
6. Letter to Dr. J. Rathje, April 17, 1947, in K. Barth, *Offene Briefe, 1945–1968*, ed. D. Koch (Zurich: Theologischer Verlag, 1984), 120.

upon a wave of my hands—or should be so. If something dangerous for the state should appear in the next number, then I will be thrown into jail . . . ! After some time, I will doubtlessly be very homesick for this grotesquely elevated life." On August 14, 1909, he was able to report to his parents, *"Now the second and last number of* Chr. W. *that appears with my name on it also is ready for the printer."* The editorial credit in both issues is, in fact, *"Responsible Editor by proxy: Karl Barth V.D.M. [Verbi Dei Minister] Marburg"* (cols. 789 and 814).

Regarding the *"Brief Communique,"* its publication was delayed because Barth got in touch with Rade to clarify the source of the text and perhaps also because of the title with which Tiedje was to be introduced. Rade responded on August 8, 1909, with a postcard *"by express":*[7] *"L. H. B.* Modersmaalet, *Nr. 180—Hadersleben, August 5. One difficulty is that we cannot describe our friend publicly as a 'Candidate' for legal reasons because he has not yet passed an examination. . . . Well, you handle it in a way that you find and think best."* On August 12, Rade sent another express postcard[8] to congratulate Barth on *"Number 33"* but missed *"the communique about Tiedje: it had to appear; the notice about* Modersmaalet *was in this case completely irrelevant. Now you certainly bring the news in Number 34; make it very plain. Call him simply a candidate in philosophy, or perhaps it would be even better to leave out any title, as he has done in his writing. I am, of course, very curious about no. 34: tota tua erit"* [it's all up to you].

The author of our series of articles about "the situation in North Schleswig" gave his name in an open letter to the editor of the Hadersleben newspaper *Modersmaalet* (no. 180): Johannes Tiedje, in the pastorate at Oesby. We share this with our readers in the certainty that they will continue to base their judgment on the matter itself.

---

7. Not cited in *Bw.* R.
8. Not cited in *Bw.* R.

Index of Scripture and Other Ancient Sources

Index of Names

Achelis, Ernst Christian, 89, 246–47, 249n6
  Fritz Barth and, 246, 248
  Karl Barth's response to, 259, 260, 261,
    262, 263, 266
  response of, to Karl Barth, 244, 246,
    252–56
Aeschbacher, Robert, 85, 245–46
Alexander IV, Pope, 9, 12, 15–16, 19, 20,
    24, 25
Ammundsen, Valdemar, 299
Amsler, Hermann, 69–70, 71
Anrich, G., 82n60
Anselm of Canterbury, 282
Aratus, 151
Aristotle, 162n176, 277, 278, 279, 280, 286,
    288, 296
Athanasius, 161, 225
Augustine, 151

Baentsch, Bruno, 268
Barth, Heinrich, 47n16, 84, 273–74, 296–98
Barth, Johann Friedrich ("Fritz"), 1, 6, 72,
    165n179
  Achelis and, 246, 248
  at Christian Students' Conferences,
    84, 86
  courses taught by, 1, 6, 72, 106
  Einleitung in das Neue Testament by, 175
  Karl's correspondence with, 33, 88, 106,
    109, 244–45, 273
  Karl's disagreement with, 245–48
  and Rade, 227
  Zofingia membership of, 46, 47
Barth, Karl
  and the Academic Evangelical-
    Theological Society, 88–89
  Achelis's response to, 246, 252–56
  and alcohol, 44, 49, 63–66
  Bern studies of, 1, 173, 177, 227
  and Christian Students' Conferences,
    84–87
  at *Die Christliche Welt*, 109, 227–28, 229,
    244, 268–71, 299–301
  church history studies of, 6, 72, 105,
    106, 109, 173–75, 177

on the cosmological proof for God,
    272–96
criticism received by, 109, 169n191,
    172n200
Drews's response to, 246–47, 256–59
and the Free Students, 272–73
Fritz's correspondence with, 33, 88, 106,
    109, 244–45, 273
Fritz's disagreement with, 245–48
Heinrich Barth's response to, 296–98
induction of, in Geneva, 247
on the Lord's Prayer, 89–104
Marburg studies of, 105, 175, 244,
    294n70
Markus's correspondence with, 49
on modern theology, 236–39, 249–52,
    259–66
on Plato and Socrates, 87n21
and Rade, 227, 228, 229, 235n17, 244,
    245, 246, 247, 248, 266–67, 299–300,
    301
religious history studies of, 1
responding to Achelis and Drews,
    259–66
as reviewer, 227–29
self-criticism of, 100n62
studying with Harnack, 105–9, 169n191,
    172n200, 179
on Swiss politics, 52–54
synoptic Gospel studies of, 33
at Tübingen, 173
at *Zeitschrift für Theologie und Kirche*,
    244–67
on *Zeitschrift für wissenschaftliche
    Theologie*, 268–71
Zofingia membership of, 44–45, 46, 47,
    48–50, 65n91, 70, 174, 175, 242
Barth, Markus, 49
Barth, Peter, 47n16
von Baur, Ferdinand Christian, 80n53, 111,
    166, 178, 186, 187, 190, 192, 270
Beck, J. T., 178, 186, 192
Becker, J. A., 277, 296
Bengel, J. A., 90, 91, 92
Benoît, L., 55

Index of Subjects

Abraham, 197, 198, 204–6
the absolute *vs.* the relative, 18, 168, 257,
  277, 280, 287, 296–97
Academic Evangelical-Theological
  Society, 88
academic study. *See* education, theological
Acts. *See also* Paul, missionary sermon of;
  Pauline missionary communities
  authorship of, 110–13, 128, 140, 144–45,
    150, 152, 155–56, 163, 164–65
  church organization in, 136, 138–39,
    143–45, 170
  dating of, 138, 146, 152
  factuality of, 124, 126, 127, 131–32,
    139–41, 143–46, 147–48, 165–70
  Judaism depicted in, 111, 122–23, 133,
    135
  miracles in, 119, 120
  Paul's stature in, 113, 170–72
  "union Paulinism" in, 130–31, 136
  "We-Source" of, 112, 113, 118–19, 125,
    128, 143, 147
Actus B. Francisci et Sociorum, 10, 13–14,
  17, 19, 21, 22, 23, 25–26, 29
Aeterni Patris, 274
agnosticism, 18, 252, 269–71, 275
alcohol, 44, 46n8, 47n14, 62n80, 63–66, 67
Alexandrians, 215. *See also* Clement of
  Alexandria *in the index of names;*
  Origen *in the index of names*
allegory, 150
analogy
  Kantian, 288–90
  of religious perspective, 295, 298
  of Wobbermin, 290–91
Ananias of Damascus, 129, 164
anarchy, 52
anti-colonial movements, 86
antinomies, 283–86, 291, 292, 297–98
Antioch in Pisidia, 115–16, 118, 121, 132,
  138–39, 148, 160
Apocrypha, second-century, 211–13
apokatastasis, 189
Apostles' Creed, 176
Aquila, 122, 123

Areopagus speech, 121, 147, 150–52, 160
Arianism, 225
Aryan people, 2
ascension, 181–82
Asia Minor, 143–44, 171
  descent into hell traditions in, 196–201,
    206
Athens, 121–22, 141–42, 148, 150
Augsburg Confession, 75, 81
authority
  apostolic, 198
  biblical, 74
  Christian political, 82
  divine *vs.* human, 75, 78
  and individualism, 249, 253, 257, 265
  of Jesus, 36, 38, 262, 263, 265
  worldly, 76–77, 78

Bamidbar Rabbah, 195
baptism, 81, 82n60, 145–46, 185
  and the Holy Spirit, 156, 157
Barnabas, 115, 116–17, 129, 138–39, 165
Basel
  Reformed Church in, 234–35
  Zofingia chapter in, 45, 46, 47, 50, 56, 71
Basel Mission, 4
Belgian Mission Church, 242–43
Bereshit Rabbah, 195
Bern
  Academic Evangelical-Theological
    Society of, 88–89
  Barth's studies in, 1, 173, 177, 227
  faculty of, 81n54, 86, 87
  Philadelphia in, 55n51
  Zofingia in, 44–46, 47n18, 48–50, 56n59,
    58–60, 62n80, 65n91, 65n92, 67–68,
    70–71
Beroea, 120–21, 141, 150
Bible
  authority of, 73, 74, 78–79
  Catholic doctrines not found in, 77
  history of religions view of, 78–79
  vs. human authority, 75–76, 78, 80
  inspiration of, 79
  orthodox view of, 78

315

spirits
  bodies and, 27, 30
  identity of, 187–89, 190
  in Luke, 183
  in 1 Peter, 185, 186, 187–89, 190
stigmata of Francis of Assisi, 1, 6–32
  and act of stigmatization, 10–14,
    23, 29
  analysis of, 31–32
  comparing sources on, 17–26
  date of, 19–20
  descriptions of, 14–17
  historical-critical approach to, 26–30
  rationalizations of, 27–28, 31
  science and, 7, 27, 28, 29, 30–31
  sources on, 8–10
  witnesses to, 9, 14, 15, 25–26
student life, 85. *See also* education,
    theological; Zofingia
subjectivism, 253, 257, 261, 265
  papal writings condemning, 274n4
substance, 280–82, 284, 289–90, 291,
    298
Sunday observance, 66–67, 144
supernatural theology, 25, 27, 128, 276,
    277, 282, 294–95, 298
Switzerland
  equality in, 54
  politics in, 52, 53–54
  Reformation in, 72–74
  Rütli oath and, 55n52
  Zofingia and, 44, 46, 47n19, 54n46,
    58n61, 61–63, 65n90
Synoptic Gospels. *See also individual
    Gospels*
  centurion at Capernaum in, 33–43
  dating of, 42
  dogmatic tendencies of, 40, 42
  eschatology in, 36–37, 38, 39, 41
  Jesus in, 156
  and John, 42, 43
  two-source theory of, 34, 41–42
  and "Ur-Mark," 40, 41

Talmudic literature, 101, 104
Testaments of the Twelve Patriarchs, 179,
    212, 213
text criticism, 88–104
theologians, formation of. *See* education,
    theological
theology. *See also* modern theology
  essence of, 257–58
  historical *vs.* systematic, 270–71
  as science, 257–58, 260n24, 269–70
  of the supernatural, 25, 27, 128, 275–78,
    282, 294–95, 298
theonomy, 253, 261
Thessalonica, 120, 141

thinking, 295, 297, 298. *See also*
  cosmological proof for God's
    existence
  vs. knowing, 292
  limits of, 293
  synthetic judgments and, 280
Thomism, 276. *See also* Thomas Aquinas *in
    the index of names*
Timothy, 117, 121, 129, 130, 140
trial of Paul, 125–27, 148, 160, 164
Troas, 119, 125, 141, 143–44
truth, 255–56
  and dogmatics, 269
  double, 276
  and goodness, 298
  and human limitations, 295–96
  scholastic definition of, 279–80
Tübingen, Barth at, 173, 174–75, 178n15
Tübingen School, 107, 108, 111–12, 113,
    122, 126, 129–30, 135–36, 166–67,
    269–70
Tyre, 125

"union Paulinism," 130–31, 136
universalism
  of Christianity, 111, 113
  in soteriology, 222–23
University of Bern. *See* Bern; Zofingia

value judgments, 255–56, 264
Vatican Council (1870), 274
Vedas, 2–4

wilderness generation, 195
World Federation of Christian Students, 86

Zähringia, 59n65, 60, 65n92, 70
Zeitschrift für Theologie und Kirche, 229,
    244, 248
Zeitschrift für wissenschaftliche Theologie,
    268–71
Zofingia, 32n131, 44–71, 242
  amicitia and, 46, 49, 54n46, 71n114
  Basel chapter of, 45, 46, 47, 50, 56, 71
  Bern chapter of, 44–46, 47n18, 48–50,
    56n59, 58–60, 62n80, 65n91, 65n92,
    67–68, 70–71
  colors and, 47, 48, 49, 62–63, 70–71
  drinking in, 44, 46n8, 47n14, 62n80,
    63–66, 67, 70, 71
  Foxes in, 65n90, 66n95
  French-speaking chapters of, 55–56, 57,
    62, 67, 71
  idealism in, 45, 46–47, 49, 54–56, 59–60,
    63–64, 70, 71
  "Ordinary Sessions" of, 56n59
  origin of, 44
  and other student fraternities, 58–59

CPSIA information can be obtained
at www.ICGtesting.com
Printed in the USA
LVHW041717301122
733922LV00001B/1

9 780664 264383